Fodor's 2010

D0089889

CANCÚN, COZUMEL & THE YUCATÁN PENINSULA

Where to Stay and Eat
for All Budgets

Must-See Sights
and Local Secrets

Ratings You Can Trust

Fodor's Travel Publications   New York, Toronto, London, Sydney, Auckland
www.fodors.com

FODOR'S CANCÚN, COZUMEL & THE YUCATÁN PENINSULA 2010
Editor: Joanna G. Cantor

Writers: Michele Joyce, Coco Krumme, Marlise Kast, Maribeth Mellin

Production Editor: Evangelos Vasilakis
Maps & Illustrations: David Lindroth, *cartographers*; Bob Blake, Rebecca Baer, *map editors*; William Wu, *information graphics*
Design: Fabrizio LaRocca, *creative director*; Guido Caroti, Siobhan O'Hare, *art directors*; Tina Malaney, Chie Ushio, Ann McBride, Jessica Walsh, *designers*; Melanie Marin, *senior picture editor*
Cover Photo: (Chac Mool, Cancún): Corbis
Production Manager: Amanda Bullock

COPYRIGHT
Copyright © 2010 by Fodor's Travel, a division of Random House, Inc.

Fodor's is a registered trademark of Random House, Inc.

All rights reserved. Published in the United States by Fodor's Travel, a division of Random House, Inc., and simultaneously in Canada by Random House of Canada, Limited, Toronto. Distributed by Random House, Inc., New York.

No maps, illustrations, or other portions of this book may be reproduced in any form without written permission from the publisher.

ISBN 978-1-4000-0845-2

ISSN 1051-6336

SPECIAL SALES
This book is available at special discounts for bulk purchases for sales promotions or premiums. Special editions, including personalized covers, excerpts of existing books, and corporate imprints, can be created in large quantities for special needs. For more information, write to Special Markets/Premium Sales, 1745 Broadway, MD 6-2, New York, New York 10019, or e-mail specialmarkets@randomhouse.com.

AN IMPORTANT TIP & AN INVITATION
Although all prices, opening times, and other details in this book are based on information supplied to us at press time, changes occur all the time in the travel world, and Fodor's cannot accept responsibility for facts that become outdated or for inadvertent errors or omissions. So **always confirm information when it matters,** especially if you're making a detour to visit a specific place. Your experiences—positive and negative—matter to us. If we have missed or misstated something, **please write to us.** We follow up on all suggestions. Contact the Cancún, Cozumel & the Yucatán Peninsula editor at editors@fodors.com or c/o Fodor's at 1745 Broadway, New York, NY 10019.

PRINTED IN THE UNITED STATES OF AMERICA

10 9 8 7 6 5 4 3 2 1

Be a Fodor's Correspondent

Your opinion matters. It matters to us. It matters to your fellow Fodor's travelers, too. And we'd like to hear it. In fact, we need to hear it.

When you share your experiences and opinions, you become an active member of the Fodor's community. That means we'll not only use your feedback to make our books better, but we'll publish your names and comments whenever possible. Throughout our guides, look for "Word of Mouth," excerpts of your unvarnished feedback.

Here's how you can help improve Fodor's for all of us.

Tell us when we're right. We rely on local writers to give you an insider's perspective. But our writers and staff editors—who are the best in the business—depend on you. Your positive feedback is a vote to renew our recommendations for the next edition.

Tell us when we're wrong. We're proud that we update most of our guides every year. But we're not perfect. Things change. Hotels cut services. Museums change hours. Charming cafés lose charm. If our writer didn't quite capture the essence of a place, tell us how you'd do it differently. If any of our descriptions are inaccurate or inadequate, we'll incorporate your changes in the next edition and will correct factual errors at fodors.com immediately.

Tell us what to include. You probably have had fantastic travel experiences that aren't yet in Fodor's. Why not share them with a community of like-minded travelers? Maybe you chanced upon a beach or bistro or B&B that you don't want to keep to yourself. Tell us why we should include it. And share your discoveries and experiences with everyone directly at fodors.com. Your input may lead us to add a new listing or highlight a place we cover with a "Highly Recommended" star or with our highest rating, "Fodor's Choice."

Give us your opinion instantly at our feedback center at www.fodors.com/feedback. You may also e-mail editors@fodors.com with the subject line "Cancún, Cozumel & the Yucatán Peninsula Editor." Or send your nominations, comments, and complaints by mail to Cancún, Cozumel & the Yucatán Peninsula Editor, Fodor's, 1745 Broadway, New York, NY 10019.

You and travelers like you are the heart of the Fodor's community. Make our community richer by sharing your experiences. Be a Fodor's correspondent.

¡Buen Viaje!

Tim Jarrell, Publisher

CONTENTS

Fodor's Features

MAPS

WHAT'S WHERE

CANCÚN 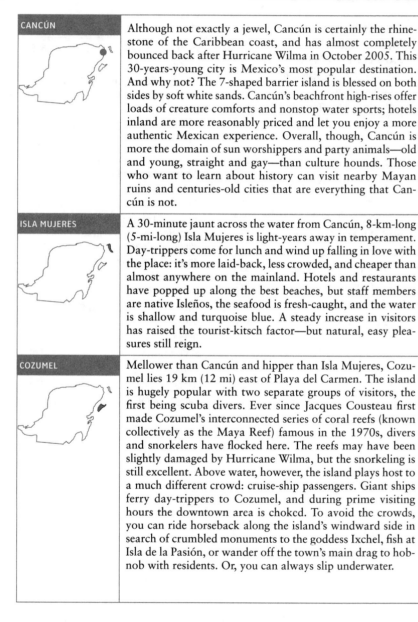	Although not exactly a jewel, Cancún is certainly the rhinestone of the Caribbean coast, and has almost completely bounced back after Hurricane Wilma in October 2005. This 30-years-young city is Mexico's most popular destination. And why not? The 7-shaped barrier island is blessed on both sides by soft white sands. Cancún's beachfront high-rises offer loads of creature comforts and nonstop water sports; hotels inland are more reasonably priced and let you enjoy a more authentic Mexican experience. Overall, though, Cancún is more the domain of sun worshippers and party animals—old and young, straight and gay—than culture hounds. Those who want to learn about history can visit nearby Mayan ruins and centuries-old cities that are everything that Cancún is not.
ISLA MUJERES	A 30-minute jaunt across the water from Cancún, 8-km-long (5-mi-long) Isla Mujeres is light-years away in temperament. Day-trippers come for lunch and wind up falling in love with the place: it's more laid-back, less crowded, and cheaper than almost anywhere on the mainland. Hotels and restaurants have popped up along the best beaches, but staff members are native Isleños, the seafood is fresh-caught, and the water is shallow and turquoise blue. A steady increase in visitors has raised the tourist-kitsch factor—but natural, easy pleasures still reign.
COZUMEL	Mellower than Cancún and hipper than Isla Mujeres, Cozumel lies 19 km (12 mi) east of Playa del Carmen. The island is hugely popular with two separate groups of visitors, the first being scuba divers. Ever since Jacques Cousteau first made Cozumel's interconnected series of coral reefs (known collectively as the Maya Reef) famous in the 1970s, divers and snorkelers have flocked here. The reefs may have been slightly damaged by Hurricane Wilma, but the snorkeling is still excellent. Above water, however, the island plays host to a much different crowd: cruise-ship passengers. Giant ships ferry day-trippers to Cozumel, and during prime visiting hours the downtown area is choked. To avoid the crowds, you can ride horseback along the island's windward side in search of crumbled monuments to the goddess Ixchel, fish at Isla de la Pasión, or wander off the town's main drag to hobnob with residents. Or, you can always slip underwater.

THE CARIBBEAN COAST

The dazzling white sands and glittering blue-green waters of the Riviera Maya beckon to sun worshippers and spa-goers as well as snorkelers, divers, and bird-watchers. Although sugary beaches are the principal draw here, the seaside ruins of Tulum, jungle-clad pyramids at Cobá, and several other Mayan sites are all nearby. This swatch of coast between Cancún and Tulum is popular with developers; jungle lodges and campgrounds now coexist with extravagant spa resorts. The town of Playa del Carmen is almost as big as Cancún, although it has a more authentic Mexican feel. Nature lovers can head farther south, to the pristine beaches of the Costa Maya or to the Reserva de la Biosfera Sian Ka'an, with more than a million acres of wild coastline and jungle.

YUCATÁN AND CAMPECHE STATES

Mérida, the capital city of Yucatán State, is the cultural hub of the entire peninsula. Bustling with traffic and swelteringly hot for much of the year, Mérida's restaurants, hotels, shops, and museums bring visitors back year after year. Weekends, when downtown streets are closed to cars and free shows are held on the main square, are especially magical. Outside of Mérida, villages offer charming shops and restaurants and shell-strewn beaches along the remote north coast. The state's major claim to fame, however, is its spectacular Mayan sites, including Chichén Itzá and Uxmal. Mellow and almost completely unvisited by tourists, Campeche is a world unto itself. Campeche City's historic colonial district is a lovely place to stroll.

Yucatán Peninsula

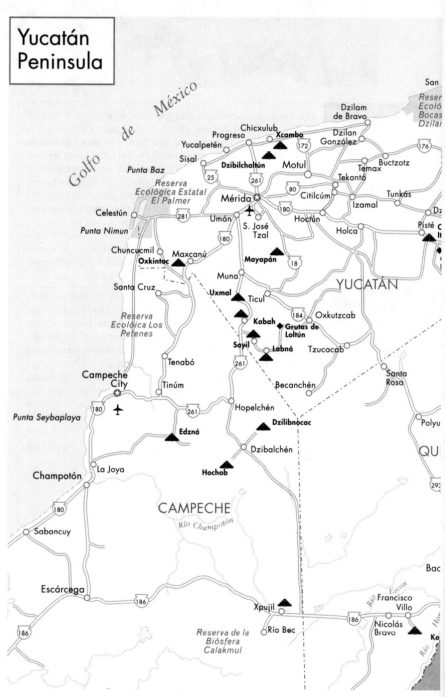

Golfo de México

San

Reser
Ecoló
Bocas
Dzilar

Dzilam
de Bravo

Chicxulub
Progreso
Yucalpetén   Xcambó   Dzilan
                                    González
Sisal   172   176

Punta Baz   Dzibilchaltún   Motul   Buctzotz
                                                Temax
        Reserva   Tekantó
        Ecológica Estatal   25   261
        El Palmer   Mérida   Citilcúm   Tunkás
Celestún   80   Izamal
                    Umán   180   Da
Punta Nimun   S. José   Hoctún   Holca   Pisté
                    Tzal   It
Chuncucmil   Maxcanú   180
    Oxkintoc   Mayapán   18

Santa Cruz   Muna   YUCATÁN
                    Uxmal   Ticul
    Reserva   184   Oxkutzcab
    Ecolóica Los   Kabah
    Petenes   Grutas de
                              Loltún
                    Sayil   Labná   Tzucacab
            Tenabó   261
Campeche   Santa
City   Tinúm   Rosa
        180   Becanchén
Punta Seybaplaya   261   Polyu
                    Hopelchén
                    Dzilibnocac   QU
            Edzná
                    Dzibalchén
        La Joya   293
Champotón   Hochob
    180
    Sabancuy   CAMPECHE
                    Río Champotón

                                        Bac

Escárcega   Río   Francisco
    186   186   Villo
186   Xpujil   Nicolás
            Reserva de la   Río Bec   Bravo   Ko
            Biósfera
            Calakmul

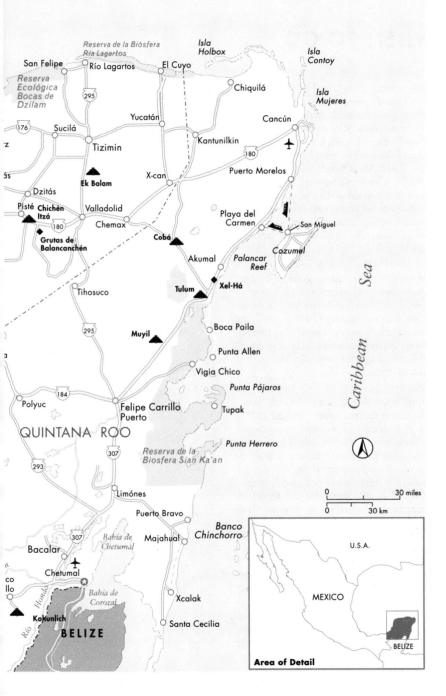

WHEN TO GO

High season along the Mexican Caribbean runs from mid-December through Easter (or the week after). The most popular vacation times are *Semana Santa* (Holy Week, the week leading up to Easter) and the weeks around Christmas and New Year's. Most hotels are booked well in advance for these holidays, when prices are at their highest and armies of travelers swarm popular attractions. Resorts popular with college students (i.e., any place with a beach) tend to fill up in the summer months and during spring-break season (generally March through April).

Off-season price changes are considerable at the beach resorts, but are less pronounced in Mérida, Campeche, and other inland regions. To avoid crowds and high prices, the best times to go are September through early December, May, and June, although May and June can be terribly hot and humid.

Climate
From November through March, winter temperatures hover around 27°C (80°F). Occasional winter storms called *nortes* can bring blustery skies and sharp winds that make air temperatures drop and swimming unappealing. A light- to medium-weight jacket or heavy sweater or shawl is recommended for travel in December or January, just in case. During the spring (especially April and May), there's a period of intense heat that tapers off in June. The hottest months, with temperatures reaching up to 43°C (110°F), are May, June, and July. The primary rainy season, July through the end of September, also is hot and humid. The rains that farmers welcome in summer threaten occasional hurricanes later in the season, primarily mid-September through mid-November. (Officially, the Caribbean tropical storm and hurricane season starts in June, but bad weather rarely arrives before September.) Inland regions tend to be 10° to 15° warmer than the coast.

Forecasts

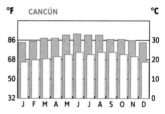

ABOUT
THIS BOOK

Our Ratings

Sometimes you find terrific travel experiences and sometimes they just find you. But usually the burden is on you to select the right combination of experiences. That's where our ratings come in.

As travelers we've all discovered a place so wonderful that its worthiness is obvious. And sometimes that place is so experiential that superlatives don't do it justice: you just have to be there to know. These sights, properties, and experiences get our highest rating, **Fodor's Choice,** indicated by orange stars throughout this book.

Black stars highlight sights and properties we deem **Highly Recommended,** places that our writers, editors, and readers praise again and again for consistency and excellence.

By default, there's another category: any place we include in this book is by definition worth your time, unless we say otherwise. And we will.

Disagree with any of our choices? Care to nominate a place or suggest that we rate one more highly? Visit our feedback center at www.fodors.com/feedback.

Budget Well

Hotel and restaurant price categories from ¢ to $$$$ are defined in the opening pages of each chapter. For attractions, we always give standard adult admission fees; reductions are usually available for children, students, and senior citizens. Want to pay with plastic? **AE, D, DC, MC, V** following restaurant and hotel listings indicate whether American Express, Discover, Diners Club, MasterCard, and Visa are accepted.

Restaurants

Unless we state otherwise, restaurants are open for lunch and dinner daily. We mention dress only when there's a specific requirement and reservations only when they're essential or not accepted—it's always best to book ahead.

Hotels

Hotels have private bath, phone, TV, and air-conditioning and operate on the European Plan (aka EP, meaning without meals), unless we specify that they use the Continental Plan (CP, with a continental breakfast), Breakfast Plan (BP, with a full breakfast), or Modified American Plan (MAP, with breakfast and dinner), or are all-inclusive (including all meals and most activities).

We always list facilities, but not whether you'll be charged an extra fee to use them, so when pricing accommodations, find out what's included.

Many Listings
★ Fodor's Choice
★ Highly recommended
⊠ Physical address
✛ Directions
🏚 Mailing address
☎ Telephone
🖷 Fax
⊕ On the Web
✍ E-mail
🎟 Admission fee
☉ Open/closed times
Ⓜ Metro stations
🖃 Credit cards

Hotels & Restaurants
🏨 Hotel
🛏 Number of rooms
✧ Facilities
🍽 Meal plans
✗ Restaurant
🖎 Reservations
⌖ Smoking
🍷 BYOB
✗🏨 Hotel with restaurant that warrants a visit

Outdoors
⛳ Golf
⛺ Camping

Other
🅒 Family-friendly
⇨ See also
⊠ Branch address
☞ Take note

IF YOU LIKE

Spas

There are dozens of spa resorts scattered throughout the Yucatán peninsula; most of them are along the coast. Here decadent body treatments are offered in luxurious seaside settings. Some incorporate indigenous healing techniques into their services, using *temazcal* (an ancient Mayan sweat-lodge ritual), and plant extracts in aromatherapy facials. Others feature seawater and marine algae in mineral-rich thalassotherapy treatments; still others go the high-tech route with cutting-edge flotarium tanks and guided Pilates sessions. You won't have any trouble getting your pampering fix here—especially in the areas around Playa del Carmen and the rest of the Riviera Maya—but you'll likely pay top dollar for it.

Spas here that get the most consistent raves include Punta Tanchacté's **Paraíso de la Bonita Resort and Thalasso,** where you can soak away stress in specially built saltwater pools; **Maroma** in Punta Maroma, with its relaxing, womb-like flotation tanks; and **Ikal del Mar,** in Punta Bete, where you can follow up your Mayan massage with a sumptuous Yucatecan meal. **Spa del Mar,** at Cancún's Le Meridien hotel, is justifiably famous for its seaweed hydrotherapy; and at the **Hotel El Rey del Caribe Spa,** also in Cancún, it's hard to imagine a sweeter way to end the day than a honey massage.

Diving and Snorkeling

The turquoise waters of the Mexican Caribbean coast are strewn with stunning coral reefs, underwater canyons, and sunken shipwrecks—all teeming with marine life. The visibility can reach 100 feet, so even on the surface you'll be amazed by what you can see.

Made famous decades ago by Jacques Cousteau, Cozumel is still considered one of the world's premier diving destinations. The **Maya Reef,** just off the western coast, stretches some 32 km (20 mi)—and more than 100 dive operators on the island offer deep dives, drift dives, wall dives, night dives, wreck dives, and dives focusing on ecology and underwater photography.

Farther south, the town of Tankah is known for its **Gorgonian Gardens,** a profusion of soft corals and sponges that's created an underwater Eden. Near the border of Belize, Mexico's largest coral atoll, **Banco Chinchorro,** is a graveyard of vessels that have foundered on the corals over the centuries. Experienced divers won't want to miss Isla Contoy's **Cave of the Sleeping Sharks.** Here, at 150 feet, you can see the otherwise dangerous creatures "dozing" in a state of relaxed nonaggression.

The freshwater *cenotes* (sinkholes) that punctuate Quintana Roo, Yucatán, and Campeche states are also favorites with divers and snorkelers. Many of these are private and secluded even though they lie right off the highways; others are so popular that they've become tourist destinations. At **Hidden Worlds Cenote Park** (on the highway between Xel-ha and Tankah), for example, you can float through cavernous sinkholes filled with otherworldly stalactites, stalagmites, and rock formations.

Mayan Ruins

The ruins of ancient Mayan cities are magical; and they're scattered all across the Yucatán. Although **Chichén Itzá**, featuring the enormous and oft-photographed El Castillo pyramid, is the most famous of the region's sites, **Uxmal** is the most graceful. Here the perfectly proportioned buildings of the Cuadrángulo de las Monjas (Nun's Quadrangle) make a beautiful "canvas" for facades carved with snakes and the fierce visages of Mayan gods. At the more easterly **Ek Balam**, workers on makeshift scaffolding brush away centuries of accumulated grime from huge monster masks that protect the mausoleum of a Mayan king. On the amazing friezes, winged figures dressed in full royal regalia gaze down.

At **Cobá**, the impressive temples and palaces—including a 79-foot-high pyramid—are surrounded by thick jungle, and only sparsely visited by tourists. In contrast, nearby **Tulum** is the peninsula's most-visited archaeological site. Although the ruins here aren't as architecturally arresting, their location—on a cliff top overlooking the blue-green Caribbean—makes Tulum unique among major Mayan sites.

Farther afield, in Campeche state, the elaborate stone mural of **Balamkú** is hidden deep within another temple, sheltered from the elements for more than a millennium. Thousands of structures lie buried under the profuse greenery of Mexico's largest eco-corridor at the **Reserva de la Biosfera Calakmul**, where songbirds trill and curious monkeys hang from the trees. These and other intriguing cities have been extensively excavated for your viewing pleasure, and throughout the peninsula, too-symmetrical "hills" hide mysterious mounds that only future generations will be privileged to explore.

Exotic Cuisine

Pickled onions tinged a luminous pink, blackened habanero chiles floating seductively in vinaigrette, lemonade spiked with the fresh green plant called *chaya*. Yucatecan cuisine is different from that of any other region in Mexico. In recent years, traditional dishes made here with local fruits, chilies, and spices have also embraced the influence of immigrants from such places as Lebanon, France, Cuba, and New Orleans. The results are deliciously sublime.

Among the best-known regional specialties are *cochinito pibíl* and *pollo pibíl* (pork or chicken pit-baked in banana leaves). Both are done beautifully at **Hacienda Teya**, an elegant restaurant outside Mérida that was once a henequen hacienda. The *poc chuc* (marinated pork served with pickled onions and a plateful of other condiments) is delicious at **El Príncipe Tutul-Xiu**, an off-the-beaten-path and very authentic restaurant in the ancient Yucatán town of Maní. *Papadzules*—crumbled hard-boiled eggs rolled inside tortillas and drenched in a sauce of pumpkin seed and fried tomatoes—are a specialty at **Labná**, in Cancún's El Centro district.

In Campeche, a signature dish is *pan de cazón*, a casserole of shredded shark meat layered with tortillas, black beans, and tomato sauce; the best place to order it is **La Pigua**, in Campeche City. The dish known as *tixin-xic* (fish marinated in sour orange juice and chiles and cooked over an open flame) is the dish of choice at Isla Mujeres' **Playa Lancheros Restaurant**.

Some of the Yucatán's tastiest treats come in liquid form. *Xtabentún*, a thick liqueur of fermented honey and anise, can be sipped at room temperature, poured over ice, or mixed with a splash of sparkling water.

GREAT ITINERARIES

CANCÚN AND DAY TRIPS

Cancún is the place where you'll likely start your visit, and if sunbathing, water sports, and parties that last until the wee hours of the morn are what you're after, you won't need to set foot outside the Zona Hotelera (or even your resort). If you're staying for a week or so, though, you should definitely check out some of the attractions that are easy day-tripping distance from Cancún: nature parks, Mayan ruins, and some of the world's best snorkeling and diving are all just a short drive or boat trip away and will leave you feeling immensely more satisfied with your vacation.

Days 1 and 2: Arrival and Cancún

After arriving at your hotel, spend your first day or two doing what comes naturally: lounging at the hotel pool, playing in the waves, parasailing, and going out for dinner and drinks. If you start to feel restless your second day, you can head to the Museo de Arte Popular, catch an evening performance at El Embarcadero, or take a ride into El Centro (Cancún city) and browse the shops and open-air markets along Avenida Tulum, and grab some authentic and delicious Mexican food while you're there.

Day 3: Cozumel or Isla Mujeres

Spend the day visiting one of the islands off Mexico's Caribbean coast. If beachcombing and a laid-back meal of fresh seafood under a palapa sounds like your bag, take a ferry from Puerto Juárez and head for Isla Mujeres; once you're there, chill on Playa Norte, or rent a moped and hit one of the beach clubs on the southeastern coast (stopping at the Tortugranja turtle farm along the way). If you like underwater sea life, drive or take a bus south from Cancún to Puerto Morelos, where you can catch a boat over to Cozumel. There are more than 100 scuba and snorkeling outfits on the island, all of which run trips out to the spectacular Maya Reef.

Day 4: Playa del Carmen and Xcaret

In the morning, grab your bathing suit and a towel, take a taxi to the Xcaret bus station near Playa Caracol, and grab a 9:45 bus to this magical nature park. You can easily spend an entire day here snorkeling through underwater caves; visiting the butterfly pavilion, sea-turtle nursery, and reef aquarium; and (if you reserve a spot early) bonding with dolphins. Alternatively, get up early and take a rental car south along Carretera 307 toward Playa del Carmen, about an hour and a half away. Once you arrive, head to Avenida 5 along the waterfront, where you can choose from dozens of places to lunch (if you want to splurge, try the ceviche or the namesake specialty at Blue Lobster). Then spend the afternoon either wandering among the shops and cafés and watching the street performers, or else jump in the car and head 10 minutes south of town to Xcaret.

Days 5 and 6: Tulum and Cobá

If you have the time, it's worth spending a day at each of these beautiful Mayan-ruin sites near Playa del Carmen; each is entirely different from the other. Cobá, which is about a half-hour's drive west from Playa, is a little-visited but spectacular ancient city that's completely surrounded by jungle; you can climb atop a 79-foot-high temple, explore pyramids and ball courts, all while listening to the calls of exotic birds and howler monkeys in the trees. Tulum, the only major Mayan site built right on the water, has less stunning architecture, but a dazzling location overlooking the Caribbean. After picking

through the ruins, you can take a path down from the cliffs and laze for a while on the fabulous beach below. Be warned, though: since Tulum is just a 45-minute drive south from Playa, it's the Yucatán's most popular Mayan site. You won't have much privacy here.

YUCATÁN AND THE MAYAN INTERIOR

If you have more than a week to spend on the peninsula, you're in luck. You'll have time to visit some of the most beautiful—and famous—ruin sites in the country, and to explore some authentically Mexican inland communities that feel worlds away from the touristy coast.

For Days 1 to 6, follow the itinerary outlined above in **Cancún and Day Trips.**

Day 7: Valladolid and Chichén Itzá

Get up early, check out of your hotel, and make the drive inland along Carretera 180 toward the world-renowned Chichén Itzá ruins. Stop en route for a late breakfast or early lunch in Valladolid, about 2½ hours from Cancún; one of the best places to go is the casual eatery at Cenote Zaci, where you can also swim in the lovely jade-green sinkhole. Continue another half hour to Chichén Itzá and check into one of the area hotels (the Hacienda Chichén is a terrific choice). Then spend the afternoon exploring the site before it closes at 5 PM. Climb El Castillo; check out the former marketplace, steam bath, observatory, and temples honoring formidable Mayan gods. Chill for an hour or two before the light-and-sound show, then turn in after dinner at your hotel.

Days 8 and 9: West to Mérida

Have a substantial breakfast at your hotel before checking out. Then either take an easterly detour for an on-the-hour tour at the limestone caverns of Grutas de Balancanchén, or head immediately west on Carretera 180 for the hour-long drive to Mérida. After checking into a hotel in the city (Villa Mercedes is an especially delightful choice), wander the zócalo and surrounding streets, take a horse-drawn carriage to Parque Centenario or to see the mansions along Paseo de Montejo, and then have a drink and a meal before returning to your hotel for the evening. Spend the next day shopping, visiting museums, and enjoying Mérida's vibrant city scene.

Day 10: Uxmal and the Ruta Puuc

Wake up early and drive south to the gorgeous ruins at Uxmal. You'll want to spend two to three hours exploring the site, which includes the mysterious, 125-foot-high Pyramid of the Magician. Afterward, you can return to Mérida, stopping first for lunch at Cana Nah near the ruins. Or, if you're spending the night in Uxmal, you'll have time after lunch to either lounge by your hotel's pool or tour some or all of the Ruta Puuc sites—Kabah, Labná, Sayil, and the Grutas de Loltún. The first three are Mayan ruins, the latter, a fascinating underground system of caves that once hid Mayans from invading Spaniards.

Days 11 and 12: East to Cancún and Departure

The drive from Mérida or Uxmal back to Cancún will take you some five or six hours on Carretera 180, so if you're flying out of Cancún airport the same day, get an early start. Otherwise, if you can afford to take your time, stop at the lovely town of Izamal on the way back; you can take a horse-drawn carriage tour of artisans' shops, visit the stately cathedral, or climb to the top of crumbling Kinich Kakmó pyramid. Arrive in Cancún in the afternoon, take a last swim on the sugarsand beach before dinner, and get a good night's sleep at your hotel before your departure the next day.

Tips

Since both the hotel/spa and restaurant at the JW Marriott have received a Fodor's Choice designation, you might splurge for this fabulous accommodation in the center of Cancún's Hotel Zone. You can also choose to stay in more rustic, reasonably priced lodgings in the downtown area—such as the charming Hotel El Rey del Caribe.

If possible, try to arrange days 8 and 9, in Mérida, during a weekend. Saturday evening and all day Sunday the city offers free concerts and folk dancing; in squares near the main plaza vendors sell crafts and homemade snacks, and the streets are closed to cars.

Despite this full itinerary, take every opportunity to rest—or at least get out of the sun—during the heat of the day between noon and 3 PM.

Driving is the best way to see the peninsula, especially if your time is limited. However, there's nothing on this itinerary that can't be accessed by either bus or taxi.

ON THE CALENDAR

WINTER December	**Fiesta de la Concepción Inmaculada** *(Feast of the Immaculate Conception)* is observed for six days in the villages across the Yucatán, with processions, dances, fireworks, and bullfights culminating on the feast day itself, December 8. **Fiesta de la Virgen de Guadalupe** *(Festival of the Virgin of Guadalupe)* is celebrated throughout Mexico on December 12. The **Procesión Acuática** highlights festivities at the fishing village of Celestún, west of Mérida. **Navidad** *(Christmas)* is celebrated throughout the Yucatán. Among the many events are *posadas,* during which families gather to eat and sing, and lively parades with colorful floats and brass bands, culminating December 24, on **Nochebuena** *(Holy Night).*
January	**El Día de los Reyes** *(Three Kings' Day / Feast of the Epiphany),* January 6, is the day children receive gifts brought by the Three Kings (instead of Santa Claus). El Día de los Reyes coincides with Mérida's **Founding Day.** Traditional gift-giving is combined with parades and fireworks. On **El Día de San Antonio Abad** *(St. Anthony the Abbot Day),* January 17, animals are taken to churches to be blessed.
February–March	**Carnaval** festivities take place the week before Lent, with parades, floats, outdoor dancing, music, and fireworks; they're especially spirited in Mérida, Cozumel, Isla Mujeres, Campeche, and Chetumal.
SPRING March–May	Parades are held on Benito Juárez's birthday, **Aniversario de Benito Juárez,** March 21, to honor the national hero. On the *equinoxes (March 20 or 21 and September 22 or 23),* shadows on the steps of the temple at Chichén Itzá create the image of a snake. **Semana Santa** is the most important holiday in Mexico. Reenactments of the Passion, family parties and meals, and religious services are held during this week leading up to Easter Sunday. Many businesses are closed on Labor Day, **Día del Trabajo** (May 1), as nearly everyone gets the day off. Celebrated throughout Mexico by masons and construction workers, the **Fiesta de la Santa Cruz,** or Holy Cross Day (May 3), is feted by the population at large in Celestún, Yucatán, and in Hopelchén, Campeche, with cockfights, dances, and fireworks. **Cinco de Mayo,** May 5, is the Mexican national holiday commemorating Mexico's defeat of the French army at Puebla in 1862. **El**

		Día de la Madre (*Mother's Day*), May 10, honors mothers with the usual flowers, kisses, and visits. Since 1991 the **Cancún Jazz Festival,** held the last weekend in May, has featured such top musicians as Wynton Marsalis and Gato Barbieri.
SUMMER	August	**Founder's Day,** August 17, celebrates the founding of Isla Mujeres with six days of races, folk dances, music, and regional cuisine.
FALL	September	**Fiesta de San Román** attracts thousands of devout Catholics to Campeche to view the procession carrying the Black Christ of San Román—the city's best-loved saint—through the streets. The two-week celebration culminates on September 28. *Vaquerías (traditional cattle-branding parties)* attract cowboy (and cowgirl) types to rural towns for bullfights, fireworks, and music throughout September. **Día de Independencia** (*Independence Day*) is celebrated throughout Mexico with fireworks and parties beginning at 11 PM on September 15, and continuing on the 16th. **Fiesta de Cristo de las Ampollas** (*Feast of the Christ of the Blisters*) is an important religious event that takes place September 17 to 27, with daily mass and processions during which people dress in typical clothing; dances, bullfights, and fireworks take place in Ticul and other small villages.
	October	Ten days of festivities and a solemn parade mark the **Fiesta del Cristo de Sitilpech,** during which the Christ image of Sitilpech village is carried to Izamal. The biggest dances (with fireworks) are toward the culmination of the festivities on October 28.
	November	**Día de los Muertos** (*Day of the Dead*), called Hanal Pixan in Mayan, is a joyful holiday during which graves are refurbished and symbolic meals are prepared to lure the spirits of family members back to earth for the day. Deceased children are associated with All Saints Day, November 1, while adults are feted on All Souls Day, November 2.

Cancún

Beach of Hotel Camino Real (Zona Hotelera), Cancún

WORD OF MOUTH

"Cancún is safe, but . . . use common sense. The bus system is easy, cheap and convenient. Walking is good also. We did the bar-hopping tour which ended at about 2 AM and we just walked back to our hotel. No problem. Please do not hibernate at your hotel. Get out, do some sightseeing, and check out some local bars/restaurants. If you don't, you're going to miss a lot."

–KVR

WELCOME TO CANCÚN

TOP REASONS TO GO

★ **Dancing the night away:** Salsa, cumbia, reggae, mariachi, hip-hop, and electronic music dizzy the air of the Zona Hotelera's many nightclubs.

★ **Exploring the nearby Mayan ruins:** Trips to remarkable sites like Tulum, Cobá, and Chichén Itzá can easily be accomplished in a day.

★ **Getting wild on the water:** Rent Jet Skis, a windsurfer, or a kayak and skim across the sea or Laguna Nichupté.

★ **Browsing for Mexican crafts:** The colorful stalls of Mercado Veintiocho will certainly hold something that catches your eye.

★ **Indulging in local flavor:** Dishes like *poc chuc* (a pork dish with *achiote* and onions) *and lime soup,* and drinks like tamarind margaritas pay respect to traditional cuisine.

1 El Centro. Cancún's mainland commercial center, known as El Centro, provides an authentic glimpse into modern-day Mexico. A colorful alternative to the Zona Hotelera, many of the restaurants scattered throughout this downtown area offer surprising bursts of culture and Mexican flavor. With more than 500,000 permanent residents living here, the shops, cafés, and open-air markets cater mainly to locals. Although the majority of tourists choose to bask on the beaches of Cancún, those who venture into the heart of El Centro will be glad they did–prices are much more reasonable and the food is outstanding.

2 The Zona Hotelera Norte. A separate northern strip called Punta Sam, north of Puerto Juárez, is sometimes referred to as the Zona Hotelera Norte (Northern Hotel Zone). This area is quieter than the main Zona, but there are some smaller hotels, marinas, and restaurants. This is also a good launching point for those heading to the nearby Isla Mujeres.

3 The Zona Hotelera. Ideal for those wanting to stay local, the Hotel Zone is structured along a 22-km

(14-mi) stretch known as Kukulcán Boulevard. On the Caribbean side, dozens of resorts and condominiums tightly line the beachfront like a row of Legos. On the inland side, Laguna Nichupté is home to water sports, shopping malls, seafood restaurants, and golf courses. Located at the northern tip of this main thoroughfare is a pack of nightclubs, discos, and bars–a nighttime favorite for Spring Breakers.

GETTING ORIENTED

Cancún is a great place to experience 21st-century Mexico. Over the past three decades it has turned into the Miami of the south, with international investors pouring money into property development. The main attractions for most travelers to Cancún lie along the Zona Hotelera–a 22½-km (14-mi) barrier island shaped roughly like the numeral 7. Off the eastern side is the Caribbean; to the west is a system of lagoons, the largest being Laguna Nichupté. Downtown Cancún–El Centro–is 4 km (2½ mi) west of the Zona Hotelera on the mainland.

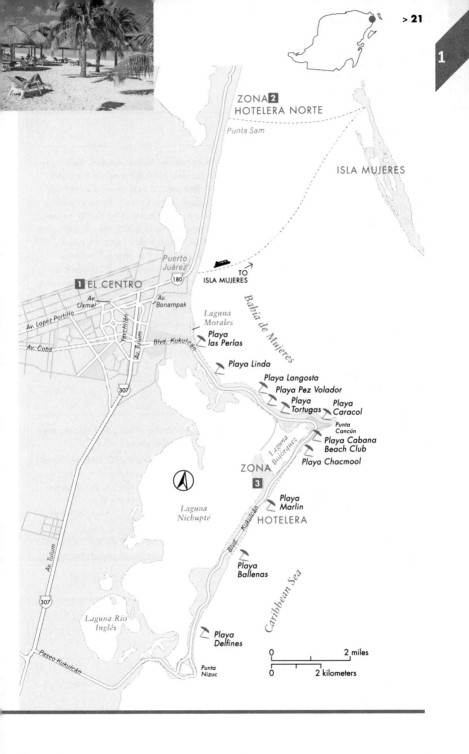

ZONA 2
HOTELERA NORTE

Punta Sam

ISLA MUJERES

Puerto Juárez

1 EL CENTRO

180

TO →
ISLA MUJERES

Av. Uxmal

Av. Bonampak

Av. López Portillo

Yaxchilán

Blvd. Kukulcán

Av. Tulum

Av. Cobá

307

Laguna Morales

Playa las Perlas

Bahía de Mujeres

Playa Linda

Playa Langosta

Playa Pez Volador

Playa Tortugas

Playa Caracol

Punta Cancún

Playa Cabana Beach Club

Playa Chacmool

Laguna Bojórquez

ZONA
3

Playa Marlin

HOTELERA

Laguna Nichupté

Blvd. Kukulcán

Playa Ballenas

Av. Tulum

Caribbean Sea

307

Laguna Río Inglés

Playa Delfines

Paseo Kukulcán

Punta Nizuc

```
0                    2 miles
├────────┬────────┤
0                    2 kilometers
```

CANCÚN PLANNER

When to Go, How Long to Stay

There's a lot to see and do in Cancún–if you can force yourself away from the beach, that is. Understandably, many visitors stay here a week, or even longer, without ever leaving the silky sands and seductive comforts of their resorts. If you're game to do some exploring, though, it's a good idea to allow an extra two or three days, so you can day-trip to nearby ecoparks and archaeological sites.

High season for Cancún starts at the end of November and lasts until the first week in April. Between December 15 and January 5, however, hotel prices are at their highest, and may rise as much as 30% to 50% above regular rates. Although costs drop from August to October, travelers might return home waterlogged rather than tan. For those who are not limited to peak-season travel, lower prices and pleasant weather are available from October 1 to December 15. Keep in mind that winter's strong north winds tend to eat away at the beaches, uprooting surface sea kelp. Less sand and choppy waters may result in overcrowded swimming pools.

If you plan to visit during Christmas, Spring Break, or Easter, you should book at least three months in advance.

On Mexico Time

Mexicans are far more relaxed about time than their counterparts north of the border. Although *mañana* translates as "tomorrow," it is often used to explain why something is not getting accomplished. In this context, *mañana* means, "Relax–it'll get taken care of ... eventually." Since the devastating hit of Hurricane Wilma in 2005, the reconstruction of Cancún has redefined Mexico as a fast-track country. Although smaller villages in Yucatán may still embrace the *mañana* mentality, the pace throughout Cancún and Quintana Roo is certainly quickening. It is still a good idea, however, to anticipate that many set appointments will start 30 minutes behind schedule.

The trick to enjoying life on Mexican time is: don't rush. And be sure to take advantage of the siesta break between 1 and 4 PM. How else are you going to stay up late dancing?

Tour Options

The companies listed here can book tours and also arrange for plane tickets and hotel reservations.

Intermar Cancún Caribe (✉ *Av. Tulum 290, at Blvd. Pioneros, Sm 8* ☎ *998/881–0000* ⊕ *travel2mexico.juniper.es*) offers tours such as snorkeling at Xel-Ha, shopping on Isla Mujeres, or exploring the ruins at Chichén Itzá.

Mayaland Tours (✉ *Calle Robalo 30, Sm 3* ☎ *998/887–0870* ⊕ *www.mayaland.com*) runs tours to Mérida, the Uxmal ruins, and the flamingo park at Celestún. Self-guided tours to Tulum and Cobá can also be arranged; the agency provides a car, maps, and an itinerary.

Olympus Tours (✉ *Av. Yaxchilán, Lote 13, Sm 17, Mza 2* ☎ *998/881–9030* ⊕ *www.olympus-tours.com*) specializes in tours around Cancún and can book your reservations to Xcaret, Xel-Ha, and other local adventure parks.

1

Booking Your Hotel Online

A growing number of Cancún hotels are now encouraging people to make their reservations online. Some allow you to book rooms on their Web sites; even hotels without their own sites usually offer reservations via online booking agencies, such as ⊕ *www.docancun.com*, ⊕ *www.cancuntoday. net,* and ⊕ *www.travel-center.com.* Since hotels customarily work with several different agencies, it's a good idea to shop around online for the best rates before booking.

Besides being convenient, booking online can often get you a 10% to 20% discount on room rates. The downside, however, is that there are occasional breakdowns in communication between booking agencies and hotels. You may arrive at your hotel to discover that your Spanish-speaking front-desk clerk has no record of your Internet reservation or has reserved a room that's different from the one you specified. To prevent such mishaps from ruining your vacation, be sure to print out copies of all your Internet transactions, including receipts and confirmations, and take them with you.

When booking a hotel online, be sure to ask if the hotel is currently undergoing renovation. Early-morning construction can be a painful wakeup call for Cancún party animals.

Dining and Lodging Prices

WHAT IT COSTS IN DOLLARS

	¢	$	$$	$$$	$$$$
Restaurants	under $5	$5–$10	$10–$15	$15–$25	over $25
Hotels	under $50	$50–$75	$75–$150	$150–$250	over $250

Restaurant prices are based on the median entrée price at dinner. Hotel prices are for a standard double room in high season.

How's the Weather?

The sun shines an average of 253 days a year in Cancún. The months between December and April have nearly perfect weather; temperatures hover at around 84°F during the day and 64°F at night. May through September are much hotter and more humid; temperatures can reach upwards of 97°F.

The rainy season starts mid-September and lasts until mid-November–which means afternoon downpours that can last anywhere from 30 minutes to two hours. The streets of El Centro often get flooded during these storms, and traffic can grind to a halt. During these months there are also occasional tropical storms, with high winds and rain that may last for days.

Need More Information?

The **Cancún Convention and Visitors Bureau** (CVB ⊠ *Blvd. Kukulcán, Km 9, Zona Hotelera* ☎ *998/881–2745* ⊕ *www.cancun.info*) has lots of information about area accommodations, restaurants, and attractions.

The **Mexican Association of Travel Agencies** (AMAV ⊠ *Blvd. Kukulcán, Km 9, Cancún Convention Center, Zona Hotelera* ☎ *998/887–1670*) can refer you to local travel agents who'll help plan your visit to Cancún.

Updated by
Marlise Kast

Cancún is a great place to experience 21st-century Mexico. There isn't much that's quaint or historical in this distinctively modern city, many of whose residents have embraced the accoutrements of urban middle-class life—cell phones, cable TV—that are found all over the world.

Beaches	★★★★★
Nightlife	★★★★★
Dining	☆☆★★★
Lodging	★★★★★
Shopping	☆★★★★
Activities	☆☆☆★★

Most locals live on the mainland, in the part of the city known as El Centro, but many work in the posh Zona Hotelera, the barrier island where most resorts are located. Boulevard Kukulcán is the main drag in the Zona Hotelera, and because the island is so narrow—less than 1 km (½ mi) wide—you would be able to see both the Caribbean and the Nichupté Lagoon on either side if it weren't for the hotels. Kilometer markers alongside Boulevard Kukulcán indicate where you are. The first marker (Km 1) is near downtown on the mainland; Km 20 lies at the south end of the Zone at Punta Nizuc. The area in between consists entirely of hotels, restaurants, shopping complexes, marinas, and time-share condominiums.

Cancún is not the sort of place you can get to know on foot, although there's a bicycle-walking path that starts downtown at the beginning of the Zona Hotelera and continues through to Punta Nizuc. The beginning of the path parallels a grassy strip of Boulevard Kukulcán decorated with reproductions of ancient Mexican art, including the Aztec calendar stone, a giant Olmec head, the Atlantids of Tula, and a Mayan Chacmool (reclining rain god).

South of Punta Cancún, Boulevard Kukulcán becomes a busy road and is difficult for pedestrians to cross. It's also punctuated by steeply inclined driveways that turn into the hotels, most of which are set at least 100 yards from the road. The lagoon side of the boulevard consists of scrubby stretches of land alternating with marinas, shopping centers, and restaurants. ■TIP→Because there are so few sights, there are no orientation tours of Cancún: just do the local bus circuit to get a feel for the island's layout. The buses run 24 hours a day and you'll rarely have to wait more than five minutes.

When you first visit El Centro, the downtown layout might not be self-evident. It's not based on a grid but rather on a circular pattern. The whole city is divided into districts called Super Manzanas (abbreviated Sm in this book), each with its own central square or park. The main streets curve around the manzanas, and the smaller neighborhood streets curl around the parks in horseshoe shapes. Be prepared to be frustrated. Local maps often look like a ball of yarn, and asking for directions rarely gets you anywhere. Few people seem to know exactly where anything is, even the locals who live in El Centro. When exploring on foot, expect to get lost at least once and enjoy it—you may just find yourself stumbling upon a courtyard café or a lively cantina.

Initially, tourists may feel out of their comfort zone when moving from Zona Hotelera to the bustle of El Centro. Here locals roam the streets, taking great pride in living in an authentic cultural quarter rather than in a zone of mass tourism. When driving, be sure to have a designated navigator pointing you in the right direction. Smaller side streets are one-way only, often looping back to the point from which you came. Main streets are paved with uneven cobblestones and tend to maneuver around circular islands generally known by their enormous landmarks. At times you may find yourself running in circles, especially near the roundabouts that branch off in eight directions.

In general, walks through downtown are somewhat unpleasant, with whizzing cars, corroding pathways, and overgrown weeds. Sidewalks disappear for brief moments, forcing pedestrians to cross grassy inlets and thin strips of land separating four lanes of traffic. Far from wheelchair-friendly, El Centro can be quite dangerous for the passive pedestrian. Be extremely careful when crossing busy roads, especially during rush hour, when traffic officers take to the streets.

Avenida Tulum is the main street–actually a four-lane road with two northbound and two southbound lanes. The inner north and south lanes, separated by a meridian of grass, are the express lanes. Along the express lanes, smaller roads lead to the outer lanes, where local shops and services are located. ■ TIP➜ **This setup makes for some amazing traffic snarls, and it can be quite dangerous crossing at the side roads. Instead, cross at the speed bumps placed along the express lanes that act as pedestrian walkways.**

Avenidas Bonampak and Yaxchilán are the other two major north–south streets that parallel Tulum. The three major east–west streets are avenidas Cobá, Uxmal, and Chichén. They are marked along Tulum by huge traffic circles, each set with a piece of sculpture. West of Avenida Tulum to Yaxchilán is where you can find authentic Mexican food at some of the best hole-in-the-wall cantinas. East of Tulum to Avenida Bonampak is considered the more upscale area of El Centro, where business executives tend to roam during lunch hour.

Numbers in the text correspond to numbers in the margin and on the Cancún map.

GETTING HERE AND AROUND

The Aeropuerto Internacional Cancún is 16 km (9 mi) southwest of the heart of Cancún and 10 km (6 mi) from the Zona Hotelera's southernmost point. While there are direct flights from some major U.S. cities, most flights transfer in Mexico City.

To get to or from the airport, you can take taxis or *colectivos* (vans). Although buses are allowed into the airport, they will only take you as far as the bus station downtown (where you will have to transfer to a public bus to get to the Zona Hotelera). Taxi rides within the Zona Hotelera cost $6 to $10; between the Zona Hotelera and El Centro they run $8 and up; and to the ferries at Punta Sam or Puerto Juárez, fares are $15 to $20 or more.

Autobuses del Oriente, or ADO, is one of the oldest bus lines in Mexico and offers regular service to Puerto Morelos and Playa del Carmen every 15 minutes from 4 AM until midnight. Playa Express has express buses that leave from a small terminal across from the main bus station every 10 minutes for Puerto Morelos and Playa del Carmen. Mayab Bus Lines has first- and second-class buses leaving for destinations along the Riviera Maya every hour.

Although driving in Cancún isn't recommended, exploring the surrounding areas on the peninsula by car is. The roads within a 100-km (62-mi) radius are excellent. If you're heading south on Carretera 307 toward Playa del Carmen, keep in mind that access to some beach towns–like Punta Brava, Punta Maroma, and Punta Bete–is limited due to the construction of major resorts along the coast. Although technically public, some beaches can now only be accessed via a hotel entrance.

ESSENTIALS

Bus Contacts Autobuses del Oriente (ADO) (☎ *998/884–5542*). **Playa Express** (☎ *998/887–6782*). **Mayab Bus Lines** (☎ *998/884–5542*). **Terminal de Autobuses** (✉ *Avs. Tulum and Uxmal, Sm 23* ☎ *998/884–5542* ⊕ *www. ticketbus.com.mx*).

Currency Exchange Banamex (✉ *Av. Tulum 19, next to City Hall, Sm 5* ☎ *998/881–6403*). **Banorte** (✉ *Av. Tulum 21, Sm 2* ☎ *998/887–6815* ✉ *Plaza Flamingos, Blvd. Kukulcán, Km 11, Zona Hotelera* ☎ *998/883–1653*). **HSBC** (✉ *Plaza Caracol, Blvd. Kukulcán, Km 8.5, Zona Hotelera* ☎ *998/883–4652*).

Internet Internet B@r (✉ *Forum-by-the-Sea, Blvd. Kukulcán, Km 9.5, Zona Hotelera* ☎ *998/883–1042*). **Infonet** (✉ *Plaza las Americas, Av. Tulum, Sm 4 and Sm 9* ☎ *998/887–9130*). **Internet Café** (✉ *Av. Tulum 10, behind Comercial Mexicana, across from bus station, Sm 2* ☎ *998/887–3168*).

Mail and Shipping Correos (Post Office) (✉ *Avs. Sunyaxchén and Xel-Há, Sm 26* ☎ *998/884–1418*). **DHL** (✉ *Av. Tulum 29, Sm 5* ☎ *998/892–8449*). **Federal Express** (✉ *Av. Tulum 31, Sm 23* ☎ *998/887–4003*). **Mas Mail Center Inc.** (✉ *Av. Xpuhil 3, behind Mercado 28, Sm 27* ☎ *998/887–4918*).

Medical Assistance Hospital Amat (emergency hospital) (✉ *Av. Náder 13, Sm 2* ☎ *998/887–4422*). **Hospital Americano** (✉ *Retorno Viento 15, Sm 4* ☎ *998/884–6133*). **Hospital de las Americas** (✉ *Avs. Bonampak and Nichupté, next to Plaza las Américas, Sm 7* ☎ *998/881–3400, 998/881–3434 for emergencies*). **Municipal Police** (☎ *998/884–1913*). **Red Cross** (✉ *Avs. Xcaret and Labná, Sm 21* ☎ *998/884–1616*). **Tourist Assistance Office** (☎ *998/884–8073*). **Green Angels (for highway breakdowns)** (☎ *078*).

Rental Cars Adocar Rental (✉ *Plaza Nautilus, Blvd. Kukulcán, Km 3.5, Zona Hotelera* ☎ *998/849–4233* ⊕ *www.adocarrental.com*). **Buster Renta Car** (✉ *Hotel Holiday Inn Arenas, Blvd. Kukulcán, Km 2.5, Zona Hotelera* ☎ *998/882–2800* ⊕ *www.busterrentacar.com*). **Caribetur Rent a Car** (✉ *Plaza Tropical, Av. Tulum 192, Local 16, Sm 4* ☎ *998/880–9167 or 01800/821–8854* ⊕ *www.caribetur.com*). **Mónaco Rent a Car** (✉ *Av. Yaxchilán 65, Lote 5, Sm 25* ☎ *998/884–7843* ⊕ *www.monacorentacar.com*).

EXPLORING

The best way to explore Cancún is by hopping on one of the public buses that run between Zona Hotelera and El Centro. The cost is 75¢ no matter the distance you travel. Don't be alarmed if a man in a clown suit roams the aisle in search of money. At night the buses come alive with all sorts of amateur performers, from accordionists to jugglers, hoping to earn them a few pesos.

TOP ATTRACTIONS

4 El Centro. Nearly two decades ago, downtown Cancún was the place to be after a day at the beach. The once-barren Hotel Zone had very limited dining options, so tourists strolled the active streets of Avenida Tulum, Xachilan, and Parque de las Palapas. With the emergence of luxury resorts and mass tourism, a major shift brought the focus back to the Hotel Zone. Today many tourists are unaware that the downtown area even exists, while others consider "downtown" to be the string of flea markets near the Convention Center. In reality, El Centro's malls and markets offer a glimpse of Mexico's urban lifestyle. Avenida Tulum, the main street, is marked by a huge sculpture of shells and starfish in the middle of a traffic circle. This iconic Cancún sculpture, which many locals refer to as "el ceviche," is particularly dramatic at night when the lights are turned on. The centro is also home to many restaurants and bars, as well as **Mercado Veintiocho** (Market 28)–an enormous crafts market just off avenidas Yaxchilán and Sunyaxchén. For bargain shopping, hit the stores and small strip malls along Avenida Tulum. While the Hotel Zone becomes increasingly dense and overcrowded, El Centro is booming with the development of Puerto Cancún. Construction of this downtown subset has been carefully designed to focus on the resident rather than the tourist. Shopping centers, marinas, golf courses, and over 2,500 condos are taking shape, making El Centro's bustling Avenida Bonampak the next "Blvd. Kukulcán."

3 La Casa del Arte Popular Mexicano. This entrancing folk-art museum is a

Fodor's Choice

★

must for anyone interested in Mexican culture and handicrafts. Located on the second floor of El Embarcadero marina, this museum looks fairly small from the outside. Inside however, it is brimming with original works by the country's finest artisans, which are arranged in fascinating tableaux. The collection represents different regions of Mexico–from nativity scenes sculpted out of Oaxaca's clays to the intricate *arbol de la vida* (tree of life) sculptures crafted in Metepec, Estado de México. Children will love the toy room, which includes an impressive display of *alebrijes* (dreamworld animals). In addition to the handicrafts, there are scenes set up throughout the museum to give visitors an idea of traditional Mexican life. The mannequins used in these re-creations, which include a church and a market setting, were actually modeled on real people that the museum director met during her trips through Mexico. Be sure to visit the museum's shop, which sells masks and figurines. ■TIP➔ **Other marina complex attractions include the Teatro Cancún, helicopter tours, a small restaurant, and ticket booths for boat tours and other attractions.** ⊠ *Blvd. Kukulcán, Km 4.5, Zona Hotelera* ☎ *998/849–4332 or*

Take a Tour

BOAT TOURS

Day cruises to Isla Mujeres generally include snorkeling, a trip to the center of town, and lunch. Cancun Lover's Cruise runs daily cruises through Laguna Nichupté and to Isla in a glass-bottom boat. Kolumbus Tours offers excursions to Isla Mujeres and Isla Contoy on replica boats of the *Pinta*, the *Niña*, and the Bermudian sloop of war *Cosario*. Sea Passion Catamaran offers both a day trip and night trip (which includes a lobster-tail and fish dinner on the beach) in 60-foot and 75-foot catamarans to Isla Mujeres.

Cancun Lover's Cruise (⊠ *Playa Tortuga/Fat Tuesday Marina, Blvd. Kukulcán, Km 6.5, Zona Hotelera* ⊕ *www. thelobsterdinner.com/*). **Kolumbus Tours** (⊠ *Punta Conoco 36, Sm 24* ☏ *998/884–5333 or 800/715–3375* ⊕ *www.kolumbustours.com*). **Sea Passion Catamaran** (⊠ *El Embarcadero, next to Museo del Arte Popular Mexicano, Blvd. Kukulcán, Km 4.5, Zona Hotelera* ☏ *998/849–5573* ⊕ *www. seapassion.net*).

BREATHING BUBBLE TOURS

If you like the idea of scuba diving but don't have time to get certified, check out B.O.B. (Breathing Observation Bubble) Cancún. Instead of using scuba gear, you can sit on a machine resembling an underwater motor scooter, and steer your way through the reef while wearing a pressurized helmet that lets you breathe normally. It's safe and requires minimal exertion. The two-hour tour through the Bahía de Mujeres costs $75 per person and includes a DVD of your adventure. Tours leave at 9, 11:30, 2, and in the summer also at 4:30.

B.O.B. (Breathing Observation Bubble) Cancún (⊠ *El Embarcadero, Blvd. Kukulcán, Km 4.5, Local E-3, Zona Hotelera* ☏ *998/849–4440 or 998/849–7284*).

HELICOPTER TOURS

If you want to view the Zona Hotelera by air, TOFLY7 operates a helicopter tour daily from the El Embarcadero complex next to the pier. The tour lasts 15 minutes and costs $89 per person. A maximum of three people are allowed in each helicopter.

TOFLY7 (⊠ *El Embarcadero, stairs to office are next to Museo del Arte Popular Mexicano, Blvd. Kukulcán, Km 4.5, Zona Hotelera* ☏ *998/849–5471 or 998/147–8088* ⊕ *www.tofly7.com*).

SUBMARINE TOURS

Aquaworld's *Sub See Explorer* is a "floating submarine"–a glass-bottom boat that submerges halfway into the water. On a 2½-hour cruise ($40) you can experience the beauty of Cancún's reef and watch the exotic fish while staying dry. Tours leave on the hour from 9 AM to 3 PM daily and include refreshments.

AquaWorld's Sub See Explorer (⊠ *Blvd. Kukulcán, Km 15.1, Zona Hotelera* ☏ *998/848–8327* ⊕ *www. aquaworld.com.mx*).

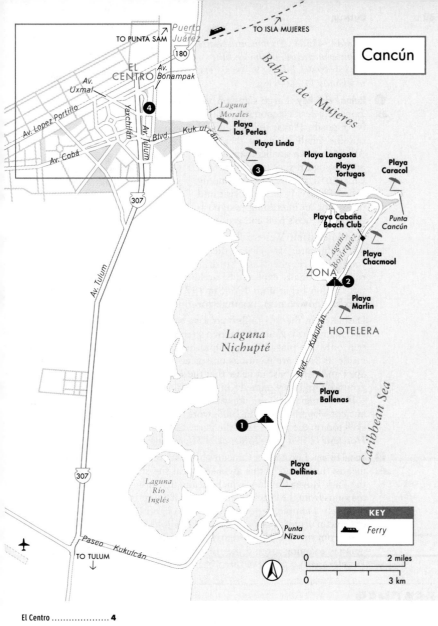

Cancún

998/849–5583 ⊕*www.museoarte*
popularmexicano.org/main.htm
🖃*$5* ⊘ *Weekdays 9* AM–7 PM,
weekends 11 AM–6 PM.

❶ **Ruinas del Rey.** Large signs on the
 Zona Hotelera's lagoon side, roughly opposite Playa Delfines, point
out the small Ruins of the King.
Although much smaller than famous
archaeological sites like Tulum and
Chichén Itzá, this site, commonly
called El Rey, is worth a visit and
makes for an interesting juxtaposi-
tion of Mexico's past and present.

BUSES MADE EASY

In conjunction with the Cancún
tourist board, Autocar and Publi-
car have published an excellent
pocket guide called "TheMAP"
that shows all the bus routes to
points of interest in Cancún and
the surrounding area. The map is
free and is easiest to find at the
airport. Some of the mid-range
hotels carry copies, and if you're
lucky you may find one on a bus.

First entered into Western chronicles
in a 16th-century travelogue, then sighted in 1842 by American explorer
John Lloyd Stephens and his draftsman, Frederick Catherwood, the
ruins were finally explored by archaeologists in 1910, though excavations didn't begin until 1954. In 1975 archaeologists, along with the
Mexican government, began restoration work on the 47 structures.

Dating from the 3rd to 2nd century BC, El Rey is notable for having
two main plazas bounded by two streets–most other Mayan cities contain only one plaza. The pyramid here is topped by a platform, and
inside its vault are paintings on stucco. Skeletons interred both at the
apex and at the base indicate that the site may have been a royal burial
ground. Originally named Kin Ich Ahau Bonil, Mayan for "king of the
solar countenance," the site was linked to astronomical practices in the
ancient Mayan culture. In 2006, workmen unearthed an ancient Mayan
skeleton on the outskirts of the park. ⊠*Blvd. Kukulcán, Km 17, Zona
Hotelera* 🕾*998/849–2880* 🖃*$3.50; free on Sun.* ⊘*Daily 8–4:30.*

❷ **Yamil Lu'um.** Located on Cancún's highest point (the name Yamil Lu'um
 means "hilly land"), this archaeological site stands on the grounds of
the Park Royal Cancún, which means that nonguests can only access
the ruins from the beach side. Although it comprises two structures–one
probably a temple, the other probably a lighthouse–this is the smallest
of Cancún's ruins. Discovered in 1842 by John Lloyd Stephens, the ruins
date from the late 13th or early 14th century. Keep your eyes out for
iguanas roaming around the ruins. ⊠*Blvd. Kukulcán, Km 12, Zona
Hotelera* 🕾*No phone* 🖃*Free* ⊘*Daily 9–5.*

BEACHES

Cancún Island is one long continuous beach shaped like the number
"7." It is virtually impossible to find a bad beach in Cancún; they all
have turquoise waters and powdery white sand. Unlike most nontropi-
cal beaches that are composed of grainy silica, the sand in Cancún is
made up of microscopic star-shaped fossils called disco-aster. The light
and fluffy texture stays cool underfoot, even when the sun is beating
down during prime tanning hours. By law, the entire coast of Mexico is

ECOTOURS

1

The 500,000-acre Reserva Ecológica El Edén, 48 km (30 mi) northwest of Cancún, is in the area known as Yalahau. The reserve was established by one of Mexico's leading naturalists, Arturo Gómez-Pompa, and his nephew, Marco Lazcano-Barrero, and is dedicated to research and conservation. It offers excursions for people interested in exploring wetlands, mangrove swamps, sand dunes, savannas, and tropical forests. Activities include bird-watching, animal-tracking, stargazing, and archaeology. You must call to make an appointment before you visit the site; rates are $75 per person for a full-day visit. If you're not into roughing it, these trips aren't for you.

Eco Colors runs adventure tours to the wildlife reserves at Isla Holbox and Sian Ka'an, El Edén, and to remote Mayan ruin sites. The company also offers bird-watching, kayaking, camping, and biking excursions around the peninsula. They operate day trips (from $48 to $205), three-day trips ($336 to $400), and seven-day trips (from $780 to $1,500). MayaSites Travel Services offers educational eco-tours for families to a variety of Mayan ruins–including five-day trips to Chichén Itzá during the spring equinox (rates start at $1,100 per person). The outfit also operates custom tours for small groups to ruins throughout the Maya Riviera. Naturama runs ecological tours to 20 different areas, including Isla Contoy, Xcaret, and Xel-Há. Rates range from $54 per person for a jungle tour to $200 per person for the SeaTrek excursion that includes swimming with dolphins.

Eco Colors (⊠ *Calle Camarón 32, Sm 27* 🖼️ *998/884–9580* ⊕ *www.ecotravelmexico.com*). **MayaSites Travel Services** (⊠ *1217 Truman Av. SE, Albuquerque, NM* 🖼️ *505/255–2279 or 877/620–8715* ⊕ *www.mayasites. com*). **Reserva Ecológica El Edén** (🖼️ *998/880–5032*). **Naturama** (⊠ *Blvd. Kukulcán, Km 9, Zona Hotelera* 🖼️ *998/883–3320* ⊕ *www. naturama.com.mx*).

federal property and open to the public. In reality, security guards discourage locals from using the beaches outside hotels. Some all-inclusives distribute neon wristbands to guests and do not let those without a wristband access the beach via the hotel. Everyone is welcome to walk along the beach as long as long as you enter and exit from one of the public points–the problem is that these points are often miles apart. One way around the situation is to find a hotel open to the public, go into the lobby bar for a drink or snack, and afterward go for a swim. Beaches that are not utilized by hotels have seaweed on their shores. All beaches can be reached by public transportation; just let the driver know where you are headed.

For those with young children, it is best to head to the beaches facing Bahía de Mujeres at the top of the "7." They tend to be less crowded and more sheltered than beaches on the Caribbean side. Wide beaches and shallow waters make the northern tip ideal for those wanting to snorkel or swim. Forming the right side of the "7" are beaches facing the Caribbean Sea. Here riptides and currents can be somewhat dangerous, especially when the surf is high. For snorkeling, it is best to head to the southern end of Blvd. Kukulcán near the Westin Hotel.

Although it is generally reserved for water sports, swimming is also allowed in the salt-water lagoon. Keep in mind that motorized Jet Skis and speedboats rule the waters by day and approximately 25 adult crocodiles wade the banks by night.

Most hotel beaches have lifeguards, but as with all ocean swimming, use common sense—even the calmest-looking waters can have currents and riptides. Overall, the beaches on the windward stretch of the island—those facing the Bahía de Mujeres—are best for swimming. Farther out, the undertow can be tricky.

In December, strong north winds bring an increase in wave size that often eats away at the sand banks. Unexpected drop-offs along the shoreline can be dangerous, especially when visibility is poor due to murky waters. At times the coast guard will "shut down" the ocean due to high winds, causing all water sports to be put on hold. On the flip side, whitecaps are always a pleasant sight for the experienced kite-boarder, sailor, or windsurfer.

The beaches listed here are organized by location, beginning on the northwest side of the "7" facing Bahia de Mujeres, and continuing down along the Caribbean side toward Punta Nizuc.

■TIP→ Don't swim when the red or black danger flags fly; yellow flags indicate that you should proceed with caution, and green or blue flags mean the waters are calm.

ℭ **Playa las Perlas** (Pearl Beach) is the first beach on the drive heading east from El Centro along Boulevard Kukulcán. Located at Km 2.5, between Cancún mainland and the bridge, it's a relatively small beach on the protected waters of the Bahía de Mujeres and is popular with locals. There are several restaurants lining the beach; however, most of the water-sports activities are available only to those staying at the nearby resorts, such as Imperial las Perlas or the Blue Bay Getaway.

At Km 4 on Boulevard Kukulcán, **Playa Linda** is where the ocean meets the freshwater of Laguna Nichupté to create the Nichupté Channel. Restaurants and changing rooms are available near the Playa Linda launching dock. There's lots of boat activity along the channel, and the ferry to Isla Mujeres leaves from the adjoining Embarcadero marina, so the area isn't safe for swimming—although it's a great place to people-watch and there's a 300-foot rotating scenic tower nearby that offers a 360-degree view.

Fodor'sChoice Small, placid **Playa Langosta**, which has an entrance at Boulevard Kukul-
★ cán's Km 5, has calm waters that make it an excellent place for a swim.
ℭ There is a dock that juts out in the middle of the water, but swimming areas are marked off with ropes and buoys. The safe waters and gentle waves make this a popular beach with families as well as Spring Break-ers. Next to the beach is a small building with a restaurant, an ice-cream shop, and an ATM.

The calm surf and relaxing shallows of **Playa Pez Volador** make it an aquatic playground for families with young children. Marked by a huge

Mexican flag at Km 5.5, the wide beach is popular with locals, as many tourists tend to head to the more active Playa Langosta. Occasionally, sea grass washes ashore here, but by early morning it has already been cleared away by the staff of the neighboring Casa Maya Hotel.

Playa Tortugas, the last "real" beach along the east–west stretch of the Zona Hotelera, eroded greatly after Hurricane Wilma. There's still a small stretch of sand at the entrance located around Km 6.5 (next to Fat Tuesday) on Boulevard Kukulcán. The water is deep and the swimming is excellent; many people come here to sail, snorkel, kayak, paraglide, and use Wave Runners. Don't be fooled by the name–this spot is seldom frequented by *tortugas* (turtles).

Playa Caracol, the outermost beach in the Zona Hotelera, is near Plaza Caracol and the Xcaret dock. Located at Km 8.5, the whole area has been eaten up by development–in particular the high-rise condominium complex next to the entrance. This beach is also hindered by the rocks that jut out from the water marking the beginning of Punta Cancún, where Boulevard Kukulcán turns south. There are several hotels along here and a few sports rental outfits. This is also the launching point for trips to Contoy Island.

Heading down from Punta Cancún onto the long, southerly stretch of the island, **Playa Chacmool** is the first beach on the Caribbean's open waters. When accessing the beach from Boulevard Kukulcán, walk directly across the street from Señor Frog's. As in the case of Playa Caracol, development has greatly encroached on Chacmool's shores. There are a lot of rocks and little sand, but it's close to several shopping centers and the party zone, so there are plenty of restaurants nearby. The short strand to the south has gentler waters and fewer rocks. Changing rooms are also available to the public. The shallow clear water makes it tempting to walk far out into the ocean, but be careful–there's a strong current and undertow.

Those who want to be pampered in the sand head to **Playa Cabaña Beach Club.** Located at Km 9 behind The City Discotheque, this is a place where tourists can enjoy the full resort experience without booking into a hotel. Facilities include 32 beach cabanas, each equipped with misting machines and a personalized sound system. The $10 entrance fee also includes access to the multilevel swimming pool, sun deck, restaurant, and sushi bar. Craving a dip in the ocean? Just walk down the short flight of stairs that leads directly to what's commonly known as City Beach or Playa Gaviota Azul (Blue Seagull Beach). Here the waves break up to 6 feet during the winter months, making it one of the few surfing spots in Cancún. Chances are, you'll never want to leave your cabana. ⊠*Blvd. Kukulcán, Km 9, Zona Hotelera* ☎*998/848–8380* ⊕*www. playacabana.com* ⊠$*10* ⊗*9–5:30.*

Playa Marlin, at Km 13 along Boulevard Kukulcán, is a seductive beach in the heart of the Zona

Hotelera, accessible via a road next to Kukulcán Plaza. Despite its turquoise waters and silky sands, the waves are strong and the currents are dangerous. If this beach is crowded, you can walk in either direction to find quieter spots. Sun umbrellas and beach chairs are available for $5 per day. There is also a small tent where one can rent boogie boards, snorkel equipment, and motorized sports equipment. Although there are currently no public facilities, you can always walk over to Kukulcán Plaza if you need a restroom.

Playa Ballenas (Whale Beach) is located at Km 14 between Le Meridien Cancún Resort & Spa and Cancún Palace. This small stretch of sand and crystal water between the two hotels is open to the public. There are often jet-skiers zooming through the water here, and the strong wind makes the surf rough. Parking and beach access are available at Calle Ballenas.

Located near Ruinas del Rey at Km 20 where Boulevard Kukulcán curves into a hill, **Playa Delfines** is the final beach. Hotels have yet to dominate this small section of coastline, and there's an incredible look-out over the ocean; on a clear day you can see at least four shades of blue in the water, though swimming is treacherous unless one of the green flags is posted. Here you'll find plenty of sand (unlike many of the beaches that were hit by Hurricane Wilma) and surfers. It's one of the few places in Cancún where you can take surfing lessons. Although decent waves roll in during hurricane season, seldom do they hit "epic" status. At best, you might find choppy, inconsistent surf at Playa Delfines, Playa Chacmool, and City Beach. Those seeking more than just a ripple should avoid the northern beaches, where Isla Mujeres lies just off shore.

WHERE TO EAT

Cancún attracts chefs–as well as visitors–from around the globe, so the area has choices to suit just about every palate (from Provençal cuisine to traditional Mexican and American diner fare). Both the Zona Hotelera and El Centro have plenty of great places to eat. Menus at the more upscale spots change on a regular basis, usually every three to six months, so expect to be pleasantly surprised.

There are some pitfalls–restaurants that line avenidas Tulum and Yaxchilán are often noisy and crowded, and gas fumes make it hard to enjoy alfresco meals. Many of the finer restaurants and boutiques that were once there have since moved to Avenida Bonampak, making it the continuation of Boulevard Kukulcán. In a hunt for fast-track, high-visibility restaurants (and discos), many Cancún residents and tourists are steadily turning to Bonampak.

Zona Hotelera chefs often cater to what they assume is a visitor preference for bland food; one key to eating well is to find the local haunts, most of which are in El Centro. The restaurants in the Parque de las Palapas, just off Avenida Tulum, serve expertly prepared Mexican food. In 2008, Parque renovations brought in a handful of contemporary restaurants, all fighting to make Las Palapas Cancún's first, authentic zócalo (central plaza). The cluster of hostels and food markets make this area especially popular with backpackers and students. Famous for its taco scene, El Centro's Avenida Yaxchilán caters mainly to large groups and budget travelers. The atmosphere can get a bit shady at

CLOSE UP

Cancún's History

1

The first known settlers of the area, the Maya, arrived in what is now Cancún centuries ago, and their descendants remain in the area to this day. During the golden age of the Mayan civilization (also referred to as the Classic Period), when other areas on the peninsula were developing trade routes and building enormous temples and pyramids, this part of the coast remained sparsely populated. Consequently, Cancún never developed into a major Mayan center; excavations have been done at the El Rey ruins (in what is now the Zona Hotelera), showing that the Mayan communities that lived here around AD 1200 simply used this area for burial sites. Even the name given to the area was not inspiring: In Mayan, Cancún means "nest of snakes."

When Spanish conquistadores began to arrive in the early 1500s, much of the Mayan culture was already in decline. Over the next three centuries the Spanish largely ignored coastal areas like Cancún–which consisted mainly of low-lying scrub, mangroves, and swarms of mosquitoes–and focused on settling inland where there was more economic promise.

Although it received a few refugees from the War of the Castes, which

engulfed the entire region in the mid-1800s, Cancún remained more or less undeveloped until the middle of the 20th century. By the 1950s, Acapulco had become the number-one tourist attraction in the country–and had given the Mexican government its first taste of tourism dollars. When Acapulco's star began to fade in the late '60s, the government hired a market-research company to determine the perfect location for developing Mexico's next big tourist destination–and the company picked Cancún.

In April 1971, Mexico's President, Luis Echeverria Alvarez, authorized the Ministry of Foreign Relations to buy the island and surrounding region. With a $22 million development loan from the World Bank and the Inter-American Development Bank, the transformation of Cancún began. At the time there were just 120 residents in the area, most of whom worked at a coconut plantation; by 1979 Cancún had become a resort of 40,000, attracting more than 2 million tourists a year. That was only the beginning: today, more than 500,000 people live in Cancún, and the city has become the most lucrative source of tourist income in Mexico.

---

night. Deeper into the city center, you can find fresh seafood and traditional fare at dozens of small, reasonably priced restaurants in the Mercado Veintiocho (Market 28). The locals, however, rarely eat here during the day because of the high volume of tourists.

Dress is casual in Cancún, but many restaurants do not allow bare feet, short shorts, bathing suits, or no shirt. At upscale restaurants, pants, skirts, or dresses are favored over shorts at dinnertime. Unless otherwise stated, restaurants serve lunch and dinner daily. Large breakfast and brunch buffets are among the most popular meals in the Zona Hotelera. With prices ranging from $10 to $25 per person, they are a good value–if you eat on the late side, you won't need to eat again until dinner.

As of May 2008, smoking is prohibited in restaurants, bars, hotels, and other enclosed public spaces throughout Mexico. Business owners who do not adhere to the new law can be subjected to heavy fine–or even up to 36 hours in jail. Some venues in Cancún have begun constructing designated smoking areas, which may be separate rooms or open-air terraces.

The success or failure of many restaurants is dependent on how Cancún is doing as a whole. The city is currently undergoing a great deal of development, with properties being sold and major renovations being planned. Some of the restaurants listed here may have changed names, or menus, by the time you visit.

ZONA HOTELERA

$$$
ARGENTINE
✗**Cambalache.** This Argentinean steak house is rustic yet elegant with its dark wooden tables and arched brick ceilings. The house cocktail, *clericot,* made from red wine, sparkling cider, and fresh fruit, is prepared at your table. For starters, try the traditional *empanadas* (turnovers stuffed with spinach and cheese). Although tenderloin steak is the most popular choice here, the lamb threaded on skewers and grilled over a brick fire is also delicious. Be sure to leave room for *alfajor* (a crisp pastry dessert layered with caramel and pecans). The tango music coupled with views of Coral Negro market give this restaurant an international flair, and help you forget that you're inside a shopping mall. With enough room for 350 people, the dining room tends to get rather loud at night, and there's no outdoor seating. ⊠ *Blvd. Kukulcán, Km 9 at Plaza Forum, Zona Hotelera* ☎*998/883–0902* ▭*AE MC, V.*

$$$–$$$$
ITALIAN
✗**Casa Rolandi.** The secret to this restaurant's success is its creative handling of Swiss and Italian cuisine. Be sure to try the *carpaccio di pesce* (thin slices of fresh raw fish), the cheese fondue, or the mesquite-grilled rib eye. Appetizers are also tempting: there's puff bread from a wood-burning oven and a huge salad and antipasto bar. The beautiful dining room and attentive service might make you want to stay for hours, and there are pleasant lagoon views from the spacious terrace. ⊠*Plaza Caracol, Blvd. Kukulcán, Km 8.5, Zona Hotelera* ☎*998/883–2557* ▭*AE, MC, V.*

$$$
ITALIAN
✗**Cenacolo.** Reliably good pizza and pasta, handmade in full view of patrons, have made this fine Italian restaurant a favorite. Appetizers include a salmon carpaccio that practically melts in your mouth and a light calamari. One of the restaurant's best features is its extensive wine cellar. Although it's located inside a mall, the restaurant's main dining room is elegant, with stained-glass panels on the ceiling and live piano music. ⊠*Kukulcán Plaza, Blvd. Kukulcán, Km 13, Zona Hotelera* ☎*998/885–3603* ▭*AE, MC, V.*

$$$$
INTERNATIONAL
✗**Club Grill.** The Club Grill has re-created the upscale ambience of the swank 1960s. Guests can commence the night with a vanilla martini in the adjoining lounge while listening to the smooth sounds of live jazz. A five-course tasting menu, paired with boutique wines, changes monthly. The dining room here is romantic and quietly elegant–with rich wood, fresh flowers, crisp linens, and courtyard views–and the classic dishes

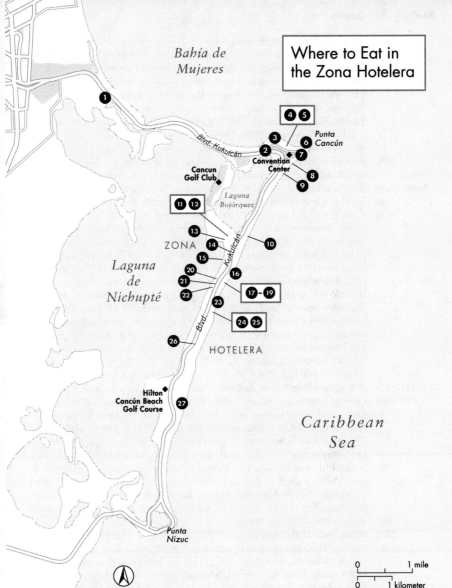

Where to Eat in the Zona Hotelera

Bahía de Mujeres

Punta Cancún

Blvd. Kukulcán

Cancun Golf Club

Laguna Bojórquez

Convention Center

ZONA

Laguna de Nichupté

Kukulcán

Blvd.

HOTELERA

Hilton Cancún Beach Golf Course

Caribbean Sea

Punta Nizuc

0   1 mile
0   1 kilometer

have a distinctly international flavor. The contemporary menu changes every three months, but might include starters like caramelized scallops and truffle corn soup, or main courses like chipotle-roasted duck or grilled Chilean sea bass. Like a waiters' ballet, the delivery of domed platters is synchronized among the servers, making the entire dining experience an unforgettable one. Reservations are recommended. ⊠ *Ritz-Carlton Cancún, Blvd. Kukulcán, Km 13.5, Retorno del Rey 36, Zona Hotelera* ☎ *998/881–0822* ⊟ *AE, D, DC, MC, V* ⊘ *Closed Mon. No lunch.*

$$$$
MEDITERRANEAN
Fodor'sChoice
★

✕ **Fantino.** Reflecting Mexico's rich Spanish heritage, this Mediterranean restaurant lives up to its reputation as one of the country's finest. Grandeur is at its peak in this ballroom setting, with long-stemmed roses and hand-painted ceiling frescos that subtly match the fine English china. Each guest, referred to by name, is treated to the melodious sounds of live piano music. Velvet walls mounted with candelabras are only overshadowed by the red satin curtains and ocean views. Each course is paired with its own wine, individually selected by Chef Andreas Schatzschneider. Designed to play with the senses, his appetizers moisten the palate in preparation for the seven-course tasting menu. Divine dishes include foie gras with artichoke hearts, duck prosciutto with truffles, and herb-crusted lamb with potato-bean timbale. All ingredients are hand selected from local farms or air-freighted to the hotel. Just when you think you've seen it all, the waiter wheels over a candy cart, featuring 10 glass towers of handmade sweets. Reservations recommended. ⊠ *Ritz-Carlton Cancún, Blvd. Kukulcán, Km 13.5, Zona Hotelera* ☎ *998/881–0822* ⊟ *AE, D, DC, MC, V* ⊘ *Closed Sun. No lunch.*

$$$–$$$$
ITALIAN

✕ **Gustino Italian Beachside Grill.** From the moment you walk down the dramatic staircase to enter this restaurant, you know you're in for a memorable dining experience. The dining room has sleek leather furniture, artistic lighting, and views of the wine cellar and open-air kitchen. The *ostriche alla provenzale* (black-shelled mussels in a spicy tomato sauce) appetizer is a standout, as are the salmon-stuffed ravioli and seafood risotto entrées. The service here is impeccable; the saxophone music adds a dash of romance. A private dinning area can hold up to 14 guests. ⊠ *JW Marriott Resort, Blvd. Kukulcán, Km 14.5, Zona Hotelera* ☎ *998/848–9600 Ext. 6849, 6851* ⚑ *Reservations essential* ⊟ *AE, MC, V* ⊘ *No lunch.*

$$$$
MEXICAN

✕ **Hacienda el Mortero.** As one of Cancún's first restaurants, the main draw at this restaurant is the setting: a replica of a 17th-century traditional hacienda, complete with courtyard fountain, flowering garden, and a strolling mariachi band. Although there's nothing outstanding on the traditional Mexican menu, the tortilla soup is very good and the chicken fajitas and rib-eye steaks are tasty. Fish lovers may also like the *pescado Veracruzana* (fresh grouper prepared Veracruz-style with olives, garlic, and fresh tomatoes). This is a popular restaurant for large groups, so be warned: it can get boisterous, especially once guests begin sampling the 110 types of tequila. ⊠ *NH Krystal Cancún, Blvd. Kukulcán, Km 9, Zona Hotelera* ☎ *998/848–9800 Ext. 778* ⊟ *AE, MC, V* ⊘ *No lunch.*

1

$$$ ✗**Hacienda Sisal.** Constructed to resemble a sprawling hacienda, this res-
MEXICAN taurant is warm and intimate, with comfortable high-backed chairs and
Mexican paintings. Menu highlights include the goat cheese and mango
salad, Tampico chicken breast, New York steak with stuffed pepper, and
annatto-seasoned grilled pork chops. Traditional dances from Mexico
and various regions of the Caribbean are performed here several nights
a week in the restaurant's El Patio section. There is a breakfast buffet
from 8 to 2 on Sunday, which is the only day on which Hacienda Sisal
opens early. ✉*Royal Sands Resort, Blvd. Kukulcán, Km 13.5, Zona
Hotelera* ☎*998/848–8200* ▱*MC, V* ⊗*No lunch.*

$$$$ ✗**Harry's.** Situated on the lagoon across from the Ritz-Carlton, this steak
STEAK house is easy to spot by the line of luxury cars at valet parking. High-
profile locals and visitors alike are drawn to the Vegas-meets-Beverly
Hills style of this flashy and contemporary establishment. Dominated
by onyx and marble, the interior is dimly lit; cedar beams and railings
add a touch of warmth. For two years, the creators traveled the world
in search of the best trends in culinary art. The result is a spectacular
menu featuring glazed duck, king salmon, Maine lobster, and USDA
Kobe beef served with aged Vermont cheddar cheese. If you can get past
the glass meat cooler in the lobby, the concept is impressive–all steaks
are aged in-house for 21 to 28 days, and then grilled and broiled to
perfection. Be sure to save room for Mini Indulgences, six tasty desserts
served in shot glasses. The waitstaff deliver a tower of cotton candy with
the check. All the stone indoors creates echoes; the outdoor seating is
recommended. ✉ *Blvd. Kukulcán, Km, 14.2 across from Ritz-Carlton,
Zona Hotelera* ☎*998/840–6550* ▱*AE, D, DC, MC, V.*

$$$ ✗**La Capilla.** Nestled in the belly of a brick cavern, this Argentine steak
STEAK house is dimly lit with wrought-iron chandeliers dramatically suspended
from wooden beams. The flavorful menu features Kobe beef carpaccio,
lobster tail, *arrachera* steak, and herb-crusted rack of lamb. Centering
the circular dining area is Cancún's most extensive salad bar, with exotic
cheeses, grilled vegetables, Italian prosciutto, and seven types of olive
oil. The creations of Chef Javier Carcamo are served on iron skillets
with skewered vegetables and roasted garlic that spreads like butter.
Be sure to check out the international wine cave, home to more than
200 types of wine. Vegetarians may want to look elsewhere; you can
smell the grill from the moment you walk in the door. Reservations recommended. ✉*CasaMagna Marriott, Blvd. Kukulcán, Km 14.5, Zona
Hotelera* ☎*998/881–2000 Ext. 16* ▱*AE, MC, V.*

$$$$ ✗**La Casa de las Margaritas.** With folk art and traditional textiles adorn-
MEXICAN ing every inch of space, this restaurant is a festive (though not exactly
tranquil) place to enjoy a Mexican meal. Appetizers include yummy
pork tamales and tortilla soup; for a main course, try apple and jala-
peño chicken, beef fajitas, or shrimp flambé. The rich *tres leches* (three
milk) cake makes a fine finish. Evening entertainment varies here,
and may include folkloric dancers and mariachi or accordion players.
✉*La Isla Shopping Village, Blvd. Kukulcán, Km 12.5, Zona Hotelera*
☎*998/883–3222* ▱*AE, MC, V.*

$$$ ✗**La Destileria.** Be prepared to have your perceptions of tequila changed
MEXICAN forever. In what looks like an old-time Mexican hacienda, you can

sample from a list of 120 varieties–in shots or superb margaritas–and also visit the on-site tequila museum and store. The traditional Mexican menu focuses on fresh fish and seafood; other highlights include the *molcajete de arrachera* (a thick beef stew served piping hot in a mortar), and the Talla-style fish fillet that follows a traditional recipe from Acapulco. Be sure to leave room for the caramel crepes–a signature Mexican dessert. Reservations are recommended. ✉*Blvd. Kukulcán, Km 12.65, across from Plaza Kukulcán, Zona Hotelera* ☎*998/885–1086 or 998/885–1087* ⊟*AE, MC, V.*

WORD OF MOUTH

"Try La Destileria: very good adult menu with local items and a gourmet twist plus a solid kids' menu–very kid-friendly (even has a playroom with constant cartoon videos and playground equipment!), most tolerant wait staff (in a country where kids are generally well tolerated as it is)."   –jw2

$$$$
MEXICAN
★
☾
✕**La Mansion.** A meal at this family-friendly Mexican steak house is as much about the experience as it is about the food. The attention to detail–cowhide-covered menus, cutting boards signed by celebrities–makes even a drink at the bar memorable. The poblano pepper cream soup, a local favorite that has been on the menu for more than 50 years, is a smooth starter; move on to the mouthwatering *cabreria* beef, served with creamed spinach and crispy potatoes. Steaklovers can sizzle their steaks to perfection on personal *parilla* grills–otherwise the kitchen will cook them to order. If you're feeling daring, try *machitos* (deep-fried small cow intestines) or *jamon pata negra* (cured ham presented in its entirety). For an after-dinner drink, try Café Mansion, a mix of brandy, Licor 43 and coffee that's set aflame tableside. La Mansion is also one of the few restaurants in Mexico that does not charge a corkage fee, and a good wine shop, La Destileria, is right down the road. There's live music nightly and a children's playroom with an onsite babysitter. ✉*Blvd. Kukulcán Km 9, Zona Hotelera* ☎*998/883–2304* ⊟*AE, MC, V.*

$$$–$$$$
ITALIAN
✕**La Dolce Vita.** This grande dame of Cancún restaurants delivers on the promise of its name (which means "the sweet life" in Italian). Whether you dine indoors or on the terrace overlooking the lagoon, the candlelighted tables adorned with fine linen and china and discreet waiters will make you feel as if you've been transported to Italy. The Italian fare

WORD OF MOUTH

"La Dolce Vita is excellent! A seafood Italian restaurant. They have great fresh seafood. They have this dish where they bake fish (snapper, I think) inside a puff pastry. It is to die for!"   –egreen

includes homemade pizzas and pastas such as bolognese-style lasagna, veal ravioli, and calamari steak in shrimp and lobster sauce. The wine list is excellent. Be patient when waiting for your order, though–good food takes time to prepare. ✉*Blvd. Kukulcán, Km 14.5, Zona Hotelera* ☎*998/885–0161 or 998/885–0150* ⊕*www.cancunitalianrestaurant.com* ⊕*AE, D, MC, V.*

$$$$
MEXICAN

✕**La Joya.** The dramatic interior of this restaurant has three levels of stained-glass windows, a fountain, artwork, and beautiful furniture from central Mexico. The food is traditional but creative: the grilled beef prepared Tampíqueña-style is especially popular, as is the catch of the day wrapped in maguey leaves. Performances by folkloric dancers and a mariachi band add to the ambience. There's a designated cigar lounge, making La Joya one of the few remaining restaurants in Cancún where smoking is permitted. ⊠*Fiesta Americana Grand Coral Beach, Blvd. Kukulcán, Km 9.5, Zona Hotelera* ☎*998/881–3200 Ext. 4201* ▤*AE, D, DC, MC, V.*

$$$–$$$$
ITALIAN

✕**La Madonna.** This dramatic-looking restaurant is a great place to enjoy a selection of 180 martinis and cigars, as well as Italian food "with a creative Swiss twist." Guests are dwarfed by a massive reproduction of the *Mona Lisa* and towering Greek sculptures that frame the three-story restaurant. For starters, try the pan-seared mozzarella wrapped in prosciutto. You can also enjoy classics like lasagna, fettuccine with shrimp in a grappa sauce, Black Angus wrapped with bacon, and three-cheese ravioli. The lychee martini is a tad expensive but worth it. ⊠*La Isla Shopping Village, Blvd. Kukulcán, Km 12.5, Zona Hotelera* ☎*998/883–4837* ⊕*www.lamadonna.com.mx* ⌦*Reservations essential* ▤*AE, MC, V.*

$$$–$$$$
ECLECTIC

✕**Laguna Grill.** Intricate tile work adorns this restaurant's floors and walls, and a natural stream divides the open-air dining room, which overlooks the lagoon. Delectable menu options such as an Asian-inspired mojito shrimp entrée and fettuccini with lobster satays match the beautiful setting. Their newly added vegetarian selections include organic soba pasta with teriyaki sautéed vegetables. For dessert there's a Bailey's crème brûlée and a dairy-free fruit dish topped with coconut foam. ⊠*Blvd. Kukulcán, Km 15.6, Zona Hotelera* ☎*998/885–0267* ⊕*www.lagunagrill.com.mx* ▤*AE, D, MC, V.*

$$$$
MEDITERRANEAN
Fodor's Choice
★

✕**Le Basilic.** If heaven had a restaurant, this would be it. Arched bay windows, checkered marble floors, live classical music, and exquisite garden views create the backdrop for this ideal spot for couples. The 14 chestnut tables surround a sunken gazebo where long-stemmed orchids bloom under glass. The dishes here—created by French chef Henri Charvet—are served beneath silver domes by pleasant tuxedoed waiters. The menu changes every four months, but it is always comprised of French-Mediterranean cuisine, from fresh tuna and sea scallops to seared duck and roasted lamb. As a keepsake, guests are presented with a box of French truffles and elegant recipe cards recapping the bill of fare. The dress code is elegant and reservations are recommended. ⊠*Fiesta Americana Grand Coral Beach, Blvd. Kukulcán, Km 9.5, Zona Hotelera* ☎*998/881–3200 Ext. 4220, 4221, 4223* ▤*AE, D, DC, MC, V* ⊘*Closed Sun. No lunch.*

$$$–$$$$
JAPANESE

✕**Mikado.** Sit around the *teppanyaki* tables and watch the utensils fly as the showmen chefs here prepare steaks, seafood, and vegetables. The menu includes Thai as well as Japanese specialties such as futo rolls, seafood curry, and panfried sea bass. The sushi, tempura, grilled salmon, and beef teriyaki are feasts fit for a shogun. Unlike most restaurants in Cancún, however, there is no outdoor seating or scenic view. ⊠*CasaMagna*

Marriott, *Blvd. Kukulcán, Km 14.5, Zona Hotelera* ☎998/881–2036 ⚑*Reservations essential* 🟰*AE, MC, V* ✪*No lunch.*

$$$$ ✕**Mitachi Seaside Grill.** The moonlight on the water, the sounds of the
SEAFOOD   surf, and the superbly attentive staff all serve to make this restaurant feel like a sanctuary. The beachfront setting is the star attraction here, but the menu includes a good variety, ranging from surf and turf to grouper fillet. The simple lunch menu of panini and salads transforms by night into delectable dishes like pistachio-and-almond-encrusted Chilean sea bass. With 24-hour notice, couples can enjoy the fixed "Romantic Menu," which includes three courses, a bottle of wine, and a private table in the sand. Live Latin jazz can be heard Tuesday through Sunday from December to July. Make sure you eat on a calm night–high winds may leave you with sandy sushi. ✉*Hilton Cancún, Blvd. Kukulcán, Km 17, Retorno Lacandones, Zona Hotelera* ☎998/881–8047 🟰*AE, MC, V.*

$$$–$$$$ ✕**Mocambo.** A strong draw at this beachfront Mexican seafood res-
SEAFOOD   taurant is the $20 all-you-can-eat buffet, which includes all the beer you can drink. The buffet special is valid Monday and Tuesday from 1 to 5 PM. From the menu, locals tend to go for the lobster in a curry-based mango sauce or the Cozumel shrimp in pineapple sauce. ✉*Blvd. Kukulcán, Km 9.5, Zona Hotelera* ☎998/883–0398 🟰*AE, MC, V* ✪*No breakfast.*

$$$–$$$$ ✕**Paloma Bonita.** Replicating three regions of Mexico, this vibrant set-
MEXICAN   ting features stone fountains, handcrafted furniture, and colorful linens imported from the western state of Michoacan. Waiters dressed in sombreros dance between the tables while women in traditional costumes serve olive bread from wicker baskets. This is one of the best places in the Hotel Zone to get authentic Mexican cuisine–so be adventurous! Traditional fare like chicken with two *moles* (thick sauces with chocolate and chiles) is fabulous here–and if you're unsure about what to order, the waiter explains the different chiles used in many of the dishes. Treat your palate to *queso fundido Oaxaca* (a specialty of bubbling cheese dripping from a stone pot onto handmade tortillas). The glass-enclosed patio with its water view is a great place to linger over tequila–or to try the tamarindo margaritas. The live music here varies between mariachi and Norteño style. Unlike the neighboring nightclubs, this lively atmosphere will remind you that you are in Mexico. Meals are on the heavy side though, so come with an appetite. ✉*Dreams Cancún Resort & Spa, Punta Cancún, Blvd. Kukulcán, Km 9, Zona Hotelera* ☎998/848–7082 Ext. 769500 🟰*AE, MC, V* ✪*No lunch.*

$$$–$$$$ ✕**Puerto Madero.** Modeled after the dock warehouses that have been
STEAK   converted into modern restaurants in the famed Argentine port city
Fodor'sChoice   Puerto Madero, this steak and seafood house gets rave reviews from
★   locals. It is the small touches–like fresh bread served in leather baskets, or martini reserves chilled in miniature ice buckets–that make this an unforgettable dining experience. The grilled octopus bathed in olive oil is exceptional and the Big Rib Eye generously serves two people. The Alaskan halibut steak, also a crowd pleaser, is prepared with white wine, shallots, and fresh pepper. No matter what you order, be sure to request a side of *papas infladas,* inflated potatoes that crackle on your

1

tongue. Adding to the cosmopolitan ambience is a fun-loving staff, most of whom have been there longer than 15 years. If the restaurant is too loud inside, ask for a table outside on the patio overlooking the lagoon. Reservations are recommended on weekends. ⊠ *Blvd. Kukulcán, Km 14.1, Zona Hotelera* ☎*998/885–2829* ⊟*AE, MC, V.*

$$$$
STEAK
✕**Rio Churrascaria Steak House.** It's easy to overlook this Brazilian restaurant because of its generic, unimpressive exterior–but make no mistake, it's one of the best steak houses in the Zona Hotelera. The waiters here walk among the tables carrying different mouthwatering meats that have been slow-cooked over charcoal on skewers. Besides Angus beef, there are also cuts of pork, chicken, and sausages, as well as crocodile, ostrich, and quail. Simply point out what you'd like; the waiters slice it directly onto your plate. If you are not a true carnivore, you won't be happy here. ⊠*Blvd. Kukulcán, Km 3.5, Zona Hotelera* ☎*998/849–9040* ⊟*AE, MC, V.*

$
MEXICAN
✕**Santos Mariscos.** A tribute to the masked wrestling champion El Santo, this Mexican cantina is colorfully decorated with retro furnishings like rainbow lawn chairs and sculptures of the Virgin Mary holding plastic roses. A bright red bar dominates the downstairs, and there is an upstairs dining area and a small outdoor patio where guests can watch nature videos on the Discovery Channel as cars cruise Boulevard Kukulcán. Frequented by locals who live in Hotel Zone, this eatery serves great shrimp tacos with seven types of sauces. For those who want an alternative to the traditional flour tortilla, try the fried cheese taco. The tamarindo margaritas are also very refreshing. Located just south of La Isla Shopping Village, this cantina is marked by a string of Christmas lights dangling over the patio. This is not a fine dining restaurant, so don't be surprised if the one waiter on staff serves your table in stages. ⊠*Blvd. Kukulcán, Km 12.7, Zona Hotelera* ☎*998/840–6300* ⊟*AE, MC, V.*

$$–$$$
THAI
✕**Thai Lounge.** Expect a truly unique dining experience from the moment you walk into this garden oasis. After all, not many restaurants have a dolphin aquarium in the bar area. The individual huts with thatched roofs provide an intimate setting to sample spicy Thai dishes like roasted duck in coconut red curry, and the house favorite, a deep-fried fish fillet prepared with ginger, garlic, and a tamarind chile sauce. Reservations are recommended. ⊠*Plaza la Isla shopping center Blvd. Kukulcán, Km 12.5, Zona Hotelera* ☎*998/883–1401* ⊟*AE, MC, V* ☉*No breakfast or lunch.*

EL CENTRO

$–$$
VEGETARIAN
✕**100% Natural.** You'll be surrounded by plants and modern Mayan sculptures when you eat at this open-air restaurant. The menu has soups, salads, fresh fruit drinks, and other vegetarian items, though egg dishes, sandwiches, grilled chicken and fish, and Mexican and Italian specialties are also available. The neighboring 100% Integral shop sells whole wheat breads and other goodies. ⊠*Av. Sunyaxchén 62, Sm 25, El Centro* ☎*998/884–0102* ⊟*AE, MC, V.*

$$$
ARGENTINE
✕**Bandoneon.** From the moment you enter the restaurant, you might think you've taken a "right" turn and ended up in Buenos Aires. Every detail replicates the streets of Argentina, right down to the cobblestone

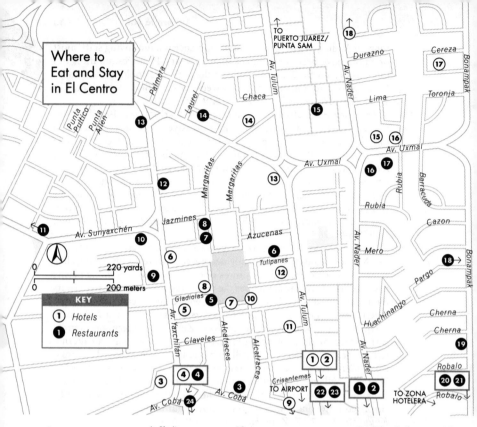

Where to Eat and Stay in El Centro

KEY
① Hotels
● Restaurants

Restaurants

Bandoneon	**20**
duMexique	**18**
El Cejas	**11**
El Oasis	**24**
El Principio	**21**
El Rincón Yucateco	**14**
El Tacolote	**3**
Iki Resto Bar	**5**
La Guadalupana	**1**
La Habichuela	**8**
La Parrilla	**12**
La Pasteleria–Crepería	**4**

La Placita	**13**
La Troje	**23**
Labná	**7**
John Gray's Downtown	**22**
Locanda Paolo	**20**
Mesón del Vecindario	**17**
100% Natural	**10**
Perico's	**9**
Rolandi's	**2**
Roots Jazz Club	**6**
Ty-Coz	**15**
Yamamoto	**16**

Hotels

Ambiance Suites Cancún	**9**
Antillano	**11**
Cancún Inn El Patio	**17**
Courtyard Marriott	**1**
Hostel Chacmool	**8**
Hotel Colonial	**12**
Hotel El Rey del Caribe	**15**
Hotel Kin Mayab	**13**

Hotel Plaza Caribe	**14**
Hotel Plaza Kokai	**16**
Hotel Sol Y Luna	**10**
Hotel Xbalamqué Resort & Spa	**6**
Los Girasoles	**3**
Maria de Lourdes	**5**
Oasis América & Sens Cancún	**2**
Radisson Hotel Hacienda Cancún	**18**
Suites Albatros Hotel	**4**
Suites Cancún Centro	**7**

floors, the dramatic tango music, and the indoor market that offers wine and pasta. In the center of the restaurant are two enormous lighthouse structures, guarding more than 100 Argentinean wines. The overwhelming menu includes starters like smoked marlin and charcoal-grilled provolone cheese. In addition to beef, Bandoneon also serves pasta, fish, and chicken. The sizzling rib-eye steak is extremely tender and succulent, but if you're health-conscious, ask for a leaner cut. If you still have room for dessert, try the brandy-soaked cake roll with caramel filling and dark chocolate sauce. With 160 seats, this place can get a bit chaotic at times, and reservations are recommended. ⊠ *Av. Bonampak at Nichupté, El Centro* ☎ *998/889–9500* ⊟ *AE, MC, V.*

$$$ ✕ **duMexique.** Discreetly located on the bustling Avenida Bonampak, this
FRENCH hidden gem shows no resemblance to a restaurant. Chef Alain Grimond and his wife Sonya have converted their home into an intimate dinner-party setting to create a dining experience unlike any other. Doubling as a gallery, the dining room features modern art, a grand piano, and a crystal chandelier that casts spectrums of light onto the pristine ceiling. Accommodating only 20 guests per evening, the restaurant begins the ritual with martinis in the tropical garden, decorated with tiki torches, dark rattan furniture, glass lanterns, and micro-suede cushions. The French menu (featuring five appetizers, five entrées, and four desserts) changes daily and is never repeated. Selections might include duckling with risotto or entrecôte with wine sauce. By calling ahead, you can request soufflé *de huitlacoche,* a delicacy made from mushrooms that grow on cornstalks. A fusion for the eye and palate, each course is a masterpiece of presentation. Be sure to visit the kitchen, where the awards of master chef Grimond are on display. ⊠ *Av. Bonampak 109, Sm 3, El Centro* ☎ *998/884–5919* ⚑ *Reservations essential* ⊟ *MC, V* ⊙ *Closed Mon. No lunch.*

$$ ✕ **El Cejas.** The seafood is fresh at this open-air eatery, and the clientele
SEAFOOD is lively–often joining in song with the musicians who stroll among the tables. If you've had a wild night, try the *vuelva a la vida,* or "return to life" (conch, oysters, shrimp, octopus, calamari, and fish with a hot tomato sauce). The ceviche and the spicy shrimp soup are also good, though the quality can be inconsistent. ⊠ *Mercado Veintiocho, right inside entrance on Avenida Xel-Ha side, Locales 90–100, Sm 26, El Centro* ☎ *998/887–1080* ⊟ *MC, V.*

$$ ✕ **El Oasis.** This appropriately named eatery offers a welcome escape
SEAFOOD from El Centro's busy streets. A small wooden bridge leads the way into a *palapa* (open-air hut), which is colorfully decorated with turquoise chairs, mosaic flooring, seashell lamps, and a bamboo bar. Diners can relax to the sounds of a cascading waterfall, skirted by palm trees and tropical plants. House specials include grilled seafood with rice, fish fillet with coconut cream, and shrimp with mango, tamarind, and guava salsa. This spot is popular with the locals; menus are in Spanish, and the staff doesn't speak much English. ⊠ *Prol. Yaxchilan, Sm 17, Mza 2, Lote 3, El Centro* ☎ *998/884–4106* ⊟ *No credit cards.*

$$$ ✕ **El Principio.** Despite its rather simple decor, this small and rustic bistro
ITALIAN restaurant, a lunch-hour favorite among Cancún execs, is arguably the best place in town for pasta. The owner, José Campos Frias, is a thirty-

something cooking genius. His dishes fuse traditional Italian cuisine with his grandmother's Mexican recipes. The salmon and mango salad with cilantro dressing is a meal in itself. Those with hearty appetites should try the exotic oriental spaghetti or the meatball panini in chipotle sauce. The portions here are enormous (two people often share one entrée). There are only eight tables, so it gets crowded at times; takeout is also available. Lunch is served beginning at 1 PM. ⊠ *Ave. Bonampak 227, Sm 4, El Centro* ☎998/892–8499 ▤*MC, V* ⊘*Closed Mon.*

$ ✕**El Rincón Yucateco.** It's so small that the tables spill out onto the street–
MEXICAN but that makes it a great place to people-watch. The traditional Yucatecan dishes here are outstanding; the *panuchos* (puffed corn tortillas stuffed with black beans and topped with shredded pork), the *sopa de lima* (shredded chicken in a tangy broth of chicken stock and lime juice), and the *cochinita pibil* (a slow-roasted pork dish) should not be missed. ⊠*Av. Uxmal 35, Sm 23, El Centro* ☎998/892–2459 ▤*No credit cards* ⊘*Closed Sun.*

$–$$ ✕**El Tacolote.** A great place to stop for lunch, this popular *taquería* (taco
MEXICAN stand) sells delicious fajitas, grilled kebabs, burritos, and all kinds of tacos. The salsa, which comes free with every meal, is fresh and *muy picante* (very hot). Ask for the two-person *parrillada*, a hearty sampler of barbecued meat, which comes with all the beer you can guzzle in one hour. A mariachi band plays nightly at 8. ⊠*Av. Cobá 19, Sm 22, El Centro* ☎998/887–3045 ▤*AE, MC, V.*

$$$ ✕**Iki Resto Bar.** Framing the town square of Parque de las Palapas, this
ASIAN chic, Zen-like utopia, from the owners of the renowned Laguna Grill,
Fodor's Choice dares to go where few restaurants have gone before. The thatched tem-
★ ple beckons you into its velvet sanctuary, discreetly lit with beaded lamps, Buddha candles, and teardrop crystal globes. The main lounge features a tropical tributary, a glowing cobalt bar, antique Victorian furniture, and a wine wall complete with a sliding ladder. Slow-spinning palm fans twirl overhead while the sounds of chill music ties together this eclectic setting. Those seeking a bit more privacy can hide away in the Balinese cabaña, sinfully adorned with overstuffed pillows and bamboo flooring. Blending styles in both decor and cuisine, Iki showcases contemporary Asian-infused dishes like oriental potstickers and coconut cream soup, all with a pinch of Latin flavor. The shrimp siva wrap, rolled in spinach and topped with red curry, is deliciously exotic. The young, hip staff also serves sweet conclusions like chocolate cake with green-tea ice cream. ⊠*Alcatraces 39, Sm 22, in front of Parque de las Palapas, El Centro* ☎998/884–7024 ⚐*Reservations essential* ▤*AE, MC, V* ⊘*Closed Sun. No lunch; open late.*

$$$ ✕**John Gray's Downtown.** This urban bistro, chef John Gray's fourth and
CONTINENTAL newest eatery, brings a touch of New York into the heart of El Centro.
★ Warehouse meets Zen in the informal yet sophisticated dining room, which has hardwood floors, exposed air ducts, dim light from dangling light bulbs, red velvet cushions, and a chicle tree enclosed in glass. Lack of detail on the chalkboard menu might deliver a pleasant surprise: the nondescript "duck" came on a bed of sweet potatoes, topped with chile, chipotle, and tequila sauce. The goat cheese pizza and Portobello mushrooms are excellent starters–follow with swordfish in brandy and

1

cream. You can watch the chefs at work in the open kitchen; there's also a lounge area with chilled-out music and powerful martinis. ⊠*Av. Xpuhil, Sm 19, Mz 2, Lt 24, El Centro* ☎998/883–9800 ⊟*AE, MC, V* ⊗*Closed Sun.*

$$

MEXICAN

✕**La Guadalupana.** This lively cantina serves steak, fajitas, tacos, and other traditional Mexican dishes to an appreciative, if sometimes noisy, local crowd. One wall is decorated with caricatures, mostly of political figures and famous bullfighters–very appropriate since it's on the bottom floor of Cancún's bullring. This is a good place to practice your Spanish. A mariachi band places nightly at 6. ⊠*Av. Bonampak, Plaza de Toros, Sm 4, El Centro* ☎998/887–0660 ⊟*AE, MC, V* ⊗*Closed Sun.*

$$$–$$$$

CARIBBEAN

★

✕**La Habichuela.** Elegant yet cozy, the much-loved Green Bean has an indoor dining room, as well as an outdoor area full of Mayan sculptures and local trees and flowers. Don't miss the famous *crema de habichuela* (a rich, cream-based seafood soup) or the *cocobichuela* (lobster and shrimp in a light curry sauce served inside a coconut). Finish off your meal with Xtabentun, a Mayan liqueur made with honey and anise. ⊠*Av. Margaritas 25, Sm 22, El Centro* ☎998/884–3158 ⊕*www. lahabichuela.com* ⊟*AE, MC, V.*

$$$

MEXICAN

✕**La Parrilla.** With its flamboyant live mariachi music and energetic waiters, this place is a Cancún classic. The menu isn't fancy, but it offers good, basic Mexican food. Two reliably tasty choices are the mixed grill (chicken, steak, shrimp) and the grilled Tampiqueña-style steak; choose from a wide selection of tequilas to accompany your meal. Reservations are recommended. ⊠*Av. Yaxchilán 51, Sm 22, El Centro* ☎998/887–6141 ⊟*AE, MC, V.*

$$

CAFÉ

✕**La Pasteleteria-Crepería.** This small café and bakery has comfortable *equipales* (rustic Mexican chairs) to plop into as you sample terrific soups, salads, and crepes (the turkey-breast crepe makes a perfect lunch), as well as a variety of sumptuous pastries baked on-site. ⊠*Av. Cobá 7, Sm 25, El Centro* ☎998/884–3420 ⊟*AE, MC, V.*

$$

MEXICAN

✕**La Placita.** The menu is simple but tasty at this colorfully decorated, casual downtown Cancún fixture, which offers indoor and outdoor seating. The mixed grill of sausage, steak, and pork chops is a stand-out, as are the glorious barbecued ribs and the tequila shrimp. A local favorite for 13 years is the *arrachera* (flank steak) served with a basket of warm tortillas. A selection of tasty pastas and salads is also available. A cold beer makes a perfect accompaniment. ⊠*Av. Yaxchilán 12, Sm 22, El Centro* ☎998/884–0407 ⊟*AE, MC, V.*

$–$$

ECLECTIC

Fodor's Choice

★

✕**La Troje.** From the moment you enter the garden patio, you'll feel as if you've tapped into a local hideaway. Potted ferns hang from wooden beams in this charming setting that's fashioned around oak trees that pierce through the bamboo roof. A brick staircase leads into the main dining area, where Chef Ana Cano and her two daughters prepare homemade pastas, pizzas, baguettes, and crepes. The colorful menu features 21 different salads, all with the distinctive flavors of fruits, nuts, cheeses, and tangy dressings. For a local favorite, try the grilled chicken stuffed with spinach, apricots, and cream cheese. Early birds can enjoy the full breakfast menu, which includes blended smoothies and fresh-squeezed juices. Although the prices are unbeatable, the service tends to be somewhat brisk. ⊠ *Av. Acanceh, Sm 15, El Centro* 🕾 *998/887–9556* ⊟ *MC, V* ⊘ *Closed Sun.*

$$
MEXICAN
★
✕ **Labná.** Yucatecan cuisine reaches new and exotic heights at this Mayan-themed restaurant, with fabulous dishes prepared by chef Elviro Pol. The *papadzules* (tortillas stuffed with eggs and covered with pumpkin sauce) are a delicious starter; for an entrée, try the *poc chuc* (tender pork loin in a sour orange sauce) or *longaniza de Valladolid* (traditional sausage from the village of Valladolid). Finish off your meal with some *guayaba* (guava) mousse, and Xtabentun-infused Mayan coffee. An all-you-can-eat buffet ($10) is served weekday afternoons from 1 to 5:30. You may want to linger and enjoy the trio that performs traditional Mexican music Friday through Sunday evenings. ⊠ *Av. Margaritas 29, Sm 22, El Centro* 🕾 *998/892–3056* ⊟ *AE, MC, V.*

$$$
ITALIAN
✕ **Locanda Paolo.** Flowers and artwork lend warmth to this sophisticated restaurant, and the staff is attentive without being fussy. The Italian-fusion cuisine–which blends both Japanese and Italian creations–includes black pasta with calamari and steamed lobster in garlic sauce. Despite the formal setting, the staff is laid-back and seems to know everyone who walks in the door. On any given night, many of chef Paolo Ceravolo's dishes are specials that do not appear on the menu; most are colorful and innovative, such as hot, coiled bread rolls interlaced with piquant mushrooms and eggplant. The international wines are a major draw for locals, as are the specialty lasagnas, which are revised every four months. ⊠ *Av. Bonampak 145, on corner of Calle Jurel, Sm 3, El Centro* 🕾 *998/887–2627* ⊟ *AE, DC, MC, V.*

$$
ECLECTIC
✕ **Mesón del Vecindario.** This sweet little restaurant, tucked away from the street, resembles a Swiss A-frame house. The menu has all kinds of cheese and beef fondues along with terrific salads, crepes, vegetarian empanadas, and baked goods. This is one of the few restaurants in El Centro that offers patio seating with a view of trees. ⊠ *Av. Uxmal 23, Sm 3, El Centro* 🕾 *998/884–8900* ⊟ *AE, MC, V* ⊘ *Closed Sun.*

$$$–$$$$
MEXICAN
✕ **Perico's.** Okay–it's a tourist trap. But it's really fun. Bar stools here are topped with saddles, and waiters dressed as revolutionaries serve flaming drinks and desserts while mariachi and marimba bands play (loudly). Every so often everyone jumps up to join the conga line; your reward for galloping through the restaurant and nearby streets is a free shot of tequila. With 370 seats, this place brings in vacationers by the busload. The Mexican menu is passable, but the real reason to come is the nonstop party. For a photo-op, stop in the lobby, where you can try on authentic Mexican clothing and pose with props like sombreros and maracas. ⊠ *Av. Yaxchilán 61, Sm 25, El Centro* 🕾 *998/884–3152* ⊟ *www.pericos.com.mx* ⊕ *AE, MC, V.*

$–$$
PIZZA
✕ **Rolandi's.** A Cancún landmark for more than 30 years, Rolandi's continues to draw crowds with its scrumptious wood-fired pizzas. There are 20 varieties to choose from–if you can't make up your mind, try the one with Roquefort cheese. Homemade pasta dishes like the veal-stuffed ravioli or seafood calzone are also very good. ⊠ *Av. Cobá 12, Sm 5, El Centro* 🕾 *998/884–4047* ⊕ *www.rolandi.com* ⊟ *AE, MC, V.*

$$
CAFÉ
✕ **Roots Jazz Club.** Locals and tourists mingle here to enjoy contemporary jazz and flamenco music (piped in during the afternoon but live

at night). The performances are the main attraction, but there's also an eclectic, international menu of salads, soups, sandwiches, and pastas. The tables nearest the window, along the quaint pedestrian street Tulipanes, are the best place to tuck into your *chíchí* (chicken breast stuffed with ham and veggies) or German sausage, since the air tends to get smoky closer to the stage. ⊠ *Av. Tulipanes 26, Sm 22, El Centro* ☎ *998/884–2437* ▭ *MC, V* ⊘ *Closed Sun. and Mon. No lunch.*

¢ **✕ Ty-Coz.** Tucked behind the Comercial Mexicana grocery store and

CAFÉ across from the bus station on Avenida Tulum, this inexpensive restaurant serves croissants and freshly brewed coffee that make for a delicious breakfast. At lunchtime, stop in for a huge baguette sandwich stuffed with all the deli classics. Lunches are a combination of sandwiches and salads served on freshly baked baguettes. Pictures of France adorn the walls of the small dining room. ⊠ *Av. Tulum, Sm 2, El Centro* ☎ *998/884–6060* ▭ *No credit cards.*

$$–$$$ **✕ Yamamoto.** The sushi here is some of the best in the area, and there's a

JAPANESE menu of traditional Japanese dishes (like chicken teriyaki and tempura) for those who prefer their food cooked. The dining room is tranquil, with Japanese art and bamboo accents–but you can also call for delivery to your hotel room. ⊠ *Av. Uxmal 31, Sm 3, El Centro* ☎ *998/887–3366, 998/860–0269 for delivery service* ▭ *AE, D, DC, MC, V.*

WHERE TO STAY

You might find it bewildering to choose between Cancún's many hotels, not least because brochures and Web sites make them sound–and look– almost exactly alike. For luxury and amenities, the Zona Hotelera is the place to stay. Boulevard Kukulcán, the district's main thoroughfare, is artfully landscaped with palm trees, sculpted bushes, waterfalls, and tiered pools. The hotels pride themselves on delivering endless opportunities for fun; most have water sports, golf, tennis, kids' clubs, fitness centers, spas, shopping, entertainment, dining, and tours and excursions (along with warm, attentive Mexican service). None of this comes cheap, however; hotels here are expensive. In the modest Centro, local color outweighs facilities. The hotels there are more basic and much less expensive than those in the Zona.

Cancún has been experiencing a wave of new development in recent years, and as a result, many hotels have been renovated or are changing hands. Hurricane Wilma, which battered Cancún in late 2005, accelerate this process. You may find that some hotels listed here are slightly different when you visit from what they were when the original reviews were written–some may even have different names.

PRICES

Many hotels have all-inclusive packages, as well as theme-night parties complete with food, beverages, activities, and games. Mexican, Italian, and Caribbean themes seem to be the most popular. Take note, however, that the larger the all-inclusive resort, the blander the food. (It's difficult to provide inventive fare when serving hundreds of people.) For more memorable dining, you may need to leave the grounds–and if you're paying for an all-inclusive package, you'll effectively be paying for meals twice if you do so. Expect high prices for food and drink in most hotels. Many of the more exclusive hotels are starting to enforce a "no outside food or drink" policy–so be discreet when bringing outside food or drinks into your room or they may be confiscated.

Many of the larger and more popular all-inclusives will no longer guarantee an ocean-view room when you book your reservation. If this is important to you, then check that all rooms have ocean views at your chosen hotel, or book only at places that will guarantee a view. Be sure to bring your confirmation information with you to prove you paid for an ocean-view room. Also be careful with towel charges, since many of the resorts have started charging up to $25 for towels not returned. Be sure your returns are duly noted by the pool staff. When checking out, make sure the hotel hasn't tacked on excessive phone or minibar expenses, as some tend to do.

ISLA BLANCA/PUNTA SAM/PUERTO JUÁREZ

The area north of Cancún is slowly being developed into an alternative hotel zone, known informally as Zona Hotelera Norte. This is an ideal area for a tranquil beach vacation, since the shops, restaurants, and nightlife of Cancún are about 45 minutes away by cab.

$$$$ 🏨 **Excellence Playa Mujeres.** North of mainland Cancún, this adults-only resort has redefined the all-inclusive concept. Gone are the days of wristbands and buffets, and in their place are double-story suites, each with a private terrace and hydro pool. Upon arrival, guests are greeted curbside with champagne and refreshing towels, fragranced with a hint of lavender. In the lobby, onyx pillars jet from two-toned marble floors, overshadowed only by a massive stained-glass mural illuminated from above. Every room has a terrace and hot tub. Included in the eight international restaurants are a sushi bar, a lobster house, and New York–style deli. Reminiscent of a Greek temple, the wellness spa features private relaxation rooms, heated waterbeds, and a 12-step hydrotherapy circuit. Dotting the seven swimming pools are hammocks and cabanas, and a man-made river winding throughout the entire property. For those seeking a break from the sun, there are classes available in cooking, Spanish language, dancing, archery, and air-rifle shooting. Attached to the hotel grounds are an 18-hole golf course and a junglelike habitat housing wild jaguars. As if that weren't enough, the hotel offers sunset excursions on its private yacht. Although Hotel Exellence bills itself as Playa Mujeres, it's actually located in the town of Punta Sam. It's a 15-minute drive from El Centro proper, and 30 minutes from the heart of the Zona Hotelera. **Pros:** beautifully sculpted grounds; relaxation spa. **Cons:** repetitive restaurant menus; far removed from activity outside resort. ⊠ *Prolongacíon Bonampak, s/n, Punta Sam, Lote Terrenos 001, MZ. 001, Sm 003, Zona Continental de Isla Mujeres* 🕾 *998/872–8600* ⊕ *www.excellence-resorts.com* ↘ *450 rooms* ⚸ *In-room: Safe, refrigerator, DVD, Wi-Fi. In-hotel: 8 restaurants, room service, bars, golf course, tennis courts, pools, gym, spa, beachfront, diving, water sports, laundry facilities, parking (free), no children under 18, no-smoking rooms* ⊟ *AE, MC, V* ⦿ *AI.*

1

$–$$ 🏨 **Hacienda Punta Sam.** Surrounded by trees, and set on a narrow beach just minutes from the Puerto Juárez docks, this hotel feels far away from the bustle of the Zona Hotelera. The rooms on the top floor are the most spacious, as they have high ceilings covered with thatched roofs. None of them have ocean views, but there is a nice seaside vista from the shared upper balcony that leads to the rooms on the top floor. There are no TVs or radios here, other than those in the sports bar, so plan on catching up on your reading and soaking up the sun. Mainly couples stay here, but children are also welcome. An all-inclusive rate is available. You must book online. **Pros:** great place to escape from the Hotel Zone; inexpensive. **Cons:** not luxurious; no ocean view from rooms; no elevator. ⊠ *Carretera Puerto Juárez–Punta Sam, Km 3.5, Punta Sam* ☎ *998/843–0348* 🛏 *42 rooms* ♿ *In-room: No phone, safe, no TV. In-hotel: Restaurant, bar, pool, beachfront, airport shuttle, parking, pets allowed, no-smoking rooms* ⊟ *No credit cards* 🍴 *AI, EP.*

ZONA HOTELERA

$$$ 🏨 **Ambiance Villas Kin Ha.** This condo hotel is a wonderful place for families, due to its tranquil beach and relaxed atmosphere. Sandwiched between the looming Presidente InterContinental Cancún Resort and the towering Las Olas Cancún Residence & Spa, this is a low-rise, multibuilding complex with lots of palm trees and plants on its grounds. Rooms are simply decorated with light-wood furniture and brightly colored artwork that brightens up the white walls. The suites have spacious dining–living rooms, large terraces, and well-equipped kitchens. There are free organized children's activities here for ages 3 to 12. **Pros:** all rooms have balconies. **Cons:** beach suffered from erosion caused by Hurricane Wilma. ⊠ *Blvd. Kukulcán, Km 8.5, Zona Hotelera* ☎ *998/891–5400* ⊕ *www.kinhabeach.com* 🛏 *80 rooms, 50 suites* ♿ *In-room: Safe, kitchen (some), refrigerator (some). In-hotel: 2 restaurants, pool, gym, beachfront, no elevator, children's programs (ages 3–12), laundry facilities, Internet terminal, Wi-Fi, parking (free), no-smoking rooms* ⊟ *AE, MC, V* 🍴 *EP, BP, AI.*

$$$$ 🏨 **AQUA Cancun.** You won't find raucous spring breakers or screaming
Fodor's Choice   kids at this Mexican-owned Grupo Posadas property, which mostly
★   attracts luxury-minded thirtysomething sun worshippers. Instead, expect soothing hues, large airy rooms, and resident DJ Gottardo Dorado's tunes perfecting the Zen vibe. MB Restaurant (by Michelle Bernstein) and Siete are both top-notch dining experiences. Splurge for a suite–they come equipped with freestanding circular Jacuzzi tubs and Aqua Lounge access, where you can enjoy complimentary Continental breakfast, refreshments, and cocktails throughout the day, and hors d'oeuvres in the evening. Escape the sun in a beach or poolside cabana for a $100 fee, which includes a heavenly foot massage. **Pros:** huge suites; all rooms have oceanfront views; extensive spa services. **Cons:** aromatherapy scents in public spaces can be strong; sliding glass patio doors do not have screens; south-facing rooms had construction views at this writing. ⊠ *Blvd. Kukulcán, Km 12.5, Zona Hotelera* ☎ *998/881–7600 or 888/782–9722* ⊕ *www.feel-aqua.com* 🛏 *335 rooms, 36 suites* ♿ *In-room: Safe, refrigerator, DVD, Wi-Fi. In-hotel:*

3 restaurants, room service, bars, pools, gym, spa, beachfront, laundry service, Wi-Fi, parking (free), no-smoking rooms ▤*AE, MC, V.*

$$–$$$ ⌨**Aquamarina Beach Hotel Cancún.** This family-friendly hotel is just a 10-minute walk from El Embarcadero marina and the Museo del Arte Popular Mexicano. The recently remodeled rooms are modest and plainly decorated, but all have balconies. Outside, you'll find a restaurant, two bars, two pools, a small play area for children, and a no-frills miniature golf course. There is a small dock jutting out from the beach here, so it is not a particularly great area for swimming. Stairs lead to an upper level concrete area that has two Jacuzzis and a couple of Ping-Pong tables. Mexican vacationers make up the largest percentage of guests here, followed by British and American tourists. **Pros:** many recreational activities for kids and adults; conveniently located; affordable. **Cons:** small beach; no Internet in rooms; at this writing, west-facing rooms had construction view. ⊠*Blvd. Kukulcán, Km 4.5, Zona Hotelera* ☎*998/849–4606* ⊕*www.aquamarinabeach.com* ↩*172 rooms* ⌖*In-room: Safe. In-hotel: 2 restaurants, room service, bars, pools, beachfront, water sports, laundry service, Internet terminal, parking (free), no-smoking rooms* ▤*AE, MC, V* ⏣*AI, EP.*

$$$ ⌨**Avalon Baccara Cancún.** Amid the towering resorts with sleek, modern interiors that line the Zona Hotelera, the Avalon Baccara stands out for its small size and rustic Mexican design. Converted from a house into a hotel, this wine-color property has 27 unique units that mainly attract couples. Adorning the lobby are arched doorways, Mexican artifacts, and terra-cotta tiles. A billiard table and quiet lounging area are available for those who want a break from Cancún's party zone. Although all different sizes, the rooms generally follow the overall rustic theme of the hotel, which means that most are decorated with carved wooden furniture, bright colors, and traditional artwork. The suites have balconies with hot tubs, as well as living rooms, dining areas, and kitchens. Some even have wood floors, which are charming, but creaky. **Pros:** refreshing home-setting far unlike all-inclusive–resort style; artistically unique. **Cons:** hard beds; small pool and patios; some rooms lack Internet access. ⊠*Blvd. Kukulcán, Km 11.5, Zona Hotelera* ☎*998/881–3900* ⊕*www.avalonvacations.com* ↩*8 rooms, 19 suites* ⌖*In-room: Safe, kitchen (some), refrigerator (some), Internet (some). In-hotel: 2 restaurants, pool, beachfront, laundry service, parking (free), no-smoking rooms* ▤*AE, MC, V* ⏣*AI, EP, MAP.*

$$$ ⌨**Avalon Grand Cancún.** Formerly a time-share property, the Avalon Grand Cancún now operates as a traditional hotel. A minimalist, modern design pervades, from the fiberglass lamps and bamboo plants in the high-ceilinged lobby to the dark wood and neutral decoration in the guest rooms. The hotel is aiming to attract families. Its overall atmosphere is low-key–even the pool activities here are much calmer than at other resorts. **Pros:** little extras for the children, such as their own "check-in" process when they arrive; guests have access to facilities at nearby sister resort Avalon Baccara. **Cons:** small beach. ⊠*Blvd. Kukulcán, Km 11.5, Zona Hotelera* ☎*998/848–9300* ⊕*www.avalon vacations.com* ↩*39 rooms, 80 suites* ⌖*In-room: Safe, kitchen (some), refrigerator, DVD (some), Internet (some). In-hotel: 2 restaurants, room*

service, bars, pools, gym, spa, beachfront, children's programs (ages infant–10), laundry service, Wi-Fi, parking (free), no-smoking rooms ⊟*AE, MC, V* ⦿*|AI, EP, AP.*

$$$–$$$$ ⊡ **Barceló Costa Cancún.** Ferries to Isla Mujeres are just steps away from this resort, as it neighbors one of Cancún's main piers, El Embarcadero. However, this location also means that the beach here is quite small and there are often boats passing by. A family-friendly hotel, there is a roomy kids' clubhouse with a small play area outside and a miniature-golf course. There are also frequent activities going on in the resort's sole pool area, which can be a drawback if you want some poolside peace and quiet. But you can always escape to the spa, where the cold-water plunge, steam room, sauna, and Jacuzzi are all free of charge. The newly remodeled suites, which come with private Jacuzzis, are a luxurious splurge. There are time-share sales people in the lobby here. **Pros:** great for kids; close to Embarcadero; good water-sports center. **Cons:** no a/c in lobby; small beach area. ⊠*Blvd. Kukulcán, Km 4.5, Zona Hotelera* ☎*998/849–7100* ⦿*www.barcelo.com* ⬐*244 rooms, 113 suites* ⟁*In-room: Safe, refrigerator (some), DVD, Internet. In-hotel: 4 restaurants, room service, bars, pool, gym, spa, beachfront, diving, water sports, bicycles, children's programs (ages 4–11), laundry facilities, laundry service, Wi-Fi, parking (free), no-smoking rooms* ⊟*AE, MC, V* ⦿*|AI.*

$$$–$$$$ ⊡ **Barceló TuCancún Beach.** Located just behind the massive Kukulcán Plaza and about a half-mile down the road from La Isla, this resort is an ideal location for mall addicts. For those who don't want to shop, however, there is the usual daytime fare to keep you occupied, such as volleyball games and water-polo matches in the activities pool. The sound does sometimes carry over into the area that houses the two quieter pools, one of which has built-in chaise longues for ultimate relaxation. This salmon-color hotel is offset by bright blue accents throughout, which complement the turquoise hues of the Caribbean that are visible as soon as you ascend the stairs to the lobby. To secure a room with these same oceanfront views, however, you will have to pay extra. And don't lose your towel card, because it will cost you $25. There are four handicapped-accessible rooms here. **Pros:** near two of Cancún's biggest malls; wide range of activities for children and adults. **Cons:** main pool area can get noisy. ⊠*Blvd. Kukulcán, Km 13.5, Zona Hotelera* ☎*998/891–5900* ⦿*www.barcelo.com* ⬐*316 rooms, 16 villas* ⟁*In-room: Safe, Wi-Fi. In-hotel: 4 restaurants, room service, bars, tennis courts, pools, spa, beachfront, diving, laundry service, Internet terminal, Wi-Fi, parking (free), no-smoking rooms* ⊟*AE, MC, V* ⦿*|AI.*

$$$–$$$$
★ ⊡ **The Bel Air Collection Cancún.** The design scheme at this strikingly chic and tranquil resort is unlike that of any other hotel that lines Boulevard Kukulcán. White furniture is offset by red and black accents, giving the entire hotel a retro look. Billowing drapery creates a wall-less passage into the open-air lobby. Neon lights in the foil-lined elevators change every two seconds, triggering sensations of peace and relaxation. In addition to the sushi bar, there are two small dining sections where you can actually cool off your feet while eating or enjoying a drink, as the tables and chairs are sitting in a low pool of water. The spa here

has a yoga–meditation room, light chambers, and high-tech machines from Europe that are used for aromatherapy and chromotherapy sessions, among other treatments. Children under the age of 12 are not permitted at this hotel, which is targeted at adults looking for a peaceful hideaway. All 19 suites have private, indoor Jacuzzis and ocean views. **Pros:** luxurious spa; aesthetically pleasing hotel. **Cons:** no kids under 12; far from party zone. ⊠*Blvd. Kukulcán, Km 20.5, Zona Hotelera* ☎*998/193–1770* ⊕*www.thebelaircollection.com* ⌨*136 rooms, 19 suites* ⚴*In-room: Safe, DVD, Wi-Fi (some). In-hotel: 2 restaurants, room service, bars, pool, gym, spa, beachfront, laundry service, Wi-Fi, parking (free), no kids under 12, no-smoking rooms* ⊟*AE, MC, V* ❑*AI, BP, EP.*

$$–$$$ ▦**Best Western Cancún Clipper Club.** Right next to the Zona Hotelera's main hub of shops and clubs, this hotel still manages to feel secluded because it is set back from Boulevard Kukulcán. Rooms are done up in bright tropical colors with rattan furniture and views of the lagoon; the quietest are Nos. 13 and 14. Suites have fully equipped kitchens, living rooms, and pull-out couches (two-bedroom suites actually consist of a one-bedroom suite and a standard room). There's a pretty pool with a large deck, which is set amid lush gardens; there's also a small children's play area. A nice detail is the red path that winds through the manicured grounds, as it makes for a nice walk while taking in views of the lagoon. **Pros:** free laundry facilities; close proximity to lots of activities. **Cons:** no beach. ⊠*Blvd. Kukulcán, Km 9, Zona Hotelera* ☎*998/891–5999* ⊕*www.clipper.com.mx* ⌨*71 rooms, 71 suites* ⚴*In-room: Safe, kitchen (some), refrigerator (some), Wi-Fi (some). In-hotel: Restaurant, room service, bar, tennis court, pool, gym, spa, laundry facilities, Internet terminal, Wi-Fi, parking (free), no-smoking rooms* ⊟*AE, MC, V.*

$$$$ ▦**Cancún Palace.** The soothing sound of running water coupled with the creamy hues and light-color walls and floors will put you immediately at ease when you enter this sophisticated minimalist hotel. All rooms come with a double hot tub and balcony, but only 70% offer an ocean view, so it's a good idea to book in advance and specify that you'd like a room facing the beach. The chic lobby bar comes alive at night from 10 to 1 with electronic and pop music, dancing, and twirling disco lights. As part of the all-inclusive package, guests may use the facilities at the Palace Resorts' sister properties, such as the Jack Nicklaus signature golf course at the Moon Palace. Other perks include the hotel's two tennis courts and a kids' club that has numerous activities for antsy teens as well. **Pros:** kids' and teens' center; two tennis courts; access to Palace Resorts' sister properties. **Cons:** some rooms lack ocean views; no water sports; at this writing, north-facing rooms had construction view. ⊠*Blvd. Kukulcán, Km 14.5, Zona Hotelera* ☎*998/881–3600* ⊕*www. palaceresorts.com* ⌨*601 rooms, 24 suites* ⚴*In-room: Safe, Wi-Fi. In-hotel: 5 restaurants, room service, bars, pool, gym, spa, beachfront, tennis court, children's programs (ages 4–17), laundry service, Wi-Fi, parking (free), no-smoking rooms* ⊟*AE, D, MC, V* ❑*AI, EP.*

$$$$ ▦**CasaMagna Marriott Cancún Resort.** Sweeping grounds and arched walkways that lead up to the six-story building will make you forget you're at a Marriott. The lobby has large windows, elegant chandeliers, and small sculptures throughout; rooms have private balconies, flat-screen TVs, and marble floors, which tend to echo at night. However, only a quarter of the rooms offer oceanfront views. The secluded gardens and beachfront gazebo are ideal for weddings. For a $15 fee, guests can enjoy the spa of neighboring JW Marriott, where amenities include chocolate body wraps and cornhusk exfoliations. The kids' club costs an additional $25 per day; the fee includes nutritional snacks, participation in a turtle-release program, and a diving class at the hotel's artificial reef. **Pros:** more culturally traditional than most Marriotts; excellent Thai restaurant. **Cons:** geared to groups and conventions, which account for 80% of the hotel's business. ⊠ *Blvd. Kukulcán, Km 14.5, Zona Hotelera* ☏ *998/881–2000 or 800/900–8800* ⊕ *www.casa magnacancun.com* ↘ *414 rooms, 38 suites* ♿ *In-room: Safe, kitchen (some), refrigerator (some), Wi-Fi. In-hotel: 3 restaurants, room service, bars, tennis courts, pool, gym, spa, beachfront, diving, water sports, children's programs (ages 4–12), laundry service, Internet terminal, Wi-Fi, parking (free), no-smoking rooms* ☐ *AE, MC, V* ⭐ *EP.*

$$ 🖵 **Club Verano Beat.** Located 5 km (3 mi) down the road from the Zona Hotelera's main hub of bars and clubs, this small hotel is best for people who want to avoid Cancún's famous party environment. Mainly frequented by Europeans and Canadians, this quiet, low-level hotel is built around a courtyard that has a small pool and towering trees. Rooms are spacious, but the closets and bathrooms are tiny. The suites, ideal for families, have dining areas, a queen bed, and a sunken bedroom with three twin beds. The stretch of beach here is quite small and located next to a marina, so we recommend visiting the closest public playa, Las Perlas, which is about a half-mile away. **Pros:** friendly staff; very quiet place. **Cons:** musty rooms; small beach. ⊠ *Blvd. Kukulcán, Km 3.5, Zona Hotelera* ☏ *998/849–4800* ↘ *94 rooms* ♿ *In-room: Kitchen. In-hotel: 2 restaurants, room service, bar, tennis court, pool, beachfront, no elevator, Wi-Fi, parking (free), no-smoking rooms* ☐ *AE, MC, V* ⭐ *AI, BP, EP.*

$$ 🖵 **Condominios Carisa y Palma.** Unlike many resorts in the area, this budget-price condo hotel is over 30 years old. Room selection varies widely, since all are different sizes and decorated in a variety of styles. Although far from luxurious, these pastel-hue rooms provide all the basic amenities. Each comes with its own kitchen and balcony, and is conveniently located near the adjoining swimming pool and tennis courts. Request one facing the ocean. **Pros:** beachfront location; five-minute walk from nightclubs and markets. **Cons:** street-side rooms with lagoon views are noisy. ⊠ *Blvd. Kukulcán, Km 9.5, Zona Hotelera* ☏ *998/883–0211 or 998/883–0287* ⊕ *www.carisaypalma.com* ↘ *122 rooms* ♿ *In-room: Safe, kitchen. In-hotel: Tennis court, pool, gym, beachfront, Internet terminal, Wi-Fi, parking (free), no-smoking rooms* ☐ *AE, MC, V.*

$$$$ 🖵 **Dreams Cancún Resort & Spa.** Surrounded on three sides by ocean, ☾ this resort provides stunning, panoramic views of the Caribbean. It stands out in other ways, too, with all the little extras (incense, umbrellas, sunscreen) that are provided in the wood, white, and turquoise guest rooms. A main draw to the hotel is Delphinus, a large aquarium

in which you can swim with dolphins; at $149 per person for 45 minutes, though, it's not cheap. The deluxe dolphin-front rooms allow you to watch performances from your private balcony. This hotel is recommended for families; there are plenty of activities to keep the

WORD OF MOUTH

"Fiesta American Grand Coral Beach has a great beach–right next to the pool there, with very, very gentle and safe tides." –RAC

children entertained if parents want to sneak off for some alone time. The kids' club here accepts children between the ages of 3 and 12, and is open for far longer than most other hotels (from 9 AM to 10 PM daily). The only catch is that parents aren't allowed to leave the hotel premises while their children are at the club. Every Sunday at 1:30, the hotel offers bilingual Catholic mass open to the public. **Pros:** dolphin aquarium; excellent beach access, family theme nights. **Cons:** swimming with dolphins costs extra; lobby extremely crowded during check-in hours. ⊠*Blvd. Kukulcán, Km 9.5, Punta Cancún, Zona Hotelera* ☎*998/848–7000* ⊕*www.dreamsresorts.com* ⇱*345 rooms, 34 suites* ⌂*In-room: Safe, DVD, refrigerator. In-hotel: 5 restaurants, room service, bars, tennis court, pools, gym, spa, beachfront, diving, water sports, bicycle tours, children's programs (ages 3–12), laundry service, Wi-Fi, parking (free), no-smoking rooms* ▤*AE, MC, V* ⦿*AI.*

$$$$
★ ⊡**Fiesta Americana Grand Coral Beach.** If luxury's your bag, you'll feel right at home at this distinctive, all-suites hotel. The vast lobby has stained-glass skylights, sculptures, plants, and mahogany furniture. The large, recently renovated suites have marble floors, small sitting rooms, and balconies overlooking the Bahía de Mujeres. The beach here is narrow, but there's a new 10,000-square-foot spa and a 660-square-foot pool surrounded by a lush exotic flower garden. The sheer size of this hotel may be daunting to some, but the guests are well attended to by the multilingual concierges. **Pros:** enormous pool with three swim-up bars; complimentary kids' club; business center has private offices. **Cons:** main lobby feels cold; too big for some. ⊠*Blvd. Kukulcán, Km 9.5, Zona Hotelera* ☎*998/881–3200* ⊕*www.fiestamericanagrand.com* ⇱*602 suites* ⌂*In-room: Safe, DVD (some), Wi-Fi, Internet. In-hotel: 5 restaurants, room service, bars, pool, gym, spa, beachfront, diving, water sports, children's programs (ages 4–12), laundry service, Internet terminal, Wi-Fi, parking (paid), no-smoking rooms* ▤*AE, D, DC, MC, V* ⦿*EP.*

$$$
⊡**Fiesta Americana Condesa Cancún.** This hotel is easily recognized by the 118-foot-tall palapa that covers its lobby. Despite the rustic roof, the rest of the architecture here is extravagant, with marble pillars, a massive swimming pool, and inner courtyards filled with lush, tropical gardens. There's also a good-size gym here and two indoor tennis courts. The spa is one of the largest in the Zona Hotelera, with 11 indoor treatment rooms and 4 outdoor ones. Activities here include pool volleyball, yoga lessons, and Tai Chi classes, and the atmosphere is more laid-back than at sister resort Fiesta Americana Grand Coral Beach. Rooms are a decent size, but not all have balconies, and ocean views cost extra. There is a large focus on groups and conventions here, which account

for about 60% of guests throughout the year. **Pros:** friendly staff; centrally located; smaller pools designated for children. **Cons:** time-share pitch; popular with tour groups. ⊠*Blvd. Kukulcán, Km 16.5, Zona Hotelera* ☎*998/881–4200* ⊕*www.fiestaamericana.com* ➪*476 rooms, 26 suites* ♿*In-room: Safe, refrigerator, Wi-Fi. In-hotel: 3 restaurants, room service, bars, tennis courts, pools, gym, spa, beachfront, diving, children's programs (ages 4–12), laundry service, Wi-Fi, parking (free), no-smoking rooms* ▤*AE, D, DC, MC, V* ⍓*AI, EP.*

$$$$ ⊞**Golden Parnassus Resort & Spa.** The rooms at this all-inclusive, adults-only resort are warmly decorated with sunset colors, flower arrangements, and rich wood furnishings; some rooms even have private hot tubs. Small sitting areas open up onto balconies with ocean or lagoon views (the ocean views are better). The beach here is small, but there's a comfortable pool area with deck chairs and palapas. The spa offers massages and facials, and there is an outdoor *temazcal* (a dome-shaped sweat lodge made from volcanic rock), which Maya believe purifies the body. There's plenty to entertain you–minigolf, a casino, windsurfing equipment, scuba lessons, and a cowboy saloon. **Pros:** guided bicycle tours; free shuttle to sister property Great Parnassus Resort & Spa; evening entertainment. **Cons:** no kids under 15; small beach; slightly dated decor. ⊠*Blvd. Kukulcán, Km 14.5, Retorno San Miguelito Lote 37, Zona Hotelera* ☎*998/885–0909* ⊕*www.parnassusresorts.com* ➪*214 rooms* ♿*In-room: Safe, refrigerator (some), Wi-Fi. In-hotel: 5 restaurants, bars, tennis courts, pools, spa, beachfront, water sports, bicycles, laundry service, Wi-Fi, gym, parking (free), no kids under 15, no-smoking rooms* ▤*AE, MC, V* ⍓*AI.*

$$$$ ⊞**GR Solaris Cancún.** More upscale than its Royal Solaris sister property in Cancún, this resort is somewhat focused on adults. A small pool and outdoor massage area are off-limits to children; this is actually the quietest spot outdoors, as activities are constantly going on at the main pool. The hotel features a spacious lobby, wrought-iron chandeliers, and a dramatic outdoor terrace. Although the hotel was built in 2004, the rooms look somewhat plain and are noticeably outdated. **Pros:** lighted tennis court; water-sports marina; fully equipped free gym. **Cons:** pool area can get noisy; rooms are nothing extraordinary. ⊠*Blvd. Kukulcán, Km 9.5, Zona Hotelera* ☎*998/848–8400* ⊕*clubsolaris.com* ➪*306 rooms* ♿*In-room: Safe, refrigerator, Wi-Fi. In-hotel: 4 restaurants, room service, bars, tennis court, pools, gym, spa, beachfront, diving, water sports, children's programs (ages 4–11), laundry service, Wi-Fi, airport shuttle, parking (free), no-smoking rooms* ▤*AE, D, MC, V* ⍓*AI.*

$$$$ ⊞**Gran Caribe Real.** There's no such thing as a standard room at this resort: the most basic option is a spacious junior suite with a sofa bed, sitting area, flat-screen TV, and balcony. Due to the high capacity of this 477-suite hotel, it may feel a bit crowded at the check-in line or at the pools, but if you're lucky (and quick), you can snag one of the chaises found around the outdoor areas. A new aqua park with a pirate ship and water slide–one for kids and one for adults–is the perfect way to cool off. Mayan-inspired artwork is found throughout the lobby and other public spaces, whereas the suites are decorated in a Mexican-colonial style that features ornate beige and gold-tone accents. Guests

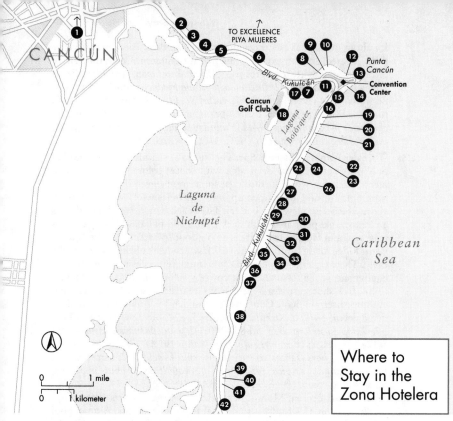

Where to Stay in the Zona Hotelera

are allowed access to the resort's sister property in Playa del Carmen, Gran Porto Real. **Pros:** wide array of land and water sports; gym has yoga and Tai Chi lessons. **Cons:** room decor uninspired; mediocre restaurants. ⊠*Blvd. Kukulcán, Km 11.5, Zona Hotelera* ☎*998/881–7300* ⊕*www.realresorts.com.mx* ↝*477 suites* �½*In-room: Safe, DVD, Wi-Fi (some). In-hotel: 6 restaurants, room service, bars, tennis court, pools, gym, spa, beachfront, diving, water sports, bicycles, children's programs (ages 4–12), laundry service, Wi-Fi, parking (free), no-smoking rooms* ▭*AE, MC, V* ⦿*AI.*

$$$–$$$$ ⊞**Gran Meliá Cancún.** This enormous beachfront hotel has been built to resemble a modern Mayan temple; its various atriums even have pyramid-shaped roof skylights. The main lobby is a sight to behold, as there is lush green vegetation everywhere. At the center is a sushi bar–café that gives the sense of being in an outdoor garden, with its wooden floors, koi ponds, central fountain, and numerous plants. Guests who want a more private stay can always upgrade to the Royal Service tower, which is more expensive but has a secluded courtyard with a pool, two Jacuzzis, and nearly 40 beds with palapa roofs overhead. Golfers will enjoy the 9-hole course. The recently remodeled YHI Spa ranks among Cancún's finest. **Pros:** one of Cancún's best spas; privacy of Royal Service tower; golf course. **Cons:** lacks intimacy due to size. ⊠*Blvd. Kukulcán, Km 16.5, Zona Hotelera* ☎*998/881–1100* ⊕*www.solmelia.com* ↝*678 rooms, 53 suites* �½*In-room: Safe, Internet, kitchen (some), DVD (some). In-hotel: 5 restaurants, room service, bars, golf course, tennis court, pools, gym, spa, beachfront, diving, water sports, children's programs (ages 5–11), laundry service, Wi-Fi, parking (free), airport shuttle, no-smoking rooms* ▭*AE, MC, V* ⦿*EP, CP, AI.*

$$$–$$$$ ⊞**Grand Oasis.** This multistructure hotel, comprised of a main building called Playa and two side buildings (Palmar I and Palmar II), is right next door to sister property and spring break mecca Oasis Cancún. The hotel pool–shared between the two hotels and one of the largest in Latin American–stretches more than a quarter of a mile and is usually full of college students during spring break. Tour groups flock to the all-inclusive resort, which offers brightly decorated rooms with Mexican wrought-iron furnishings. Playa's trapezoidal lobby is strikingly beautiful (though it's not air-conditioned), with a crystal dome and vines that drape over the six-storied balcony; every room in this building has a balcony and king-sized bed. **Pros:** enormous pool area; renovated gym; lively atmosphere. **Cons:** limited shade by pool; large grounds require fair amount of walking; rather boisterous for some. ⊠*Blvd. Kukulcán, Km 16.5, Zona Hotelera* ☎*998/881–7000* ⊕*www.hotelesoasis.com* ↝*442 rooms* �½*In-room: Safe, refrigerator, Wi-Fi (some). In-hotel: 5 restaurants, room service, bars, golf course, tennis courts, pool, gym, Internet terminal, beachfront, diving, children's programs (ages 6–12), spa, parking (no fee), no-smoking rooms* ▭*AE, MC, V* ⦿*AI.*

$$$–$$$$ ⊞**Hilton Cancún Golf & Spa Resort.** The Caribbean plays a central role at
★ this resort, with ocean views from all standard guest rooms and junior suites. Set amid 150 lush acres, the tropical setting, with palapa huts and poolside hammocks, is luxurious without seeming overly ostentatious. The landscaping incorporates a series of lavish, interconnected

swimming pools that wind through palm-dotted lawns, ending at the beach. Airy and vibrant, the rooms are pristine white with a splash of turquoise to match the sea. Some of the villas, however, only offer garden views, so make sure to specify oceanfront when booking. Guests who want to get more intimate with nature can participate in the resort's turtle-release program or work on their swing at the resort's championship 18-hole, par-72 course, where crocodile and peacock sightings are frequent. For the ultimate in pampering, the hotel's spa features a Zengarden hot tub, a bamboo relaxation lounge, poolside yoga, and massages on the beach. The children's activities cost $45 for a full day, $32 for a half-day, or $10 per hour. **Pros:** outstanding beachfront villas; tasteful decor; angled pool area gets all-day sunshine. **Cons:** only one heated pool; food quality is inconsistent. ⊠*Blvd. Kukulcán, Km 17, Zona Hotelera* ☎*998/881–8000* ⊕*www.hiltoncancun.com* ⤵*426 rooms, 23 suites, 82 villas* ⚿*In-room: Safe, DVD, Internet (some), Wi-Fi (some). In-hotel: 5 restaurants, room service, bars, golf course, tennis courts, pools, gym, spa, beachfront, diving, water sports, bicycles, children's programs (ages 4–11), laundry service, Internet terminal, Wi-Fi, parking (free), no-smoking rooms* ⊟*AE, D, DC, MC, V* ♯⃝*EP.*

$$–$$$ ⊡ **Holiday Inn Express.** Within walking distance of the Cancún Golf Club, the Convention Center, and the party zone, this hotel caters to business travelers and tourists seeking an affordable alternative to the pricey resorts. Rooms have either patios or small balconies that overlook the pool and garden areas that surround it. All rooms are subdued in shades of cream and salmon; furnishings are modern. Although not luxurious, it's perfect for families in which Dad wants to golf, Mom wants to shop, and the kids want to hit the beach—a 15-minute walk from the hotel. Breakfast, Wi-Fi, and local telephone calls are all complimentary. Those planning to spend time in the hub of hotel zone should factor taxi fares into the budget. It is a 10-minute walk from Kukulcán's nearest bus stop. **Pros:** price; good location; free shuttle to beach. **Cons:** simple rooms; no elevator; not on beach. ⊠*Paseo Pok-Ta-Pok, Lotes 21 and 22, off Blvd. Kukulcán, Km 7.5, Zona Hotelera* ☎*998/883–2200* ⊕*www.hiexpress.com/cancunmex* ⤵*119 rooms* ⚿*In-room: Wi-Fi. In-hotel: Bar, pool gym, spa, laundry service, Wi-Fi, parking (free), no-smoking rooms* ⊟*AE, MC, V* ♯⃝*BP.*

$$$ ⊡ **Hotetur Beach Paradise.** This hotel is eclectic in everything from its choice of decoration to its varied mix of guests, which include students, families, couples, and groups. In the public areas, a more modern look dominates, from the dark-wood and cream furniture in the lobby to the red chairs and pool tables in the sports bar. The guest rooms, however, are all furnished in a Mexican rustic style characterized by carved wooden furniture and bright blue, orange, and yellow accents. **Pros:** spacious standard rooms; activities like billiards, water polo, and windsurfing. **Cons:** very thin walls; gym and spa need a facelift. ⊠*Blvd. Kukulcán, Km 19.5, Zona Hotelera* ☎*998/885–2222* ⊕*www.hotetur. com* ⤵*117 rooms, 53 suites* ⚿*In-room: Safe. In-hotel: 3 restaurants, bars, tennis court, pool, gym, spa, beachfront, diving, water sports, children's programs (ages 4–12), laundry service, Wi-Fi, parking (free), no-smoking rooms* ⊟*AE, MC, V* ♯⃝*AI.*

$$$$ ⬚ **Hyatt Cancún Caribe Resort.** There is a wide variety of accommodations at the Hyatt Cancún Caribe, and all have ocean views. There are also some stunning vistas of the Zona Hotelera's glittering lights from certain areas of the hotel (as in front of rooms 3608–3616 in the Main Tower). Even the standard rooms have balconies, flat-screen TVs, and high-speed Internet access. Deluxe rooms and suites–the most luxurious of which have Jacuzzis and outdoor terraces with plunge pools–are located in the Premier Beach Front Tower and Regency Club Building. The pool area in this newer section of the property has couches and tables under a slatted roof, a swim-up bar, and a dozen poolside beds (you have to pay to rent them). The main pool area, located on the other side of the grounds, is ringed with cobblestone that looks pretty but is difficult to walk on. **Pros:** all rooms face ocean; new beachfront building; excellent pool areas. **Cons:** Internet costs extra. ✉ *Blvd. Kukulcán, Km 10.5, Zona Hotelera* ☎ *998/848–7800* ⊕ *www.cancun.caribe. hyatt.com* ⇌ *263 rooms, 23 suites* ♿ *In-room: Safe, DVD (some), Internet. In-hotel: 3 restaurants, room service, bars, pools, gym, spa, beachfront, diving, children's programs (ages 6–12), laundry service, Internet terminal, Wi-Fi, parking (free), no-smoking rooms* ▭ *AE, MC, V* ⏀ *EP, BP, CP, MAP, AP.*

$$ ⬚ **Imperial Laguna.** On a quiet residential street that skirts the edge of Laguna Nichupté, this budget hotel features plain, spacious rooms (some with kitchenettes). The hotel's greatest draw is the courtyard swimming pool, surrounded by thatched palapas, manicured hedges, and a wooden bridge. Its lagoon-side, open-air restaurant is named after the Belgian chef, Oliver, who cooks up different specials every night, ranging from baked mussels to tuna steak. In sharp contrast to the restaurant and pool, the rooms are rather so-so. Each is decorated with rattan lampshades, faux-wood furnishings, and chintz bedding. **Pros:** nicely landscaped. **Cons:** rooms are drab and can get musty. ✉ *Club de Golf, Calle Quetzal 11, turn right at Km 7.5 after golf course, Zona Hotelera* ☎ *998/883–3446 or 998/883–3448* ⊕ *www.hotelimperialcancun.com* ⇌ *62 rooms, 4 suites, 3 villas* ♿ *In-room: Kitchen (some), refrigerator. In-hotel: Restaurant, pool, Internet terminal, parking (free), no-smoking rooms* ▭ *AE, MC, V* ⏀ *EP.*

$$$$ ⬚ **JW Marriott Cancún Resort & Spa.** This is the best hotel for experiencing luxury Cancún style and service. Plush is the name of the game at the towering beach resort, where manicured lawns are dotted with an expansive maze of pools, and large vaulted windows let sunlight stream into a lobby decorated with marble floors and beautiful flower arrangements. All rooms have ocean views, private balconies, and wall-to-wall carpeting. Two of the hotel's best features are its 35,000-square-foot spa with indoor pool and its 20-foot dive pool with an artificial reef, where you can practice snorkeling and scuba diving. Like its sister property CasaMagna Marriott Cancún, the majority of guests are here on business travel. **Pros:** top-notch service; huge spa; artificial reef. **Cons:** lacks the festive mood of other hotels along the strip. ✉ *Blvd. Kukulcán, Km 14.5, Zona Hotelera* ☎ *998/848–9600 or 888/813–2776* ⊕ *www. marriott.com* ⇌ *448 rooms, 74 suites* ♿ *In-room: Safe, kitchen (some), refrigerator (some), Wi-Fi. In-hotel: 3 restaurants, room service, bars,*

Fodor'sChoice
★

tennis courts, pools, gym, spa, beachfront, diving, water sports, children's programs (ages 4–12), laundry service, Internet terminal, Wi-Fi, parking (free), no-smoking rooms ⊟AE, MC, V ⦿EP.

$$$$ ⊡ **Le Blanc Spa Resort.** An airy and modern hotel with white and beige refined minimalist decor and lots of windows, Le Blanc Spa is the most upscale of the Palace Resorts properties in Cancún. Mainly couples stay in this resort, which is restricted to guests over 18. The spa is extremely large, with 19 indoor treatment rooms and services ranging from aroma foot reflexology to chocolate body wraps. Located along both the ocean and the lagoon, this resort offers some spectacular views. However, only about 50% of the rooms have full ocean views. **Pros:** aesthetically pleasing design; excellent spa; butler service. **Cons:** no kids; pricey. ⊠ *Blvd. Kukulcán, Km 10, Zona Hotelera* ☎ *998/881–4740* ⊕ *www.leblancsparesort.com* ⇪ *260 rooms* ⋀ *In-room: Safe, DVD (some), Wi-Fi. In-hotel: 4 restaurants, room service, bars, pools, gym, spa, beachfront, diving, laundry service, Wi-Fi, parking (free), no kids under 18, no-smoking rooms* ⊟AE, D, DC, MC, V ⦿AI.

$$$$ ⊡ **Le Meridien Cancún Resort & Spa.** High on a hill and tucked away from the main boulevard, this refined yet relaxed hotel is an artful blend of art deco and Mayan styles; there's lots of wood, glass, and mirrors. The beach is small, but rooms have partial ocean views. The many thoughtful details—such as different temperatures in each of the swimming pools—make a stay here truly special. The Spa del Mar offers the latest European treatments (including seaweed hydrotherapy) in 14 treatment rooms. Business groups are starting to book here, and account for about 40% of the hotel's clientele. **Pros:** near one of Cancún's best malls; large fitness center; all rooms with ocean or lagoon views. **Cons:** expensive considering it's not all-inclusive; small beach; at this writing, south-facing rooms had construction views. ⊠ *Blvd. Kukulcán, Km 14, Retorno del Rey, Lote 37, Zona Hotelera* ☎ *998/881–2200 or 800/543–4300* ⊕ *www.cancun.lemeridien.com* ⇪ *213 rooms, 26 suites* ⋀ *In-room: Safe, DVD (some), Wi-Fi. In-hotel: 2 restaurants, bar, tennis courts, pools, gym, spa, beachfront, children's programs (ages 4–12) Wi-Fi, parking (free), no-smoking rooms* ⊟AE, MC, V ⦿BP, EP, CP.

$$$$ ⊡ **ME by Meliá Cancún.** The ME takes the chic flavor of a trendy boutique hotel and blows it up to the grand scale of a large resort. The aim here is to arouse all five senses; you'll find yourself inhaling soothing scents while listening to electronic lounge music that is played everywhere, even in the elevators. This hotel oozes hipness, from the sleek black mermaid sculptures by artist Marie France Porta to the slick bars created by nightlife gurus Rande and Scott Gerber. And if you want to literally bring a piece of ME back home with you, guest-room furnishings and artwork by Yuri Zatarain can be purchased from the on-site gallery. Also, pet owners take note—your furry friends are welcome here. **Pros:** great for young couples; amazing contemporary design; pet-friendly. **Cons:** not ideal for kids; lacks traditional Mexican flavor. ⊠ *Blvd. Kukulcán, Km 12, Zona Hotelera* ☎ *998/881–2500 or 998/881–2506* ⊕ *www.mebymelia.com* ⇪ *410 rooms, 38 suites* ⋀ *In-room: Safe, DVD (some), Internet, Wi-Fi. In-hotel: 4 restaurants, room service, bars, pools, gym, spa, beachfront, laundry service, Internet*

terminal, Wi-Fi, parking (free), some pets allowed, no-smoking rooms
⊟AE, MC, V ⦿EP.

$$$–$$$$ ⊡ **NH Krystal Cancún.** Located right in the midst of Party Center, this
hotel sits on a cul-de-sac off Kukulcán Boulevard. It's one of the few
properties in the Zona Hotelera where the standard rooms don't have
balconies and beach access is nearly nonexistent. However, the outside
courtyard has an infinity pool and a viewing platform with dramatic
columns where you can watch the waves crash below. Standard rooms
have contemporary wood furniture with dark-orange accents; the newly
added NH Romantic Rooms, which are geared to honeymooners, have
ocean-view terraces, plasma TVs, and king-size bed; appetizers and
house wine are served in the room each evening. Only half the standard
rooms have ocean views, while the other half face the street (the quieter
ones are on the ocean side). The clientele runs the gamut from fami-
lies to retired couples to students. **Pros:** in a quiet cul-de-sac near the
party zone; recently remodeled; computer and laptop rentals available.
Cons: small beach; most rooms lack balconies; very simple pool area.
⊠*Blvd. Kukulcán, Km 9, Zona Hotelera* ☎998/848–9800 ⊕*www.
nh-hotels.com* ⇆*346 rooms, 3 suites* ⬧*In-room: Safe, refrigerator,
Internet, Wi-Fi. In-hotel: 4 restaurants, room service, bars, pools, gym,
spa, beachfront, diving, water sports, children's programs (ages 5–12),
laundry service, Wi-Fi, parking (free), no-smoking rooms* ⊟AE, MC,
V AI, CP, EP, MAP.

$$$ ⊡ **Oasis Palm Beach.** Within walking distance of El Embarcadero, this
☾ all-inclusive family resort sits in prime location if you're looking to take
a boat to Isla Mujeres. The lobby has modern black and red furniture
with marble floors, although the rooms are decorated in contemporary
Mexican fashion; around a third of them have an ocean view. Guests
have access to a 9-hole, par-27 golf course at sister property Grand
Oasis Cancún. On-site amenities include a teens' and kids' club, a wide
array of water and land sports, Mexican and Caribbean theme parties
with music and dance performances, and Spanish classes if you feel
like brushing up on your language skills. **Pros:** great location; access to
Grand Oasis Cancún golf course; good for families. **Cons:** no in-room
Internet; only Jacuzzi is at the spa and costs extra. ⊠*Blvd. Kukulcán,
Km 4.5, Zona Hotelera* ☎998/848–7500 ⊕*www.hotelesoasis.com*
⇆*469 rooms, 2 suites* ⬧*In-room: Safe. In-hotel: 6 restaurants, bars,
Wi-Fi, pool, spa, beachfront, children's programs (ages 4–15), laundry
service, parking (free), no-smoking rooms* ⊟AE, MC, V ⦿AI.

$$$–$$$$ ⊡ **Omni Cancún Hotel & Villas.** After undergoing a $15 million renova-
tion in 2007, this 10-story hotel has definitely moved up a notch or two
in Cancún's hotel hierarchy. Each standard room has a balcony with
built-in benches, a marble bathroom, flat-screen TV, and radio with an
MP3 docking station. If you decide to splurge on one of the three-floor
villas that surround the hotel, you will not be disappointed. They each
have a sunken living room, fully equipped kitchen, sun terrace off the
third-floor bedroom, and parking space right outside. Your stay here
will not be complete without paying a visit to the huge, adults-only
hot-tub area with swim-up bar–it is the only one of its kind in the
entire Zona Hotelera. If you'd rather be dry when drinking, then grab

a table at the lobby bar and try one of the delicious martinis that are the house specialty. There are four handicapped-accessible rooms here. **Pros:** refurbished rooms; tons of scheduled activities. **Cons:** crowded pool area; timeshare sales pitches in the lobby. ⊠*Blvd. Kukulcán, Km 16.5, Zona Hotelera* ☎998/881–0600 ⊕*www.omnihotels.com* 312 *rooms, 19 suites, 20 villas* ♿*In-room: Safe, kitchen (some), refrigerator (some), DVD (some), Wi-Fi. In-hotel: 3 restaurants, room service, bars, tennis courts, pools, gym, spa, beachfront, children's programs (ages 5–12), laundry service, Internet terminal, Wi-Fi, parking (free), no-smoking rooms* ⊟*AE, MC, V* ⍾*AI, EP.*

WORD OF MOUTH

"The Omni Cancún is about the best place for the money in Cancún."   –Joe P.

$$$$ ⊞**Park Royal Cancún.** A resort that embraces color and art, Park Royal Cancún's pastel tropical style is reminiscent of the Miami art-deco style of the 1930s. Here, you'll find hues of turquoise and teal throughout, as well as novel sand art that decorates everything from the walls of the lobby to the lamps in the spacious guest rooms (the smallest ones encompass 434 square feet). Conveniently located across from La Isla Shopping, the hotel offers suites that can comfortably sleep up to six people. The beach here is decent-sized, but the waves can get quite rough, depending on the weather. Right next to the hotel's beach area is the small Yamil Lu'um archaeological site, which can be accessed only with hotel permission. Parents should take note that although Park Royal Cancún markets itself as a family-oriented resort, there is no kids' club and children under the age of 12 are not allowed into the à la carte restaurant. **Pros:** excellent service; on-site babysitting; spotless rooms. **Cons:** decor a bit outdated; time-share pitches can be bothersome; beach has strong undertow. ⊠*Blvd. Kukulcán, Km 12.5, Zona Hotelera* ☎998/885–1333 ⊕*www.park-royalhotels.com* 150 *rooms, 140 suites* ♿*In-room: Safe. In-hotel: 2 restaurants, bars, pools, gym, spa, beachfront, children's programs (ages 5–11), laundry service, Wi-Fi, parking (free), no-smoking rooms* ⊟*AE, MC, V* ⍾*AI.*

$$$$ ⊞**Presidente InterContinental Cancún Resort.** This landmark hotel boasts arguably the best beach in Cancún. It gained at least 20 feet more sand after Hurricane Wilma. The entire hotel has a contemporary look to it, including the swanky lobby with a tequila bar. Adults looking for even more peace and quiet can take advantage of the adults-only, quiet pool or a beachfront massage. The atmosphere here is more conservative than at many of the other resorts along the Zona Hotelera, so you're likely to have a quiet, relaxed stay. **Pros:** short walk to shops and restaurants; virtually currentless beach is great for families. **Cons:** focus on business travelers and conventions. ⊠*Blvd. Kukulcán, Km 7.5, Zona Hotelera* ☎998/848–8700 ⊕*www.intercontinental.com/cancun* 299 *rooms, 7 suites* ♿*In-room: Safe, Wi-Fi. In-hotel: 4 restaurants, room service, bars, pools, gym, beachfront, diving, water sports, children's programs (ages 9–12), laundry service, Wi-Fi, parking (no fee), no-smoking rooms* ⊟*AE, MC, V.*

$$$$ 🛎 **The Ritz-Carlton, Cancún.** Outfitted
Fodor'sChoice with crystal chandeliers, beautiful
   ★ antiques, and elegant oil paintings,
this hotel's style is so European that
you may well forget you're in Mexico. Rooms are done in understated
shades of teal, beige, and rose, with
wall-to-wall carpeting, large balconies overlooking the Caribbean,
and marble bathrooms with separate tubs and showers. For families
with small children, special rooms
with cribs and changing tables are
available. A great feature of this
resort is its Culinary Center, where
guests can participate in wine and
tequila tastings or join in cooking

> **COOKING CLASSES**
>
> **The Ritz-Carlton Culinary Center** (⊠ *Blvd. Kukulcán, Km 13.5,
> Retorno del Rey 36, Zona Hotelera*
> 🕾 *998/881-0822* ⊕ *www.ritzcarlton.com* ⊠ *$115* ⊗ *Mon.–Sat.
> 11–3 PM; wine and tequila tasting
> at 6:30)* offers two-hour cooking
> classes led by Chef Rory Dunaway.
> You can choose from six themed
> sessions, including Mexican grilling and Tuscan dinner parties.
> Courses are open to everyone but
> must be booked in advance.

classes. For an extra charge, guests can join Sunrise Boot Camp, a
morning workout program that includes yoga, a power walk on the
beach, and hydro-balance exercises in the pool. The resort's overall
atmosphere is fairly conservative, and it is one of few hotels that charges
for children's activities ($45 for a half-day program and $65 for a full-day program). **Pros:** one of the city's most elegant hotels; good restaurant variety; tennis center offers private lessons. **Cons:** conservative
atmosphere; expensive; parking costs extra. ⊠*Blvd. Kukulcán, Km
13.5, Retorno del Rey 36, Zona Hotelera* 🕾*998/881–0808* ⊕*www.
ritzcarlton.com* ⟲*365 rooms, 50 suites* ⚿*In-room: Safe, Wi-Fi. In-hotel: 6 restaurants, room service, bar, tennis courts, pools, gym, spa,
beachfront, diving, children's programs (ages 4–12), laundry service,
Internet terminal, Wi-Fi, parking (paid), no-smoking rooms* ⊟*AE, D,
DC, MC, V* ⋈*EP.*

$$$–$$$$ 🛎 **Riu Caribe.** The predominant Mayan theme in this hotel leaps out at
you in the main lobby, where you'll see pyramid-shape architectural
plans, striking stained-glass Mayan calendars on the high ceiling, and
lots of tropical vegetation. All rooms have an ocean view, and the more
spacious junior suites come with a living-room area and terrace. Unfortunately, if you want to use the Internet, the only place to do so is in the
hotel's sports bar. Strong draws here are the huge pools lined with tall
palm trees and the wide beach, which has fairly calm waters for swimming. The large open-air theater stages daily performances in Spanish
and English. **Pros:** tennis courts; large beach and pools; outdoor theater. **Cons:** no Internet in rooms or lobby; beach and pool areas can get
crowded. ⊠*Blvd. Kukulcán, Km 5.5, Zona Hotelera* 🕾*998/848–7850*
⊕*www.riu.com* ⟲*473 rooms, 68 suites* ⚿ *In-room: Safe. In-hotel:
5 restaurants, bars, beachfront, Internet terminal, water sports, children's programs (ages 4–12), tennis courts, pools, spa, gym, no-smoking
rooms, parking (free)* ⊟*AE, MC, V* ⋈*AI.*

$$$$ 🛎 **Riu Palace Las Américas.** A colossal eight-story property at the north
end of the Zona, the Palace is visually stunning and different from
the modern, minimalist resorts that dot the Zona Hotelera. Here the

decoration is a bit baroque. There are towering columns and cupolas in the lobby, and even the most basic guest rooms (all are suites) have ornate mahogany furniture and Victorian-print bedding. The daily origami ritual of swan towel folding can be rather vexing, as can the boisterous emcee directing poolside games. Each room has its own walk-in closet, sitting room, and four-bottle liquor dispenser. This resort mainly attracts guests over 40. **Pros:** spacious suites; access to sister properties Riu Cancún and Riu Caribe. **Cons:** small pools and tiny beach; not much sun by the pool or beach by late afternoon. ⊠*Blvd. Kukulcán, Km 8.5, Zona Hotelera* ☎*998/891–4300* ⊕*www.riu.com* ⇋*372 junior suites* ⌂*In-room: Safe, refrigerator, Internet. In-hotel: 6 restaurants, room service, bars, beachfront, Wi-Fi, water sports, children's programs (ages 4–12), laundry service, pools, gym, spa, no-smoking rooms* ⊟*AE, MC, V* ⭕*AI.*

$$$$ 🖼**The Royal in Cancún.** Luxury is the focus at this high-end, adults-only resort, where all 285 suites have mahogany furniture, Jacuzzis, ocean views, balconies with hammocks, and "magic boxes" that allow room service to be delivered without ever opening the door. All accommodations above the junior deluxe suite level offer guests additional perks, such as an online check-in option, a pillow menu, a Bose stereo system, a loaded iPod, and complimentary Internet service. The resort is located adjacent to sister property Gran Caribe Real, where all guests of the Royal are allowed access. Of course, this location also means that the crowds from the much larger Gran Caribe Real are right down the beach. **Pros:** two-person Jacuzzis in suites; ocean view from all suites and spa. **Cons:** adults only. ⊠*Blvd. Kukulcán, Km 11.5, Zona Hotelera* ☎*998/881–5600* ⊕*www.realresorts.com.mx* ⇋*285 suites* ⌂*In-room: Safe, DVD, Wi-Fi, Internet. In-hotel: 6 restaurants, room service, bars, golf course, tennis court, pools, gym, spa, beachfront, diving, bicycles, laundry service, Internet terminal, Wi-Fi, parking (free), no kids under age 16, no-smoking rooms* ⊟*AE, MC, V* ⭕*AI.*

$$ 🖼**Suites Sina.** On a quiet residential street off Boulevard Kukulcán,
★ these economical suites are in front of Laguna Nichupté and close to the Pok-Ta-Pok golf course. The lobby leads out to a lush garden, pool, and a small restaurant at the center. When it comes to accommodations, skip the standard rooms and upgrade to a junior or master suite, as they have lagoon views, kitchenettes, and spacious dining-living rooms. The atmosphere is relaxed and quiet, making it the perfect place to hide away from the craziness that is the Zona Hotelera; the hotel is actually located between the Hotel Zone and El Centro, though it claims to be in the heart of the Hotel Zone. **Pros:** ideally situated on the lagoon; affordable. **Cons:** 10-minute walk from beach; no elevator. ⊠*Club de Golf, Calle Quetzal 33, turn right at Km 7.5 after golf course, Zona Hotelera/El Centro* ☎*998/883–1017 or 877/666–9837* ⊕*www.cancunsinasuites. com.mx* ⇋*4 rooms, 36 suites* ⌂*In-room: Kitchen (some), refrigerator (some). In-hotel: Restaurant, room service, bar, pool, Wi-Fi, parking (free), no-smoking rooms* ⊟*AE, MC, V* ⭕*EP.*

$$$$ 🖼**The Westin Resort & Spa Cancún.** On the southern end of the Zona Hotelera, this hotel is quite secluded; you'll get privacy, but you'll have to drive to get to shops and restaurants. Subtle hints of pampering are what make this hotel so extraordinary, like the white tea mist that periodically sprays in the lobby and the "heavenly beds," so luxurious that many guests purchase them for their homes. Inside the resort, the modern is juxtaposed with the traditional, as sleek dark-wood furniture is offset by brightly colored rugs and the occasional blue or yellow wall. There are two beaches here–an expansive one on the Caribbean side and a smaller one facing Laguna Nichupté–so guests always have a place to sunbathe. Due to the quiet, isolated nature of the resort, it mainly attracts families with small children and adults in their 30s and 40s. This resort is one of the few in Cancún that allow pets. **Pros:** two beaches. **Cons:** extra charge for the use of amenities like Internet, gym, and spa. ⊠ *Blvd. Kukulcán, Km 20, Zona Hotelera* ☏ *998/848–7400* ⊕ *www.westin.com/cancun* ⇙ *379 rooms, 17 suites* ⇘ *In-room: Safe, DVD (some), Internet, Wi-Fi. In-hotel: 5 restaurants, room service, bars, tennis courts, pools, gym, spa, beachfront, diving, bicycles, children's programs (ages 4–12), laundry service, Wi-Fi, parking (no fee), some pets allowed, no-smoking rooms* ▭ *AE, DC, MC, V* ⏀ *AI, EP.*

EL CENTRO

$$ ⌂ **Ambiance Suites Cancún.** Branding itself as "your home and office,"
★ this modern hotel caters mostly to business executives. Cream leather sofas are accented with hints of cherry, establishing a daring color palette throughout the entire hotel. Thick, white duvets cover the beds, and each room comes with a plasma TV and Wi-Fi. There is a cocktail bar on the first floor and a swimming pool that forms a pleasant oasis in the property's center. The suites have an added sitting area and microwave, but only those overlooking the pool have a pleasant view. The hotel is conveniently located just two blocks from El Centro's largest shopping center, Plaza Las Américas. **Pros:** convenient location within El Centro; good value. **Cons:** unfriendly staff; no restaurant. ⊠ *Av. Tulum 227, Sm 20, El Centro* ☏ *998/892–0392* ⊕ *www.ambiancecancun.com* ⇙ *49 rooms* ⇘ *In-room: Safe, refrigerator, DVD, Wi-Fi. In-hotel: Room service, bar, pool, gym, Wi-Fi, no-smoking rooms* ▭ *AE, MC, V* ⏀ *EP.*

$ ⌂ **Antillano.** This small, well-kept hotel has a decent-sized pool surrounded by wrought-iron patio furniture, and a cozy lobby bar where you can hang with locals. Each room has wood furniture, one or two double beds, a sink area separate from the bath, and tile floors. The quietest rooms face the street–avoid the noisier ones overlooking Avenida Tulum. The lobby bar is a great place to practice Spanish. **Pros:** near bus terminal and main avenues. **Cons:** nothing fancy; rooms facing street can be noisy; no elevator. ⊠ *Av. Tulum and Calle Claveles 1, Sm 22, El Centro* ☏ *998/884–1532* ⊕ *www.hotelantillano.com* ⇙ *48 rooms* ⇘ *In-room: Wi-Fi, Internet. In-hotel: Room service, bar, pool, laundry service, Wi-Fi, parking (free), no-smoking rooms* ▭ *AE, MC, V* ⏀ *CP.*

$–$$ ⌂ **Cancún Inn El Patio.** This traditional, Mexican-style inn has been converted into a charming 15-room guesthouse. An iron gate leads off a busy street into a courtyard, delightfully landscaped with trees, flowers, and a tile fountain. Breakfast is served in a lower-level restaurant, creatively designed with arched doorways, brick walls, and wrought-iron chandeliers, giving it an intimate wine-cellar atmosphere. Upstairs, many of the large, airy rooms have Mexican rustic furniture and Talavera ceramics. Smoking and food are not allowed in the rooms but are permitted in the outdoor patio areas. The helpful staff embraces the *"mi casa es su casa"* mentality and offers expert advice on the area. **Pros:** clean and safe; great value.

> ### WORD OF MOUTH
>
> "There are plenty of buses from Cancun airport into [El Centro]. This is a completely different area from the Zona Hotelera, where all the high-end hotels are. I stayed at a place right next to the bus station from less than $50 a night. Pool included."   –gertie3751

Cons: high processing fee if you pay by credit card; major construction project across the street at this writing; no Internet. ⊠ *Av. Bonampak 51, El Centro* ☎ *998/884–3500* ⊕ *www.cancun-suites.com* ↙ *15 rooms* ♿ *In-room: Safe, no phone. In-hotel: Parking (free), no-smoking rooms* ▤ *MC, V* ¶Ol*CP.*

$$$ 🏨 **Courtyard Marriott.** The draw of this deluxe property is that it's five minutes from the International Airport. Ideal for business travelers, rooms have high-speed Internet, large desks with ergonomic chairs, MP3 docking stations, and 32-inch plasma TVs. Suites have an added lounge area, dining room, kitchenette, and private steam room. Given its location, the property is surprisingly quiet, even in the garden courtyard, outdoor swimming pool, and palapa lounge. Located on a relatively undeveloped stretch of highway, the 20-minute commute to central Cancún creates a sense of isolation from the typical energy associated with the area. On Thursday, the restaurant serves Mexican *pozole,* a delicious pork stew. **Pros:** access to beach clubs at other Marriott resorts in town; complimentary shuttle service to downtown Cancún, airport and sister properties. **Cons:** astronomical phone charges; far from Cancún center and beaches. ⊠ *Blvd. Luis Donaldo Colosio, Km 12.5, Sm 301, Carretera Cancún-Aeropuerto* ☎ *998/287–2200* ⊕ *www.marriott. com/cuncy* ↙ *195 rooms, 6 suites* ♿ *In-room: Safe, kitchen (some), refrigerator, Wi-Fi. In-hotel: Restaurant, room service, bar, pool, gym, laundry facilities, Wi-Fi, Internet terminal, parking (free), no-smoking rooms* ▤ *AE, MC, V.*

¢ 🏨 **Hostel Chacmool.** One of the cheapest and hippest places to stay in downtown Cancún, this family-run hostel offers clean rooms, a complimentary Continental breakfast, a trendy lobby bar, and a terrace with a pool table. Live entertainment is just a stone's throw away at the Parque de las Palapas, and there's no curfew if you decide to make it a late night out. Mixed-gender and female-only dorms are available; if you decide to splurge, opt for the private room with two double beds and a private bath. There's a full kitchen with purified water that guests may use; towels, lockers, and padlocks are also included in the rate. **Pros:** excellent location; no curfew; one hour Internet free. **Cons:** not much privacy in dorms; young crowd. ⊠ *Gladiolas 18, Sm 22, in front of Parque de las Palapas, El Centro* ☎ *998/887–5873* ⊕ *www. chacmool.com.mx* ↙ *30 beds* ♿ *In-room: No phone, no TV. In-hotel: Restaurant, bar, laundry facilities, Internet terminal, parking (free), no-smoking rooms* ▤ *MC, V* ¶Ol*CP.*

1

¢–$ ⌂**Hotel Colonial.** A charming fountain and garden are at the center of this hotel's colonial-style buildings. Rooms are simple but comfortable, each with a double bed, shelves, and decent-size bathroom. Not all have air-conditioning, however, so make sure to request it when you book. What the place lacks in luxury it makes up for in value and location; you are five minutes away from all the downtown concerts, clubs, restaurants, shops, and attractions. Sheltered from the bustle of downtown Cancún, the hotel is on a pleasant pedestrian-only street that's lined with great places to eat. **Pros:** good location; friendly staff. **Cons:** no meals served; no pool; no elevator. ⊠ *Av. Tulipanes 22, Sm 22, El Centro* ☎ *998/884–1535* ⊕ *www.hotelcolonialcancun.com* ⇨ *46 rooms ♿ In-room: No a/c (some), no phone. In-hotel: Internet terminal, no-smoking rooms* ☐ *MC, V.*

$ ⌂**Hotel El Rey del Caribe.** Thanks to the use of solar energy, a water-
★ recycling system, and composting toilets, this unique hotel has very little impact on the environment–and its luxuriant garden blocks the heat and noise of downtown. Hammocks hang poolside, and wrought-iron tables and chairs dot the grounds. There is artwork throughout the property, much of which was painted by the owner herself (who lives on-site). Standard rooms are small but pleasant and have kitchenettes. The newest accommodations, known as the executive rooms, are larger and have wood floors. No smoking allowed in any of the rooms. A great feature is the tiny spa, where you can book honey or chocolate massages that cost a third of what they do in the Zona Hotelera. El Centro's shops and restaurants are within walking distance. **Pros:** tranquil atmosphere; eco-friendly; affordable spa. **Cons:** simple and musty rooms; no elevator. ⊠ *Av. Uxmal 24 at Náder, Sm 2A, El Centro* ☎ *998/884–2028* ⊕ *www.reycaribe.com* ⇨ *31 rooms ♿ In-room: Safe, kitchen, Wi-Fi. In-hotel: Restaurant, pool, spa, Internet terminal, Wi-Fi, parking (free), no-smoking rooms* ☐ *MC, V* �ʘ|*BP.*

$ ⌂**Hotel Kin Mayab.** This small, two-building budget hotel is on downtown's main street, Avenida Tulum, and right down the block from the bus station. The main building houses the superior rooms, which have wood and bamboo furniture, tile floors, stone accents on the walls, and small potted plants. The standard rooms are in the back building, which is a bit quieter and more private. This hotel has a pool and a breakfast restaurant. **Pros:** location; pleasant lobby; clean rooms. **Cons:** fairly simple; on busy street; no elevator. ⊠ *Av. Tulum 75, Sm 22 El Centro* ☎ *998/884–2999* ⊕ *www.hotelkinmayab.com* ⇨ *45 rooms ♿ In-room: Safe, refrigerator (some), Wi-Fi (some). In-hotel: Restaurant, room service, pool, laundry service, Wi-Fi, parking (free), no-smoking rooms* ☐ *MC, V* ʘ|*EP.*

$$ ⌂**Hotel Plaza Caribe.** Although directly across from the bus station, this large economy hotel doesn't absorb much street noise. It has a spacious lawn in the back with a play area for children, as well as a pool and two large cages with colorful Guacamaya birds inside. Each of the hotel's standard rooms has white wooden furniture (including a small table and two chairs), a closet, and a coffeemaker. Some rooms have small windows that face the inner corridors of the building, so be sure to ask for the ones that have large windows and a pool view. The six

suites seem inappropriately named; they are really just two adjoining guest rooms. **Pros:** affordable; some thoughtful touches; new snack bar. **Cons:** tiny bathrooms; king-size beds are actually two twins pushed together; no elevator. ✉ *Av. Tulum with Av. Uxmal, Lote 19, Sm 23, El Centro* ☎ *998/884–1377* ⊕ *www.hotelplazacaribe.com* ✑ *127 rooms, 6 suites* ♿ *In-room: Safe, Wi-Fi. In-hotel: 2 restaurants, room service, bar, pool, gym,, laundry service, Internet terminal, Wi-Fi, parking (free), no-smoking rooms* ☰ *AE, D, DC, MC, V* ⦿ *EP, BP, CP, MAP.*

$$ ▦ **Hotel Plaza Kokai.** With a nautical-theme bar that has live music on weekends, and a large penthouse suite that can accommodate up to 10 guests, this place offers amenities that go above and beyond the typical budget hotel. Assuming you're not seeking the facilities of a posh resort, you'll pretty much find it all here: a sports bar with a pool table; Wi-Fi in the rooms and lobby; a decent pool area; a restaurant that prepares Mexican and international dishes; and, of course, the clean and spacious rooms. The deluxe penthouse, which comes with a fully equipped kitchen, washing machine, and terrace, costs only $200 (quite a bargain if you have a large group). **Pros:** many perks for the price; penthouse suite. **Cons:** rooms near street can be somewhat noisy. ✉ *Av. Uxmal 26, Sm 2a, El Centro* ☎ *998/193–3170* ⊕ *www.hotelkokai.com* ✑ *48 rooms, 1 suite* ♿ *In-room: Safe, Wi-Fi. In-hotel: Restaurant, bars, nightclub, pool, Wi-Fi, room service, laundry service, parking (free), no-smoking rooms* ☰ *MC, V* ⦿ *EP.*

$ ▦ **Hotel Sol Y Luna.** Reminiscent of an upscale European flat, this four-
Fodor's Choice story hotel with tangerine shutters and signature cupolas is one of the
★ jewels of Parque de las Palapas. Bearing names like Nova, Bamboo, Lotus, and Soleil, the themed rooms are uniquely designed to incorporate traces of nature. The artwork here is pure genius, ranging from rustic floor-plank paintings to plaster castings of sea life. Several bathrooms, inlaid with vibrant mosaic tiles, have freestanding stone basins and citrus-infused bath products. A small wooden bridge spans a swimming pool, which separates the main building from the hotel's check-in area. Each standard room comes with a private terrace and small lounging area. The two suites are more modern in design with olive-toned walls, microsuede sofas, and teak furnishings; they offer stunning views of the town square below. **Pros:** thoughtful, creative details for a modest price. **Cons:** no elevator; loud and creaky wooden staircase might mean restless nights if you're on a lower floor. ✉ *Calle Alcatraces 33, Mza. 9, Sm 22, in front of Parque de las Palapas, El Centro* ☎ *998/887–5528* ✑ *9 rooms, 2 suites* ♿ *In-rooms: Safe, refrigerator, Wi-Fi. In-hotel: Pool, no-smoking rooms* ☰ *AE, V* ⦿ *CP*

$$ ▦ **Hotel Xbalamqué Resort & Spa.** A refreshing retreat from the bustling
Fodor's Choice streets of El Centro, the hotel has a lobby adorned with palapa roofs,
★ exquisite waterfalls, tropical birds, and stamped flooring. It forms part of a complex that also includes a juice bar, Internet café, and three restaurants, all of which are open to the general public. Following Mayan tradition, the hotel opened La Flor De Lis, a quaint tamalería with only three tables that offers gourmet salsas and hand-rolled tamales. Guests can enjoy live music in Coffeebrary, a café–library with a bohemian atmosphere. The Xbalamqué is distinctively decorated, with Mayan-

themed murals, statues, and reliefs throughout the hotel. The newly renovated rooms are simply decorated with rustic Mexican furniture. **Pros:** only downtown hotel with (small) spa, beauty salon, and yoga studio on-site. **Cons:** street noise audible from front rooms; thin room doors offer limited security. ⊠ *Av. Yaxchilan 31, Sm 22, Mza. 18, El Centro* ☎ *998/884–9690* ⊕ *www.xbalamque.com* ↻ *80 rooms, 12 suites* ⚐ *In-room: Internet. In-hotel: 3 restaurants, room service, bar, pool, spa, Internet terminal, parking (free), no-smoking rooms* ⊟ *AE, MC, V* ⦿ *BP.*

¢–$ 🏨 **Los Girasoles.** Set back on one of El Centro's few quiet streets, this pleasant hotel is within walking distance of the city's main avenues and shopping centers. Rising out of the ground like a giant sugar cube, the pallid building comes alive with its shaded patio, vibrant rooms, and open-air staircase. Hints of Mexican decor come through in the wrought-iron headboards, local artwork, and bright bedding in hues of red and gold. Cobalt tiles frame the kitchenettes and mirrors, and there are contemporary rain showerheads in all of the bathrooms. The suites comfortably sleep up to four people. For a silent night, your best options are rooms 7 and 14. **Pros:** very affordable. **Cons:** no decent views or balconies; no elevator. ⊠ *Calle Pina 20, Sm 25, El Centro* ☎ *998/887–3990* ⊕ *www.losgirasolescancun.com.mx* ↻ *11 rooms, 6 suites* ⚐ *In-room: Wi-Fi, no phone. In-hotel: No-smoking rooms* ⊟ *No credit cards* ⦿ *EP.*

¢–$ 🏨 **María de Lourdes.** A great pool, clean and basic rooms, and bargain prices are the draws at this downtown hotel. Rooms overlooking the street are noisy, but they're brighter and airier than those facing the hallways. Downtown shops and restaurants are minutes away. This hotel attracts a mix of guests, both local and foreign: business travelers, couples, and tour groups. **Pros:** two double beds in each room; decent pool area; clean rooms. **Cons:** street noise can lead to sleepless nights; no elevator; no Internet in rooms. ⊠ *Av. Yaxchilán 80, Sm 22, El Centro* ☎ *998/884–4744* ⊕ *www.hotelmariadelourdes.com* ↻ *57 rooms* ⚐ *In-room: Refrigerator. In-hotel: Restaurant, room service, pool, laundry service, Internet terminal, no-smoking rooms* ⊟ *AE, MC, V* ⦿ *EP.*

$$$ 🏨 **Oasis América.** With 119 rooms, the Oasis América is one of the largest hotels downtown. Unlike the other Oasis properties in Cancún, most of the guests here are business travelers or part of tour groups. Rooms are average in size, and all except the ones on the sixth floor have small balconies. Rooms in the neighboring sister resort **Sens**, which cost an additional $25, are worth checking into if you like contemporary, minimalist decor. The two hotels share a small spa. If you purchase the all-inclusive package you're allowed access to the beach, restaurant, and gym at the Oasis Palm Beach and Oasis Cancún hotels in the Zona Hotelera. **Pros:** peaceful atmosphere; walking distance from main avenues; free shuttle to sister properties in Zona Hotelera. **Cons:** small bathrooms; sushi bar is seldom open; seemingly safe but old elevators. ⊠ *Av. Tulum, Lote 113, Sm 4, El Centro* ☎ *998/848–8600* ⊕ *www. oasishoteles.com* ↻ *119 rooms (Oasis América); 58 rooms (Sens)* ⚐ *In-room: Safe, Internet, Wi-Fi (some). In-hotel: Restaurant, room service, bars, pool, spa, laundry service, Wi-Fi, no-smoking rooms* ⊟ *AE, D, DC, MC, V* ⦿ *BP, AI.*

$$ ⚐ Radisson Hotel Hacienda Cancún. A stimulating change from the street on which it lies, this hacienda-style building is strikingly hip and sleek. The circular lobby is designed with illuminated onyx stone and features a martini bar, marble floors, and teak furnishings accented with olive and cream cushions. Similar in style, many of the rooms come in neutral colors and are pleasantly decorated with Mexican wall prints and wrought-iron bed frames. All rooms have balconies, and there is one handicapped-accessible unit here. Be sure to request a room overlooking the pool. The daily breakfast buffet is popular with locals, and there's a shuttle to the beach. The children's program here is available only on weekends. **Pros:** prices do not increase in high season; state-of-the-art gym equipment; business center with Internet access. **Cons:** east-facing rooms tend to have street noise. ⊠ *Av. Náder 1, El Centro* ☎ *998/881–6500* ⊕ *www.radissoncancun.com* ⟿ *233 rooms, 15 suites* ⚑ *In-room: Safe, Internet. In-hotel: Restaurant, room service, bar, tennis court, pool, gym, children's programs (ages 4–12), laundry service, Internet terminal, Wi-Fi, parking (free), no-smoking rooms* ⊟ *AE, MC, V* ❘⊙❘*EP, BP, CP, MAP, AP.*

¢ ⚐ Suites Albatros Hotel. This charming budget hotel offers pleasant but spartan rooms with double beds, private baths, and small kitchenettes that look out onto a tropical garden. There is no office or lobby but rather an informal, friendly staff that passes the time on the front steps. The bright yellow rooms sleep up to four people comfortably. Avenida Tulum is a 10-minute walk away, and there is a public bus that stops just outside the door. **Pros:** prices do not go up in high season; at this writing hotel was planning major renovations **Cons:** no luxury amenities; 1980s decor; no elevator. ⊠ *Av. Yaxchilán 154, Sm 20, across street from Red Cross, El Centro* ☎ *998/884–2242* ⊕ *www.albatroscancun.com* ⟿ *15 rooms* ⚑ *In-room: Safe, kitchen, Wi-Fi. In-hotel: Parking (free), some pets allowed, no-smoking rooms* ⊟ *No credit cards.*

¢–$ ⚐ Suites Cancún Centro. You can rent suites or rooms by the day, week, or month at this quiet hotel. Though it abuts the lively Parque de las Palapas, the property manages to maintain a tranquil atmosphere, with lovely, private rooms that open onto a courtyard and a small pool. Tile bathrooms are small but pleasant, and there are king-size as well as single beds. Suites have fully equipped kitchenettes along with sitting and dining areas. **Pros:** in the heart of downtown Cancún; near many restaurants and bars; clean and affordable. **Cons:** no elevator; not much of a social scene at hotel. ⊠ *Calle Alcatraces 32, Sm 22, next to Parque de las Palapas, El Centro* ☎ *998/887–5833 or 998/887–5655* ⊕ *www.suitescancun.com.mx* ⟿ *42 rooms, 27 suites* ⚑ *In-room: Kitchen (some), Wi-Fi. In-hotel: Pool, Wi-Fi, parking (free), no-smoking rooms* ⊟ *MC, V.*

NIGHTLIFE

We're not here to judge: we know that when you come to Cancún, you come to party. Sure, if you want fine dining and dancing under the stars, you'll find it here. But if your tastes run more toward bikini contests, all-night chug-a-thons, or cross-dressing Cher impersonators, rest assured: Cancún delivers.

BARS

ALL-PURPOSE BARS

Many of these spots daylight as restaurants, but when the sun goes down, the party kicks up with pulsating music and waiters who don't so much encourage crowd participation as demand it. Just remember that it's all in good fun.

Black Pearl Bar (⊠ *Blvd. Kukulcán, Km 9.1, Zona Hotelera* ☎ *998/883– 1301)*, a swashbuckler theme bar and grill on the waterfront, is a great place to knock back a few drinks before heading out to the nearby discos. At night the waiters here toss restaurant leftovers off the bar's deck onto the edge of the lagoon, drawing the attention of fish and a few hungry crocodiles. The bar is open until 4 AM.

At **Carlos 'n Charlie's** (⊠ *Blvd. Kukulcán, Km 9, Forum by the Sea mall, Zona Hotelera* ☎ *998/883–1862)* waiters will occasionally abandon their posts to start singing or performing comical skits. It's not unusual for them to roust everyone from their seats to join in a conga line before going back to serving food and drinks.

Fat Tuesday (⊠ *Blvd. Kukulcán, Km 6.5, Zona Hotelera* ☎ *998/849–7201)*, with its large daiquiri bar and live and piped-in disco music, is another place to dance the night away.

You can enjoy a cheeseburger in paradise, along with live music, drinks, and games, at **Jimmy Buffett's Margaritaville** (⊠ *Plaza Flamingo, Blvd. Kukulcán, Km 11.5, Zona Hotelera* ☎ *998/885–2375* ⊕ *www.marga ritaville.com.mx)*. Of course, you'll especially like this place if you're a parrothead.

Pat O'Brien's (⊠ *Plaza Flamingo, Blvd. Kukulcán, Km 11.5, Zona Hotelera* ☎ *998/883–0832)* brings the New Orleans party scene to the Zona with live rock bands and its famous cocktails balanced on the heads of waiters as they dance through the crowd. The really experienced servers can balance up to four margaritas or strawberry daiquiris at once! It's always Mardi Gras here, so the place is decorated with lots of balloons, banners, and those infamous beads given out to brave patrons.

Planet Hollywood (⊠ *Plaza la Isla, Blvd. Kukulcán, Km 12.5, Zona Hotelera* ☎ *998/883–1936)* has a nightly show incorporating aerial acrobatics and bartenders juggling liquor bottles. DJs begin playing music at 8 PM. The dance floor is warmed up by a laser light show.

A relaxing alternative to the loud discos, **Resto-Bar Bling** (⊠ *Blvd. Kukulcán, Km 13.5, in front of Plaza Kukulcán, Zona Hotelera* ☎ *998/840–6015* ☙ *Opens at 6* PM) has a chic open-air lounge bar with canopy-covered beds overlooking the lagoon. DJs spin house and chill-out tunes as the bartenders mix their famous kiwi, cucumber, or coffee martinis. The restaurant inside, which closes at 1 AM, specializes in Mediterranean cuisine and sushi.

Known for its over-the-top drinks, **Señor Frog's** (⊠ *Blvd. Kukulcán, Km 9.5, Zona Hotelera* ☎ *998/883–1092)* serves up foot-long funnel glasses

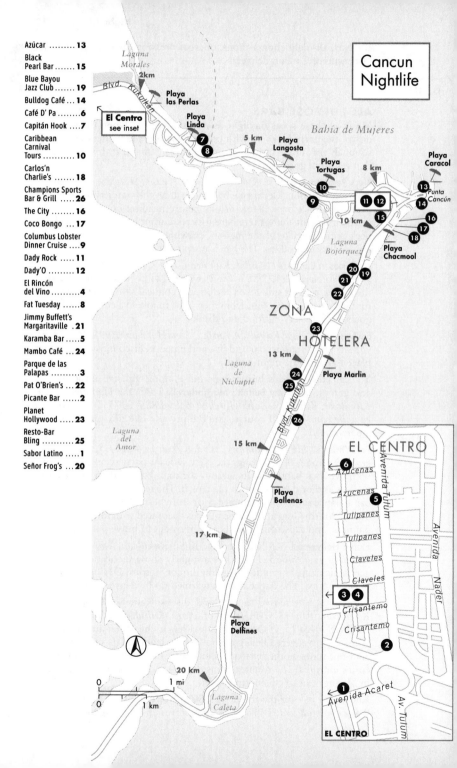

Cancun
Nightlife

*Laguna
Morales*

2km

Blvd. Kukulkán

Playa
las Perlas

El Centro
see inset

Playa
Linda

7

8

5 km

Playa
Langosta

Bahía de Mujeres

Playa
Tortugas

8 km

Playa
Caracol

10

13

Punta
Cancún

9

11 12

14

10 km

15

16

17

18

*Laguna
Bojórquez*

Playa
Chacmool

20

21 19

22

ZONA

23

HOTELERA

*Laguna
de
Nichupté*

13 km

24

Playa Marlin

25

*Laguna
del
Amor*

26

Blvd. Kukulkán

15 km

Playa
Ballenas

17 km

*Laguna
Caleta*

Playa
Delfines

20 km

0   1 mi

0   1 km

EL CENTRO

6

Azucenas

Avenida Tulum

Azucenas

5

Tulipanes

Tulipanes

Avenida Nader

Claveles

Claveles

3 4

Crisantemo

Crisantemo

2

1

Avenida Acaret

Av. Tulim

EL CENTRO

filled with margaritas, daiquiris, or beer, which you can take home as souvenirs once you've chugged them dry. Needless to say, Spring Breakers simply adore this place and often stagger back night after night.

GAY BARS

Cancún has become a popular destination for gay and lesbian travelers and there are lots of gay-friendly clubs in the area. These nightspots get especially busy during the International Gay Festival in mid-May. This celebration includes a welcome party, Caribbean cruise, beach- and bar-hopping, and sightseeing tours to area attractions.

While most Mexicans will treat gay visitors with respect, some are still uncomfortable with public displays of affection. You won't see any open advertisements for the clubs listed below and all of them have fairly discreet entrances. Very few women attend the gay clubs with strip shows.

Café D' Pa (✉ *Parque de las Palapas, Mza. 16, Sm 22, El Centro* ☎ *998/884–7615*) is a cheerful bar and restaurant offering a menu of specialty crepes; since it opens at 6 PM, it's a popular place to gather before the city's other gay bars open their doors.

A variety of drag shows with the usual lip-synching and dancing celebrity impersonations are put on every Wednesday and Thursday at **Karamba Bar** (✉ *Av. Tulum 9, Sm 22, El Centro* ☎ *No phone* ⊕ *www.karambabar.com*), a large open-air disco and club that's known for its stage performers. On Friday night the Go-Go Boys of Cancún entertain, and strip shows are on weekends. The bar opens at 10:30 PM and the party goes on until dawn. There's no cover charge.

The oldest gay bar in Cancún, **Picante Bar** (✉ *Plaza Galerias, Av. Tulum 20, Sm 5, El Centro* ☎ *No phone*) has been operating for 15 years. (It survived several raids and closures during less lenient times in the '90s.) The drag shows here tend to reflect local culture; for instance, during Carnival there is a special holiday beauty pageant followed by the crowning of "the Queen." The owner, "Mother Picante," emcees the floor show that includes Las Vegas–type dance revues, singers, and strippers. Doors open at 9 PM and close at 5 AM, and there's no cover.

SPORTS BARS

Champions Sports Bar & Grill (✉ *CasaMagna Marriott Cancún Resort, Blvd. Kukulcán, Km 14.5, Zona Hotelera* ☎ *998/881–2000 Ext. 6341*) has a giant TV screen and many smaller monitors on which to watch all kinds of sporting events. You can also play pool here and dig in to American-style bar grub.

WINE BARS

El Rincón del Vino (✉ *Alcatraces 29, Mza. 10, Sm 22, in front of Parque de las Palapas, El Centro* ☎ *998/898–3187*) is a popular wine and tapas bar where you can enjoy the sounds of live trova, rumba flamenco, and jazz music. The bar has 250 varieties of *vino* hailing from the world's top winemaking regions, and tapas like *tortilla española* (a potato omelet) and *chistorra* (a Spanish sausage). It's open from 6 to 12 Tuesday through Saturday.

DANCE CLUBS

Cancún wouldn't be Cancún without its glittering discos, which generally start jumping around 10:30 PM (though some open at around 9) and often carry on until 6 AM. As the hours roll on, clothes are peeled off and frenzied dancing seems to quake the building around and the floor beneath. Most clubs offer open bar tickets ($35 to $40) that cover admission and unlimited drinks until 3 AM; this is the way to go if you plan on having more than a couple drinks. If you stay past 3, however, you'll have to pay by the drink. You can also pay a lower cover charge of $10 to $20 and buy drinks separately. Typical prices range from $3 for a shot to $8 for a cocktail. Although every spot seems to pumping by midnight (especially during March and April), the most popular clubs include Coco Bongo, Dady O, The City, and Dady Rock.

Azúcar (⊠*Dreams Cancún Resort & Spa, Blvd. Kukulcán, Km 9.5, Zona Hotelera* ☎*998/848–7000* ▦*$10*) showcases the very best Latin American bands. Go just to watch the locals dance (the beautiful people tend to turn up here really late). Proper dress is required–no jeans or sneakers.

The City (⊠*Blvd. Kukulcán, Km 9.5, Zona Hotelera* ☎*998/848–8380* ⊕*www.thecitycancun.com*) is a giant party complex with a daytime water park; at night there's a cavernous dance floor with stadium seating and several large bars selling overpriced drinks. Dancing and live shows are the main draw, as well as a Tuesday night moonlight pool party and bikini contest. This is by far the loudest club in the Zona Hotelera, so don't be surprised if you go home with a ringing in your ears. Doors open at 10 PM.

The wild, wild **Coco Bongo** (⊠ *Blvd. Kukulcán, Km 9.5, across street from Dady'O, Zona Hotelera* ☎*998/883–5061* ⊕*www.cocobongo. com.mx* ▦*$20, $60 for open bar*) has no chairs, but there are plenty of tables that everyone dances on. There's also a popular floor show billed as "Las Vegas meets Hollywood," featuring celebrity impersonators; and an amazing gravity-defying acrobatic show with an accompanying 12-piece orchestra. After the shows, the techno gets turned up to full volume and everyone gets up to get down.

Dady'O (⊠*Blvd. Kukulcán, Km 9.5, Zona Hotelera* ☎*998/883–3333* ⊕*www.dadyo.com.mx* ▦*$20 cover, $45 for open bar*) has been around for a while, but it is still very "in" with the younger set. A giant screen projects music videos about the always-packed dance floor, while laser lights whirl across the crowd. During spring break the place gets even livelier during the Hawaiian Bikini contests.

Dady Rock (⊠*Blvd. Kukulcán, Km 9.5, Zona Hotelera* ☎*998/883–3333* ⊕*www.dadyrock.com.mx* ▦*$20, $45 for open bar*) draws a high-energy crowd that likes entertainment along with their dinner. Live bands usually start off the action, followed by DJs spinning dance tracks into the wee hours of the morning. Wet body contests are on Thursdays and hot male contests on Sundays. Winners take home $1,500 in cash and prizes. It's open Thursday through Sunday from 8 PM on.

Mambo Café (⊠*Blvd. Kukulcán, Km 13.5, Zona Hotelera* ☎*998/840–6498* ⊕*www.mambocafe.com.mx* ▦*$10, $30 for open bar*) features some of the city's hottest live bands and DJs playing tropical music, making it the ideal disco in which to practice your salsa and merengue steps.

DINNER CRUISES

Sunset boat cruises that include dinner, drinks, music, and sometimes dancing are popular in Cancún—especially among couples looking for a romantic evening and visitors who'd rather avoid the carnival atmosphere of the clubs and discos.

On the **Capitán Hook** (⊠ *El Embarcadero, Blvd. Kukulcán, Km 4.5, Zona Hotelera* ☎ *998/884–3760* ⊕ *www.capitanhook.com* ⊠ *Adults $77–$89, children $42–$48* ⊙ *7:30–10:30* PM) has a private show aboard a replica of an 18th-century Spanish galleon, then enjoy a lobster dinner and drinks as the ship cruises around at sunset. Beware of pirate attacks!

Caribbean Carnival Tours (⊠ *Playa Tortugas, next to Dos Playas hotel, Blvd. Kukulcán, Km 6.5, Zona Hotelera* ☎ *998/884–3760* ⊕ *www.can cunfuntours.com* ⊠ *$85* ⊙ *7–11* PM) start off on a large two-level catamaran at sunset. There's an open bar for the sail across to Isla Mujeres; once you reach shore, you'll join in a moonlight calypso cookout and a full dinner buffet, followed by a Caribbean carnival show.

Columbus Lobster Dinner Cruises (⊠ *Agua Tours Marina, Blvd. Kukulcán, Km 6.5, Zona Hotelera* ☎ *998/849–4748* ⊕ *www.thelobsterdinner. com.mx* ⊠ *$74–$79* ⊙ *5* PM, *8* PM) offers tranquil, couples-only cruises on a 62-foot galleon. A fresh lobster dinner is served while the sun sets over Laguna Nichupté; afterward, the boat continues to cruise so you can stargaze.

LIVE MUSIC

The Blue Bayou Jazz Club (⊠ *Blvd. Kukulcán, Km 10.5, Zona Hotelera* ☎ *998/884–0044*), the lobby bar in the Hyatt Cancún Caribe, has nightly jazz ranging from contemporary to Dixieland.

Bulldog Cafe (⊠ *Krystal Cancún hotel, Blvd. Kukulcán, Km 9, Zona Hotelera* ☎ *998/848–9800* ⊕ *www.bulldogcafe.com* ⊠ *$40*) has an all-you-can-drink bar, live rock groups, the latest dance music, and an impressive laser light show. The stage here is large, and some very well-known bands have played on it, including Guns n' Roses and Radiohead. Another, somewhat bawdier draw is the private hot tub, where you can have "the Jacuzzi bikini girls" scrub your back. Naturally, this place is popular with Spring Breakers.

Sabor Latino (⊠ *Plaza Hong Kong, Loc 31, Sm 20, El Centro* ☎ *998/898– 4006* ⊕ *www.saborlatino.com.mx* ⊙ *Opens at 10* PM, *Wed.–Sun.*) has live salsa bands and lots of locals to show you new dance moves. If you want something more structured, you can take dance lessons here.

To mingle with locals and hear great music for free, head to the **Parque de las Palapas** (⊠ *Bordered by Avs. Tulum, Yaxchilán, Uxmal, and Cobá, Sm 22, El Centro*). Every Friday night at 7:30 there's live music that ranges from jazz to salsa to Caribbean; lots of locals show up to dance. On Sunday afternoon the Cancún Municipal Orchestra plays.

SHOPPING

The *centros comerciales* (malls) in Cancún are fully air-conditioned and as well kept as similar establishments in the United States or Canada. Like their northerly counterparts, they also sell just about everything: designer clothing, beachwear (including tons of raunchy T-shirts aimed at the Spring Breaker crowd), sportswear, jewelry, music, video games, household items, shoes, and books. Some even have the same terrible mall food that is standard north of the border. Prices are fixed in shops. They're

> **AVOID TORTOISESHELL**
>
> Refrain from buying anything made from tortoiseshell. The *carey*, or hawksbill turtles from which most of it comes, is an endangered species, and it's illegal to bring tortoiseshell products into the United States and several other countries. Also be aware that there are some restrictions regarding black coral. You must purchase it from a recognized dealer.

also generally—but not always—higher than in the markets, where bargaining for better prices is a possibility. Perfumes in Cancún are considerably less expensive than you might find at home, and you'll even beat the duty-free price you would pay at the airport. Of course tequila is a bargain here as well, but make sure you buy at the supermarket rather than at a souvenir shop.

There are many duty-free stores that sell designer goods at reduced prices—sometimes as much as 30% or 40% below retail. Although prices for handicrafts are higher here than in other cities and the selection is limited, you can find handwoven textiles, leather goods, and handcrafted silver jewelry.

Shopping hours are generally weekdays 10 to 1 and 4 to 7, although more stores are staying open throughout the day rather than closing for siesta. Many shops keep Saturday morning hours, and some are now open on Sunday until 1. Centros comerciales tend to be open daily 9 AM or 10 AM to 8 PM or 9 PM.

GALLERIES

Serious collectors visit **Casa de Cultura** (⊠ *Prolongación Av. Yaxchilán, Sm 25* ☎ *998/884–8364*) for regular art shows featuring Mexican artists.

Dorfman's Art Gallery (⊠ *Inside the Royal Caribbean hotel, Blvd. Kukulcán, Km 17, Zona Hotelera* ☎ *998/881–0100 Ext. 63610*) features Mayan-inspired and environmentally themed sculptures and paintings by local artists and brothers Renato and Adán Dorfman.

El Pabilo (⊠ *Av. Yaxchilán 3, Sm 7* ☎ *998/892–4553*) is a downtown café that showcases Mexican painters and photographers on a rotating basis.

GROCERY STORES

Chedraui (⊠*Av. Tulum 57, at Av. Cobá, Centro* ☎998/884–1024 ⊠*Plaza las Americas, Av. Tulum 260, Sm 7* ☎998/887–2111) is a popular superstore with six locations.

If you're a member in the States, you can visit **Costco** (⊠*Avs. Kabah and Yaxchilán, Sm 21* ☎998/881–0250).

Mega Comercial Mexicana (⊠*Avs. Tulum and Uxmal, Sm 2* ☎998/884–3330 ⊠*Avs. Kabah and Mayapan, Sm 21* ☎998/880–9164) is one of the major Mexican grocery-store chains, with three locations. The most convenient is at Avenidas Tulum and Uxmal, across from the bus station; its largest store is farther north on Avenida Kabah, which is open 24 hours.

Sam's Club (⊠*Av. Cobá, Lote 2, Sm 21* ☎998/881–0200) has plenty of bargains on groceries and souvenirs.

Super Aki (⊠*Av. Xel-Ha, Lote 1, next to Mercado Veintiocho, Sm 28* ☎998/884–2812) is a smaller grocery store downtown.

Wal-Mart (⊠*Av. Cobá, Lote 2, Sm 21* ☎998/884–1383) is a popular shopping spot where you can find beach supplies, snacks, and necessities you forgot to pack.

■**TIP**➔ The few grocery stores in the Zona Hotelera tend to be expensive. It's better to shop for groceries downtown.

MARKETS AND MALLS

ZONA HOTELERA

Coral Negro (⊠*Blvd. Kukulcán, Km 9, Zona Hotelera*), next to the Convention Center, is an open-air market that has about 50 stalls selling crafts and souvenirs. It's open daily until late evening. Everything here is overpriced, but bargaining does work. Stalls deeper in the market tend to have better deals than those around the market's periphery.

Forum-by-the-Sea (⊠*Blvd. Kukulcán, Km 9.5, Zona Hotelera* ☎998/883–4428) is a three-level entertainment and shopping plaza in the Zona. This open-air mall features brand-name restaurants, upscale clothing boutiques, a food court, and chain stores, all in a circuslike atmosphere. For spring breakers, the main draws are the nightclubs, Coco Bongo and Hard Rock Cafe, which are identified by the massive guitar at the mall entrance. The bungee trampolines set up here during high season are especially popular with children.

★ The glittering, ultratrendy, and ultraexpensive **La Isla Shopping Village** (⊠*Blvd. Kukulcán, Km 12.5, Zona Hotelera* ☎998/883–5025) is on the Laguna Nichupté under chic, white canopies. A series of canals and small bridges is designed to give the place a Venetian look. In addition to more than 200 shops, the mall has a marina, a disco, restaurants, and movie theaters. There is also an interactive aquarium where you can swim with the dolphins and feed the sharks. A fun, inexpensive activity here is the River Ride Tour, a 20-minute boat ride around the canals and out into the lagoon that costs only $4 per person (a great time to go is right at sundown, so you can watch the sun set over the lagoon).

Located north of the Convention Center, the two-story **Plaza Caracol** (⊠*Blvd. Kukulcán, Km 8.5, Zona Hotelera* ☎998/883–4760) houses chain stores like Sunglass Island, Benetton, and Ultrafemme, along with souvenir and jewelry shops and pharmacies. Making up this contemporary mall are 150 shops, as well as a small food court, an enormous Starbucks, and the fine Italian restaurant Casa Rolandi. The Plaza is closed on weekends.

Located in from the Convention Center, **Plaza la Fiesta** (⊠*Blvd. Kukulcán, Km 9, Zona Hotelera* ☎998/883–2116) has 20,000 square feet of showroom space and more than 100,000 different products for sale. Probably the widest selection of Mexican goods in the Hotel Zone, it includes leather goods, silver and gold jewelry, handicrafts, souvenirs, and swimwear. There are some good bargains here.

Plaza Flamingo (⊠*Blvd. Kukulcán, Km 11.5, across from Hotel Flamingo Resort & Plaza, Zona Hotelera* ☎998/883–2855) is a small mall that houses around 80 different shops that sell mainly clothing, jewelry, and souvenirs. The main attractions here are the chain restaurants Jimmy Buffet's Margaritaville, Outback Steakhouse, Bubba Gump, and Pat O'Brien's, which fill up with partiers during spring break.

★ **Plaza Kukulcán** (⊠*Blvd. Kukulcán, Km 13, Zona Hotelera* ☎998/193–0161) is a large, upscale mall with around 100 shops and six restaurants. Some highlights include a bar with a bowling alley and the Luxury Avenue section of the mall, which offers brand names from Cartier, Fendi, and Burberry to Coach. While parents shop, kids can enjoy the game arcade, a play area, and Chocolate City, a theme restaurant with table games, live music, and a weekly circus show. The mall hosts art exhibits and other cultural events. If you stop in any night at 8 PM, you can watch the 10-minute, English-language light show under the Mayan stained-glass dome. If you fell in love with the European clothing chain Mango on your last trip to Paris, swing by the branch here.

Plaza El Zócalo (⊠*Blvd. Kuckulcán, Km 9, Zona Hotelera* ☎998/883–3698) may look small from the entrance, but it has about 60 stalls where you can find traditional Mexican handicrafts, silver jewelry, and handmade sandals. El Zócalo also houses four restaurants–including Mextreme, which still sports a banner announcing its claim to fame as a set in the 1980s movie *Cocktail.*

EL CENTRO

There are lots of interesting shops downtown along Avenida Tulum (between avenidas Cobá and Uxmal). The oldest and largest of Cancún's crafts markets is **Ki Huic** (⊠*Av. Tulum 17, between Bancomer and Bital banks, Sm 3* ☎998/884–3347). It's open daily 9 AM to 10 PM and houses about 100 vendors. **Mercado Veintiocho** *(Market 28),* just off avenidas Yaxchilán and Sunyaxchén, is the largest open-air market in Cancún. In addition to a few small restaurants, here you will find around 100 stalls selling many of the same items found in the Zona Hotelera but at half the price. **Ultrafemme** (⊠*Av. Tulum 111, at Calle Claveles, Sm 21* ☎998/884–1402) is a popular downtown store that carries duty-free perfume, cosmetics, and jewelry. It also has branches in the Zona Hotelera at Plaza Caracol, Plaza las Américas, Plaza

Kukulcán, and La Isla Shopping Village. The downtown store is open daily 9:30 AM to 9 PM.

Cancún Gran Plaza (⊠*Av. Nichupté, Mza. 18, Lote 1, Locales 24, 30 Y 62A, Sm 51, El Centro* ☾*9–9*) offers jewelry shops, fashion boutiques, and major department stores such as Sanborns and Wal-Mart. There are also cinemas, cafés, and restaurants in the shopping mall.

Paseo Cancún (⊠*Av. Andrés, Sm 39* ☎*998/872–3735* ⊕*www.cabi corp.com.mx*) was developed by the same company that owns La Isla in the Zona Hotelera, so it has the same open-air design with modern white canopies throughout. Here you'll find a small ice-skating rink, a movie theater, a bowling alley, a pet store, a food court, several cafés, and around 60 stores.

Parque Lumpkul (⊠*Between Av. Margaritas and Calle Azucenas, Sm 22*) is a small park with a hippy vibe. Vendors sell their wares here Wednesday through Sunday, but Friday and Saturday are the best nights to go. There are only about 20 tables, but you can find bargains on beautiful handmade jewelry with unusual stones, as well as hand-painted clothes. There are sometimes music and artistic performances on market days.

Plaza las Américas (⊠*Av. Tulum, Sm 4 and Sm 9* ☎*998/887–3863*) is the largest shopping center in downtown Cancún. Its 50-plus stores, three restaurants, two movie theaters, video arcade, fast-food outlets, and several large department stores will–for better or worse–make you feel right at home. This mall is intolerably crowded on weekends.

Plaza Las Avenidas (⊠*Av. Yaxchilán, Sm 35, N.C-2, El Centro* ☎*998/887–7552*) has gift shops, fast-food restaurants, cafés, nightclubs, and a karaoke bar. There are also a drugstore and a bakery on the premises.

Plaza Bonita (⊠*Av. Xel-Há 1 and 2, Sm 28* ☎*998/884–6812*) is a small outdoor plaza next door to Mercado Veintiocho (Market 28). It has many wonderful specialty shops carrying Mexican goods and crafts.

Plaza Cancún 2000 (⊠*Avs. Tulum and López Portillo, Sm 7* ☎*998/884–9988*) is a shopping mall popular with locals. There are some great bargains to be found here on shoes, clothes, and cosmetics. If you need a break from shopping, there is a charming ice-cream parlor nestled in this traditional colonial-town setting.

Plaza Chinatown (⊠*Sm 35, Mza. 2, Lote 6, between Labná and Av. Xcaret, El Centro* ☎*998/887–6315*) commonly referred to as Plaza Hong Kong, seems strikingly out of place with it massive pagoda structure. Here you will find Mexican handicrafts, souvenir shops, and a restaurant appropriately named Hong Kong. There is also a babysitting service available in the mall.

Plaza Hollywood (⊠*Av. Xcaret at Rubi Cancún, El Centro* ☎*998/887–3187*) is one of the newest strip malls to join El Centro. Here you will find several small boutiques and restaurants as well as a bank, post office, and Starbucks. For the wine connoisseur, there is La Europe Wine Market, which carries a wide selection of imported cheeses, meats, as well as Mexican reds.

Plaza Nayandei (⊠ *Av. Bonampak 200, Mza. 1, Lote 4B-2, Sm 4-A, El Centro* ☎998/898–3743) is a local favorite with its bars, cafés, gym, and eight restaurants. This plaza also has several good furniture stores and a yoga club for kids.

SPORTS AND THE OUTDOORS

BOATING AND SAILING

There are lots of ways to get your adrenaline going on the waters of Cancún. You can arrange to go parasailing (about $50 for 10 minutes), waterskiing ($70 per hour), or jet skiing ($70 per hour, or $80 for Wave Runners). Paddleboats, kayaks, catamarans, and banana boats are readily available, too. Jungle boat tours, which usually last from 2 to 2½ hours, are also popular. They cost around $60 per person.

AquaWorld (⊠ *Blvd. Kukulcán, Km 15.2, Zona Hotelera* ☎998/848–8300 ⊕*www.aquaworld.com.mx*) rents boats and water toys like Aqua Twister, a high-speed boat that fishtails 270 degrees. They also offer parasailing and submarine tours.

Delta Tours (⊠ *Playa Tortugas, Blvd. Kukulcán, Km 6.5, Zona Hotelera* ☎998/849–4995) has banana boats, snorkeling gear, Wave Runners, and parasails. Willing to match competitive prices, they also offer night cruises, paddy boats, catamarans, and all-inclusive tours to Isla Mujeres.

El Embarcadero (⊠ *Blvd. Kukulcán, Km 4, Zona Hotelera* ☎998/849–7343), the marina complex at Playa Linda, is the departure point for ferries to Isla Mujeres and several tour boats.

Marina Barracuda (⊠ *Blvd. Kukulcán, Km 14, in front of Ritz-Carlton, Zona Hotelera* ☎998/885–3444 ⊕*www.marinebarracuda.com*), **Marina Punta del Este** (⊠ *Blvd. Kukulcán, Km 10.3, Zona Hotelera* ☎998/883–1210), and **Marina del Rey** (⊠ *Blvd. Kukulcán, Km 15.6, in front of Grand Oasis Cancún, Zona Hotelera* ☎998/885–0363), all rent out Wave Runners and offer jungle tours that leave several times a day. Marina Punta del Este also has jungle tours that leave every hour from 9 AM to 3 PM.

FISHING

Some 500 species–including sailfish, wahoo, bluefin, marlin, barracuda, and red snapper–live in the waters off Cancún. You can charter deep-sea fishing boats starting at about $380 for four hours, $470 for six hours, and $550 for eight hours. Rates generally include a captain and first mate, gear, bait, and beverages.

Asterix Tours (⊠ *Blvd. Kukulcán, Km 5.5, Zona Hotelera* ☎998/886–4847 ⊕*www.contoytours.com*) offers nighttime "party fishing" trips that cost $65 per person and include dinner and drinks. With an emphasis on nature conservation, Asterix is the only tour company permitted to visit Isla Contoy and the underwater gardens of Isla Mujeres. Thirty-minute boat tours cost $65 per person.

Wet, Wild Water Sports

Cancún is one of the water-sports capitals of the world, and, with the Caribbean on one side of the island and the still waters of Laguna Nichupté on the other, it's no wonder. The most popular water activities are snorkeling and diving along the coral reef just off the coast.

Due to northeasterly winds, sports such as kiteboarding and windsurfing have become increasingly popular. Although waves are not as constant as those on the Pacific side, it is possible to find some decent surf in and around Cancún. During December and January, waves peak at about six feet, but it usually takes a windstorm or winter swell to make the choppy paddle worthwhile. During hurricane season, from May through November, the surf can be borderline epic on a good day. For the avid beach-break surfer, the sandbars are best at Playa Delfines, Chamol, and City Beach. Twenty miles south of Cancún are several point breaks off the coast of Puerto Morelos and Punta Brava.

If you want to view the mysterious underwater world but don't want to get your feet wet, a glass-bottom boat or "submarine" is the ticket. You can also fish, sail, jet-ski, or parasail.

Since the beaches along the Zona Hotelera can have a strong undertow, you should always respect the flags posted in the area. A black flag means you cannot swim at all. A red flag means you can swim but only with extreme caution. Yellow means approach with caution, while green means water conditions are safe. You will seldom see the green flag–even when the water is calm–so swim cautiously, and don't assume you're immune to riptides because you're on vacation. At least one tourist drowns per season after ignoring the flags.

Unfortunately, Laguna Nichupté has become polluted from illegal dumping of sewage and at times can have a strong smell. In 1993 the city began conducting a clean-up campaign that included handing out fines to offenders, so the quality of the water is slowly improving. There is very little wildlife to see in the lagoon, so most advertised jungle tours are glorified jet-ski romps where you drive around fast, make a lot of noise, and don't see many animals. American crocodiles still reside in these waters though, so do not stand or swim in the lagoon.

Although the coral reef in this area is not as spectacular as farther south, there is still plenty to see, with more than 500 species of sea life in the waters. It is actually quite common to see angelfish, parrotfish, blue tang, and the occasional moray eel. But the corals in this area are extremely fragile and currently endangered. To be a good world citizen, follow the six golden rules for snorkeling or scuba diving:

1. Don't throw any garbage into the sea, as the marine life will assume it is food, an often lethal mistake.

2. Never stand on the coral.

3. Secure all cameras and gear onto your body so you don't drop anything onto the fragile reef.

4. Never take anything from the sea.

5. Don't feed any of the marine animals.

6. Avoid sunblock or tanning lotion just before you visit the reef.

FISHING AND DIVING COMBOS

Mundo Marino (⊠ *Blvd. Kukulcán, Km 5.5, Zona Hotelera* ☎998/849–7257 *or 998/849–7258*) is the marina closest to downtown and specializes in diving and fishing, including deep-sea fishing expeditions. Prices range from $380 to $940, depending on the size of the boat and the length of the trip. They also offer small game-fishing trips that cost $220 for four hours or $330 for six hours.

Scuba Cancún (⊠ *Blvd. Kukulcán, Km 5, Zona Hotelera* ☎998/849–7508, *998/849–4736, or 998/849–5225* ⊕*www.scubacancun.com*) also offers deep-sea fishing and diving. Prices range from $550 for a four-hour fishing trip to $800 for an eight-hour expedition.

GOLF

Many hotels offer golf packages that can considerably reduce your green fees at Cancún golf courses. Cancún's main golf course is at **Cancún Golf Club at Pok-Ta-Pok** (⊠ *Blvd. Kukulcán, Km 7.5, Zona Hotelera* ☎998/883–1230 ⊕*www.cancungolfclub.com*). The club has fine views of both sea and lagoon; its 18 holes were designed by Robert Trent Jones Jr. It also has two practice greens, three tennis courts, a pro shop, and a restaurant. The green fees go from $145 to $175, and include your cart, food, and beverages; club rentals are $40, shoes $18.

The 9-hole executive course, **Gran Sol Meliá** (⊠ *Gran Melia Cancún Resort, Blvd. Kukulcán, Km 16.5, Zona Hotelera* ☎998/881–1100 ⊕*www.solmelia.com*) forms a semicircle around the property and looks out onto the lagoon. The green fee is $30, but the course is for the exclusive use of hotel guests.

There's an 18-hole championship golf course at the **Hilton** (⊠ *Hilton Cancún Golf & Spa Resort, Blvd. Kukulcán, Km 17, Zona Hotelera* ☎998/881–8016 ⊕*www.hiltoncancun.com/golf.htm*). Located along the Nichupté Lagoon, the course has a practice facility with driving range and putting green. The 16th hole overlooks the Mayan Ruinas del Rey. Green fees are $199 ($159 for hotel guests), carts included.

The newest course in Cancún is the **Playa Mujeres Golf Club** (⊠ *Playa Mujeres Beach Resort, Prolongación Bonampak, Punta Sam* ☎998/887–7322 *or 998/892–0874*). Designed by Greg Norman, this 18-hole, par-72 course is located within the 930-acre Playa Mujeres Resort that is currently being developed in Punta Sam. Practice facilities include a driving range, two putting greens, and a short game area. You can also arrange for individual and group instruction. Green fees run from $185 to $230.

Moon Spa & Golf Club (⊠ *Carretera Cancún-Chetumal, Km 340, Sm 40 [about 15 min from airport]* ☎998/881–6000 ⊕*www.palaceresorts. com*) has three 9-hole courses. The 18-hole green fee, which includes a cart, food, and drink service, costs $260. If you're staying at the Moon Palace, inquire about the hotel's all-inclusive golf package.

SNORKELING AND SCUBA DIVING

The snorkeling is best at Punta Nizuc, Punta Cancún, and Playa Tortugas, although you should be careful of the strong currents at Tortugas. You can rent gear for about $10 per day from many of the scuba-diving places as well as at many hotels.

WORD OF MOUTH

"I would suggest taking the jungle tour with Aquaworld in Cancún. You get your own mini-boat or jet ski and go around the mangroves."

–KVR

Scuba diving is popular in Cancún, though it's not as spectacular as in Cozumel. Look for a scuba company that will give you lots of personal attention: smaller companies are often better at this than larger ones. Regardless, ask to meet the dive master, and check the equipment and certifications thoroughly. ■**TIP➔A few words of caution about one-hour courses that many resorts offer for free: such courses *do not* prepare you to dive in the open ocean–only in shallow water where you can easily surface without danger. If you've caught the scuba bug and want to take deep or boat dives, prepare yourself properly by investing in a full certification course.**

☺ **Aqua Fun** (✉*Blvd. Kukulcán, Km 16.5, Zona Hotelera* ☎*998/885–2930* ⊕*www.aquafun.com.mx*) offers a two-hour tour of the mangroves that costs $66 per person and includes snorkeling at the Punta Nizuc reef.

☺ **AquaWorld** (✉*Blvd. Kukulcán, Km 15.2, Zona Hotelera* ☎*998/848–8300* ⊕*www.aquaworld.com.mx*) has a day-trip snorkeling excursion to Isla Mujeres that costs $69 per person. This operation also offers diving; a one-tank dive costs $66 and two-tank dives start at $71. Dive explorations of boat wrecks cost $79, sinkhole expeditions cost $132.

☺ **Marina Barracuda** (✉*Blvd. Kukulcán, Km 14, Zona Hotelera* ☎*998/885–2444*) has a two-hour jungle boat tour through the mangroves, which ends with snorkeling at the Punta Nizuc coral reef. The fee (starting at $66) includes snorkeling equipment, life jackets, and refreshments.

Marina Punta del Este (✉*Blvd. Kukulcán, Km 10.3, Zona Hotelera* ☎*998/883–1210*) is right in front of the Hyatt Cancún Caribe. They have dives that last from 3½ to 4 hours; $72 if you are certified and $88 for a lesson. Daily lessons begin at 8 AM and 1 PM.

☺ **Mundo Marino** (✉*Blvd. Kukulcán, Km 5.5, Zona Hotelera* ☎*998/849–7257 or 998/849–7258*) has a 2½-hour snorkeling excursion that costs $28 per person. They also offer a single-tank dive ($55), two-tank dive ($70), night dive ($70), and diving instruction course ($90).

Scuba Cancún (✉*Blvd. Kukulcán, Km 5, Zona Hotelera* ☎*998/849–7508* ⊕*www.scubacancun.com.mx*) specializes in diving trips and offers NAUI, CMAS, and PADI instruction. It's operated by Tomás Hurtado, who has more than 30 years of experience. A two-tank dive starts at $68.

Solo Buceo (✉*Blvd. Kukulcán, Km 9.5, Zona Hotelera* ☎*998/883–3979* ⊕*www.solobuceo.com*) charges $55 for one-tank dives, $70 for two-tank dives, and $90 for twilight diving every Tuesday and Thursday. They also have NAUI, FMAS, CMAS, and PADI instruction (lesson prices range from $90 to $240). The outfit also offers a full-day excursion to Cozumel, as well as dive explorations of various cenotes near Akumal. These extended trips are available from $145 every Wednesday and Friday.

Isla Mujeres

Playa Norte, Isla Mujeres

WORD OF MOUTH

"You may want to consider taking the ferry (or a tour boat) to Isla Mujeres for the day. Rent a golf cart and explore the southern end of the island (lots of things to see and do, in the water and on land). And then have a swim at Playa Norte before heading back to Cancun."

—Succeed

WELCOME TO ISLA MUJERES

TOP REASONS TO GO

★ Getting away from the crowd: Although Isla Mujeres is just across the bay from Cancún, the peace and quiet make it seem like another universe.

★ Exploring the southeastern coast: Bump along in a golf cart where craggy cliffs meet the blue Caribbean.

★ Eating freshly grilled seafood: For some reason it always tastes best under a beachfront palapa at lovely Playa Norte.

★ The chance to dive with "sleeping sharks": They dwell in the underwater caverns off Isla.

★ Taking a boat trip to Isla Contoy: On this even smaller island, more than 70 species of birds make their home.

1 The Western Coast. Midway along the western coast of Isla you can glimpse the lovely Laguna Makax. At the lagoon's southeastern end are the remains of a 19th-century mansion, Hacienda Mundaca, and the shady stretches of Playa Tiburon and Playa Lancheros. At Isla's southernmost tip is El Garrafón National Park.

2 Playa Norte. With its waist-deep turquoise waters and wide soft sands, Playa Norte is the most northerly and most beautiful beach on Isla Mujeres. Most of the island's resorts and hotels are located here; El Pueblo and the historic El Cementerio are just a short walk away.

3 El Pueblo. Directly in front of the ferry piers, El Pueblo is Isla's only town. It extends the full width of the northern end and is sandwiched between sand and sea to the south, west, and northeast. The *zócalo* (main square) here is the hub of Isleño life.

GETTING ORIENTED

Isla Mujeres is still quiet by Riviera Maya standards. It retains the small-town feel that makes it a great escape from Cancún. (Don't mention that to locals, who will tell you that the influx of big hotels has changed it forever.) Just 8 km (5 mi) long and 1 km (½ mi) wide, its landscapes include flat sandy beaches in the north and steep rocky bluffs to the south. The liveliest activities here are swimming or snorkeling, exploring the remnants of the island's past, drinking cold beer and eating fresh seafood, and lazing under thatched palapas.

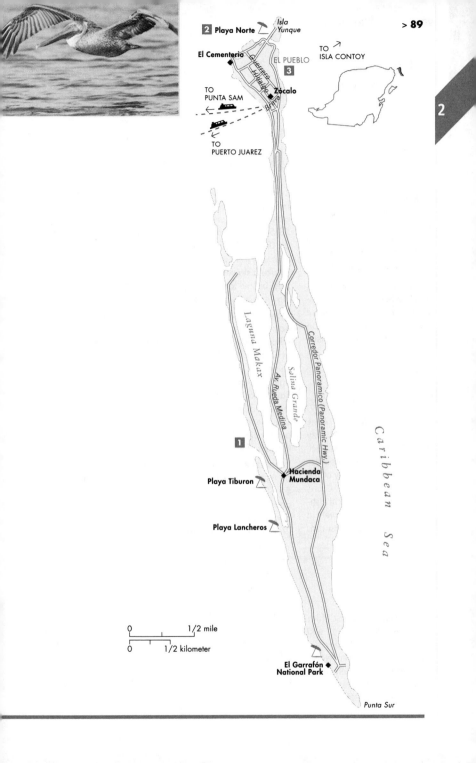

2 Playa Norte

Isla Yunque

El Cementerio

EL PUEBLO

3

TO
ISLA CONTOY

TO
PUNTA SAM

Zócalo

Guerrero

Hidalgo

Bravo

TO
PUERTO JUAREZ

2

Laguna Makax

Salina Grande

Av. Rueda Medina

Corredor Panoramico (Panoramic Hwy.)

1

**Hacienda
Mundaca**

Playa Tiburon

Playa Lancheros

Caribbean Sea

0   1/2 mile

0   1/2 kilometer

El Garrafón ◆
National Park

Punta Sur

ISLA MUJERES PLANNER

How's the Weather?

Isla enjoys its best weather between November and May, when temperatures usually hover around 80°F. June, July, and August are the hottest and most humid months, when temperatures routinely top 95°F.

The rainy hurricane season lasts from late September until mid-November, bringing frequent downpours in the afternoon as well as the occasional hairy tropical storm.

Save the Dates

Sol a Sol Regatta: late April. Founder's Day: Aug. 17. Day of the Dead celebrations: Oct. 31–Nov. 2. Immaculate Conception Feast: Dec. 1–8. Day of the Virgin de la Caridad del Cobre, the patron saint of local fishermen: Sept. 9. Book well in advance, and come if you can.

Need More Information?

The **Isla Mujeres** tourist office (⊠ *Av. Rueda Medina 130* ☎ *998/877-0307* ⊕ *www.isla-mujeres.com.mx*), open weekdays 8 to 8 and weekends 8 to noon, has lots of general information about the island.

Getting Here and Around

Isla ferries are actually speedboats that run between the main dock on the island and Puerto Juárez on the mainland. The *Miss Valentina, Ultramar,* and the *Caribbean Lady* are small air-conditioned cruisers able to make the crossing in just under 20 minutes. A one-way ticket costs $3.50, and the boats leave daily every 30 minutes from 5:30 AM to 8:30 PM, with a late ferry at 11:30 PM for those returning from partying in Cancún. You can also choose to take a slower open-air ferry; its trips take about 45 minutes, but the fare is cheap: tickets are $1.60 per person. Slow ferries run from 5 AM until 6 PM.

More expensive fast ferries to Isla's main dock also leave from El Embarcadero marina complex, and from the Xcaret office complex at Playa Caracol just across from Plaza Caracol Shopping Mall. Both are in Cancún's Zona Hotelera. The cost is between $10 and $15 round-trip, and the voyage takes about 30 minutes. Although it's not necessary to have a car on Isla, there is a car ferry that travels between the island and Punta Sam, a dock north of Puerto Juárez. The ride takes about 45 minutes, and the fare is $1.50 per person and about $18 to $26 per vehicle, depending on the size of your car.

Scooters are the most popular mode of transportation on Isla. Most rental places charge $25 to $35 a day, or $5.50 to $11 per hour, depending on the scooter's make and age. One of the most reliable rental outfits is Rentadora Ma José; rentals start at $10 per hour or $25 per day (9 AM to 5 PM) or $35 for 24 hours.

You can also rent bicycles on Isla, but keep in mind that it's hot here and the roads have plenty of speed bumps. Don't ride at night, as many roads don't have streetlights. David's Bike Rental rents bikes starting at $6 per day for beaters and $12 per day for fancy three-speeds.

Golf carts are another fun way to get around the island, especially with kids. Ciro's Motorent has an excellent choice of new flatbed golf carts, which cost from $35 to $50 for 24 hours, depending on the season. P'pe's Rentadora also has a large fleet of carts (rental prices start at $40 for 24 hours) and mopeds (rental prices start at $25 per day).

Staying Awhile

There are several Internet-based rental agencies that can help you rent a home on the island: ⊕ *www.islabeckons. com*, for example, lists fully equipped apartments and houses (and also handles reservations for hotel rooms); ⊕ *www.morningsinmexico.com* offers smaller and less expensive properties. Most rental homes have fully equipped kitchens, bathrooms, and bedrooms. You can opt for a house downtown or a more secluded one on the eastern coast.

Behaving Yourself

Life on the island moves slowly. You'll find most *isleños* are laid-back and friendly, especially if you make the effort to speak a few words of Spanish. The Virgin Mary is an important icon on the island, so it's considered respectful to cover yourself up before visiting any of the churches. Isla residents are protective of their peaceful island sanctuary, and so their attitudes toward risqué behavior (like public drunkenness and topless sunbathing) are conservative. Spring Breakers who want to party into the wee hours of the morning will find more options in Cancún.

Island Dining

Perhaps it's the fresh air and sunlight that whet the appetite, making Isla's simple meals so delicious. There's plenty of fish and shellfish, including grilled lobster. There are also pleasant variations on staples such as pasta, pizza, steak, and sandwiches. Fruit, fresh coffee, and baked goods make breakfast a treat. Like island life, meals don't need to be complicated.

WHAT IT COSTS IN DOLLARS

	¢	$	$$	$$$	$$$$
Restaurants	under $5	$5–$10	$10–$15	$15–$25	over $25
Hotels	under $50	$50–$75	$75–$150	$150–$250	over $250

Restaurant prices are based on the median entrée price at dinner. Hotel prices are for a standard double room in high season.

What to See

You can walk to Isla's historic **Cementerio** by going northwest from the ferry piers on Avenida López Mateos. Then head southeast (by vehicle) along Avenida Rueda Medina, to reach the Mexican naval base, where you can see flag ceremonies at sunrise and sunset. (Just don't take any pictures—it's illegal to photograph military sites.) Continue southeast to **Laguna Makax** on your right.

At the lagoon's southeast end, a dirt road on the left leads to the remains of the **Hacienda Mundaca**. About a block west, where Avenida Rueda Medina splits, is a statue of Ramón Bravo, Isla's first environmentalist. If you turn right (northwest), you'll reach Playa Tiburón and the Tortugranja (turtle farm). If you turn left (southwest), you'll see Playa Lancheros. Both are good swimming beaches.

Continue southeast past Playa Lancheros to **El Garrafón National Park**. Slightly farther along the same road, on the windward side of the tip of Isla, is the site of the former temple dedicated to the goddess Ixchel. Although little remains, the ocean views are still worth the stop. Follow the paved eastern perimeter road northwest back into town. Known as either the Corredor Panorámico (Panoramic Highway) or Carretera Perimetral al Garrafón (Garrafón Perimeter Highway), this is a scenic drive with a few pull-off areas.

Updated by
Marlise Kast

The minute you step off the boat, you'll get a sense of how small Isla is. The sights and properties on the island are strung along the coasts; there's not much to the interior except the two saltwater marshes, Salina Chica and Salina Grande, where Mayan inhabitants harvested salt centuries ago.

The main road is Avenida Rueda Medina, which runs the length of the island; southeast of a village known as El Colonia, it turns into Carretera El Garrafón. Smaller street names and other address details don't really matter much here.

GETTING HERE AND AROUND

Isla's only airport is for private planes and military aircraft, so the closest you'll get to the island by plane is the Aeropuerto Internacional Cancún. Take a ferry instead.

Taxis line up by the ferry dock around the clock. Fares run $2 to $3 from the ferry to hotels along Playa Norte. A taxi to the south end of the island should be about $5. You can also hire a taxi for an island tour for about $15 an hour. Or rent a bike, scooter, or golf cart to putter around at your own pace.

ESSENTIALS

Currency Exchange Cunex Money Exchange (✉ *Av. Francisco Madero 12A, at Av. Hidalgo* ☎ *998/877-0474*). **Monex Exchange** (✉ *Av. Morelos 9, Lote 4* ☎ *No phone*).

Internet Cafe Internet Isla Mujeres (✉ *Av. Francisco Madero 17* ☎ *998/877-0461*). **DigaMe** (✉ *Av. Guerrero 6, between Avs. Matamoros and Abasolo* ☎ *608/467-4202*). **Digit Centre** (✉ *Av. Juárez between Avs. Mateos and Matamoros* ☎ *998/877-2025*).

Medical Assistance Centro de Salud (✉ *Av. Guerrero de Salud* ☎ *998/877-0017*). **Farmacia Isla Mujeres** (✉ *Av. Juárez 8* ☎ *998/877-0178*). **Red Cross Clinic** (✉ *Colonia La Gloria* ☎ *998/877-0280*).

Post Office Main Post Office (✉ *Avs. Guerrero and Lopez Mateos, ½ block from market* ☎ *998/877-0085*).

Rental Cars Ciro's Motorent (✉ *Av. Guerrero Norte 1, at Av. Matamoros* ☎ *998/877-0578*). **David's Bike Rental** (✉ *Across from Pemex station, Av. Rueda Medina* ☎ *No phone*). **Gomar** (✉ *Av. Rueda Medina and Nicolas Bravo* ☎ *998/877-0541*). **P'pe's Rentadora** (✉ *Av. Hidalgo 19* ☎ *998/877-0019*). **Rentadora Ma José** (✉ *Av. Francisco Madero 25* ☎ *998/877-0130*).

Visitor and Tour Info Caribbean Realty & Travel Enterprises (✉ *Calle Abasolo 677400* ☎ *998/877-1371 or 998/877-1372* ⊕ *www.caribbean realtytravel.com*). **La Isleña Tours** (✉ *Av. Morelos, 1 block up from ferry docks* ☎ *998/877-0578*). **Viajes Prisma** (✉ *Av. Rueda Medina 9C* ☎ *998/877-0938*).

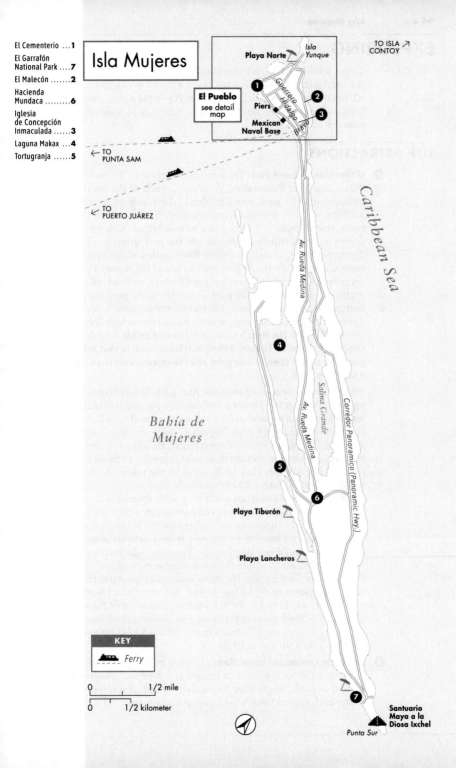

Isla Mujeres

El Pueblo
see detail
map

Playa Norte

Isla
Yunque

TO ISLA ↗
CONTOY

Piers

Mexican
Naval Base

Guerrero

Hidalgo

Bravo

← TO
PUNTA SAM

← TO
PUERTO JUÁREZ

Caribbean Sea

Av. Rueda Medina

Salina Grande

Av. Rueda Medina

Corredor Panoramico (Panoramic Hwy.)

Bahía de
Mujeres

Playa Tiburón

Playa Lancheros

Santuario
Maya a la
Diosa Ixchel

Punta Sur

KEY

Ferry

0   1/2 mile

0   1/2 kilometer

EXPLORING

To get your bearings, try thinking of the island as a long, narrow fish: the head is the southeastern tip, the northwest prong the tail. Although it's possible to explore Isla in one day, if you take your time, rent a golf cart, and spend a couple of days, you'll be able to soak up more of the nuances of island life.

TOP ATTRACTIONS

❼ El Garrafón National Park. Despite participation in the much-publicized "Garrafón Reef Restoration Program," much of the coral reef at this national marine park remains dead (the result of hurricanes, boat anchors, and too many careless tourists). There are still colorful fish, but many of them will only come near if bribed with food. Although there's no longer much for snorkelers, the park does have kayaks and a diving platform, as well as a three-floor facility with restaurants, bathrooms, and gift shops. Be prepared to spend big money here; the basic entry fee doesn't include snorkel gear, lockers, or food, all of which are pretty pricey. However, the park does offer some package deals online that include gear, lunch, and even transportation from Cancún. Another option is Dolphin Discovery, where you can swim with dolphins or bull sharks. ■TIP➔ **The Beach Club Garrafón de Castilla next door is a much cheaper alternative; the snorkeling is at least equal to that available in the park. The club is open to everyone and the entrance fee is $4. You can take a taxi from town.**

The park is home to the **Santuario Maya a la Diosa Ixchel,** the sad vestiges of a Mayan temple once dedicated to the goddess Ixchel. A lovely walkway around the area remains, but the natural arch beneath the ruin has been blasted open and "repaired" with concrete badly disguised as rocks. The views here are spectacular, though: you can look to the open ocean where waves crash against dramatic cliffs on one side, and the Bahía de Mujeres (Bay of Women) on the other. On the way to the temple there's a cutesy Caribbean-style shopping center selling overpriced jewelry and souvenirs and a park with abstract sculptures painted in bright colors. There's also an old lighthouse, which you can enter for free. Climb to the top for an incredible view to the south; the vista in the other direction is marred by a tower from a defunct amusement-park ride (Ixchel would not be pleased). The ruin, which is open daily 9 to 5:30, is at the point where the road turns northeast into the Corredor Panorámico. To visit just the ruins and sculpture park, the admission is $3. Admission to the village is free. ⊠ *Carretera El Garrafón, 6 km (3¾ mi) Mz 41, Lote 12, Sm 9, Punta Sur, southeast of Playa Lancheros* ☎ 998/193–3360 ⊕ *www.garrafon.com* ⊕ *www.dolphindiscovery.com* 🖃 *Basic entrance fee $19; tours from Cancún $29–$59; tours from Isla $44* ⊙ *Daily 8:30* AM–6:30 PM.

❸ Iglesia de Concepción Inmaculada *(Church of the Immaculate Conception).* In 1890 local fishermen landed at a deserted colonial settlement known as Ecab, where they found three identical statues of the Virgin Mary, each carved from wood with porcelain face and hands. No one

Who Was Ixchel?

Ixchel (ee-*shell*) is a principal figure in the pantheon of Mayan gods. Originally married to the earth god Voltan, Ixchel fell in love with the moon god Itzamna, considered the founder of the Mayans because he taught them how to read, write, and grow corn. When Ixchel became his consort, she gave birth to four powerful sons known as the Bacabs, who continue to hold up the sky in each of the four directions. Sometimes called Lady Rainbow, Ixchel is the goddess of childbirth, fertility, and healing. She controls the tides and all water on earth.

Often portrayed as a wise crone, she is seen wearing a skirt decorated with crossbones and a crown of serpents while carrying a jug of water. The crossbones are a symbol of her role as the giver of new life and keeper of dead souls. The serpents represent her wisdom and power to rejuvenate. The water jug alludes to her dual role as both a benign and destructive deity. Although she gives mankind the continual gift of water—the most essential element of life—according to Mayan myth, Ixchel also sent floods to cleanse the earth of wicked men who had stopped thanking the gods. She is said to give special protection to those making the sacred pilgrimage to her sites on Cozumel and Isla Mujeres.

knows for certain where the statues originated, but it's widely believed that they're gifts from the conquistadores during a visit in 1770. One statue went to the city of Izamal in the Yucatán, and another was sent to Kantunikin in Quintana Roo. The third remained on the island. It was housed in a small wooden chapel while this church was being built; legend has it that the chapel burst into flames when the statue was removed. Some islanders still believe the statue walks on the water around the island from dusk until dawn, looking for her sisters. You can pay your respects daily from 10 AM until 11:30 AM and then from 7 PM until 9 PM. ⊠*Avs. Morelos and Bravo, south side of the zócalo.*

NEED A BREAK? It's a small island, but there are several small shops selling gelato. Gelateria Monte Bianco (⊠*Av. Matamoros 20 77400* ☎*998/149–3109* ▤No credit cards) is the one to choose. The gelato here is made with the freshest fruit by an Italian couple who have lived on the island for just over a year.

② **El Malecón.** To enjoy the drama of Isla's eastern shore while soaking up some rays, stroll along this mile-long boardwalk. It's the beginning of a long-term improvement project and will eventually encircle the island. Currently, it runs from Half Moon Bay to El Colonia, with several benches and lookout points. Visit El Monumento de Tortugas (Turtle Monument) along the way. Food and souvenir vendors run the length of the boardwalk.

⑤ **Tortugranja** *(Turtle Farm).* This scientific station is run by the Mexican government in partnership with private funding. Its mission is to continue conservation efforts on behalf of the endangered sea turtle. You can see rescued turtle hatchlings in three large pools or watch the larger turtles in sea pens. There is also a small museum with an excellent display about turtles and the eco-system. From May through August you can make arrangements to join the staff in collecting and hatching eggs. ⊠*Take Av. Rueda Medina south of town; about a block southeast of Hacienda Mundaca, take right fork (smaller road that loops back north called Sac Bajo); entrance is about ½ km (¼ mi) farther, on left* ☎998/877–0595 ⊠*$3* ⊙*Daily 9–5.*

WORD OF MOUTH

"It's very easy to get around Isla Mujeres. Taxis from one end of the island to the other run you about $5. Golf cart rentals for the day are around $45 and available a few blocks from the ferry dock."

—ontariogirl

WORTH NOTING

❶ **El Cementerio.** Isla's unnamed cemetery, with its century-old colorful gravestones, is on Avenida López Mateos, the road that runs parallel to Playa Norte. Many of the tombstones are covered with carved angels and flowers; the most elaborate and beautiful mark the graves of children. Hidden among them is the tomb of the notorious Fermín Mundaca de Marechaja. This 19th-century slave trader—who's often billed more glamorously as a pirate—carved his own skull-and-crossbones gravestone with the ominous epitaph: AS YOU ARE, I ONCE WAS; AS I AM, SO SHALL YOU BE. Mundaca's grave is empty, however; his remains lie in Mérida, where he died. The monument is tough to find—ask a local to point out the unidentified marker.

❻ **Hacienda Mundaca.** A dirt drive where vendors sell mobiles, mermaid figurines, and other crafts made out of local shells marks the entrance to what's left of a mansion constructed by 19th-century slave trader–turned–pirate Fermín Mundaca de Marechaja. When the British navy began cracking down on slavers, Mundaca settled on the island. He fell in love with a local beauty nicknamed La Trigueña (The Brunette). To woo her, Mundaca built a sprawling estate with verdant gardens. Apparently unimpressed, La Trigueña instead married a young islander—and legend has it that Mundaca went slowly mad waiting for her to change her mind. He ended up dying in a brothel in Mérida.

The actual hacienda has vanished. All that remain are a rusted cannon and a ruined stone archway with a triangular pediment carved with the following inscription: HUERTA DE LA HACIENDA DE VISTA ALEGRE (Orchard of the Happy View Hacienda). The gardens are also suffering from neglect, and the animals in a small on-site zoo seem as tired as the rest of the property. Mundaca would, however, approve of the admission charge; considering what little there is to see, it's piracy. ⊠*East of Av. Rueda Medina; take main road southeast from town to S-curve at end of Laguna Makax, turn left onto dirt road* ☎*No phone* ⊠*$2* ⊙*Daily 9* AM–*5* PM.

❹ **Laguna Makax.** Pirates are said to have anchored their ships in this lagoon while waiting to ambush hapless vessels crossing the Spanish Main (the area in which Spanish treasure ships sailed). These days the lagoon houses a local shipyard and provides a safe harbor for boats

Isla's History

The name Isla Mujeres means "Island of Women," although no one knows who dubbed it that. Many believe it was the ancient Maya, who were said to use the island as a religious center for worshipping Ixchel, the Mayan goddess of rainbows, the moon, and the sea, and the guardian of fertility and childbirth. Another popular legend has it that the Spanish conquistador Hernández de Córdoba named the island when he landed here in 1517 and found hundreds of female-shaped clay idols dedicated to Ixchel and her daughters. Others say the name dates later, from the 17th century, when visiting pirates stashed their women on Isla before heading out to rob the high seas. (Legend has it that both Henry Morgan and Jean Lafitte buried treasure on Isla, although no one has ever found any pirate's gold.)

It wasn't until after 1821, when Mexico became independent, that people really began to settle on Isla. In 1847 refugees from the War of the Castes fled to the island and built its first official village of Dolores—which was welcomed into the newly created territory of Quintana Roo in 1850. By 1858 a slave trader–turned–pirate named Fermín Mundaca de Marechaja began building an estate on Isla, which took up 40% of the island. By

the end of the century the population had risen to 651, and residents had begun to establish trade—mostly by supplying fish to the owners of chicle and coconut plantations on the mainland coast. In 1949 the Mexican navy built a base on Isla's northwestern coast; around this time, the island also caught the eye of some wealthy Mexican sportsmen, who began using it as a vacation spot.

Tourism flourished on Isla during the later half of the 20th century, partly due to the island's most famous resident, Ramón Bravo (1927–98). A diver, cinematographer, ecologist, and colleague of Jacques Cousteau, Bravo was the first underwater photographer to explore the area. He discovered the now-famous Cave of the Sleeping Sharks and produced dozens of underwater documentaries for American, European, and Mexican television. Bravo's efforts to maintain the ecology on Isla has helped keep development here to a minimum. Even today, Bravo remains a hero to many *isleños* (ees-*lay*-nyos); his statue can be found beside Hacienda Mundaca where Avenida Rueda Medina changes into the Carretera El Garrafón, and there's a museum named after him on nearby Isla Contoy.

during hurricane season. It's off Avenida Rueda Medina, about 2½ km (1½ mi) south of town, about two blocks south of the naval base and some *salinas* (salt marshes).

BEACHES

In 2008, high winds and stormy seas stole nearly 30 yards of Isla's sandy beaches. Many say the beaches never fully recovered from Hurricane Wilma in 2005. The local government is now working to replenish sand and taking other measures to restore the island's stunning beaches.

★ **Playa Norte** is easy to find: simply head north on any of the north–south streets in town until you hit this superb beach. The turquoise sea is as calm as a lake here, though developers have arrived on the scene and the area no longer has a secluded feel. Enjoy a drink and a snack at one of the area's palapa bars, where wooden swings take the place of bar stools; **Buho's** is especially popular with locals and tourists who gather to chat, eat fresh seafood, drink cold beer, and watch the sunset. Lounge chairs and hammocks at **Sergio's** are free for customers, but to relax in front of **Maria del Maria** in a lounge chair will cost you $3. **Na Balam** charges a whopping $10 for one chair and umbrella.

> **NOT ALL BEACHES ARE FOR SWIMMING!**
>
> Although the beaches on the eastern side of the island (often referred to as the Caribe side) are quite beautiful, they're not safe for swimming because of the dangerous undertows; several drownings have occurred at these beaches. Another gorgeous but dangerous beach is found northeast, just kitty-corner to Playa Norte. **Playa Media Luna** (Half Moon beach) is very tempting, but the strong currents make it treacherous for swimmers.

There are two beaches between Laguna Makax and El Garrafón National Park.

Playa Lancheros is a popular spot with an open-air restaurant where locals gather to eat freshly grilled fish. The beach has grittier sand than Playa Norte, but more palm trees. The calm water makes it the perfect spot for children—although it's best if they stay close to shore, since the ocean floor drops off steeply. The souvenir stands here are fairly low-key and run by local families. There is a small pen with domesticated and quite harmless *tiburones gatos*—nurse sharks. (These sharks are much friendlier than the *tintoreras,* or blue sharks, which live in the open seas, have seven rows of teeth, and weigh up to 1,100 lbs.) You can swim with the nurse sharks or get your picture taken with them for $1.

Playa Tiburón, like Playa Lancheros, is on the west coast facing Bahía de Mujeres, and so its waters are also exceptionally calm. It's a more developed beach, with a large, popular seafood restaurant (through which you actually enter the beach). There are several souvenir stands selling the usual T-shirts as well as handmade seashell jewelry. On certain days there are women who will braid your hair or give you a henna tattoo. This beach also has two sea pens with the sleepy and relatively tame nurse sharks. Swim with them for $2.

WHERE TO EAT

Dining on Isla is a casual affair. Restaurants tend to serve simple meals: seafood, pizza, salads, and Mexican dishes, mostly prepared by local cooks. Fresh ingredients and hospitable waiters make up for the island's lack of elaborate menus and master chefs. It's cash only in most of the restaurants.

Isla's Salt Mines

The ancient salt mines, remains of which still exist in Isla's interior, were constructed during the Post-classic period of Mayan history, which lasted roughly between the years AD 1000 and 1500. Salt was an important commodity for the Maya; they used it not only for preserving and flavoring food, but for creating battle armor. Since the Maya had no metal, they soaked cotton cloth in salt until it formed a hard coating—innovative to say the least.

Today the shallow marshes where salt was long ago harvested bear modern names: Salina Chica (small salt mine) and Salina Grande (large salt mine). Unfortunately there is little to see at the salt mines today. They are simply shallow marshes with murky water and quite a few mosquitoes at dusk. Since both the island's main roads (Avenida Rueda Medina and the Corredor Panorámico) pass by them, however, you can have a look at them on your way to visiting other parts of Isla.

Locals often eat their main meal of the day during siesta hours, between 1 and 4, and then have a light dinner in the evening. Unless otherwise stated, restaurants are open daily for lunch and dinner. Some restaurants open late and close early Sunday; others are closed Monday. Most restaurants welcome children and will cater to their tastes.

Though informal, most indoor restaurants do require that you wear a shirt and shoes when dining. Some outdoor terrace and palapa restaurants also request that you wear shoes and some sort of cover-up over your bathing suit.

It's customary in Mexico for the waiter not to bring you the bill until you ask for it (*"la cuenta, por favor"*). Always check your bill to make sure you didn't get charged for something you didn't order, and to make sure the addition is correct. The "tax" on the bill is often a service charge—kind of a guaranteed tip.

EL PUEBLO

$$$
ITALIAN

✗**Angelo.** Named for Angelo Sanna, its Italian chef, this charming bistro is done up with soft lighting and a wood-fired oven. The pizzas are decent, but the meat dishes are even tastier. Try their famous wood-oven lasagna or mussels steamed in white wine. Angelo, who has lived and worked in Isla Mujeres for more than a decade, is also a great source of local information. ✉*Av. Hidalgo 14* ☎*998/877–1273* ▤*MC, V.*

$$–$$$
ECLECTIC

✗**Bamboo.** This casual restaurant, with its bright tablecloths and bamboo-covered walls, offers an seafood, steak, Asian, and Mexican dishes prepared by two different chefs. Starting at 7 AM, the first chef cooks up hearty breakfasts of omelets and hash browns with freshly brewed coffee. Later in the day, the second chef switches to steaks, tacos, and Asian-fusion-style lunches and dinners, including knockout shrimp tempura, vegetable stir-fry, and chicken satay in a spicy peanut sauce. During high season Bamboo's split personality continues: two bands play each evening, attracting locals who linger until around midnight. This restaurant has the only ATM in the area. ⊠*Plaza Los Almendros No. 477400* ☎*998/877–1355* ⊟*AE, MC, V.*

$ ✕**Café Cito.** This cheery, seashell-decorated café was one of Isla's first
CAFÉ   cafés—and it's still one of the best places to breakfast on the island. The breakfast menu includes fresh waffles, fruit-filled crepes, and egg dishes, as well as great cappuccino and espresso; lunch specials are also available daily. After your meal, be sure to head to the Soñadores del Sol shop next door; the proprietor gives great tarot readings. ⊠*Avs. Juárez and Matamoros* ☎*998/877–1470* ⊟*No credit cards.*

¢   ✕**Color de Verano.** This small café near Playa Norte is one of the cut-
CAFÉ   est on the island. It opens at 8 AM, so it's a good place to start your day. The whole place is done up with an impressive collection of cof-fee- and teapots, many imported from the owner's native France. The espresso is strong and the desserts are delicious. The *amanacer* crepe, with mango, kiwi, strawberry, and blueberries—served with vanilla ice cream—is a delicious option on a sunny day. They also offer light dinners including salads, quiches, and crepes. ⊠*Av. López Mateos 23* ☎*998/877–1264* ⊟*MC, V.*

$$ ✕**Don Chepo.** Mexican-style grilled meats (tacos, fajitas, and steaks) are
MEXICAN   the draw at this lively restaurant that resembles a small hacienda. Inside, the focal point is the large and well-stocked bar where you can chat with other visitors or enjoy the (sometimes live) mariachi music. Tables outside are perfect for watching all the downtown action on Hidalgo Street. The *arrachera,* a fine cut of beef grilled to perfection and served with rice, salad, baked potato, warm tortillas, and beans, is a reliably excellent choice as is the chile relleno. ⊠*Avs. Hidalgo and Francisco Madero* ☎*998/877–0165* ⊟*MC, V.*

$ ✕**El Patio.** With its sandy floors, rooftop terrace, and smooth jazz, this
ECLECTIC   low-key eatery is a peaceful oasis in the heart of El Pueblo's action. Chit palms and ocean grape trees decorate the open-air restaurant, each branch wrapped in fairy lights and adorned with seashell lanterns. House specialties like T-bone steak and shrimp wrapped in prosciutto are smoked over a bed of coals and served with grilled vegetables and a baked potato. The menu features over 20 vegetarian dishes including a tofu pate, soy burgers, and a spinach salad. A complimentary glass of house wine is served with dinner; you can also go for El Patio's two-for-one margaritas. ⊠ *Av. Hidalgo 17, El Pueblo* ☎*998/230–0021* ⊟*No credit cards* ⊙*Closed Sun.*

$$$ ✕**Fayne's.** The vibe at this brightly painted spot is hip and energetic.
MEXICAN   Best known for its terrific cocktails (don't miss the mango margaritas), this funky restaurant serves good island fare such as garlic shrimp, calamari stuffed with spinach, and grilled snapper. There's live music nightly. ⊠*Av. Hidalgo 12A, between Avs. Mateos and Matamoros* ☎*998/877–0528* ⊟*MC, V.*

$ ✕**Fredy's Restaurant & Bar.** This family-run restaurant specializes in sim-
MEXICAN   ple fish, seafood, and traditional Mexican dishes like fajitas and oven-baked shrimp. There isn't much here in the way of decor—they use plastic chairs and tables—but the staff is wonderfully friendly, the food is fresh, and the beer is cold. The tasty daily specials are a bargain and

attract both locals and visitors. ⊠ *Av. Hidalgo just below Av. Mateos* ☎ *998/877–1339* ⊕ *fredys.myislamujeres.com* ⊟ *MC, V.*

$$ ✕ **Jax Bar & Grill.** The downstairs of this palapa-roofed hot spot is a lively ECLECTIC sports bar that serves huge, thick, perfectly grilled burgers and with ↻ cold beer. If you're not in the mood for a burger, you can choose from over 60 items on the menu, including fish tacos, corndogs, and rib-eye steak. The satellite TV is always turned to the big game, and there's a pool game or round of darts in progress. Upstairs is a terrace where you can enjoy dishes like fresh grilled seafood and the house "bucket of beer" (five Coronas for $6) while watching the sunset. The friendly staff caters to kids and is often able to procure their favorite dishes, even if they aren't on the menu. ⊠ *Av. Adolfo Mateos 42* ☎ *998/887–1218* ⊕ *www.jaxsportfishing.com* ⊟ *AE, MC, V.*

$–$$ ✕ **L'Argentina Grill.** As famous for its location as it is for its food, this ARGENTINE boisterous restaurant offers both Mexican and Argentine dishes. There are over 150 entrées on the menu, including ostrich, lamb, wild boar, filet mignon, and honey-glazed quail. For a sample platter, try the Argentine Grill for Two. Portions are huge and revolve around meat, so this isn't a great choice for vegetarians. For a quiet table away from the lively streets, head indoors to the restaurant's lounge bar or Internet café—an ideal spot to catch up on emails between courses. ⊠ *Corner of Av. Hidalgo and Matamoros, El Pueblo* ☎ *998/214–1349* ⊟ *MC, V.*

¢ ✕ **Los Aluxes Cafe.** The perfect spot for an early-morning or late-night CAFÉ cappuccino (it opens at 6:30 AM and closes at 10 PM), this place also has terrific desserts and baked goods. The New York–style cheesecake and triple-fudge brownies are especially decadent. There's also a great selection of exotic teas, and there's locally made jewelry for sale. If you want the café's famous banana bread, get here early—the loaves usually sell out by 10 AM. ⊠ *Av. Matamoros 87 77400* ⊟ *No credit cards.*

$$ ✕ **Los Amigos.** This authentic isleño eatery really lives up to its name; once ECLECTIC you've settled at one of the street-side tables, the staff treats you like an old friend. The friendly vibe makes Los Amigos a favorite among locals, so you can expect a taste of real island life. Though it used to be known mainly for its superb pizza, the restaurant serves excellent fish, meat, and vegetarian dishes as well. The fish baked in sea salt is a good bet, as are desserts like the rich chocolate cake or flambéed crepes. ⊠ *Av. Hidalgo 19 between Avs. Matamoros and Abasolo* ☎ *998/877–0624* ⊟ *MC, V.*

¢–$ ✕ **Mañana Restaurant & Bookstore.** It's hard to miss this bright fuchsia CAFÉ restaurant with a yellow sun stretching its rays over the front door. But you won't want to miss the great breakfasts, with excellent egg dishes, fresh baguettes, and Italian coffee. Salads, homemade burgers (meat or vegetarian), and fresh fruit shakes are served at lunch. If you're in a hurry, you can grab a quick snack at the outdoor counter with its palapa roof—but since Cosmic Cosas bookstore is also here, you may want to lounge on the couch and read after your meal. ⊠ *Av. Guerrero 17* ☎ *998/877–0555* ⊟ *No credit cards* ⊘ *No dinner.*

$ ✕ **Olivia.** The delightful dishes at this Mediterranean restaurant are MEDITERRANEAN fusions of Moroccan, Greek, and Turkish flavors based on owners Fodor'sChoice Lior and Yaron Zelzer's old family recipes. Everything from the freshly ★ baked spanakopita to the flaky baklava is made from scratch in the open-air kitchen. House favorites include the *shawarma* pita wrap filled with grilled chicken, hummus, tahini, and fried eggplant or the *mafrum* (a blend of potatoes stuffed with ground beef in Moroccan red sauce). The setting is casual yet romantic, with tiki torches lighting the way to a tropical garden where rustic tables sit beneath a palapa roof. A visit to Oliva's isn't complete without a bowl of homemade cherry ice cream. ⊠*Av. Matamoros between Juarez and Medina, El Pueblo* ☎*998/877–1765* ▭*No credit cards* ✷*No lunch; closed Sun. and Mon.*

$$ ✕**Picus Cocktelería.** Kick off your shoes and settle back with a cold beer
SEAFOOD at this charming beachside restaurant right near the ferry docks. You can watch the fishing boats come and go while you wait for some of the freshest seafood on the island. The grilled fish and grilled lobster with garlic butter are both magnificent, as are the shrimp fajitas—but the real showstopper is the mixed seafood ceviche, which might include conch, shrimp, abalone, fish, or octopus. ⊠*Av. Rueda Medina, 1 block northwest of ferry docks* ☎*998/129–6011* ▭*AE.*

¢–$ ✕**Sergio's Playa Sol.** Delicious chicken nachos, creamy guacamole, and
MEXICAN savory fish kebabs are on the menu at this great beach bar at Playa Norte. You can easily spend the whole day here and stay for the sunset; there are free hammocks, beach chairs, and umbrellas for customers. ⊠*North end of Rueda Medina on Playa Norte* ☎*No phone* ▭*No credit cards.*

$$$ ✕**Sunset Grill.** The perfect place to savor the sunset, this spot has a cov-
MEXICAN ered dining terrace with large picture windows that overlook the sea.
Fodor'sChoice Soft music and candlelight add to the romantic ambience. Grab a table
★ outside and you can take a dip in the ocean between your appetizer and main course. The dinner menu has a wide range of dishes, including favorites like fried calamari, coconut shrimp, and fried snapper. The kitchen offers a lunch of Mexican favorites like tacos and quesadillas, but also fries up a great burger. Service is very good, and there's live music nightly. ⊠*Av. Rueda Medina, North End, Condominios Nautibeach, Playa Norte* ☎*998/877–0785* ▭*AE, MC, V.*

$$ ✕**Zazil Ha.** At this beachside restaurant you can dine downstairs under
MEXICAN big, shady palms or upstairs under a palapa roof. Homemade breads make breakfast a treat. Later in the day the kitchen serves innovative vegetarian fare—like salads with avocado and grapefruit, or with coconut, mango, and mint vinaigrette—as well as traditional Mexican dishes. The chicken with cilantro sauce is especially good. ⊠*Na Balam Hotel, Calle Zazil-Ha 118* ☎*998/877–0279* ▭*AE, MC, V.*

ELSEWHERE ON THE ISLAND

$ ✕**Bistro Français.** This casual café, with menu items painted on the walls
FRENCH in bright colors, serves up tasty French dishes at reasonable prices. Breakfast is particularly nice, with tasty fruit salads and practically perfect waffles. Later on in the day, try French dishes like chicken cordon bleu or coq au vin. The deck overlooks the street, so you can watch the world go by. ⊠*Av. Matamoros 29* ☎*No phone* ▭*No credit cards.*

$$$ ✕ **Casa O's.** Though it's more expensive than its neighbors, this restau-
ECLECTIC rant is worth every penny. The magic starts at the footpath, which leads
Fodor's Choice over a small stream before entering the three-tier circular dining room
★ overlooking the bay. As you watch the sunset, you can choose your
fish—salmon, tuna, snapper, or grouper—and have the chef prepare it
to your individual taste. If you prefer, pick out a lobster from the on-site
pond. Be sure to save room for key lime pie, the house specialty. The
restaurant is named for its waiters—all of whose names end in the letter
"o." ⊠ *Carretera El Garrafón s/n* ☎ *998/888–0170* ▭ *MC, V.*

$$$ ✕ **Casa Rolandi.** This hotel restaurant is casually sophisticated, with an
ECLECTIC open-air dining room leading out to a deck that overlooks the water.
★ Tables are set with beautiful linens, china, and cutlery. The northern
Italian menu here includes the wonderful carpaccio *di tonno alla Gior-
gio* (thin slices of tuna with extra-virgin olive oil and lime juice), along
with excellent pastas—even the simplest dishes such as angel-hair pasta
in tomato sauce are delicious. For something different, try the saffron
risotto or the *costolette d'agnello al forno* (lamb chops with a thyme
infusion). The sunset views are spectacular. ⊠ *Hotel Villa Rolandi,
Fracc. Laguna Mar, Sm 7, Mza. 75, Lotes 15 and 16* ☎ *998/999–2000*
▭ *AE, MC, V.*

$ ✕ **Playa Lancheros Restaurant.** If you want to savor one of the island's
MEXICAN most authentic meals, take a short taxi ride to this casual eatery under
a big palapa roof. It's right on the beach, so it's no surprise that the
kitchen takes pride in serving the freshest fish. The house specialty
is the Yucatecan *tikinchic* (fish marinated in a sour-orange sauce and
cooked in a banana leaf over an open flame). There are also delicious
tacos, fresh guacamole, and spicy salsa. The food may take a while to
arrive, so bring your swimsuit and take a dip while you wait. On Sunday there's music, dancing, and the occasional shark wrestler. ⊠ *Playa
Lancheros where Av. Rueda Medina splits into Sac Bajo and Carretera
El Garrafón* ☎ *998/877–0340* ▭ No *credit cards.*

WHERE TO STAY

Isla hotels focus on providing a relaxed, tranquil beach vacation. Many
have simple rooms with ceiling fans, but not all have air-conditioning.
(This is changing as more luxury hotels are built.) Generally speaking,
modest budget hotels can be found in town, whereas the more expensive
resorts are around Punta Norte or the peninsula near the lagoon. Local
travel agents can provide information about luxury condos and residential homes for rent—an excellent option if you're planning a long stay.

Many of the smaller hotels on the island don't accept credit cards, and
some add a 10% surcharge if you use one. Isla has also been tightening
up its cancellation policy, so check with your hotel about surcharges for
changing reservations. ■ TIP➜ **Before paying, always ask to see your room
to make sure everything is satisfactory—especially at the smaller hotels.**

A growing number of Isla hotels are now encouraging people to make
their reservations online. Some allow you to book rooms right on their
Web sites, but even hotels without their own sites usually offer reservations via online booking agencies, such as ⊕ *www.docancun.com*

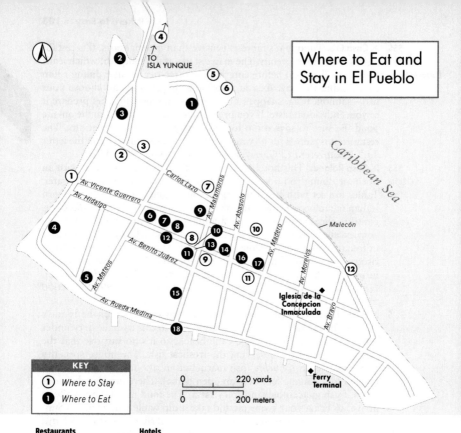

Where to Eat and Stay in El Pueblo

Caribbean Sea

Malecón

TO
ISLA YUNQUE

Carlos Lazo

Av. Vicente Guerrero

Av. Hidalgo

Av. Benito Juárez

Av. Matamoros

Av. Abasolo

Av. Matero

Av. Morelos

Av. Mateos

Av. Rueda Medina

Av. Bravo

Iglesia de la
Concepcion
Inmaculada

Ferry
Terminal

KEY

① *Where to Stay*

● *Where to Eat*

| 0 | 220 yards |
| 0 | 200 meters |

and ⊕*www.lostoasis.net.* You may see these agency Web sites listed in some of the hotel reviews below, but since hotels customarily work with several different agencies, it's a good idea to shop around online for the best rates before booking with one of them. You might also want to contact the hotel directly to inquire of any discounts or specials that may not be offered online. ■**TIP**➔ Be sure to ask if construction is taking place nearby; it's often the reason a hotel lowers its rates, but the savings may not be worth the disruption.

Booking online is certainly convenient, and can often get you a 10% to 20% discount on room rates. The bad news, though, is that there may be an occasional breakdown in communication between a booking agency and a hotel. You may arrive at the hotel to discover that your Spanish-speaking front-desk clerk has no record of your Internet reservation or has reserved a room that's different from the one you specified. If you arrive during the day, there should be time to sort out the problem. But late at night, the hotel may ask you to pay for your room before sorting out your reservation the following day. ■**TIP**➔ If you do end up booking online, be sure to print out copies of all your Internet transactions, including receipts and confirmations, and bring them with you.

EL PUEBLO

$$$$ ⌷**Avalon Reef Club.** This all-inclusive resort sits on a tiny island at the northern tip of Isla Mujeres. The location is gorgeous, and the seaside suites take advantage of this with balconies overlooking the ocean. Regular rooms in the hotel tower are small without balconies. Be warned: this is a time-share resort, and preference is given to those who bought into the "Paradise Found" program. Sales pitches are relentless, but if you can be stalwart in your refusal, you may be able to enjoy this lovely property. You can choose to pay just for your room or go with the all-inclusive option if you prefer to stay in. **Pros:** beautiful location; stunning beaches. **Cons:** constant sales pitches; some rooms lack views. ⊠*Calle Zazcil-Ha s/n 7, Isla Yunque* ☎*998/999–2050* ⊕*www. avalonvacations.com* ⊅*80 rooms, 5 suites, 60 villas* ⌂*In-room: Kitchen (some). In-hotel: Restaurant, room service, pool, gym, beachfront, Internet terminal, no-smoking rooms* ▤*AE, MC, V* ⦿|*AI, EP.*

$ ⌷**Hotel Belmar.** This hacienda-style hotel has cozy rooms that are cheerfully decorated with flowers, plants, and Mexican artwork. The beds are large and the showers have good water pressure. Front rooms have terraces that open onto the main street where you can watch all the downtown action; back rooms are quieter. You can get pizza delivered to your room from Rolandi's restaurant, which is just downstairs. **Pros:** clean and comfortable; near shops and restaurants. **Cons:** dome street noise; no elevator. ⊠*Av. Hidalgo Norte 110, between Avs. Madero and Abasolo* ☎*998/877–0430* ⊕*www.rolandi.com* ⊅*12 rooms* ⌂*In-hotel: Room service, laundry service, Wi-Fi, no-smoking rooms* ▤*AE, MC, V.*

$ ⌷**Hotel Frances Arlene.** This small hotel is a perennial favorite. Rooms surround a pleasant courtyard and are outfitted with double beds, bamboo furniture, and refrigerators. Some have kitchenettes. The Magaña family takes great care to maintain the property—signs everywhere remind you to save electricity and keep noise to a minimum. Playa Norte is a few blocks north, and downtown is a block away. This is one of the few hotels that can accommodate wheelchairs. **Pros:** reasonable rates; friendly staff. **Cons:** some street noise; not all rooms have balconies. ⊠*Av. Guerrero 7* ☎*998/877–0310* ⊕*www.francisarlene.com* ⤵*22 rooms* ♿*In-room: No a/c (some), kitchen (some), refrigerator. In-hotel: No-smoking rooms* ⊟*MC, V.*

$$–$$$ ⛅ **Hotel Playa la Media Luna.** This breezy palapa-roofed bed-and-breakfast lies along Half Moon Beach, just south of Playa Norte. Guest rooms here are done in bright Mexican colors, with king-size beds and balconies or terraces that look out over the pool and the ocean beyond; some have Jacuzzis. Continental breakfast is served in a sunny dining room. The hotel also has small, spartan rooms, with no view and no breakfast, for $60 per night. **Pros:** rooms have balconies; nearby beach is calm and shallow. **Cons:** no Internet access, no elevator. ⊠*Sección Rocas, Punta Norte, Lote 9/10* ☎*998/877–0759* ⊕*www.playamedialuna.com* ⤵*18 rooms* ♿*In-room: Safe, refrigerator. In-hotel: Restaurant, pool, beachfront, no-smoking rooms* ⊟*MC, V* ⛌⃝*CP.*

$–$$ ⛅ **Hotel Plaza Almendros.** This little hotel is right in the center of the action, close to all the restaurants and bars on Avenida Hidalgo. The rooms, built around a central patio with a pool where guests take in the sun on lounge chairs, are comfortably and simply decorated in a local style. Appliances like microwaves, coffeemakers, and toasters make the rooms great for families. There is also a computer in the lobby where you can use the Internet. **Pros:** central location; family-friendly atmosphere. **Cons:** can be noisy; basic rooms. ⊠*Av. Hidalgo, Lote 14* ☎*998/877–1217* ⊕*www.hotelplazaalmendros.com* ⤵*19 suites, 20 rooms* ♿*In-room: Safe, refrigerator. In-hotel: Pool, Internet terminal, no-smoking rooms* ⊟*MC, V* ⛌⃝*EP.*

$$ ⛅ **Hotel Roca Mar.** You can smell, hear, and see the ocean from the simply furnished, blue-and-white guest rooms at this hotel; it's right on the eastern malecón (boardwalk) and is one of the few hotels on the island that overlooks the Caribbean. Since it's tucked away at the southern end of the town square, there isn't much to distract you from the ocean—except at Carnival (the week before Lent in February or March), when the music can get loud. The freshwater pool and courtyard—filled with plants, birds, and benches—overlook the ocean, too. **Pros:** rooms are steps away from the water; friendly and helpful staff. **Cons:** basic decor; rooms lack TVs; no elevator. ⊠*Calle Nicolas Bravo and Zona Maritima* ☎*998/877–0101* ⊕*www.isla-mujeres.net/hotel rocamar* ⤵*31 rooms* ♿*In-room: No a/c (some), no phone, no TV. In-hotel: Restaurant, pool, beachfront, water sports, no-smoking rooms* ⊟*No credit cards.*

$$$ ⛅ **Hotel Secreto.** It's beautiful. It's famous. It's très, très chic. But if you're looking for a warm, inviting atmosphere, this may not be the place for you. Although the sense of reserve makes it perfect for honeymoon couples that want to be alone, singles may find it too quiet, and families with children are not made to feel welcome. Rooms have floor-to-ceiling windows, veiled king-size four-poster beds, and balconies overlooking

Half Moon Bay. Mexican artwork looks bold against the predominantly white color scheme, and a small, intimate dining room sits alongside a small ocean-side pool. This place isn't much of a secret anymore, so it's sometimes hard to get a reservation. **Pros:** accommodating staff; pool overlooks ocean; peace and quiet. **Cons:** not good for children; books up in advance; no restaurant. ⊠*Sección Rocas, Lote 11, Half Moon Beach* ☎*998/877–1039* ⊕*www.hotelsecreto.com* ⤷ *11 rooms* ⏷*In-room: Safe, refrigerator, Wi-Fi. In-hotel: Bar, pool, water sports, no-smoking rooms* ⊟*AE, MC, V* ⏏⏐*CP.*

$$$ ⌷**Ixchel Beach Hotel.** This location—on a beach with clear, calm water— is unbeatable. The rooms in this five-story lodging are actually privately owned condos, so they are all decorated differently. Even the cheapest ones have a TV, DVD player, and Wi-Fi. Some have ocean views. Rooms with garden views are steps away from the pool, snack bar, and beach. **Pros:** beautiful location, reasonable rates, complimentary beach chairs. **Cons:** small pool. ⊠*Playa Norte, Calle Guerrero, Sm 1* ☎*998/999–2010* ⊕*www.ixchelbeachhotel.com* ⤷*117 rooms* ⏷*In-room: Safe, kitchen (some), Wi-Fi. In-hotel: Restaurant, bar, pool, gym, spa, beachfront, no-smoking rooms* ⊟*AE, MC, V.*

$–$$ ⌷**Los Arcos.** In the heart of downtown, this hotel is a terrific value.
★ The comfortable suites are all cheerfully decorated with Mexican-style furnishings. Each has a small kitchenette with a microwave and fridge, a fully tiled bathroom with great water pressure, a small sitting area, and a king-size bed. The large and sunny balconies on the front have views of the street, whereas those at the back are more private. The pleasant and helpful staff is an added bonus. The hotel management encourages online booking. **Pros:** reasonable rates; spacious rooms; near restaurants and shops. **Cons:** some linens feel worn; sparse furnishings; no elevator. ⊠*Av. Hidalgo 58, between Abasolo and Matamoros* ☎*998/877–1343* ⊕*www.suites-los-arcos.myislamujeres.com* ⤷*12 rooms* ⏷*In-room: Safe, kitchen. In-hotel: Internet terminal, no-smoking rooms* ⊟*MC, V.*

$$$$ ⌷**Na Balam.** Elegant without being pretentious, this tranquil hotel is
Fodor'sChoice a true sanctuary. Each guest room in the main building has a thatched
★ palapa roof, Mexican folk art, a large bathroom, an eating area, and a spacious balcony or patio facing the ocean. The beach here is private, with its own bar serving snacks and drinks. Across the street are eight more spacious rooms surrounding a pool, a garden, and a meditation room where yoga classes are held. **Pros:** excellent restaurant; beautiful beach. **Cons:** not all rooms are on the beach; no elevator. ⊠*Calle Zazil-Ha 118* ☎*998/881–4770* ⊕*www.nabalam.com* ⤷ *33 rooms* ⏷*In-room: Safe, no phone, no TV. In-hotel: Restaurant, bar, pool, beachfront, no-smoking rooms* ⊟*AE, MC, V.*

¢ ⌷**Poc-Ná.** This coed youth hostel is one of El Pueblo's best deals. Half the rooms are dorm-style and have fans; the others are private and air-conditioned. To promote community spirit, the hostel hosts movie nights, board and card games, and regular parties. There is also a "beach bar," which is not actually on the beach but is open to the public nightly. The hostel is within walking distance of Playa Norte and all the downtown shops, restaurants, and bars. **Pros:** convivial; unbeatable price.

Cons: party atmosphere; rooms not that clean; no elevator. ⊠ *Av. Matamoros 15* 🕾*998/877–0090* ⇆*187 beds* ♿ *In-room: No a/c (some), no phone, no TV (some). In-hotel: Restaurant, bar, Internet terminal, no-smoking rooms* ⊟*MC, V* ⏻❘*CP.*

$ 🖥 **Sea Hawk Divers Rooms.** Catering largely to scuba divers, this hotel is half a block from Playa Norte. Lovely rooms above the dive shop have queen-size beds, brightly tiled bathrooms, and huge private balconies that face either the ocean or the garden patio. There are also two studio suites with full kitchenettes and large outdoor decks perfect for private breakfasts. The third-floor terrace, open to all, is a great place to watch the sunset. Diving and deep-sea fishing trips are offered at the shop. This hotel encourages online booking. **Pros:** laid-back atmosphere; lively common areas; great packages. **Cons:** not the place for non-divers; rooms lack TVs; no elevator. ⊠ *Calle Carlos Lazo, just before Buho's restaurant* 🕾*998/877–1233* ⊕*www.isla-mujeres. net/seahawkdivers/index.htm* ⇆ *8 rooms, 2 studio suites* ♿ *In-room: No phone, kitchen (some), no TV. In-hotel: Water sports, no-smoking rooms* ⊟*MC, V.*

WORD OF MOUTH

"We did find that the south end of the island is much quieter than the north but you would also have to cab it to Hildago [Avenue], which is where most of the restaurants are located. There are some beautiful resorts on that end of the island though. We took a golf cart ride down that way even though we stayed on the north end." –PamT

ELSEWHERE ON THE ISLAND

$ 🖥 **Hotel & Beach Club Garrafón de Castilla.** The snorkeling at this small family-owned hotel is better than what you're likely to experience at El Garrafón National Park next door; the reef is less crowded, and there are more fish. Rooms have double beds and balconies overlooking the water; some have refrigerators. Decorations are minimal, but the overall effect is bright, cheery, and comfortable. **Pros:** one of the best locations on the island; great for snorkeling and diving. **Cons:** taxi-ride away from downtown; no Internet; no elevator. ⊠ *Carretera Punta Sur, Km 6* 🕾*998/877–0107* ⇆*12 rooms* ♿ *In-room: No phone, refrigerator (some), no TV. In-hotel: Beachfront, diving, water sports, no-smoking rooms* ⏻*No credit cards* ⏻❘*CP.*

$$$$ 🖥 **Hotel Villa Rolandi.** A private yacht delivers you to the hotel's lagoon
FodorśChoice dock from Cancún's Embarcadero Marina. Each elegant suites has an
★ ocean view, a king-size bed, and a sitting area that leads to a balcony with a heated whirlpool bath. Italian marble floors, vaulted ceilings, and stained glass archways create a feeling of decadence. Showers have *six* adjustable heads and can be converted into saunas. Both the restaurant and the infinity pool overlook the Bahía de Mujeres; a path leads down to an intimate beach. For additional pampering, try Thalassotherapy, an ancient form of natural healing that utilizes hot sea water, at the spa. The hotel runs onsite cooking classes and can arrange whale shark swimming expeditions. For the best view, ask for a second- or third-floor room. **Pros:** attentive staff; great ocean views; luxurious touches

like fragrant towels and bathrobes. **Cons:** expensive; pool and beach can get crowded; young children not allowed. ⊠*Fracc. Laguna Mar, Sm 7, Mza. 75, Lotes 15 and 16, Carretera Sac-Bajo* ☎*998/999–2000* ⊕*www.villarolandi.com* ↝ *35 suites* 🔑*In-room: Safe. In-hotel: Restaurant, room service, pool, gym, spa, water sports, beachfront, laundry service, no kids under 13, no-smoking rooms* ⊟*AE, MC, V* ⦿*MAP.*

$$$$ 🎬 **Isla Mujeres Palace.** At this all-inclusive hotel you can forget about ever leaving the property and take advantage of the restaurants, the beach, and the pool. All of the spacious rooms are decorated in a modern Mexican style. Each room has its own Jacuzzi, either inside the room or on the balcony, from which you can view the ocean below. The service is excellent; each building has its own attentive butler. If you stay for more than three nights, a tour of the island or a snorkeling trip is included in the price of your stay. In the evening, there are music and dance performances. **Pros:** family-friendly environment; comfortable rooms. **Cons:** far from downtown. ⊠*Carretera Garrafón, Km 4.5, Mza. 62, Sm 8* ☎*998/999–2020, 800/346–8225 in U.S.* ⊕*www. islamujerespalace.com* ↝*62 rooms* 🔑*In-room: Safe, refrigerator, Wi-Fi. In-hotel: Restaurant, room service, pool, bar, beachfront, spa, no-smoking rooms* ⊟*AE, MC, V* ⦿*AI.*

$$–$$$ 🎬 **Villa La Bella.** It can be difficult to get reservations at this romantic spot tucked away on the eastern coast—it's often booked months in advance—but most agree it's worth the effort. All rooms here have funky designs, fantastic sea views, and are equipped with king-size beds, conch-head showers, ceiling fans, and refrigerators. A restaurant, spa, and small pool mean you don't have to leave the property unless you feel like exploring the island. It's a bit of a hike to downtown, but you can arrange for a taxi or a golf-cart rental. This hotel gets lots of wind! **Pros:** welcoming owners; relaxing atmosphere; tasty breakfasts. **Cons:** taxi-ride from downtown; kids not allowed. ⊠*Carretera Perimetral al Garrafón* ☎*998/888–0342* ⊕*www.villalabella.com* ↝*6 rooms* 🔑*In-room: No a/c (some), no phone, refrigerator, no TV. In-hotel: Restaurant, pool, laundry service, spa, no kids under 18, no-smoking rooms* ⊟*MC, V* ⦿*BP.*

$$$–$$$$ 🎬 **Villa Vera Puerto Isla Mujeres.** Yachties love this hideaway at Isla's main yacht club. Rooms are awash in rose and blue, and have cozy seating areas. The recently remodeled beach club is surround by a garden and includes a large pool and swim-up bar. Paths lead to the dock and the lagoon, where a shuttle boat ferries you to a beach club that faces Cancún. Families are warmly welcomed. There is a discount when you book online. **Pros:** family-friendly atmosphere; pretty pool. **Cons:** pricey restaurant; no elevator. ⊠*Puerto de Abrigo, Laguna Makax* ☎*998/287–3340 or 800/508–7923* ⊕*www.puertoislamujeres.com* ↝*17 suites, 4 villas* 🔑*In-room: Kitchen (some). In-hotel: Restaurant, pools, beachfront, Wi-Fi, no-smoking rooms* ⊟*AE, MC, V* ⦿*EP.*

NIGHTLIFE

Isla Mujeres has begun to develop a healthy nightlife with a variety of clubs from which to choose.

BARS

La Adelita (⊠ *Av. Hidalgo Norte 12A* ☎ *998/877–0528*) is a popular spot for enjoying reggae, salsa, and Caribbean music while trying out a variety of tequilas and cigars.

Jax Bar & Grill (⊠ *Av. Adolfo Mateos 42, near lighthouse* ☎ *998/887–1218*) has live music, cold beer, good bar food, and satellite TV that's always turned to whatever game happens to be on at the time.

DANCE CLUBS

Bar OM (⊠ *Av. Matamoros, Lote 19, Mza. 15* ☎ *998/820–4876*) is an eclectic lounge bar offering wine, organic teas, and self-serve draft-beer taps at each table. Chill out to the sounds of acid jazz, bossa nova, and reggae.

Buho's (⊠ *Cabañas María del Mar, Av. Arq. Carlos Lazo 1* ☎ *No phone*) remains the favorite restaurant on Playa Norte for a relaxing sunset drink—although the drinks have started to become overpriced.

You can dance the night away with the locals at **Nitrox** (⊠ *Av. Guerrero 11* ☎ *998/887–0568*). Wednesday night is ladies' night, Friday is Latin night, and the weekend is a blend of disco, techno, and house. It's open Wednesday through Sunday from 9 PM until 3 AM.

La Peña (⊠ *Av. Guerreo s/n Centro, opposite church square* ☎ *998/845–7384*), just across from the downtown main square, is the only downtown bar that overlooks the Caribbean. There's a lovely terrace bar that serves a variety of sinful cocktails and a DJ who sets the mood with techno, salsa, reggae, and dance music. It is the only downtown bar that overlook the Caribbean. The owners recently added a movie lounge and a courtyard restaurant to the lively scene.

SHOPPING

Aside from seashell art and jewelry, Isla produces few local crafts. The streets are filled with souvenir shops selling cheap T-shirts, garish ceramics, and seashells glued onto a variety of objects. But amid all the junk, you may find good Mexican folk art, hammocks, textiles, and silver jewelry. Most stores are small family operations that don't take credit cards, but everyone gladly accepts American dollars. Stores that do take credit cards sometimes tack on a fee to offset the commission they must pay. Hours are generally Monday through Saturday 10 to 1 and 4 to 7, although many stores stay open during siesta hours (1 to 4).

GET YOUR CULTURE ON

Isleños celebrate many religious holidays and festivals in El Pueblo's zócalo, usually with live entertainment. Carnival, held annually in February, is spectacular fun. Other popular events include the springtime regattas and fishing tournaments. Founder's Day, August 17, marks the island's official founding by the Mexican government. Isla's cemetery is among the best places to mark the Día de los Muertos (Day of the Dead) on November 1. Families decorate the graves of loved ones with marigolds and their favorite objects from life, then hold all-night vigils to commemorate their lost loved ones.

Casa de la Cultura (⊠ *Av. Guerrero and Av. Abasolo* ☎ *998/877–0639*) has art, drama, yoga, and folkloric-dance classes year-round. It's open weekdays 9 AM to 4 PM.

BOOKS

Cosmic Cosas (⊠ *Av. Guerrero 17* ☎ *998/877–0555*) is the island's only English-language bookstore and is found in **Mañana Restaurant & Bookstore.** This friendly shop offers two-for-one trades (no Harlequin romances) and rents out board games. You can have something to eat and then settle in on the couch for some reading.

CRAFTS

Artesanías Arcoiris (⊠ *Avs. Hidalgo and Juárez* ☎ *No phone*) has Mexican blankets and other handicrafts. The staffers here also braid hair. Look for Mexican ceramics and onyx jewelry at **Artesanías Lupita** (⊠ *Av. Hidalgo 13* ☎ *No phone*). Many local artists display their works at the **Artesanías Market** (⊠ *Avs. Matamoros and Arq. Carlos Lazo* ☎ *No phone*), where you can find plenty of bargains. For custom-made clothing, visit **Hortensia**—the last stall on the left after you come through the market entrance. You can choose from bright Mexican fabrics and then pick a pattern for a skirt, shirt, shorts, or a dress; Hortensia will sew it up for you within a day or two. You can also buy off-the-rack designs. **Casa del Arte Mexicano** (⊠ *Av. Hidalgo 16* ☎ *No phone*) has a large selection of Mexican handicrafts, including ceramics and silver jewelry. **De Corazón** (*Boutique* ⊠ *Av. Abasolo between Avs. Hidalgo and Guerrero* ☎ *998/877–1211*) has a wide variety of jewelry, T-shirts, and personal-care products. **Gladys Galdamez** (⊠ *Av. Hidalgo 14* ☎ *998/877–0320*) carries Isla-designed and -manufactured clothing and accessories for both men and women, as well as bags and jewelry.

GROCERY STORES

For fresh produce, the **Mercado Municipal** (⊠ *Av. Guerrero Norte near post office* ☎ *No phone*) is your best bet. The Municipal Market is open daily until noon. **Mirtita Grocery** (⊠ *Av. Juárez 6, at Av. Bravo* ☎ *No phone*) is a good place to find American products like Kraft Dinners, Cheerios, and Ritz Crackers. **Super Express** (⊠ *Av. Morelos 3,* *in plaza* ☎*No phone*), Isla's main grocery store, is well stocked with all the basics.

JEWELRY

Jewelry on Isla ranges from tasteful creations to junk. Bargains are available, but beware of street vendors—most of their wares, especially the amber, are fake. **Gold and Silver Jewelry** (⊠*Av. Hidalgo 58* ☎*No phone*) specializes in precious stones such as sapphires, tanzanite, and amber in a variety of settings. **Joyería Maritz** (⊠*Av. Hidalgo between Avs. Morelos and Francisco Madero* ☎*998/877–0526*) sells jewelry from Taxco (Mexico's silver capital) and crafts from Oaxaca at reasonable prices. **Van Cleef & Arpels** (⊠*Avs. Juárez and Morelos* ☎*998/877–0331*) stocks rings, bracelets, necklaces, and earrings with precious stones set in 18K gold. Many of the designs are innovative; prices are often lower than in the United States. You can also check out the Van Cleef sister store, the **Silver Factory** (⊠*Avs. Juárez and Morelos* ☎*998/877–0331*), which has a variety of designer pieces at reduced prices.

SPORTS AND THE OUTDOORS

BOATING

Villa Vera Puerto Isla Mujeres (⊠*Puerto de Abrigo, Laguna Makax* ☎*998/287–3340* ⊕*www.puertoislamujeres.com*) is a full-service marina for vessels up to 175 feet. Services include a fuel station, a 150-ton lift, customs assistance, 24-hour security, and laundry and cleaning services. Docking prices depend on the size of your boat and how long you stay. If you prefer to sleep on land, the Villa Vera Puerto Isla Mujeres resort is steps away from the docks.

Serious Diving (*DigaMe Internet* ⊠*Av. Guerrero between Matamoros and Abasolo* ☎*No Phone* ⊕*www.islawhalesharks.com*) will take you into the heart of whale shark territory, where you can swim with these gentle creatures. Owner Ramon Guerrero Garcia is a professional diver who has dedicated over 20 years to researching whale sharks. Included in the six-hour boat trip are beverages, a light snack, and snorkel gear. Tours are approximately five hours long, cost $125, and must be pre-booked online. Ramon is available to answer questions nightly from 7 to 8 at DigaMe Internet.

FISHING

Captain Anthony Mendillo Jr. (⊠*Av. Arq. Carlos Lazo 1* ☎*998/877–0759*) provides specialized fishing trips from December to June aboard his 41-foot vessel, the *Keen M.* He charges $1,000 for a daylong trip for four people. **Jax Sport Fishing** (⊠ *Av. Adolfo Mateos 42, near lighthouse* ☎*998/877–1254*) offers a 29-foot custom charter boat for $850 per full day. Captain Michael has over 20 years experience in offshore fishing. **Sea Hawk Divers** (⊠*Av. Arq. Carlos Lazo* ☎*998/877–1233* ⊕*www.sea-hawk-divers.myislamujeres.com*) runs fishing trips—for

In Search of the Dead

El Día de los Muertos (the Day of the Dead) is often billed as "Mexican Halloween," but it's much more than that. The festival, which takes place November 1 and November 2, is a hybrid of pre-Hispanic and Christian beliefs that honors the cyclical nature of life and death. Local celebrations are as varied as they are dynamic, often laced with warm tributes and dark humor.

To honor departed loved ones at this time of year, families and friends create *ofrendas*, altars adorned with photos, flowers, candles, liquor, and other items whose colors, smells, and potent nostalgia are meant to lure spirits back for a family reunion. The favorite foods of the deceased are also included, prepared extra spicy so that the souls can absorb the essence of these offerings. Although the *ofrendas* and the colorful *calaveritas* (skeletons made from sugar that are a treat for Mexican children) are common everywhere, the holiday is

observed in so many ways that a definition of it depends entirely on what part of Mexico you visit.

In a sandy Isla Mujeres cemetery, Marta, a middle-age woman wearing a tidy pantsuit and stylish sunglasses, rests on a fanciful tomb in the late-afternoon sun. "She is my sister," Marta says, motioning toward the teal-and-blue tomb. "I painted this today." She exudes no melancholy; rather she's smiling, happy to be spending the day with her sibling.

Nearby, Juan puts the final touches—vases made from shells he's collected—on his father's colorful tomb. A glass box holds a red candle and a statue of the Virgin Mary, her outstretched arms pressing against the glass as if trying to escape the flame. "This is all for him," Juan says, motioning to his masterpiece, "because he is a good man."

—David Downing

barracuda, snapper, and smaller fish—that start at $250 for a half day. **Sociedad Cooperativa Turística** (✉ *Av. Rueda Medina at Contoy Pier* ☎ *No phone*) is a fishermen's cooperative that rents boats for a maximum of four hours and six people ($120). An island tour with lunch costs $20 per person.

SNORKELING AND SCUBA DIVING

Most area dive spots are described in detail in *Dive Mexico* magazine, available in many local shops. The coral reefs at El Garrafón National Park have suffered tremendously for a variety of factors, some unavoidable (hurricanes) and some all too avoidable (boats dropping anchors onto soft coral, a practice now outlawed). Some good snorkeling can be had near Playa Norte on the north end.

Isla is a good place for learning to dive, since the snorkeling is close to shore. Offshore, there is excellent diving and snorkeling at Xlaches (pronounced *ees*-lah-chayss) reef, due north on the way to Isla Contoy. One of Contoy's most alluring dives is the **Cave of the Sleeping Sharks,** east of the northern tip. The cave was discovered by an island fisherman, Carlos Gracía Castilla, and extensively explored by Ramón Bravo, a local diver, cinematographer, and Mexico's foremost expert on sharks. The cave is a fascinating 150-foot dive for experienced divers only.

At 30 feet to 40 feet deep and 3,300 feet off the southwestern coast, the coral reef known as **Los Manchones** is a good dive site. During the summer of 1994 an ecological group hoping to divert divers and snorkelers from El Garrafón commissioned the creation of a 1-ton, 9¾-foot bronze cross, which was sunk here. Named the Cruz de la Bahía (Cross of the Bay), it's a tribute to everyone who has died at sea. Another option is the Barco L-55 and C-58 dive, which takes in sunken World War II boats just 20 minutes off the coast of Isla.

> ### THE WHOLE PACKAGE
>
> **Sea Passion** (☎ *998/877–0798* ⊕ *www.seapassion.net*) offers one-of-a-kind tours that include sailing on a 75-foot catamaran from Cancún to Isla Mujeres, snorkeling, shopping, and lunch at a private beach club. This all-day tour includes food and drink and costs $79 to $89 per person. Other packages are also available.

DIVE SHOPS

Most dive shops offer a variety of dive packages with rates variable on the time of day, the reef visited, and the number of tanks. A PADI-affiliated dive shop, **Aqua Adventures** (⊠ *Plaza Almendros 10* ☎ *998/877–1615* ⊕ *www.diveislamujeres.com*) offers dives to shipwrecks and sleeping shark caves. A one-tank dive goes for $40 and a two-tank dive costs $64. **Coral Scuba Dive Center** (⊠ *Av. Matamoros 13A* ☎ *998/877–0763* ⊕ *www.coralscubadivecenter.com*) has a variety of dive packages. Fees start at $55 for one-tank dives and go up to $65 for two-tank dives and shipwreck dives. The PADI-affiliated shop also offers snorkeling trips. **Cruise Divers** (⊠ *Avs. Rueda Medina and Matamoros* ☎ *998/877–1190*) offers two-tank reef dives starting at $49 and a resort course (a quickie learn-to-scuba course) for $69. The company also organizes nighttime dives. **Sea Hawk Divers** (⊠ *Av. Arq. Carlos Lazo* ☎ *998/877–1233* ⊕ *www.sea-hawk-divers.myislamujeres. com*) runs reef dives from $45 (for one tank) to $65 (for two tanks). Special excursions to the more exotic shipwrecks cost from $75 to $95. The PADI courses taught here are highly regarded. For nondivers there are snorkel trips that depart at 9:30 and 2:30 daily.

SIDE TRIP TO ISLA CONTOY

30 km (19 mi) north of Isla Mujeres.

A national wildlife park and bird sanctuary, Isla Contoy (Isle of Birds) is just 6 km (4 mi) long and less than 1 km (about ½ mi) wide. The island is a protected area—the number of visitors is carefully regulated in order to safeguard the flora and fauna. Isla Contoy has become a favorite among bird-watchers, snorkelers, and nature lovers who come to enjoy its unspoiled beauty.

Shhh . . . Don't Wake the Sharks

The underwater caverns off Isla Mujeres attract a dangerous species of shark—though nobody knows exactly why. Stranger still, once the sharks swim into the caves they enter a state of relaxed nonaggression seen nowhere else. Naturalists have two explanations, both involving the composition of the water inside the caves—it contains more oxygen, more carbon dioxide, and less salt. According to the first theory, the decreased salinity causes the parasites that plague sharks to loosen their grip, allowing the remora fish (the sharks' personal vacuum cleaner) to eat the parasites more easily. Perhaps the sharks relax in order to facilitate the cleaning, or maybe their deep state of relaxation is a side effect of having been scrubbed clean.

Another theory is that the caves' combination of fresh- and saltwater may produce euphoria, similar to the effect scuba divers experience on extremely deep dives. Whatever the sharks experience while "sleeping" in the caves, they pay a heavy price for it: a swimming shark breathes automatically and without effort (water is forced through the gills as the shark swims), but a stationary shark must laboriously pump water to continue breathing. If you dive in the Cave of the Sleeping Sharks, be cautious: many are reef sharks, the species responsible for the largest number of attacks on humans. Dive with a reliable guide and be on your best diving behavior.

More than 70 bird species—including gulls, pelicans, petrels, cormorants, cranes, ducks, flamingos, herons, doves, quail, spoonbills, and hawks—fly this way in late fall, some to nest and breed. Although the number of species is diminishing—partly as a result of human traffic—Isla Contoy remains a treat for bird-watchers.

The island is rich in sea life as well. Snorkelers will see brilliant coral and fish. Manta rays, which average about 5 feet across, are visible in the shallow waters. Surrounding the island are large numbers of shrimp, mackerel, barracuda, flying fish, and trumpet fish. In December, lobsters pass through in great (though diminishing) numbers, on their southerly migration route.

Sand dunes inland from the east coast rise as high as 70 feet above sea level. Black rocks and coral reefs fringe the island's east coast, which drops off abruptly 15 feet into the sea. The west coast is fringed with sand, shrubs, and coconut palms. At the north and the south ends, you find nothing but trees and small pools of water.

GETTING HERE AND AROUND

The trip to Isla Contoy takes about 45 minutes to 1½ hours, depending on the weather and the boat; the cost is between $38 and $50. Everyone landing on Isla Contoy must purchase a $5 authorization ticket; the price is usually included in the cost of a guided tour. The standard tour begins with a fruit breakfast on the boat and a stopover at Xlaches reef on the way to Isla Contoy for snorkeling (gear is included in the price). As you sail, your crew trolls for the lunch it will cook on the beach—you may be in for anything from barracuda to snapper (beer and soda are also included). While the catch is being barbecued, you have time to explore the island, snorkel, check out the small museum and biological station, or just laze under a palapa.

The island is officially open to visitors daily from 9 to 5:30; overnight stays aren't allowed. Other than the birds and the dozen or so park rangers who live here, the island's only residents are iguanas, lizards, turtles, hermit crabs, and boa constrictors. You can read more about Isla Contoy by visiting a Web site devoted to the island: ⊕*www.islacontoy.org.*

Sociedad Cooperativa Isla Mujeres (⊠ *Contoy Pier, Av. Rueda Medina* ☎*998/877–1363*) offers daily boat trips from Isla Mujeres to Isla Contoy Pier at Rueda Medina. Groups are a minimum of 6 and a maximum of 12 people.

Captain Ricardo Gaitan (⊠ *Contoy Pier, Av. Rueda Medina* ☎*998/877–0798*), a local Isla Contoy expert, also provides an excellent tour for large groups (6 to 20 people) aboard his 36-foot boat *Estrella del Norte.*

Cozumel

Reef near San Miguel de Cozumel

WORD OF MOUTH

"We've been to Cozumel 3 times. It's our favorite Island and we've been to many. We thought the snorkeling was better than St. John, but not as good as Grand Cayman. . . .

There are many cruise ships during the day. Most of the passengers center around the Mercado for shopping and the Senor Frogs/Carlos and Charlies bars. There are plenty of places to go to get away from them until the ships leave."

—KVR

WELCOME TO COZUMEL

TOP REASONS TO GO

★ **Scuba dive the Great Maya Reef:** A Technicolor profusion of fish, coral, and other underwater creatures resides in this 600-mi-long reef, stretching from Cozumel to Central America.

★ **Utterly unwind:** Lounge poolside, stroll along a white sand beach, or explore the gardens at Chankanaab. You can spend hours just sitting in the main plaza (or at a sidewalk café) watching island life pass by.

★ **Taste local flavor:** On Sunday nights at San Miguel's Plaza Central, join the families and couples who gather for music and dancing. Visit during Carnival, the spring Fería del Cedral, or any national holiday, and you'll find parades, processions, and seasonal treats sold at food stands.

★ **Contemplate the Maya:** Explore the temples dedicated to Ixchel, the Mayan goddess of fertility and the moon, at San Gervasio, and study the exhibits on Mayan culture past and present at the Museo de Cozumel.

1 The Northwest Coast. Broad beaches and the island's first golf course lie at the northwest tip of Cozumel. The sand gives way to limestone shelves jutting over the water; hotels that don't have big beaches provide ladders down to excellent snorkeling spots, where parrot fish crunch on coral.

2 San Miguel. Cozumel's only town, where cruise ships loom from the piers and endless souvenir shops line the streets, still retains some of the flavor of a Mexican village. On weekend nights musical groups and food vendors gather in the main square, attracting a lively crowd.

3 The Southwestern Beaches. Proximity to Cozumel's best reefs makes the beaches south of San Miguel a home base for divers. A parade of hotels, beach clubs, commercial piers, and dive shops lines the shore here.

4 The Southern Nature Parks. Cozumel's natural treasures are protected both above and below the sea. At Faro Celarain Eco Park, mangrove lagoons and beaches shelter nesting sea turtles. Parque Chankanaab, one of Mexico's first marine parks, is superb for snorkeling. Parque Marino Nacional Arrecifes de Cozumel encompasses the coral reefs along the southwest edge of the island.

5 The Windward Coast. The rough surf of the Caribbean pounds against the limestone shore here, creating pocket-size beaches perfect for solitary sunbathing. The water can be rough, though, so pay attention to the tides, currents, and sudden drop-offs in the ocean floor.

1 THE
NORTHWEST
COAST

Punta Molas

Punta Norte

Isla de
Pasión

Playa
Santa
Pilar

Playa
San
Juan

◆ Cozumel
Country Club

San
Gervasio ◆

✈ Airport

Plaza
Central

Av. Benito Juárez

SAN
MIGUEL

Panta
Lanqosta

2

Av. Rafael Melgar

Commerical
Pier

TO PUERTO
MORELOS

3

Playa
San
Juan

Parque
◆ Chankanaab

Playa San
Francisco

Playa Sol

El Cedral

Punta
Francesca ◆

Playa del
Palancar

Laguna
Colombia

4

◆ Faro Celarain
Eco Park

Laguna
Chunchataab

M A Y A   R E E F

GETTING
ORIENTED

3

A 490-square-km
(189-square-mi) island
19 km (12 mi) east of
the Yucatán peninsula,
Cozumel is mostly flat,
with an interior covered by
parched scrub, low jungle,
and marshy lagoons. White
beaches with calm waters
line the island's leeward
(western) side, which is
fringed by a spectacular
reef system; the windward
(eastern) side, facing the
Caribbean Sea, has rocky
strands and powerful surf.

5 THE
WINDWARD
COAST

Playa de
San Martín

Playa
Bonita

Playa Paradíso

0 ├───┤ 4 miles

0 ├───┤ 4 kilometers

COZUMEL PLANNER

Easy Riding

A vehicle comes in handy on Cozumel, but driving can be tricky. Locals get around on bicycles and mopeds, often piled high with relatives and friends. Though they're adept at weaving around faster, bigger vehicles, you'll need to keep careful watch to make sure you don't hit them. This is especially important on roads around the cruise-ship piers and on major cross streets. Separate lanes for scooters on the busy southwest coast reduce the hazards somewhat.

How's the Weather?

Weather conditions are more extreme here than you might expect on a tropical island. *Nortes*—winds from the north— blow through in December, churning the sea and making air and water temperatures drop. If you visit during this time, bring a shawl or jacket for the chilly 65°F evenings. Summers, on the other hand, can be beastly hot and humid. The windward side is calmer in winter than the leeward side, and the interior is warmer than the coast.

Booking Your Hotel Online

A growing number of Cozumel hotels encourage people to make their reservations online. Some allow you to book rooms through their own Web sites, and those without one usually offer reservations via online booking agencies, such as ⊕ *www.cozumel-hotels.net*, ⊕ *www.cometocozumel. com*, or ⊕ *www.cozumel.net*. Since hotels customarily work with several different agencies, it's a good idea to shop around online for the best rates.

Besides being convenient, booking online can often get you a 10% to 20% discount on room rates. The downside, though, is that there are occasional breakdowns in communication. You may arrive to discover that your Spanish-speaking front desk clerk has no record of your Internet reservation or has reserved a room that's different from the one you specified. To prevent such mishaps from ruining your vacation, be sure to bring copies of all your Internet transactions, including receipts and confirmations, with you.

Need More Information?

The Web site ⊕ *www.cozumelmycozumel.com*, edited by full-time residents of the island, has insider tips on activities, sights, and places to stay and eat. There's a bulletin board, too, where you can post questions.

Dining and Lodging Prices

WHAT IT COSTS IN DOLLARS

	¢	$	$$	$$$	$$$$
Restaurants	under $5	$5–$10	$10–$15	$15–$25	over $25
Hotels	under $50	$50–$75	$75–$150	$150–$250	over $250

Restaurant prices are based on the median entrée price at dinner. Hotel prices are for a standard double room in high season.

Updated by
Maribeth
Mellin

It's all about the water here—the shimmering, clear-as-glass aquamarine sea that makes you want to kick off your shoes, slip on your fins, and dive right in. Once you come up for air, though, you'll find that Mexico's largest Caribbean island is pretty fun to explore on land, too.

3

Despite a severe lashing by Hurricane Wilma in October 2005, by 2009 nearly everything was back to normal. Remodeled and upgraded hotels and businesses are better than ever.

Cozumel is 53 km (33 mi) long and 15 km (9 mi) wide, and its main paved roads are excellent. The dirt roads, however, are another story; they're too deeply rutted for most rental cars. Streets in congested neighborhoods and remote areas flood quickly in heavy rains and are tough to navigate in heavy traffic no matter the weather. The island's windward side and rapidly developing interior lack the infrastructure to handle severe storms.

Cozumel's main road is Avenida Rafael E. Melgar, which runs along the island's western shore. South of San Miguel, the road is known as Carretera Chankanaab or Carretera Sur; it runs past hotels, shops, and the international cruise-ship terminals. South of town, the road splits into two parallel lanes, the right lane reserved for slower motor-scooter and bicycle traffic. After Parque Chankanaab, the road passes several excellent beaches and a cluster of resorts. At Cozumel's southernmost point the road turns northeast; beyond that point, it's known simply as "the coastal road." North of San Miguel, Avenida Rafael E. Melgar becomes Carretera Norte along the North Hotel Zone and ends near the Cozumel Country Club.

Alongside Avenida Rafael E. Melgar in San Miguel is the 14-km (9-mi) walkway called the *malecón*. The sidewalk by the water is relatively uncrowded; the other side, packed with shops and restaurants, gets clogged with crowds when cruise ships are in port. Avenida Juárez, Cozumel's other major road, stretches east from the pier for 16 km (10 mi), dividing town and island into north and south.

San Miguel is laid out in a grid. *Avenidas* are roads that run north or south; they're numbered in increments of five. A road that starts out as an "avenida norte" turns into an "avenida sur" when it crosses Avenida Juárez. *Calles* are streets that run east–west; those north of Avenida Juárez have even numbers (Calle 2 Norte, Calle 4 Norte), whereas those to the south have odd numbers (Calle 1 Sur, Calle 3 Sur).

Plaza Central, or *la plaza,* the heart of San Miguel, is directly across from the docks. Residents congregate here in the evening, especially on weekends, when free concerts begin at 8. Shops and restaurants abound in the square. Heading inland (east) takes you away from the tourist zone and toward the residential sections. The heaviest commercial district is concentrated between Calle 10 Norte and Calle 11 Sur to beyond Avenida Pedro Joaquin Coldwell.

GETTING HERE AND AROUND

The Aeropuerto Internacional de Cozumel is 3 km (2 mi) north of San Miguel and receives a few international and domestic flights. Flights to Cancún may be considerably less expensive. From the Cancún airport you can take a bus to Playa del Carmen and then take the ferry to Cozumel. The trip should cost less than $20 and take about three hours if everything runs on schedule. Flights between Cancún and Cozumel began again in 2008 after a long hiatus.

WORD OF MOUTH

"Cozumel is NOTHING like Cancun. It has a wonderful small town feel, only with amazing water views. The people are so friendly."

—TC

At the airport, the *colectivo,* a van that seats up to eight, takes arriving passengers to their hotels; the fare is about $7 to $20 per person. Passenger-only ferries to and from Playa del Carmen leave approximately every hour on the hour from early morning until late night. The trip takes 45 minutes and costs about $14 each way. Car ferries leave from Puerto Morelos and Calica.

Bus service on Cozumel is basically limited to San Miguel, so a rental car is recommended. Though it's tempting to drive on Cozumel's dirt roads (which lead to uncrowded beaches), most car-rental companies have a policy that voids your insurance once you leave the paved roadway.

Cabs wait at all the major hotels, and you can hail them on the street. The fixed rates run about $3 within town; $8 to $20 between town and either hotel zone; $10 to $30 from most hotels to the airport; and about $20 to $40 from the northern hotels or town to Parque Chankanaab or Playa San Francisco. The cost from the Puerto Maya cruise-ship terminal by El Cid La Ceiba to San Miguel is about $10.

ESSENTIALS

Currency Exchange American Express (⊠ *Punta Langosta, Av. Rafael E. Melgar 599* ☎ *987/869–1389*). **Promotora Cambiaria del Centro** (⊠ *Av. 5 Sur between Calles 1 Sur and Adolfo Rosado Salas* ☎ *No phone*).

Ferry Contacts Passenger-only ferry from Playa del Carmen (☎ *987/872– 1578 or 987/869–2223*). **Car ferry from Puerto Morelos** (☎ *987/872–0950*). **Car ferry from Calica** (☎ *987/872–7688*).

Internet Calling Station (⊠ *Av. Rafael E. Melgar 27, at Calle 3 Sur* ☎ *987/ 872–1417*). **The Crew Office** (⊠ *Av. 5, No. 201, between Calle 3 Sur and Av. Rosada Salas* ☎ *987/869–1485*). **CreWorld Internet** (⊠ *Av. Rafael E. Melgar and Calle 11 Sur* ☎ *987/872–6509*).

Mail and Shipping Correos (⊠ *Calle 7 Sur and Av. Rafael E. Melgar* ☎ *987/872–0106*). **DHL** (⊠ *Av. Salas 7* ☎ *987/872–3110*).

Medical Assistance Air Ambulance (☎ *987/872–4070*). **Centro Médico de Cozumel** ([*Cozumel Medical Center*] ⊠ *Calle 1 Sur 101 and Av. 50* ☎ *987/ 872–5664 or 987/872–5370*). **Police** (⊠ *Anexo del Palacio Municipal* ☎ *987/ 872–0092*). **Red Cross** (⊠ *Calle Adolfo Rosada Salas and Av. 20 Sur* ☎ *987/872–1058, 065 for emergencies*).

Recompression Chambers **Buceo Médico Mexicano** (⊠ *Calle 5 Sur 21B* ☎ *987/872–1430 24-hr hotline*). **Cozumel Recompression Chamber** (⊠ *San Miguel Clinic, Calle 6 Norte between Avs. 5 and 10* ☎ *987/872–3070*).

Rental Cars **Aguila Rentals** (⊠ *Av. Rafael E. Melgar 685* ☎ *987/872–0729*). **CP Rentals** (⊠ *Av. 10 Norte, between Calles 2 and 4* ☎ *987/878–4055*). **Fiesta** (⊠ *Calle 11, No. 598* ☎ *987/872–0433*).

Visitor and Tour Info **Fidecomiso and the Cozumel Island Hotel Association** (⊠ *Calle 2 Norte and Av. 15* ☎ *987/872–7585* ⊕ *www.islacozumel.com.mx*).

3

EXPLORING

Outside its developed areas, Cozumel consists of sandy or rocky beaches, quiet coves, palm groves, lagoons, swamps, scrubby jungle, and a few low hills (the highest elevation is 45 feet). Brilliantly feathered tropical birds, lizards, armadillos, coatimundi (raccoonlike mammals), deer, and small foxes populate the undergrowth and mangroves. Several minor Mayan ruins dot the island's eastern coast, including El Caracol, an ancient lighthouse.

TOP ATTRACTIONS

❷ **Museo de la Isla de Cozumel.** Cozumel's island museum is housed on two floors of a former hotel. It has displays on natural history—with exhibits on the island's origins, endangered species, topography, and coral-reef ecology—as well as the pre-Columbian and colonial periods. The photos of the island's transformation over the 20th and 21st centuries are especially fascinating, as is the exhibit of a typical Mayan home. Guided tours are available. ⊠ *Av. Rafael E. Melgar, between Calles 4 and 6 Norte* ☎ *987/872–1475* ⊡ *$3* ⊙ *Daily 9–5.*

> **NEED A BREAK?** On the terrace off the second floor of the Museo de la Isla de Cozumel, the **Restaurante del Museo** (☎ *987/872–0838*) serves breakfast and lunch from 7 to 2. The Mexican fare is enhanced by a great waterfront view, and the café is as popular with locals as tourists.

❺ **Parque Chankanaab.** Chankanaab (which means "small sea") is a national park with a saltwater lagoon, an archaeological park, and a botanical garden. Scattered throughout are reproductions of a Mayan village, and of Olmec, Toltec, Aztec, and Mayan stone carvings. You can enjoy a cool walk along pathways leading to the sea, where parrot fish and sergeant majors swarm around snorkelers.

You can swim, scuba dive, or snorkel at the beach. There's plenty to see: underwater caverns, a sunken ship, crusty old cannons and anchors, and a sculpture of la Virgen del Mar (Virgin of the Sea). To preserve the ecosystem, park rules forbid touching the reef or feeding the fish.

Dive shops, restaurants, gift shops, a snack stand, and dressing rooms with lockers and showers are right on the sand. A small museum has exhibits on coral, shells, and the park's history, as well as some sculptures. ⊠ *Carretera Sur, Km 9* ☎ *987/872–2940* ⊡ *$16* ⊙ *Daily 8–5.*

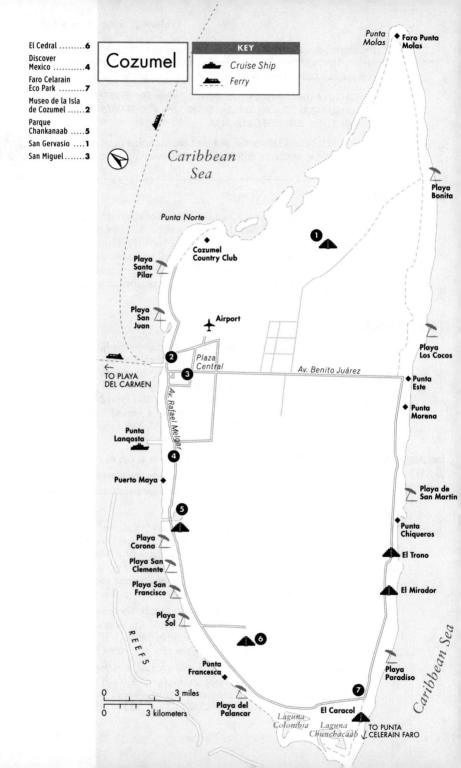

Cozumel

KEY

🚢 *Cruise Ship*

⛴ *Ferry*

*Caribbean
Sea*

*Punta
Molas* ◆ **Faro Punta
Molas**

**Playa
Bonita**

Punta Norte

◆ **Cozumel
Country Club**

**Playa
Santa
Pilar**

**Playa
San
Juan**

✈ **Airport**

**Playa
Los Cocos**

2
*Plaza
Central*

3

← *Av. Benito Juárez*

**TO PLAYA
DEL CARMEN**

◆ **Punta
Este**

◆ **Punta
Morena**

Av. Rafael Melgar

**Punta
Lanqosta**

4

Puerto Maya ◆

**Playa de
San Martín**

5

◆ **Punta
Chiqueros**

**Playa
Corona**

🔺 **El Trono**

**Playa San
Clemente**

**Playa San
Francisco**

🔺 **El Mirador**

**Playa
Sol**

R
E
E
F
S

🔺 **6**

**Punta
Francesca** ◆

**Playa
Paradíso**

7

0 ___ 3 miles

0 ___ 3 kilometers

**Playa del
Palancar**

*Laguna
Colombia*

El Caracol

*Laguna
Chunchacáab*

**TO PUNTA
CELERAIN FARO**

Caribbean Sea

❶ **San Gervasio.** Surrounded by a forest, these temples make up Cozumel's largest remaining Mayan and Toltec site. San Gervasio was the island's capital and ceremonial center, dedicated to the fertility goddess Ixchel. Its classic- and postclassic-style buildings and temples were continuously occupied from AD 300 to 1500. Typical architectural features include limestone plazas and arches atop stepped platforms, as well as stelae and bas-reliefs. Be sure to see the temple "Las Manitas," with red handprints all over its altar. Plaques clearly describe each structure in Mayan, Spanish, and English. ⊠*From San Miguel take cross-island road (follow signs to airport) east to San Gervasio access road; turn left and follow road 7 km (4½ mi)* ☎*$5.75* ☉*Daily 7–4.*

WORD OF MOUTH

"Our last time in Cozumel, we got a cab driver who took us all over . . . showed us parts of Cozumel we had never seen in our MANY cruises there. The driver could tell us about things and one of us did not have to watch the road—we could ALL look at the scenery. The driver must keep his eye on the road and the other WILD drivers! We never rent cars on cruises—let the driver, who knows where to go, take us all over!" —bonniejns

❸ **San Miguel.** Wait until the cruise ships sail toward the horizon before visiting San Miguel, Cozumel's only town. Then stroll along the *malecón* (boardwalk) and take in the ocean breeze. The waterfront has been taken over by large shops selling jewelry, imported rugs, leather boots, and souvenirs to cruise-ship passengers. The northern end of the malecón, past Calle 10 Norte, is a pleasant area lined with sculptures of Mayan gods and goddesses that draws more locals than tourists. The town feels more traditional as you head inland to the pedestrian streets around the plaza, where family-owned restaurants and shops cater to locals and savvy travelers. The plaza and surrounding buildings underwent a total makeover in 2008. The central *kiosko* (bandstand) and clock tower remained the same, but there's less greenery and the dilapidated Plaza Sol building facing the plaza was completely rebuilt, with new spaces for shops. The artisan's market behind the building was refreshed as well, and now has more space and sunlight.

WORTH NOTING

❻ **El Cedral.** Spanish explorers discovered this site, once the hub of Mayan life on Cozumel, in 1518. Later it became the island's first official city, founded in 1847. Today it's a farming community with small well-tended houses and gardens. Conquistadors tore down much of the Mayan temple, and during World War II the U.S. Army Corps of Engineers destroyed the rest to make way for the island's first airport. All that remains of the Mayan ruins is one small structure with an arch. Nearby is a green-and-white cinder-block church, decorated inside with crosses shrouded in embroidered lace; legend has it that Mexico's first Mass was held here. Vendors display embroidered blouses, hammocks, and other souvenirs at stands around the main plaza. ⊠*Turn at Km 17.5 off Carretera Sur or Av. Rafael E. Melgar, then drive 3 km (2 mi) inland to site* ☎*No phone* ☎*Free* ☉*Daily dawn–dusk.*

④ ⊛ ★ Discover Mexico. New to the island in 2007, this ingenious attraction allows visitors to learn about Mexico's archaeological sites, important architectural landmarks, and cultures. A gorgeous film about Mexico runs continuously, and exhibits display collector-quality textiles, pottery, and painted figurines. Outdoors are scale models of temples, pyramids, monasteries, and Mexico City's main square, the Zócalo. An outdoor café serves tasty fruit sorbets and light meals. The gift shop has the island's finest array of Mexican folk art. Expect to spend about two hours to fully experience the entire exhibit. A combo entry ticket includes admissions to Discover Mexico and Parque Chakanaab. The price is $34 or adult and $24 for children ⊠ *Carretera Sur, Km 5.5* ☎ *987/875–2820* ⊕ *www.discovermexico.org* ≦ *$10 adults and children* ⊗ *Mon.–Sat. 8–6.*

> **COZUMEL BY TOUR**
>
> Tours of the island's sights, including the San Gervasio ruins, El Cedral, Parque Chankanaab, and the Museo de la Isla de Cozumel, cost about $50 a person and can be arranged through travel agencies. **Fiesta Holidays** (⊠ *Calle 11 Sur 598, between Avs. 25 and 30* ☎ *987/872–0923*), which has representatives in many hotels, sells several tours. Another option is to take a private tour of the island via taxi, which costs about $60 for a half-day tour.

❼ ⊛ Faro Celarain Eco Park. This 247-acre national preserve at Cozumel's southernmost tip is a protected habitat for numerous birds and animals, including crocodiles, flamingos, egrets, and herons. Cars aren't allowed, so you'll need to use park transportation (rented bicycles or park shuttles) to get around here. From observation towers you can spot crocodiles and birds in **Laguna Colombia** or **Laguna Chunchacaab.** Or visit the ancient Mayan lighthouse, **El Caracol,** designed to whistle when the wind blows in a certain direction. At the park's (and the island's) southernmost point is the **Faro de Celarain,** a lighthouse that is now a museum of navigation. Climb the 134 steps to the top; it's a steamy effort, but the views are incredible. Beaches here are wide and deserted, and there's great snorkeling offshore. Snorkeling equipment is available for rent, as are kayaks, and there are restrooms at the museum and by the beach. Without a rental car, expect to pay about $40 for a round-trip taxi ride from San Miguel. ⊠ *Southernmost point of Carretera Sur and coastal road* ☎ *987/872–2940 or 987/872–8462* ≦ *$10* ⊗ *Daily 9–5.*

BEACHES

Cozumel's beaches vary from sandy treeless stretches to isolated coves to rocky shores. Most of the development on the island is on the leeward (western) side, where the coast is relatively sheltered by the mainland. Beach clubs line the southwest coast; a few charge admission despite the fact that Mexican beaches are public property. However, admission is usually free, as long as you buy food and drinks. Beware of tour buses in club parking lots—they indicate that hordes of cruise-ship passengers have taken over the facilities. Clubs offer typical tourist fare: souvenir

Cozumel's History

Cozumel's name is believed to have come from the Mayan "Ah-Cuzamil-Peten" ("land of the swallows"). For the Maya, who lived here intermittently between about AD 600 and 1200, the island was not only a center for trade and navigation, but also a sacred place. Pilgrims from all over Mesoamerica came to honor Ixchel, the goddess of fertility, childbirth, the moon, and rainbows. Viewed as the mother of all other gods, Ixchel was often depicted with swallows at her feet. Mayan women, who were expected to visit Ixchel's site at least once during their lives, made the dangerous journey from the mainland by canoe. Cozumel's main exports were salt and honey; at the time, both were considered more valuable than gold.

In 1518 Spanish explorer Juan de Grijalva arrived on Cozumel, looking for slaves. His tales of treasure inspired Hernán Cortés, Mexico's most famous Spanish explorer, to visit the island the following year. There he met Geronimo de Aguilar and Gonzales Guerrero, Spanish men who had been shipwrecked on Cozumel years earlier. Initially enslaved by the Maya, the two were later accepted into their community. Aguilar joined forces with Cortés, helping set up a military base on the island and using his knowledge of the Maya to defeat them. Guerrero died defending his adopted people; the Maya still consider him a hero. By 1570 most Mayan islanders had been massacred by Spaniards or killed by disease. By 1600 the island was abandoned.

In the 17th and 18th centuries, pirates found Cozumel to be the perfect hideout. Two notorious buccaneers, Jean Laffite and Henry Morgan, favored the island's safe harbors and hid their treasures in the Mayan catacombs and tunnels. By 1843 Cozumel had again been abandoned. Five years later, 20 families fleeing Mexico's brutal War of the Castes resettled the island; their descendants still live on Cozumel.

By the early 20th century the island began capitalizing on its abundant supply of *zapote* (sapodilla) trees, which produce chicle, prized by the chewing-gum industry (think Chiclets). Shipping routes began to include Cozumel, whose deep harbors made it a perfect stop for large vessels. Jungle forays in search of chicle led to the discovery of ruins; soon archaeologists began visiting the island as well. Meanwhile, Cozumel's importance as a seaport diminished as air travel grew, and demand for chicle dropped off with the invention of synthetic chewing gum.

For decades Cozumel was another backwater where locals fished, hunted alligators and iguanas, and worked on coconut plantations to produce *copra*, the dried kernels from which coconut oil is extracted. Cozumeleños subsisted largely on seafood, still a staple of the local economy. During World War II the U.S. Army built an airstrip and maintained a submarine base here, accidentally destroying some Mayan ruins. Then in the 1960s the underwater explorer Jacques Cousteau helped make Cozumel a vacation spot by featuring its incredible reefs on his television show. Today Cozumel is among the world's most popular diving locations.

shops, *palapa* (thatch-roof) restaurants, kayaks, and cold beer. A cab ride from San Miguel to most of the beach clubs costs about $15 each way. Reaching beaches on the windward (eastern) side is more difficult, but the solitude is worth the effort.

LEEWARD BEACHES

Wide sandy beaches washed with shallow waters are typical at the far north and south ends of Cozumel's west coast. The topography changes between the two, with small sandy coves interspersed with limestone outcroppings. ■ TIP➜ Generally, the best snorkeling is wherever piers or rocky shorelines provide a haven for sergeant majors and angelfish. Shore diving and snorkeling aren't as good as they were before Hurricane Wilma, though they're improving gradually. You're best off taking a boat tour to the reefs to see swarms of fish.

Playa Santa Pilar runs along the northern hotel strip and ends at Punta Norte. Long stretches of sand and shallow water encourage leisurely swims. The privacy diminishes as you swim south past hotels and condos.

Playa San Juan, south of Playa Santa Pilar, has a rocky shore with no easy ocean access. It's usually crowded with guests from nearby hotels. The wind can be strong here, which makes it popular with windsurfers.

A small parking lot on the side of Carretera Sur just south of town marks the entrance to **Playa Caletita**. There's a rock ledge here and fairly easy access into the water.

The **Money Bar Beach Club** (✉ *Carretera Sur, Km 6* ☎ *987/857–1000 www.moneybarbeachclub.com*) has opened at the wildly popular Dzul Ha beach in place of the former simple facilities. A water sports center offers rental scuba and snorkeling gear, kayaks, and small sailboats as well as showers and lockers. You can buy one of various packages, which include meals, massage, and snorkel tours, or you can just rent a snorkel and mask and check out the angel fish gliding over Dzul Ha reef before lunching under the peaked palapas shading the Miramar Terrace. Happy regulars and visitors come to sip frothy cocktails during the daily sunset happy hour and linger into the night.

Uvas (✉ *Carretera Sur, Km 8.5* ☎ *987/872–3539*) started out with a sexy, South Beach–style attitude but now caters to cruise-ship tours. Facilities include lockers, restrooms with showers, a dive shop, and a shop that rents see-through kayaks for paddling.

Playa San Francisco was one of the first beach clubs on the coast. The inviting 5-km (3-mi) stretch of sandy beach, which extends along Carretera Sur south of Parque Chankanaab at about Km 14, is among the longest and finest on Cozumel. Encompassing beaches known as Playa Maya and Santa Rosa, it's typically packed with cruise-ship passengers in high season. On Sunday locals flock here to eat fresh fish and hear live music. Amenities include two outdoor restaurants, a bar, dressing rooms, gift shops, volleyball nets, beach chairs, and water-sports equipment rentals. Divers use this beach as a jumping-off point for the San

Francisco reef and Santa Rosa wall. The abundance of turtle grass in the water, however, makes this a less-than-ideal spot for swimming.

Carlos'n Charlie's Beach Club (⊠ *Carretera Costera Sur Km 14* ☎*987/564– 0960)* abuts Playa San Francisco. It's a rowdy, bawdy affair with a restaurant and bar where waiters break into song and draw customers into line dances. The food is typical of the chain—burgers, barbecued ribs, tacos—and alcohol flows generously. The beach is shallow and the water not always clear, and the scene best suits youthful fun seekers.

☽ The club at **Paradise Beach** (⊠ *Carretera Sur, Km 14.5* ☎*987/871–9010*
★ ⊕*www.paradise-beach-cozumel.net*) has cushy lounge chairs and charges $10 per person for full-day use of kayaks, snorkel gear, a trampoline, and a climbing wall that looks like an iceberg in the water. Food is expensive, though. There's no charge to enter.

☽ **Mr. Sancho's Beach Club** (⊠ *Carretera Sur, Km 15* ☎*987/876–1629* ⊕*www.*
★ *mrsanchos.com*) always has a party going on: scores of holidaymakers come here to swim, snorkel, and drink buzz-inducing concoctions out of pineapples. Seemingly every water toy known to man is here; kids shriek happily as they hang onto banana boats dragged behind speedboats. Guides lead horseback and ATV rides into the jungle and along the beach, and the restaurant holds a lively, informative tequila seminar at lunchtime. Grab a swing seat at the beach bar and sip a mango margarita, or settle into the 30-person hot tub. Showers and lockers are available, and there are souvenirs aplenty for sale.

★ South of the resorts lies the mostly ignored (and therefore serene) **Playa Palancar** (⊠ *Carretera Sur* ☎*987/878–5238*). The deeply rutted and potholed road to the beach is a sure sign you've left tourist hell. Offshore is the famous Palancar Reef, easily accessed by the on-site dive shop. There's also a water-sports center, a bar-café, and a long beach with hammocks hanging under coconut palms. The aroma of grilled fish with garlic butter is tantalizing. Playa del Palancar keeps prices low and rarely feels crowded.

WINDWARD BEACHES

The east coast of Cozumel presents a splendid succession of mostly deserted rocky coves and narrow powdery beaches poised dramatically against the turquoise Caribbean. ■TIP➜**Swimming can be treacherous here if you go out too far—in some parts a deadly undertow can sweep you out to sea in minutes.** But the beaches are perfect for solitary sunbathing. Several casual restaurants dot the coastline; they all close after sunset.

Punta Chiqueros, a half-moon-shaped cove sheltered by an offshore reef, is the first popular swimming area as you drive north on the coastal road (it's about 12 km [8 mi] north of Parque Punta Sur). Part of a longer beach that some locals call Playa Bonita, it has fine sand, clear water, and moderate waves. This is a great place to swim, watch the sunset, and eat fresh fish at the restaurant, also called Playa Bonita.

Not quite 5 km (3 mi) north of Punta Chiqueros, a long stretch of beach begins along the Chen Río Reef. Turtles come to lay their eggs on the section known as **Playa de San Martín** (although some locals call

The Quieter Cozumel

Blazing-white cruise ships parade in and out of Cozumel as if competing in a big-time regatta. Rare is the day there isn't a white behemoth looming on the horizon. Typically, hundreds of day-trippers wander along the waterfront, packing franchise jewelry and souvenir shops and drinking in tourist-trap bars. Precious few explore the beaches and streets favored by locals.

Travelers staying in Cozumel's one-of-a-kind hotels experience a totally different island. They quickly learn to stick close to the beach and pool when more than two ships are in port (some days the island gets six). If you're lucky enough to stay overnight, consider these strategies for avoiding the crowds.

1. Time your excursions. Go into San Miguel for early breakfast and errands, then stay out of town for the rest of the day. Wander back after you hear the ships blast their departure warnings (around 5 or 6 PM).

2. Dive in. Hide from the hordes by slipping underwater. But be sure to choose a small dive operation that travels to less popular reefs.

3. Drive on the wild side. Rent a car and cruise the windward coast, still free of rampant construction. You can picnic and sunbathe on private beaches hidden by limestone outcroppings. Use caution when swimming; the surf can be rough.

4. Frequent the "other" downtown. The majority of Cozumel's residents live and shop far from San Miguel's waterfront. Avenidas 15, 20, and 25 are packed with taco stands, stationery stores (or *papelerías*), farmacias, and neighborhood markets. Driving here is a nightmare. Park on a quieter side street and explore the shops and neighborhoods to glimpse a whole different side of Cozumel.

---

it Chen Río, after the reef). During full moons in May and June the beach is sometimes blocked by soldiers or ecologists to prevent poaching of the turtle eggs. Directly in front of the reef is a small bay with clear waters and surf that's relatively mild, thanks to a protective rock formation. This is a particularly good spot for swimming when the water is calm. A restaurant, also called **Chen Río**, serves cold drinks and decent seafood.

★ About 1 km (½ mi) to the north of Playa San Martín, the island road turns hilly, providing panoramic ocean views. **Coconuts,** a hilltop restaurant, is an additional lookout spot, and serves good food. The adjacent **Ventanas al Mar** hotel is the only hotel on the windward coast and attracts locals and travelers who value solitude. Locals picnic on the long beach directly north of the hotel. When the water's calm there's good snorkeling around the rocks beneath the hotel.

Surfers and boogie-boarders have adopted **Punta Morena,** a short drive north of Ventanas al Mar, as their official hangout. The pounding surf creates great waves, and the local restaurant serves typical surfer food (hamburgers, hot dogs, and french fries). Vendors sell hammocks by the side of the road. The owners allow camping here.

The beach at **Punta Este** has been nicknamed Mezcalitos, after the much-loved restaurant here. **Mezcalito Café** serves seafood and beer and can get pretty rowdy. Punta Este is a typical windward beach—great for beachcombing but unsuitable for swimming.

The sandy road beside Mezcalitos leading to the wild northeast coast was closed at press time. Rumors abound as to this area's future—some say there will be a small-scale resort here soon, while others hope it will become an ecological reserve. A small Navy base is the only permanent settlement on the road for now, though some of the scrub jungle is divided into housing lots.

WHERE TO EAT

Dining options on Cozumel reflect the island's nature: breezy and relaxed with few pretensions (casual dress and no reservations are the rule here). Most restaurants emphasize fresh ingredients, simple presentation, and amiable service. Nearly every menu includes seafood; for a regional touch, go for *pescado tixin-xic* (fish spiced with achiote and baked in banana leaves). Only a few tourist-area restaurants serve regional Yucatecan cuisine, though nearly all carry standard Mexican fare like tacos, enchiladas, and huevos rancheros. Budget meals are harder and harder to find, especially near the waterfront. The best dining experiences are usually in small, family-owned restaurants that seem to have been here forever.

Many restaurants accept credit cards; café-type places generally don't.

■ TIP→ **Don't follow cab drivers' dining suggestions; they're often paid to recommend restaurants.**

ZONA HOTELERA SUR

$$$ ✕**Alfredo di Roma.** The opportunity to dine graciously amid crystal and ITALIAN candlelight (and blessedly cool air-conditioning) is just one reason to book a special dinner at Alfredo's. The pastas are made fresh daily and cheeses are flown in from Italy so the chef can prepare authentic fettuccini Alfredo tableside to rousing music from the accordion player. The octopus salad, pasta puttanesca, and grilled sea bass are all superb, and the wine cellar is the largest on the island. Book a table for early evening and enjoy the sunset view through wall-length windows. ⊠*Presidente InterContinental Cozumel, Carretera Chankanaab, Km 6.5* ☎*987/872–9500* ⬧*Reservations essential* ▤*AE, MC, V* ⊗*No lunch.*

SAN MIGUEL

¢–$ ✕**Casa Denis.** This little yellow house near the plaza has been satisfy-MEXICAN ing cravings for Yucatecan *pollo pibíl* (spiced chicken baked in banana ★ leaves) and other local favorites since 1945. *Tortas* (sandwiches) and tacos are a real bargain, and you'll start to feel like a local if you spend an hour at one of the outdoor tables, watching shoppers dash about. ⊠*Calle 1 Sur 132, between Avs. 5 and 10* ☎*987/872–0067* ▤*No credit cards.*

Island Dining

The aromas of sizzling shrimp, grilled chicken and steak, spicy sauces, and crisp pizza fill the air of San Miguel in the evening. Waiters deliver platters of enchiladas, tacos, and fajitas to sidewalk tables along pedestrian walkways, while people stroll along eyeing others' dinners before deciding where to stop for a meal. At rooftop restaurants, groups gather over Italian feasts; along the shoreline, lobster and the catch of the day are the delicacies of choice. There's no shortage of dining choices on Cozumel, where entrepreneurs from the U.S., Switzerland, and Italy have decided to make a go of their dreams. Foods familiar to American taste buds abound. In fact, it can be hard to find authentic regional cuisine. Yucatecan dishes such as *cochinita pibíl* (pork with achiote spice), *queso relleno* (Gouda cheese stuffed with ground meat), and *sopa de lima* (lime soup) rarely appear on tourist-oriented menus but are served at small family-owned eateries in San Miguel. Look for groups of local families gathered at wobbly tables in tiny cafés to find authentic Mexican cooking. Even the finest chefs tend to emphasize natural flavors and simple preparations rather than fancy sauces and experimental cuisine. Trends aren't important here. There are places where you can wear your finest sundress or silky Hawaiian shirt and dine by candlelight, for sure. But clean shorts and shirts with buttons are considered dress-up clothing suitable for most establishments. At the finer restaurants, guitarists or trios play soft ballads while customers savor lobster salad, filet mignon, and chocolate mousse. But the most popular dining spots are combination restaurant-bars in the Carlos'n Charlie's style, where diners fuel up on barbecued ribs and burgers before burning those calories away on the dance floor.

$$
✕ Casa Mission. Part private home and part restaurant, this estate evokes
MEXICAN a country hacienda in mainland Mexico. The on-site botanical garden
☾ has mango and papaya trees and a small zoo with caged birds. The setting, with tables lining the veranda, outshines the food. Stalwart fans rave about huge platters of fajitas and grilled fish. It's out of the way, so you'll need to take a cab. ⊠ *Av. Juárez and Calle 55A* ☎*987/872–1641* ⊟*AE, MC, V* ⊘*No lunch.*

$
✕ **Cocos Cozumel.** Start the day with a bountiful breakfast at this cheery
CAFÉ café where the coffee is strong and the egg dishes will remind you of U.S. coffeeshop fare. If you've come early enough to beat the heat, sit at a table under the front awning and watch the town come to life. The restaurant is open 6 AM to noon. ⊠ *Av. 5 Sur 180* ☎*987/872–0241* ⚇*Reservations not accepted* ⊟*No credit cards* ⊘*Closed Mon., Sept., and Oct. No dinner.*

¢–$
✕ **El Foco.** Locals fuel up before and after partying at this traditional
MEXICAN *taquería* (it's open until midnight, or until the last customer leaves). The soft tacos stuffed with pork, chorizo, cheese, or beef are cheap and filling; the graffiti on the walls and the late-night revelers provide the entertainment. ⊠ *Av. 5 Sur 13B, between Calles Adolfo Rosado Salas and 3 Sur* ☎*987/872–5980* ⊟*No credit cards.*

$$–$$$ ✕**Guido's.** Chef Yvonne Villiger
ITALIAN works wonders with fresh fish—if
★ the wahoo with capers and black
olives is on the menu, don't miss
it. But Guido's is best known for
its pizzas baked in a wood-burning
oven, which makes sections of the
indoor dining room rather warm.
Sit in the pleasantly overgrown
courtyard instead, and order a
pitcher of sangria to go with the
puffy garlic bread. ⊠ *Av. Rafael E.
Melgar 23, between Calles 6 and 8
Norte* ☎ *987/872–0946* ▭ *MC, V*
⊘ *Closed Sun.*

WORD OF MOUTH

"The restaurants in Cozumel
were fabulous and CHEAP. Our
favorite meal was at Kinta. For
$78 USD for 3 adults, we had
2 mixed drinks, 3 bottled waters,
1 appetizer, 3 entrees, 2 desserts,
and 1 dessert coffee. And it was
delicious. We ate there the last
night and wished we had tried
it earlier." —beanweb24

3

$–$$ ✕**Kinta.** Both locals and visitors rave about this little café, which is
MEXICAN owned by former Guido's chef Kris Wallenta. It's easy to overlook the
★ entrance (look for a bright orange facade on the west side of the street),
but once you've discovered the blissfully air-conditioned dining room,
romantic outdoor garden, and impressive menu, you'll likely return.
Wallenta rushes about the open kitchen, whipping up savory black
bean soup, a chile relleno filled with vegetable ratatouille and Chi-
huahua cheese, panko-crusted shrimp, and a tender filet mignon with
*huitlaoche*a corn truffle) and cheese. Hand-crushed mojitos, fruity sangria, and virgin *limomenta* (lemonade with mint) add a refreshing lilt,
and the bread pudding with Mexican chocolate and *cajeta* (caramel
sauce) is a fitting end to a stellar meal. ⊠ *Av. 5 between Calles 2 and
4* ☎ *987/869–0544* ▭ *MC, V* ⊘ *Closed Mon.*

$$ ✕**La Choza.** A fire destroyed this cherished landmark in the summer
MEXICAN of 2008, but the owners had the new place up and running by that
★ December. Still purely Mexican in design and cuisine—with the dining
room set beneath a soaring palapa—the family-owned restaurant is a
favorite for *pollo con mole poblano* (chicken in chocolate, cinnamon,
and chiles) and chile relleno *de camarón* (chile stuffed with shrimp).
Leave room for the chilled chocolate or lemon pie. Locals fill the restau-
rant at lunchtime for the economical fixed-price *comida corrida* (meal
of the day). ⊠ *Av. 10 between Calle Adolfo Rosado Salas and Av. 3*
☎ *987/872–0958* ▭ *AE, MC, V.*

$$$ ✕**La Cocay.** This casually sophisticated dining room is one of the most
ECLECTIC exciting dining venues on the island, thanks to the creative chef. The
Fodor'sChoice menu changes frequently, but you can expect to find salad with mixed
★ baby lettuces, salmon pâté, and entrées like seared sashimi-grade tuna.
Such fare may be the norm in L.A. or Honolulu but is hard to find on
Cozumel. Consider sharing several small plates, such the blue cheese
phyllo rolls, the *empanaditas* (tiny empanadas) with goat cheese and
caramelized apple, and the figs with prosciutto. There are reasonably
priced wines by the glass from Argentina, Chile, and Mexico. ⊠ *Calle
8 Norte between Avs. 10 and 15* ☎ *987/872–5533* ▭ *AE, MC, V*
⊘ *Closed Sun., no lunch.*

$$$ ╳**La Veranda.** Romantic and intimate, this wooden Caribbean house has
CARIBBEAN comfortable rattan furniture, soft lighting, and a terrace that's perfect
for evening cocktails (it's also a popular wedding venue). You can start
with Roquefort quesadillas, then move on to shrimp curry, jerk chicken,
or a seafood-stuffed poblano chile. ⊠ *Calle 4 Norte 140, between Avs.
5 and 10 Norte* ☎ *987/872–4132* ⊟ *AE, MC, V.*

$$-$$$ ╳**Pancho's Backyard.** Marimbas play beside the bubbling fountain in
MEXICAN this gorgeous courtyard behind one of Cozumel's best folk-art shops.
★ Though Pancho's is always busy, the waitstaff is amazingly patient
and helpful. Cruise-ship passengers seeking a taste of Mexico pack the
place at lunch; dinner is a bit more serene. The menu is definitely geared
toward tourists (written in English with detailed descriptions and prices
in dollars), but regional ingredients make even the standard steak stand
out when it's flavored with smoky chipotle chiles. Other stellar dish-
es include the cilantro cream soup and shrimp flambéed with tequila.
⊠ *Av. Rafael Melgar between Calles 8 and 10 Norte* ☎ *987/872–2141*
⊟ *AE, MC, V* ☉ *Dinner only on Sun.*

$$$ ╳**Pepe's Grill.** This nautical-theme eatery has model boats, ships' wheels,
STEAK and weather vanes covering the walls—appropriate because it's popular
with the cruise-ship crowds. The upstairs dining room's tall windows
allow for fantastic sunset views. The chateaubriand, T-bone steaks, and
prime rib please American palates, though the meat isn't up to steakhouse standards. Long waits for tables aren't uncommon. ⊠ *Av. Rafael
E. Melgar and Calle Adolfo Rosado Salas* ☎ *987/872–0213* ⌕ *Reservations not accepted* ⊟ *AE, MC, V* ☉ *No lunch.*

$ ╳**Plaza Leza.** The outdoor tables here are a wonderful place to linger;
MEXICAN you can watch the crowds in the square while savoring Mexican dishes
like *poc chuc* (tender pork loin in a sour-orange sauce), enchiladas, and
lime soup. Breakfast is available here as well. For more privacy, there's
also a somewhat secluded inner patio. ⊠ *Calle 1 Sur, south side of Plaza
Central* ☎ *987/872–1041* ⊟ *MC, V.*

$ ╳**Rock 'n Java Caribbean Café.** The extensive breakfast menu here
CAFÉ includes whole wheat French toast and cheese crepes. For lunch or
dinner try the vegetarian tacos or linguine with clams, or choose from
more than a dozen salads. Scrumptious pies, cakes, and pastries are
baked here daily. You can enjoy your healthy meal or sinful snack while
enjoying a sea view through the back windows. Used books are piled
on shelves along one wall, and the bulletin board by the front door is
an interesting read. ⊠ *Av. Rafael E. Melgar 602-6* ☎ *987/872–4405*
⊟ *MC, V* ☉ *No dinner Sat.*

WINDWARD COAST

$-$$ ╳**Coconuts.** The T-shirts and bikinis hanging from the palapa roof at
MEXICAN this windward-side hangout are a good indication of its party-time
★ atmosphere. Jimmy Buffett tunes play in the background while crowds
down *cervezas* (beers). The scene is more peaceful if you choose a
palapa-shaded table on the rocks overlooking the water. The calamari
and garlic shrimp are good enough to write home about. Assign a
designated driver and hit the road home before dark (remember, there
are no streetlights). ⊠ *East-coast road near junction with Av. Benito*

Juárez ☎*No phone* ⊟*No credit cards* ⊗*No dinner.*

$ ✗**Playa Bonita.** Locals gather on
MEXICAN Sunday afternoons at this casual beach café. The water here is usually calm, and families alternate between swimming and lingering over long lunches of fried fish. Weekdays are quieter; this is a good place to spend the day if you want access to food, drinks, and showers but aren't into the rowdy beachclub scene. ⊠*East-coast road* ☎*987/872–4868* ⊟*No credit cards* ⊗*No dinner.*

WORD OF MOUTH

"The Northern hotel zone is the best for shore snorkeling. The Southern zone has sandy beaches but no reefs close to shore. At the North end there is a beautiful wall covered in coral that has made an outstanding comeback since hurricane Wilma."   —TC

WHERE TO STAY

Small, one-of-a-kind hotels have long been the norm in Cozumel. Glamour and glitz are nearly nonexistent—though designer toiletries and fine linens are starting to appear in a few resorts. The emphasis remains on relaxed comfort and reasonable rates (though prices are rising). Most of Cozumel's hotels are on the leeward (west) and south sides of the island; there is one peaceful hideaway on the windward (east) side. The larger resorts are north and south of San Miguel; the less-expensive places are in town. Divers and snorkelers tend to congregate at the southern properties close to the best reefs. Swimmers and families prefer the hotels to the north, where the water is usually calm and shallow. Note that the beaches at some places may be rocky. Bring along swim shoes for easier water entries.

ZONA HOTELERA NORTE

$$$ ⊞ **Coral Princess Hotel and Resort.** Good snorkeling off the rocky shoreline ⟳ makes this a north coast favorite. The hotel was completely remodeled in 2006 with a new restaurant, bar, and gym. The suites have one or two bedrooms, a kitchen, and a balcony or terrace. These large rooms are often taken by time-share owners, especially in summer, though there's no pressure to attend a sales demo. Most of the studio-size hotel rooms overlook the jungle; try to get an ocean-view room on an upper floor for the best views and sea breezes. Housekeeping service is optional and costs an extra $1.50 per day. **Pros:** excellent snorkeling right off beach; decent, well-priced meals; family-friendly. **Cons:** can be noisy; some rooms lack bathtubs. ⊠*Carretera Costera Norte, Km 2.5* ☎*987/872–3200 or 800/253–2702* ⊕*www.coralprincess.com* ⮑*110 rooms, 26 suites* ⬠*In-room: Safe, kitchen (some), refrigerator. In-hotel: Restaurant, room service, bar, pools, gym, diving, water sports, laundry service, parking (free), no-smoking rooms* ⊟*AE, MC, V* ⫙*BP.*

$$$–$$$$ ⊞ **Playa Azul Golf and Beach Resort.** This romantic boutique hotel has ★ bright and airy rooms facing the ocean or the gardens. Inside the rooms are mirrored niches, wicker and pale-wood furnishings, and sun-filled

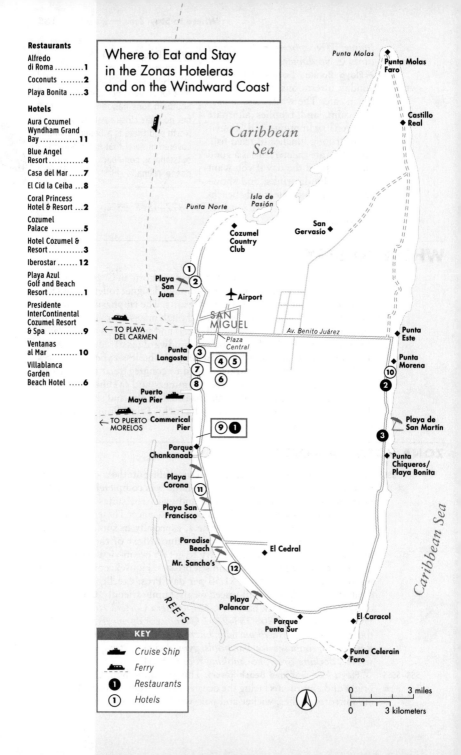

Where to Eat and Stay in the Zonas Hoteleras and on the Windward Coast

Restaurants

Alfredo
di Roma **1**

Coconuts **2**

Playa Bonita **3**

Hotels

Aura Cozumel
Wyndham Grand
Bay **11**

Blue Angel
Resort **4**

Casa del Mar **7**

El Cid la Ceiba ...**8**

Coral Princess
Hotel & Resort ...**2**

Cozumel
Palace **5**

Hotel Cozumel &
Resort **3**

Iberostar **12**

Playa Azul
Golf and Beach
Resort **1**

Presidente
InterContinental
Cozumel Resort
& Spa **9**

Ventanas
al Mar **10**

Villablanca
Garden
Beach Hotel **6**

Caribbean Sea

Punta Molas

Punta Molas
Faro

Castillo
Real

Isla de
Pasión

Punta Norte

San
Gervasio

Cozumel
Country
Club

Playa
San
Juan

Airport

SAN
MIGUEL

Plaza
Central

Av. Benito Juárez

Punta
Este

Punta
Morena

Punta
Langosta

Playa de
San Martín

← TO PLAYA
DEL CARMEN

Puerto
Maya Pier

← TO PUERTO
MORELOS

Commerical
Pier

Punta
Chiqueros/
Playa Bonita

Parque
Chankanaab

Playa
Corona

Playa San
Francisco

Paradise
Beach

El Cedral

Mr. Sancho's

Playa
Palancar

Parque
Punta Sur

El Caracol

Punta Celerain
Faro

REEFS

Caribbean Sea

KEY

🚢 *Cruise Ship*

⛴ *Ferry*

1 *Restaurants*

① *Hotels*

0   3 miles

0   3 kilometers

terraces. None of the rooms have bathtubs, and the best are the corner suites on the upper floors. Small palapas shade lounge chairs on the beach, and you can arrange snorkeling and diving trips at the hotel's own dock. Golf fees are included in the room rates; some guests hit the course daily. A freestanding spa at the hotel's entrance offers body and beauty treatments. The small Chan Ka'an dinner restaurant is a lovely spot for a quiet evening. Make reservations in advance in case there's a reception or other function taking place. **Pros:** small and intimate feel; excellent spa; no green fees. **Cons:** unheated pool and no hot tub; may be too quiet for some; rocky beach. ⊠ *Carretera Costera Norte, Km 4* ☎ *987/869-5160* ⊕ *www.playa-azul.com* ⤶ *34 rooms, 16 suites, 1 house* ⅏ *In-room: Safe, Internet. In-hotel: 2 restaurants, room service, bars, pool, beachfront, diving, water sports, spa, laundry service, parking (free), no-smoking rooms* ☐ *AE, MC, V* ⏀ *BP.*

ZONA HOTELERA SUR

$$$$ 🏨 **Aura Cozumel Wyndham Grand Bay.** Opened in 2008, this elegant, all-inclusive boutique hotel raises the standard for the southern coast's string of all-inclusive resorts. Four low-rise buildings face a meandering pool with separate areas linked by a lazy river. Swim-up suites have direct patio access to the ground-level pool, while third-story solarium suites have narrow rooftop lap pools. The design throughout the seven suite categories is sleekly contemporary, with dark-wood furnishings and contrasting sea-blue textiles, flat-screen TVs, iPod docks, and Egyptian cotton sheets. The hotel is adjacent to the 402-room Wyndham Cozumel Resort and Spa (formerly the Reef Club); both face a long beach with shallow water. Aura guests have use of the spa, restaurants, and facilities at both hotels. **Pros:** high-tech, luxurious suite amenities (rare on Cozumel); intimate, sophisticated ambience. **Cons:** far from town; offshore snorkeling not very good; no kids. ⊠ *Carretera Costera Sur, Km 12.9* ☎ *987/872-9300 or 866/551-2872* ⊕ *www.auraresorts. com* ⤶ *87 suites* ⅏ *In-room: Safe, refrigerator, DVD, Wi-Fi. In-hotel: 2 restaurants, room service, bars, pools, gym, beachfront, diving, water sports, laundry service, Wi-Fi, parking (no fee), no kids under 18, no-smoking rooms* ☐ *MC, V* ⏀ *AI.*

$$ 🏨 **Blue Angel Resort.** These moderately priced rooms are just right for wet, sandy divers who need to stash a lot of damp gear, take a powerful hot shower, and rush back to the beach. The hotel sits beside the sea on a limestone shelf, just a short walk from town. The owners also run the adjacent Blue Angel dive shop. Lazing here in a beachside hammock after a perfect morning dive is the quintessential Cozumel experience. **Pros:** friendly, repeat clientele; clean; close to town. **Cons:** nondivers may feel out of place; hard mattresses; erratic hot water. ⊠ *Carretera Sur, Km 2.2* ☎ *987/872-0188 or 866/779-9986* ⊕ *www.blueangelresort. com* ⤶ *22 rooms* ⅏ *In-room: Safe, refrigerator (some). In-hotel: Restaurant, pool, beachfront, diving, water sports, laundry service, no-smoking rooms* ☐ *MC, V* ⏀ *BP.*

$$ 🏨 **Casa del Mar.** Rooms vary considerably at this three-story hotel, which caters mostly to divers. Some are decorated with Mexican artwork and have large TVs and coffeemakers; only a few have bathtubs. Request

a room with a balcony facing the water for the view and light—other rooms tend to be dark. The bi-level cabanas, which sleep three or four, are a good deal. In addition to an in-house dive shop, the property has dive-gear storage areas. The narrow beach is across the street, and has palapas shading hammocks, a wooden sundeck with lounge chairs, and steps leading into the water. The hotel also offers a shuttle to the Nacho Cocom beach club. Food at the restaurant is decent (breakfasts are best). **Pros:** good dive shop; optional, reasonably priced all-inclusive plan. **Cons:** air-conditioning weak in some rooms; nondivers may feel out of place. ⊠*Carretera Sur, Km 4* ☎*987/872–1900 or 888/577–2758* ⊕*www.casadelmarcozumel.com* ↻*98 rooms, 8 cabanas* ⌂*In-hotel: Restaurant, bars, pool, diving, laundry service, Internet terminal, parking (free), no-smoking rooms* ⊟*AE, MC, V* ⟋⊙*EP*

$$$$ ⊡**Cozumel Palace.** This gorgeous all-inclusive hotel is part of the popular Palace Resorts chain. Within walking distance of San Miguel, the hotel faces the water but lacks a beach. Instead, an infinity pool seems to flow into the sea, and stairs lead from the property into a fairly good snorkeling area. The romantic rooms are airy, white enclaves with double whirlpool tubs and hammocks on most balconies. The chain has vacation ownership and club programs, so you may feel a bit hassled by sellers. Owners can use the facilities at the Palace Resort in Playa del Carmen on the mainland. The rate includes spa and golf discount vouchers and unlimited free calls to the U.S. and Canada. **Pros:** in-room hot tubs; good honeymoon hideaway. **Cons:** sales pressure; slow elevators. ⊠*Av. Rafael E. Melgar, Km 1.5* ☎*987/872–9430 or 800/635–1836* ⊕*www. palaceresorts.com* ↻*175 rooms* ⌂*In-room: Safe, refrigerator. In-hotel: 3 restaurants, room service, bars, pools, gym, spa, diving, water sports, children's programs (ages 4–12), laundry service, Wi-Fi, parking (free), no-smoking rooms* ⊟*AE, DC, MC, V* ⟋⊙*AI.*

$$$ ⊡**El Cid la Ceiba.** A favorite among divers and frequent Cozumel visitors, this compact property was originally built in 1978 beside a shady ceiba (a tree sacred to the Maya). The hotel was completely remodeled in 2006 with an eye to casual comfort (lots of towels, fold-out couches facing TVs, large dining tables). Most rooms overlook the ocean; the best have separate living rooms, kitchenettes, and enormous bathrooms with deep tubs and separate showers. The lobby and a small pool area separate the two towers, one facing a generous beach and the other above a smaller patch of sand bordering a shallow saltwater lagoon with a waterfall. **Pros:** great Mexican food in restaurant and reasonably priced all-inclusive option available; good snorkeling offshore. **Cons:** massive cruise ships nearby mar sea view; pool scene can be rowdy. ⊠*Carretera Chankanaab, Km 4.5* ☎*987/872–0844 or 800/525–1925* ⊕*www.elcid.com* ↻*60 rooms* ⌂*In-room: Safe, kitchens (some). In-hotel: Restaurant, room service, bars, tennis, 2 pools, gym, spa, beachfront, diving, water sports, no-smoking rooms* ⊟*MC, V* ⟋⊙*EP, AI.*

$$ ⊡**Hotel Cozumel and Resort.** On sunny days in high season, families and ♻ revelers surround the enormous pool at this hotel close to town; activity directors enliven the crowd with games and loud music. The scene is quieter at the beach club, accessed via a tunnel that looks like an underground aquarium, but there isn't an actual beach, just a rocky shoreline.

SCOOTING AROUND

Scooters are popular here, but also extremely dangerous because of heavy traffic, potholes, and hidden stop signs; accidents happen all too frequently. Mexican law requires all riders to wear helmets (it's a $25 fine if you don't).

If you do decide to rent a scooter, drive slowly, check for oncoming traffic, and don't ride when it's raining or if you've been drinking. Scooters rent for about $25 per day or $15 for a half day, including insurance.

MOPED RENTALS

Ernesto's Scooter Rental (⊠ *Carretera Costera Sur, Km 4* ☎ *987/872–3152*).

Rentadora Cozumel (⊠ *Avenida Juárez and Calle 10 77600*).

Rentadora Marlin (⊠ *Av. 5 and Calle 1 Sur 77600* ☎ *987/872–1586*).

The large rooms are reminiscent of a moderate chain hotel, with cool tile floors, comfy beds, and bathtub-shower combos. The hotel was originally all-inclusive; now there's a less-expensive BandB package that includes a bountiful buffet breakfast but no other meals or drinks. The hotel is close to downtown San Miguel, so you might want to skip the pricier AI plan and sample various nearby restaurants. **Pros:** 10-minute walk from town; near grocery stores and restaurants; recently added 10 fully handicap-accessible rooms. **Cons:** rocky beach area; poolside entertainment sometimes loud and annoying. ⊠ *Carretera Sur, Km 1.7* ☎ *987/872–9020* ⊕ *www.hotelcozumel.us* ↩ *181 rooms* ♿ *In-room: Safe. In-hotel: 2 restaurants, room service, bar, pools, gym, beachfront, diving, water sports, children's program (ages 5–12), laundry service, parking (free), no-smoking rooms* ☰ *MC, V* ☉ *AI, BP.*

$$$ 🏨 **Iberostar.** Jungle greenery surrounds this all-inclusive resort at
☾ Cozumel's southernmost point. Rooms are small but pleasant; each has wrought-iron details, one king-size or two queen-size beds, and a terrace or patio with hammocks. Rooms with king beds have more space, but there still aren't any dressers, so you may need to stash some necessities in the closet or a small suitcase. There isn't much privacy— pathways through the resort wind around the rooms—but this is the most enjoyable all-inclusive on the south coast. **Pros:** large pool area with plenty of lounge chairs. **Cons:** murky water; so-so food without much variety. ⊠ *Carretera Chankanaab, Km 17, past El Cedral turn-off* ☎ *987/872–9900 or 888/923–2722* ⊕ *www.iberostar.com* ↩ *306 rooms* ♿ *In-room: Safe. In-hotel: 3 restaurants, bars, tennis courts, pools, gym, spa, beachfront, diving, water sports, bicycles, children's programs (ages 4–12), parking (free)* ☰ *AE, MC* ☉ *AI.*

$$$$ 🏨 **Presidente InterContinental Cozumel Resort and Spa.** Cozumel's loveliest
☾ resort is a thoroughly modern, sophisticated property. The expansive
Fodor's Choice lawns and beaches are bordered by a marina to the north and undevel-
★ oped jungle to the south, making the hotel feel ultraprivate and seclud-
ed. Soft white sand covers the limestone shelf beside a small cove and the shores in front of the two hotel wings. Ground-level suites facing

the sea have large terraces, outdoor rain showers, and indoor bathtubs, whereas those in the upper floors have whirlpool tubs with sea views (and separate showers in the large bathrooms). Rooms have sleek dark-wood furnishings and a calm cream-and-brown color scheme. Special touches include gourmet coffeemakers, iPod docks, and complimentary Wi-Fi. The main palapa-covered restaurant is best for breakfast and lunch by the sea. The Mandara Spa is the island's largest, with sublime treatments and a *temazcal* (Mayan sweat lodge). Bellmen greet you like an old friend, waiters quickly learn your preferences, and housekeepers are quick to provide whatever you need. **Pros:** secluded and spacious feel; high-quality beds and linens; professional service. **Cons:** may be too quiet for partiers; far from town. ⊠ *Carretera Chankanaab, Km 6.5* ☎ *987/872–9500 or 800/327–0200* ⊕ *www.intercontinentalcozumel. com* ⟳ *173 rooms, 47 suites* ⚑ *In-room: Safe, DVD, Wi-Fi. In-hotel: 2 restaurants, room service, bars, tennis courts, pools, gym, spa, beachfront, diving, water sports, children's programs (ages 4–12), laundry service, Wi-Fi, parking (free), some pets allowed, no-smoking rooms* ⊟ *AE, DC, MC, V* �‖ *EP.*

$$ ⛉ **Villablanca Garden Beach Hotel.** The architecture at this hotel is unusual—several low-rise buildings framing generous lawns house the guestrooms, the largest of which have white Moorish facades and archways separating the living and sleeping areas. All rooms have sunken bathtubs; some have terraces or balconies shaded with red awnings. Though the grounds are lovely, some of the facilities are budget-hotel quality; rooms vary, so test the air-conditioning, fan, and hot water before settling in, and ask to see another room if you're not satisfied. The sea is across the street from the rooms, gardens, and pool, and there's a dock for dive boats. Three dive shops and several restaurants are nearby. Guests tend to return annually, often with dive groups. ■ **TIP→The hotel sometimes offers incentives such as complimentary breakfast for booking directly on their Web site. Pros:** lush gardens around pool; good value. **Cons:** spotty hot water and weak water pressure; loud a/c. ⊠ *Carretera Chankanaab, Km 3* ☎ *987/872–0730* ⊕ *www.villablanca.net* ⟳ *25 rooms and suites, 1 penthouse, 3 villas* ⚑ *In-room: Kitchen (some), refrigerator (some). In-hotel: Restaurant, tennis court, pool, bicycles, laundry service, Wi-Fi, parking (free), no-smoking rooms* ⊟ *AE, MC, V* �‖ *EP.*

SAN MIGUEL

$$ ⛉ **Casa Mexicana.** A dramatic staircase leads up to this hotel's windswept lobby, and distinctive rooms are decorated in subtle blues and yellows. Some face the ocean and Avenida Rafael E. Melgar; others overlook unattractive downtown streets behind the hotel or the indoor terrace where breakfast is served. Splurge on a waterfront room if you can, as the balcony is a great place to hang out and enjoy the sea view and malecón scene. Rooms have bathtubs (hard to find downtown) and are immaculate and comfy. The rate includes a full breakfast buffet, and the lobby bar overlooking the street is a great place for sunset drinks. Two sister properties, Hotel Bahía and Suites Colonial, offer less expensive suites with kitchenettes (the Bahía has some ocean views; the

Colonial is near the square). **Pros:** great downtown location near restaurants and shops; friendly staff (especially bartenders); substantial breakfast. **Cons:** no beach; tiny pool; some street noise. ✉ *Av. Rafael E. Melgar Sur 457, between Calles 5 and 7* ☎ *987/872–9090 or 877/228–6747* ⊕ *www.casamexicanacozumel.com* ➹ *90 rooms* ♿ *In-room: Safe, Internet. In-hotel: Bar, gym, pool, Wi-Fi, laundry service, no-smoking rooms* ▭ *AE, D, MC, V* ⦿ *BP.*

WORD OF MOUTH

"Casa Mexicana is a lovely modern hotel across from one of cruise line docks. It was carefully designed and is a charming place to stay in town. The extensive breakfast buffet is included and is in a lovely open garden deck. There is a nice, though small, pool on the first floor that looks out to the sea and ships. It was interesting to watch the thousands of passengers going to and from their ships. We walked around, ate, and shopped. The town wasn't too exciting, and we did not see any more of the island. We understand that it is quite beautiful, and we would like to return at another time."   —justretired

$$ 🏨 **Hacienda San Miguel.** At this small inn, with its two-story buildings set around a lush courtyard, you can have Continental breakfast delivered to your room. The second-floor rooms get far more air and light than those at ground level, which can be humid and musty. All have coffeemakers, purified water, and bathrobes. The town house has a full kitchen and two bedrooms. The plaza is five blocks south, and the closest beach is a 10-minute walk north. Guests get discounts at the affiliated Mr. Sancho's Beach Club. You can use the office phone, but won't be able to hook up your laptop (when the office staff aren't busy, they'll let you check your email on their computer). **Pros:** quiet but central; plenty of great restaurants nearby; courtyard gardens make it feel like a private home. **Cons:** musty smell in some rooms; a/c can be noisy; no pool. ✉ *Calle 10 Norte 500, at Av. 5* ☎ *987/872–1986 or 866/712–6387* ⊕ *www.haciendasanmiguel. com* ➹ *7 studios, 3 suites, 1 town house* ♿ *In-room: Safe, kitchen, no phone* ▭ *MC, V* ⦿ *CP.*

$$ 🏨 **Hotel Flamingo.** You get a lot for your pesos at this budget hotel, which includes a rooftop sundeck with a view of the water. Three blocks from the ferry in the heart of downtown, it isn't close to the good beaches, but guests tend to share rental-car costs and offer each other rides around town. The hotel can arrange treatments with the nearby Spa Aroma day spa. The Aqua Bar has live music on weekends (keep this in mind when choosing your room's location). The rooms vary in size; all have two double beds that can be pushed together to make one huge bed. Some superior (larger upstairs rooms) in front have balconies but can be noisy. Breakfast is included and dive packages are available. **Pros:** close to restaurants and shops; staff and guests share budget travel tips; friendly bartender. **Cons:** street and bar noise; limited street parking. ✉ *Calle 6 Norte 81, near Cozumel Museum* ☎ *987/872–1264 or 800/806–1601* ⊕ *www.hotelflamingo.com* ➹ *16 rooms, 1 penthouse* ♿ *In-room: Safe, kitchen (some). In-hotel: Restaurant, room service, bar, laundry service, Wi-Fi, no-smoking rooms* ▭ *MC, V* ⦿ *BP.*

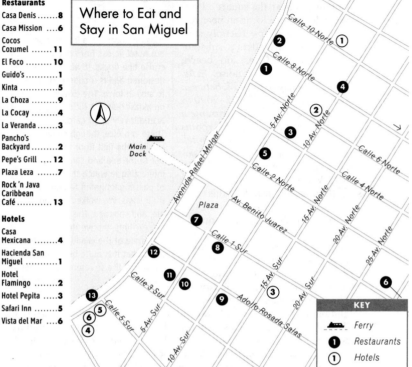

Where to Eat and Stay in San Miguel

¢ **Hotel Pepita.** Despite being more than 50 years old, the Pepita is one of the best budget hotels on the island. The blue-and-white facade is painted frequently, as are the rooms. Wooden shutters cover screened windows that keep out the bugs (who thrive happily among the court-yard's many plants and shrubs). Cable TV, refrigerators, and air-conditioning are surprising pluses given the low room rates. Shelves in the lobby are stacked high with novels in several languages, and German and Dutch are as common as Spanish and English during conversations over free coffee around the long wooden table in the courtyard. There are no kitchen facilities, but plenty of small markets and cafés nearby. **Pros:** untouristy neighborhood; amiable staff. **Cons:** buggy (keep doors closed); no phones in rooms; some staff speak Spanish only. ⊠*Av. 15 Sur 120* ☎*987/872–0098* ⊋*20 rooms* ⌂*In-room: Refrigerator. In-hotel: No-smoking rooms* ⊟*No credit cards* ⓄⅠ*EP.*

¢ **Safari Inn.** Above the Aqua Safari dive shop on the waterfront, this small hotel has comfy beds, powerful hot-water showers, air-conditioning, and the camaraderie of fellow scuba fanatics. The owner also operates Condumel, a small, comfortable condo complex that's perfect for setting up house for one night, a week, or longer. Rates are reasonable and the setting is peaceful, with excellent snorkeling. **Pros:** above an excellent dive shop; immaculately clean; in middle of town action. **Cons:** some street noise; no in-room phones or TV. ⊠*Av. Rafael E.*

Melgar and Calle 5 Sur ☎987/872–0101 ⊕*www.aquasafari.com* ⤙12 *rooms* ♿*In-room: No phone, no TV. In-hotel: Diving, water sports, no-smoking rooms* ▤*MC, V* ⎮○⎮*EP.*

$$ 🖼 **Vista del Mar.** This cozy inn on the downtown waterfront is reasonably priced compared to those right on the beach. The soft beige, brown, and white walls are decorated with shells and beach stones; mosquito nets drape over the beds at night. Room 405 has a spot-on view of the sea. Making your way through the crowds in front of the hotel can be a hassle. On the other hand, it's amusing to watch the sweating shoppers from a deck chair beside the hot tub overlooking a shopping arcade. Metal hurricane shutters on street-facing windows help cut the noise but make rooms dark as night. **Pros:** near restaurants, plaza, and shops; lots of amenities for price. **Cons:** no beach; can be noisy. ⊠*Av. Rafael E. Melgar 45, between Calles 5 and 7* ☎987/872–0545 ⊕*www.hotel vistadelmar.com* ⤙20 *rooms* ♿*In-room: Safe, refrigerator. In-hotel: Pool, laundry service, no-smoking rooms* ▤*MC, V* ⎮○⎮*CP.*

WINDWARD COAST

$$ 🖼 **Ventanas al Mar.** The lights of San Miguel are but a distant glow
★ on the horizon when you look west from the only hotel on the windward coast. Turn east, though, and you can watch shooting stars flash through the nighttime sky over the foaming sea. Escape is complete at this small, eco-friendly inn that runs on solar power; there are no phones, no computer hookups. The rooms are commodious and comfortable, and have kitchenettes with sinks and coffeemakers; mini-refrigerators are available on request. Two-story suites have a bedroom and full bath upstairs and a trundle sleeper sofa and half-bath downstairs. Rates ($164 to $184) are significantly higher but a bargain when shared by four people. A full breakfast is served in the open-air lobby; lunches and early dinners are available at Coconuts, next door. Sea turtles nest on the long beach beside the hotel in summer, and tropical fish and anemones gather by the rocky point in front of the rooms. **Pros:** blissful solitude; long beach great for sunset walks. **Cons:** limited food and drink options; driving at night not advisable as coastal road is not lighted. ⊠*East-coast road north of Coconuts* ☎987/105–2684 ⊕*www.ventanasalmar.com.mx* ⤙16 *rooms* ♿*In-room: No phone, refrigerator (some), no TV. In-hotel: Beachfront, water sports, parking (free), no-smoking rooms* ▤*No credit cards* ⎮○⎮*BP.*

NIGHTLIFE

Discos and trendy clubs are not Cozumel's scene. In fact, some visitors complain that the town seems to shut down completely by midnight. Perhaps it's the emphasis on sun and scuba diving that sends everyone to bed early. (It's hard to be a night owl when your dive boat leaves first thing in the morning.) Cruise-ship passengers mobbing the bars seem to party more than those staying on the island, so the rowdiest action sometimes takes place in the afternoon, when revelers pull out the stops before reboarding. Dance and music clubs come and go; check for new clubs around the pedestrian streets in San Miguel.

BARS

Sports fans come to bet on their favorite teams, watch the games, and catch the ESPN news at **All Sports** (⊠*Av. 5 Norte and Calle 2* ☎*987/869–2246*).

Carlos 'n Charlie's and Señor Frog's (⊠*Av. Rafael E. Melgar at Punta Langosta* ☎*987/872–0191*) are members of the Carlos Anderson chain of rowdy restaurant-bars that attract crowds. The *Animal House* ambience includes loud rock music and a libertine, anything-goes dancing scene that seems to have special allure to the cruising set.

Lively, rowdy **Fat Tuesdays** (⊠*Av. Juárez between Av. Rafael E. Melgar and Calle 3 Sur* ☎*987/872–5130*) draws crowds day and night for frozen daiquiris, ice-cold beers, and blaring rock.

SPRING FESTIVAL

If you're here in April, you can see some traditional dance during the **Fería del Cedral**, a fair held in the settlement of El Cedral around the last weekend in April. The festival begins with a dawn prayer vigil and there are religious ceremonies throughout the week. Other festivities begin in mid-morning and last long into the night. Parking is available in dirt lots, and there are plenty of taxis available. To get here, turn at Km 17.5 off Carretera Sur or Avenida Rafael E. Melgar, then drive 3 km (2 mi) inland to site.

For a more sophisticated scene with mojitos and great cigars, check out **Havana Blue** (⊠*Av. Rafael E. Melgar and Calle 10 Norte, 2nd fl.* ☎*987/869–1687*) in the flashy Forum shopping mall.

Martinis and high-end tequilas are on order at **1.5 Tequila Lounge** (⊠*Av. Rafael Melgar at Calle 11 Sur* ☎*987/872–4421*) on the south end of downtown. The waterfront location and classy lounge ambience set it apart from the rowdier bars, though the scene does get pretty wild here as well.

Viva Mexico (⊠*Av. Rafael E. Melgar* ☎*987/872–0799*) sometimes has a DJ who spins Latin and American dance music into the wee hours. There's also an extensive snack menu. This place is wildly popular anytime of day or night. The best seats are near the second-story railing overlooking the waterfront.

Wet Wendy's Margarita House (⊠ *Av. 5 Norte between Calle 2 and Av. Juárez*) pleases fun-seeking travelers with frosty margaritas and quirky drinks like the frozen Creamsicle (a piña colada mixed with orange soda). Finger food and full meals soak up the alcohol so you can stay for hours.

DANCE CLUBS

Cozumel's oldest disco, **Neptune Dance Club** (⊠*Av. Rafael E. Melgar and Av. 11* ☎*987/872–1537*), underwent a complete makeover in 2008. It now has dance floors and bars on two levels and upgraded sound systems. The music ranges from disco to salsa; Latin-music bands draw crowds of locals.

LIVE MUSIC

Sunday evenings from 8 to 10, locals head for the zócalo to hear maria-
chis and island musicians playing tropical tunes.

The band at the **Hard Rock Cafe** (⊠ *Av. Rafael E. Melgar between Av.
Juárez and Calle 2, 2nd fl.* ☎*987/872–5273*) often rocks until near
dawn. Air-conditioning is a major plus.

MOVIES

Locals say the best place on sweltering afternoons is **Cinepolis** (⊠ *Av.
Rafael E. Melgar ⊹ Behind Chedruai Supermarket* ☎*987/869–0799*).
The modern, multiscreen theater shows current hit films in Spanish and
English and has afternoon matinees and nightly shows.

SHOPPING

Cozumel's main souvenir-shopping area is downtown along Avenida
Rafael E. Melgar and on some side streets around the plaza. There are
also clusters of shops at **Plaza del Sol** (⊠ *East side of main plaza*) and
Vista del Mar (⊠ *Avenida Rafael E. Melgar 45*). Malls at the cruise-ship
piers aim to please passengers seeking jewelry, perfume, sportswear, and
low-end souvenirs at high-end prices.

Most downtown shops accept U.S. dollars; many goods are priced in
dollars. To get better prices, pay with cash or traveler's checks—some
shops tack a hefty surcharge on credit-card purchases. Shops, restaurants, and streets are always crowded between 10 AM and 2 PM, but
get calmer in the evening. Traditionally, stores are open from 9 to 1
(except Sunday) and 5 to 9, but those nearest the pier tend to stay
open all day, particularly during high season. Most shops are closed
Sunday morning.

■TIP➔When you shop in Cozumel, be sure you don't buy anything made
with black coral. Not only is it overpriced, it's also an endangered species, and you may be barred from bringing it to the United States and other
countries.

MARKETS

There's a **crafts market** (⊠ *Calle 1 Sur, behind plaza*) in town that sells a
respectable assortment of Mexican wares. It's the best place to practice
your bartering skills while shopping for blankets, T-shirts, hammocks,
and pottery. For fresh produce, fish, chiles, and a taste of local life, try
the **Mercado Municipal** (⊠ *Calle Adolfo Rosado Salas between Avs. 20
and 25 Sur* ☎*No phone*), open Monday through Saturday 8 to 5.

SHOPPING MALLS

Forum Shops (⊠ *Av. Rafael E. Melgar and Calle 10 Norte* ☎*987/869–
1687*) is a flashy marble-and-glass mall with jewels glistening in glass
cases and an overabundance of eager salesclerks. Diamonds International and Tanzanite International have shops in the Forum and all over

A Ceremonial Dance

Women regally dressed in embroidered, lace-trim dresses and men in their best guayabera shirts carry festooned trays on their heads during the Baile de las Cabezas de Cochino (dance of the pig's head) at the Fería del Cedral, held in El Cedral. The trays are festooned with trailing ribbons, *papeles picados* (paper cutouts), piles of bread, and, in some cases, the head of a barbecued pig.

The pig is a sacrificial offering to God, who supposedly saved the founders of this tiny Cozumel settlement. According to legend, the tradition began during the 19th-century War of the Castes, when Yucatán's Maya rose up against their oppressors. The enslaved Maya killed most of the mestizos in the mainland village of Sabán. Casimiro Cardenas, a wealthy young man, survived while clutching a small wooden cross. He promised he would establish an annual religious festival once he found a new home.

Today the original religious vigils and novenas blend into the more secular fair, which usually runs through the last weekend in April. Festivities include horse races, bullfights, and amusement-park rides, and stands selling hot dogs, corn on the cob, and cold beer. Celebrations peak during the ritualistic dance, which is usually held on the final day.

The music begins with a solemn cadence as families enter the stage, surrounding one member bearing a multitiered tray. The procession proceeds in a solemn circle as the participants proudly display their costumes and offerings. Gradually, the beat quickens and the dancing begins. Grabbing the ends of ribbons trailing from the trays, children, parents, and grandparents twirl in ever-faster circles until the scene becomes a whirling blend of grinning, sweaty faces and bright colors.

Avenida Rafael E. Melgar, as does Roger's Boots, a leather store. There's a Havana Blue bar upstairs, where shoppers select expensive cigars.

Puerto Maya (⊠ *Carretera Sur at southern cruise dock*) is a mall geared to cruise-ship passengers, with branches of many of downtown's most popular shops, restaurants, and bars. It's close to the ships at the end of a huge parking lot.

Punta Langosta (⊠ *Av. Rafael E. Melgar 551, at Calle 7*), a fancy multi-level shopping mall, is across the street from the cruise-ship dock. An enclosed pedestrian walkway leads over the street from the ships to the center, which houses several jewelry and sportswear stores. The center is designed to lure cruise-ship passengers into shopping in air-conditioned comfort and has reduced traffic for local businesses.

SPECIALTY STORES

CLOTHING
Several trendy sportswear stores line Avenida Rafael E. Melgar between Calles 2 and 6. **Exotica** (⊠ *Av. Juárez at plaza* ☎ *987/872–5880*) has high-quality sportswear and shirts with nature-theme designs.

Island Outfitters (⊠ *Av. Rafael E. Melgar, at plaza* ☎*987/872–0132*) has high-quality sportswear, beach towels, and sarongs.

Mr. Buho (⊠ *Av. Rafael E. Melgar between Calles 6 and 8* ☎*987/869–1601*) specializes in white-and-black clothes and has well-made guayabera shirts and cotton dresses.

CRAFTS

The showrooms at **Anji** (⊠ *Av. 5 between Calles Adolfo Rosado Salas and 1 Sur* ☎*987/869–2623*) are filled with imported lamps, carved animals, and clothing from Bali.

At **Balam Mayan Feather** (⊠ *Av. 5 and Calle 2 Norte* ☎*987/869–0548*) artists create intricate paintings on feathers from local birds.

Bugambilias (⊠ *Av. 10 Sur between Calles Adolfo Rosado Salas and 1 Sur* ☎*987/872–6282*) sells handmade Mexican linens.

★ **Los Cinco Soles** (⊠ *Av. Rafael E. Melgar and Calle 8 Norte* ☎*987/872–0132*) is the best one-stop shop for crafts from around Mexico. Several display rooms, covering almost an entire block, are filled with clothing, furnishings, home-decor items, and jewelry.

Latin music CDs and English-language novels are displayed at **Fama** (⊠ *Av. 5 between Calle 2 and plaza* ☎*987/872–2050*), which also has sandals, swimsuits, and souvenirs.

At Cozumel's best art gallery, **Galería Azul** (⊠ *Calle 10 Sur, between Av. Salas and Calle 1* ☎*987/869–0963*), artist Greg Deitrich displays his engraved blown glass along with paintings, jewelry, and other works by local artists.

Indigo (⊠ *Av. Rafael E. Melgar 221* ☎*987/872–1076*) carries a large selection of purses, belts, vests, and shirts from bright blue, purple, and green Guatemalan fabrics. They also have wooden masks.

Librería del Parque (⊠ *Av. 5 at plaza* ☎*987/872–0031*) is Cozumel's best bookstore; it carries the *Miami Herald, USA Today,* and English- and Spanish-language magazines and books, and also sells phone cards.

El Porton (⊠ *Av. 5 Sur and Calle 1 Sur* ☎*987/872–5606*) has a collection of masks and unusual crafts.

Antiques and high-quality silver jewelry are the draws at **Shalom** (⊠ *Av. 10, No. 25* ☎*987/872–3783*).

Viva Mexico (⊠ *Av. Rafael E. Melgar and Calle Adolfo Rosada Salas* ☎*987/872–0791*) sells souvenirs and handicrafts from all over Mexico; it's a great place to find T-shirts, blankets, and trinkets.

GROCERY STORES

The grocery store **Chedraui** (⊠ *Carretera Chankanaab, Km 1.5 and Calle 15 Sur* ☎*987/872–3655*) is open daily 8 AM to 10 PM, and also carries clothing, kitchenware, appliances, and furniture.

JEWELRY

Diamond Creations (⊠ *Av. Rafael E. Melgar Sur 131* ☎*987/872–5330*) lets you custom-design pieces of jewelry from a collection of loose diamonds, emeralds, rubies, sapphires, or tanzanite. The shop and its affiliates, Tanzanite International and Silver International, have multiple

Continued on page 154

COZUMEL DIVING & SNORKELING

First comes the giant step, a leap from a dry boat into the warm Caribbean Sea. Then the slow descent to white sand framed by rippling brain coral and waving purple sea fans. If you lean back, you can look up toward the sea's surface. The water off Cozumel is so clear you can see puffy white clouds in the sky even when you're submerged 20 feet under.

With more than 30 charted reefs whose depths average 50–80 feet and water temperatures around 24°C–27°C (75°F–80°F) during peak diving season (June–August, when hotel rates are coincidentally at their lowest), Cozumel is far and away *the* place to dive in Mexico. More than 60,000 divers come here each year.

Because of the diversity of coral formations and the dramatic underwater peaks and valleys, divers consider Cozumel's Palancar Reef (promoters now call it the Maya Reef) to be one of the top five in the world. Sea turtles headed to the beach to lay their eggs swim beside divers in May and June. Fifteen-pound lobsters wave their antennae from beneath coral ledges; they've been protected in Cozumel's National Marine Park for so long they've lost all fear of humans. Long, green moray eels still appear rather menacing as they bare their fangs at curious onlookers, and snaggle-toothed barracuda look ominous as they swim by. But all in all, diving off Cozumel is relaxing, rewarding, and so addictive you simply can't do it just once.

Hurricane Wilma damaged the reefs somewhat during her 2005 attack and rearranged the underwater landscape. Favorite snorkeling and diving spots close to shore were affected, and the fish may not be as abundant as they were in the past.

SCUBA DIVING

The water is so warm and clear—around 80 degrees with near-100-foot visibility most of the year—that diving feels nearly effortless. There's no way anyone can do all the deep dives, drift dives, shore dives, wall dives, and night dives in one trip, never mind the theme dives focusing on ecology, archaeology, sunken ships, and photography.

Many hotels and dive shops offer introductory classes in a swimming pool. Most include a beach or boat dive. Resort courses cost about $60–$80. Many dive shops also offer full open-water certification classes, which take at least four days of intensive classroom study and pool practice. Basic certification courses cost about $350, while advanced and specialty certification courses cost about $250–$500. You can also do your classroom study at home, then make your training and test dives on Cozumel.

DIVING SAFELY There are more than 100 dive shops in Cozumel, so look for high safety standards and documented credentials. The best places offer small groups and individual attention. Next to your equipment, your dive master is the most important consideration for your adventure. Make sure he or she has PADI or NAUI certification (or FMAS, the Mexican equivalent). Be sure to bring your own certification card; all reputable shops require customers to show them before diving. If you forget, you may be able to call the agency that certified you and have the card number faxed to the shop.

Keep in mind that much of the reef off Cozumel is a protected National Marine Park. Boats aren't allowed to anchor in certain areas, and you shouldn't touch the coral or take any "souvenirs" from the reefs when you dive there. It's best to swim at least three feet above the reef—not just because coral can sting or cut

you, but also because it's easily damaged and grows very slowly; it has taken 2,000 years to reach their present size.

There's a reputable recompression chamber at the **Buceo Médico Mexicano** (✉ Calle 5 Sur 21B ☎ 987/872–1430 24-hr hotline). The **Cozumel Hyperbarics Chamber** (✉ San Miguel Clinic, Calle 6 between Avs. 5 and 10 ☎ 987/872–3070) is also a fully equipped recompression center. These chambers, which aim for a 35-minute response time from reef to chamber, treat decompression sickness, commonly known as "the bends," which occurs when you surface too quickly and nitrogen bubbles form in the bloodstream. Recompression chambers are also used to treat nitrogen narcosis, collapsed lungs, and overexposure to the cold.

You may also want to consider buying dive-accident insurance from the U.S.-based **Divers Alert Network (DAN)** (☎ 800/446–2671, 919/684–9119 ⊕ www. diversalertnetwork.org) before embarking on your dive vacation. DAN insurance covers dive accidents and injuries, and their emergency hotline can help you find the best local doctors, hyperbaric chambers, and medical services. They can also arrange for airlifts.

3

IN FOCUS COZUMEL DIVING & SNORKELING

DIVE SITES

Cozumel's reefs stretch for 32 km (20 mi), beginning at the international pier and continuing to Punta Celarain at the island's southernmost tip. Following is a rundown of Cozumel's main dive destinations.

Chankanaab Reef. This inviting reef lies south of Parque Chankanaab, about 350 yards offshore. Large underground caves are filled with striped grunt, snapper, sergeant majors, and butterfly fish. At 55 feet, there's another large coral formation that's often filled with crabs, lobster, barrel sponges, and angelfish. If you drift a bit farther south, you can see the Balones de Chankanaab, balloon-shaped coral heads at 70 feet. This is an excellent dive site for beginners.

Colombia Reef. Several miles off Palancar, the reef reaches 82–98 feet and is best suited for experienced divers. Its underwater structures are as varied as those of Palancar Reef, with large canyons and ravines to explore. Clustered near the overhangs are large groupers, jacks, rays, and an occasional sea turtle.

Felipe Xicotencatl (C-53 Wreck). Sunk in 2000 specifically for scuba divers, this 154-foot-long minesweeper is located on a sandy bottom about 80 feet deep near Tormentos and Chankanaab. Created as an artificial reef to decrease some of the traffic on the natural reefs, the ship is open so divers can explore the interior and is gradually attracting schools of fish.

Maracaibo Reef. Considered one of the most difficult reefs, Maracaibo is a thrilling dive with strong currents and intriguing old coral formations. Although there are shallow areas, only advanced divers who can cope with the current should attempt Maracaibo.

Palancar Reef. About 2 km (1 mi) offshore, Palancar is actually a series of varying coral formations with about 40 dive locations. It's filled with winding canyons, deep ravines, narrow crevices, archways, tunnels, and caves. Black and red coral and huge elephant-ear, and barrel sponges are among the attractions. At the section called Horseshoe, a series of coral heads form a natural horseshoe shape. This is one of the most popular sites for dive boats and can become crowded.

Paraíso Reef. About 330 feet offshore, running parallel to the international cruise-ship pier, this reef averages 30–50 feet. It's a perfect spot to dive before you head for deeper drop-offs such as La Ceiba and Villa Blanca. There are impressive formations of star and brain coral as well as sea fans, sponges, sea eels, and yellow rays. It's wonderful for night diving.

Paseo El Cedral. Running parallel to Santa Rosa reef, this flat reef has gardenlike valleys full of fish, including angelfish, grunt, and snapper. At depths of 35–55 feet, you can also spot rays.

San Francisco Reef. Considered Cozumel's shallowest wall dive (35–50 feet), this 1-km (½-mi) reef runs parallel to Playa San Francisco and has many varieties of reef fish. You'll need to take a dive boat to get here.

Santa Rosa Wall. North of Palancar, Santa Rosa is renowned among experienced divers for deep dives and drift dives; at 50 feet there's an abrupt yet sensational drop-off to enormous coral overhangs. The strong current drags you along the tunnels and caves, where there are huge sponges, angelfish, groupers, and rays—and sometime even a shark or two.

Tormentos Reef. The abundance of sea fans, sponges, sea cucumbers, arrow crabs, green eels, groupers, and other marine life—against a terrifically colorful backdrop—makes this a perfect spot for underwater photography. This variegated reef has a maximum depth of around 70 feet.

Yucab Reef. South of Tormentos Reef, this relatively shallow reef is close to shore, making it an ideal spot for beginners. About 400 feet long and 55 feet deep, it's teeming with queen angelfish and sea whip swimming around the large coral heads. The one drawback is the strong current, which can reach two or three knots.

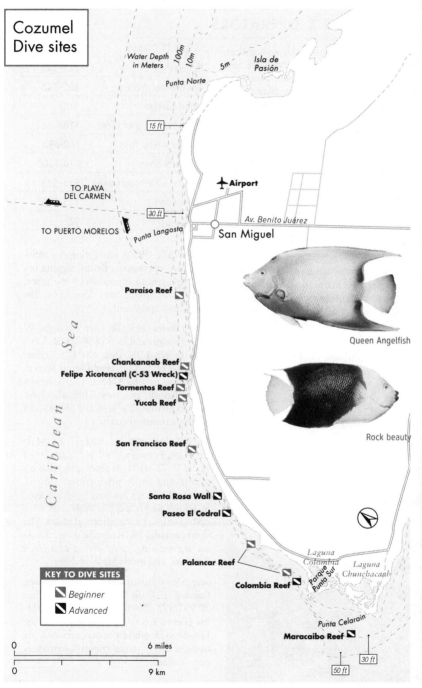

Cozumel Dive sites

Water Depth in Meters

100m 10m 5m

Isla de Pasión

Punta Norte

15 ft

3

IN FOCUS COZUMEL DIVING & SNORKELING

✈ **Airport**

TO PLAYA DEL CARMEN

TO PUERTO MORELOS

30 ft

Punta Langosta

Av. Benito Juárez

San Miguel

Paraíso Reef

Sea

Queen Angelfish

Chankanaab Reef
Felipe Xicotencatl (C-53 Wreck)
Tormentos Reef
Yucab Reef

Caribbean

San Francisco Reef

Rock beauty

Santa Rosa Wall
Paseo El Cedral

Palancar Reef

Laguna Colombia

Laguna Chunchacaab

Colombia Reef

Parque Punta Sur

KEY TO DIVE SITES

◣ *Beginner*
◣ *Advanced*

Punta Celarain

Maracaibo Reef

30 ft

0 —————————— 6 miles
0 —————————— 9 km

50 ft

DIVE SHOPS & OPERATORS

It's important to choose a dive shop that suits your expectations. Beginners are best off with the more established, conservative shops that limit the depth and time you spend underwater. Experienced divers may be impatient with this approach, and are better suited to shops that offer smaller group dives and more challenging dive sites. More and more shops are merging these days, so don't be surprised if the outfit you dive with one year has been absorbed by another the following year. Recommending a shop is dicey. The ones listed below are well-established and are recommended by experienced Cozumel divers.

■ TIP→Dive shops handle more than 1,000 divers per day; many run "cattle boats" packed with lots of divers and gear. It's worth the extra money to go out with a smaller group on a fast boat, especially if you're experienced.

Because dive shops tend to be competitive, it's well worth your while to shop around. Many hotels have their own on-site operations, and there are dozens of dive shops in town. **ANOAAT** (Aquatic Sports Operators Association;

WHAT IT COSTS	
Regulator & BC	$15–$25
Underwater camera	$35–$45
Video camera	$75
Pro videos of your dive	$160
Two-tank boat trips	$60-$90
Specialty dives	$70-$100
One-tank afternoon dives	$35–$45
Night dives	$35–$45
Marine park fee	$2

☎ 987/872–5955) has listings of affiliated dive operations. Before signing on, ask experienced divers about the place, check credentials, and look over the boats and equipment.

Aldora Divers (✉ Calle 5 Sur between Av. Rafael Melgar and Av. 5 ☎ 987/872–3397, or 210/569–1203 from the U.S.) offers reef dives on fast boats and offers accommodations in Villa Aldora, a 12-bedroom inn just north of town. They also have trips to pristine dive sites and shipwrecks off the windward coast.

Aqua Safari (✉ Av. Rafael E. Melgar 429, between Calles 5 and 7 Sur ☎ 987/872–0101) is among the island's oldest and most professional shops. Owner Bill Horn has long been involved in efforts to protect the reefs and stays on top of local environmental issues. The shop provides PADI certification, classes on night diving, deep diving and other interests, and individualized dives.

Sergio Sandoval of **Aquatic Sports and Scuba Cozumel** (✉ Calle 21 Sur and Av. 20 Sur ☎ 987/872–0640) gets rave reviews from his clients, many of them guests at the Flamingo Hotel. His boats carry only six to eight divers so the trips are extremely personalized.

Blue Angel (✉ Carretera Sur Km. 2.3 ☎ 987/872–1631 or 866/779–9986) offers combo dive and snorkel trips so families who don't all scuba can still stick together. Along with dive trips to local reefs, they offer PADI courses.

Del Mar Aquatics (✉ Casa Del Mar Hotel Carretera Sur, Km 4 ☎ 987/872–5949) has been in operation since 1987 and offers dive trips, certification, and fishing trips.

Dive Cozumel-Yellow Rose (✉ Calle Adolfo Rosado Salas 85, between Avs. Rafael E. Melgar and 5 Sur ☎ 987/872–4567, or 866/319–2649) specializes in cave diving for highly experienced divers, along with regular open-water dives. Classes in cavern and other technical diving specialties are also available. Tours are made on a customized 48-foot boat, for a maximum of 12 people.

Eagle Ray Divers (✉ La Caleta Marina, near the Presidente InterContinental hotel ☎ 987/872–5735 or 866/465–1616) offers snorkeling trips (the three-reef trip lets nondivers explore beyond the shore) and dive instruction. As befits their name, the company keeps track of the eagle rays that appear off Cozumel from December to February and

Grouper

runs trips for advanced divers to walls where the rays congregate. Beginners can also see rays around some of the reefs.

Pepe Scuba (✉ Carretera Costera Norte, Km 2.5 ☎ 987/872–6740) operates out of the Coral Princess Hotel and offers boat dives and several options for resort divers. They also have dive packages available for people staying at the hotel.

Dive magazines regularly rate **Scuba Du** (✉ at the Presidente InterContinental hotel ☎ 987/872–9505, or 310/684–5556 from the U.S.) among the best dive shops in the Caribbean. Along with the requisite Cozumel dives, the company offers an advanced divers trip to walls off Punta Sur.

SNORKELING

Snorkeling equipment is available at nearly all hotels and beach clubs as well as at Parque Chankanaab, Playa San Francisco, and Parque Punta Sur. Gear rents for less than $10 a day. Snorkeling tours run about $60 and take in the shallow reefs off Palancar, Chankanaab, Colombia, and Yucab.

☾ Cozumel Sailing (✉ Carretera Norte at Puerto Abrigo ☎ 987/869–2312, or 866/694–4194) offers sailing tours with open bar, lunch, snorkeling, and beach time for $80. Sunset cruises aboard the

trimaran *El Tucan* are also available; they include unlimited drinks and live entertainment and cost about $30 or $20 for non-drinkers. They also offer boat rentals.

Fury Catamarans (✉ Carretera Sur beside Casa del Mar hotel ☎ 987/872–5145) runs snorkeling tours from its 45-foot catamarans. Rates begin at about $55 per day and include equipment, a guide, soft drinks, beer, and margaritas and a beach party with lunch.

locations along the waterfront and in the shopping malls—in fact, you can't avoid them.

Look for silver, gold, and coral jewelry—especially bracelets and earrings—at **Joyería Palancar** (⊠*Av. Rafael E. Melgar Norte 15* ☎*987/872–1468*).

Luxury Avenue (Ultrafemme) (⊠*Av. Rafael E. Melgar 341* ☎*987/872–1217*) sells high-end goods including watches and perfume.

Pama (⊠*Av. Rafael E. Melgar Sur 9* ☎*987/872–0090*), near the pier, carries imported jewelry, perfumes, and glassware.

Innovative designs and top-quality stones are available at **Van Cleef and Arpels** (⊠*Av. Rafael E. Melgar Norte across from ferry* ☎*987/ 872–6540*).

SPORTS AND THE OUTDOORS

Most people come to Cozumel for the water sports—especially scuba diving, snorkeling, and fishing. Services and equipment rentals are available throughout the island, especially through major hotels and watersports centers at the beach clubs.

If you're curious about what's underneath Cozumel's waters but don't like getting wet, **Atlantis Submarine** (⊠*Carretera Sur, Km 4, across from Hotel Casa del Mar* ☎*987/872–5671*) runs 1½-hour submarine rides that explore the Chankanaab Reef and surrounding area; tickets for the tours are $79 for adults and $45 for children. Even divers enjoy going down 100 feet below sea level. Claustrophobes may not be able to handle the sardine-can conditions.

FISHING

The waters off Cozumel swarm with more than 230 species of fish, making this one of the world's best deep-sea fishing destinations. During billfish migration season, from late April through June, blue marlin, white marlin, and sailfish are plentiful, and world-record catches aren't uncommon.

Deep-sea fishing for tuna, barracuda, wahoo, and dorado is good year-round. You can go bottom-fishing for grouper, yellowtail, and snapper on the shallow sand flats at the island's north end and fly-fish for bonefish, tarpon, snook, grouper, and small sharks in the same area. Regulations forbid commercial fishing, sportfishing, spear fishing, and collecting marine life in certain areas around Cozumel. It's illegal to kill certain species within marine reserves, including billfish, so be prepared to return some prize catches to the sea. Most sport fishing boats are located in the Puerto Abrigo marina just north of San Miguel. A new marina is under construction on the south side, beside the Presidente Intercontinental resort.

CHARTERS

You can charter high-speed fishing boats for about $420 per half-day or $600 per day (with a maximum of six people). Your hotel can help arrange daily charters—some offer special deals, with boats leaving from their own docks.

Albatros Deep Sea Fishing (☎987/872–7904 or 888/333–4643) offers full-day trips that include boat and crew, tackle and bait, and lunch with beer and soda starting at $575 for up to 6 persons.

All equipment and tackle, lunch with beer, and the boat and crew are also included in **Ocean Tours'** (☎987/872–9530 Ext. 8) full-day rates, which start at $550.

3 Hermanos (☎987/872–6417 or 987/876–8931) specializes in deep-sea and fly-fishing trips. Their rates for a half-day deep-sea fishing trip start at $350; a full day is $450. They also offer scuba-diving trips, and their boats are available for group charters (a great way to snorkel and cruise around at your own pace) for $400 for up to 6 passengers.

GOLF

The **Cozumel Country Club** (⊠Carretera Costera Norte, Km 5.8 ☎987/872–9570 ⊕www.cozumelcountryclub.com.mx) has an 18-hole championship golf course. The gorgeous fairways amid mangroves and a lagoon are the work of the Nicklaus Design Group and have been declared an Audubon nature reserve. The green fee is $149 and includes a shared golf cart. The full package with rental clubs and balls is $169. Many hotels offer golf packages here.

☾ If you're not a fan of miniature golf, the challenging **Cozumel Mini-Golf** (⊠Calle 1, Sur 20 ☎987/872–6570) might turn you into one. The jungle-theme course has banana trees, birds, two fountains, and a waterfall. You can choose your music from a selection of more than 800 CDs and order your drinks via walkie-talkie; they'll be delivered as you try for that hole in one. Admission is $7 for adults, $5 for kids; it's open Monday through Saturday 10 AM to 11 PM and Sunday 5 PM to 11 PM.

HORSEBACK RIDING

Aventuras Naturales (⊠Av. 35, No. 1081 ☎987/872–1628 or 858/366–4632 ⊕www.aventurasnaturalascozumel.com) runs a two-hour guided horseback tour through the jungle to El Cedral. Prices start at $35. Groups are small and the guides fun and informative. The company also has hiking tours and a full-day action tour combining biking, horseback riding, and snorkeling for $65 per person.

Rancho Buenavista (⊠Carretera Perimetral, Km 32.5 ☎987/872–1537) provides four-hour rides through the jungle starting at $65 per person.

KAYAKING

Located at Uvas beach club, **Clear Kayak** (✉ *Carretera Sur, Km 8.5* ☎ *987/872–3539*) runs what are called "dry-snorkeling" tours in see-through kayaks (imagine what the fish must be thinking). Paddling around with water seeming to flow past your toes is great fun, and there's time for real snorkeling as well. Tours, which cost $45 for adults and $33 for children, include entrance fee, two domestic drinks, and a 45-minute kayak trip; a more-expensive tour includes lunch.

The Caribbean Coast

Xcaret

WORD OF MOUTH

"Tulum is wonderful. The ruins can be done easily in an hour or two max. It's best to do that early anyway and [have] a leisurely afternoon [at the beaches] south of Tulum—it will give you a whole new appreciation for how beautiful that area is. Renting a car for one day gives you the most options."

—jette

WELCOME TO THE CARIBBEAN COAST

TOP REASONS TO GO

★ Visiting the only Mayan site that overlooks the Caribbean: The ruins at Tulum, only an hour south of Playa del Carmen, are a dramatic remnant of a sophisticated pre-Columbian people.

★ Casting for bonefish: These elusive shallows-dwellers, off the Chinchorro Reef near the Reserva de la Biosfera Sian Ka'an, can match wits with even the most seasoned fly-fisher.

★ Indulging in a decadent massage or body treatment: The Riviera Maya is flush with luxurious spa resorts that will make you ooh and aah.

★ Diving or snorkeling with parrot fish and spotted eagle rays: The Puerto Morelos Maritime National Park, a marine preserve, is just off the Yucatán's east coast, so you get that classic Caribbean aquamarine water with a bevy of sea creatures.

★ Exploring the inland jungle: South of Rio Bec, the forests grow thick, and you might glimpse howler monkeys, coatimundi, and Yucatán parrots.

1 **The Riviera Maya.** The coastal communities along the Caribbean vary widely: some are sleepy fishing villages, others are filled with glitzy resorts, and one—Tulum—is an ancient Mayan port city. The pyramids at Cobá are surrounded by jungle, where birds and monkeys call overhead. The beaches along this stretch are stunning, and are heralded by scuba divers, snorkelers, anglers, bird-watchers, and beachcombers.

2 **Reserva de la Biosfera Sian Ka'an.** The 1.6 million acres of this reserve—now more than 20 years old—protects thousands of wildlife species. Its mass is split between the Riviera Maya and the Costa Maya and encompasses *cenotes* (sinkholes), coastal mangrove forests, and dense inland vegetation, resplendent with monkeys, coatimundis, and jaguars.

3 **The Costa Maya.** Once a no-man's-land stretching south of Felipe Carrillo Puerto to Chetumal, the Costa Maya is now being eyed by developers. Although the newly built port of Puerto Costa Maya attracts droves of cruise-ship passengers, it is still possible to enjoy a sleepy, sun-baked, and inexpensive Mexican vacation here.

184

Caobas

Rio Bec

Kohunlich

CAMPECHE

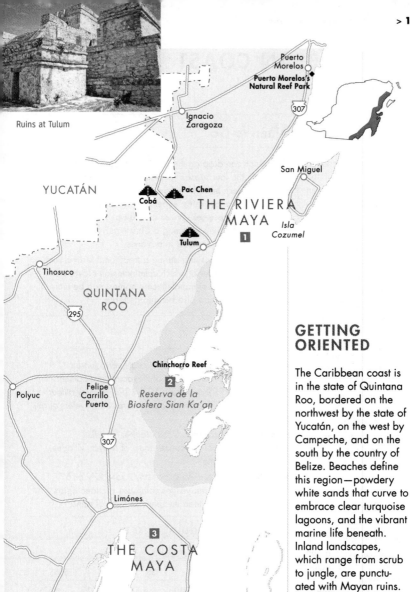

Ruins at Tulum

Puerto
Morelos

**Puerto Morelos's
Natural Reef Park**

307

Ignacio
Zaragoza

San Miguel

YUCATÁN

Pac Chen

Cobá

**THE RIVIERA
MAYA**

*Isla
Cozumel*

Tulum

1

4

Tihosuco

**QUINTANA
ROO**

295

Chinchorro Reef

2

*Reserva de la
Biosfera Sian Ka'an*

Polyuc

Felipe
Carrillo
Puerto

307

Limónes

3

**THE COSTA
MAYA**

Ucum

Chetumal

186

*Mexico
Belize*

*Golfo de
Honduras*

GETTING ORIENTED

The Caribbean coast is in the state of Quintana Roo, bordered on the northwest by the state of Yucatán, on the west by Campeche, and on the south by the country of Belize. Beaches define this region—powdery white sands that curve to embrace clear turquoise lagoons, and the vibrant marine life beneath. Inland landscapes, which range from scrub to jungle, are punctuated with Mayan ruins.

THE CARIBBEAN COAST PLANNER

A Sample Itinerary

Five days will give you enough time to explore many of the best parts of the Caribbean Coast. If you use Playa del Carmen as a base, you can try the following itinerary:

Start with a daylong visit to the Xcaret eco-park. Spend the morning of Day 2 at the gorgeous cliff-side ruins of Tulum; in the afternoon, cool off at Xel-Há or at one of the numerous cenotes along Carretera 307. On Day 3, explore the beaches at Paamul and Xpu-há and continue on to Akumal and Yalkú. Spend Day 4 at the Mayan village of Pac Chen in the morning and, after lunch, head for the ruins at Cobá. On Day 5, take a tour of the Reserva de la Biosfera Sian Ka'an.

Need More Information?

For additional information on attractions, lodging, dining, and services in the Caribbean Coast, check out ⊕ *www.locogringo. com*, ⊕ *www.yucatantoday. com*, ⊕ *www.sac-be.com*, and ⊕ *www.playamayanews.com*.

When to Go

Hotel rates can drop on the Caribbean Coast by as much as 50% in the low season (September to approximately mid-December). In high season, however, it's virtually impossible to find low rates, especially in Playa del Carmen. During Christmas week, prices can rise as much as $100 a night—so if you're planning a Christmas vacation, you'd do well to book six months in advance.

Keep in mind that visiting during a traditional festival such as the Day of the Dead (which culminates on November 2 after three nights of candlelit ceremonies) can be more expensive—but it can also be unforgettable.

Tour Options

Alltournative (⊠ *Carrertera Chetumal-Puerto Juárez Km 287, Lote 13 Sur, in front of Playacar development* ☎ *984/803–9999 and 800/507–1092* ⊕ *www.alltour native.com*) offers eco-friendly adventures for travelers of all ages and fitness levels.

Hilario Hiller (⊠ *La Jolla, Casa Nai Na, 3rd fl.* ☎ *984/875–9066*) customizes tours of Mayan villages, ruins, and the jungle.

Maya Sites Travel Services (☎ *505/255–2279 or 877/ 620–8715* ⊕ *www.mayasites.com*) uses archaeologists and other experts to lead inexpensive tours of ruins.

Dining and Lodging Prices

WHAT IT COSTS IN DOLLARS

	¢	$	$$	$$$	$$$$
Restaurants	under $5	$5–$10	$10–$15	$15–$25	over $25
Hotels	under $50	$50–$75	$75–$150	$150–$250	over $250

Restaurant prices are per person, for a main course at dinner, excluding tax and tip. Hotel prices are for a standard double room in high season.

Updated by
Marlise Kast

Mexico's stretch of Caribbean coastline is divided into two major areas. The stretch from Punta Tanchacté to Punta Allen—called the Riviera Maya—has the most sites and accommodations, and includes some of the Yucatán's most beautiful ruins. The more southern stretch, from Punta Allen to Chetumal, has been dubbed the Costa Maya.

This is where civilization thins out and you can find the most alluring landscapes, including the pristine jungle wilderness of the Reserva de la Biosfera Sian Ka'an. The Río Bec Route starts west of Chetumal and continues into Campeche.

ABOUT THE RESTAURANTS

Restaurants here vary from quirky beachside affairs with outdoor tables and *palapas* (thatch roofs) to more elaborate and sophisticated establishments. Dress is casual at most places, so leave your tie and jacket at home. Smaller cafés and fish eateries may not accept credit cards or traveler's checks, especially in remote beach villages. Bigger establishments and those in hotels normally accept plastic. Unlike restaurants in Playa del Carmen, those in Puerto Morelos do not factor *propinas* (tips) into the bill. Depending on the service, a 10% to 15% gratuity is usually standard. It's best to order fresh local fish—grouper, dorado, red snapper, and sea bass—rather than shellfish like shrimp, lobster, and oysters, since the latter are often flown in frozen from the Gulf.

ABOUT THE HOTELS

Many resorts are in remote areas; if you haven't rented a car and want to visit local sights or restaurants, you may find yourself at the mercy of the hotel shuttle service (if there is one) or waiting for long stretches of time for the bus or spending large sums on taxis. Smaller hotels and inns are often family-run; a stay in one of them will give you the chance to mix with the locals.

THE RIVIERA MAYA

It takes patience to discover the treasures along this part of the coast. Beaches and towns aren't easily visible from the main highway—the road from Cancún to Tulum is 1 to 2 km (½ to 1 mi) from the coast. Thus there's little to see but dense vegetation, lots of billboards, many roadside markets, and signs marking entrances to various hotels and attractions.

Still, the treasures—which include spectacular white-sand beaches and some of the peninsula's most beautiful Mayan ruins—are here, and they haven't been lost on resort developers. In fact, the Riviera Maya, which stretches from Punta Tanchacté in the north down to Punta Allen in the south, currently has about 23,512 hotel rooms. This frenzy of building has affected many beachside Mayan communities, which have had to relocate to the inland jungle. The residents of these settlements, who

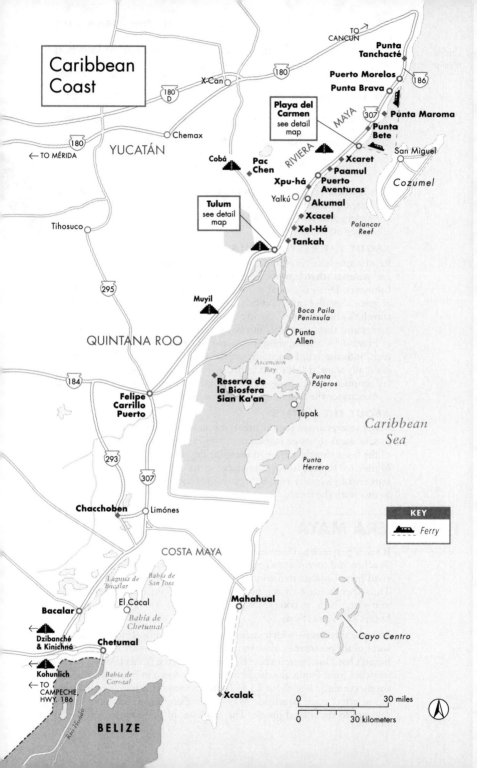

mainly work in the hotels, have managed to keep Yucatecan traditions—including food, music, and holiday celebrations—alive in the area. Wildlife has also been affected by the development of coastal resorts. Thanks to the federal government's foresight, however, 1.6 million acres of coastline and jungle have been set aside for protection as the *Reserva de la Biosfera Sian Ka'an*. Whatever may happen elsewhere along the coast, this preserve is a haven for the wildlife and the travelers who seek the Yucatán of old.

PLAYA DEL CARMEN

68 km (42 mi) south of Cancún.

Once upon a time, Playa del Carmen was a fishing village with a ravishing deserted beach. The villagers fished and raised coconut palms, and the only foreigners who ventured here were those catching ferries to Cozumel. These days, the beach is far from deserted, although it is still delightful, with alabaster-white sand and turquoise-blue waters. In fact, Playa has become one of Latin America's fastest-growing communities, with a population of more than 135,000 and a pace almost as hectic as that of Cancún. Hotels, restaurants, and shops multiply here faster than you can say "Kukulcán." Some are branches of Cancún eateries whose owners have taken up permanent residence in Playa, while others are owned by American and European expats who came here years ago. It makes for a varied, international community.

La Quinta Avenida is considered the town's main thoroughfare. Running parallel to the beach, Fifth Avenue is a colorfully tiled pedestrian walkway full of street performers. Ducking into the little shops or people-watching from a corner café is virtually mandatory. Avenida Juárez, running perpendicular to the beach, is the main commercial strip. Many travelers stop here to stock up on supplies—its banks, grocery stores, and gas stations are the last ones until Tulum.

The ferry pier, where the hourly boats arrive from and depart for Cozumel, is a busy part of town. The streets leading from the dock have shops, restaurants, cafés, a hotel, and food stands. If you take a stroll north along Playa Mamitas, you'll find the serious sun worshippers.

GETTING HERE AND AROUND

Almost everyone who arrives in this region by air flies into Cancún's *Aeropuerto Internacional.* Buses traveling south from Cancún stop at Playa del Carmen's bus terminal at Avenida 20 and Calle 12. Buses headed to Cancún from Playa del Carmen use the main bus terminal at Avenida Juárez and Avenida 5. ADO runs express, first-class, and second-class buses to major destinations. You can hire taxis in Cancún to go as far as Playa del Carmen, but the price is steep—about $55 for the one-hour drive. Shared vans from Cancún airport generally cost $80 for a six-person van, or $120 for a 10-person van; if you're traveling with a group or even find some other Playa-bound travelers at the airport, a van can be a good way to go.

ESSENTIALS

Bus Contacts ADO (☏ *983/832–5110* ⊕ *www.ado.com.mx*).

Currency Exchange Banamex (⊠*Av. Juárez between Avs. 20 and 25* ☎*984/ 873-0825* ⊠*Av. 10 at 12* ☎*984/873-2947*). **Bancomer** (⊠*Av. Juárez between Calles 25 and 30* ☎*984/873-0356*).

Internet Cyberia Internet Café (⊠*Calle 4 and Av. 15*). **El Point** (⊠*Av. 5 between 24 and 26 Norte* ☎*984/803-3412* ⊠*Av. 10 between 12 and 15* ☎*984/803-0897* ⊠*Av 10 between 2 and 4 Norte* ☎*984/803-1268*). **24 Com Center** (⊠*Av. 24, between Calle 1 and Calle 8* ☎*984/803-5778*).

Mail and Shipping Correos (⊠*Av. Juárez, next to police station* ☎*983/873-0300*).

Medical Assistance Centro de Salud (⊠*Av. Juárez and Av. 15* ☎*984/873-1230 Ext. 147*).

Visitor and Tour Info Playa del Carmen tourist information booth (⊠*Av. Juárez by police station, between Calles 15 and 20* ☎*984/873-2804 in Playa del Carmen, 888/955-7155 in U.S., 604/990-6506 in Canada*). **Tierra Maya Tours** (⊠*Av. 5 and Calle 6* ☎*984/873-1385*).

EXPLORING

The **Tres Ríos Eco Park** (⊠*Carretera Cancún–Tulum, Km 54* ☎*998/850– 4849* 🎟*$18* ☉*Daily 9–5*), located 11 km (7 mi) north of Playa, is a great place to get a sense of this region's ecology and natural wonders. Three rivers converge in the expansive 800-acre property (a lush rarity in the dry Yucatán landscape), and you can explore them by kayaking, canoeing, or snorkeling. You can also take horseback rides along the beach or bike along jungle paths. Keep an eye out for birds and animals. If you're lucky, you might spot a white-fronted parrot, or even a coati. Day Passes can be purchased at the main entrance or at Hacienda Tres Rios Resort, located near the park gate.

The excellent 32-acre **Xaman Ha Aviary** (⊠*Paseo Xaman-Ha, Mza 13-A Lote 1, Playacar* ☎*984/873–0330*), in the middle of the Playacar development, is home to more than 30 species of native birds. It's open daily 9 to 5, and admission is $20.

WHERE TO EAT

$$–$$$ ✕**Alux Restaurant & Lounge.** Although this restaurant is 15 to 20 min-
ECLECTIC   utes from downtown, its location in an underground cavern makes it extremely popular. A candlelit rock stairway leads to a setting that's part Carlsbad Caverns, part *The Flintstones*. Some of the "cavernous" rooms are for lounging, some for drinking, some for eating, some for dancing. Creative lighting casts the stalactites and stalagmites in pale shades of violet, blue, and pink. Although the food seems mediocre compared to the atmosphere, you shouldn't miss this one-of-a-kind place. ⊠*Av. Juárez, Colonial Ejidal* ☎*984/803–2936* ▭*MC, V* ☉*No lunch*.

$$ ✕**Babe's Noodles & Bar.** Photos and paintings of old Hollywood pinup
ECLECTIC   models decorate the walls and are even laminated onto the bar of this
★   Swedish-owned Asian restaurant, known for its fresh and interesting fare. Everything is cooked to order—no prefab dishes here. Try the spring rolls with peanut sauce, or the sesame noodles, made with chicken or pork, veggies, lime, green curry, and ginger. In the Buddha Garden you can sip a mojito or sit at the bar and watch the crowds on nearby

5th Avenue. The lemonade, blended with ice and mint, is incredibly refreshing. If the place is crowded, head to their second location on Avenida 5 between calles 28 and 30. ⊠ *Calle 10 between Avs. 5 and 10* ☎ *984/120–2592* ⊠ *Av. 5 between Calles 28 and 30* ☎ *984/803–0056* ⊟ *No credit cards.*

$$–$$$ ✕ **Blue Lobster.** You can choose your dinner live from a tank here, and if it's
SEAFOOD grilled, you pay by the weight—a small lobster costs $20, while a monster will set you back $100. At night, the candlelit dining room draws a good crowd. People come not only for the lobster but also for the ceviche, mussels, and jumbo shrimp. Ask for a table on the terrace overlooking the street. ⊠ *Calle 12 and Av. 5* ☎ *984/873–1360* ⊟ *AE, MC, V.*

¢ ✕ **Café Sasta.** This sweet little café serves fantastic coffee drinks (cap-
CAFÉ puccino, espresso, mocha blends), teas, bagel sandwiches, and baked goods. The flan is sinfully delicious and the staff is very pleasant. ⊠ *Av. 5 between Calles 8 and 10* ☎ *No phone* ⊟ *No credit cards.*

$ ✕ **Casa Tucan.** The refined Italian, Swiss, and Greek dishes at this side-
VEGETARIAN walk restaurant are top-notch. Everything on the menu is fresh; even the herbs are homegrown. The spanakopita and lasagna are especially good. There's additional seating on the rooftop terrace. ⊠ *Calle 4 between Avs. 10 and 15* ☎ *984/873–0283* ⊟ *MC, V.*

$–$$ ✕ **CH Super Carnes.** Follow your nose to this grill house, where locals
STEAK gather for some of the best-tasting steak in town. Far from romantic, the open-air restaurant is filled with the sounds of mariachi music blaring from the radio; bright piñatas and a mounted bull's head hang above the plastic tables and chairs. The main draws are the huge cuts of beef, pork, and chicken served with baskets of corn tortillas, baked potatoes, and ripe avocados. Be sure to try their refreshing *horchata* (a beverage made with rice and cinnamon). The restaurant is also a butcher shop and many of Playa's restaurants buy their meat here. ⊠ *Calle 1 between Avs. 20 and 25* ☎ *984/130–6053 or 984/803–4727* ⊟ *No credit cards.*

$$$$ ✕ **Di Vino.** Centrally located in the heart of 5th Avenue, this Italian res-
MEDITERRANEAN taurant serves food inspired by the regional cuisines of Naples, Rome, Milan, and Venice. A *gelato* trolley lends an authentic taste, as do the rough brick walls, wooden floors, square umbrellas, and chalkboard inscribed with the daily specials. All breads and pastas, which include spinach ravioli and zucchini *tagliolini* (long, thin noodles), are made from scratch. The fresh crab is delicious, as is the grilled sea bass served with strawberry and balsamic vinaigrette. The desserts here are said to be the best in Playa: chocolate mousse, stuffed crepes, and three types of biscotti. Large groups can reserve the Imperial Table for 18; the street-level patio is the best place to sit if you want to people-watch. There's a buffet breakfast from 7 to 11 daily, and the bar is open until 2 AM. ⊠ *Av. 5 and Calle 12, Playa del Carmen* ☎ *984/803–1270* ⊟ *AE, MC, V.*

$$$$ ✕ **Glass Bar.** Located just off La Quinta Avenida, this authentic Italian
ITALIAN restaurant focuses less on the wine *glass* than on what it holds. A grid-
Fodor's Choice shaped wine wall cradles over 350 Italian reds—no surprise, as this is
★ one of Mexico's leading importers of vino. The decor is a mix of modern and classic, with high-backed leather chairs, steel ceiling fans, and dark wood furnishings, all imported from Naples. Street-level seating is

covered with two enormous umbrellas so you can dine outdoors even during rainy season. Everything from grilled lamb and roasted duck to homemade pasta and fresh fish is on the menu. One standout appetizer is a plate with three types of carpaccio (tuna, beef, and octopus), flavorfully bathed in cold-pressed olive oil from Italy's Garda region. If you aren't sure what to order, just ask owner Nicola Iorio, who has a talent for determining what you'll most enjoy. ⊠ *Calle 10 between Avs. 1 and 5* ☎ *984/803–1676* ⊟ *AE, MC, V.*

¢–$ ✕ **Hot.** This café is a great place to get an early start before a full day of
CAFÉ sightseeing, shopping, or even sunbathing. It opens at 7 AM and whips up great egg dishes (the chili-and-cheese omelet is particularly good), baked goods, and hot coffee. Everything, including delicious bagels and bread, is made on the premises. Salads and sandwiches are available at lunch. ⊠ *Calle 14 Norte, between Avs. 5 and 10* ☎ *984/116–3020* ⊟ *No credit cards.*

¢–$ ✕ **Java Joe's.** This is one of Playa's favorite coffee spots, where you
CAFÉ can buy your joe by the cup or by the kilo. You can also indulge in Joe's "hangover special"—an English muffin, Canadian bacon, and a fried egg—if you've had a Playa kind of night. There are also 16 types of bagels to choose from, along with other baked goodies and pastries. ⊠ *Calle 10 between Avs. 5 and 10* ☎ *984/876–2694* ⊟ *No credit cards.*

$$$ ✕ **John Gray's Place.** After the success of his restaurant in nearby Puerto
ECLECTIC Morelos, chef John Gray opened this small place in the heart of Playa
Fodor's Choice del Carmen. Stop in for a drink at the well-stocked downstairs bar or
★ head upstairs, past the glass-encased wine wall, to enjoy some of the finest dining in the city. Start your meal with the decorative shrimp sushi or ahi tuna. The pasta in rich cheese sauce with grilled shrimp and truffle oil is an excellent entrée, as is the grilled duck bathed in chipotle and honey sauce. The menu is constantly changing, so ask about the daily specials. ⊠ *Calle Corazón, just off Av. 5, between Calles 12 and 14* ☎ *984/803–3689* ⊟ *AE, MC, V* ⊘ *Closed Sun. No lunch.*

$$$$ ✕ **La Casa del Agua.** This eatery features four separate levels, each with its
SEAFOOD own atmosphere. From the street-level bistro, a dramatic staircase leads to a small cocktail bar where candelabras drip onto the wooden floors. A stone waterfall is the focal point in the dining rooms illuminated by wrought-iron chandeliers. The open layout provides nearly every table with an ocean breeze. Among the favorites is a seared hamachi served over asparagus and tomato with a sauce of oil, lime, wasabi, jalapeño, and ginger. Those who prefer a local catch should try the fish fillet in a Mediterranean-style vinaigrette. ⊠ *Av. 5 and Calle 2* ☎ *984/803–0232* ⊕ *www.lacasadelagua.com* ⊟ *MC, V.*

$$$ ✕ **La Palapa Hemingway.** A mural of Che Guevara brandishing a knife
CARIBBEAN and fork looms larger than life in this palapa-shaded seafood restaurant, which takes its theme from the Cuban revolution. The grilled shrimp, fish, and steaks are good choices, as are the fresh salads, pastas, and chicken dishes. ⊠ *Av. 5 between Calles 12 and 14* ☎ *984/803–0003 or 984/803–0004* ⊟ *MC, V.*

$$$ ✕ **La Parrilla.** Reliably tasty Mexican fare is the draw at this boister-
MEXICAN ous, touristy restaurant. The smell of sizzling *parrilla mixta* (a grilled,

marinated mixture of lobster, shrimp, chicken, and steak) can make it difficult to resist grabbing one of the few available tables. The margaritas here are strong, and there's often live music. ⌧*Av. 5 and Calle 8* ☎*984/873–0687* ▭*AE, MC, V.*

$$$$
ECLECTIC
✕**Negrosal.** An isolated location and alluring atmosphere make "Black Salt" a local favorite. Inspired by the female form, the decor integrates damask chairs cinched by corsets, candles shaded by black lace, and table legs shaped to resemble those of a ballerina. The restaurant's lighting subtlety changes color every few minutes, and a glass flooring allows you to peek down at the extensive wine cellar. Playing with contradictions, the menu features sweet and salty combinations like lobster tail topped with a corn and pineapple sauce. Every dish, including the tequila duck tacos and the grilled sea bass, is served under a silver dome. Be sure to try the house cocktail: black champagne covered with floating rose pedals. ⌧*Calle 16 between Avs. 1 and 5* ☎*984/803–2448* ⊕*www.negrosal.com* ▭*AE, MC, V* ⊗*No lunch.*

$$$$
ASIAN
✕**Playasia.** With something to appeal to all five senses, Playasia's jungle setting offers a waterfall for sight, a DJ for sound, bamboo for touch, flowers for smell, and sushi for taste. The focus of the open-air courtyard is an illuminated koi pond around which stand six tree houses hung with strands of fairy lights. Asian specialties are served with a tropical twist, such as the battered shrimp rolled in coconut. A local favorite is the blackened sea bass sautéed in a thick marmalade. From the top-level palapa bar, sushi fans can try one of the 10 signature rolls. Be sure to leave room for the tempura cheesecake dribbled with chocolate and mango puree. ⌧*Av. 5 between Calles 10 and 12* ☎*984/879–4749* ▭*AE, MC, V* ⊗*No lunch.*

$$$$
ARGENTINE
✕**Sur.** This two-story enclave of food from the Pampas region of Argentina is a trendy spot. Dine outside on the garden terrace or in the intimate upstairs dining room. Entrées come with four sauces, dominant among them *chimichurri,* made with oil, vinegar, and finely chopped herbs. You can start off with meat or spinach *empanadas* or Argentine sausage, followed by a sizzling half-pound *churrasco* (top sirloin steak), and finish your meal with apple crisp served with chilled cream. ⌧*Av. 5 between Calles 12 and 14* ☎*984/803–2995* ▭*AE, D, MC, V.*

$$$–$$$$
ECLECTIC
✕**Ula-Gula.** As original as its name, this rooftop restaurant boldly experiments with a variety of textures, colors, and flavors. Chef Luis Aguilar puts together such ingenious appetizers as the carrot cannelloni in a warm Brie sauce. Unusual combinations in the entrées include the shrimp tempura with mango sorbet. For dessert, don't miss the liquid chocolate cake with chilled grapefruit—a truly exceptional dish. The decor is just as imaginative. Votive candles embedded in the stucco

WORD OF MOUTH

"Playa del Carmen is a hopping, very busy small city right on a fabulous (most of it) beach. There are many small hotels on or near the beach, and lots of restaurants, shopping and nightlife. For some reason Playa is very popular with Europeans. The north end of Playa is exploding with construction. What was jungle a few years ago is now covered with new condos."
–zootsi

4

walls guide you up a wooden staircase. Over the tables are cone-shaped lamps made of rolled parchment paper. More lively than the secluded restaurant is the street level bar by the same name. ⊠ *Av. 5 and Calle 10* ☎ *984/879–3727* ⊟ *AE, MC, V* ⊘ *No lunch.*

$$–$$$ ✕ **Yaxche.** One of Playa's best restaurants has reproductions of stelae
MEXICAN (stone slabs with carved inscriptions) from famous ruins, and murals of Mayan gods and kings. Mayan dishes such as *halach winic* (chicken in a spicy four-pepper sauce) are superb, and you can finish your meal with a Café Maya (made from Kahlúa, brandy, vanilla, and Xtabentun, the local liqueur flavored with anise and honey). Watching the waiter pour and light Café Maya from its silver demitasse is almost as seductive as the drink itself. ⊠ *Calle 8 and Av. 5* ☎ *984/873–2502* ⊟ *AE, MC, V.*

WHERE TO STAY

PLAYA DEL CARMEN

$$ 🏨 **Aventura Mexicana.** This small inn, three blocks from the beach, is a work of art, with burnt-orange and ocher color schemes, batik wall hangings, and rustic wood-frame beds. Rooms have balconies overlooking the garden and pool area, which also has a thatch-roof restaurant. A *temazcal* (sweat lodge) ceremony led by a shaman costs $70. **Pros:** spotless; friendly staff; spacious rooms. **Cons:** uncomfortable beds; unimaginative breakfasts. ⊠ *Calle 24 between Avs. 5 and 10* ☎ *984/873–1876* ⊕ *www.aventuramexicana.com* ⤞ *49 rooms* ⚷ *In-room: Safe, kitchen (some), refrigerator. In-hotel: 2 restaurants, bar, 2 pools, parking (free), Wi-Fi, no-smoking rooms* ⊟ *MC, V* ⚑ *CP.*

$$–$$$ 🏨 **Blue Parrot Hotel.** Once of Playa's first hotels, the Blue Parrot opened in 1984; its success has led to the opening of two sister properties, Blue Parrot Suites and Blue Parrot 5th Avenue. The spacious rooms at the original hotel have luxurious details such as mahogany-and-glass sliding doors and chic Tommy Bahama accessories. The hotel complex includes a restaurant and a bar, adjoined by a common room beneath a towering beachfront palapa, where amber sconces sit atop *zapote* beams for a romantic effect. You can happily kick off your shoes here—the floor is made of sand. **Pros:** Yucatán bath products; lively bar; spic-and-span facilities. **Cons:** drab decor in suites; poor service; beach views only on top floor. ⊠ *Calle 12 Norte* ☎ *984/206–3350* ⊕ *www.blueparrot.com* ⤞ *39 rooms* ⚷ *In-room: Safe, refrigerator. In-hotel: Restaurant, bar, beachfront, no-smoking rooms* ⊟ *AE, MC, V* ⚑ *EP.*

$ 🏨 **Casa Tucan.** For the price, it's hard to beat this warm, eclectic hotel a few blocks from the beach. Mexican fabrics decorate the cheerful rooms and apartments, and the property has a yoga palapa, a TV bar, a book exchange, and a specially designed pool that's used for onsite diving instruction. Guestrooms have Wi-Fi access, and there's also an Internet café. This is one of the only hotels in Playa del Carmen that offers parking. **Pros:** multilingual staff; onsite car rental agency; exceptional restaurant. **Cons:** some rooms lack a/c. ⊠ *Calle 4 between Avs. 10 and 15* ☎ *984/873–0283* ⊕ *www.casatucan.de* ⤞ *24 rooms, 4 apartments, 10 cabanas* ⚷ *In-room: No a/c (some), no phone, no TV. In-hotel: Restaurant, bar, pool, diving, parking (free), no-smoking rooms* ⊟ *MC, V* ⚑ *EP*

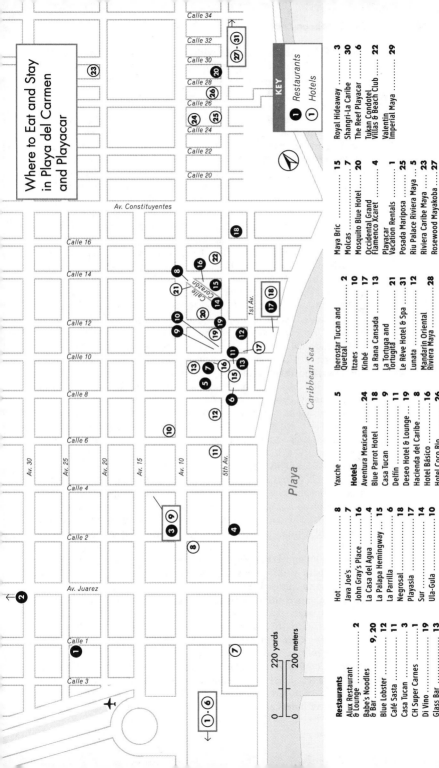

Where to Eat and Stay in Playa del Carmen and Playacar

KEY

- 1 Restaurants
- 1 Hotels

Caribbean Sea

Playa

$ ⌧**Delfín.** The Delfín is covered with ivy and looks fresh and smart. Sea breezes cool the bright rooms, where mosaics lend touches of color. Some rooms have wonderful ocean views. The management is exceptionally helpful. **Pros:** quiet setting; central location. **Cons:** no common areas; no restaurant or bar; lots of steps to climb (and no elevator). ⌧*Av. 5 and Calle 6* ☎ *984/873–0176* ⊕*www.hoteldelfin.com* ⤳*12 rooms* &*In-room: Safe, refrigerator, no phone. In-hotel: Wi-Fi, no-smoking rooms* ⊟*MC, V* ⦿*EP.*

$$$ ⌧**Deseo Hotel & Lounge.** This adults-only hotel is known for its cutting-edge design. A great stone stairway cuts through the stark modern main building; the steps lead to a minimalist, white-on-white open-air lobby, with huge blue daybeds for sunning, a trendy bar, and a pool illuminated with purple lights. Each of the guest rooms has a king-size bed, soft lighting, and clothesline hung with flip-flops, earplugs (the bar has a DJ), bananas, and a beach bag. Suites have large balconies with draping hammocks. Each room is outfitted with a noisemaker, so you can fall asleep to the sound of chirping crickets and awake to the sound of whistling birds. **Pros:** contemporary decor; friendly staff,; comfortable beds; films shown nightly. **Cons:** small rooms; kids not allowed; noisy at night. ⌧*Av. 5 and Calle 12* ☎*984/879–3620* ⊕*www.hoteldeseo.com* ⤳*12 rooms, 3 suites* &*In-room: Safe, Wi-Fi. In-hotel: Room service, bar, pool, no kids under 18, no-smoking rooms* ⊟*AE, MC, V* ⦿*CP.*

Fodor's Choice ★

$$ ⌧**Hacienda del Caribe.** This hotel evokes an old Yucatecan hacienda—albeit a colorful one—with wrought-iron balconies, stained-glass windows, and Talavera tile work. Rooms have unique details like headboards with calla lily motifs and painted tile sinks. The beach is half a block away. **Pros:** creative architecture and decor; near beach and bus depot. **Cons:** street noise; musty bathrooms. ⌧*Calle 2 between Avs. 5 and 10* ☎*984/873–3130* ⊕*www.haciendadelcaribe.com* ⤳*29 rooms, 5 suites* &*In-room: Safe. In-hotel: Pool, no-smoking rooms* ⊟*AE, MC, V* ⦿*EP.*

$$$ ⌧**Hotel Básico.** This ultrahip hotel has won awards for its innovative design. You'll find imaginatively recycled materials throughout the hotel, from the used tires laid down to create the spongy lobby floor to the rooftop lounge chairs made from boxes that were once pickup truck beds. The roof also has two small pools made of recycled oil tanks, and a small bar where Playa's young and trendy meet up with hotel guests for late-night drinks. Guest rooms, though equipped with plasma TVs and DVD players, are designed to look very basic, with plain cement walls, exposed plumbing, and floating beds. All come with retro amenities like beach balls, swim fins, and Polaroid cameras. **Pros:** innovative and eco-friendly design; great rooftop lounge. **Cons:** limited storage space in rooms; not family-friendly; late-night noise. ⌧*Av. 5 at Calle 10 Norte* ☎*984/879–4448* ⊕*www.hotelbasico.com* &*In-room: Refrigerator, DVD. In-hotel: Restaurant, room service, bar, Wi-Fi, laundry service, no-smoking rooms* ⊟*AE, MC, V.*

$$ ⌧**Hotel Coco Rio.** A tropical garden beckons near the entry to this small hotel on a tree-lined street in Playa's north end. Spacious, sunny rooms with king- or queen-size beds are painted in soft pastels; the large bathrooms have bidets and mosaic tiles. It's the details, along with a super price, that make this hotel a real deal. If you want to splurge a bit, get a junior suite with a private balcony. Unfortunately, the ocean view has been blocked by recent construction. **Pros:** pleasant staff; charming setting. **Cons:** some rooms better than others; weak water pressure. ⊠ *Calle 26 between Avs. 5 and 10* ☎ *984/879–3361* ⊕ *www.hotelcocorio. com* ➟ *12 rooms, 5 suites* ⬧ *In-room: Safe, refrigerator. In-hotel: No-smoking room* ☐ *MC, V.*

$$–$$$ ⬚ **Itzaes.** Although this colonial-style hotel has amenities geared to business travelers, divers also like to stay here because of it's two blocks from the beach. The lobby, which opens onto a vine-draped atrium, is a bit hard to see from the street; as you enter, though, you'll notice several inviting sitting areas and a tapas bar. Rooms have tile floors, two double beds each, desks, and hair dryers. There is also a solarium for those who like to start sunning themselves immediately. **Pros:** stunning rooftop pool; reasonably priced rooms; lovely overhead garden in lobby. **Cons:** no room service; many steps to climb and no elevator. ⊠ *Av. 10 and Calle 6* ☎ *984/873–2397* ⊕ *www.itzaes.com* ➟ *14 rooms, 2 suites* ⬧ *In-room: Refrigerator, Internet. In-hotel: Pool, no-smoking rooms* ☐ *AE, MC, V* ⦿ *CP.*

$$ ⬚ **Kinbé.** This boutique hotel, whose decor is an interesting fusion of Mayan and contemporary styles, is set in a tropical garden steps from the beach. Even if you don't stay here, visit the impressive lobby where an onyx bridge crosses an illuminated pool that is filled by a three-story waterfall. The newly designed rooms are divided into four themes, which are pictured on their Web site: Pretty (the smallest, with one double bed), Garden (two levels), Moody (two beds or a king), and Rugiada (king bed). Each has a private balcony with either garden or ocean views. The unique furnishings include suspended bookshelves, triangular desks, and coiled floor lamps with flower-shaped light bulbs. For extra space, opt for the two-level Garden room. **Pros:** great value; discounted rates at nearby Zenzi Beach Club and DiVino restaurant; in-room spa treatments. **Cons:** small rooms; rustic decor is not family-friendly; strict cancellation policy. ⊠ *Calle 10 north between Avs. 1 and 5, Playa del Carmen* ☎ *984/873–0441 or 984/873–0443* ⊕ *www.kinbe.com* ➟ *19 rooms, 10 suites* ⬧ *In-room: Safe, refrigerator, Wi-Fi. In-hotel: Pool, spa, laundry service, Wi-Fi, no-smoking rooms* ☐ *MC, V* ⦿ *EP.*

$$ ⬚ **La Rana Cansada.** Close to the downtown action yet far enough away to have a peaceful feel, this little hotel has all the creature comforts. There's a full kitchen that guests may use, a lending library and reading room, and a bar. Guests gather nightly under the large palapa, where you'll also find the reception desk and sitting area. The rooms are small and simply furnished with high ceilings. If partying isn't your thing, ask for an upstairs room away from the bar. **Pros:** great bar; free purified drinking water. **Cons:** hard beds; no hot water; poor ventilation. ⊠ *Calle 10 between Avs. 5 and 10* ☎ *984/873–0389* ⊕ *www.ranacansada.com* ➟ *14 rooms, 1 suite* ⬧ *In-room: No phone, no TV (some), kitchen (some). In-hotel: Bar, no-smoking rooms* ☐ *MC, V* ⦿ *EP.*

$$ ⬚ **La Tortuga and Tortugita.** European couples often choose this inn, which is located on a quiet side street. Mosaic stone paths wind through the gardens, and colonial-style hardwood furnishings gleam throughout.

Rooms are small but have balconies and are well equipped. The interior was recently underwent extensive renovations. **Pros:** some rooms have rooftop terraces; gorgeous grounds; outstanding breakfast. **Cons:** showers tend to overflow; flat pillows; kids not allowed. ⊠ *Calle 14 and Av. 10* ☎ *984/873–1484 or 800/822–3274* ⊕ *www.hotellator tuga.com* ⇆ *45 rooms, 6 junior suites* ⟁ *In-room: Safe. In-hotel: Restaurant, room service, pool, Wi-Fi, no kids under 16, no-smoking rooms* ☐ *AE, MC, V* ⎰*CP.*

WORD OF MOUTH

"I would also have to recommend La Tortuga . . . such a lovely property and excellent service . . . not a far walk to the beach, and reasonably priced. Rooms are basic, but clean. Nice restaurant by the pool for breakfast, and close to everything in Playa." –Elizabeth27

$$$ ⚃ **Le Rêve Hotel & Spa.** If you're seeking privacy and serenity, you'll will appreciate the luxury at this new beachfront boutique hotel just outside Playa. Expect polished service and thoughtful touches such as homemade soaps and posh bedding. Stylish rooms were built without significantly disturbing trees and other natural surroundings. For the ultimate indulgence, book a beach bungalow, which includes a private patio and infinity plunge pool. Playa del Carmen is just a 10-minute drive away. **Pros:** beautiful pool area; great restaurant. **Cons:** not family-friendly; no airport shuttle. ⊠ *Playa Xcalacoco Fraccion 2A, Playa del Carmen, Quintana Roo,* ☎ *984/109–5660* ⇆ *25 rooms* ⟁ *In-room: No TV. In-hotel: Restaurant, room service, bar, pool, gym, spa, beachfront, laundry service, parking (free), no kids under 16, no-smoking rooms* ☐ *MC, V* ⎰*EP.*

$$$–$$$$ ⚃ **Lunata.** An elegant entrance, Spanish-tile floors, and hand-tooled fur-
★ niture from Guadalajara greet you at this classy inn. Guest rooms have sitting areas and terraces and are filled with dark hardwood furnishings and interesting local crafts. The service is personal and gracious. Breakfast is laid out in the garden each day. Rooms with garden views tend to be quieter than those overlooking La Quinta Avenida. The staff can book excursions to Coba, Tulum, Xcaret, Chichen Itza, and Xel-Ha. **Pros:** prime location; impeccable rooms; intimate setting. **Cons:** street-facing rooms tend to be noisy; mediocre breakfast; hard beds; no elevator. ⊠ *Av. 5 between Calles 6 and 8* ☎ *984/873–0884* ⊕ *www. lunata.com* ⇆ *10 rooms* ⟁ *In-room: Refrigerator. In-hotel: Laundry service, Wi-Fi, no-smoking rooms* ☐ *AE, MC, V* ⎰*CP.*

$$$$ ⚃ **Mandarin Oriental Riviera Maya.** This extraordinary resort blends Mayan and Asian traditions, particularly at the 25,000-square-foot spa, which is both literally and figuratively at the center of the place. After a welcoming cup of freshly brewed tea in the lobby, you consult with a "lifestyle guru" who recommends a personalized regimen. Shaded by paper parasols, you are escorted to the Mandala Garden, where a circular path blooms with Chinese and Mexican herbs. Your guru will choose herbs based on your consultation and infuse them into aromatic teas and massage oils. The spa accommodates honeymooners with numerous treatments for couples. Winding paths extend over the mangroves, leading to the bungalows suites, all of which rise above

the lush vegetation. Standard rooms have Asian influences like rice-paper walls, onyx sinks, and rain-forest showers. Service is exceptional, with three staff members to every guest. **Pros:** golf carts available for exploring property; attentive staff; innovative architecture. **Cons:** organized excursions are pricey; murky ocean water is strewn with seaweed; spa treatments are overpriced. ☒ *Carretera Federal 307, Km 298.8* ☎ *984/877–3888* ⊕ *www.mandarinoriental.com* 📞 *128 rooms* ♿ *In-room: Safe, Wi-Fi. In-hotel: 4 restaurants, room service, bar, pools, spa, gym, beachfront, diving, water sports, children's program (ages 4–12), laundry service, Wi-Fi, no-smoking rooms* 🚭 *AE, MC, V* ⑩ *EP.*

$ **Maya Bric.** Though it's in the middle of La Quinta Avenida, this three-story hotel is surprisingly quiet. The small, brightly colored rooms have double beds and private baths and open onto the garden and small pool. There is a communal dining area, as well as a gazebo where guests can escape the sun. **Pros:** affordable. **Cons:** extra charge for a/c; no elevator and long staircases. ☒ *Av. 5 between Calles 8 and 10* ☎ *984/873–0011* ⊕ *www.mayabric.com* 📞 *27 rooms* ♿ *In-room: No a/c (some), safe, no phone, no TV. In-hotel: Restaurant, Wi-Fi, pool, no-smoking rooms* 🚭 *MC, V* ⑩ *EP.*

$–$$ **Molcas.** This colonial-style hotel, steps from the ferry dock, has been in business since the early 1980s. Over the past few decades it has aged gracefully. Rooms have dark-wood furniture and face the pool, the sea, or the street. The second-floor pool area is glamorous, with white umbrellas. Although it's in the heart of town, the hotel is well insulated from noise, and the price is reasonable. **Pros:** affordable rates; near beach. **Cons:** no-frills rooms; no soap in bathrooms; pool bar seldom open. ☒ *Av. 5 and Calle 1 Sur* ☎ *984/873–0070* ⊕ *www.molcas.com.mx* 📞 *25 rooms* ♿ *In-room: Refrigerator. In-hotel: Bar, pool, beach-front, Wi-Fi, no-smoking rooms* 🚭 *MC, V* ⑩ *EP.*

$$$$ **Mosquito Blue Hotel.** Modern, exotic, and elegant, this hotel has Indonesian decor, mahogany furniture, and soft lighting. Standard rooms have king-size beds, marble bathrooms, and patios that open onto the pool or garden area. The courtyard bar, near one of the pools, is a soothing spot—it's sheltered by a thatch roof and pastel walls. The 4,000-square-foot spa offers services like Mayan healing baths and an aroma therapeutic oxygen bar. For some beach time, spend a day at sister property, Mosquito Beach Hotel, where sun beds, showers, and service are on hand. **Pros:** access to Mosquito Beach Hotel; spotless rooms; access to nearby fitness center. **Cons:** billiards area tends to get loud at night; kids not allowed. ☒ *Calle 12 between Avs. 5 and 10* ☎ *984/873–1245* ⊕ *www.mosquitoblue.com* 📞 *44 rooms, 1 suite* ♿ *In-room: Safe, refrigerator, room service, Wi-Fi. In-hotel: Restaurant, bar, pools, spa, Wi-Fi, some pets allowed, laundry service, no kids under 16, no-smoking rooms* 🚭 *AE, MC, V* ⑩ *EP.*

$$$$ **Occidental Grand Flamenco Xcaret.** In such an enormous all-inclusive hotel it's surprising to find the excellent, personal service that you have here. The staff members go out of their way to make your stay pleasing, beginning with a glass of champagne at registration and helpful concierge service. Guests staying in the larger and pricier Royal Club rooms have even more personalized service—there's a small reception

office serving these 45 rooms exclusively. The hotel has a small artificial beach and walking access to Xcaret park; one-day park admission is included in the price of the room. **Pros:** pleasant lagoon; good teen club; excellent buffet. **Cons:** small beach; squawking parrots in the lobby; parts of resort get crowded. ✉ *Carretera Federal 307, off Puerto Juárez, Km 282* ☎ *984/871–5400* ⊕ *www.occidental-hoteles.com* ↘ *724 rooms, 45 suites* ⟳ *In-room: Safe, refrigerator, Wi-Fi. In-hotel: 11 restaurants, room service, tennis courts, pools, gym, spa, beachfront, diving, children's programs (ages 4–12), laundry service, no-smoking rooms* ▭ *AE, MC, V* ⍩ *AI.*

$–$$ ⌂ **Posada Mariposa.** Not only is this Italian-style property in the quiet north end of town impeccable and comfortable, it's also a great value. Set around a garden, the recently renovated rooms have queen-size beds, luxurious bathrooms, and shared patios. Suites have full kitchens. A small handicrafts and art boutique is attached to the hotel. The beach is five minutes away. **Pros:** cozy setting, good shuttle service, rustic decor. **Cons:** hard beds; no pool; ocean view blocked by new hotels. ✉ *Av. 5 No. 314, between Calles 24 and 26* ☎ *984/873–3886* ⊕ *www.posada-mariposa. com* ↘ *18 rooms, 4 suites* ⟳ *In-room: No phone, safe, refrigerator. In-hotel: Wi-Fi, no-smoking rooms* ▭ *MC, V.*

$$ ⌂ **Riviera Caribe Maya.** It may not have the bells and whistles of other hotels, but this small property is very pleasant. It's in a quiet neighborhood and two blocks from the beach. Rooms have tile floors, cedar furnishings, and spacious baths; suites also have hot tubs. Amenities include a beach club where lounge chairs can be rented for just a dollar; beach towels are free. **Pros:** breezy rooms; outstanding pool area. **Cons:** hard mattresses. ✉ *Av. 10 and Calle 30* ☎ *984/873–1193* ⊕ *www.hotelrivieramaya.com* ↘ *22 rooms, 3 suites* ⟳ *In-room: Safe, refrigerator. In-hotel: Restaurant, room service, pool, diving, laundry service, Wi-Fi, no-smoking rooms* ▭ *MC, V* ⍩ *EP*

$$$$ ⌂ **Rosewood Mayakoba.** Marking the entrance to this peaceful oasis is a
Fodor's Choice   platinum gate. Meandering trails lead through the 1,600-acre grounds
★   to the main building, where a spiraling limestone staircase descends to a network of lagoons. Here you set sail on a thatch-roofed boat to your private sanctuary. Lily-strewn waters create an exotic labyrinth, leading to 128 suites with jungle or ocean views. In keeping with the contemporary Mexican motif, the villas are crafted from indigenous materials such as wood and limestone. Some suites have garden showers and private plunge pools, boat dock, and rooftop sundecks. The golf course is the newest stop on the PGA tour. Despite its elegant atmosphere, the resort is welcoming to families and offers free accommodations to children under 12. **Pros:** 24-hour butler service; private plunge pools; extraordinary spa. **Cons:** poor concierge service; limited food options. ✉ *Carretera Federal, Km 298* ☎ *984/875–8000* ⊕ *www. rosewoodmayakoba.com* ↘ *128 suites* ⟳ *In-room: Safe, DVD, Wi-Fi. In-hotel: 2 restaurants, room service, bar, golf course, pools, spa, gym, beachfront, diving, water sports, children's program (ages 4–11), Wi-Fi, no-smoking rooms* ▭ *AE, MC, V.*

$$$$ ⌂ **Shangri-La Caribe.** Although this resort's location used to be considered the outskirts of Playa, it's now simply the northern end of the downtown area. Still, the property is relatively tranquil, with a tropical garden and attractive whitewashed bungalows. Rooms have comfortable beds, tile floors, baths, and balconies or patios with hammocks that look out over the sea. The restaurants serve Mexican and international fare. **Pros:** private patios with hammocks; excellent service; outstanding breakfast. **Cons:** credit cards not accepted for all hotel services; no evening entertainment; long walk to center. ⊠ *Calle 38 between Av. 5 and Zona Playa*

WORD OF MOUTH

"Playa del Carmen is getting more developed and built up, but it's still a smaller town [than Cancún]. It's easy to wander just a couple blocks off the main drag and find wonderful little authentic (and cheap) restaurants. It's also much more pedestrian friendly. Even with an early morning departure [from Cancún airport], I'd opt for Playa."   –JeanH

⌖ *Reservations: Turquoise Reef Group, Box 2664, Evergreen, CO* ☎ *984/873–0611 or 800/538–6802* ⊕ *www.shangrilacaribe.net* ⤳ *121 cabanas* ⚙ *In-room: Safe. In-hotel: 2 restaurants, pools, beachfront, diving , no-smoking rooms* ☰ *AE, MC, V* ⦿ *MAP.*

$$$ 🏨 **Tukan Condotel Villas & Beach Club.** The immense jungle garden at the entrance to this hotel leads to a lobby and sitting area and separates it from the hustle and bustle of Quinta Avenida. The small, simple rooms and suites are well separated from one another and have private terraces, tile floors, and painted wood furniture. (Make sure you choose a newly painted room—mold spreads fast in the tropics.) The garden has a lovely pool. The buffet breakfast and other meals are served at the Tukan Maya restaurant next door. **Pros:** ideal location; casual atmosphere; free parking. **Cons:** must reserve breakfast in advance; cold-water Jacuzzi; 10-minute walk to beach club. ⊠ *Av. 5 between Calles 14 and 16* ☎ *984/873–1255* ⊕ *www.tukanhotels.com* ⤳ *113 rooms, 37 suites* ⚙ *In-room: Safe. In-hotel: Bar, restaurant, parking (free), pool, public Wi-Fi, no-smoking rooms* ☰ *AE, MC, V* ⦿ *AI, BP.*

$$$ 🏨 **Valentin Imperial Maya.** Nestled in the thriving mangrove forests of Playa del Secreto, this adults-only, all-inclusive resort is one of the few hotels that still embraces Mexican tradition. Look for brick archways and terra-cotta walkways inlaid with mosaic tile. In typical hacienda fashion, the extravagant lobby features a pipe organ, a grand piano, and more than a dozen wrought-iron chandeliers suspended above marble floors. Wooden paths lead to private *palafitos* (structures on stilts), where couples can enjoy romantic dinners. Jazz or classical music echoes throughout the 75 acres of unspoiled grounds. Standard rooms are richly decorated with teak furnishings and include sitting areas with plasma TVs and terraces with spacious hot tubs. The surf at the beach can be somewhat rough but there are two enormous swimming pools, one with an artificial island. **Pros:** impeccable service; enormous pool; authentic Mexican coffee. **Cons:** evening entertainment disappointing; not for kids. ⊠ *Carretera Federal 307, Km 311.5* ☎ *994/206–3660, 800/232–8316 in U.S.* ⊕ *www.valentinmaya.com* ⤳ *408 rooms* ⚙ *In-room: Safe, refrigerator, Wi-Fi. In-hotel: 8 restaurants, room service,*

bar, tennis courts, pools, spa, gym, beachfront, diving, water sports, no kids under 18, Wi-Fi, no-smoking rooms ⊟*AE, MC, V* ⏏*AI.*

PLAYACAR

$$$$ ⊡ **Iberostar Tucan and Quetzal.** This unique all-inclusive resort has preserved its natural surroundings—among the resident animals are flamingos, turtles, toucans, and monkeys. Landscaped pool areas surround the open-air restaurant and reception area. Spacious rooms have cheerful color schemes and patios overlooking dense vegetation. **Pros:** oceanfront rooms; tropical setting; separate areas for families and singles. **Cons:** food lacks variety. ⊠*Fracc. Playacar, Playacar* ☎*984/877–2000* ⊕*www.iberostar.com* ⟿*700 rooms* ⚐*In-room: Safe, refrigerator. In-hotel: 5 restaurants, room service, bars, tennis courts, pools, gym, spa, beachfront, diving, water sports, children's programs (ages 4–12), laundry service, Wi-Fi, parking (free), no-smoking rooms* ⊟*AE, D, MC, V* ⏏*AI.*

$$$ ⊡ **Playacar Vacation Rentals.** You can rent a furnished condo or house on the beach at this upscale resort area. Units have from one to four bedrooms as well as air-conditioning and maid service; they start at $168 a night (for a one-bedroom). There's a five-night minimum stay during high season, and reservations must be made at least six months in advance. The rest of the year the minimum stay is three nights. **Pros:** luxury accommodations; gated beach community; refreshing alternative to all-inclusive resorts. **Cons:** minimum stay in peak season, must book far in advance. ⊠*Av. 10 Sur between Avs. 1 and 3, Playacar* ☎*984/873–0418* ⊕*www.playacarvacationrentals.com* ⚐*In-room: Kitchen. In-hotel: Pools, no-smoking rooms* ⊟*MC, V* ⏏*EP.*

$$$$ ⊡ **Riu Palace Riviera Maya.** This enormous all-inclusive takes luxury seriously: room service is available 24 hours a day. The size and glitz of the hotel feel somewhat excessive, however: oversized columns at the entrance; enormous crystal chandeliers; gold details; and fountains. Still, the beach is breathtaking and the service is exceptional. You are permitted to use the amenities of any of Riu Palace's six sister hotels throughout Playa del Carmen. **Pros:** sports bar open nonstop; friendly staff; lots of scheduled activities. **Cons:** need to make dinner reservations in advance at certain restaurants; no poolside service; hallways echo at night. ⊠*Av. Xaman-Ha, Lote 1, Playacar* ☎*984/877–2280* ⊕*www.riu.com* ⟿*460 rooms* ⚐*In-room: Safe, refrigerator. In-hotel: 6 restaurants, room service, bars, tennis court, pools, gym, spa, beachfront, children's programs (ages 4–12), laundry service, parking (free), no-smoking rooms* ⊟*AE, MC, V* ⏏*AI.*

$$$$ ⊡ **Royal Hideaway.** Located on a stretch of beach, this 13-acre resort has exceptional amenities and superior service. Art and artifacts from around the world fill the lobby, and streams, waterfalls, and fountains dot the grounds. Rooms are in two- and three-story colonial-style villas, each with its own concierge. Gorgeous rooms have two queen-size beds, sitting areas, and ocean-view terraces. **Pros:** romantic setting; attentive service; the ultimate in pampering. **Cons:** not family-friendly; beach never fully recovered from hurricane damage. ⊠*Fracc. Playacar, Lote 6, Playacar* ☎*984/873–4500 or 800/858–2258* ⊕*www.royalhideaway.com* ⟿*192 rooms, 8 suites* ⚐*In-room: Wi-Fi. In-hotel: 5* restaurants, bars, tennis courts, pools, spa, beachfront, water sports, bicycles, Internet terminal, laundry service, parking (free), no kids under 13, no-smoking rooms ☐AE, MC, V ⎮◯⎮AI.

$$$ ⊡ **The Reef Playacar.** At this all-inclusive family resort, cascading water-falls, exotic flowers, and wooden walkways are sheltered beneath a thick jungle canopy. Connected by bamboo paths are three-story villas, each one containing no more than 10 rooms. Rattan furnishings and sunny decks add to the tropical feel of the rooms. There are free dance lessons and fitness classes for resort guests throughout the day; for an extra charge, the onsite dive shop can arrange diving, snorkeling, sail-ing, or windsurfing courses. Wave runners, kayaks, and boogie boards are also available. While parents get pampered at the spa, kids can share a banana split at the ice-cream parlor or burn off energy at the children's disco. **Pros:** family-friendly atmosphere; plenty of outdoor activities; nightly entertainment. **Cons:** pricey spa; dim lighting in rooms; high-pressure sales pitch to purchase timeshare properties. ⊠*Av. Xaman-Ha, Retorno Sayil, Playacar* ☏*984/873–4120* ⊕*www.thereefplayacar. com* ⤳*197 rooms, 3 suites* � &*In-room: Safe, refrigerator. In-hotel: 3 restaurants, bars, tennis courts, pools, gym, spa, beachfront, diving, water sports, children's program (ages 4–12), laundry service, Wi-Fi, parking (free), no-smoking rooms* ☐AE, MC, V ⎮◯⎮AI.

NIGHTLIFE

★ Inside a cavern, **Alux** (⊠*Av. Juárez, Mza. 217, Lote 2, Colonial Eijidal, Playa del Carmen* ☏*984/803–2936*) has a bar, disco, and restaurant. Live DJs spin everything from smooth jazz to electronica until 2 AM.

Bali (⊠*Calle 12 Norte, Playa del Carmen* ☏*984/803–2863*) is the area's largest dance club, accommodating up to 800 people. The mul-tilevel club offers the latest hits mixed by resident spinmaster DJ Carlos. The cover charge is $10.

Bar Ranita (⊠*Calle 10 between Avs. 5 and 10* ☏*984/873–0389*), a cozy alcove, is run by a Swedish couple who really know how to party. The prices are unbeatable, and the margaritas pack a powerful punch!

El Cielo (⊠*Calle 12 between Avs. 1 and 5, Playa del Carmen* ☏*984/141–3731*) is the area's newest party spot. This trendy venue is divided into a street-level bar, a rooftop terrace, and a dance club. Each section has its own DJ spinning everything from house and hip-hop to disco and techno. The patent-leather sofas are a great place to chill out.

★ Classic films are projected on the wall as DJs spin disco nightly at the **Deseo Lounge** (⊠*Av. 5 at Calle 12, Playa del Carmen* ☏*984/879–3620* ⊕*www.hoteldeseo.com*), a rooftop bar and local hot spot.

Diablito Cha Cha Cha (⊠*Calle 12 between Avs. 5 and 1, Playa del Car-men* ☏*984/803–3695*) is a popular palapa bar. The open-air setting is the perfect place to people-watch while a DJ spins until 3 AM.

Kartabar (⊠*Calle 12 at Av. 1, Playa del Carmen* ☏*984/873–2228*) has a laid-back vibe. The sweet scent of strawberry, mint, apple, and rose waft from the hookah pipes as belly dancers weave between the tables. The house martini is sinfully divine.

At **Mambo Cafe** (⊠ *Calle 6 between Avs. 5 and 10, Playa del Carmen* ☎ *984/879–2304*) a dance review begins at 9:30 every night, followed by live salsa music. A younger crowd of locals and tourists typically fills the dance floor.

SHOPPING

Avenida 5 between Calles 4 and 10 is the best place to shop along the coast. Boutiques sell folk art and textiles from around Mexico, and clothing stores carry lots of sarongs and beachwear made from Indonesian batiks. A shopping area called Calle Corazon, between calles 12 and 14, has a pedestrian street, art galleries, restaurants, and boutiques.

BOOKS

★ **Mundo Librería–Bookstore** (⊠ *1 Sur No. 189 between Avs. 20 and 25* ☎ *984/879–3004, 984/109–1566 at Plaza las Americas in Playa del Carmen*) has an extensive selection of books on Mayan culture, along with used English-language books. Profits from all English-language books here are donated to Mexican schools to buy textbooks.

CLOTHING

★ The retro '70s-style fashions at **Blue Planet** (⊠ *Av. 5 between Calles 10 and 12* ☎ *984/803–1504*) are great for a day at the beach. **Crunch** (⊠ *Av. 5 between Calles 6 and 8* ☎ *984/873–1240*) sells high-style evening gowns, swimsuits, and sportswear for women. **Xbaal** (⊠ *Av. 5 and Calle 14* ☎ *984/803–4107*) is filled with attractive men's and women's cotton shirts, woven skirts, and stylish sundresses.

CRAFTS

At **La Hierbabuena Artesanía** (⊠ *Av. 5 between Calles 8 and 10* ☎ *984/873–1741*), owner Melinda Burns offers a collection of fine Mexican clothing and crafts.

★ **La Calaca** (⊠ *Av. 5 between Calles 12 and 14* ☎ *984/873–0174*) has an eclectic selection of wooden masks, whimsically carved angels and devils, and other crafts. **Maya Arts Gallery** (⊠ *Av. 5 between Calles 6 and 8* ☎ *984/879–3389*) has an extensive collection of *huipiles*, the embroidered cotton dresses worn by Mayan women in Mexico and Guatemala.

JEWELRY

Ambar Mexicano (⊠ *Av. 5 between Calles 4 and 6* ☎ *984/873–2357*) has amber jewelry crafted by a local designer who imports the amber from Chiapas. The **Opal Mine** (⊠ *Av. 5 between Calles 4 and 6* ☎ *984/879–5041* ⊠ *Av. 5 and Calle 12* ☎ *984/803–3658*) has fire, white, pink, and orange opals from Jalisco State. You can buy loose stones or commission pieces of custom jewelry. **Santa Prisca** (⊠ *Av. 5 between Calles 2 and 4* ☎ *984/873–0960*) has silver jewelry, flatware, trays, and decorative items from the town of Taxco. Some pieces are set with semiprecious stones.

MALLS

Centro Maya (⊠ *Carretera Federal 2100* ☎ *984/803–9057*) has Soriana, Mexico's large retail outlet, and more than 50 other stores. **Paseo del Carmen** (⊠ *Av. 10 and Calle 1* ☎ *984/803–3789*) is an open-air shopping mall with a number of boutiques, including Diesel, Ultrafemme, and

American Apparel. Caffeine junkies can get their fix at the Starbucks that dominates the center of the mall. Area Body Zone, a large fitness club, has aerobics classes open to the public. A cobblestone path makes this mall one of the area's most popular and pleasant shopping destinations. **Plaza Las Américas** (⊠ *Carretera Federal* ☎ *984/109–2161*) is a family-friendly mall featuring restaurants, shops, and cinemas.

SPORTS AND THE OUTDOORS

ADVENTURE TOURS

Alltournative (⊠ *Carretera Federal 307, Km 287, in front of Playacar development, Playa del Carmen* ☎ *984/803–9999* ⊕ *www.alltournative. com*) will have you feeling like Indiana Jones in no time. Trips, which range in price from $82 to $125, focus on ecological preservation and Mexican culture. You can kayak through a lagoon, snorkel in a cenote, or zip-line above a lush jungle. The company also organizes trips to Mayan communities.

South of Playa del Camen, **Punta Venado** (⊠ *Carretera Federal 307, Km 278, Calica* ☎ *998/887–1191 or 800/503–0046* ⊕ *www.puntavenado. com*) offers adventure tours in all-terrain vehicles, on mountain bikes, or in jeeps. The 2.5 mi of isolated coastline are perfect for horseback riding, snorkeling, and kayaking. Packages range from $48 to $90.

Yucatán Sky Explorer (⊠ *Playa del Carmen Airport, Playa del Carmen* ☎ *984/873–1626* ⊕ *www.playatoursdirect.com*) will take you on an exhilarating aerial tour above the Caribbean's turquoise waters. The ultralight airplane comfortably seats one person plus the licensed pilot. The 25-minute trips cost $99 per person.

GOLF

Playa del Carmen's golf course is an 18-hole, par-72 championship course designed by Robert von Hagge. The green fee is $180; there's also a special twilight fee of $120. Information is available from the **Casa Club de Golf** (☎ *984/873–0624 or 998/881–6088*). The **Golf Club at Playacar** (⊠ *Paseo Xaman-Ha and Mza. 26, Playacar* ☎ *984/873–4990* ⊕ *www.palaceresorts.com*) has an 18-hole course; the green fee is $190 and the twilight fee $130.

HORSEBACK RIDING

Two-hour horseback rides along beaches and jungle trails are run by **Rancho Loma Bonita** (*Carretera Federal 307 between Km 317 and Km 316* ☎ *998/887–5465*). The $84 fee includes transportation, insurance, guides, lunch, drinks, and the use of the property's swimming pool and playground. Children under 5 are free.

SCUBA DIVING

The PADI and SSI-affiliated **Abyss** (⊠ *Av. 1 between Calles 10 and 12* ☎ *984/873–2164* ⊕ *www.abyssdiveshop.com*) offers introductory courses and dive trips ($50 for one tank, $70 for two tanks). The friendly staff at **Diversity Diving** (⊠ *Calle 24, between Avs. 5 and 10, Playa del Carmen* ☎ *984/803–1042* ⊕ *www.diversitydiving.com*) takes you snorkeling at three different locations: open ocean, cenote, and lagoon. The trips cost $85 per person and includes lunch, beverages, snorkeling gear, park entrance and a guide.

Mexico Blue Dream (⊠ *Between Av.1 and Mamitas Beach, Playa del Carmen* ☎ *984/803–0660* ⊕ *www.mexicobluedream.com*) provides custom tours to Cozumel, Yal-Ku, Akumal, and nearby cenotes. Four-tank dives start at 136; boats departing five times daily. The oldest shop in town, **Tank-Ha Dive Center** (⊠ *Calle 10 between Av 5 and 10, Playa del Carmen* ☎ *984/873–0302* ⊕ *www.tankha.com*), has PADI-certified teachers and runs diving and snorkeling trips to the reefs and caverns. A one-tank dive costs $45; for a two-tank trip it's $75. Dive packages are also available.

★ **Yucatek Divers** (⊠ *Av. 15 Norte between Calles 2 and 4, Playa del Carmen* ☎ *984/803–2836* ⊕ *www.yucatek-divers.com*), which is affiliated with PADI, specializes in cenote dives, dive packages, and dives for those with disabilities. Introductory courses start at $95 for a one-tank dive and go as high as $390 for a four-day beginner course in open water.

SKYDIVING
Thrill seekers can take the plunge high above Playa in a tandem sky dive (where you're hooked up to the instructor the whole time). **Sky-Dive** (⊠ *Plaza Marina 32Playa del Carmen* ☎ *984/873–0192* ⊕ *www. skydive.com.mx*) even videotapes your trip so you have proof that you did it. Jumps take place every hour, and cost $230. Reserve at least one day in advance.

PUNTA BETE

10 km (6 mi) north of Playa del Carmen; 55 km (34 mi) south of Cancun.

Dividing Punta Maroma from Punta Bete is a river that spills into the sea. South of the split, Punta Bete consists of a 7-km-long (5½-mi-long) beach dotted with bungalow hotels and thatch-roofed restaurants, isolated because it backs into dense forest. The road to paradise isn't an easy one, however. Leading to the treasured beach is a 2-km (1-mi) pitted path with potholes the size of swimming pools. Lining both sides of this gutted trek is a jungle that provide refuge to green parrots and squirrel monkeys. Just as you begin to smell the ocean, the road forks—the left leading to more affordable accommodations and the right to luxury hotels. For those who don't mind getting sand in their suitcase, there is a beachfront campsite where you can hang your hammock for less than $5 a night.

GETTING HERE AND AROUND
There is no public transportation in Punte Bete and taxis seldom pass. The best way to reach this beautiful beach area is by car. If you're heading south from Cancun, take Carretera 307to the east turnoff at Km 296. The road here is marked by a large Coca Cola sign. Continue 3 km (2 mi) along a jungle road until the road splits, running parallel to the beach. The north (left) fork leads to a string of hotels and resorts, while the south (right) fork will eventually meet with Paradise Point Resort. From here, you can walk along the beach to Playa del Carmen in just under 1½ hours.

WHERE TO STAY

$ 🖼 **Cocos Cabañas.** Tranquillity and seclusion are the name of the game in these cozy bungalows a stone's throw from the beach. Although small, the bungalows are colorful and bright; each has a bath, a netting-draped queen- or king-size bed, hammocks, and a terrace that leads to a garden. Breakfast, lunch, and dinner are served at the Grill Bar, whose menu includes fresh fish dishes and Mexican and international fare. **Pros:** the ultimate in relaxation; friendly staff; gorgeous beach. **Cons:** rough journey to get here; a bit of a drive from Playa del Carmen. ⊠*Playa Xcalacoco, Carretera 307, Km 42 (turn east at Coca-Cola Factory)* ☎*998/874–7056* ⊕*www.travel-center.com* ↩*5 bungalows, 1 room* ⌂*In-room: No a/c (some), no phone, no TV. In-hotel: Restaurant, pool, beachfront, no-smoking rooms* ⊟*No credit cards* ⅋O⅋*EP*

$$$$ 🖼 **Petit Lafitte Seaside Bungalow Resort.** This warm, family-friendly resort
Ↄ is named after a pirate known to have frequented local waters; small cannons on the sundeck point toward the ocean. Guest quarters are in multi-unit cabañas—if you crave privacy, opt for one of the newer ones on the beach's tranquil north end. All units have balconies, and some are practically flush with the ocean for wonderful views. The simple rooms have tile floors and are decorated in shades of blue and white. An onsite ecological zoo and a game room with Ping-Pong and billiards will appeal to children. **Pros:** peaceful atmosphere; on-site library; kids love the small zoo. **Cons:** construction noise from neighboring resorts; uncomfortable beds. ⊠*Carretera 307, Km 295* ☎*984/877–4000* ⊕*www.petitlafitte.com* ↩*46 rooms* ⌂*In-room: Safe, refrigerator. In-hotel: Restaurant, bar, pool, beachfront, water sports, laundry service, Wi-Fi, no-smoking rooms* ⊟*AE, MC, V* ⅋O⅋*MAP.*

$$$$ 🖼 **The Tides.** This romantic jungle lodge epitomizes understated luxury and sophistication. Visitors cherish the privacy and serenity of the villas, all of which have intricately carved woodwork and plunge pools adorned with votive candles and rose petals. Pampering touches include sumptuous Egyptian-cotton sheets, Swiss piqué robes, and Molton Brown soaps and shampoos. Located beside the sea and near temple ruins, the spa delicately fuses Mayan healing lore and ancient techniques into its treatments. The restaurant's chef, Cupertino Ortiz, adds Mediterranean touches to a menu featuring dishes like seared scallops, braised beef, and lobster. Those who prefer not to leave their room can order up a bottle from the wine cellar or try organic fusion cuisine available through room service. Guests booking the top suites are provided with a private butler and chauffeur. The bumpy road to luxury is cushioned by the hotel's string of Land Rovers—they'll also bring you here in a private helicopter, for an additional charge. The hotel is 9 km (5½ mi) north of Playa del Carmen. **Pros:** private pools; delicious dining options. **Cons:** hidden service charges; construction noise from neighboring projects; overpriced drinks. ⊠*Playa Xcalacoco, Fracc. 7* ☎*984/877–3000 or 888/230–7330* ⊕*www.tidesrivieramaya.com* ↩*29 villas, 1 suite* ⌂*In-room: DVD, Wi-Fi, safe. In-hotel: Restaurant, bar, pool, gym, spa, beachfront, diving, laundry service, parking (free), no kids under 16, no-smoking rooms* ⊟*AE, MC, V* ⅋O⅋*EP.*

4

PUNTA MAROMA

23 km (14 mi) north of Playa del Carmen.

On a bay where the winds don't reach the waters, this gorgeous beach remains calm even on blustery days. To the north you can see the land curve out to another beach, Playa del Secreto. To the south, the curve that leads eventually to Punta Bete is visible. Punta Maroma is located at km 51 off of Carretera 307.

WHERE TO STAY

$$$$ ⊡ **Maroma.** At this elegant hotel, peacocks wander jungle walkways and the scent of flowers fills the air. Rooms, which have small sitting areas, are filled with whimsical decorative items and original artwork. The king-size beds are draped in mosquito netting that adds a romantic touch. A full breakfast is served on each room's private terrace; the restaurant ($$$–$$$$) excels at such dishes as lobster bisque and honeyed rack of lamb. Off Carretera 307, this stunning hotel is marked only by a faded peacock mural. **Pros:** outstanding spa; exceptional service; great place to escape the crowds. **Cons:** no nightlife or entertainment; difficult to find from the highway. ⊠ *Carretera 307, Km 51* ☎ *998/872–8200* ⊕ *www.maromahotel.com* ⟲ *52 rooms, 14 suites, 1 villa* ⌂ *In-room: Safe, Wi-Fi. In-hotel: 3 restaurants, room service, bar, pool, gym, spa, beachfront, water sports, laundry service, airport shuttle, no kids under 12, no-smoking rooms* ⊟ *AE, MC, V* ⦿ *BP.*

PUNTA BRAVA

24 km (15 mi) north of Playa del Carmen.

Punta Brava is also known as South Beach. It's a long, winding beach strewn with seashells. In an effort to calm the powerful waves, Punta Brava resorts have built artificial sandbars along the shore. Not only are these burlap sacks an eyesore, but they have also eliminated one of the few spots in the area where bodysurfing was once possible.

WHERE TO STAY

$$$$ ⊡ **El Dorado Royale.** This beachfront resort has been overshadowed by the newer resorts, but the staff is friendly and the location—amid 500 acres of lush jungle—is just as alluring as ever. Showcased in the extravagant lobby are a crystal chandelier and an infinity pool made of marble. Junior suites have small sitting rooms, king-size beds, hot tubs, and ocean-facing terraces. Swim-up casitas with dome roofs have oceanfront terraces. Seven restaurants, such as La Fondue, serve exceptional dishes. There's free shuttle service to Cancún and Playa del Carmen for those who stay in casitas. **Pros:** on-site health bar with fruit smoothies and health foods; sprawling property; on-site ATM. **Cons:** gym crowded in the morning; slow room service; rocky beach. ⊠ *Carretera 307, Km 45* ☎ *998/872–8030* ⊕ *www.eldorado-resort.com* ⟲ *522 rooms, 117 casitas* ⌂ *In-room: DVD (some), safe. In-hotel: 7 restaurants, room service, bars, tennis courts, pools, spa, beachfront, water sports, bicycles, laundry service, public Wi-Fi, no kids under 18, no-smoking rooms* ⊟ *AE, MC, V* ⦿ *AI.*

PUERTO MORELOS

32 km (20 mi) north of Playa del Carmen.

The sleeping beauty is awakening. For years Puerto Morelos was known only for being the coastal town where the car ferry departed for Cozumel. Over the past decade, this cargo port has morphed into the gateway to the Riviera Maya. About halfway between Cancún and Playa del Carmen, Puerto Morelos makes a great base for exploring the region. The town itself is small but colorful, with a central plaza surrounded by shops and restaurants. The pace is slow, the vibe is relaxed, and the atmosphere bohemian enough to attract a cluster of artists, painters, and poets. Its trademark is a leaning lighthouse.

Puerto Morelos's greatest appeal lies out at sea: the superb coral reef only 1,800 feet offshore is an excellent place to snorkel and scuba dive. This thriving reef and the surrounding mangrove forests are a protected national park, meaning trips can only be made with licensed guides. The park is home to 36 species of birds, making it a great place for bird-watchers. (The mangroves are also a haven for mosquitoes—bring repellant, especially after dusk.)

Environmental laws and building restrictions keep growth under tight control. This has prevented Puerto Morelos from becoming the next Cancún or Playa del Carmen—which many locals consider a blessing. Although these are not the turquoise waters of Cancún, they are calm and safe. The sand may not be as immaculate as elsewhere, but you can walk for miles and see only a few people.

EXPLORING

There are plenty of beaches in Puerto Morelos; the best is two blocks north of the square. They're rarely crowded, except on Sundays, when Cancun locals visit the area for a weekend escape.

⟳ The biologists running the **Croco-Cun** (⊠ *Carretera 307, Km 31* ☎ *998/ 850–3719* ⊕ *www.crococunzoo.com*), an animal farm just north of Puerto Morelos, have collected specimens of many of the reptiles and some of the mammals indigenous to the area. They offer immensely informative tours—you may even get to handle a baby crocodile or feed a deer. Be sure to wave hello to the 500-pound crocodile secure in his deep pit. The farm is open daily 9 AM to 5 PM. Admission is $20.

South of Puerto Morelos, the 150-acre **Yaax Che Jardín Botánico del Dr. Alfredo Barrera Marín** (*Dr. Alfredo Barrera Marín Botanical Garden* ⊠ *Carretera 307, Km 33* ☎ *983/832–1666 or 998/206–9233* ⊕ *www. ecosur.mx/jb/YaaxChe*) is the largest botanical garden in Mexico. Named for a local botanist, the garden exhibits the peninsula's plants and flowers, which are labeled in English, Spanish, and Latin. The park features a 40-meter suspension bridge, three observation towers, and a library equipped with reading hammocks. There's also a tree nursery, a remarkable orchid and epiphyte garden, an authentic Mayan house, and an archaeological site. A nature walk goes directly through the mangroves for some great birding. More than 220 species have been identified here (be sure to bring the bug spray, though). Spider monkeys can usually be spotted in the afternoons, and a tree-house lookout offers

4

a spectacular view—but the climb isn't for those afraid of heights. The park is open Monday to Saturday throughout the year, 8 to 4 November through April and 9 to 5 May through October. Admission is $7.

WHERE TO EAT

$$$
MEXICAN

✕ **El Pirata.** A popular spot for breakfast, lunch, dinner, or just a drink from the bar, this open-air restaurant seats you at the center of the action on Puerto Morelos's town square. If you have a hankering for American food, you can get a good hamburger with fries here; there are also great daily specials. If you're lucky, they might include *pozole*, a broth made from cracked corn, pork, chiles, and bay leaves and served with tostada shells. ⌧ *Av. Rafael E Melgar, Lote 4* ☎ *998/251–7948* ▭ *MC, V.*

> **A SACRED JOURNEY**
>
> In ancient times Puerto Morelos was a point of departure for pregnant Mayan women making pilgrimages by canoe to Cozumel, the sacred isle of the fertility goddess, Ixchel. Remnants of Mayan ruins survive along the coast here, although none of them have been restored.

$–$$
ASIAN

✕ **Hola Asia.** This small, open-air restaurant is a local favorite that serves up generous portions of tasty Chinese, Japanese, and Thai food. Be sure to sample the most popular dish in the place, General Tso's Chicken, a sweet and sour chicken with a dash of spice. The lunch buffet only costs $5, including a soft drink. The rooftop bar offers minty mojitos and stunning ocean views. ⌧ *Av. Tulum 1* ☎ *998/871–0679* ⊕ *www.holaasia.com* ▭ *MC, V* ⊘ *Closed Tues. No lunch.*

$$$
INTERNATIONAL
Fodor's Choice
★

✕ **John Gray's Kitchen.** This former Ritz-Carlton chef's current restaurant, which is located right next to the jungle, draws a regular crowd of Cancún and Playa locals. Using only the freshest ingredients—from local fruits and vegetables to seafood right off the pier—Gray works his magic in a comfortable and contemporary setting that feels more Manhattan than Mayan. Don't miss the delicious tender roasted duck breast with tequila, *chipotle*, and honey. Another great option when it's available is the *boquinete*, a local white fish grilled to perfection and served with mango salsa. ⌧ *Av. Niños Heroes, Lote 6* ☎ *998/871–0665* ▭ *MC, V* ⊘ *Closed Sun. No lunch.*

$
MEXICAN

✕ **La Suegra.** *La suegra* means "mother-in-law," and this new restaurant is named for Maria Ramirez, the mother-in-law of famed chef John Gray. An accomplished chef herself, Maria Ramirez creates dishes like grilled fish, pork chops, and ceviche escargot, all served with steak fries and coleslaw. Early risers can start the day with Maria's delicious *huevos rancheros*. The palapa-covered patio overlooks one of the largest reefs in the world, making this an ideal spot to drop by for a slice of homemade cheesecake or linger over a refreshing lemonade. ⌧ *Av. Rafael Melgar Lote 6, No. 181, Mz. 3, Sm, Puerto Morelos* ☎ *998/845–9419* ▭ *MC, V* ⊘ *Closed Sun; no dinner*

$$$
ITALIAN

✕ **L'Oazis.** The earthy atmosphere of this Italian restaurant is balanced by the sweet spirit of its Canadian owners, Martine and Flavio. The place has a bohemian feel, with ceramic lamps, bamboo railings, and candleholders made from bits of glass. House specialties include the balsamic-marinated tuna, which looks like a steak but has the grilled flavor of nothing you've ever tasted. The seafood linguini, topped with a pyramid of jumbo shrimp, is bathed in a white wine and tomato sauce. All meals come with wild rice, rosemary potatoes, or grilled eggplant. Ask for an inside table, as street traffic and mosquitoes tend to be bothersome. ✉*Av. Tulum and Av Javier Rojo Gomez* ☎*998/228–3733* ▭*No credit cards* ☉*Closed Mon. No lunch.*

¢ ✕**Le Café D'Amancia.** This colorful local hangout on the corner of the
ECLECTIC main plaza is the best place in town to grab a seat and a cup of coffee and a pastry to munch as you watch the world go by. The fruit smoothies are also delicious. Or take your food upstairs and use one of the café's computers for $2 per hour. ✉*Av. Tulum, Lote 2* ☎*998/206–9242* ▭*No credit cards.*

¢ ✕**Loncheria El Tio.** More like a hole in the wall than a restaurant, this
MEXICAN short-order eatery is never empty and almost never closed. Yucatecan specialties such as *salbutes* (flour tortillas with shredded turkey, cabbage, tomatoes, and pickled onions) or *panuchos* (beans, chicken, avocado, and pickled onions on flour tortillas) will leave you satisfied, and you'll still have pesos left in your pocket. This is a great place to chuckle at the overdramatic *telenovelas* (soap operas) blaring from the TV in the corner. ✉*Av. Rafael E. Melgar, Lote 2, across from main dock* ☎*998/233–4634* ▭*No credit cards.*

$$$ ✕**Los Pelicanos.** Enjoy the fresh, well-prepared seafood on the shaded
SEAFOOD patio at this family-owned restaurant in the heart of town. Try the fresh fish prepared *al ajo* (in a delicious garlicky, butter sauce). On a small dock, the restaurant offers a variety of four-hour day trips that include fishing, snorkeling, and cooking at the restaurant. If you want to take one of these tours, call a day in advance. ✉*Av. Rafael E. Melgar, Lote 2, in front of beach, on corner of Av. Tulum* ☎*998/871–0014* ▭*MC, V.*

$$–$$$ ✕**Posada Amor.** This restaurant, the oldest in Puerto Morelos, has
MEXICAN retained a loyal clientele for nearly three decades. In the palapa-cov-
★ ered dining room with its picnic-style wooden tables and benches, the gracious staff serves up terrific Mexican and seafood dishes, including a memorable whole fish dinner and a rich seafood bisque. The daily brunch is also delicious. Live music, including Spanish guitar, can be heard every night at the patio bar. ✉*Avs. Javier Rojo Gómez and Tulum* ☎*998/871–0033* ▭ *MC, V.*

WHERE TO STAY

¢ ⛺**Acamaya Reef Cabanas and RV Park.** North of Puerto Morelos, this RV park and campground sits right on the beach. There are six cabañas here, four of which have private baths, and three of which have air-conditioning ($100 per night). There are also 10 RV sites, 50 tent sites, and a small restaurant. **Pros:** a 20-minute walk along the beach brings you right into town. **Cons:** cabañas are pricey for what you get. ✉*Carretera 307, Km 29* ☎*998/871–0131* ⊕*www.acamayareef.com* ⌇*50 tent sites, $15 per person, per day; 10 RV sites with full hookups, $30 to $40 per day; 6 cabañas, $100 for 2 people per night* ⌂*Flush toilets, full hookups, showers, picnic tables, food service, electricity, public telephone, general store, play area, swimming (ocean)* ▭*DC, MC, V* ⊙*EP.*

$$$$ ⬚ **Ceiba del Mar Hotel & Spa.** Rooms at this secluded beach resort north of town are in six thatch-roofed buildings, all with ocean-view terraces. Painted tiles, wrought-iron work, and bamboo details in the rooms complement the hardwood furnishings from Guadalajara. There's also butler service, and your Continental breakfast is discreetly delivered to your room through a hidden closet chamber. **Pros:** delicious coconut ice cream; excellent service; romantic setting. **Cons:** few restaurants nearby. ⊠ *Costera Norte* ☎ *998/872–8060 or 877/545–6221* ⊕ *www. ceibadelmar.com* ⬚ *88 rooms, 7 suites* ⬚ *In-room: Safe, Wi-Fi. In-hotel: 2 restaurants, bar, tennis court, 2 pools, spa, beachfront, diving, laundry service, Wi-Fi, no-smoking rooms* ⊟ *AE, MC, V* ⓘ *CP.*

$$$$ ⬚ **Excellence Riviera Cancún.** A grand entrance leads to a Spanish marble
Fodor's Choice   lobby, where bellmen in pith helmets await. Rooms are similarly opu-
★   lent: all have hot tubs, ornate Italianate furnishings, and private balco-
nies. Located 15 minutes from Cancún Airport, the property is centered around a luxurious spa and six meandering pools. After a relaxing spa treatment, sip margaritas under a beachside palapa or experience local culture at the traditional *temazcal* sauna. **Pros:** caters to honeymoon-ers; plenty of pool lounging space; rooms have private hot tubs for two. **Cons:** bland food; far from town; no kids. ⊠ *Carretera Federal 307, Mza. 7, Lote 1* ☎ *998/872–8500* ⊕ *www.excellence-resorts.com* ⬚ *440 rooms* ⬚ *In-room: Safe, DVD, refrigerator, Internet. In-hotel: 8 restaurants, room service, bars, tennis courts, pools, gym, spa, beach-front, diving, water sports, no kids under 18, no-smoking rooms* ⊟ *AE, MC, V* ⓘ *AI.*

$–$$ ⬚ **Hotel Ojo de Agua.** This peaceful, family-run beachfront hotel is a great bargain. Half the rooms have kitchenettes; all are painted in cheer-ful colors with simple furniture and ceiling fans. Third-floor units have private balconies, with views of the sea or gardens. The beach offers superb snorkeling directly out front, including the Ojo de Agua, an underwater sinkhole shaped like an eye. **Pros:** spotless rooms, spec-tacular ocean views. **Cons:** slow service in restaurant, poor mainte-nance, low water pressure. ⊠ *Av. Javier Rojo Gómez, Sm 2, Lote 16* ☎ *998/871–0027* ⊕ *www.ojo-de-agua.com* ⬚ *36 rooms* ⬚ *In-room: Safe, kitchen (some). In-hotel: Restaurant, pool, beachfront, Internet terminal, parking (free), no-smoking rooms* ⊟ *AE, MC, V.*

$$ ⬚ **Hotelito y Studios Marviya.** Close to the town center and to the beach, this hotel has a great location. Breezy rooms and studios have king-size beds and large tile baths. Terraces have hammocks and views of the ocean or mangroves. You have use of a large kitchen and a lounge. The grounds include a walled courtyard and a fragrant garden. If you want a little extra pampering, you can book an appointment with the onsite massage therapist. **Pros:** bicycles available; multilingual staff; commu-nal kitchen. **Cons:** rooms must be paid for online in advance. ⊠ *Avs. Javier Rojo Gómez and Ejercito Mexicano* ☎ *998/871–0049* ⊕ *www. marviya.com* ⬚ *6 rooms* ⬚ *In-room: No a/c, no phone, kitchen, refrig-erator, Wi-Fi, no TV. In-hotel: Bar, Wi-Fi, water sports, no-smoking rooms* ⊟ *MC, V* ⓘ *CP.*

¢   ⬚ **Posada Amor.** In the early 1970s, the founder of this small, cozy downtown hotel dedicated it to the virtues of love *(amor)*. Although he's since passed away, the founding philosophy has been upheld by his wife and children, who now run the property. Rooms are clean, small, and simple; all have private baths. The on-site restaurant serves delicious meals, the specialty being fresh fish, and on Sunday the breakfast buffet is not to be missed. The helpful staff makes you feel right at home. **Pros:** excellent food; friendly staff; family-run business. **Cons:** no towels; rooms can get musty and some lack a/c; no elevator. ⊠ *Avs. Javier Rojo Gómez and Tulum* ☎ *998/871–0033* ➴ *13 rooms* ᏔᏔ *In-room: No a/c (some), no phone, no TV. In-hotel: Restaurant, bar, Wi-Fi, no-smoking rooms* ☰ *MC, V* ⏐❙⏐ *EP.*

> ### LOCAL GOODNESS
>
> **Jungle Market & Spa** (⊠ *Calle 2* ☎ *998/208–9148* ⊕ *www.maya echo.com*) is a nonprofit organization that generates income for Mayan women and their families. The Jungle Market features traditional dances, regional foods, and handmade crafts sold by Mayan women dressed in embroidered dresses. Between December and April the market takes place Sunday from 9:30 to 2. The spa offers traditional Mayan treatments such as hot-stone massages and aloe vera body wraps. It's open Wednesdays and Fridays from 10:30 to 4.

SHOPPING

BOOKS

Alma Libre Bookstore (⊠ *Av. Tulum* ☎ *998/871–0713* ⊕ *www.almalibre books.com*) has more than 20,000 titles in stock. You can trade in your own books for 25% of their cover prices here and replenish your holiday reading list. It's open October through June, Tuesday through Saturday 10 to 3 and 6 to 9, and on Sunday 4 to 9. Owners Robert and Joanne Birce are also great sources of information on local happenings.

CRAFTS AND FOLK ART

★ The **Colectivo de Artesanos de Puerto Morelos** (*Puerto Morelos Artists' Cooperative* ⊠ *Avs. Javier Rojo Gómez and Isla Mujeres* ☎ *No phone*) is a series of palapa-style buildings where local artisans sell their jewelry, hand-embroidered clothes, hammocks, and other items. You can sometimes find real bargains. It's open daily from 8 AM until dusk.

SPORTS AND THE OUTDOORS

ADVENTURE TOURS

Selvática (⊠ *Carretera 307, Km 321, 19 km from turnoff* ☎ *998/898– 4312* ⊕ *www.selvatica.com.mx*), just outside the center of Puerto Morelos, offers tours over the jungle on more than 3 km (2 mi) of zip-lines. The entire tour will take you a little over two hours, so you'll be glad to have a snack afterward in the on-site cafeteria. Mountain-biking tours are also available. If you want a taste of all the activities, you can go on a four-hour zip-line, biking, and swimming tour for $95. Advance reservations are required.

FISHING

If you want to fish beyond the reef, you can take this four-hour trip (for up to four people) on a luxury Bayliner for $350 for the boat. **Pelicanos** (⊠ *Av. Rafael E. Melgar, Lote 277580* ☎ *998/871–0014*), a downtown restaurant, offers four-hour tours that include fishing, snorkeling, and cooking up the catch of the day. The tour cost is either $250 for a 27-foot boat or $300 for a 31-foot boat. Drinks and snacks on the boat are included.

SCUBA DIVING

Almost Heaven Adventures (⊠*Javier Rojo Gomez, Mza. 2, Lote 10* ☎998/871–0230 ⊕*www.almostheavenadventures.com*), the oldest dive shop in the area, is the only one owned and operated by locals. Snorkeling trips cost $55, and two tank reef dives cost $75. Night tours are especially popular in the summer, so book at least a day in advance. **Diving Dog Tours** (☎998/201–9805 or 998/848–8819 ⊕*www.puerto morelosfishing.com*) runs snorkeling trips at various sites on the Great Mesoamerican Reef for $30 per person.

PUNTA TANCHACTÉ

8 km (5 mi) north of Puerto Morelos.

The Riviera Maya region technically starts at Punta Tanchacté (pronounced tan-chak-*te*), also known as Peten Pich (pronounced like "peach"), with small hotels on long stretches of beach caressed by turquoise waters. It's quieter here than in Cancún, and you can walk for miles with only the birds for company.

WHERE TO STAY

$$$$ ⌷**Azul Hotel and Beach Resort.** On a secluded beach, this all-inclusive ☾ hotel has ocean views, lush grounds, and palapa-covered walkways. Rooms are filled with Mayan designs and tasteful art, and have two twin beds or one double, as well as a tiny bathroom. The property also caters to families with children: there are shallow pools just for children, and cribs and strollers are on hand for guests. For an extra fee, a shuttle transports you to nearby Puerto Morelos, Cancún, or Playa del Carmen. **Pros:** intimate setting; excellent service; romantic beach dinners. **Cons:** smallish rooms; mediocre menu; crowded during spring. ⊠*Carretera 307, Km 27.5* ☎998/872–8080 ⊕*www.karismahotels. com/azul* ⤢*98 rooms* ☾*In-room: Safe, refrigerator, Wi-Fi. In-hotel: 4 restaurants, room service, bars, pools, beachfront, diving, water sports, children's programs (ages 4–12), laundry service, no-smoking rooms* ⊟*AE, MC, V* ⏀*AI.*

$$$$ ⌷**Zoëtry Paraíso de la Bonita.** Eclectic is the byword at this luxurious
Fodor'sChoice hotel, which is now managed by Zoëtry Wellness & Spa Resorts. A
★ pair of stone dragons guard the entrance, and the spacious two-room suites—all with sweeping sea and jungle views—are decorated with Indian, African, Indonesian, and Caribbean furnishings. The restaurants, which are among the best in the Riviera Maya, adroitly blend Asian and Mexican flavors. The knockout spa has thalassotherapy treatments, some of which take place in specially built saltwater pools. **Pros:** attentive staff; tasteful room design; delicious breakfast. **Cons:** no evening entertainment; no nightlife; expensive compared to other properties. ⊠*Carretera 307, Km 328* ☎998/872–8300 or 998/872–8314 ⊕*www.zoetryparaisodelabonita.com/Paraiso/* ⤢*90 suites* ☾*In-room: Safe, Wi-Fi. In-hotel: 3 restaurants, bar, tennis court, pools, gym, spa,*

beachfront, water sports, laundry service, airport shuttle, parking (free), no kids under 13, no-smoking rooms ☰AE, MC, V ⦿CP.

XCARET

☺ *11 km (6½ mi) south of Playa del*
Fodor'sChoice *Carmen.*
★
⚐ Once a sacred Mayan city and
port, Xcaret (pronounced *ish*-car-
et) is now a 250-acre ecological
theme park on a gorgeous stretch
of coastline. It's the coast's most
heavily advertised attraction, billed
as "nature's sacred paradise," with
a network of buses, its own published magazines, and a collection
of stores.

NAVIGATING THE PARK

You can easily spend at least a
full day at Xcaret. The park is big,
so it's a good idea to check the
daily activities against a map of
the park to organize your time.
Plan to be in the general area of
an activity before it is scheduled
to begin. You'll beat the crowds
and avoid having to run across
the park.

Among the most popular attrac-
tions are the Paradise River raft tour that takes you on a winding,
watery journey through the jungle; the Butterfly Pavilion, where thousands of butterflies float dreamily through a botanical garden while
New Age music plays in the background; and an ocean-fed aquarium
where you can see local sea life drifting through coral heads and sea
fans.

The park has a Wild Bird Breeding Aviary, nurseries for both abandoned flamingo eggs and sea turtles, and a series of underwater caverns
that you can explore by snorkeling or snuba (a hybrid of snorkeling
and scuba). A replica Mayan village includes a colorful cemetery with
catacomb-like caverns underneath; traditional music and dance ceremonies (including performances by the famed *Voladores de Papantla*—the
Flying Birdmen of Papantla) are performed here at night. But the star
show is the evening "Spectacular Mexico Night Show," which tells the
history of Mexico through song and dance.

The list of Xcaret's attractions goes on and on: you can visit a dolphi-
narium, a bee farm, a manatee lagoon, a bat cave, an orchid and bro-
meliad greenhouse, an edible-mushroom farm, and a small zoo. You
can also visit a scenic tower that takes you 240 feet up in the air for a
spectacular view of the park.

■TIP➜ **Although Xcaret has 11 restaurants, many visitors bring their own
lunches and take advantage of picnic tables scattered throughout the park.**
The entrance fee covers only access to the grounds and the exhibits; all
other activities and equipment—from sea treks and dolphin tours to
lockers and swim gear—are extra. You can buy tickets from any travel
agency or major hotel along the coast. ☎*984/871–5200, 998/883–0470
in Cancun* ⊕*www.xcaret.com* ✉*$59* ⊙*Daily 8:30* AM*–10* PM.

A CRESCENT-SHAPE LAGOON

Beachcombers, campers, and snorkelers are fond of **Paamul** (pronounced paul-*mool*), a crescent-shaped lagoon with clear, placid waters sheltered by a coral reef, that's 21 km (13 mi) south of Playa del Carmen. Shells, sand dollars, and even glass beads—some from the sunken, 18th-century pirate ship *Mantanceros*, which lies off nearby Akumal—wash onto the sandy parts of the beach. In June and July you can see one of Paamul's chief attractions: sea-turtle hatchlings. If you'd like to stay on this piece of paradise, the hotel below is a solid option.

⌕ **Cabañas Paamul**, a rustic hostelry, sits on a perfect white-sand beach. Ten bungalows have two double beds each, a/c, Wi-Fi, and hammocks; farther along the beach are 12 even more private cabanas. There is also a swimming pool. The property includes 220 RV sites ($30 a day), as well as tent sites ($10 a day). An on-site, full-service dive shop conducts PADI- and NAUI-certification courses. **Pros:** on the beach; some lovely views; nice open-air restaurant. **Cons:** need car to get around; some rooms need repainting. ⌂ *Carretera 307, Km 85* ☎ *984/875–1053* ⊕ *www.paamul-cabanas.com and www.scubamex.com* ⌕ *12 suites, 10 cabanas, 220 RV sites, 30 campsites* ♿ *In-room: No phone, no TV, Wi-Fi. In-hotel: Restaurant, bar, pool, beachfront, diving, laundry service, no-smoking rooms* ▤ *MC, V.*

PUERTO AVENTURAS

26 km (16 mi) south of Playa del Carmen.

GETTING HERE AND AROUND

Puerto Aventuras is a 20-minute drive south of Playa del Carmen along Carrertera 307. Taxis from Playa del Carmen cost about $15.

ESSENTIALS

Currency Exchange **Asesores Turisticos Cambiarios** (⌂ *Carrertera Chetumal-Cancún, Km 269.5* ☎ *984/873–5177*)

Internet **Café C@fe** (⌂ *Plaza Marina F-4C* ☎ *984/873–5728*).

EXPLORING

While the rest of the coast has been caught up in a development furor, the small community of **Puerto Aventuras** has been quietly doing its own thing. It's become a popular vacation spot, particularly for families—although it's certainly not the place to experience authentic Yucatecan culture. The 900-acre self-contained resort is built around a 95-ship marina. It has a beach club, golf course, tennis courts, restaurants, and a great dive center. Children may enjoy the dolphin training center or the nautical museum.

The **Museo CEDAM** displays coins, sewing needles, nautical devices, clay dishes, and other artifacts from 18th-century sunken ships. All recoveries were made by members of the Mexican Underwater Expeditions Club, founded in 1959 by Pablo Bush Romero. ⌂ *North end of marina* ☎ *984/873–5000* ⊕ *www.puertoaventuras.com* ⌕ *Donation* ⏱ *Daily 10–1 and 3:30–5:30.*

WHERE TO EAT

$$ ✕**Café Olé International.** The laid-back hub of Puerto Aventuras is a ter-
SEAFOOD race café with a varied menu. The coconut shrimp is a good choice, as is
the chicken with a chimichurri sauce made from red wine, garlic, onion,
and fine herbs. If you're lucky, the nightly specials might include locally
caught fish in garlic sauce. Each Sunday during high season, musicians
from around the world play until the wee hours. ⊠ *Across from Omni
Puerto Aventuras hotel* ☎*984/873–5125* ▤*MC, V.*

WHERE TO STAY

$$$ ⊡**Aventura Spa Palace.** This 85-acre all-inclusive resort is so big, and
has so many activities, that you may have trouble finding a reason to
leave. The grounds are stunning, with a meditation pond, yoga hut,
labyrinthine Zen path, and botanical gardens. Combining relaxation
and fitness, the resort offers an indoor swimming pool with sound
therapy and private coves where guests can snorkel. There's also a
100-foot climbing tower, an obstacle fitness trail, and a virtual spinning room. There are plenty of good restaurants and an enormous spa
with more treatments than you can imagine. All rooms have hot tubs
and balconies. **Pros:** breakfast delivered to your door; access to neighboring golf course; onsite cooking classes. **Cons:** lots of sales pitches
for timeshares; beach is artificial; no kids. ⊠ *Km 72, Carrertera Can-
cún-Tulum* ☎*984/875–1100 or 800/346–8225* ⊕*www.palaceresorts.
com* ⌥*1,213 rooms, 45 suites* ♿*In-room: Safe, refrigerator, Wi-Fi.
In-hotel: 7 restaurants, room service, pools, spa, gym, tennis courts,
golf course, water sports, no kids under 18, no-smoking rooms* ▤*AE,
MC, V* ⦿*AI.*

$$$$ ⊡**Catalonia Royal Tulum.** This lavish all-inclusive resort was designed
around the surrounding jungle. The marble-floor lobby has bamboo
furniture and a central waterfall underneath a giant palapa roof. Rooms
have pleasant wood furniture and private terraces with views of the
lush foliage. Three large pools, separated from the outdoor hot tubs
by an island of palm trees, look out onto the spectacular beach. The
food is exceptional and varied, with everything from Spanish tapas
to fruit smoothies. The hotel is in the community of Xpu-há. **Pros:**
excellent beach; great diving classes; enthusiastic staff. **Cons:** pressure
to join in activities; no kids; no elevator. ⊠ *Carretera 307, Km 264.5,
Xpu-há* ☎*984/875–1800* ⌥*288 rooms* ♿*In-room: Safe, refrigerator.
In-hotel: 4 restaurants, room service, bars, pools, gym, beachfront,
water sports, no kids under 18, laundry service, no-smoking rooms*
▤*AE, MC, V* ⦿*AI.*

$$$$ ⊡**Omni Puerto Aventuras.** Simultaneously low-key and elegant, this
resort is a great place for some serious pampering. Each room has a
sitting area, terrace, hot tub, and an ocean or pool-view. The beach is
steps away, and the pool seems to flow right into the sea. A golf course
and the marina are within walking distance. Breakfast and a newspa-
per arrive at your room every morning by way of a cubbyhole to avoid
disturbing your slumber. **Pros:** pretty beach; sushi restaurant; decent
golf course. **Cons:** food could be better; no elevator. ⊠ *Carretera 307,
Km 269.5* ☎*984/875–1950 or 800/843–6664* ⊕*www.omnihotels.com*
⌥*30 rooms* ♿*In-room: Safe, refrigerator, Wi-Fi. In-hotel: Restaurant,*

Continued on page 196

ANCIENT ARCHITECTS: THE MAYA

As well as developing a highly accurate calendar (based on their careful study of astronomy), hieroglyphic writing, and the mathematical concept of zero, the Maya were also superb architects. Looking at the remains of their ancient cities today, it's hard to believe that Maya builders erected their immense palaces and temples without the aid of metal tools, the wheel, or beasts of burden—and in terrible heat and difficult terrain. Centuries later, these feats of ceremonial architecture still have the power to dazzle.

Calakmul

Preclassic Period: PETEN ARCHITECTURE

Between approximately 2000 BC and AD 100, the Maya were centered around the lowlands in the south-central region of Guatemala. Their communities were family-based, and governed by hereditary chiefs; their worship of agricultural gods (such as Chaac, the rain god), who they believed controlled the seasons, led them to chart the movement of heavenly bodies. Their religious beliefs also led them to build enormous temples and pyramids—such as El Mirador, in the Guatemalan lowlands— where sacrifices were made and ceremonies performed to please the gods.

The structures at El Mirador, as well as at the neighboring ruin site of Tikal, were built in what is known today as the Peten style; pyramids were steeply pitched, built on stepped terraces, and decorated with large stucco masks and ornamental (but sometimes "false" or unclimbable) stairways. Peten-style structures were also often roofed with corbeled archways. The Maya began to move northward into the Yucatán during the late part of this period, which is why Peten-style buildings can also be found at Calakmul, just north of the Guatemalan border.

Early Classic Period: RÍO USUMACINTA ARCHITECTURE

The Classic Period, often referred to as the "golden age" of the Maya, spanned the years between about AD 100 and AD 1000. During this period, Maya civilization expanded northward and became much more complex. A distinct ruling class emerged, and hereditary kings began to rule over the communities—which had grown into densely populated jungle cities, filled with towering, increasingly impressive-looking palaces and temples.

During the early part of the Classic period, Maya architecture began to take on some distinctive characteristics, representative of what is now called the Río Usumacinta style. Builders placed their structures on hillsides or crests, and the principal buildings were covered with bas-reliefs carved in stone. The pyramid-top temples had vestibules and rooms with vaulted ceilings, and many chamber walls were carved with scenes recounting important events during the reign of the ruler who built the pyramid. Some of the most stunning examples of Río Usumacinta architecture that can be seen today are at the ruins of Palenque, near Chiapas.

Chicanná

Mid-Classic Period: RÍO BEC AND CHENES ARCHITECTURE

It was during the middle part of the Classic Period (roughly between AD 600 and AD 800) that the Maya presence exploded into the Yucatán Peninsula. Several Maya settlements were established in what is now Campeche state, including Chicanná and Xpujil, near the southwest corner of the state. The architecture at these sites was built in what is now known as the Río Bec style. As in the earlier Peten style, Río Bec pyramids had steeply pitched sides and ornately decorated foundations. Other Río Bec-style buildings, however, were long, one-story affairs incorporating two or sometimes three tall towers. These towers were typically capped by large roof combs that resembled mini-temples.

During the same part of the Classic Period, a different architectural style, known as Chenes, developed in some of the more northerly Maya cities, such as Hochob. While some Chenes-style structures share the same long, single-story construction as Río Bec buildings, others have strikingly different characteristics—like doorways carved in the shape of huge Chaac faces with gaping open mouths.

Late Classic Period: PUUC AND NORTHEAST YUCATÁN ARCHITECTURE

Chichén Itzá

Some of the Yucatán's most spectacular Mayan architecture was built between about AD 800 and AD 1000. By this time, the Maya had spread into territory that is now Yucatán state, and established lavish cities at Labná, Kabah, Sayil, and Uxmal—all fine examples of the Puuc architectural style. Puuc buildings were beautifully proportioned, often designed in a low-slung quadrangle shape that allowed for many rooms inside. Exterior walls were kept plain to show off the friezes above—which were embellished with stone-mosaic gods, geometric designs, and serpentine motifs. Corners were edged with gargoyle-like, curved-nose Chaac figures.

The fusion of two distinct Maya groups—the Chichén Maya and the Itzás—produced another striking architectural style. This style, known as Northeast Yucatán, is exemplified by the ruins at Chichén Itzá. Here, columns and grand colonnades were introduced. Palaces with row upon row of columns carved in the shape of serpents looked over grand patios, platforms were dedicated to the planet Venus, and pyramids were raised to honor Kukulcán (the plumed serpent god borrowed from the Toltecs, who called him Quetzalcoátl). Northeast Yucatán structures also incorporated carved stone Chacmool figures—reclining statues with offering trays carved in their midsections for sacrificial offerings.

Uxmal

▼
Between 2000 BC and AD 100, the Maya are based in lowlands of south-central Guatemala, and governed by hereditary chiefs.

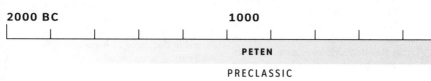

2000 BC   **1000**

PETEN

PRECLASSIC

Postclassic Period: QUINTANA ROO COAST ARCHITECTURE

Although Maya culture continued to flourish between AD 1000 and the early 1500s, signs of decline also began to take form. Wars broke out between neighboring city-states, leaving the region vulnerable when the Spaniards began invading in 1521. By 1600, the Spanish had dominated the Maya empire.

Mayan architecture enjoyed its last hurrah during this period, mostly in the region along the Yucatán's Caribbean coast. Known as Quintana Roo Coast architecture, this style can be seen today at the ruins of Tulum. Although the struc-

tures here aren't as visually arresting as those at earlier, inland sites, Tulum's location is breathtaking: it's the only major Maya city overlooking the sea.

Tulum

KEY TO ARCHITECTURE

- Peten
- Rio Usumacinta
- Rio Bec & Chenes
- Puuc & NE Yucatán
- Quintana Roo Coast

YUCATÁN

Chichén Itzá

Uxmal · Cobá

Kabah · Sayil · Labná · Tulum

Hochob · QUINTANA ROO

CAMPECHE

Xpujil · Chicanná · Calakmul

CHIAPAS

Palenque · El Mirador · Tikal

GUATEMALA · BELIZE

Caribbean Sea

▼ Maya civilization expands northward. Distinct ruling class emerges, and hereditary kings take charge.

▼ Maya settlements established on Yucatán Peninsula, including what is now Campeche State.

▼ Conflicts between city-states leave region weak when Spaniards invade. By 1600, the Spanish dominate the Maya.

100 AD — **600** — **1000** — **1600**

| RIO USUMACINTA | RIO BEC | PUUC | QUINTANA ROO COAST |

———CLASSIC——— POSTCLASSIC

room service, bars, golf course, pool, gym, beachfront, diving, parking (free), no-smoking rooms ⊟AE, MC, V ⎮◎⎮CP.

$$ 🏮**Organic Yoga.** It's all about yoga at this small beachfront hotel. Manager Leon Shlecter makes sure you're well looked-after at this relaxed property. Rooms in stand-alone bungalows are basic, with simple furniture and double beds. There's good, inexpensive food at Café del Mar on the beach morning, noon, and night. The hotel is in the nearby community of Xpu-há. **Pros:** reasonable rates; on the beach; tasty food. **Cons:** basic decor; linens are a little worn. ⊠*Carretera 307, Km 257, turn at dirt road next to Sirenis Hotel, follow signs to B&B, Xpu-há* 🕿*984/128–4260 or 984/105–8633* ⊕*www.organicyogamexico.com* ⇥*16 rooms, 4 cabanas* ⚘*In-room: No phone, refrigerator. In-hotel: Restaurant, bar, laundry service, beachfront, Wi-Fi, no-smoking rooms* ⊟*No credit cards* ⎮◎⎮CP.

NIGHTLIFE

Puerto Aventuras is lower-key than nearby Playa del Carmen. There are a few good places to have a sunset drink, but if you want to dance until the sun comes up, a quick trip to Playa is your best bet.

Gringo Dave's (⊠*On marina* 🕿*281/414–5229*) is a fun place to go for an evening drink.

SPORTS AND THE OUTDOORS

Puerto Aventuras is known for its diving and snorkeling. The reef here invites exploration. You can find tennis and golf as well. There is also a dolphin facility where you can spend some time in the water.

Aquanuts (⊠*Center Complex, by marina* 🕿*984/873–5041*) is a full-service dive shop that specializes in open-water dives, multitank dives, and certification courses. Dives start at $45 and courses at $445.

Dolphin Discovery (⊠*Mza. 23, Plano 1, Lote 11, Centro Comercial Marina Puerto Aventuras* 🕿*984/873–5954* ⊕*www.dolphindiscovery.com*) offers interactive programs with dolphins. You can also get up close and personal with manatees and sting rays. Programs start at $70 and are available daily from 9 to 11 AM and 1 to 3 PM.

EN ROUTE The Maya-owned and operated eco-park of **Cenotes Kantún Chi** has cenotes and a few beautiful underground caverns that are great for snorkeling and diving, as well as some small Mayan ruins and a botanical garden. The place is low key, so it's a nice break from the rather commercial feel of Puerto Aventuras. Bring mosquito repellent. ⊠*Carretera 307, 3 km (2 mi) south of Puerto Aventuras, Km 22 from Playa del Carmen* 🕿*984/873–0021* ⊕*www.kantunchi.com* ⌑*$39 for cenote and cave tour; $19 for access to cenote only* ⊙*Daily 9–5:30.*

AKUMAL

37 km (23 mi) south of Playa del Carmen; 104 km (65 mi) south of Cancún.

In Mayan, Akumal (pronounced ah-koo-*maal*) means "place of the turtle," and for hundreds of years this beach has been a nesting ground for turtles. The season is June through August, and the best place to see them is on Half Moon Bay. Akumal first attracted international attention in 1926, when explorers discovered the *Mantanceros*, a Spanish galleon that sank there in 1741.

Today Akumal is probably the most Americanized community on the coast. It consists of three areas: Half Moon Bay, with its pretty beaches, terrific snorkeling, and large number of rentals; Akumal proper, a large resort with a market, grocery stores, laundry facilities, and a pharmacy; and Akumal Aventuras, to the south, with more condos and homes. The original Mayan community has been moved to a planned location across the highway.

GETTING HERE AND AROUND
You can hire taxis in Cancún to go as far as Akumal, but the price is steep unless you have many passengers.

ESSENTIALS
Currency Exchange TSA Akumal (⊠ *Carrertera 307* ☏ *984/875–9030*).

EXPLORING

Fodor'sChoice
★
Aktun-Chen is Mayan for "the cave with cenote inside." These amazing underground caves, estimated to be about 5 million years old, are the area's largest. You walk through the underground passages, past stalactites and stalagmites, until you reach the cenote with its various shades of deep green. There is also a canopy tour and one cenote where you can swim. You don't want to miss this one. ⊠ *Carretera 307, Km 107* ☏ *984/109–2061* ⊕ *www.aktunchen.com* ⊠ *$24, including 1-hr tour* ⊗ *Daily 9–5.*

Xcacel (pronounced *ish*-ka-shell) is one of the few remaining nesting grounds for the endangered Atlantic green and loggerhead turtles. For years this stretch of coastline 7 km (4½ mi) south of Akumal was a federally protected zone, until it was sold—illegally—in 1998 to a Spanish conglomerate. The new owners immediately tried to railroad through an elaborate development plan that would have destroyed the turtle nesting grounds. This prompted Greenpeace, in cooperation with biologists, scientists, and locals, to fight an international campaign, which they won, to save the turtles. You can visit the turtle center or offer to volunteer there. The Friends of Xcacel Web site (⊕ *www.turtles.org/xcacel.htm*) has more information.

☾ Brought to you by the people who manage Xcaret, **Xel-Há** (pronounced shel-*hah*) is a natural aquarium made from coves, inlets, and lagoons cut from the limestone shoreline. The name means "where the water is born," and a natural spring here flows out to meet the saltwater, creating a perfect habitat for tropical marine life. There's still enough here to impress novice snorkelers, although there seem to be fewer fish each year, and the mixture of fresh and saltwater can cloud visibility.

Scattered throughout the park are small Mayan ruins, including Na Balaam, known for a yellow jaguar painted on one of its walls. Low wooden bridges over the lagoons allow for leisurely walks around the park, and there are spots to rest or swim.

Xel-Ha gets overwhelmingly crowded, so come early. The grounds are well equipped with bathrooms, restaurants, and a shop. At the entrance you will receive specially prepared sunscreen that won't kill the fish;

other sunscreens are prohibited. For an extra charge, you can "interact" (not swim) with dolphins. There's also an all-inclusive package with a meal, a towel, a locker, and snorkel equipment for $75. Other activities like scuba diving, and an underwater walk, are available at an additional cost and should be reserved at least a day in advance. ☎984/875–6000, 998/884–7165, or 800/009–3542 ⊕ *www.xelha. com* ☽ *Daily 8:30–6.*

Devoted snorkelers may want to walk the unmarked dirt road to **Yalkú,** a couple of miles north of Akumal in Half Moon Bay. A series of small lagoons that gradually reach the ocean, Yalkú is an ecopark that's home to schools of parrot fish in superbly clear water with visibility to 160 feet. The entrance fee is about $7.50. You can rent snorkeling equipment in the parking lot for $10 and a locker for $2. The park is open daily 8 to 5:30.

WORD OF MOUTH

"I absolutely love Akumal, although it can be crowded at times. They have great restaurants, bars and shops all within walking distance and it's just a great friendly atmosphere. I was there about a month ago and it was much more crowded than it was in previous trips, so I guess it's becoming a lot more popular, but who can blame people for that?"

—ewesthoff

WHERE TO EAT

$$$ ✕ **La Cueva del Pescador.** Dig your toes in the sand floor at this simple res-
SEAFOOD   taurant and enjoy the catch of the day. Their *ceviche,* a mix of shrimp, octopus, and fish "cooked" with lime juice and flavored with cilantro, is one of the best around because the ingredients are so fresh. All the servings are generous, so a soup and an entrée might be perfect for two. If you really have a big appetite, try the seafood medley of lobster, octopus, and shrimp. ⊠ *Half Moon Bay Rd, at plaza* ☎984/875–9002 ▤ *No credit cards.*

$$–$$$ ✕ **Que Onda.** A Swiss-Italian couple created this northern Italian res-
ITALIAN   taurant at the end of Half Moon Bay. Dishes are served under a palapa and include great homemade pastas, shrimp flambéed in cognac with a touch of saffron, and vegetarian lasagna. Que Onda also has a neighboring seven-room hotel that's creatively furnished with Mexican and Guatemalan handicrafts. ⊠ *Caleta Yalkú, Lotes 97–99; enter through Club Akumal Caribe, turn left, and go north to end of road at Half Moon Bay* ☎984/875–9101 ▤ *MC, V* ☽ *Closed Tues.*

¢–$ ✕ **Turtle Bay Café & Bakery.** This funky café has delicious (and healthy)
CAFÉ   breakfasts, lunches, and dinners; the smoothies, homemade ice cream, and fresh baked goods are especially yummy. It has a garden where you can sit and drink coffee, and its location by the ecological center makes it the closest thing Akumal has to a downtown. ⊠ *Half Moon Bay Rd., at Plaza* ☎984/875–9138 ▤ *MC, V.*

WHERE TO STAY

$$ ▦ **Casa Carolina.** This small hotel is a great place stay if you want to dive, snorkel, kayak, or just relax in one of the hammocks. Bob Villier and Caroline Wexler are gracious hosts. Rooms are spacious and decorated simply with colorful tiles and hand-woven blankets.

Each has a kitchenette, though you don't have to worry about breakfast since it's included in the room rate. **Pros:** on a nice beach, diving lessons available. **Cons:** no restaurant, no air-conditioning. ⊠*Carretera Mahahual-Xcalak, Km 48* ☎*610/616–3862 in U.S.* ⊕*www.casacarolina.net* ⤢*4 rooms* ⚪*In-room: No a/c. In-hotel: Beachfront, no-smoking rooms* ⊟*No credit cards* ⦿*CP.*

$$–$$$ 🖫**Club Akumal Caribe & Villas Maya.** Back in the 1960s, Pablo Bush Romero established this resort as a

WORD OF MOUTH

"The Club Akumal Caribe is a small gem. Much of the Mayan Rivera is lined with large, all-inclusive hotels. Akumal has not been developed in the same way. Besides the Caribe, there are a few other small hotels and several condos. We loved the bungalow—private and quiet even though it was steps from the beach and restaurant."   –justretired

place for his diving buddies to crash. It still has pleasant accommodations and a congenial staff. Rooms have rattan furniture and ocean views. The bungalows are surrounded by gardens and have lots of beautiful Mexican tiles. The one-, two-, and three-bedroom villas are on Half Moon Bay. If you want the babysitting service, ask about it when you book your room. **Pros:** reasonable rates; on the beach; easy snorkeling. **Cons:** basic decor; sometimes a bit noisy; no elevator. ⊠*Carretera 307, Km 104* ☎*984/875–9012, 800/351–1622 in U.S.* ⊕*www.hotelakumalcaribe.com* ⤢*22 rooms, 40 bungalows, 4 villas, 1 condo* ⚪*In-room: Kitchen (some), refrigerator, no TV (some), Wi-Fi. In-hotel: 3 restaurants, bar, pool, beachfront, diving, no-smoking rooms* ⊟*AE, MC, V* ⦿*EP.*

$$$$ 🖫**Gran Bahía Príncipe.** This all-inclusive is one of the best in the area. Rooms are spacious and decorated in bright colors. Most offer ocean views. Junior suites also have private hot tubs. As with many all-inclusives, there are several buffet eateries and an à la carte restaurant. The difference here is that food is tasty in all of them. There is also a little market area, disco, spa, and gym. **Pros:** on the beach; attentive staff; good food. **Cons:** beach is rocky. ⊠*Carrertera Chetumal-Akumal, Km 250* ☎*984/875–5000, 866/282–2442 in U.S.* ⊕*www.bahiaprincipeusa.com* ⤢*72 rooms, 360 suites* ⚪*In-room: Safe, refrigerator, Wi-Fi. In-hotel: 4 restaurants, bars, pools, spa, beachfront, water sports* ⊟*AE, MC, V* ⦿*AI.*

$$ 🖫**Vista Del Mar.** Each small room in the main building here has an ocean view, a private terrace, and colorful Guatemalan-Mexican accents. Next door are more expensive condos with Spanish-colonial touches. The spacious one-, two-, and three-bedroom units have full kitchens, living and dining rooms, and oceanfront balconies. **Pros:** on beach; great ocean views; well-kept grounds. **Cons:** beach is a little rocky; beds aren't very comfortable. ⊠*Carretera 307, Km 104, at south end of Half Moon Bay* ☎*984/875–9060* ⊕*www.akumalinfo.com* ⤢*16 rooms, 14 condos* ⚪*In-room: No phone, kitchen (some), refrigerator. In-hotel: Restaurant, pool, beachfront, diving, Wi-Fi, no-smoking rooms* ⊟*MC, V.*

SHOPPING

Galería Lamanai Carribean Arts & Crafts (✉*Carrertera 307, Km 104* ☎*984/875–9055*) is a laid-back gallery under a palapa roof. There's a real mix of folk art and fine art from Mexican and international artists.

Mexicarte (✉*Carrertera 307* ☎*984/875–9115*) is a little shop that sells high-quality crafts from around the country.

SPORTS AND THE OUTDOORS

★ The **Akumal Dive Center** (✉*About 10 min north of Club Akumal Caribe* ☎*984/875–9025* ⊕*www.akumaldivecenter.com*) is the area's oldest and most experienced dive operation, offering reef or cenote diving, fishing, and snorkeling. Dives cost from $36 (one tank) to $120 (four tanks); a three-hour fishing trip for up to four people runs $150. Take a sharp right at the Akumal arches and you'll see the dive shop on the beach.

TSA Travel Agency and Bike Rental (✉*Carretera 307, Km 104, next to Ecology Center* ☎*984/875–9030* ⊕*www.akumaltravel.com*) rents bikes for a 3½-hour jungle-biking adventure. The cost is $45 per person.

EN ROUTE

Hidden Worlds Cenotes Park. This park was made semi-famous when it was featured in a 2002 IMAX film, *Journey into Amazing Caves,* which was shown at theaters across North America. The park, which was founded by Florida native Buddy Quattlebaum in 1998, contains some of the Yucatán's most spectacular cenotes. You can explore these startlingly clear freshwater sinkholes, which are full of fantastic stalactites, stalagmites, and rock formations, on guided diving or snorkeling tours. To get to the cenotes, you ride in a jungle buggy through dense tropical forest from the main park entrance. You can also ride the skycycle, a cable bicycle that glides over the abundant Mayan rain forest. Prices start at $25 for snorkeling tours ($20 for children) and go up to $100 for diving tours. Canopying on the 600-foot zip-line will set you back $10. Be sure to bring your bug spray. ✉*1.5 km (0.9 mi) south of Xel-Há on Carretera 307* ☎*984/115–4514 or 984/120–1977* ⊕*www.hiddenworlds.com* ☉*Mon.–Sat. 9–5; snorkeling tours between 9 and 3, and diving tours at 9 and 1.*

TULUM

Fodor'sChoice
★
🔺
61 km (38 mi) southwest of Playa del Carmen.

Tulum, which means "wall" in Mayan, is a quickly growing town built near the spectacular ruins that draw most visitors here. But its charm extends past the famous ruins: pristine beaches, $10 cabanas, and open-air markets explain the town's increasing popularity with travelers. The town is divided into three main sections: the archaeological site, the *pueblo* (town), and the *zona hotelera* (hotel zone).

The Tulum site itself is the Yucatán Peninsula's most-visited Mayan ruin, attracting more than 2 million people annually. Though most of the architecture is of unremarkable post classic (1000–1521) style, the amount of attention that Tulum receives is not entirely undeserved. Its location—on a beach known for its sugar-white sand, by the blue-green Caribbean—is breathtaking.

Carretera 307, the main thoroughfare, runs through the pueblo and is lined with dozens of food stalls, souvenir shops, budget hotels, and nightlife spots. If you stay in this part of town, you'll be close to the ruins, though you'll sacrifice a beach view. You can walk the 1 mi to the park entrance, or catch one of the shuttles that pass every few minutes.

A mile east of Carretera 307 you'll find the more relaxed zona hotelera,a string of rustic cabanas, colorful cafés, and palapa boutiques line the beach. This secluded area is growing rapidly and now has Internet cafés, organic restaurants, luxury accommodations, and holistic centers and spas. A number of eco-resorts, which rely on wind turbines, solar renewable energy, recycled water, generators, and/or candlelight, have sprung up along Tulum's coastline. Beaches south of the hotel zonetend to be less rocky and more secluded than the northern beaches, although it is almost impossible to find a bad stretch of sand in Tulum.

Buses do not serve the hotel zone, so travelers must rely on taxis, cars, or bikes to get around. Although the area is generally safe, walking around at night is not recommended because there are no sidewalks or streetlamps in this part of town. If you plan on driving, watch carefully for the large beach crabs that cross the roads after dark.

GETTING HERE AND AROUND
Off Careterra 307, Tulum is a 10-minute drive from Akumal and a 45-minute drive from Playa del Carmen. You can hire taxis in Cancún to go as far as Tulum, but the price is approximately $75 unless you have many passengers.

ESSENTIALS
Currency Exchange Asesores Turísticos Cambiarios del Caribe (*Av. Tulum s/n Pueblo Tulum* ☎ *984/871–2078*).

Internet El Point (⊠ *Avs. Tulum and Alfa* ☎ *984/877–3044*).

Mail and Shipping Main Post Office (⊠ *Av. Tulum and Satelite* ☎ *984/871–2001*).

EXPLORING
Tulum is one of the few Mayan cities known to have been inhabited when the conquistadores arrived in 1518. In the 16th century it functioned as a safe harbor for trade goods from rival Mayan factions; it was considered neutral territory, where merchandise could be stored and traded in peace. The city reached its height when traders, made wealthy through the exchange of goods, for the first time outranked Mayan priests in authority and power. When the Spaniards arrived, they forbade the Mayan traders to sail the seas, and commerce among the Maya died.

Tulum has long held special significance for the Maya. A key city in the League of Mayapán (AD 987–1194), it was never conquered by the Spaniards, although it was abandoned about 75 years after the conquest. For 300 years thereafter it symbolized the defiance of an otherwise subjugated people; it was one of the last outposts of the Maya during their insurrection against Mexican rule in the War of the Castes, which began in 1846. Uprisings continued intermittently until 1935, when the Maya ceded Tulum to the Mexican government.

■TIP➔At the entrance to the ruins you can hire a guide for $25, but keep in mind that some of their information is more entertainment than historical accuracy. (Disregard that stuff about virgin sacrifices atop the altars.) Although you can see the ruins in two hours, you might want to allow extra time for a swim or a stroll on the beach.

The first significant structure is the two-story **Templo de los Frescos,** to the left of the entryway. The temple's vault roof and corbel arch are examples of classic Mayan architecture. Faint traces of blue-green frescoes outlined in black on the inner and outer walls refer to ancient Mayan beliefs (the clearest frescoes are hidden from sight now that you aren't allowed to enter the temple). Reminiscent of the Mixtec style, the frescoes depict the three worlds of the Maya and their major deities, and are decorated with stellar and serpentine patterns, rosettes, and ears of maize and other offerings to the gods. One scene portrays the rain god seated on a four-legged animal—probably a reference to the Spaniards on their horses.

The largest and most famous building, the **Castillo** (Castle), looms at the edge of a 40-foot limestone cliff just past the Temple of the Frescoes. Atop it, at the end of a broad stairway, is a temple with stucco ornamentation on the outside and traces of fine frescoes inside the two chambers. (The stairway has been roped off, so the top temple is inaccessible.) The front wall of the Castillo has faint carvings of the Descending God and columns depicting the plumed serpent god, Kukulcán, who was introduced to the Maya by the Toltecs. To the left of the Castillo is the **Templo del Díos Descendente**—so called for the carving of a winged god plummeting to earth over the doorway.

A few small altars sit atop a hill at the north side of the cove with a good view of the Castillo and the sea. ✉ *Carretera 307, Km 133, Tulum* 🕾 *983/837–2411* 🖅 *$5 entrance, $3 parking, $3 video fee, $1 shuttle from parking to ruins* ☉ *Daily 8–5.*

WHERE TO EAT

$ ╳**Charlie's.** This eatery is a happening spot where local children display
MEXICAN their artwork. Wall murals are made from empty wine bottles, and painted chili peppers adorn the dining tables. There's a charming garden in back with a stage for live salsa and rock. The chicken tacos and black-bean soup are especially good here, and the *chili rellenos* are a house favorite. Attached to the restaurant is a wonderful boutique selling jewelry, clothing, and souvenirs. ✉ *Avs. Tulum and Jupiter, next to bus station, downtown* 🕾 *984/871–2573* 🖃 *MC, V* ☉ *Closed Mon.*

$$ ╳**El Pequeño Buenos Aires.** Owner and chef Sergio Patrone serves deli-
ARGENTINE cious *parrilladas* (a mixed grill made with marinated chicken, beef, and pork) at this Argentine-inspired restaurant. There are excellent empanadas as well as a nice selection of wines. If you have a sweet tooth, be sure to try the trilogy chocolate cake. White tablecloths add a sophisticated touch, even though you're eating under a palapa roof. ✉ *Av. Tulum 42, downtown* 🕾 *984/871–2708* 🖃 *MC, V.*

$$–$$$ ╳**Ginger.** With its red walls, exotic menu, martini bar, and metropoli-
ECLECTIC tan vibe, this chic restaurant has taken Tulum dining to a whole new
Fodor'sChoice level. Flavorful starters include tropical ceviche, goat cheese tart, and
★ spinach salad with camembert and green apple. Select from entrées like

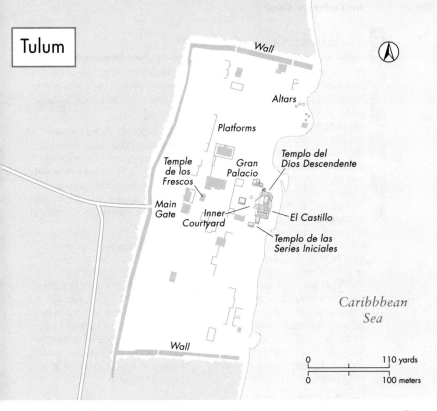

Tulum

Wall

Altars

Platforms

Temple de los Frescos

Gran Palacio

Templo del Dios Descendente

Main Gate

Inner Courtyard

El Castillo

Templo de las Series Iniciales

Caribbbean Sea

Wall

| 0 | | 110 yards |
| 0 | | 100 meters |

the coconut-crusted salmon with mango ginger sauce or grouper filet topped with passion fruit. Save room for the sweet fruit flambé and vanilla ice-cream. This is a great spot to relax with a martini, listen to chill-out music and meets some locals. ⊠ *Av. Polar Ponignte between Satelite and Centauro, downtown Tulum* ☎ *984/116–4033* ▭ *No credit cards* ⊗ *Closed Tues., no lunch.*

$$–$$$ ╳ **La Vita e Bella.** Italian tourists travel miles out of their way to eat
ITALIAN at this utterly rustic, authentically Italian place, where wooden tables and chairs are set on a sandy floor. Overhead is a DJ hut where blues, jazz and salsa are played nightly. The menu offers 6 pasta dishes, and 14 types of pizza prepared in a brick oven with toppings like squid, lobster, and Italian sausage. There are wine, beer, and margaritas to sip with your supper. Save room for the tiramisu and chocolate crepes— they are heavenly. ⊠ *Carretera Tulum Ruinas, Km 1.5, Zona Hotelera* ☎ *984/877–8145* ▭ *No credit cards.*

$ ╳ **Taqueria el Mariachi.** For traditional Mexican food, this eatery fits the
MEXICAN bill. The fajitalike *arracheras* (grilled beef or pork with onions, bell peppers, and tomatoes) is also a winner. ⊠ *Avs. Tulum and Orion, downtown* ☎ *984/106–2032* ▭ *No credit cards.*

$–$$ ╳ **Trece Lunas.** Early birds can start their day with a power breakfast at
CAFÉ this Zen-inspired coffee house. The cheese omelet, served with grilled vegetables and seven-grain bread, is sure to satisfy any appetite. Late

Caribbean Coastal History

The Mayan culture is the enduring backdrop for Mexico's Caribbean coast. Archaeologists have divided this civilization, which lasted some 3,000 years, into three main periods: preclassic and late preclassic (2000 BC–AD 100, together), classic (AD 100–1000), and postclassic (AD 1000–1521). Considered the most advanced civilization in the ancient Americas, the Maya are credited with several major breakthroughs: a highly accurate calendar based on astronomical study; the mathematical concept of zero; hieroglyphic writing; and extraordinary ceremonial architecture. Although the Maya's early days were centered around the lowlands in the south-central region of Guatemala, Mayan culture spread north to the Yucatán Peninsula sometime around AD 987. Tulum, which was built during this period, is the only ancient Mayan city constructed right on the water.

Until the 1960s, Quintana Roo (a Mexican territory, not a state) was considered the most savage coast in Central America. The Caste Wars of the Yucatán, which began in 1847 and ended with a half-hearted truce in 1935, herded hardy Maya to this remote region. With the exception of *chicleros*, (men who tapped *zapote* or chicle trees for the Wrigley

Chewing Gum Corporation), few non-Maya roamed here. Whites and *mestizos* were unwelcome because it was not safe.

By the 1950s the Mexican government began giving tracts of land to the *chicleros* in hopes of colonizing Quintana Roo. At that time there were no roads. A few *cocals*, or coconut plantations, were scattered throughout the peninsula, headed by a handful of Mayan families.

In 1967 the Mexican government sought a location for an international tourist destination with the finest beaches, the most beautiful water, and the fewest hurricanes. A stretch of unpopulated sand at the northeast tip of the Yucatán Peninsula fit the bill. Soon after identifying Cancún as the fortunate winner, that locale, Quintana Roo became Mexico's 31st state.

The 1980s saw an initial surge in tourism with the advent of the Riviera Maya in 2000, this 96-km (60-mi) region stretching south from Puerto Morelos to Tulum developed into one of the world's most popular beach destinations, with Playa del Carmen the fastest growing city in Latin America.

rises can enjoy the lunch or dinner menu comprised of fish, chicken, and beef. There is also a wide selection of vegetarian dishes such as the Caribbean Salad prepared with mango and coconut dressing. Coffee is served all day. Check out the attached gift shop, which sells selling organic soaps, incense, and handmade journals. ⊠ *Carretera Tulum—Boca Paila, Km 3.5, Zona Hotelera* ☎*984/115–5122* ⊟*No credit cards.*

WHERE TO STAY

$$$$ ⚷ **Azulik Eco-Resort.** Billed as a high-end barefoot resort, Azulik will soothe your senses. The charming hardwood villas are perched right at the ocean's edge; each has a private deck on the ocean side and floor-to-ceiling windows on the jungle side (with bamboo curtains when privacy

is needed). There is no electricity here, so guests must rely on romantic candlelight to get around after dark. Hand-carved soaking tubs made from hollowed out tree trunks add a natural feeling to this tropical paradise. Insect repellant is a must. Note that though you'll give a credit card number when you reserve your room, you must pay in cash. **Pros:** spacious rooms; relaxing atmosphere. **Cons:** not family-friendly; hard beds; jungle setting attracts mosquitoes. ☒*Carretera Tulum Ruinas, Km 5, Zona Hotelera* ☎*01800/123–3278 in Mexico, 888/898–9922 in U.S.* ⊕*www.azulik.com* ➵*15 villas* ♿*In-room: No a/c, no phone, no TV. In-hotel: Spa, beachfront, no kids under 18, no-smoking rooms* ▭*No credit cards* ⊙*EP.*

$$ 　▦**Cabañas Copal.** The smell of incense wafts through the grounds of this hippy-esque eco-hotel where guests can choose to rough it or stay in relative luxury. Dirt or cement floor cabanas are sheltered from the elements by mosquito nets and thatch roofs; some have shared baths (¢), and there's no electricity. The rooms in the central building are bigger and more elegant, with hardwood floors, hand-carved furniture, and a kind of primitive whirlpool bath. At night thousands of candles light the meandering pathways; by day, local artists set up tables to sell their crafts. A variety of wellness and exercise programs are available, including yoga and dream classes, and the spa offers Mayan massage, among other treatments. **Pros:** on the beach; eco-friendly; clothing optional. **Cons:** clothing optional; showers use salt water; some cabañas share bathrooms. ☒*Carretera Tulum Ruinas, Km 5, turn right at fork in highway; hotel is less than 1 km (½ mi) on right, Zona Hotelera* ☎*984/8079–5164* ⊕*www.cabanascopal.com* ➵*47 rooms* ♿*In-room: No a/c, no phone, no TV. In-hotel: Restaurant, bar, beachfront, water sports, Wi-Fi, no elevator, no-smoking rooms* ▭*MC, V* ⊙*EP.*

$$$$ 　▦**Eurostars Blue Tulum.** From the lush tropical plants and crashing waterfall at the hotel entrance to the gorgeous rooms with private hot tubs, this all-inclusive offers luxury and relaxation everywhere you look. There are nearly 100 rooms, but the hotel is divided into smaller buildings that give it a very personal atmosphere. Rooms are spacious and have high-tech touches like flat-screen TVs, iPod docks, DVD players, and a selection of DVDs (just fill out the request form). The restaurants feature international chefs who will prepare whatever suits you, whether or not it is on the menu. The staff is happy to provide different kinds of pillows and bath products upon request. **Pros:** incredible service and attention to detail; beautiful grounds. **Cons:** not on beach; no elevator. ☒*Carretera Tulum Ruinas, Lote 47* ☎*984/871–1000* ⊕*www.eurostarshotels.com* ➵*96 rooms* ♿*In-room: Safe, refrigerator, DVD, Wi-Fi. In-hotel: 3 restaurants, bar, room service, Wi-Fi, pool, spa, gym, beachfront, laundry service, water sports, no-smoking rooms* ▭*AE, MC, V* ⊙*CP, AI.*

Fodor's Choice
★

$$$ 　▦**La Vita e Bella Beachfront Bungalows.** Perched on sand dunes above the sea, this small Italian resort has lodgings that are rustic but also very comfortable. The 10 roomy bungalows have wooden floors, palapa roofs, balconies with hammocks, and wide ocean views; most have queen-size beds. Smaller, less expensive cement-floored cabanas are also available—they're set farther away from the beach but are

near the sandy-floored restaurant. **Pros:** beautiful beach; laid-back atmosphere; nice restaurant. **Cons:** electricity is limited; mosquitoes at dusk; cash only. ⊠ *Carretera Tulum Ruinas, Km 1.5, Zona Hotelera* ☎ *www.lavitae-bella-tulum.com* ⤳ *10 bungalows, 10 cabanas* ⊘ *In-room: No a/c, no phone. In-hotel: Restaurant, bar, water sports, no-smoking rooms* ⊟ *No credit cards* ◉ *EP.*

WORD OF MOUTH

"We stayed in Tulum last February and snorkeled a couple of cenotes and then took a boat out to the reef off of Half Moon Bay in Akumal. Great snorkeling."   –jaleha

$$$ ★ **Las Ranitas.** Built for ecological sustainability, Las Ranitas (the Little Frogs) generates its own electricity through wind-powered generators and solar panels. Each chic and very private room has gorgeous tile and fabric from Oaxaca. Terraces overlook gardens and ocean, and jungle walkways lead to the breathtaking beach. The pièce de résistance is the on-site restaurant's French chef, who whips up tasty French and Mexican cuisine. There is a library where guests can borrow or exchange books in five languages. Yoga classes are also available. **Pros:** on beach; attractive rooms; lots of privacy. **Cons:** a bit pricey for what you get; inconsistent service. ⊠ *Carretera Tulum–Boca Paila, Km 9; last hotel before Reserva de la Biosfera Sian Ka'an, Zona Hotelera* ☎ *984/877–8554* ☎ *www.lasranitas.com* ⤳ *18 rooms, 5 suites* ⊘ *In-room: No a/c, no phone, no TV. In-hotel: Restaurant, pool, beachfront, tennis courts, water sports, Wi-Fi, no-smoking rooms* ⊟ *No credit cards* ◉ *CP.*

$$$ **Mezzanine.** Music lovers will enjoy this small, hip hotel where DJs mix lounge and house music on the patio. On Friday evenings this is the place to be, as guest musicians entertain until 2 AM. Each of the four attractive suites, decorated with dark modern furniture and splashes of bright color, offers an ocean view. The other rooms are on the ground floor and are pleasant but have no view. There's Wi-Fi access in the restaurant and lounge. **Pros:** tasty food; helpful staff; two-for-one margaritas daily from 1 to 4. **Cons:** pool area gets crowded; some rooms lack view; noisy on weekends. ⊠ *Carretera Tulum–Boca Paila, Km 1.5, Zona Hotelera* ☎ *984/131–1596* ☎ *www.mezzanine.com.mx* ⤳ *9 rooms* ⊘ *In-room: No a/c, no phone, safe. In-hotel: Restaurant, bar, pool, beachfront, bicycles, Wi-Fi, no-smoking rooms* ⊟ *MC, V* ◉ *EP.*

$$$ **Fodor's**Choice ★ **Ocho Tulum.** This is one of the few eco-friendly resorts that can guarantee hot water and 24-hour electricity. Wind turbines and solar panels power the resorts 22 cabanas, which are built from locally-sourced materials and have ceiling fans, mosquito nets, and private terraces with ocean views. Stone bathrooms have duel showerheads and come with citrus bath soaps and tote bags you can take to the beach. The hotel offers beach beds for sunning, kayaks, and kiteboarding lessons. The palapa restaurant serves delicious Mexican and Caribbean cuisine. A yoga center and a luxurious spa are recent additions. **Pros:** attentive staff; environmentally conscious; incredible restaurant; family-friendly. **Cons:** periodic sound of wind turbines can be annoying; two roaming

dogs may bother some guests. ⊠ *Carretera Tulum-Boca Paila, Km 8, Tulum, Zona Hotelera* ☎ *998/282–8399* ⊕ *www.ochotulum.com* ➾ *22 rooms* ⌂ *In-room: No a/c, no TV, no phone. In-hotel: Restaurant, bar, room service, beachfront, water sports, spa, Wi-Fi, parking, no-smoking rooms* ☐ *MC, V* |O| *CP.*

$$$ 🏨**Tierras Del Sol.** Situated on a long, secluded beach, this charming resort has eight cabanas, each with a private balcony and ocean view. The colorful rooms are decorated with local artwork and furnishings such as Mexican blankets, macramé chairs, and handmade hammocks. A stone pathway meanders through the jungle setting, past a small bar and library, before spilling onto a brilliantly white beach. The palapa restaurant serves traditional Mexican and international dishes. Pros: reliable electricity; peaceful atmosphere; rooms sleep three people. Cons: jungle setting attracts iguanas and mosquitoes; waves can get rough on windy days. ⊠ *Carretera Tulum–Boca Paila Km 10, Tulum, Zona hotelera* ☎ *984/807–9387* ⊕ *www.tierrasdelsol.com* ➾ *8 rooms* ⌂ *In-hotel: Restaurant, bar, parking, laundry service, beachfront, water sports, Wi-Fi, no-smoking rooms* ☐ *No credit cards* |O| *EP.*

¢ 🏨**Weary Traveler Hostel, Cafe and Bar.** Tulum is backpacker central, and if you're roughing it, this is one of the cheapest, most convenient spots to hang your hat. Most rooms are shared, with either bunk or twin beds and a private bath. Furnishings are basic but neat. You have use of a communal television, pool table, and kitchen, and there are picnic tables in a central area for eating and meeting. A simple but plentiful breakfast is included in the price of the room. There's also a cheap Internet café, and the bus station is one block away. The staff can organize snorkeling tours upon request. **Pros:** reasonable rates; friendly atmosphere; great location. **Cons:** rustic furniture; noise from bar. ⊠ *Av. Tulum, between Avs. Jupiter and Acuario, downtown* ☎ *984/871–2390* ➾ *20 rooms, 66 beds* ⌂ *In-room: No a/c (some), no phone, kitchen, no TV. In-hotel: Restaurant, bar, Internet terminal, no-smoking rooms* ☐ *No credit cards* |O| *BP.*

$$–$$$ 🏨**Zamas.** On the wild, isolated *Punta Piedra* (Rock Point), this hotel has ocean views as far as the eye can see. The romantically rustic cabañas— with mosquito nets over comfortable beds, spacious, tile bathrooms, and bright Mexican colors—are nicely distanced from one another. The restaurant, one of the area's best, has an eclectic Italian-Mexican-Yucatecan menu. **Pros:** great restaurant; unspoiled views. **Cons:** rocky beach; on noisy street; no elevator. ⊠ *Carretera Tulum–Boca Paila, Km 5, Zona Hotelera* ☎ *984/877–8523, 415/387–9806 in U.S.* ⊕ *www.zamas.com* ➾ *24 cabanas* ⌂ *In-room: No a/c, no phone, safe. In-hotel: Restaurant, bar, beachfront, Wi-Fi, water sports, no-smoking rooms* ☐ *AE, MC, V* |O| *EP.*

SPORTS AND THE OUTDOORS

Punta Piedra Bike Rental (⊠ *Carretera Tulum–Boca paila, Km 4, Tulum, Zona Hotelera* ☎ *984/116–4296* ☉ *Daily 7:30–7*) is a small shack that rents equipment by the day; boogie boards cost 5, bikes are 8, and snorkel gear is 5. The owner, Felix, can also organize two-hour snorkeling tours for 25. Cash only. **Volis-Nah Kite School** (⊠ *Carretera Tulum–Coba, Km 2, Tulum, downtown* ☎ *984/130–1596 or 984/745–4555* ⊕ *www.*

extremecontrol.net) offers four-hour kitesurfing lessons and equipment for $190. Led by IKO Instructor, Marco Cristofanelli, courses take place at Tulum's El Paraiso Beach and must be booked 24-hours in advance. Those who stay at Kite Hotel "Volis Nah" receive a 10% discount on kitesurfing courses. To get here, exit Carretera 307 at Km 2 and head west on the road towards Coba. Volis-Nah is on the left just beyond the intersection, next to Super Sanfrancisco Market. The school's hours literally change with the wind, so call ahead to be sure they're open.

COBÁ

Fodor's Choice
★
⚠︎

50 km (31 mi) northwest of Tulum.

Mayan for "water stirred by the wind," **Cobá** flourished from AD 800 to 1100, with a population of as many as 55,000. Now it stands in solitude, and the jungle has overgrown many of its buildings. ■ TIP➔**Cobá is often overlooked by visitors who opt for better-known Tulum. This site is less crowded, giving you a chance to immerse yourself in ancient culture. Cobá is open daily from 8 to 5, and costs $4.50 to enter.** Cobá exudes stillness, the silence broken only by the occasional shriek of a spider monkey or the call of a bird. Processions of huge army ants cross the footpaths as the sun slips through openings between the tall hardwood trees, ferns, and giant palms.

Near five lakes and between coastal watchtowers and inland cities, Cobá (pronounced ko-*bah*) exercised economic control over the region through a network of at least 16 *sacbéob* (white-stone roads), one of which measures 100 km (62 mi) and is the longest in the Mayan world. The city once covered 70 square km (27 square mi), making it a noteworthy sister state to Tikal in northern Guatemala, with which it had close cultural and commercial ties. It is noted for its massive temple-pyramids, one of which is 138 feet tall, the largest and highest in northern Yucatán. The main groupings of ruins are separated by several miles of dense vegetation, so the best way to get a sense of the immensity of the city is to scale one of the pyramids. ■ TIP➔**It's easy to get lost here, so stay on the main road.** Don't be tempted by the narrow paths that lead into the jungle unless you have a qualified guide with you.

The first major cluster of structures, to your right as you enter the ruins, is the **Cobá Group,** whose pyramids are around a sunken patio. At the near end of the group, facing a large plaza, is the 79-foot-high temple, which was dedicated to the rain god, Chaac. Some Mayans still place offerings and light candles here in hopes of improving their harvests. Around the rear, to the left, is a restored ball court, where a sacred game was once played to petition the gods for rain, fertility, and other blessings.

Farther along the main path to your left is the **Chumuc Mul Group,** little of which has been excavated. The principal pyramid here is covered with the remains of vibrantly painted stucco motifs (*chumuc mul* means "stucco pyramid"). A kilometer (½ mi) past this site is the **Nohoch Mul Group** (Large Hill Group), the highlight of which is the pyramid of the same name, the tallest at Cobá. It has 120 steps—equivalent to 12 stories—and shares a plaza with Temple 10. The Descending

God (also seen at Tulum) is depicted on a facade of the temple atop
Nohoch Mul, from which the view
is excellent.

Beyond the Nohoch Mul Group is
the **Castillo,** with nine chambers
that are reached by a stairway.
To the south are the remains of a
ball court, including the stone ring
through which the ball was hurled.
From the main route, follow the
sign to **Las Pinturas Group,** named
for the still-discernible polychrome
friezes on the inner and outer walls
of its large, patioed pyramid. An
enormous stela here depicts a man standing with his feet on two prone
captives. Take the minor path for 1 km (½ mi) to the Macanxoc Group,
not far from the lake of the same name. The main pyramid at Macanxoc
is accessible by a stairway.

WORD OF MOUTH

"At Cobá you can rent bikes and
ride to all the ruins, which is very
fun. We have been twice and
once you get away from the main
areas, you feel like you are in the
jungle all alone. Cobá is also next
a lake full of crocodiles and you
can eat at a really good restaurant located across the street and
watch the crocs swim around."
—Suru11

GETTING HERE AND AROUND

Cobá is a 45-minute drive northwest of the city of Tankah, where most
of the accommodations are located, along a road that leads straight
through the jungle. Buses depart to and from Cobá for Playa del Carmen and Tulum at least twice daily. Taxis from Tulum are about $20.

**OFF THE
BEATEN
PATH**

Pac Chen is a Maya jungle settlement of 125 people who still live in
round thatch huts. There's no electricity or indoor plumbing, and the
roads aren't paved. The inhabitants, who primarily make their living
farming pineapple, beans, and plantains, still pray to the gods for good
crops.

■ **TIP→** You can only visit Pac Chen (pronounced "*pak chin*") on trips organized by Alltournative, an eco-tour company based in Playa del Carmen. The
unusual, soft-adventure experience is definitely worth your while. Alltournative pays the villagers by the number of tourists it brings in, though
no more than 80 people are allowed to visit on any given day. This
money has made the village self-sustaining, and has given the people
an alternative to logging and hunting, which were their main means of
livelihood before.

The half-day tour starts with a trek through the jungle to a cenote where
you grab onto a harness and Z-line to the other side. Next is the Jaguar cenote, set deeper into the forest, where you must rappel down the
cavelike sides into a cool underground lagoon. You'll eat lunch under
an open-air palapa overlooking another lagoon, where canoes await.
The food includes such Mayan dishes as grilled *achiote* (annatto seed)
chicken, fresh tortillas, beans, and watermelon.

WHERE TO EAT

¢–$

MEXICAN

✕**El Bocadito.** The restaurant closest to the Cobá ruins is run by a gracious Mayan family that serves simple, traditional cuisine. A three-
course fixed-price lunch costs $6. Look for such classic dishes as *pollo
pibíl* and *cochinita pibíl*. There are also a few bare-bones rooms for

$10 a night for those who want to stay close to the ruins. ⊠ *On road to Cobá ruins, ½ km from ruin-site entrance* ☎985/852–0052 ⊟No *credit cards* ⊘*No dinner.*

$$$ ✕**Restaurante Oscar y Lalo.** A couple of miles outside Tankah, alone
ECLECTIC on Carretera 307, sits this wonderful palapa restaurant with a pebble floor and a peaceful garden. The seafood is excellent here, although a bit pricey; Lalo's Special, a dish made with local lobster, shrimp, conch, and fish, and the chicken fajitas, prepared for two to 10 people, are standouts. The ceviche made of fresh fish, lobster, and caracol with citrus juice is also exceptional. ⊠ *Carretera 307 at Km 3 from Xel-Ha, look for large billboard and Mayan sculptures* ☎984/115–9965 or 984/807–2919 ⊟MC, V.

WHERE TO STAY

If you plan on staying in the area, nearby Tankah is your best option. In ancient times Tankah was an important Mayan trading city. Over the past few centuries it has lain mostly dormant. That's beginning to change, though. A number of small, reasonably priced hotels have cropped up here over the past few years, and several expats who own villas in the area rent them out year-round. To reach the coastal road in Tankah, turn east off Carretera 307 (a faded green sign marks the turning point). At the end of the long pitted road, turn left (north) where a string of villas and small hotels parallel the beach. Tankah is approximately 90 minutes south of Cancun.

$$$ ⌸**Blue Sky Hotel and Restaurant.** Guest quarters here have one-of-a-kind
★ touches, such as Cuban oil paintings, Guatemalan bedspreads, hand-blown vases, inlaid-silver mirrors, and chairs hand-tooled from native *chichén* wood. Rooms come with sofa beds, stereos, terraces, ocean view—and, of course—sky-blue painted ceilings. To cool off, guests can take a dip in the swimming pool, or head out to sea with a kayak and snorkel gear, compliments of the hotel. **Pros:** on beach; excellent restaurant. **Cons:** need car to get around. ⊠ *Bahía Tankah, past Casa Cenote* ☎984/807–7285 ⊕*www.blueskymexico.com* ➬*6 rooms, 2 suites* ⌂*In-room: No phone, refrigerator, no TV, Wi-Fi. In-hotel: Restaurant, pool, beachfront, water sports, Wi-Fi , no-smoking rooms* ⊟MC, V ⊺CP.

$$ ⌸**Casa Tropical.** This two-story villa has been divided into two units, one upstairs, one down. The cozy casita downstairs is less expensive and right on the beach; the larger upstairs unit has a rooftop patio with sweeping ocean views. Both are decorated with Haitian artwork and come with a queen-size bed, a fully equipped kitchen, a stereo, and an ample supply of books. There are also kayaks and beachside hammocks where you can sip a margarita and watch for exotic birds (you might see a roseate spoonbill fly past). The beach here has excellent snorkeling, with many small inlets. **Pros:** reasonable rates; on the beach; secluded. **Cons:** simple rooms; maid service only twice a week; need car to get around. ⊠ *Tankah 3, Lote 3* ☎215/966–8644 in U.S. ⊕*www.casat-ropical.com* ➬*2 units* ⌂*In-room: No phone, no TV, kitchen. In-hotel: Beachfront, water sports, no elevator, no-smoking rooms* ⊟*No credit cards* ⊺EP.

$$$ ▦ **Maya Jardin.** Available by the week or month, this five-bedroom villa can comfortably sleep up to 14 guests. You and your traveling companions may rent three, four, or five bedrooms by the week, with a maximum of three guests per room. The villa has many thoughtful details, like the very private outdoor shower in one room and the door leading directly to the heated pool in another. Rooms are decorated in subdued colors and have blackout curtains for guests who want to stay in bed even after the sun rises over the water. In addition to the regular kitchen, there's an outdoor kitchen for beachside grilling. Kayaks are on hand to use at no additional charge. **Pros:** on beach; clean and comfortable rooms; friendly owners. **Cons:** need car to get around; must rent minimum three rooms and stay for at least a week. ✉ *Lote 4B, Bahia de Soliman* ☎ *984/120–5098, 509/540–4880 in U.S.* ⊕ *www.mayajardin. com* ➫ *5 rooms* ⚬ *In-room: Safe. In-hotel:Pool, beachfront, Wi-Fi, no-smoking rooms* ⊟ *AE, MC, V* ⦵*EP.*

4

RESERVA DE LA BIOSFERA SIAN KA'AN

☾ *15 km (9 mi) south of Tulum to Punta Allen turnoff and within Sian*
Fodor'sChoice *Ka'an; 252 km (156 mi) north of Chetumal.*

★ The Sian Ka'an ("where the sky is born," pronounced see-*an* caan) region was first settled by the Maya in the 5th century AD. In 1986 the Mexican government established the 1.3-million-acre Reserva de la Biosfera Sian Ka'an as a protected area. The next year it was named a UNESCO World Heritage Site. The Riviera Maya and Costa Maya split the biosphere reserve; Punta Allen and north belong to the Riviera Maya, and everything south of Punta Allen is part of the Costa Maya.

The Sian Ka'an reserve constitutes 10% of the land in Quintana Roo, and covers 100 km (62 mi) of coastline. Hundreds of species of local and migratory birds, fish, other animals and plants, and fewer than 1,000 residents (primarily Maya) share this area of freshwater and coastal lagoons, mangrove swamps, cays, savannas, tropical forests, and a barrier reef. There are approximately 27 ruins (none excavated) linked by a unique canal system—one of the few of its kind in the Mayan world in Mexico. This is one of the last undeveloped stretches of North American coast. There's a $4 entrance charge. To visit the sites, you must take a guided tour.

Many species of the once-flourishing wildlife have fallen into the endangered category, but the waters here still teem with rooster fish, bonefish, mojarra, snapper, shad, permit, sea bass, and crocodiles. Fishing the flats for wily bonefish is popular, and the peninsula's few lodges also run deep-sea fishing trips.

To explore on your own, follow the road past Boca Paila to the secluded 35-km (22-mi) coastal strip of land that's part of the reserve. You'll be limited to swimming, snorkeling, and camping on the beaches, as there are no trails into the surrounding jungle. The narrow, extremely rough dirt roads down the peninsula are filled with monstrous potholes which are completely impassable after a rainfall. Don't attempt it unless

CLOSE UP

Caste Wars

When Mexico achieved independence from Spain in 1821, the Maya didn't celebrate. The new government didn't return their lost land or treat them with respect. In 1847 a Mayan rebellion began in Valladolid. The Indians were rising up against centuries of being relegated to the status of "lower caste" people. Hence the conflict was called the Guerra de las Castas, or "War of the Castes." A year later, they had killed hundreds and the battle raged on.

Help for the embattled Mexicans arrived with a vengeance from Mexico City, Cuba, and the United States. By 1850 the Maya had been mercilessly slaughtered, their population plummeting from 500,000 to 300,000. Survivors fled to the jungles and held out against the government until its troops withdrew in 1915. The Maya controlled Quintana Roo from Tulum, their headquarters, and finally accepted Mexican rule in 1935.

you have four-wheel drive. Most fishing lodges along the way close for the rainy season in August and September, and accommodations are hard to come by. The road ends at Punta Allen, a fishing village whose main catch is spiny lobster, which was becoming scarce until ecologists taught the local fishing cooperative how to build and lay special traps to conserve the species. There are several small, expensive guesthouses. If you haven't booked ahead, start out early in the morning so you can get back to civilization before dark.

EXPLORING

Several kinds of tours, including bird-watching by boat and night kayaking to observe crocodiles, are offered on-site through the **Sian Ka'an Visitor Center** (☎998/884–3667, 998/884–9580, or 998/871–0709 ⊕*www.cesiak.org*), which also offers five rooms with shared bath and one private suite for overnight stays. Prices range from $70 to $100, and meals are separate. The visitor center's observation tower offers the best view of the Sian Ka'an Biosphere from high atop their deck and wood bridge.

This photogenic archaeological site at the northern end of the *Reserva de la Biosfera Sian Ka'an* is underrated. Once known as Chunyaxché, it's now called by its ancient name, **Muyil** (pronounced mool-*hill*). It dates from the late preclassic era, when it was connected by road to the sea and served as a port between Cobá and the Mayan centers in Belize and Guatemala. A 15-foot-wide *sacbé*, built during the postclassic period, extended from the city to the mangrove swamp and was still in use when the Spaniards arrived.

Structures were erected at 400-foot intervals along the white limestone road, almost all of them facing west, but there are only three still standing. At the beginning of the 20th century the ancient stones were used to build a chicle (gum arabic) plantation, which was managed by one of the leaders of the War of the Castes. The most notable site at Muyil today is the remains of the 56-foot **Castillo**—one of the tallest on the Quintana Roo coast—at the center of a large acropolis. During excavations of the Castillo, jade figurines representing the moon and fertility goddess Ixchel were found. Recent excavations at Muyil have uncovered some smaller structures.

The ruins stand near the edge of a deep-blue lagoon and are surrounded by almost impenetrable jungle—so be sure to bring insect repellent. You can drive down a dirt road on the side of the ruins to swim or fish in the lagoon. The bird-watching is also exceptional here. ⊕*muyil.smv. org/* ⚱*$4, free Sun.* ⊘*Daily 8–5.*

WHERE TO EAT AND STAY

$$$$ 🏨**Boca Paila Fishing Lodge.** Home of the "grand slam" (fishing lingo for catching three different kinds of fish in one trip), this charming lodge has nine cottages, each with a/c, two double beds, couches, bathrooms, and screened-in sitting areas. Boats and guides for fly-fishing and bonefishing are provided; you can rent tackle at the lodge. Meals consist mainly of fresh fish dishes and Mayan specialties. A 50% deposit is required, and while week long stays are preferred, shorter stays are accepted based on availability. **Pros:** on beach; attentive staff; great fishing. **Cons:** not much to do in area besides fish. ⊠*Boca Paila Peninsula* ⊡*Reservations: Frontiers, Box 959, Wexford, PA 15090* ☎*724/935–1577 or 800/245–1950* ⊕*www.bocapailamexico.com* ⤙*9 cottages* ⚹*In-room: No phone, no TV, Wi-Fi. In-hotel: Restaurant, bar, beachfront, water sports, laundry service, Wi-Fi, no-smoking rooms* ⊟*MC, V* ⦿⎮*AI.*

$$$$ 🏨**Casa Blanca Lodge.** This lodge is on a rocky outcrop on remote Punta
★   Pájaros Island, which is reputed to be one of the best places in the world for light-tackle saltwater fishing. An open-air, thatch-roof bar welcomes anglers with drinks, fresh fish dishes, fruit, and vegetables at the start and end of the day. Only weeklong packages can be booked from March through July. Rates include a charter flight from Cancún, all meals, a boat, and a guide; nonfishing packages are cheaper. A 50% prepayment is required. **Pros:** remote location, comfortable rooms. **Cons:** there's a minimum stay, far from anywhere else. ⊠*Punta Pájaros* ⊡*Reservations: Frontiers, Box 959, Wexford, PA 15090* ☎*724/935–1577, 800/245–1950 for Frontiers* ⊕*www.frontierstravel.com* ⤙*9 rooms* ⚹*In-room: No phone, no TV. In-hotel: Restaurant, bar, beachfront, water sports, laundry service* ⊟*MC, V* ⦿⎮*AI.*

THE COSTA MAYA

The coastal area south of Punta Allen is more purely Mayan than the stretch south of Cancún. Fishing collectives and close-knit communities carry on ancient traditions here, and the proximity to Belize lends a Caribbean flavor, particularly in Chetumal, where you'll hear both Spanish and a Caribbean *patois*. A multimillion-dollar government initiative is attempting to support eco-tourism and sustainable development projects here, which will perhaps prevent resorts from taking over quite as much of the landscape.

CHETUMAL

328 km (283 mi) southeast of Playa del Carmen.

At times, Chetumal feels more Caribbean than Mexican; this isn't surprising, given its proximity to Belize. A population that includes Afro-Caribbean and Middle Eastern immigrants has resulted in a mix of music (reggae, salsa, calypso) and cuisines (Yucatecan, Mexican, and Lebanese). Although Chetumal's provisions are modest, the town has a number of parks on a waterfront that's as pleasant as it is long: the Bay of Chetumal surrounds the city on three sides. Tours are run to the fascinating nearby ruins of Kohunlich, Dzibanché, and Kinichná, a trio dubbed the "Valley of the Masks."

GETTING HERE AND AROUND

Chetumal's airport, Aeropuerto de Chetumal, lies on its southwestern edge. Mexicana Airlines flies from Mexico City to Chetumal five times a week. Chetumal's main bus terminal, at Avenida Salvador Novo 179, is served mainly by ADO. Caribe Express also runs buses regularly from Mexico City and other distant destinations. Omnibus Cristóbal Colón has buses that run to Palenque and San Cristóbal.

ESSENTIALS

Bus Contacts ADO (☎ *983/832–5110* ⊕ *www.ado.com.mx*). **Caribe Express** (☎ *983/832–7889*). **Omnibus Cristóbal Colón** (☎ *983/832–5110*).

Mail and Shipping Main Post Office (⊠ *Calle Plutarco E. Calles s/n*).

Medical Assistance General Hospital (⊠ *Av. Andrés Quintana Roo 399, between Isla Cancún and J. Sordia* ☎ *983/832–1932*). **Hospital Morelos** (⊠ *Av. Juárez, between Efraín and Héroes de Chapultepec* ☎ *983/ 832–4598*).

Visitor and Tour Info Chetumal tourist information booths (⊠ *Calles Cinco de Mayo and Carmen Ocho* ☎ *983/832–6647* ⊠ *Calle 22 de Enero and Av. Reforma* ☎ *983/832–6647*).

EXPLORING

The **Museo de la Cultura Maya**, a sophisticated interactive museum dedicated to the complex world of the Maya, is outstanding. Displays, which have explanations in Spanish and English, trace Mayan architecture, social classes, politics, and customs. The most impressive display is the three-story Sacred Ceiba Tree. The Maya use this symbol to explain the relationship between the cosmos and the earth. The first floor represents the roots of the tree and the Mayan underworld, called Xibalba. The middle floor is the tree trunk, known as Middle World, home to humans and all their trappings. The top floor is the leaves and branches and the 13 heavens of the cosmic otherworld. ⊠ *Av. Héroes and Calle Mahatma Gandhi* ☎ *983/832–6838* ⊡ *$5* ⊙ *Mon.–Thurs. 9–7, Fri.–Sun. 9–8.*

Paseo Bahía, Chetumal's main thoroughfare, runs along the water for several miles. A walkway runs parallel to this road and is a popular gathering spot at night. If you follow the road it turns into the Carretera Chetumal–Calderitas, and after 16 km (11 mi) leads to the small ruins of **Oxtankah**. Archaeologists believe this city's prosperity peaked between AD 200 and 600. ⊡ *$3* ⊙ *Daily 8–5.*

WHERE TO EAT AND STAY

¢–$
CAFÉ
✗**Expresso Cafe.** At this bright, modern café, you can look out over the placid Bay of Chetumal while you enjoy fresh salads, sandwiches, and chicken dishes, and your choice of 15 kinds of coffee. ⊠ *Calle 22 at Blvd Bahía* ☎*983/833–3013* ▤*No credit cards.*

$–$$
PIZZA
★
✗**Sergio's Restaurant & Pizzas.** Locals rave about this restaurant's grilled steaks, barbecued chicken (made with the owner's special sauce), and garlic shrimp, along with smoked-oyster and seafood pizzas. The restaurant feels fancier than most other local joints, and the staff is gracious. When you order the delicious Caesar salad for two, a waiter prepares it at your table. You can also order takeout or delivery. ⊠*Av. Alvaro Obregón 182, at Av. 5 de Mayo* ☎*983/832–2991* ▤*D, MC, V.*

¢
🏨**Hotel Marlon.** This comfortable hotel with a pastel color scheme is one of the best deals in town. There's plenty of cool air and hot water. The pool is good, the restaurant is great, and the bar is small but sweet. The staff demonstrates what traditional Mexican hospitality is all about. **Pros:** reasonable rates, friendly staff. **Cons:** uncomfortable beds, courtyard pool doesn't get much use. ⊠*Av. Juárez 8777700* ☎*983/832–9411 or 983/832–9522* ⤵*50 rooms* ⚐*In-room: Wi-Fi. In-hotel: Restaurant, bar, pool, Wi-Fi, no-smoking rooms* ▤*AE, MC, V* ❙◯❙*EP.*

$$
🏨**Los Cocos.** The rooms at this hotel are painted in subdued pastels. Some have balconies or outside sitting areas. There's a pool in a large pleasant garden, the waterfront is within easy walking distance. There are also suites and villas available. **Pros:** reasonable rates, friendly staff, clean rooms. **Cons:** uncomfortable beds, dated decor. ⊠*Av. Héroes 134, at Calle Chapultepec* ☎*983/832–0544* ⊕*www.hotelloscocos.com.mx* ⤵*176 rooms* ⚐*In-room: Refrigerator (some), Wi-Fi. In-hotel: Restaurant, bar, pool, Internet, no-smoking rooms* ▤*AE, MC, V* ❙◯❙*EP.*

XCALAK

55 km (34 mi) southwest of Chetumal.

It's quite a journey to get to Xcalak (pronounced *ish*-ka-lack), but it's worth the effort. This national reserve is on the tip of a peninsula that divides Chetumal Bay from the Caribbean. Flowers, birds, and butterflies are abundant here, and the terrain is marked by savannas, marshes, streams, and lagoons dotted with islands. There are also fabulously deserted beaches. Visitor amenities are few; the hotels cater mostly to rugged types who come to bird-watch on Bird Island or to dive at Banco Chinchorro, a coral atoll and national park some two hours northeast by boat.

During the month of April, Xcalak hosts the annual **Costa Maya Blues Festival** (⊕*www.costamayablues.com*). The weekend event takes place on the waterfront, with all proceeds donated to a hurricane relief fund.

WHERE TO EAT AND STAY

$
SEAFOOD
Fodor'sChoice
★
✗**The Leaky Palapa.** Nobody expected the kind of sophisticated flavors that the Leaky Palapa brought to town. But this little palapa, commonly called by its former name, Conchita's, is done up in twinkling lights and has quickly become *the* place for both tourists and locals to meet, enjoy

a beer, and sample tasty food. There are seafood options like the delicious lobster bisque, and there are surprises like incredible hamburgers (made with chipotle peppers and guacamole) and memorable pastas (in season there's a delicious shrimp and lobster pasta). Canadian owners Linda and Marla believe in using local ingredients as much as possible. ⊠ *Leona Vicario s/n, beside the port captain's office* ☎ *No phone* ☲ *No credit cards* ☉ *No lunch; closed Fri.*

$$ **☷ Sin Duda.** Situated on a lovely beach, this property has several parts:
★ a house divided into two suites; two apartments; and one studio apartment set in the jungle. The three suites share a kitchen, dining room, library, and sun deck. The studio, which the owners call a treehouse for adults, offers more privacy; apartments 7 and 8 are larger and better for families. All guest quarters are adorned with Mexican pottery and other collectibles. **Pros:** solar powered; very private. **Cons:** getting here isn't easy; owner's dogs may bark at night; no children under 8. ⊠ *Xcalak Peninsula, 60 km (33 mi) south of Majahual, 5½ km (4 mi) north of Costa de Cocos* ☎ *415/568–9925 in U.S.* ⊕ *www.sindudavillas. com* ⌨ *3 rooms, 1 studio, 2 apartments* ⚭ *In-room: No a/c, no phone, kitchen, no TV. In-hotel: Beachfront, water sports, no-smoking rooms* ☲ *No credit cards* ☉ *CP.*

BACALAR

⛟ *40 km (25 mi) northwest of Chetumal.*

Founded in AD 435, Bacalar (pronounced *baa*-ka-lar) is one of Quintana Roo's oldest settlements. There is a mix of freshwater and saltwater in Laguna de Bacalar because it is fed by cenotes. This mixing intensifies the color, which earned the lagoon the nickname *Lago de los Siete Colores* (Lake of the Seven Colors). Drive along the lake's southern shores to enter the affluent section of the town of Bacalar, with elegant waterfront homes.

EXPLORING

The alliance between the sister cities Dzibanché and Kinichná was thought to have made them the most powerful cities in southern Quintana Roo during the Mayan classic period (AD 100–1000). The fertile farmlands surrounding the ruins are still used today as they were hundreds of years ago, and the winding drive deep into the fields makes you feel as if you're coming upon something undiscovered.

Archaeologists have been making progress in excavating more and more ruins, albeit slowly. At **Dzibanché** ("place where they write on wood," pronounced zee-ban-*che*), several carved wooden lintels have been discovered; the most perfectly preserved sample is in a supporting arch at the **Plaza de Xibalba** (Plaza of Xibalba). Also at the plaza is the **Templo del Búho** (Temple of the Owl), atop which a recessed tomb was found, the second discovery of its kind in Mexico (the first was at Palenque in Chiapas). In the tomb were magnificent clay vessels painted with white owls—messengers of the underworld gods. More buildings and three plazas have been restored as excavation continues. Several other plazas are surrounded by temples, palaces, and pyramids, all in the Petén style. The carved stone steps at **Edificio 13** and **Edificio 2** (Buildings 13 and

2) still bear traces of stone masks. A copy of the famed lintel of **Templo IV** (Temple IV), with eight glyphs dating from AD 618, is housed in the Museo de la Cultura Maya in Chetumal. (The original was replaced in 2003 because of deterioration.) Four more tombs were discovered at **Templo I** (Temple I). ☎*No phone* 🎟️*$4* ⊙*Daily 8–5.*

After you see Dzibanché, make your way back to the fork in the road and head to **Kinichná** (House of the Sun, pronounced kin-itch-*na*). At the fork, you'll see the restored **Complejo Lamai** (Lamai Complex), administrative buildings of Dzibanché. Kinichná consists of a two-level pyramidal mound split into Acropolis B and Acropolis C, apparently dedicated to the sun god. Two mounds at the foot of the pyramid suggest that the temple was a ceremonial site. Here a giant Olmec-style jade figure was found. At its summit, Kinichná affords one of the finest views of any archaeological site in the area. ☎*No phone* 🎟️*$4* ⊙*Daily 8–5.*

Fuerte de San Felipe Bacalar *(San Felipe Fort)* is a 17th-century stone fort built by the Spaniards using stones from the nearby Mayan pyramids. It was constructed as a haven against pirates and marauding Indians, though during the War of the Castes it was a Mayan stronghold. Today the monolithic structure, which overlooks the enormous Laguna de Bacalar, houses government offices and a museum with exhibits on local history (ask for someone to bring a key if museum doors are locked). ☎*No phone* ⊕*www.bacalarmosaico.com/pages/activities/fort. htm* 🎟️*$4.75* ⊙*Tues.–Thurs. 9–7, Fri.–Sun. 9–8.*

★ **Kohunlich** (pronounced *ko*-hoon-lich) is renowned for the giant stucco masks on its principal pyramid, the **Edificio de los Mascarones** (Mask Building). It also has one of Quintana Roo's oldest ball courts and the remains of a great drainage system at the **Plaza de las Estelas** (Plaza of the Stelae). Masks that are about six feet tall are set vertically into the wide staircases at the main pyramid, called **Edificio de las Estelas** (Building of the Stelae). First thought to represent the Mayan sun god, they are now considered to be composites of the rulers and important warriors of Kohunlich. Another giant mask was discovered in 2001 in the building's upper staircase.

In 1902 loggers came upon Kohunlich, which was built and occupied during the classic period by various Mayan groups. This explains the eclectic architecture, which includes the Petén and Río Bec styles. Although there are 14 buildings to visit, it's thought that there are at least 500 mounds on the site waiting to be excavated. Digs have turned up 29 individual and multiple burial sites inside a residence building called **Temple de Los Viente-Siete Escalones** (Temple of the Twenty-Seven Steps). This site doesn't have a great deal of tourist traffic, so it's surrounded by thriving flora and fauna. ✉*42 km (26 mi) west of Chetumal on Carretera 186* ☎*No phone* 🎟️*$4* ⊙*Daily 8–5.*

WHERE TO EAT

$ ✕**Chepe's.** Bacalar's mayor José Contreras, known as Chepe, runs this
SEAFOOD little taco shop. The most famous tacos here are made with a delicious house *cochinita pibíl* (slow-roasted pork). If you are still a little sleepy when the restaurant opens at 7 AM, the spicy *habanero* salsa should

wake you right up. Get here early, because the handmade taquitos are gone before lunchtime. ☎983/102–4251 ▭No credit cards.

$$
SEAFOOD

✕**Restaurant Cenote Azul.** Here you can linger over fresh fish and a beer while gazing out over the deep blue waters or enjoy a swim off the dock. A giant, all-inclusive resort keeps threatening to open here; try to visit before the tranquility is gone. ⊠Carretera Chetumal-Cancún, Km 34 ☎983/834–2460 ▭AE, MC, V.

WHERE TO STAY

$$$$
Fodor'sChoice
★

⛴**Explorean Kohunlich.** At the edge of the Kohunlich ceremonial grounds, this ecological resort gives you the chance to have an adventure without giving up life's comforts. Daily excursions include trips to nearby ruins, lagoons, and forests for bird-watching, mountain biking, kayaking, rock climbing, and hiking. You return in the evening to luxurious, Mexican-style suites filled with natural textiles and woods. All guest quarters are strung along a serpentine jungle path; they're very private and have showers that open onto small back gardens. The pool and outdoor hot tub have views of the distant ruins. **Pros:** attentive staff; tours included room rate. **Cons:** expensive rates. ⊠Carretera Chetumal–Escarega, Km 5.65, same road as ruins ☎55/5201–8350 in Mexico City, 877/397–5672 ⊕www.theexplorean.com ⟿40 suites ⌂In-room: No TV. In-hotel: Restaurant, bar, pool, bicycles, no kids under 18, no elevator, no-smoking rooms ▭AE, MC, V ⎜ⓄⅠAI.

$

⛴**Hotel Laguna.** This brightly colored, eclectic hotel outside Bacalar is reminiscent of a lakeside summer camp. The main building resembles a lodge; cabins are on a hill overlooking the water. Rooms are spartan but comfortable. A garden path leads down to a dock-restaurant area where you can swim or use the canoes. The place is well manicured and maintained by a friendly, knowledgeable staff. **Pros:** wonderful water views; close to town. **Cons:** plain rooms; no a/c. ⊠Carretera 307, Km 40 ☎983/834–2205 ⟿3 cabins, 29 rooms ⌂In-room: No a/c (some), no phone, no TV. In-hotel: Restaurant, pool, no-smoking rooms ▭MC, V.

$$$
★

⛴**Rancho Encantado.** On the shores of Laguna Bacalar, 30 minutes north of Chetumal, the enchanting Rancho Encantado consists of Mayan-themed casitas (cottages). Each one has traditional furnishings, a patio, a hammock, a refrigerator, a sitting area, and a bathroom. Breakfast and dinner are included in the room rate (no red meat is served). You can swim and snorkel off the private dock leading into the lagoon or tour the ruins in southern Yucatán, Campeche, and Belize. Pick a room close to the water or your nights will be marred by the sound of trucks zooming by. Guided tours in English can also be organized to visit local ancient sites. **Pros:** great location on lagoon; breakfast and dinner included; friendly staff. **Cons:** some traffic noise; need car to get around. ⊠Off Carretera 307, Km 3, look for turnoff sign ⎔Reservations: 470 East Riverside Dr., Truth or Consequences, NM 77930 ☎983/101–3358, 800/505–6294 in U.S. ⊕www.encantado.com ⟿12 casitas, 1 suite ⌂In-room: No phone, refrigerator, no TV. In-hotel: Restaurant, bar, no-smoking rooms ▭AE, MC, V ⎜ⓄⅠMAP.

MAHAHUAL

143 km (89 mi) northwest of Chetumal via Carretera 186 and Carretera 307.

Prior to a devastating 2007 hurricane, most travelers overlooked the small fishing village of Mahahual (pronounced ma-ha-*wal*). Though there are still only has about 200 residents, post-hurricane renovations have put the village on the map; it now has its own pier as well as a smattering of hotels, restaurants, and shops. The new cement boardwalk along the beach has made Mahahual an ideal spot for a sunset stroll. The crystal-clear waters and unspoiled beaches are delightful for snorkeling, diving, and fishing.

WHERE TO STAY

$$ **Arenas.** Across the street from the beach, rooms here have exceptional ocean views. Private balconies are made of wood that seems to just have been tied together à la Robinson Crusoe. Rooms are spacious, decorated with modern furniture, and quite comfortable. **Pros:** great location near restaurants and shops. **Cons:** no elevator. ⊠ *Av. Mahahual, Mza. 27, Lote 7* ☎ *983/834–5832* ⊕ *www.hotelarenasmx.com* ☞ *13 rooms* ⟨ *In-room: Wi-Fi. In-hotel: No-smoking rooms* ▤ *MC, V.*

$ **Balamku.** While vacationing in the area, Canadian expats Carol Tumer and Alan Knight missed their turnoff to Punta Allen and ended up spending the night in Mahahual. The next day they bought the property and built this stunning small hotel. They have exceeded all expectations in their ecologically sustainable practices. In addition to generating power with solar panels and wind generators, they use water-saving toilets and they compost all of the waste from the hotel. Since they have no septic tanks underground, they make sure that none of their waste leaks into the sea. All the cool and spacious rooms here face a quiet stretch of beach. They have tile floors and Mexican and Guatemalan bedding and handicrafts. Breakfast and kayaking equipment are included in the cost of the room. **Pros:** beachfront location; comfortable rooms; staff makes you feel at home. **Cons:** need car to get around; restaurant only serves breakfast; rooms lack a/c. ⊠ *Av. Mahahual, Km 5.7* ☎ *983/839–5332* ⊕ *www.balamku.com* ☞ *10 rooms* ⟨ *In-room: No a/c, Wi-Fi, no TV. In-hotel: Restaurant, beachfront, water sports, no-smoking rooms* ▤ *No credit cards* ⫣ *BP.*

$–$$ **Hotel Castillo.** Located on a pristine beach, this small hotel is a paradise for families, water sports enthusiasts, and anyone looking to relax. Each room has a private balcony and ocean view; several can accommodate up to five people. Theres a designated childrens play area. Hotel guests can enjoy complimentary boat rides or pay extra to join a tour of Banco Chinchorro, the largest coral reef in the Caribbean. The onsite restaurant serves European and Mexican cuisine alongside fresh fruit direct from the hotel's tropical garden. **Pros:** owners catch and prepare fresh fish; family-friendly. **Cons:** no hot showers; 6 mi from main village. ⊠ *From Carretera 307, turn east after Mahahual and continue along coast road for 11.6 Km toward Xcalak, Mahahual* ☎ *983/110–5918* ⊕ *www.hotel-castillo.com* ☞ *7 rooms, 1 suite* ⟨ *In-*

room: No a/c, no phone, no TV. In-hotel: Wi-Fi, bar, restaurant, water sports, no-smoking rooms ☐*No credit cards* ⦿*EP.*

$$ 🖼**Maya Luna.** This small lodging on the beach, far from the boardwalk, is a quiet place to relax and enjoy the sand and the sun. Cabanas are simple concrete rooms with palapa roofs. All have private roof decks where you can sit back and enjoy the view. The Dutch owners are often in their small restaurant with its framed photos of Frida Kahlo, Pancho Villa, Emelio Zapata, and other Mexican notables lining the walls. The restaurant serves breakfast for guests, but people who aren't staying here often shows up between 3:30 and 8 for well-prepared seafood. **Pros:** beachfront location; nice restaurant; relaxed atmosphere. **Cons:** no a/c. ✉*Av. Mahahual, Km 4* ☎*983/836–0905* ⊕*www.hotelmaya luna.com* ⮞*5 rooms* ♿*In-room: No a/c. In-hotel: Restaurant, Wi-Fi, no-smoking rooms* ☐*No credit cards.*

$$ 🖼**Mayan Beach Garden.** Located 12 mi north of Mahahual, this charming bed and breakfast has two types of rooms: beachfront cabanas and two-story beach-view suites. Cabanas have full kitchens, king beds, and private decks with hammock and lounge chairs. Inspired by the ancient ruin Yaxchilan, the beach-view rooms have Mayan artwork, and unique touches like hand-painted sinks and wood-framed mirrors in the large bathrooms—as well as king beds and sleeper sofas. The BB uses solar power and recycled rain water, providing guests with electricity and hot water 24 hours a day. Cooking classes, diving tours, and fishing trips can be arranged upon request. **Pros:** optional all-inclusive plan available; beautiful garden restaurant; ATM on-site. **Cons:** minimum three-night stay during high season; $50 deposit required for reservation. ✉*21.5 km, N. Carretera Costera Mahahual-Punta Herrera, Mahahual 77940* ☎*983/132–2603, 206/905–9665 in U.S.* ⊕*www.mayanbeach garden.com* ⮞*2 cabanas, 3 rooms, 1 suite* ♿*In-room: No a/c (some), no phone, safe, kitchen, Wi-Fi (some). In-hotel: Restaurant, bar, spa, water sports, beachfront, laundry service, no-smoking rooms* ☐*AE, D, MC, V* ⦿*BP, AI.*

$ 🖼**Posada Pachamama.** This simple, charming little hotel is just across the street from the beach on Mahahual's main boardwalk. Rooms are friendly with bright colors and Mexican art craft accents. The owners are an Italian couple who, while friendly, let guests do their own thing. **Pros:** beachfront location; good rates; near restaurants and shops. **Cons:** no a/c. ✉*Calle Huachinango s/n* ☎*983/134–3049* ⊕*www.posada pachamama.net* ⮞*6 rooms* ♿*In-room: No a/c. In hotel: No-smoking rooms* ☐*MC, V.*

SPORTS AND THE OUTDOORS
ADVENTURE TOURS

Yolanda Ros (✉*Hotel Mayaluna, Carretera Mahahual Xcalak, Km 4* ☎*983/ 103–4739* ⊕*www.tortugazul.com*) is experienced in all kinds of outdoor adventure. She offers personalized biking, kayaking, and horseback tours in the area for groups of up to eight people. Tours range from $25 to $160.

SCUBA DIVING

Dreamtime Dive Resort (⊠ *Av. Mahahual s/n, Km 2.5* ☎ *983/700–5824, 904/730–4337 in U.S.* ⊕ *www.dreamtimediving.com*) offers snorkeling tours and night dives managed by some of the most experienced divers in the area. Single-tank dives cost $40; two-tank dives are $75.

FELIPE CARRILLO PUERTO

156 km (97 mi) north of Chetumal.

Formerly known as Chan Santa Cruz, Felipe Carrillo Puerto—the Costa Maya's first major town—is named for the man who became governor of Yucatán in 1920 and who was hailed as a hero after instituting a series of reforms to help the impoverished *campesinos* (peasants). Not far away is Chacchoben, a little-explored archaeological site.

GETTING HERE AND AROUND

The entire 382-km (237-mi) coast from Punta Sam near Cancún to the main border crossing to Belize at Chetumal is traversable on Carretera 307—a straight, paved highway. A few years ago only a handful of gas stations serviced the entire state of Quintana Roo, but now—with the exception of the lonely stretch from Felipe Carrillo Puerto south to Chetumal—they are plentiful.

EXPLORING

Interesting **Chacchoben** (pronounced *cha*-cho-ben) is one of the more recent archaeological sites to undergo excavation. An ancient city that was a contemporary of Kohunlich and the most important trading partner with Guatemala north of the Bacalar Lagoon area, the site contains several newly unearthed buildings that are still in good condition. The lofty **Templo Uno,** the site's main temple, was dedicated to the Mayan sun god Itzamná, and once held a royal tomb. (When archaeologists found it, though, it had already been looted.) Most buildings were constructed in the early classic period around AD 200 in the Petén style, although the city could have been inhabited as early as 200 BC. The inhabitants made a living by growing cotton and extracting chewing gum and copal resin from the trees. ⊠ *Carretera 307, turn right on Carretera 293 south of Cafetal, continue 9 km (5½ mi) passing Lázaro Cardenas town* ☎ *No phone* ⊠ *$3.70; additional $3 to use video cameras* ⊗ *Daily 8–5.*

WHERE TO STAY

¢ ⊞ **El Faisán y El Venado.** The price is right at this simple, comfortable hotel. The restaurant (¢–$) does a brisk business with locals because it's very central and has good Yucatecan specialties such as *poc chuc* (pork marinated in sour-orange sauce), *bistec a la yucateca* (Yucatecan-style steak), and *pollo pibíl.* Try the refreshing agua Jamaica, a hibiscus infused iced tea. A trio performs traditional Mexican music nightly and appetizers are free with your meal.**Pros:** best place to stay in town. **Cons:** simple rooms; staff speaks little English. ⊠ *Av. Benito Juárez, Lote 781* ☎ *983/834–0043* ⊷ *36 rooms* ⊘ *In-room: No a/c (some), refrigerator. In-hotel: Restaurant* ⊟ *MC, V.*

Yucatán and Campeche States

WITH CHICHÉN ITZÁ

Chac-Mool, Temple of the Warriors, Chichén Itzá

WORD OF MOUTH

"Both Uxmal and Chichen are fascinating. Try to stay overnight at Chichen, so you'll be able to enter first thing in the morning to avoid crowds. I can highly recommend a stay at the Hacienda Chichen. If you're driving from Merida to Uxmal, you might consider continuing south and west to Campeche. I liked Merida, but I loved Campeche. A beautiful, charming, lively, historic small city on the Gulf."

—robertino

WELCOME TO YUCATÁN AND CAMPECHE

TOP REASONS TO GO

★ Visiting spectacular Mayan ruins: Chichén Itzá and Uxmal are two of the largest, most beautiful sites in the region.

★ Living like a wealthy *hacendado*: You can stay in a restored *henequen* (sisal) plantation-turned-hotel and delight in its old-world charm.

★ Browsing at fantastic craft markets: This region is known for its handmade *hamacas* (hammocks), piñatas, and other local handicrafts.

★ Swimming in the secluded, pristine freshwater cenotes: These sinkholes, like portals to the underworld, are scattered throughout the inland landscape.

★ The chance to taste the diverse flavors of Yucatecan food: Mérida has 50-odd restaurants, which serve up local specialties like fish stews and Mayan-originated dishes like *pollo pibíl* (chicken cooked in banana leaves).

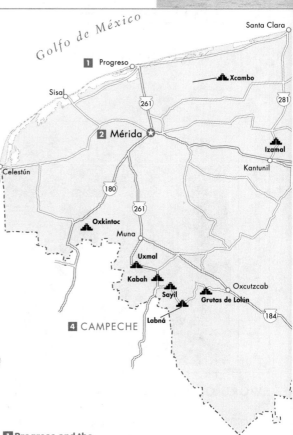

1 Progreso and the Northern Coast. Outside the unpretentious town of Progreso, empty beaches stretch for miles in either direction—punctuated only by fishing villages, estuaries, and salt flats. Bird-watchers and nature lovers gravitate to rustic Celestún and Río Lagartos, home to one of the hemisphere's largest colonies of pink flamingos.

2 Mérida. Fully urban, and bustling with foot and car traffic, Mérida was once the main stronghold of Spanish colonialism in the peninsula. Tucked among the restaurants, museums and markets are grand, old, beautifully ornamented mansions and buildings that recall the city's heyday as the wealthiest capital in Mexico.

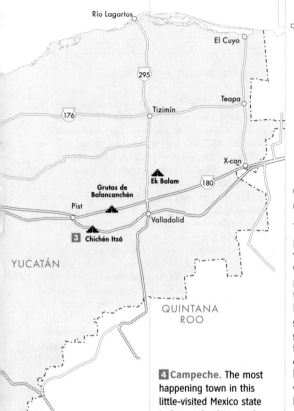

Río Lagartos
El Cuyo
295
Teapa
Tizimín
176
X-can
Grutas de
Balancanchén
Ek Balam
180
Pist
Valladolid
3 Chichén Itzá
YUCATÁN
QUINTANA
ROO

GETTING ORIENTED

5

Yucatán State's topography has more in common with that of Florida and Cuba—with which it was probably once connected—than with central Mexico. Exotic plants like wild ginger and spider lilies grow in the jungles; vast flamingo colonies nest at coastal estuaries. Human history is evident everywhere here—in looming Franciscan missions, thatchroofed adobe huts, and the majestic ruins of ancient Maya cities. Campeche State, the Yucatán Peninsula's least-visited corner, is the perfect place for adventure. Its colonial communities have retained an air of innocence, and its protected biospheres, farmland, and jungles are relatively unspoiled. Campeche City, the state's most accessible spot, makes a good hub for exploring other areas, many of which have only basic restaurants and primitive lodgings.

4 **Campeche.** The most happening town in this little-visited Mexico state is Campeche City, a colonial enclave with brightly painted buildings and the dreamy airs of bygone times. The rest of the state is traversed by two-lane highways, which lead to Mayan villages where three-wheeled bike-taxis rule the road and women dress in embroidered *huipiles.* Far to the south, along the Guatemalan border, the Reserva de la Biosfera Calakmul is home to thousands of birds, butterflies, and plants—but only hosts about a dozen visitors a day.

3 **Chichén Itzá and the Mayan Interior.** Yucatán's spectacular Mayan ruins are famous all over the world. The best-known, Chichén Itzá, draws thousands of visitors every year. Farther south is the less-known but beautiful (and typically far less crowded) site of Uxmal. Many smaller archaeological sites—some hardly visited— lie along the Ruta Puuc south of Mérida.

YUCATÁN AND CAMPECHE STATES PLANNER

When to Go

As with many other places in Mexico, the weeks around Christmas and Easter are peak times for visiting Yucatán State. Making reservations up to a year in advance is common.

If you like music and dance, Mérida hosts its *Otoño Cultural*, or Autumn Cultural Festival, during the last week of October and first week of November. El festival de Mérida, which celebrates the founding of the city, also runs through nearly the entire month of January. Over the course of January, a thousand artists participate in nearly two hundred free events (⊕ www.merida.gob.mx/festival). During both of these events, music concerts, dance performances, and art exhibits take place almost nightly at theaters and open-air venues around the city.

Thousands of people, from international sightseers to Mayan shamans, swarm Chichén Itzá on the vernal equinox (the first day of spring). On this particular day the sun creates a shadow that looks like a snake—meant to evoke the ancient Maya serpent god, Kukulcán—that moves slowly down the side of the main pyramid. If you're planning to witness it, make your travel arrangements many months in advance.

Getting Here and Around

Mérida is the hub of the Yucatán Peninsula and a good base for exploring the rest of the state. From there, highways radiate in every direction. To the east, Carreteras 180 *cuota* and 180 *libre* are, respectively, the toll and free roads to Cancún. The toll road (which costs about $30 from Cancún to Merida; ⊕ www.sct.gob.mx) has exits for the famous Chichén Itzá ruins and the low-key colonial city of Valladolid; the free road passes these and many smaller towns. Heading south from Mérida on Carretera 261 (Carretera 180 until the town of Umán), you come to Uxmal and the Ruta Puuc, a series of small ruins (most have at least one outstanding building) of relatively uniform style. Carretera 261 north from Mérida takes you to the port and beach resort of Progreso. To the west, the laid-back fishing village of Celestún—which borders on protected wetland— can be accessed by a separate highway from Mérida.

■ TIP→ **If you're independent and adventurous, hiring a rental car is a great way to explore. Be sure to check the lights and spare tire before taking off, carry plenty of bottled water, fill up the gas tank whenever you see a station, and try to avoid driving at night.**

How Long to Stay

You should plan to spend at least five days in the Yucatán. It's best to start your trip with a few days in Mérida; the weekends, when streets are closed to traffic and there are lots of free outdoor performances, are great times to visit. You should also budget enough time to day-trip to the sites of Chichén Itzá and Uxmal; visiting Mérida without traveling to at least one of these sites is like driving to the beach and not getting out of the car.

How's the Weather?

Rainfall is heaviest in the Yucatán between June and October, bringing with it an uncomfortable humidity. The coolest months are December to February, when it can get chilly in the evening; April and May are usually the hottest. Afternoon showers are the norm June through September; hurricane season is late September through early November.

About the Restaurants

Expect a superb variety of cuisines—primarily Yucatecan, of course, but also Lebanese, Italian, French, Chinese, vegetarian, and Mexican—at very reasonable prices. Reservations are advised for the pricier restaurants on weekends and in high season. Beach towns, such as Progreso, Río Lagartos, and Celestún, tend to serve fresh, simply prepared seafood. The regional cuisine of Campeche is renowned throughout Mexico. Specialties include fish and shellfish stews, cream soups, shrimp cocktail, squid and octopus, and *panuchos* (chubby rounds of fried cornmeal covered with refried beans and topped with onion and shredded turkey or chicken).

Mexicans generally eat lunch in the afternoon—certainly not before 2. If you want to eat at noon, call ahead to verify hours. In Mérida the locals make a real event of late dinners, especially during the summer. Casual, but neat, dress is acceptable at all restaurants. Avoid wearing shorts or casual sandals in the more expensive places, and anywhere at all—especially in the evening—if you don't want to look like a tourist.

Dining and Lodging Prices

WHAT IT COSTS IN DOLLARS

	¢	$	$$	$$$	$$$$
Restaurants	under $5	$5–$10	$10–$15	$15–$25	over $25
Hotels	under $50	$50–$75	$75–$150	$150–$250	over $250

Restaurant prices reflect the median entrée price at dinner. Hotel prices are for a standard double room in high season.

About the Hotels

Yucatán State has around 8,500 hotel rooms—a little over a third of what Cancún has. Try to check out the interior before booking a room; in general the public spaces in Mérida's hotels are prettier than the sleeping rooms. Most hotels have air-conditioning, and even many budget hotels have installed it in at least some rooms—but it's best to ask ahead.

■TIP→If you plan to spend most of your time enjoying downtown Mérida, stay near the main square or along Calle 60. If you're a light sleeper, however, opt for one of the high-rises along or near Paseo Montejo, about a 20-minute stroll (but an easy cab ride) from the main square.

Inland towns such as Valladolid and Ticul are good options for a look at the slow-paced countryside. There are several charming hotels near the major archaeological sites Chichén Itzá and Uxmal, and a couple of foreign-run bed-and-breakfasts in Progreso, which previously had only desultory digs. Campeche City has a few interesting lodgings converted from old homes (and in some cases mansions).

MÉRIDA

Updated by
Michele Joyce

Travelers to Mérida are a loyal bunch, who return again and again to their favorite restaurants, neighborhoods, and museums. The hubbub of the city can seem frustrating—especially if you've just spent a peaceful few days on the coast or visiting Mayan sites—but as the cultural and intellectual hub of the peninsula, Mérida is rich in art, history, and tradition.

A two- to three-hour group tour of the city, including museums, parks, public buildings, and monuments, costs $20 to $35 per person. Free guided tours are offered daily by the Municipal Tourism Department. These depart from City Hall, on the main plaza, at 9:30 AM.

If you need extra orientation, be sure to stop in at the tourism offices, where you will find friendly, helpful staff. After recent scandals involving scam artists who hang official looking "tourist guide" badges around their necks, the tourism office staff warns tourists not to trust people offering themselves as guides.

There have also been recent reports of vendors increasing the prices of their art and crafts by the hundreds, claiming that the value of their wares is far greater than it really is. Most vendors are honest, so just be sure to shop around and acquaint yourself with the kinds of crafts, and the levels of quality, that are available. Once you have an idea of what's out there, you'll be much better able to spot fraud, and you may even have some fun bargaining.

■ TIP→Most streets in Mérida are numbered, not named, and most run one-way. North–south streets have even numbers, which descend from west to east; east–west streets have odd numbers, which ascend from north to south. Street addresses are confusing because they don't progress in even increments by blocks; for example, the 600s may occupy two or more blocks. A particular location is therefore usually identified by indicating the street number and the nearest cross street, as in "Calle 64 and Calle 61," or "Calle 64 between Calles 61 and 63," which is written "Calle 64 x 61 y 63."

GETTING HERE AND AROUND

Mérida's airport, Aeropuerto Manuel Crescencio Rejón, is 7 km (4½ mi) west of the city on Avenida Itzáes. Getting there from the downtown area usually takes 20 to 30 minutes by taxi. Numerous airlines, including Aerocaribe, Aeroméxico, and Mexicana fly from Cancún, Mexico City, Villahermosa, and other cities. Continental flies daily nonstop from Houston.

For travel outside the city, ADO and UNO have direct buses to many coastal cities and ruins; they depart from the first-class CAME bus station. Regional bus lines to intermediate or more out-of-the-way destinations leave from the second-class terminal. City buses charge about 40¢ (4 pesos); having the correct change is helpful but not required.

Regular taxis in Mérida charge beach-resort prices. The minimum fare is $3, which should get you from one downtown location to another.

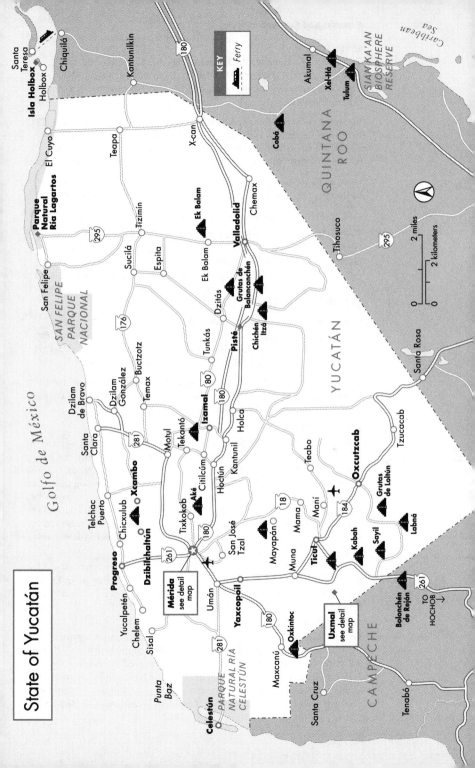

State of Yucatán

ESSENTIALS

Bus Contacts Autobuses de Occidente (✉ *Calle 69, between 68 and 70, Centro* ☏ *999/924–8391 or 999/924–9741* ⊕ *www.ado.com.mx*). **CAME** (First Class Terminal) (✉ *Calle 70 No. 555, between Calle 69 and 71, Centro* ☏ *999/924–9130*).

Currency Exchange Banamex (✉ *Calle 59 No. 485Centro* ☏ *01800/021–2345 toll-free in Mexico* ⊕ *www.banamex.com*). **Banorte** (✉ *Prolongación Paseo de Montejo No. 497Itzimna* ☏ *999/926–6060* ⊕ *www.banorte.com*). **HSBC** (✉ *Paseo Montejo 467A, Centro* ☏ *999/942–2378* ⊕ *www.hsbc.com*).

Internet La Vía Olimpo (✉ *Calle 62 No. 502, Centro* ☏ *999/923–5843*). **Café La Habana** (✉ *Calle 59 No. 511-A, at Calle 62, Centro* ☏ *999/928–6502*).

Mail and Shipping Correo (✉ *Calles 65 and 56, Centro* ☏ *999/928–5404*).

Medical Assistance Star Médica (✉ *Calle 26 No. 199, between Avs. 15 and 16, Alta Brisa* ☏ *999/930–2800* ⊕ *www.starmedica.com*). **Centro Médico de las Américas** (✉ *Calle 54 No. 365, between Calle 33A and Av. Pérez Ponce, Centro* ☏ *999/926–2111* ⊕ *www.centromedicodelasamericas.com.mx*). **Clínica Santa Helena** (✉ *Calle 14 No. 81, between Calles 5 and 7, Col. San Antonio Cinta* ☏ *999/943–1334 or 999/943–1335*).

Rental Cars Avis (✉ *Fiesta Americana, Calle 60 No. 319-C, near Av. Colón, Centro* ☏ *999/925–2525 or 999/920–1101* ⊕ *www.avis.com*). **Budget** (✉ *Holiday Inn, Av. Colón 498, at Calle 60, Centro* ☏ *999/920–4395 or 999/925–6877 Ext. 516* ✉ *Airport* ☏ *999/946–1323* ⊕ *www.budget.com*).

Visitor and Tour Info Municipal Tourism Department (✉ *Calles 61 and 60, Centro* ☏ *999/930–3101*). **Municipal Tourist Information Center** (✉ *Calle 62, ground floor of Palacio Municipal, Centro* ☏ *999/928–2020 Ext. 133*).

EXPLORING

The *zócalo,* or main square, is in the oldest part of town—the Centro Histórico. On Saturday nights and Sundays practically the entire population of the city gathers in the parks and plazas surrounding the zócalo to socialize and watch live entertainment. Cafés along this route are perfect places from which to watch the parade of people as well as folk dancers and singers. Calle 60 between Parque Santa Lucía and the main square gets especially lively; restaurants here set out tables in the streets, which quickly fill with patrons enjoying the free hip-hop, tango, salsa, or jazz performances.

Every Sunday, from 8 AM to 12:30 PM, downtown streets are closed for pedestrians and cyclists. The route begins at the Parque de la Ermita, and travels through the Plaza Grande, out on to the Paseo Montejo (⊕ *www.merida.gob.mx/biciruta*).

TOP ATTRACTIONS

❷ **Casa de Montejo.** Francisco de Montejo—father and son—conquered the peninsula and founded Mérida in 1542; they built their stately "casa" 10 years later. In the late 1970s it was restored by banker Agustín Legorreta, converted to a branch of Banamex bank, and now sits on the south side of the plaza. It is the city's finest—and oldest—example of colonial plateresque architecture, a Spanish architectural style popular

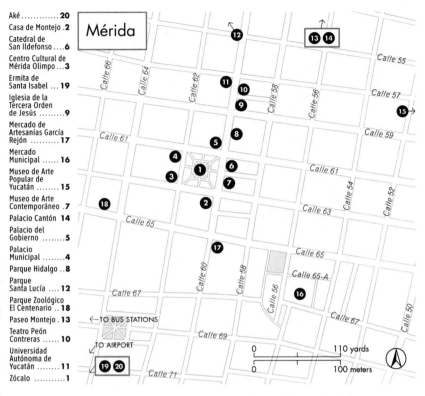

in the 16th century and typified by the kind of elaborate ornamentation you'll see here. A bas-relief on the doorway—the facade is all that remains of the original house—depicts Francisco de Montejo the younger, his wife, and daughter, as well as Spanish soldiers standing on the heads of the vanquished Maya. Even if you have no banking to do, step into the building to glimpse the leafy inner patio. ⊠ *Calle 63, Centro* ⊙ *Weekdays 9–5 and Saturdays 9–1.*

❻ **Catedral de San Ildefonso.** Begun in 1561, St. Ildefonso is believed to be the oldest cathedral in the Americas. It took several hundred Mayan laborers, working with stones from the pyramids of the ravaged Mayan city, 36 years to complete it. Designed in the somber Renaissance style by an architect who had worked on the Escorial in Madrid, its facade is stark and unadorned, with gunnery slits instead of windows, and faintly Moorish spires. Inside, the black Cristo de las Ampollas (Christ of the Blisters)—at 7 meters (23 feet) tall, perhaps the tallest Christ in Mexico—occupies a side chapel to the left of the main altar. The statue is a replica of the original, which was destroyed during the revolution in 1910; this is also when the gold that typically decorated Mexican cathedrals was carried off. According to one of many legends, the Christ figure burned all night yet appeared the next morning unscathed—except that it was covered with the blisters for which it is named. You can

Take a Tour

Mérida has more than 50 tour operators, and it could be said that they generally take you to the same places. Since there are so many reputable and reasonably priced operators, there's no reason to opt for the less-predictable *piratas* ("pirates") who sometimes stand outside tour offices offering to sell you a cheaper trip and don't necessarily have much experience or your best interests at heart.

ARCHAEOLOGICAL TOURS

Amigo Travel is a reliable operator offering group and private tours to the major archaeological sites and also to Celestún, the town known for the massive flamingo colonies living in its river. Amigo has transfer–accommodation packages and well-crafted tours, like their Campeche and Yucatán combo, and have adopted a pace that allows you to actually enjoy the sites you visit.

If you don't have your own wheels, but like the freedom afforded by traveling in your own, a great option for seeing the ruins of the Ruta Puuc is the unguided **ATS** tour that leaves Mérida at 8 AM from the second-class bus station (Terminal 69, ATS line). The tour stops for a half hour each at the ruins of Labná, Xlapak, Sayil, and Kabah, giving you just enough time to scan the plaques, poke your nose into a crevice or two, and pose before a pyramid for your holiday card picture. You get almost two hours at Uxmal before heading back to Mérida at 2:30 PM. The trip costs $10 per person (entrance to the ruins isn't included) and is worth every penny.

Ecoturismo Yucatán has a good mix of day and overnight tours. Their Calakmul tour includes several nights camping in the biosphere reserve for nature spotting, as well as visits to Calakmul, Chicanná, and other area ruins. The one-day biking adventure packs in biking as well as brief visits to two archaeological sites, a cave, and two cenotes.

CITY TOURS BY BUS

Within Mérida, a fun way to get around, to get a feel for the city layout—and to hear some of its history—is to spend some time on the red, open-roof, double-decker **Turibus**. You buy your ticket ($10) onboard the bus, and you can get on and off at the seven bus stops as you please. The complete bus route is 1 hour and 45 minutes. Buses operate from 9:05 AM until 9 PM, and stop at the Holiday Inn, Fiesta Americana, and Hyatt hotels, clustered near one another on Paseo Montejo; the plaza principal, downtown; Palacio Cantón; the old barrio of Izimná, east of Prolongación Paseo Montejo; the Gran Plaza shopping center (with multiplex theater); and the Monument to the Flag, near the Paseo Montejo hotels.

CITY TOURS BY CARRIAGE

One of the best ways to get a feel for the city of Mérida is to hire a *calesa*—a horse-drawn carriage. The gentle clip-clop of hooves is transporting. You can hail one of these at the main square or, during the day, at Palacio Cantón, site of the archaeology museum on Paseo Montejo. Choose your horse and driver carefully as some of the horses look dispirited, but others are fairly well cared for. Drivers charge about $15 for an hour-long circuit around downtown and up Paseo de Montejo, pointing out notable buildings, and providing a little historic background along the way, and $22 for an extended tour.

hear the pipe organ play at the 11 AM Sunday mass. ✉ *Calles 60 and 61, Centro* ☎ *No phone* ⊙ *Daily 7–11:30 and 4:30–8.*

WORD OF MOUTH

"I should add here that Merida is totally genuine and not particularly touristy. Or perhaps a better way of saying it is that the size of the city makes tourists less noticeable."   —robertino

③ Centro Cultural de Mérida Olimpo. Referred to as simply Olimpo, this is the best venue in town for free cultural events. The beautiful porticoed cultural center was built adjacent to City Hall in late 1999, occupying what used to be a parking lot. The marble interior is a showcase for top international art exhibits, classical-music concerts, conferences, and theater and dance performances. The adjoining 1950s-style movie house shows classic art films by directors like Buñuel, Fellini, and Kazan. There is also a planetarium with 90-minute shows explaining the solar system ($3; Tuesday through Sunday at 11, noon, 5, and 7; be sure to be there 15 minutes early, since nobody is allowed to sneak in once the show has begun), a bookstore, and a wonderful cybercafé-restaurant. ✉ *Calle 62 between Calles 61 and 63, Centro* ☎ *999/942–0000* ⊕ *www.merida.gob.mx/planetario* ✉ *Free* ⊙ *Tues.–Sun. 10–10.*

⑬ Paseo Montejo. North of downtown, this 10-block-long street was *the* place to reside in the late 19th century, when wealthy plantation owners sought to outdo each other with the opulence of their elegant mansions. Mansion owners typically opted for the decorative styles popular in New Orleans, Cuba, and Paris—imported Carrara marble, European antiques—rather than any style from Mexico. The broad boulevard, lined with tamarind and laurel trees, has lost much of its former panache; some of the mansions have fallen into disrepair. Many are now used as office buildings; others have been or are being restored as part of a citywide, privately funded beautification program. The street is a lovely place to explore on foot or in a horse-drawn carriage.

⑩ Teatro Peón Contreras. This 1908 Italianate theater was built along the same lines as grand turn-of-the-20th-century European theaters and opera houses. In the early 1980s the marble staircase, dome, and frescoes were restored. Today, in addition to performing arts, the theater houses the **Centro de Información Turística** (Tourist Information Center), which provides maps, brochures, and details about attractions in the city and state. The theater's most popular attraction, however, is the café-bar spilling out into the street facing Parque de la Madre. It's crowded every night with people enjoying the balladeers singing romantic and politically inspired songs. ✉ *Calle 60 between Calles 57 and 59, Centro* ☎ *Tourist Information Center 999/924–9290, theater 999/923–7344 and 999/924–9290* ⊙ *Tourist Information Center daily 8–9.*

⑪ Universidad Autónoma de Yucatán. Pop into the university's main building—which plays a major role in the city's cultural and intellectual life—to check the bulletin boards just inside the entrance for upcoming cultural events. The folkloric ballet performs on the patio of the main building most Fridays between 9 and 10 PM ($5). You'll easily find this imposing Moorish-inspired building, which dates from 1711, with its crenellated

CLOSE UP

Take a Tour

CITY TOURS BY FOOT
The Mérida English-Language Library
(⇨ see Browsing for Books, below)
conducts home and garden tours (2½
hours costs $20) every Wednesday
morning. Meet at the library at 10 AM.

Amigo Travel (⊠ Av. Colón
508C, Col. García Ginerés, Mérida
☎ 999/920–0104 or 999/920–0103
⊕ www.amigoyucatan.com). **ATS**
(⊠ Calle 69 No. 544, between
Calles 68 and 70, Centro, Mérida

☎ 999/923–2287). **Ecoturismo
Yucatán** (⊠ Calle 3 No. 235, between
Calles 32A and 34, Col. Pensiones,
Mérida ☎ 999/920–2772 ⊕ www.
ecoyuc.com). **Mayaland Tours**
(⊠ Calle Robalo 30, Sm 3, Cancún ☎ 998/887–2495 in Cancún,
01800/719–5465 toll-free from
elsewhere in Mexico, 800/235–4079
⊕ www.mayaland.com). **Turibus**
(☎ 55/5563–6693 in Mexico City
⊕ www.turibus.com.mx).

ramparts and arabesque archways. ⊠ *Calle 60 between Calles 57 and 59, Centro* ☎ *999/924–8000 operator, 999/924–6429, art and culture programming* ⊕ *www.uady.mx/sitios/cultura/ballet.html.*

❶ **Zócalo.** Méridians traditionally refer to this main square as the Plaza de la Independencia, or the Plaza Principal. Whichever name you prefer, it's a good spot from which to begin a tour of the city, in which to watch music or dance performances, or to chill in the shade of a laurel tree when the day gets too hot. The plaza was laid out in 1542 on the ruins of T'hó, the Mayan city demolished to make way for Mérida, and is still the focal point around which the most important public buildings cluster. *Confidenciales* (S-shape benches) invite intimate tête-à-têtes; lampposts keep the park beautifully illuminated at night. ⊠ *Bordered by Calles 60, 62, 61, and 63, Centro.*

WORTH NOTING

❷⓪ **Aké,** a compact archaeological site 35 km (22 mi) southeast of Mérida, offers the unique opportunity to see architecture spanning two millennia in one sweeping vista. Standing atop a ruined Mayan temple built more than a thousand years ago, you can see the incongruous nearby sight of workers processing sisal in a rusty-looking factory, which was built in the early 20th century. To the right of this dilapidated building are the ruins of the old Hacienda and Iglesia de San Lorenzo Aké, both constructed of stones taken from the Mayan temples.

Experts estimate that Aké was populated between around 200 BC and AD 900; today many people in the area have Aké as a surname. The city seems to have been related to the very important and powerful one at present-day Izamal; in fact, the two cities were once connected by a *sacbé* (white road) 13 meters (43 feet) wide and 33 km (20 mi) long. All that's excavated so far are two pyramids, one with rows of columns (35 total) at the top, very reminiscent of the Toltec columns at Tula, north of Mexico City. ⌐$2.20 ☉ *Daily 9–5.*

❶⑨ **Ermita de Santa Isabel.** At the southern end of the city stands the restored and beautiful Hermitage of St. Isabel. Built circa-1748 as part of a Jesuit monastery also known as the Hermitage of the Good Trip, it served as a resting place for colonial-era travelers heading to Campeche. It is one of the most peaceful places in the city, with an interesting, inlaid-stone facade (although the church itself is almost always closed), and is a good destination for a ride in a horse carriage. Behind the hermitage are its huge and lush tropical gardens, with a waterfall and footpaths; they're usually unlocked during daylight hours. ⊠ *Calles 66 and 77, La Ermita* ☎ *No phone* ☎ *Free* ⊙ *Church open only during mass.*

WORD OF MOUTH

"[Our] last day in Merida was a Sunday, the best day in the city because the streets are closed—activities and vendors are all over the Zócalo. The Zócalo has free Wi-Fi which was pretty cool, so I was able check e-mail on my iPhone and use Internet." —Nicci

⑨ Iglesia de la Tercera Orden de Jesús. Just north of Parque Hidalgo is one of Mérida's oldest buildings and the first Jesuit church in the Yucatán. It was built in 1618 from the limestone blocks of a dismantled Mayan temple, and faint outlines of ancient carvings are still visible on the west wall. Although a favorite place for society weddings due to its antiquity, the church interior is not ornate.

The former convent rooms in the rear of the building now host the **Pinoteca Juan Gamboa Guzmán,** a small but interesting art collection. The most engaging pieces here are the striking bronze sculptures of indigenous Maya crafted by celebrated 20th-century sculptor Enrique Gottdiener Soto. On the second floor are about 20 forgettable oil paintings—mostly of past civic officials of the area. ⊠ *Calle 59 between Calles 58 and 60, Centro* ☎ *999/924–5233* ☎ *$3* ⊙ *Tues.–Sat. 9–5, Sun. 10–5.*

⑰ Mercado de Artesanías García Rejón. Although many deal in the same wares, the shops or stalls of the García Rejón Crafts Market sell some quality items, and the shopping experience here can be less of a hassle than at the municipal market. You'll find reasonable prices on palm-fiber hats, hammocks, leather sandals, jewelry, and locally made liqueurs; persistent but polite bargaining may get you even better deals. ⊠ *Calles 60 and 65, Centro* ☎ *No phone* ⊙ *Weekdays 9–6, Sat. 9–4, Sun. 9–1.*

⑯ Mercado Municipal. Sellers of chiles, herbs, crafts, trinkets, and fruit fill this pungent and labyrinthine municipal market. In the early morning the first floor is jammed with housewives and restaurateurs shopping for the freshest seafood and produce. The stairs at Calles 56 and 57 lead to the second-floor Bazar de Artesanías Municipales, on either side, where you'll find local pottery, embroidered clothes, men's guayabera dress shirts, hammocks, and straw bags. Note that most prices are inflated, and vendors expect you will bargain—one way to begin is to politely request a discount. ⊠ *Calles 56 and 67, Centro* ☎ *No phone* ⊙ *Mon.–Sat. dawn–dusk, Sun. 8–3.*

⑦ Museo de Arte Contemporáneo. Originally designed as an art school and used until 1915 as a seminary, this enormous, light-filled building now showcases the works of contemporary Yucatecan artists such as Gabriel Ramírez Aznar and Fernando García Ponce, as well as a variety of temporary exhibits. ⊠*Pasaje de la Revolución 1907, between Calles 58 and 60 on main square, Centro* ☎*999/928–3236 or 999/928–3258* ⊕*www.macay.org* ⊠*Free* ⊙ *Wed. and Thurs., 10–5:30, Fri. and Sat. 10–7:30.*

⑮ **Museo de Arte Popular de Yucatán** (*Museum of Popular Art of the Yucatán* ⊠*Calle 50 No. 487, between 57 and 59* ☎*999/928–5263* ⊠*$2* ⊙*Tues.–Sat. 9:30–6:30*), facing the Plaza Mejorada, is funded by the Banamex Cultural Foundation and offers a comprehensive introduction to the different kinds of Mexican art craft including ceramics, textiles, stone work, cardboard art, woodwork, and glass. Even if you don't want to see the whole museum, take a look in the gift shop, which sells all sorts of crafts like shawls, baskets, dolls, and masks. Prices are a bit high, but so is the quality of the crafts; even if you don't buy anything here, a look around will inform your purchases at area markets.

⑭ **Palacio Cantón.** The most compelling of the mansions on **Paseo Montejo,** this stately palacio was built as the residence for a general between 1909 and 1911. Designed by Enrique Deserti, who also did the blueprints for the Teatro Peón Contreras, the building has a grandiose air that seems more characteristic of a mausoleum than a home: there's marble everywhere, as well as Doric and Ionic columns and other Italianate Beaux-Arts flourishes. The building also houses the air-conditioned **Museo de Antropología e Historia,** which introduces visitors to ancient Mayan culture. Temporary exhibits sometimes brighten the standard collection. ⊠*Paseo Montejo 485, at Calle 43, Paseo Montejo* ☎*999/923–0469* ⊠*$5* ⊙*Tues.–Sat. 9 AM–8 PM, Sun. 9–2.*

❺ **Palacio del Gobierno.** Visit the seat of state government to see Fernando Castro Pacheco's murals of the bloody history of the conquest of the Yucatán, painted in bold colors in the 1970s and influenced by the Mexican muralists José Clemente Orozco and David Alfaro Siquieros. On the main balcony (visible from outside on the plaza) stands a reproduction of the Bell of Dolores Hidalgo, on which Mexican independence rang out on the night of September 15, 1810, in the town of Dolores Hidalgo in Guanajuato. On the anniversary of the event, the governor rings the bell to commemorate the occasion. ⊠*Calle 61 between Calles 60 and 62, Centro* ☎*999/930–3101* ⊠*Free* ⊙*Daily 9 AM–9 PM.*

❹ **Palacio Municipal.** The west side of the main square is occupied by City Hall, a 17th-century building trimmed with white arcades, balustrades, and the national coat of arms. Originally erected on the ruins of the last surviving Mayan structure, it was rebuilt in 1735 and then completely reconstructed along colonial lines in 1928. It remains the headquarters of the local government, and houses the municipal tourist office. ⊠*Calle 62 between Calles 61 and 63, Centro* ☎*999/928–2020* ⊙*Palacio daily 9–8; Tourist Information Center weekdays 8–8, Sat. 9–1.*

NEED A BREAK?
The homemade ice cream and sorbet at **El Colón** have been a tradition since 1907. It's one way that locals keep cool. The tropical fruit flavors, like *chico zapote* (a brown fruit native to Mexico that has a flavor a little like cinnamon and comes from a tree that is used in chewing-gum production), served up in a pyramid-shaped scoop are particularly delicious and

refreshing. The shop also sell cookies and fresh candies—the meringues are exceptional. ⊠ *Calle 62 No. 500, at Calle 59 and Calle 61, Centro* ☎ *999/928-1497* ▤ *No credit cards.*

8 **Parque Hidalgo.** A half block north of the main plaza is this small cozy park, officially known as Plaza Cepeda Peraza. Historic mansions, now reincarnated as hotels and sidewalk cafés, line the south side of the park; at night the area comes alive with marimba bands and street vendors. On Sunday the streets are closed to vehicular traffic, and there's free live music performed throughout the day. ⊠ *Calle 60 between Calles 59 and 61, Centro* ☎ *No phone.*

12 **Parque Santa Lucía.** The rather plain park at calles 60 and 55 draws crowds with its Thursday-night music and dance performances (shows start at 9); on Sunday, couples also come to dance to a live band, and enjoy food from carts set up in the plaza. The small church opposite the park dates to 1575 and was built as a place of worship for the Maya, who weren't allowed to worship at just any Mérida temple. ⊠ *Calles 60 and 55, Centro* ☎ *No phone.*

18 **Parque Zoológico El Centenario.** Mérida's greatest children's attraction, this ☾ large amusement complex features playgrounds, rides (including ponies and a small train), a rollerblading rink, snack bars, and cages with more than 300 native animals as well as exotics such as lions, tigers, and bears. It also has picnic areas, pleasant wooded paths, and a small lake where you can rent rowboats. The French Renaissance–style arch (1921) commemorates the 100th anniversary of Mexican independence. ⊠ *Av. Itzáes between Calles 59 and 65, entrances on Calles 59 and 65, Centro* ☎ *No phone* ⊕ *www.merida.gob.mx/centenario/* ☜ *Free* ☾ *Zoo Tues.–Sun. 6–6.*

WHERE TO EAT

With more than 250 restaurants (not to mention the markets and street-food stands) there are plenty of dining options to choose from in Mérida. Regional dishes and Middle Eastern cuisine are staples, but the flavors and preparations don't stop there. You can even find places serving hamburgers and sandwiches if you're craving something familiar.

¢ ✕ **Alameda.** The waiters are brusque, the building is old, and the decor

MIDDLE EASTERN couldn't be plainer. But you'll find good, hearty, and cheap fare at this always-popular spot. The most expensive main dish here costs about $4—but side dishes are extra. Middle Eastern and standard Yucatecan fare share the menu with vegetarian specialties: meat-free dishes include tabbouleh and spongy, lemon-flavor spinach turnovers. Shopkeepers linger over grilled beef shish kebab, pita bread, and coffee; some old couples have been coming in once a week for decades. An English-language menu, which has explanations as well as translations, is essential even for Spanish speakers. Alameda closes at 5 PM. ⊠ *Calle 58 No. 474, near Calle 57, Centro* ☎ *999/928–3635* ▤ *No credit cards* ☾ *No dinner.*

$$$ ✕ **Alberto's Continental Patio.** Though locals say this eatery has lost some

MIDDLE EASTERN of its star power, it's still a dependable place for shish kebab, fried *kibbe* (meatballs of ground beef, wheat germ, and spices), hummus, tabbouleh, and other Lebanese dishes. The strikingly handsome dining spot dates to 1727 and is adorned with some of the original stones from the Mayan temple it replaced, as well as mosaic floors from Cuba. Even if you choose to have lunch or dinner elsewhere, stop in for almond pie and Turkish coffee in the romantic, candlelit courtyard. ⊠*Calle 64 No. 482, at Calle 57, Centro* ☎*999/928–5367* ▤*MC, V.*

$ ✗**Amaro.** The open patio of this

VEGETARIAN historic home glows with candlelight in the evening; during the day things look a lot more casual. Meat, fish, and shellfish are served here in moderation, but the emphasis is on vegetarian dishes like eggplant curry and chaya soup (made

WORD OF MOUTH

"We love Albertos. We always eat there when we are in Merida. The first time we visited the restaurant, we were early diners and it was very quiet . . . the owner, Alberto, greeted us, gave us a personal tour of the eye-boggling restaurant. There were "lilies de noche" he called them—night-blooming, fragrant flowers at each table that began to open as we dined. Very romantic. Last year, as we finished eating, a large group had hired a mariachi band to serenade and perform for their table, and we spent a delightful half hour enjoying a few more drinks and watching a wonderful performance. Great place!" –parrmt

from a green plant similar to spinach), and healthful juices. Prices are reasonable and the service is always excellent. If you're missing your favorite comfort foods, get your fix with a side order of mashed potatoes or french fries. Amaro stays open until 2 AM from Monday to Saturday. Expect live music Monday through Saturday between 9 PM and midnight. ⊠*Calle 59 No. 507, between Calles 60 and 62, Centro* ☎*999/928–2451* ⊕*www.restauranteamaro.com* ▤*V.*

$ ✗**Café La Habana.** A gleaming wood bar, white-jacketed waiters, and

MEXICAN the scent of cigarettes contribute to the Old European feel at this overwhelmingly popular spot, a branch of a Mexico City café that has been around since the 1950s. Overhead, brass-studded ceiling fans swirl the air-conditioned air. Sixteen specialty coffees are offered (some spiked with spirits like Kahlúa or cognac), and the menu has light snacks as well as some entrées, including tamales, fajitas, and enchiladas. The waiters are friendly, and there are plenty of them, although service is not always brisk. Both the café and upstairs Internet joint are open 24 hours a day; free Wi-Fi is available downstairs for laptop-toting customers. ⊠*Calle 59 No. 511A, at Calle 62, Centro* ☎*999/928–6502* ▤*MC, V.*

$$ ✗**Café Lucía.** Opera music floats above black-and-white tile floors in

ITALIAN the dining room of this century-old restaurant in the Hotel Casa Lucía near the main plaza. Pizzas and calzones are the linchpins of the Italian menu; luscious pecan pies, cakes, and cookies beckon from behind the glass dessert case. The original art on the walls is for sale; however, the paintings by the late Oaxacan artist Rodolfo Morales are not, so don't bother asking. ⊠*Calle 60 No. 474A, Centro* ☎*999/928–0704* ⊕*www.casalucia.com.mx* ▤*AE, MC, V.*

¢–$ **✕ Dante's.** Couples, groups of students, and lots of families crowd this
CAFÉ bustling coffeehouse on the second floor of one of Mérida's largest
bookshops. The house specialty is crepes: there are 18 varieties with
either sweet or savory fillings. Light entrées such as sandwiches, burgers, pizzas, and *molletes*—large open-face rolls smeared with beans
and cheese and then broiled—are also served, along with cappuccino, specialty coffees, beer, and wine. A small theater puts on evening
comic sketches and live music from time to time, and free children's
programs on Sunday mornings. ✉ *Prolongación Paseo Montejo 138B,
Paseo Montejo* ☎ *999/927–7676* ▭ *MC, V.*

$$$ **✕ Eladio's.** Part bar, part restaurant, and part theater, this lively, recently
MEXICAN remodeled venue is often crammed with local families and couples.
There's an ample dance floor and a free, supervised children's play area
where children can play for free—you can also buy ceramic figures for
them to paint while you dance. There's a full menu of tasty Yucatecan
dishes like *papadzules* (hard-boiled eggs wrapped in warm tortillas and
covered with a thick pumpkin-seed sauce) and *sopa de lima* (turkey
soup with vegetables, tortilla strips, and lime). Free appetizers, which
are actually just smaller portions of the dishes on the menu, come with
your suds. From 2 to 6:30 PM there's live salsa, cumbia, and other Latino
tunes, punctuated by stage-show-style talking. At 7:30 most families
disappear, and singles and couples arrive to watch whatever football or
boxing match is on TV. ✉ *Calle 24 No. 101C, at Calle 59, Col. Itzimná*
☎ *999/927–2126* ⊕ *www.eladios.com.mx.*

$ **✕ El Gran Café.** Brought to you by the owners of Café La Habana, this
MEXICAN café has a great deal more space and is more popular with families.
Black and white photos of the original Café La Habana, in Mexico
City, adorn the walls, and an old-fashioned cash register adds to the
'50s feel, but the automatic doors, free Wi-Fi, and air-conditioning
remind you what century we're in. On weekends the place fills up early
with breakfasters and brunchers. Friday, Saturday, and Sunday there's a
nice breakfast buffet with tasty Mexican and international fare. There
are a number of tasty coffee drinks, included some spiked with liquor
and a delicious white chocolate concoction. Like Café La Habana, El
Gran is open 24/7. ✉ *Calle 47 No. 486, at Calle 56 and 58, Centro*
☎ *999/923–2273* ▭ *MC, V.*

$$ **✕ Hacienda Teya.** Once a henequen-producing site, this beautiful haci-
MEXICAN enda just outside the city serves some of the best regional food around.
Fodor's Choice It has attracted some big names, like Vicente Fox (back when he was
★ president) and even Hillary Clinton. Most patrons are well-to-do Méridians enjoying a leisurely lunch, so you don't want to wear your beach
clothes; in fact, men wearing tank tops are asked to change. It's open
from noon to 6 daily (though most Mexicans don't show up until after
3), and a guitarist serenades the tables between 2 and 5 on weekends.
After a fabulous lunch of *cochinita pibíl* (pork baked in banana leaves)
or *queso relleno* (cheese stuffed with ground pork and beef and slath-
ered in a tasty white sauce with tomatoes), take a stroll through the
surrounding orchards and botanical gardens. If you find yourself wanting to spend the night, you can—the hacienda has six handsome suites
($$), which are often available on short notice, although they need

5

to be reserved in advance over long weekends and holidays. ⊠ *12.5 km (8 mi) east of Mérida on Carretera 180, Kanasín* ☎ *999/988–0800* ⊕ *www.haciendateya.com* ☐ *AE, MC, V* ⊘ *No dinner.*

$$ ✕ **La Bella Epoca.** The coveted, tiny
ECLECTIC   private balconies at this elegantly restored mansion overlook Parque Hidalgo. You'll need to call in advance to reserve one for a 7 PM or 10 PM seating; tables that overlook the park go especially fast. On weekends, when the street below is closed to traffic and tables are set up outside, it's especially pleasant to survey the park while feasting on Mayan dishes like *sikil-pak* (a dip with ground pumpkin seeds, charbroiled tomatoes, and onions) or succulent *pollo pibíl* (chicken baked in banana leaves). ⊠ *Calle 60 No. 497, between Calles 57 and 59, Centro* ☎ *999/928–1928* ☐ *AE, MC, V* ⊘ *No lunch.*

WORD OF MOUTH

"I chose to dine at La Casa de Frida specifically because I had read a review that praised its *chiles en nogada* . . . and I found it praiseworthy indeed! I began with an appetizer of crêpes with *cuitlachoche* that was so delicious that I couldn't bring myself to stop eating . . . unfortunately, I was too full to do proper justice to the *chiles en nogada.* Even so, just thinking of that evening brings back memories of that entrée and its intensely flavorful and rich walnut sauce—wow! My server always seemed to appear out of nowhere at exactly the right time." —kja

$ ✕ **La Casa de Frida.** Chef-owner Gabriela Praget puts a healthful, cosmo-
MEXICAN   politan spin on Mexican fare at her restaurant. This is a great place to
Fodor'sChoice   sample foods from around Mexico. Praget prepares all the dishes herself
★   and is usually on hand to greet guests. Traditional dishes like duck in a dark, rich mole sauce (made with chocolate and chiles) share the menu with gourmet vegetarian cuisine: potato and cheese tacos, ratatouille in puff pastry, and crepes made with *cuitlachoche* (a delicious trufflelike corn fungus). The flavors here are so divine that diners have been known to hug Praget after a meal. The dining room—a casual covered patio decorated with plants, copies of Frida Kahlo self-portraits, several Frida dolls, and other art—is a comfortable place to enjoy a leisurely meal. ⊠ *Calle 61 No. 526, at Calle 66, Centro* ☎ *999/928–2311* ☐ *No credit cards* ⊘ *Closed Sun. No lunch.*

$ ✕ **La Tradición.** This family restaurant is popular among locals—in fact,
MEXICAN   many say it's their favorite restaurant in town. It's also one of the most formal places that serves the region's cuisine, but you'll still fit right in if you're wearing jeans. Proprietor Albino Medina is a third-generation chef and restaurant owner in his family. Dishes are prepared with charcoal stove, like your grandma might have made, if you were from around here. The kitchen standards of cleanliness are so strict that the restaurant has received recognition from Secretary of Tourism. Just about everything you'll try is tasty, but you might not want to pass up the cream of chaya soup (made from fresh chaya, a leafy green) since you won't find it in many other restaurants. ⊠ *Calle 60 No. 293, at Calle 25, Col. Alcalá Martin* ☎ *999/925–2526* ☐ *MC, V.*

$ ✕ **La Vía Olimpo.** Lingering over coffee and a book is a pleasure at this
CAFÉ   smart Internet café; the outdoor tables are a great place to watch the

CLOSE UP

Yucatecan Cuisine

Yucatecan food is surprisingly diverse, and milder than you might expect. Anything that's too mild, however, can be spiced up in a jiffy with one of many varieties of chile sauce. The sour orange chile—large, green, and only slightly sour—is native to the region, and is also used to give many soups and sauces a unique flavor.

Typical snacks like *panuchos* (small, thick, fried rounds of cornmeal stuffed or topped with beans and sprinkled with shredded meat and cabbage), *empanadas* (turnovers of meat, fish, potatoes, or, occasionally, cheese or beans), and *salbutes* (fried tortillas smothered with diced turkey, pickled onion, and sliced avocado) are ubiquitous. You'll find them at lunch counters (*loncherías*), in the market, and on the menus of restaurants specializing in local food.

Some recipes made famous in certain Yucatecan towns have made their way to mainstream menus. *Huevos motuleños*, presumably a recipe from the town of Motul, are so tasty they're found on breakfast menus throughout

the region, and even elsewhere in Mexico. The recipe is similar to *huevos rancheros* (fried eggs on soft corn tortillas smothered in a mild red sauce) with the addition of sliced ham, melted cheese, and peas. Likewise, *pollo ticuleño*, which originated in Ticul, is served throughout the Yucatán. It's a delicious casserole of layered tomato sauce, mashed potatoes or cornmeal, crispy tortillas, chicken, cheese, and peas.

Tixin-Xic (pronounced teak-en-*sheek*) is fun to say and even better to eat. This coastal delicacy consists of butterflied snapper rubbed with salt and achiote (an aromatic paste made from the ground seeds of the annatto plant, and used to color food red as well as to subtly season it), grilled over a wood fire, and garnished with tomatoes and onions. As throughout Mexico, *aguas frescas*—fruit-flavored waters—are refreshing on a typically hot day, as are the dark beers Montejo and Leon Negro. Xtabentún is a sweet, thick, locally made liqueur made of anise and honey.

5

nonstop parade—or the free Sunday performances—on the main square. In the air-conditioned dining room you can feast on turkey sandwiches, burgers and fries, or *poc chuc* (slices of pork marinated in sour-orange sauce and spices). Crepes are also popular, and there are lots of salads and juices if you're in the mood for something light. Crowds keep this place hopping from 7 AM to 11 PM daily. Spirits are served, and you'll get an appetizer, like a basket of chips with freshly made guacamole, with most drink orders. ⊠ *Calle 62 No. 502, between Calles 63 and 61, Centro* ☎ *999/923–5843* ▭*MC, V*

$ ✕**Los Almendros.** This classic Yucatecan eatery has been a favorite with

MEXICAN locals since the 1960s when the owners opened their first restaurant in nearby Ticul. The Mérida branch has been here since 1972, and many say it's still the best place to eat in town. The restaurant is actually separated in two buildings called Los Almendros and Gran Almendros. The menu and prices are the same, but the atmosphere and schedules are slightly different—Los Alemdros has a more casual feel, while the Gran Almendros's high Colonial ceilings create a slightly more elegant atmosphere—so take a look around to see where you'd like to sit before settling in. The *combinado yucateco* (Yucatecan combination plate) is a great way to try different dishes: *cochinita pibíl* (slow roasted pork), *longaniza asada* (grilled pork sausages), *escabeche de Valladolid* (turkey with chiles, onions, and seasonings in an acidic sauce), and *poc-chuc* (tender grilled pork). In fact, they invented some dishes that have become Yucatecan classicsincluding the *poc-chuc* and the cheese soup which is also spectacular. ✉ *Calle 57 No. 50, facing Parque La Mejorada, Col. Centro* ☎ *999/928–5459 or 999/923–8135* ▤ *AE, MC, V.*

> ## MARKET SNACKS
>
> The simple market in **Parque Santa Ana** (✉ *Calle 60, between 45 and 47, Centro* ☎ *No phone*) is a popular breakfast spot where you will find locals happily starting their day with regional dishes and fresh juices at plastic tables. The *tamales* are good. The *tortas de cochinita*, pork sandwiches flavored with a few drops of sour-orange chile sauce are heavenly. Most vendors here close around 1:30 in the afternoon, but some reopen to sell snacks between 7 PM and midnight.

$ ✗**Ristorante & Pizzería Bologna.** You can dine alfresco or inside at this
ITALIAN   beautifully restored old mansion, a few blocks off Paseo Montejo. Tables have fresh flowers and cloth napkins; walls are adorned with pictures of Italy, and there are plants everywhere. Most menu items are ordered à la carte; among the favorites are the shrimp pizza and pizza *diabola,* topped with salami, tomato, and chiles. The beef fillet—served solo or covered in cheese or mushrooms—is served with baked potato and a medley of mixed sautéed vegetables. ✉ *Calle 21 No. 117A, near Calle 24, Col. Izimná* ☎ *999/926–2505* ▤ *AE, MC, V.*

¢   ✗**Wayan'e.** Friendly owner Mauricio Loría presides over this oasis of
MEXICAN   carnivorous delights (mostly tortas, Mexico's answer to the sandwich, though tacos are also served) at the crossroads of several busy streets. In addition to ham and cheese tortas, there are pork loin in smoky chipotle-chile sauce, chorizo sausage, turkey strips sautéed with onions and peppers, and several other delicious combos guaranteed to go straight to your arteries. Non-meat-eaters can try some unusual combos, like chopped cactus pads sautéed with mushrooms, or scrambled eggs with chaya or string beans. The place is casual and unassuming, with plastic tables and chairs, but most diners gather around the counter where the food is handed over. The storefront, which is almost always busy but still quick and efficient, closes at 3 PM on weekdays and 2 PM on Saturday. ✉ *Felipe Carrillo Puerto 11A No. 57C, at Calle 4, Col. Itzimná* ☎ *999/938–0676* ⊜ *Reservations not accepted* ▤ *No credit cards* ⊘ *Closed Sun., no dinner.*

WHERE TO STAY

Mérida has a wide range of lodging choices, from old haciendas and privately owned, converted colonial homes to big corporate hotels. Generally, you will find smaller hotels in the downtown area, within walking distance of most sights; nights are inevitably a little louder here, especially if your room faces the street. A few larger chain hotels around the Paseo de Montejo offer quiet rooms and are still near major streets, and only a short ride from downtown.

$$ ★ ☰ **Casa del Balam.** This pleasant hotel has an excellent location two blocks from the zócalo in downtown's best shopping area. The rooms here include colonial touches, like carved cedar doors and rocking chairs on the wide verandas, but they also have modern-day conveniences like double-paned windows to keep out the noise. The rich decor and thoughtful details, like the hand-painted plates, make this place seem more like a home than a hotel; the open central patio is a lovely spot for a meal or a drink. Guests have access to a golf and tennis club about 15 minutes away by car. **Pros:** easy walk to many sights; spacious rooms; tasty food (particularly at breakfast). **Cons:** slow elevator; street noise can be a problem. ⊠ *Calle 60 No. 488, Centro* ☎ *999/924–8844 or 800/624–8451* ⊕ *www.casadelbalam.com* ⇨ *44 rooms, 7 suites* ♿ *In-hotel: Restaurant, room service, bar, pool, parking (no fee), no-smoking rooms* ☰ *AE, D, DC, MC, V* ⏁ *EP.*

$–$$ ☰ **Casa Mexilio.** This eclectic B&B is four blocks from the main square. Middle Eastern wall hangings, French tapestries, and colorful tile floors crowd the public spaces; individually decorated rooms have tile sinks and folk-art furniture. Some find this inn private and romantic, although others may find it a bit too intimate for their liking. The grottolike pool is surrounded by ferns, and the light-filled penthouse, up four dozen steps, has an excellent city view from its oversize balcony. A two-night minimum stay is required. **Pros:** pleasant courtyard; easy walk to downtown attractions; excellent room prices. **Cons:** small bathrooms; some linens look dated; no children allowed; no parking. ⊠ *Calle 68 No. 495, between Calles 57 and 59, Centro* ☎ *999/928–2505, 800/538–6802 in U.S. and Canada* ⊕ *www.mexicoholiday.com* ⇨ *8 rooms, 1 penthouse* ♿ *In-room: No phone, no TV, Wi-Fi (some). In-hotel: Restaurant, bar, pool, no children under 16, no-smoking rooms* ☰ *AE, MC, V* ⏁ *CP.*

¢–$ ★ ☰ **Dolores Alba.** The newer wing of this comfortable, cheerful hotel has spiffy rooms with quietly powerful air-conditioning, comfortable beds, and amenities like large TVs, balconies, and telephones. The older (and cheaper) rooms also have air-conditioning, but they have fans, too, which newer rooms do not. The pool is surrounded by lounge chairs and shaded by giant trees, and there's a comfortable restaurant and bar at the front of the property. There's a small discount if you book on their Web site. **Pros:** great room prices; nice pool and clean rooms; short walk to the zócalo. **Cons:** mediocre breakfast; no Internet access from rooms. ⊠ *Calle 63 No. 464, between Calles 52 and 54, Centro* ☎ *999/928–5650* ⊕ *www.doloresalba.com* ⇨ *100 rooms* ♿ *In-room: Safe. In-hotel: Restaurant, bar, pool, parking (free), Wi-Fi, Internet terminal, no-smoking rooms* ☰ *MC, V* ⏁ *EP.*

$$ ☰ **Fiesta Americana Mérida.** The facade of this posh hotel echoes the grandeur of the mansions on Paseo Montejo. The spacious lobby—with groupings of plush armchairs where guests often lounge—is filled with colonial accents and gleaming marble; above is a 300-foot-high stained-glass roof. The tasteful and subdued guest room, inspired by late-19th-century design, have extras like balconies, bathtubs, hair-dryers, and coffeemakers. Some rooms face the street and have a little

5

more noise, while others face a dull inner courtyard with the hotel pool, so be sure to specify which you'd prefer. Downstairs you'll find a department store, a couple of restaurants (including a Chili's), souvenir shops, and myriad other shops and services. Occasionally there are events at the hotel, including dinner shows and dances for children, so be sure to inquire whether anything is in the works at the front desk. **Pros:** comfortable beds; exceptionally varied and tasty breakfast buffet; powerful air-conditioning. **Cons:** a taxi ride away from downtown; very small bathtubs. ⊠ *Av. Colón 451, Paseo Montejo* ☎*999/942–1111 or 800/343–7821* ⊕*www.fiestaamericana.com* ⇗*323 rooms, 27 suites* ⌂*In-room: Safe, Internet. In-hotel: Restaurant, room service, bar, tennis court, pool, gym, spa, laundry service, parking (free), no-smoking rooms* ▭*AE, D, MC, V* ⎮⊘⎮*CP, EP.*

$$ ⊡**Gran Hotel.** Cozily situated on Parque Hidalgo, this legendary 1901 hotel does look its age, with extremely high ceilings, wrought-iron balcony and stair rails, and ornately patterned tile floors. The period decor is so classic that you expect a mantilla-wearing Spanish señorita to appear, fluttering her fan, at any moment. The old-fashioned sitting room has formal seating areas and lots of antiques and plants. A renovation in 2004 enlarged some guest rooms and replaced tiny twin beds with doubles. Wide interior verandas on the second and third floors provide pretty outside seating. Porfirio Díaz, a former Mexican president, stayed in one of the corner suites, which have small living and dining areas. The downstairs boutique sells high-quality clothes, including wedding dresses, made from natural fibers. **Pros:** beautiful antique decorations (especially in public areas); located in the middle of downtown bustle, sights, and shops. **Cons:** downtown noise; no elevator makes upstairs rooms quite a hike. ⊠*Calle 60 No. 496, Centro* ☎*999/923–6963* ⇗*25 rooms, 7 suites* ⌂*In-hotel: Restaurant, room service, laundry service, parking (free), some pets allowed, no-smoking rooms* ▭*MC, V* ⎮⊘⎮*EP*

$$$$ ⊡**Hacienda Xcanatun.** The furnishings at this beautifully restored 18th
★ century henequen hacienda include African and Indonesian antiques, locally made lamps, and comfortable, oversized couches and chairs from Puebla. The cool and spacious rooms come with cozy sleigh beds, fine sheets, and fluffy comforters, and are impeccably decorated with art from Mexico, Cuzco, Peru, and other places the owners have traveled. Bathrooms are luxuriously large. The restaurant serves a standard breakfast as well as French and Caribbean dishes with Yucatan accents and ingredients for lunch and dinner, while the hacienda's spa cooks up innovative treatments such as cacao-and-honey massages. **Pros:** good restaurant; expansive gardens; poolside bar service. **Cons:** a drive from the city; pricey. ⊠*Carretera 261, Km 12, 13 km (8 mi) north of Mérida* ☎*999/941–0213 or 888/883–3633* ⊕*www.xcanatun.com* ⇗*18 suites* ⌂*In-room: Safe, no TV. In-hotel: Restaurant, room service, bars, pools, spa, laundry service, parking (free), Wi-Fi, no-smoking rooms* ▭*AE, MC, V* ⎮⊘⎮*CP.*

$$ ⊡**Holiday Inn.** The most light-filled hotel in Mérida, the Holiday Inn has floor-to-ceiling windows throughout the colorful lobby and tiled dining room. Rooms and suites face an open courtyard and have comfy

furnishings and marble bathrooms. Amenities include ironing boards, hair dryers, coffeemakers, alarm clocks, and more. Be sure to ask about special rates, which can save you quite a bit. **Pros:** spacious rooms; nice breakfast buffet. **Cons:** about a mile from downtown; pool too small for serious swimming. ⊠ *Av. Colón 468, at Calle 60, Paseo Montejo* ☎ *999/942–8800 or 800/465–4329* ⊕ *www.ichotelsgroup.com* ↘ *197 rooms, 15 suites* ⅄ *In-room: Wi-Fi. In-hotel: Restaurant, room service, bar, gym, tennis court, pool, laundry service, Wi-Fi, parking (free), no-smoking rooms* ▤ *AE, DC, MC, V* �†⊙† *EP.*

¢–$ ⊞ **Hostal del Peregrino.** This recently restored old home is now part upscale hostel, part inexpensive hotel. Private rooms downstairs have few amenities but wonderfully restored *piso de pasta*—tile floors with intricate designs. Upstairs are shared coed dorm rooms with separate showers and toilets, and an open-air bar and TV lounge for hanging out in the evening with fellow guests. Hostel staff can help arrange tours. **Pros:** inexpensive; easy walk downtown; staff can arrange tours and Spanish tutoring. **Cons:** spacious but basic rooms; kitchen and lounge areas can get noisy. ⊠ *Calle 51 No. 488, between Calles 54 and 56, Centro* ☎ *999/924–5491* ⊕ *www.hostaldelperegrino.com* ↘ *7 private rooms, 3 dorm rooms* ⅄ *In-room: Wi-Fi. In-hotel: Restaurant, bar, no-smoking rooms* ▤ *MC, V* †⊙† *CP.*

$–$$ ⊞ **Hotel María del Carmen.** Innocuous as you please, this hotel caters to business travelers, tour groups, and those who desire secure parking and a familiar environment. Rooms have lacquered furniture and ornate Chinese lamps. The main square is about five long blocks away. **Pros:** spacious rooms; big pool. **Cons:** slow service; rooms facing street are noisy; children under 12 not allowed. ⊠ *Calle 63 No. 550, between Calles 68 and 70, Centro* ☎ *999/930–0390 or 800/528–1234* ⊕ *www. hotelmariadelcarmen.com.mx* ↘ *86 rooms, 4 suites* ⅄ *In-hotel: Restaurant, room service, bar, pool, laundry service, parking (free), Wi-Fi, no children under 12, no-smoking rooms* ▤ *AE, MC, V* †⊙† *EP.*

$$ ⊞ **Hyatt Regency Mérida.** The city's first deluxe hotel is still among its
★ most elegant. Rooms are regally decorated, with russet-hue quilts and rugs set off by blond-wood furniture and cream-color walls. There's a top-notch business center, and a beautiful marble lobby. Upper-crust Méridians recommend Spasso Italian restaurant as a fine place to have a drink in the evening; for an amazing seafood extravaganza, don't miss the $20 seafood buffet at Peregrina bistro on Friday afternoons from 1 to 5. **Pros:** attentive service; reasonably priced compared to neighboring hotels; popular restaurant. **Cons:** just off the Paseo Montejo but far from downtown. ⊠ *Calle 60 No. 344, at Av. Colón, Paseo Montejo* ☎ *999/942–0202, 999/942–1234, or 800/233–1234* ⊕ *merida.regency. hyatt.com.mx* ↘ *296 rooms, 4 suites* ⅄ *In-room: Safe, Internet, Wi-Fi. In-hotel: 2 restaurants, room service, bars, tennis courts, pool, gym, laundry service, parking (free), no-smoking rooms* ▤ *AE, DC, MC, V* †⊙† *BP, EP.*

$$ ⊞ **Maison LaFitte.** Jazz and tropical music float quietly above this hotel's two charming patios, where you can sip a drink near the fountain or swim in the small pool. Rooms are simple here and the bathrooms a bit cramped, but the staff is friendly and the location—a few blocks from

the central plaza and surrounded by shops and restaurants—is ideal. Thursday through Saturday evenings a trio entertains on the pretty outdoor patio. While there is no spa, the hotel does offer in-room massages. **Pros:** pretty patio areas; parking makes staying downtown much easier; attentive staff. **Cons:** street noise almost as loud as courtyard fountain; small rooms. ✉ *Calle 60 No. 472, between Calles 53 and 55, Centro* ☎ *999/923–9159* 🖷 *800/538–6802 in U.S. and Canada* ⊕ *www. maisonlafitte.com.mx* �‍*30 rooms* ⚲ *In-room: Safe, Wi-Fi. In-hotel: Restaurant, bar, room service, pool, Internet terminal, laundry service, parking (free), no-smoking rooms* ⊟ *AE, MC, V* ⦿ *BP.*

$$ 🖼 **Marionetas.** Attentive proprietors Daniel and Sofija Bosco, who are
★ originally from Argentina and Macedonia, have created this lovely B&B on a quiet street seven blocks from the main plaza. From the Macedonian lace dust ruffles and fine cotton sheets and bedspreads to the quiet, remote-controlled air-conditioning and pressurized showerheads (there are no tubs), every detail and fixture here is of the highest quality. You'll delight in the carefully chosen folk-art decoration throughout. You'll need to book your reservation well in advance. You can pick up the Wi-Fi signal in some rooms but not others, so let the staff know if you'll be bringing a laptop when you book. **Pros:** intimate feel; personal attention from proprietors and staff; courtyard and pool area are a calm escape from the bustling Mérida streets. **Cons:** reservations can be hard to come by in high season; restaurant only serves breakfast. ✉ *Calle 49 No. 516, between Calles 62 and 64, Centro* ☎ *999/928–3377 or 999/923–2790* ⊕ *www.hotelmarionetas.com* �‍*8 rooms, 1 suite* ⚲ *In-room: Safe. In-hotel: Restaurant, bar, Wi-Fi, Internet terminal, no elevator, no-smoking rooms* ⊟ *MC, V* ⦿ *BP.*

$ 🖼 **Medio Mundo.** A Lebanese-Uruguayan couple runs this hotel in a residential area downtown. The house has been brightly painted and has Mediterranean accents and spacious rooms off a long passageway. The original thick walls and tile floors are well preserved; spacious rooms have custom-made hardwood furniture. A large patio in the back holds the breakfast nook, a small kidney-shaped swimming pool, and an old mango tree. There's also a pond with a delightful waterfall and fountain surrounded by fruit and flowering trees. For a small fee you can have a nice daily breakfast. A small gift shop is also on hand for crafts. **Pros:** great location; friendly staff; reasonable rates. **Cons:** breakfast costs extra and no other meals are served; guests' comings and goings can be noisy at night. ✉ *Calle 55 No. 533, between Calles 64 and 66, Centro* 🖷 *999/924–5472* ⊕ *www.hotelmediomundo.com* �‍*12 rooms* ⚲ *In-room: No a/c (some), no phone, no TV. In-hotel: Restaurant, pool, laundry service, parking (paid), no-smoking rooms* ⊟ *MC, V* ⦿ *BP, EP.*

¢ 🖼 **Posada Toledo.** This beautiful centuries-old house has retained its elegance with high ceilings, floors of patterned tile, and carved, colonial-style furniture. The guest rooms themselves are less impressive, and the furnishings (and their condition) vary more than the rates reflect, so be sure to inspect your shabby-chic room before checking in. Room 5 is an elegant two-room suite that was originally the mansion's master bedroom. Rooms on the second floor are newer and somewhat more modern. If you're a light sleeper, ask for a room away from the courtyard. The restaurant only serves breakfast. **Pros:** inexpensive; friendly staff. **Cons:** room quality varies; sound from courtyard audible from nearby rooms; small bathrooms. ⊠ *Calle 58 No. 487, at Calle 57, Centro* ☎ *999/923–1690* ⤵ *21 rooms, 2 suites* ♿ *In-hotel: Restaurant, parking (fee)* ▭ *MC, V* ⊙*EP.*

MAKING YOURSELF AT HOME

There are a few Internet agencies that can help you rent a home if you plan on staying in the area for a while. At ⊕ *www.bestofyucatan. com,* you can find some stunningly remodeled old Mérida homes, and haciendas remodeled by artists John Powell and Josh Ramos.

$$ ⚏**Presidente InterContinental.** A salmon-color replica of a 19th-century French-colonial mansion, the Presidente is a bit of a hike from the main plaza but sits right next to the Santiago church and public square, where a big, live band attracts whirling couples on Tuesdays at 9 PM. Rooms are spacious, beautifully decorated with modern furniture, and have remote-control cable TV, blow dryers, and spacious closets. The small swimming pool in the central courtyard is pleasant for relaxing, but far from private, as many of the rooms face the pool area. **Pros:** spacious rooms; comfortable beds; good value. **Cons:** far from main plaza. ⊠ *Calle 59 No. 589, at Calle 76, Barrio Santiago* ☎ *999/924–3899 or 999/924–3099* ⊕ *www.hotel residencial.com.mx* ⤵ *64 rooms, 2 suites* ♿ *In-room: Wi-Fi. In-hotel: Restaurant, room service, bar, pool, laundry service, parking (free), Wi-Fi, no-smoking rooms* ▭ *MC, V* ⊙*EP.*

$$$–$$$$ ⚏**Villa María.** This spacious colonial home was converted to a hotel in 2004. Most rooms are airy and spacious, with loft bedrooms hovering near the 20-foot ceilings. But it's the large patio restaurant ($–$$) that really shines. Stone columns and lacy-looking Moorish arches frame the tables here, along with a lightly spraying central fountain; it's a lovely place to enjoy such European-Mediterranean fare as squash-blossom ravioli garnished with crispy spring potatoes, roast pork loin, or savory French onion soup. For dessert there's crème brûlée, ice cream, or warm apple–almond tart. Breakfast is fine, but less impressive than lunch or dinner. **Pros:** easy walk to downtown sights; romantic architecture and decoration. **Cons:** street noise can be a problem; pool too small for serious swimming. ⊠ *Calle 59 No. 553, at Calle 68, Centro* ☎ *999/923–3357* ⊕ *www.villamariamerida.com* ⤵ *10 rooms, 2 suites* ♿ *In-room: Safe, Wi-Fi. In-hotel: Restaurant, room service, bar, parking (free), no elevator, no-smoking rooms* ▭ *AE, MC, V* ⊙*EP.*

NIGHTLIFE

Mérida has an active and diverse cultural life, which features free government-sponsored music and dance performances many evenings, as well as sidewalk art shows in local parks. Thursday at 9 PM Méridians enjoy an evening of outdoor entertainment at the **Serenata Yucateca.** At **Parque Santa Lucía** (calles 60 and 55) you'll see trios, the local orchestra, and soloists performing compositions by Yucatecan composers. On Saturday evenings after 7 PM, the **Noche Mexicana** (corner of Paseo

Montejo and Calle 47) hosts different musical and cultural events; more free music, dance, comedy, and regional handicrafts can be found at the **Corazón de Mérida,** on Calle 60 between the main plaza and Calle 55. Between 8 PM and 1 AM, multiple bandstands throughout this area (which is closed to traffic) entertain locals and visitors with an ever-changing playbill, from grunge to classical.

On Sunday, six blocks around the zócalo are closed off to traffic, and you can see performances—often mariachi and marimba bands or folkloric dancers—at Plaza Santa Lucía, Parque Hidalgo, and the main plaza. For a schedule of current performances, consult the tourist offices, the local newspapers, or the billboards and posters at the Teatro Peón Contreras or the Centro Cultural Olimpo.

BARS AND DANCE CLUBS

Mérida has always been a great city to walk in by day and dance in by night. Méridians love music, and they love to dance, but since they also have to work, many discos are open only on weekend nights, or Thursday through Sunday. ■ TIP➡Be aware that it's becoming more and more common for discos, and even restaurants with live music and "comedy" acts, geared to young people to invite customers onstage for some rather shocking "audience participation" acts. Since these are otherwise fine establishments, we can only suggest that you let your sense of outrage be your guide. Locals don't seem to mind.

★ Popular with the local *niños fresa* (which translates as "strawberry children," meaning upper-class youth) as well as some middle-age professionals, the indoor-outdoor lounge **El Cielo** (✉ *Prolongación Paseo Montejo between Calles 15 and 17, Col. México* ☎ *999/944–5127* ⊕ *www.elcielobar.com*) is one of the latest minimalist hot spots where you can drink and dance to party or lounge music videos. It's open Wednesday through Saturday nights after 9:30 PM. Their first-floor restaurant, Sky, serves sushi beginning at 1 daily, except on Mondays when it's closed.

Mambo Café (✉ *Calle 21 No. 327, between Calles 50 and 52, Plaza las Américas, Fracc. Miguel Hidalgo* ☎ *999/987–7533* ⊕ *www.mambo cafe.com.mx*) is the best place in town for dancing to DJ-spun salsa, merengue, cumbia, and disco tunes. You might want to hit the john during their raunchy audience-participation acts between sets. It's open from 9 PM until 3 AM Wednesday, Friday, and Saturday.

El Nuevo Tucho (✉ *Calle 60 No. 482, between Calles 55 and 57, Centro* ☎ *999/924–2323*) has cheesy cabaret-style entertainment beginning at 4 PM, with no drink minimum and no cover. In fact, despite the music and comedy, this is not just a place for young people or for dancing. Families dine here as well. There's music for dancing in this cavernous—sometimes full, sometimes empty—venue. Drinks come with free appetizers.

Pancho's (✉ *Calle 59 No. 509, between Calles 60 and 62, Centro* ☎ *999/923–0942* ⊕ *www.panchosmerida.com*), open daily 6 PM–2:30 AM, has a lively bar and a restaurant. It also has a small dance floor that attracts locals and visitors for a mix of live salsa and English-language pop music.

If dancing to the likes of Los Panchos and other romantic trios of the 1940s is more your style, don't miss this Tuesday-night ritual at **Parque de Santiago** (⊠ *Calles 59 and 72, Centro* ☎ *No phone*), where old folks and the occasional young lovers gather for dancing under the stars at 8:30 PM.

Fodor'sChoice ★ Enormously popular and rightly so, the red-walled **Slavia** (⊠ *Calle 29 No. 490, at Calle 58* ☎ *999/926–6587*) is an exotic Middle Eastern beauty. There are all sorts of nooks where you can be alone yet together with upscale Méridians, most of whom simply call this "the Buddha Bar." Arabian music in the background, low lighting, beaded curtains, embroidered tablecloths, mirrors, and sumptuous pillows and settees surrounding low tables produce a fabulous Arabian-nights vibe you won't find anywhere else in Mérida. It's open daily 7 PM–2 AM.

Tequila Rock (⊠ *Prolongación Paseo Montejo at Av. Campestre* ☎ *999/883–3147*) is a disco where salsa and Mexican and American pop are played Wednesday through Saturday. It's popular mainly with those between 18 and 25.

FILM

Cine Colón (⊠ *Av. Reforma 363A, Colón* ☎ *999/925–4500*) functions as a theater on Friday, Saturday, and Sunday. Box-office hits are shown at the recently restored **Cine Fantasio** (⊠ *Calle 59 No. 492, at Calle 60, Centro* ☎ *999/923–5431 or 999/925–4500*), which has just one screen, but is the city's nicest theater. **Cine Hollywood** (⊠ *Calle 50 Diagonal 460, Fracc. Gonzalo Guerrero* ☎ *999/920–1411*) is within the popular Gran Plaza mall and offers VIP rooms, with waiter service. International art films are shown most days at noon, 5, and 8 PM at **Teatro Mérida** (⊠ *Calle 60 between Calles 59 and 61, Centro* ☎ *999/924–7687 or 999/924–9990*).

FOLKLORIC SHOWS

Paseo Montejo hotels such as the Fiesta Americana, Hyatt Regency, and Holiday Inn stage dinner shows with folkloric dances; check with concierges for schedules.

★ The **Ballet Folklórico de Yucatán** (⊠ *Calles 57 and 60, Centro* ☎ *999/923–1198* ⊕ *www.uady.mx/sitios/cultura/ballet.html*) presents a combination of music, dance, and theater every Friday at 9 PM at the university; tickets are $5. (Performances are every other Friday in the off-season, and there are no shows from August 1 to September 22 and the last two weeks of December.)

SHOPPING

Mérida has something for everyone when it comes to shopping, from the souvenir junkies to the most discriminating of market trollers. Crafts at very reasonable prices can be found in the markets, parks, and plazas, and local art can be picked up at one of the many galleries, for the art scene here is burgeoning. If you're looking for a more standard shopping experience, or need to stock up on goods like new tennis shoes or a pair of jeans, there are also a few shopping malls in town.

MALLS

Mérida has several shopping malls, but the largest and nicest, **Gran Plaza** (⊠ *Calle 50 Diagonal 460, Fracc. Gonzalo Guerrero* ☎ *999/944–7657* ⊕ *www.granplaza.com.mx*), has more than 90 shops and a multiplex theater. It's just outside town, on the highway to Progreso (called Carretera a Progreso beyond the Mérida city limits). Tiny **Pasaje Picheta** is on the north side of the town square on Calle 61. It has a bus ticket information booth and an upstairs art gallery, as well as souvenir shops and a food court. **Plaza Américas** (⊠ *Calle 21 No. 331, Col. Miguel Hidalgo* ☎ *No phone*) is a pleasant mall where you'll find the Cineopolis movie theater complex.

MARKETS

The **Mercado Municipal** (⊠ *Calles 56 and 67, Centro*) has lots of things you won't need, but which are fascinating to look at: songbirds in cane cages, mountains of mysterious fruits and vegetables, dippers made of hollow gourds (the same way they've been made here for a thousand years). There are also lots of crafts for sale, including hammocks, sturdy leather *huaraches,* and piñatas in every imaginable shape and color. ■TIP➜Guides often approach tourists near this market. They expect a tip and won't necessarily bring you to the best deals. You're better off visiting some specialty stores first to learn about the quality and types of hammocks, hats, and other crafts; then you'll have an idea of what you're buying—and what it's worth—if you want to bargain in the market. Also be wary of pickpockets within the markets.

Sunday brings an array of wares into Mérida; starting at 9 AM, the Handicrafts Bazaar, or **Bazar de Artesanías** (⊠ *At main square, Centro*), sells lots of *huipiles* (traditional, white embroidered dresses) as well as hats and costume jewelry. As its name implies, popular art, or handicrafts, are sold at the **Bazar de Artes Populares** (⊠ *Parque Santa Lucía, at Calles 60 and 55, Centro*) beginning at 9 AM on Sunday. If you're interested in handicrafts, **Bazar García Rejón** (⊠ *Calles 65 and 62, Centro*) has rows of indoor stalls that sell items like leather goods, palm hats, and handmade guitars.

SPECIALTY STORES
BOOKS

Amate Books (⊠ *Calle 60 and Calle 51* ☎ *999/924–2222* ⊕ *www.amate books.com* ⊙ *Closed Mon.*), this one a new branch of an old Oaxacan bookstore, stocks books on all kinds of Mexican themes—from art and cooking to archaeology and language—in English. This cool building with high ceilings and old ceramic-tile floors is a beautiful setting in which to browse, meet people, and ask questions about local goings on, especially if you have the good fortune of stopping in when manager Kai Delvendahl is in. He's an archaeologist, a Maya specialist, and is very knowledgeable about the area.

CLOTHING

You might not wear a guayabera to a business meeting as some men in Mexico do, but the shirts are cool, comfortable, and attractive; for a good selection, try **Camisería Canul** (⊠ *Calle 62 No. 484, between*

BROWSING FOR BOOKS

Librería Dante has a great selection of colorful books on Mayan culture, although only a few are in English. There are many locations throughout town, including most of the malls, and there's also a large, happening shop–café–performance venue on Paseo Montejo. The Mérida English Library has novels and nonfiction in English; you can read in the library for five days without having to pay the $18 annual membership fee, and they host a gathering every Monday evening where you can meet people and practice Spanish. The giveaway

"Yucatán Today," in English and Spanish, has good maps of the state and city and lots of useful information for travelers.

Librería Dante (⊠ *Calle 62 No. 502, at Calle 61 on main plaza, Centro, Mérida* ☎ *999/928–2611* ⊕ ⊠ *Calle 17 No. 138B, at Prolongación Paseo Montejo, Centro, Mérida* ☎ *999/927–7676).* **Mérida English Library** (⊠ *Calle 53 No. 524, between Calles 66 and 68, Centro, Mérida* ☎ *999/924–8401* ⊕ *www.meridaenglishlibrary.com).*

Calles 57 and 59, Centro ☎ *999/923–0158* ⊕ *www.camiseriacanul. com).* Custom shirts take a week to construct, in sizes 4 to 52.

Guayaberas Jack (⊠ *Calle 59 No. 507A, between Calles 60 and 62, Centro* ☎ *999/928–6002)* has an excellent selection of guayaberas (18 delicious colors to choose from!) and typical women's cotton *filipinas* (house dresses), blouses, dresses, classy straw handbags, and lovely rayon *rebozos* (shawls) from San Luis Potosí. Guayaberas can be made to order, allegedly in less than a day, to fit anyone from a year-old baby to a 240-pound man, and anything in the shop can be altered or custom made. Everything here is of fine quality, and is often quite different from the clothes sold in neighboring shops. Prices are higher that in neighboring shops, but everything here is excellent quality and much of it is different from what you'll find elsewhere. The store has a small branch near the Fiesta Americana Mérida, but the branch does not have as much variety as the downtown location. You can browse and make purchases on their Web site as well. **Mexicanísimo** (⊠ *Calle 60 No. 496, at Parque Hidalgo, Centro* ☎ *999/923–8132* ⊕ *www.guayaberasjack. com.mx)* sells sleek, clean-lined clothing made from natural fibers for both women and men.

JEWELRY

Shop for malachite, turquoise, and other semiprecious stones set in silver at **Joyería Kema** (⊠ *Calle 60 No. 502-B, between Calles 61 and 63, at main plaza, Centro* ☎ *999/923–5838).* Beaders and other creative types flock to **Papagayo's Paradise** (⊠ *Calle 62 No. 488, between Calles 57 and 59, Centro* ☎ *999/993–0383),* where you'll find loose beads and semiprecious stones; lovely necklaces and earrings; and Brussels-lace-trimmed, hand-embroidered, tatted, and crocheted blouses. This small but exceptional store also sells men's handkerchiefs and place mats. **Tane** (⊠ *Hyatt Regency, Calle 60 No. 344, at Av. Colón, Paseo Montejo* ☎ *999/942–0202* ⊕ *www.tane.com.mx)* is an outlet for exquisite (and

Hamacas: A Primer

Yucatecan artisans are known for creating some of the finest *hamacas,* or hammocks, in the country. For the most part, the shops of Mérida are the best places in Yucatán to buy these beautiful, practical items— although if you travel to some of the outlying small towns, like Tixkokob, Izamal, and Ek Balam, you may find cheaper prices—and enjoy the experience as well.

One of the first decisions you'll have to make when buying a hamaca is whether to choose one made from cotton or nylon; nylon dries more quickly and is therefore well suited to humid climates, but cotton is softer and more comfortable (though its colors tend to fade faster). You'll also see that hamacas come in both double-threaded and single-threaded weaves; the double-threaded ones are sturdiest because they're more densely woven.

Hamacas come in a variety of sizes, too. A *sencillo* (cen-*see*-oh) hammock is meant for just one person (although most people find it's a rather tight fit); a *doble* (*doh*-blay), on the other hand, is very comfortable for one but crowded for two. *Matrimonial* or king-size hammocks accommodate two; and *familiares* or *matrimoniales especiales* can theoretically sleep an entire family. (Yucatecans tend to be smaller than Anglos are, and also lie diagonally in hammocks rather than end-to-end.)

For a good-quality king-size nylon or cotton hamaca, expect to pay about $35; sencillos go for about $22. Unless you're an expert, it's best to buy a hammock at a specialty shop, where you can climb in to try the size. The proprietors will also give you tips on washing, storing, and hanging your hammock. There are lots of hammock stores near Mérida's municipal market on Calle 58, between calles 69 and 73.

expensive) silver earrings, necklaces, and bracelets, some incorporating ancient Mayan designs.

LOCAL GOODS AND CRAFTS

A great place to purchase hammocks is **El Aguacate** (⊠ *Calle 58 No. 604, at Calle 73, Centro* ☎ *999/928–6429* ⊕ *www.hamacaselaguacate.com. mx*), a family-run outfit with many sizes and designs. Closed Sunday. Visit the government-run **Casa de las Artesanías Ki-Huic** (⊠ *Calle 63 No. 503A, between Calles 64 and 62, Centro* ☎ *999/928–6676*) for folk art from throughout Yucatán. There's a showcase of hard-to-find traditional filigree jewelry in silver, gold, and gold-dipped versions. **Casa de los Artesanos** (⊠ *Calle 62 No. 492, between Calles 59 and 61, Centro* ☎ *999/923–4523*), half a block from the main plaza, sells mainly small ceramic pieces, including more modern, stylized takes on traditional designs. The **Casa de Cera** (⊠ *Calle 74A No. 430E, between Calles 41 and 43, Centro* ☎ *999/920–0219*) is a small shop selling signed collectible indigenous beeswax figurines. Closed Sunday and afternoons after 3 PM. **El Hamaquero** (⊠ *Calle 58 No. 572, between Calles 69 and 71, Centro* ☎ *999/923–2117*) has knowledgeable personnel who let you try out the hammocks before you buy. Closed Sundays. **El Mayab**

(⊠*Calle 58 No. 553-A, at Calle 71, Centro* ☎*999/924–0853*) has a multitude of hammocks and is open on Sundays until 2 PM. **Miniaturas** (⊠*Calle 59 No. 507A, Centro* ☎*999/928–6503*) sells a delightful and diverse assortment of different crafts, but specializes in miniatures. **El Sombrero Popular** (⊠*Calle 65, between Calles 54 and 56, Centro* ☎*999/923–9501*) has a good assortment of men's hats—especially *jipis*, better known as Panama hats, which cost between $12 and $65. The elder of this father-and-son team has been in the business for 40 years. Closed Sunday. **Tequilería Ajua** (⊠*Calle 59 No. 506, at Calle 62, Centro* ☎*999/924–1453*) sells tequila, brandy, and mezcal as well as *Xtabentún*—a locally made liqueur flavored with anise and honey, which some claim is a aphrodisiac—and thick liqueurs made of local fruit from 10 AM to 9 PM.

You can get hammocks made to order—choose from standard nylon and cotton, super-soft processed sisal, Brazilian-style (six-stringed), or crocheted—at **El Xiric** (⊠*Calle 57-A No. 15 y 16, Pasaje Congreso, Centro* ☎*999/924–9906*). You can also get Xtabentún, as well as jewelry, black pottery, woven goods from Oaxaca, T-shirts, and souvenirs.

SPORTS AND THE OUTDOORS

It's possible to either watch or participate in sports, from baseball to bullfights, while you're in town.

BASEBALL

Baseball is played with enthusiasm between February and July at the **Centro Deportivo Kukulcán** (⊠*Calle 6 No. 315, Circuito Colonias, Col. Granjas* ⊹*Across street from Pemex gas station and next to Santa Clara brewery* ☎*999/940–0676 or 999/940–4261*). There are also tennis courts, soccer courts, and an Olympic pool. It's most common to buy your ticket at the on-site ticket booth the day of the game. A-league volleyball and basketball games and tennis tournaments are also held here.

BULLFIGHTS

Bullfights are held sporadically from late September through February, though the most famed *matadors* begin their fighting season in November at **Plaza de Toros** (⊠*Av. Reforma near Calle 25, Col. García Ginerés* ☎*999/925–7996*). Seats in the shade generally go for around $50, but can cost as much as $150, depending on the fame of the bullfighter. You can buy tickets at the bullring or in advance at OXXO convenience stores. Check with the tourism office for the current schedule, or look for posters around town.

GOLF

The 18-hole championship golf course at **Club de Golf de Yucatán** (⊠*Carretera Mérida–Progreso, Km 14.5* ☎*999/922–0053* ⊕*www.golfyucatan. com*) is open to the public. It is about 16 km (10 mi) north of Mérida on the road to Progreso; green fees are about $100, carts are an additional $40, and clubs can be rented. The pro shop is closed Monday, but the golf course is open seven days a week.

TENNIS

There are two cement public courts at **Estadio Salvador Alvarado** (⊠ *Calle 11 between Calles 62 and 60, Paseo Montejo* ☎ *999/925–4856*). Cost is $2 per hour during the day and $2.50 at night, when the courts are lighted. At the **Fiesta Americana Mérida** (⊠ *Av. Colón 451, Paseo Montejo* ☎ *999/920–2194*), guests have access to one unlit cement court. The one cement tennis court at **Holiday Inn** (⊠ *Av. Colón 498, at Calle 60, Colón* ☎ *999/942–8800*) is lighted at night. The **Hyatt Regency Mérida** (⊠ *Calle 60 No. 344, Colón* ☎ *999/942–0202*) has two lighted cement outdoor courts.

IZAMAL

68 km (42 mi) east of Mérida.

In the beautiful town of Izamal, you may not find too many sights, but you will almost certainly be taken by the town's color and aging architecture. Although unsophisticated, Izamal is a charming and neighborly alternative to the sometimes frenetic tourism of Mérida. Hotels are humble, and the few restaurants offer basic fare. For those who enjoy a quieter, slower-pace vacation, Izamal is worth considering as a base. The city has recently been refurbished, and the downtown area shines with remodeled buildings and bright yellow paint that contrasts strikingly with the blue sky.

One of the best examples of a Spanish colonial town in the Yucatán, Izamal is nicknamed *Ciudad Amarilla* (Yellow City), because its most important buildings are painted a golden ocher. It's also sometimes called "the City of Three Cultures," because of its combined pre-Hispanic, colonial, and contemporary influences.

GETTING HERE AND AROUND

The drive to Izamal from Mérida takes less than an hour; take Highway 180 and follow the signs. *Calesas* (horse-drawn carriages) are stationed at the town's large main square, fronting the lovely cathedral, day and night. The drivers charge about $5 an hour for sightseeing; many will also take you on a shopping tour for whichever items you're interested in buying (for instance, hammocks or jewelry). Pick up a brochure at the visitor center for details.

ESSENTIALS

Currency Exchange Banorte (⊠ *Calle 28 No. 300B97540* ☎ *988/954–0425* ⊕ *www.banorte.com*).

Visitor and Tour Info Izamal Tourism Department (⊠ *Calle 30 No. 323, between Calles 31 and 31-A, Centro* ⊕ *www.izamal.travel/* ☎ *988/954–0009*).

EXPLORING

★ **Ex-Convento y Iglesia de San Antonio de Padua.** Facing the main plaza, this enormous 16th-century *former monastery and church of St. Anthony of Padua* is perched on—and built from—the remains of a Mayan pyramid devoted to Itzámná, god of the heavens. The monastery's ocher-painted church, where Pope John Paul II led prayers in 1993, has a gigantic atrium (supposedly second in size only to the Vatican's) facing a colonnaded facade and rows of 75 white-trimmed arches. The Virgin of the

Immaculate Conception, to whom the church is dedicated, is the patron saint of the Yucatán. A statue of Nuestra Señora de Izamal, or Our Lady of Izamal, was brought here from Guatemala in 1562 by Bishop Diego de Landa. Miracles are ascribed to her, and a yearly pilgrimage takes place in her honor. Frescoes of saints at the front of the church, once plastered over, were rediscovered and refurbished in 1996.

The monastery and church are now illuminated in a light-and-sound show of the type usually shown at the archaeological sites. You can catch a Spanish-only narration and the play of lights on the nearly 500-year-old structure at 8:30 PM Tuesday, Thursday, Friday, and Saturday—buy tickets ($4.50) on-site at 8.

Diagonally across from the massive cathedral, the small **municipal market** is worth a wander. It's a lot less frenetic than markets at major cities like Mérida. On the other side of the square, **Hecho a Mano** (⊠*Calle 31 No. 308, Centro* ☎*988/954–0344)* sells a nice collection of framed photographs and handicrafts.

Centro Cultural y Artesanal Izamal. Banamex has set up this small, well-organized popular art museum right on the main plaza. There are all kinds of high-quality crafts on display, from textiles and ceramics to papier mâché and woodwork. You can also take home a souvenir from the gift shop. The center also has small café, a mini-spa that offers massages, and a pleasant patio at the foot of the Kabul pyramid. ⊠*Calle 31 s/n, Centro* ⊕*www.fundacionhaciendas.com* ⊠*Free* ☉*Mon.–Sat. 10–8, Sun. 10–5.*

Kinich Kakmó pyramid is the largest pre-Hispanic building in the Yucatán, and it is all that remains of the royal Mayan city that flourished here between AD 250 and 600. Dedicated to Zamná, Mayan god of the dew, the enormous structure is the largest of its kind in the state, covering about 10 acres. More remarkable for its size than for any remaining decoration, it's nonetheless an impressive monument, and you can scale it from stairs on the south face for a view of the cathedral and the surrounding countryside. The entrance is $2.

WHERE TO EAT AND STAY

¢ ✕**Los Mestizos.** This humble restaurant has brightly painted walls,

MEXICAN and even the ceiling fans are painted a bright orange. The short menu includes regional fare such as *salbutes* and *panuchos*—both typical appetizers of fried cornmeal, the latter stuffed with beans—as well as chicken and turkey dishes. There's a bit of a view of the church beyond the marketplace from the outdoor terrace. ⊠*Calle 33 s/n, behind market, Centro* ☎*988/954–0289* ⊟*No credit cards.*

$ ⊞**Hacienda San Antonio Chalanté.** You can't beat the price of a room and breakfast at this refurbished, yet still authentic, hacienda just outside of Izamal. The rooms are ample and comfortable, but the real joy here is exploring the grounds. There are horses, a pool, and a garden that has been well cared for, and if you venture away from the hacienda you can explore, and find things that few others have seen. **Pros:** breakfast included in room price (dinner is optional). **Cons:** some rooms lack air-conditioning. ⊠*Domicilio Conocido, Sudzal* ☎*999/132–7441, 813/636–8200 in U.S.* ⊕*www.haciendachalante.com* ↩*10 rooms*

&In-room: *No a/c (some). In-hotel: Restaurant, pool, no-smoking rooms* ⊟*No credit cards* †◯|*BP.*

¢–$ **Macanché.** Each freestanding guest room here has its own theme decor: the Asian room has a Chinese checkers board and origami decorations; the safari room has artifacts from Mexico and Africa. All have screened windows and are surrounded by exuberant gardens of bamboo, bird of paradise, and bougainvillea. Some have skylights, or hammock chairs on a front porch. The restaurant offers salads and other health-conscious fare. **Pros:** good restaurant and breakfast included; nice limestone pool surrounded by plants; great room price. **Cons:** far from central plaza. ✉*Calle 22 No. 305, between Calles 33 and 35* ☎*988/954–0287* ⊕*www.macanche.com* ➴*12 bungalows, 2 cabins* &*In-room: No a/c (some), no phone, refrigerator (some), no TV. In-hotel: Restaurant, bar, pool, bicycles, laundry service, parking (no fee), Wi-Fi, no-smoking rooms* ⊟*No credit cards* †◯|*BP.*

UXMAL AND THE RUTA PUUC

Passing through the large Mayan town of Umán on Mérida's southern outskirts, you enter one of the Yucatán's least populated areas. The highway to Uxmal (ush-*mal*) and Kabah is relatively free of traffic and runs through uncultivated low jungle. The forest seems to become denser beyond Uxmal, which was connected to a number of smaller ceremonial centers in ancient times by *sacbé* (white roads). Several of these satellite sites—including Kabah, with its 250 masks; Sayil, with its majestic, three-story palace; and Labná, with its iconic, vaulted *puerta* (gateway)—are open to the public along a route known as the Ruta Puuc, which winds its way eastward through the countryside.

The last archaeological site on the Ruta Puuc is the Grutas de Loltún, Yucatán's most mysterious and extensive cave system. You can make a loop to all these sites, ending in the little town of Oxcutzcab, or in somewhat larger Ticul, which produces much of the pottery (and the women's shoes) you'll see around the peninsula. If you want to use your video camera at any of the sites, $3 also buys you a pass for the day that you can use at all of the sites you visit.

UXMAL

Fodor'sChoice   *78 km (48 mi) south of Mérida on Carretera 261.*
★
🚌   **GETTING HERE AND AROUND**

There's daily transportation on the ATS bus line to Uxmal, Labná, Xlapak, Sayil, Kabah, and Uxmal. For about $10 you can get transportation to each of these places, with 20 to 30 minutes to explore the lesser sites and nearly two hours to see Uxmal. If you plan to drive yourself, take Highway 180 south out of Mérida, and then get on Highway 261 in Uman. This will take you south all the way to Uxmal. In addition to standard tours, Mayaland Tours also offers "self-guided tours," which means that you set out on your own, but they provide a road map, itinerary, and rental car, and set up lodgings at the archaeological sites.

When you consider the price of lodgings and a rental car if purchasing them separately, this is a pretty sweet deal.

EXPLORING

If Chichén Itzá is the most expansive Mayan ruin in Yucatán, **Uxmal** is arguably the most elegant. The architecture here reflects the late classical renaissance of the 7th to 9th centuries and is contemporary with that of Palenque and Tikal, among other great Mayan cities of the southern highlands.

The site is considered the finest and most extensively excavated example of Puuc architecture, which embraces such details as ornate stone mosaics and friezes on the upper walls, intricate cornices, rows of columns, and soaring vaulted arches.

You could easily spend a couple of days exploring the ruins, though keep in mind that the only entertainment offered outside the ruins is provided by hotels and the odd restaurant.

Although much of Uxmal hasn't been restored, the following buildings in particular merit attention:

At 125 feet high, the **Pirámide del Adivino** is the tallest and most prominent structure at the site. Unlike most other Mayan pyramids, which are stepped and angular, the Temple of the Magician has a softer and more refined round-corner design. This structure was rebuilt five times over hundreds of years, each time on the same foundation, so artifacts found here represent several different kingdoms. The pyramid has a stairway on its western side that leads through a giant open-mouthed mask to two temples at the summit. During restoration work in 2002 the grave of a high-ranking Mayan official, a ceramic mask, and a jade necklace were discovered within the pyramid. Continuing excavations have revealed exciting new finds that are still being studied.

West of the pyramid lies the **Cuadrángulo de las Monjas**, considered by some to be the finest part of Uxmal. The name was given to it by the conquistadores because it reminded them of a convent building in Old Spain (*monjas* means nuns). You may enter the four buildings; each comprises a series of low, gracefully repetitive chambers that look onto a central patio. Elaborate and symbolic decorations—masks, geometric patterns, coiling snakes, and some phallic figures—blanket the upper facades.

Heading south, you'll pass a small ball court before reaching the **Palacio del Gobernador**, which archaeologist Victor von Hagen considered the most magnificent building ever erected in the Americas. Interestingly, the palace faces east, while the rest of Uxmal faces west. Archaeologists believe this is because the palace was built to allow observation of the planet Venus. Covering five acres and rising over an immense acropolis, it lies at the heart of what may have been Uxmal's administrative center.

Apparently the house of an important person, the recently excavated **Cuadrángalo de los Pájaros** (Quadrangle of the Birds), located between the above-mentioned buildings, is composed of a series of small chambers. In one of these chambers, archaeologists found a statue of the royal, by the name of Chac (as opposed to Chaac, the rain god), who apparently dwelt there. The building was named for the repeated pattern of birds, which decorates the upper part of the building's frieze.

Today you can watch a sound-and-light show at the site that recounts Mayan legends. The colored light brings out details of carvings and mosaics that are easy to miss when the sun is shining. The show is performed nightly in Spanish; earphones ($2.50) provide an English translation. ■ TIP➔In the summer months, tarantulas are a common sight at the ruins and around the hotels that surround the ruins. ✉ *Site, museum, and sound-and-light show $19.50; parking $1; use of video camera $2 (keep this receipt if visiting other archaeological sites along the Ruta Puuc on the same day)* ⊘*Daily 8–5; sound-and-light show just after dusk (at 7 PM in winter or 8 PM in summer, tickets to only the show $3); official English language tour guide $55.*

WHERE TO EAT

$　✕**Cana Nah.** Although this large, recently remodeled roadside spot
MEXICAN　mainly caters to the groups visiting Uxmal, locals recommend it as the most formally established and hygienic eatery in the area, and the friendly owners are happy to serve small parties. The basic menu includes local dishes like lime soup and *pollo pibíl*, and such universals as fried chicken and vegetable soup. Approach the salsa on the table with a bit of caution: it's made almost purely of habanero chiles. After your meal you can laze in one of the hammocks out back under the trees or dive into the property's large rectangular swimming pool. There's a small shop as well, selling pieces of popular art including figurines of *los aluxes,* the mischievous "lords of the jungle" that Mayan legend says protect farmers' fields. ✉*Carretera Muna–Uxmal, 4 km (2½ mi) north of Uxmal* ☎*999/910–3829* ▱*No credit cards.*

WHERE TO STAY

$$$$　🏨**Hacienda Uxmal.** The first hotel built in Uxmal, this pleasant colonial-style building was looking positively haggard before a recent facelift, when sheets, towels, and furnishings were finally replaced. Now rooms are furnished simply, but with high-quality wooden pieces. Still in good shape are the lovely floor tiles, ceramics, and iron grillwork. The rooms are fronted with wide, furnished verandas; the courtyard has two pools surrounded by gardens. Each room has an ample bathroom with tub, comfortable beds, and coffeemaker. Some can accommodate a hammock, and some also have a hot tub. Ask about packages that include free or low-cost car rentals, or catching a ride in the comfortable minivan that makes trips to Mérida, Chichén, or Cancún. **Pros:** good service; good restaurant; pretty gardens. **Cons:** fairly close (5-minute walk) to Uxmal ruins, but you could be closer. ✉*Carretera 261, Km 78* ☎*997/976–2012 or 800/235–4079* ⊕*www.mayaland.com* ⇗*80 rooms, 7 suites* ⚒*In-hotel: Restaurant, room service, bar, pools, laundry service, parking (free), no-smoking rooms* ▱*AE, MC, V.*

$$$$　🏨**Lodge at Uxmal.** The outwardly rustic, thatch-roof buildings here have red-tile floors, doors and rocking chairs carved from polished hardwood, and local weavings. The effect is comfortable yet luxuriant; the property feels sort of like a peaceful ranch. All rooms have bathtubs

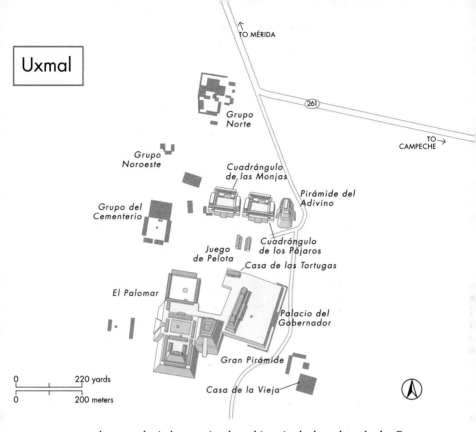

Uxmal

TO MÉRIDA

(261)

TO →
CAMPECHE

Grupo Norte

Grupo Noroeste

Cuadrángulo de las Monjas

Pirámide del Adivino

Grupo del Cementerio

Cuadrángulo de los Pájaros

Juego de Pelota

Casa de las Tortugas

El Palomar

Palacio del Gobernador

Gran Pirámide

Casa de la Vieja

0 — 220 yards
0 — 200 meters

and screened windows; suites have king-size beds and spa baths. **Pros:** directly across from Uxmal entrance; simple, beautiful rooms; big pools. **Cons:** no room phones; mediocre restaurant; expensive. ⊠ *Carretera Uxmal, Km 78* ☎ *997/976–2010 or 800/235–4079* ⊕ *www.mayaland. com* ⇨ *40 suites* ⚬ *In-hotel: 2 restaurants, bar, pools, laundry service, parking (free), no-smoking rooms* ⊟ *AE, MC, V.*

$$ **Misión Uxmal.** This hotel is a little different from the others that surround the ruins. It's farther away, but the ruins are visible in the distance from the rooms and balconies. You can watch the ruins light up with the sound-and-light show at night, and the fog roll across the jungle over the ruins in the morning. It's such a spectacular sight that hotel guests fill their room balconies, and nearly everyone snaps away with their camera. The hotel itself is comfortable. Rooms have ceramic-tile floors, big windows, and comfortable beds. There's a restaurant with lackluster meals, mainly buffets. Hotel staff is friendly, and is happy to accommodate those interested in specialized tours. There are special holiday packages at Christmas and Halloween. **Pros:** different view of ruins and jungle; relatively low price. **Cons:** not walking distance from ruins (hotel provides transport); occasional noise from passing cars; drab restaurant. ⊠ *Carrertera Mérida-Campeche, Km 78* ☎ *55/55209–1700, 01800/900–3800 toll-free in Mexico* ⊕ *www.hoteles*

mision.com ⟿82 rooms ☺ In-room: Wi-Fi. In-hotel: Restaurant, bar, pool, spa, no-smoking rooms ⊟MC, V ❢⊙⎮AI, EP.

$$
FodorsChoice
★
⚏**Villas Arqueológicas Uxmal.** Rooms at this pretty two-story former Club Med property are small, like hobbit holes, but bright and functional, with wooden furniture and cozy twin beds that fit nicely into alcoves, and a number of them have garden views. Since rooms are petite, guests tend to hang out in the comfy library with a giant-screen TV and lots of reading material, or at thatch-shaded tables next to the pool. The indoor restaurant ($), which may seem classy or old-Europe fussy depending on your taste, serves both regional fare and international dishes. With museum-quality reproductions of Mayan statues throughout (even in the pool), it's several times less expensive than, and equally as charming as, the other options, which are just a stone's throw from the ruins. While you can't connect a laptop to the Internet, you can borrow a computer in the hotel office for a couple of dollars an hour. **Pros:** upgraded beds and other improvements; walking distance to ruins; nice pool. **Cons:** rooms could be more spacious; restaurant food is just OK. ✉Carretera 261, Km 76 ☏997/974–6020 or 800/258–2633 ⟿40 rooms, 3 suites ☺In-room: Safe, no TV. In-hotel: Restaurant, bar, tennis court, pool, laundry service, parking (free), no-smoking rooms ⊟AE, MC, V.

KABAH

⛰ 23 km (14 mi) south of Uxmal on Carretera 261.

The most important buildings at Kabah, which means "lord of the powerful hand" in Mayan, were built between AD 600 and 900, during the later part of the classic era. A ceremonial center of almost Grecian beauty, it was once linked to Uxmal by a sacbé, at the end of which looms a great independent arch—now across the highway from the main ruins. The 151-foot-long **Palacio de los Mascarones,** or Palace of the Masks, boasts a three-dimensional mosaic of 250 masks of inlaid stones. On the central plaza, you can see ground-level wells called *chultunes,* which were used to store precious rainwater. The site officially opens at 8 AM, but the staff doesn't usually show up until 9. ⛏$3 ⊙Daily 8–5.

SAYIL

⛰ 9 km (5½ mi) south of Kabah on Carretera 31 E.

Experts believe that Sayil, or "place of the red ants," flourished between AD 800 and 1000. It's renowned primarily for its majestic **Gran Palacio.** Built on a hill, the three-story structure is adorned with decorations of animals and other figures, and contains more than 80 rooms. The structure recalls Palenque in its use of multiple planes, columned porticoes, and sober cornices. Also on the grounds is a stela in the shape of a phallus—an obvious symbol of fertility. ⛏$3 ⊙Daily 8–5.

LABNÁ

🔺 *9 km (5½ mi) south of Sayil on Carretera 31 E.*

The striking monumental structure at Labná (which means "old house" or "abandoned house") is a fanciful corbeled arch (also called the Mayan arch, or false arch), with elaborate latticework and a small chamber on each side. One theory says the arch was the entrance to an area where religious ceremonies were staged. The site was used mainly by the military elite and royalty. 🎟*$3* ⊙*Daily 8–5.*

GRUTAS DE LOLTÚN

🕓 *19 km (12 mi) northeast of Labná.*

★ The Loltún ("stone flower" in Mayan) is one of the largest and most
🔺 fascinating cave systems on the Yucatán Peninsula. Long ago, Mayan ceremonies were routinely held inside these mysterious caves; artifacts found inside date as far back as 800 BC. The topography of the caves themselves is fascinating: there are stalactites, stalagmites, and limestone formations known by such names as Ear of Corn and Cathedral. Illuminated pathways meander a little over a kilometer through the caverns, most of which are quite spacious and well ventilated (claustrophobics needn't worry). Nine different openings allow air and some (but not much) light to filter in. ■**TIP→You can enter only with a guide. Although these guides were once paid a small salary, they are now forced to work for tips only—so be generous.** Scheduled tours are at 9:30, 12:30, 3, and 4 (in Spanish), and 11 and 2 (in English). 🎟*$5.50, parking $1* ⊙*Daily 9–5.*

TICUL

27 km (17½ mi) northwest of the Loltún Caves; 28 km (17 mi) east of Uxmal, 100 km (62 mi) south of Mérida.

One of the larger cities in the Yucatán (with a population of around 20,000), and a busy market town, Ticul is a good base for exploring the Puuc region—if you don't mind rudimentary hotels and a limited choice of simple restaurants. Many descendants of the Xiu Dynasty, which ruled Uxmal until the conquest, still live here. Industries include fabrication of *huipiles* (blouses) and shoes, as well as much of the pottery you see around the Yucatán. It also has a handsome 17th-century church.

GETTING HERE AND AROUND

Ticul is an easy drive south of Mérida, along the Ruta Puuc. Follow México 180 from Mérida to Umán, where you will get on the México 261 to Muná. From Muná, simply follow the signs to Ticul, by way of the México 184.

ESSENTIALS

Currency Exchange Banamex (☎*01800/226–2639 toll-free in Mexico* ✉*Calle 26 No. 199D* ⊕*www.banamex.com*).

Yucatán's History

Francisco de Montejo's conquest of Yucatán took three gruesome wars over a total of 24 years. "Nowhere in all America was resistance to Spanish conquest more obstinate or more nearly successful," wrote the historian Henry Parkes. In fact the irresolute Maya, their ancestors long incorrectly portrayed by archaeologists as docile and peace-loving, provided the Spaniards and the mainland Mexicans with one of their greatest challenges. Rebellious pockets of Mayan communities held out against the *dzulo'obs* (dzoo-loh-obs)—the upper class, or outsiders—as late as the 1920s and '30s.

If Yucatecans are proud of their heritage and culture, it's with good reason. Although in a state of decline when the conquistadores clanked into their world with iron swords and fire-belching cannons, the Maya were one of the world's greatest ancient cultures. As mathematicians and astronomers they were perhaps without equal among their contemporaries; their architecture in places like Uxmal was as graceful as that of the ancient Greeks.

To "facilitate" Catholic conversion among the conquered, the Spaniards superimposed Christian rituals on existing beliefs whenever possible, creating the ethnic Catholicism that's alive and well today. (Those defiant Maya who resisted the new ideology were burned at the stake, drowned, and hanged.) Having procured a huge workforce of free indigenous labor, Spanish agricultural estates prospered like mad. Mérida soon became a thriving administrative and military center, the gateway to Cuba and to Spain. By the 18th century, huge maize and

cattle plantations were making the *hacendados* incredibly rich.

Insurrection came during the War of the Castes in the mid-1800s, when the enslaved indigenous people rose up with long-repressed furor and massacred thousands of non-Indians. The United States, Cuba, and Mexico City finally came to the aid of the ruling elite, and between 1846 and 1850 the Indian population of Yucatán was effectively halved. Those Maya who did not escape into the remote jungles of neighboring Quintana Roo or Chiapas or get sold into slavery in Cuba found themselves, if possible, worse off than before under the dictatorship of Porfirio Díaz.

The hopeless status of the indigenous people—both Yucatán natives and those kidnapped and lured with the promise of work from elsewhere in Mexico—changed little as the economic base segued from one industry to the next. After the thin limestone soil failed to produce fat cattle or impressive corn, entrepreneurs turned to dyewood and then to *henequen* (sisal), a natural fiber used to make rope. After the widespread acceptance of synthetic fibers, the entrepreneurs used the sweat of local labor to convert gum arabic from the peninsula's prevalent *zapote* tree into European vacations and Miami bank accounts. The fruits of their labor can be seen today in the imposing French-style mansions that stretch along Mérida's Paseo Montejo.

EXPLORING

★ **Arte Maya** (⊠*Calle 23 No. 30197860* ☎*997/972–1669* ⊕*www.arte maya.com.mx*) is a ceramics workshop that produces museum-quality replicas of archaeological pieces found throughout Mexico. The workshop also creates souvenir-quality pieces that are more affordable and more easily transported.

Iglesia de San Antonio de Padua. This pretty, faded, red colonial church is typical of the Yucatán colonial churches. It has been weathered and ransacked on more than one occasion, but the Black Christ altarpiece is original. The best view might be from the outside, where you can take in the facade, including its three towers, and the slow pace of the town as families ride by in carts attached to bicycles, and locals mill around in traditional Mayan dress. ⊠*On the zócalo, Centro.*

OFF THE BEATEN PATH

Mayapán. Those who are enamored of Yucatán and the ancient Maya may want to take a 42-km (26-mi) detour east of Ticul (or 43 km [27 mi] from Mérida) to Mayapán, the last of the major city-states on the peninsula that flourished during the postclassic era. It was demolished in 1450, presumably by war. It is thought that the city, with an architectural style reminiscent of Uxmal, was as big as Chichén Itzá, and there are more than 4,000 mounds, which might lend truth to this. At its height, the population could have been well over 12,000. A half-dozen mounds have been excavated, including the palaces of Mayan royalty and the temple of the benign god Kukulcán, where stucco sculptures and murals in vivid reds and oranges have been uncovered. The ceremonial structures that were faithfully described in Bishop Diego de Landa's writings will look like they have jumped right out of his book when the work is completed. ⊠*Off road to left before Telchaquillo; follow signs* ☎*$4* ⊙*Daily 8–5.*

WHERE TO EAT AND STAY

$ ✕**El Príncipe Tutul-Xiu.** About 15 km (9 mi) from Ticul in the little town of Maní, this large open restaurant under a giant palapa roof is a great place for lunch or an early dinner (it closes at 7 PM). Though you'll find the same Yucatecan dishes here as elsewhere—*pollo pibíl*, lime soup—the preparation is excellent and portions are generous. Best of all is the *poc chuc*—little bites of pork marinated in sour orange, garlic, and chilies and grilled over charcoal. ⊠*Calle 26 No. 210, between Calles 25 and 27* ☎*997/978–4086* ⊟*MC, V.*

MEXICAN
★

¢–$ ✕**Los Almendros.** One of the few places in town open from 9 AM until 9 PM, "the Almonds" is a good place to sample tasty, well-prepared regional fare, served with handmade tortillas. The restaurant has been so successful that there are now branches in Merida and Cancun, but this is the original. The *combinado yucateco* gives you a chance to try poc-chuc and *cochinita pibíl* (two pork dishes) as well as *pavo relleno* (stuffed turkey) and sausage. The owners claim to have invented *poc-chuc* right here. The newish building at the edge of town is often full of tour groups—or completely empty. There's a pool out back where you can swim—but do as mama says and wait at least a half-hour after eating—especially if you order a big plate like the *combinado.* ⊠*Calle 22 s/n, at Carretera Ticul–Chetumal* ☎*997/972–0021* ⊟*No credit cards.*

MEXICAN

5

$ ✕**Pizzería La Góndola.** The wonderful smells of fresh-baked bread and
PIZZA pizza waft from this small corner establishment between the market
and the main square. Scenes of Old Italy and the Yucatán adorn bright
yellow walls; clients pull their padded folding chairs up to yellow-tile
tables, or take their orders to go. Pizza is the name of the game here,
although tortas and pastas are also for sale. ⊠*Calle 23 No. 208, at
Calle 26A* ☎*997/972–0112* ▬*No credit cards* ⊗*Daily 1–5* PM.

¢ **Plaza.** While they get no points for creativity as far as their name
is concerned, the Plaza does have a convenient location about a block
from the main plaza. It has clean bathrooms and firm mattresses, hammock hooks, telephones, fans, and TV. A café serves breakfast, which at
least gets you out of your extremely plain room. **Pros:** downtown location; clean rooms. **Cons:** no frills; church bells might keep you up late
or wake you early; 6% surcharge for paying with credit card. ⊠*Calle
23 No. 202, between Calles 26 and 26A* ☎*997/972–0484* ⊕*www.
hotelplazayucatan.com* ⥅*25 rooms, 5 suites* ♿*In-hotel: Restaurant,
parking (free), no-smoking rooms* ▬*MC, V.*

OXCUTZCAB

22 km (14 mi) southeast of Ticul; 122 km (76 mi) south of Mérida.

This market town, hungry for tourism, is a good alternative to Ticul
for those who want to spend the night in the Puuc area. Strangers will
greet you as you walk the streets. Even the teenagers here are friendly
and polite. Oxcutzcab (osh-coots-*cob*) supplies much of the state with
produce: avocados, mangoes, mameys, papayas, watermelons, peanuts,
and citrus fruits are all grown in the surrounding region and sold daily
at the cheerful municipal market, directly in front of the town's picturesque Franciscan church. Pedicabs line up on the opposite side of
the market, ready to take you on a three-wheeled tour of town for just
a few pesos. The town's coat of arms tells the etymology of the name
Oxcutzcab. In Mayan, Ox means *ramon* (twigs cut for cattle fodder);
kutz is tobacco, also grown in the area; and *cab* is honey. It's a sweet
little town.

WHERE TO STAY

¢ **Hotel Puuc.** This two-story, motel-style property opened in 2004.
Rooms are plain but clean, with comfy beds, découpage scenes of
Puuc-area ruins, and blond-wood furniture. Each has a shower and
toilet crammed into a tiny room around the corner from a sink. Noise
from the street, the front desk, and other rooms creeps in through thin
walls. The international food at Peregrino Restaurant ($) is as simple
as the guest rooms, but portions are generous and the waitstaff, like
most of the town, is friendly. **Pros:** cheap; clean rooms. **Cons:** plain
rooms; street noise can be a problem. ⊠*Calle 55 No. 80, at Calle 44*
☎*997/975–0103* ⥅*24 rooms* ♿*In-hotel: Restaurant, laundry service,
parking (free)* ▬*No credit cards.*

YAXCOPOIL

50 km (31 mi) north of Uxmal on Carretera 261.

Yaxcopoil (yash-co-po-*il*), a restored 17th-century hacienda, makes for a nice change of pace from the ruins. The main building, with its distinctive Moorish double arch at the entrance, has been used as a film set and is the best-known *henequen* plantation in the region. The greathouse's rooms—including library, kitchen, dining room, drawing room, and salons—are fitted with late-19th-century European furnishings. You can tour these, along with the chapel, and the storerooms and machine room used in the processing of *henequen*. In the museum you'll see pottery and other artifacts recovered from the still-unexplored, classic-era Mayan site for which the hacienda is named. The hacienda has restored a one-room guesthouse ($) for overnighters and will serve a Continental breakfast and simple dinner of traditional tamales and *horchata* (rice-flavored drink) by prior arrangement. You can reserve the guest cottage by visiting the property's Web site. ✉ *Carretera 261, Km 186* ☎ *999/900–1193* ⊕ *www.yaxcopoil.com* 🖅 *$5* ⊗ *Mon.–Sat. 8–6, Sun. 9–1.*

WHERE TO STAY

$$$$ 🛏 **Hacienda Temozón.** These luxurious Starwood accommodations may seem far from any town or city, but they're actually quite close to the ruins of Uxmal, the Ruta Puuc, and even Mérida. The converted henequen estate exudes luxury and grace, with mahogany furnishings, carved wooden doors, intricate mosaic floors in tile and stone, and a general air of genteel sophistication. It is such a special place that you will find pictures of former U.S. presidents who have stayed here hanging in the library. The rooms have ceilings that are more than 20 feet high, with multiple ceiling fans, comfortable high beds with piles of pillows, armoires, and twin hammocks. Modern lighting and quiet, remote-controlled air-conditioning units add creature comforts to most rooms. Horseback riding and bike use are available. You can also catch a ride to a nearby cenote in a donkey-pulled trolley. **Pros:** gorgeous grounds; beautiful rooms. **Cons:** expensive; you'll need to drive to get to nearby ruins and cities. ✉ *Carretera 261, Km 182, Temozón Sur* ☎ *999/923–8089 or 888/625–5144* ⊕ *www.haciendasmexico.com* 🛏 *26 rooms, 1 suite* ⚐ *In-room: Safe, no TV, air-conditioning (some), Internet. In-hotel: Restaurant, room service, bar, tennis court, pool, concierge, laundry service, spa, parking (no fee)* 🖃 *AE, MC, V* ⑩ *EP.*

OXKINTOC

▲ *50 km (31 mi) south of Mérida on Carretera 180.*

The archaeological site of Oxkintoc (osh-kin-*tok*) is 5 km (3 mi) east of Maxcanú, off Carretera 180, and contains the ruins of an important Mayan capital that dominated the region from about AD 300 to 1100. Little was known about Oxkintoc until excavations began here in 1987. Structures that have been excavated so far include two tall pyramids and a palace with stone statues of several ancient rulers. ✉ *Off Carretera 184, 1½ km (1 mi) west of Carretera 180* 🖅 *$2.70* ⊗ *Daily 8–5.*

THE MAYAN INTERIOR

120 km (74 mi) east of Mérida.

The area around Chichén Itzá is dotted with sleepy towns in which you may feel like you have stepped back in time; however, many people stay in Mérida and day-trip to the ruins. Near Chichén Itzá, in the picturesque town of Valladolid, with a cenote and a beautiful 16th-century church, things seem to move at a slower pace. The small town of Pisté is little more than an outpost, a place where visitors to Chichén Itzá can rest at small hotels.

GETTING HERE AND AROUND

Although you can get to Chichén Itzá along the shorter Carretera 180, there's a more scenic and interesting alternative. Head east on Carretera 281 through Tixkokob, a Mayan community famous for its hammock weavers, and continue through Citilcúm and Izamal. From there, continue on through the small, untouristy towns of Dzudzal and Xanaba en route to Kantunil. There you can hop on the toll road or continue on the free road that parallels it through Holca and Libre Unión, both of which have very swimmable cenotes.

VALLADOLID

161 km (100 mi) from Mérida; 44½ km (28 mi) east of Chichén Itzá.

The second-largest city in Yucatán State, Valladolid (vay-ah-do-*lid*), is a picturesque provincial town that's been growing popular among travelers en route to or from Chichén Itzá (or Río Lagartos, to the north). Francisco de Montejo founded Valladolid in 1543 on the site of the Mayan town of Sisal. The city suffered during the War of the Castes—when the Maya in revolt killed nearly all Spanish residents—and again during the Mexican Revolution.

Despite its turbulent history, Valladolid's downtown has many colonial and 19th-century structures. On Sunday evenings at 8 PM the city's orchestra plays elegant, stylized *danzón*—waltzlike dance music to which unsmiling couples (think tango: no smiling allowed) swirl around the bandstand of the main square. Valladolid is renowned for its *longaniza en escabeche*—a sausage dish made with pork, beef, or venison, served in many of the restaurants facing the square. In the shops and market you can also find good buys on sandals, baskets, and Xtabentún liqueur.

GETTING HERE AND AROUND

The drive from Mérida to Valladolid via the toll road (the tolls come to about $11) takes about two hours. The free road (México 295) cuts through several small towns where speed bumps, street repairs, and traffic can increase the travel time significantly. ADO and UNO have direct buses from Mérida to Valladolid, and other Mexican cities. They depart from the first-class CAME bus station. Most buses that come into Valladolid actually stop just outside of town, where you have to get on a second bus, a city bus. This is included in the price of your ticket.

ESSENTIALS

Bus Contacts Autobuses de Occidente (☎ *999/924–8391 or 999/924–9741* ⊕ *www.ado.com.mx*).

Currency Exchange Banamex (✉ *Calle 41 No. 206* ☎ *01800/226–2639 toll-free in Mexico* ⊕ *www.banamex.com*).

Medical Assistance Clínica San Juan (✉ *Calle 40, No. 238* ☎ *985/856–2174*).

Post Office Correo (✉ *Calle 40 No. 194, between Calle 39 and Calle 41* ☎ *985/85–2623*).

Visitor and Tour Info Municipal Tourist Information Center (✉ *Palacio Municipal* ☎ *No phone* ⊙ *Mon.–Sat. 9–8, Sun. 9–1*).

EXPLORING

On the west side of the city's main plaza is the large **Iglesia de San Servacio,** which was pillaged during the War of the Castes.

★ Three long blocks away is the 16th-century, terra-cotta-color **Ex-Convento y Iglesia San Bernadino,** a Franciscan church and former monastery. ■ TIP➔ **If the priest is around, ask him to show you the 16th-century frescoes, protected behind curtains near the altarpiece. The lack of proportion in the human figures shows the initial clumsiness of indigenous artisans in reproducing the Christian saints.**

The large, round, and beautiful sinkhole at the edge of town, **Cenote Zací** (✉ *Calles 36 and 37* ☎ *985/856–2107*), is sometimes crowded with tourists and local boys clowning it up; at other times, it's deserted. Leaves from the tall old trees surrounding the sinkhole float on the surface, but the water itself is quite clean. If you're not up for a dip, visit the adjacent handicraft shop or have a bite or a drink at the well-loved, thatch-roof restaurant overlooking the water.

Five kilometers (3 mi) west of the main square and on the old highway to Chichén Itzá, you can swim with the catfish in lovely, mysterious

Ⓒ **Cenote X-Keken** *(Cenote Dzitnup)*, which is in a cave lighted by a small
★ natural skylight; admission is $3, and guides offer tours for tips.

WHERE TO STAY

$ 🏨 **Ecotel Quinta Real.** This salmon-color hotel is a mix of colonial and modern Mexico. Each whitewashed room is accented with one brightly colored wall; wrought-iron ceiling and wall fixtures; and substantial, hand-carved furniture. Junior suites have balconies (overlooking the parking area), wet bars, living/dining area, king beds, and spa baths. Of the standard rooms, the nicest have terraces overlooking the orchard. The Ecotel also has a game room, an arboretum with local flora, and an uninspiring, fenced-in area for ducks. You can borrow racquets and tennis balls to use on the cement court. The main restaurant ($–$$) has a substantial menu ranging from nachos and pizza to filet mignon and lobster. **Pros:** short walk to central plaza; Wi-Fi. **Cons:** not as central as some hotels; unexciting restaurant. ✉ *Calle 40 No. 160A, at Calle 27* ☎🖷 *985/856–3476* ⊕ *www.ecotelquintaregia.com.mx* ⬖ *106 rooms, 8 suites* ⚿ *In-room: Safe, Wi-Fi. In-hotel: Restaurant, room service, bar, tennis court, pool, laundry service, parking (free), Wi-Fi, no-smoking rooms* ▭ *AE, MC, V.*

Continued on page 276

The towering **El Castillo** pyramid, nearly 80-feet high, is the most striking structure at Chichén Itzá. Each side of the pyramid has 91 steps, which, with the addition of the topmost platform, equal 365, one for each day of the calendar year. At the vernal and autumnal equinoxes, thousands of people gather to watch as the shadow of the serpent god Kukulcán seems to slither down the side of the pyramid.

CHICHÉN ITZÁ

Carvings of ball players adorn the walls of the *juego de pelota*.

One of the most dramatically beautiful of the ancient Maya cities, Chichén Itzá draws some 3,000 visitors a day from all over the world. Since the remains of this once-thriving kingdom were discovered by Europeans in the mid 1800s, many of the travelers who make the pilgrimage here have been archaeologists and scholars, who study the structures and glyphs and try to piece together the mysteries surrounding them. While the artifacts here give fascinating insight into the Maya civilization, they also raise many, many unanswered questions.

The name of this ancient city, which means "the mouth of the well of the Itzás," is a mystery in and of itself. Although it likely refers to the valuable water sources at the site (there are several sinkholes here), experts have little information about who might have actually founded the city—some structures, likely built in the 5th century, pre-date the arrival of the Itzás who occupied the city starting around the late 8th and early 9th centuries. The reason why the Itzás abandoned the city, around 1224, is also unknown. The role that this center then took is still being evaluated.

Of course, most of the visitors that converge on Chichén Itzá come to marvel at its beauty, not ponder its significance. This ancient metropolis, which encompasses 6 square km (2½ square mi), is known around the world as one of the most stunning and well-preserved Maya sites in existence.

The sight of the immense ❶ **El Castillo** pyramid, rising imposingly yet gracefully from the surrounding plain, has been known to produce goose pimples on sight. El Castillo (The Castle) dominates the site both in size and in the sym-

CHICHÉN ITZÁ

The spiral staircased El Caracol was used as an astronomical observatory.

7 Casa Roja

8 Casa del Venado

Anexo de las Monjas

11

Templo del Osario

Grupo de las Monjas

10

6

9 El Caracol

13 Templo de los Panales Cuadrados

Akab Dzib

12

Structures at the Grupo de las Monjas have some of the site's most exquisite carvings and masks.

Xtaloc Sinkhole

5

Cenote Xtaloc

← TO OLD CHICHÉN ITZÁ

Juego de Pelota

THE CULT OF KUKULCÁN

Although the Maya worshipped many of their own gods, Kukulcán was a deity introduced to them by the Toltecs—who referred to him as Quetzacóatl, or the plumed serpent. The pyramid of El Castillo, along with many other structures at Chichén Itzá, was built in honor of Kukulcán.

El Mercado

14

Plaza de Mil Columnas

15

Plaza de Mil Columnas

Temazcal

Juego de Pelota

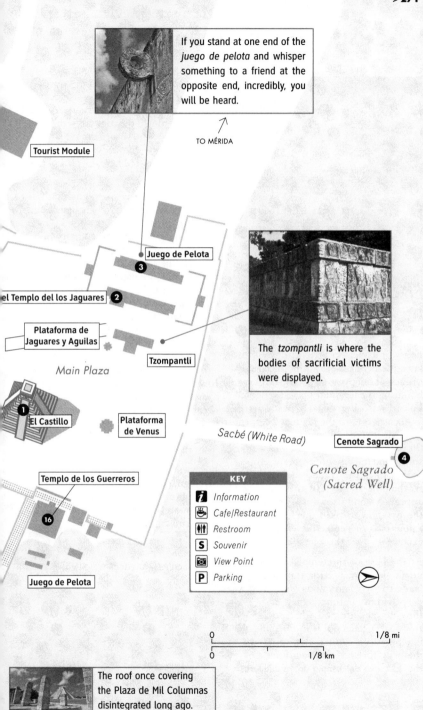

If you stand at one end of the *juego de pelota* and whisper something to a friend at the opposite end, incredibly, you will be heard.

TO MÉRIDA

Tourist Module

Juego de Pelota
3

el Templo del los Jaguares **2**

Plataforma de Jaguares y Aguilas

Main Plaza

Tzompantli

The *tzompantli* is where the bodies of sacrificial victims were displayed.

1
El Castillo

Plataforma de Venus

Sacbé (White Road)

Cenote Sagrado
4

Cenote Sagrado (Sacred Well)

Templo de los Guerreros

16

KEY	
🛈	Information
☕	Cafe/Restaurant
🚻	Restroom
S	Souvenir
📷	View Point
P	Parking

Juego de Pelota

0 ⸺ 1/8 mi
0 ⸺ 1/8 km

The roof once covering the Plaza de Mil Columnas disintegrated long ago.

5

IN FOCUS CHICHÉN ITZÁ

MAJOR SITES AND ATTRACTIONS

Rows of freestanding columns at the site have a strangely Greek look.

metry of its perfect proportions. Open-jawed serpent statues adorn the corners of each of the pyramid's four stairways, honoring the legendary priest-king Kukulcán (also known as Quetzalcóatl), an incarnation of the feathered serpent god. More serpents appear at the top of the building as sculpted columns. At the spring and fall equinoxes, the afternoon light strikes the trapezoidal structure so that the shadow of the snake-god appears to undulate down the side of the pyramid to bless the fertile earth. Thousands of people travel to the site each year to see this phenomenon.

At the base of the temple on the north side, an interior staircase leads to two marvelous statues deep within: a stone jaguar, and the intermediate god Chacmool. As usual, Chacmool is in a reclining position, with a flat spot on the belly for receiving sacrifices. On the ❷Anexo del Templo de los Jaguares

(Annex to the Temple of the Jaguars), just west of El Castillo, bas-relief carvings represent more important deities. On the bottom of the columns is the rain god Tlaloc. It's no surprise that his tears represent rain—but why is the Toltec god Tlaloc honored here, instead of the Maya rain god, Chaac?

That's one of many questions that archaeologists and epigraphers have been trying to answer, ever since John Lloyd Stephens and Frederick Catherwood, the first English-speaking explorers to discover the site, first hacked their way through the surrounding forest in 1840. Scholars once thought that the symbols of foreign gods and differing architectural styles at Chichén Itzá proved it was conquered by the Toltecs of central Mexico. (As well as representations of Tlaloc, the site also has a *tzompantli*—a stone platform decorated with row upon row of sculpted human skulls, which is a distinctively Toltec-style structure.) Most experts now agree, however, that Chichén Itzá was only influenced—not conquered—by Toltec trading partners from the north.

Just west of the Anexo del Templo de los Jaguares is another puzzle: the auditory marvel of Chichén Itzá's main ball court. At 490 feet, this ❸ **Juego de Pelota**

The flat part of a reclining Chacmool statue is where sacrificial offerings were laid.

Although the rules of the game that were played on the ball court aren't known, it's thought that players had to pass some sort of ball through high stone loops.

The walls of the ball field are intricately carved.

is the largest in Mesoamerica. Yet if you stand at one end of the playing field and whisper something to a friend at the other end, incredibly, you will be heard. The game played on this ball court was apparently something like soccer (no hands were used), but it likely had some sort of ritualistic significance. Carvings on the low walls surrounding the field show a decapitation, blood spurting from the victim's neck to fertilize the earth. Whether this is a historical depiction (perhaps the losers or winners of the game were sacrificed?) or a symbolic scene, we can only guess.

On the other side of El Castillo, just before a small temple dedicated to the planet Venus, a ruined *sacbé,* or white road leads to the ❹ **Cenote Sagrado** (Holy Well, or Sinkhole), which was also probably used for ritualistic purposes. Jacques Cousteau and his companions recovered about 80 skeletons from this deep, straight-sided, subsurface pond, as well as thousands of pieces of jewelry and figures of jade, obsidian, wood, bone, and turquoise. In direct alignment with this cloudy green cenote, on the other side of El Castillo, the ❺**Xtaloc sinkhole** was kept pristine, undoubtedly for bathing and drinking. Adjacent to this water source

TIPS

To get more in-depth information about the ruins, hire a multilingual guide at the ticket booth. Guides charge about $35 for a group of up to 7 people. Tours generally last about two hours. ◷ *$9.80* ◷ Ruins daily 8–5, museum Tues.–Sun. 9–4.

is a steam bath, its interior lined with benches along the wall like those you'd see in any steam room today. Outside, a tiny pool was used for cooling down during the ritual.

The older Mayan structures at Chichén Itzá are south and west of Cenote Xtaloc. Archaeologists have been restoring several buildings in this area, including the ❻ **Templo del Osario** (Ossuary Temple), which, as its name implies, concealed several tombs with skeletons and offerings. Behind the smaller ❼ **Casa Roja** (Red House) and ❽ **Casa del Venado** (House of the Deer) are the site's oldest structures, including ❾ **El Caracol** (The Snail), one of the few round buildings built by the Maya, with a spiral staircase within. Clearly built as a celestial observatory, it has eight tiny windows precisely aligned with the points of the compass rose. Scholars now know that Maya priests studied the planets and the stars; in fact, they were able to accurately predict the orbits of Venus and the moon, and the appearance of comets and eclipses. To modern astronomers, this is nothing short of amazing.

The Maya of Chichén Itzá were not just scholars, however. They were skilled artisans and architects as well. South of El Caracol, the ❿ **Grupo de las Monjas** (The Nunnery complex) has some of the site's

The doorway of the Anexo de las Monjas represents an entrance to the underworld.

most exquisite façades. A combination of Puuc and Chenes styles dominates here, with playful latticework, masks, and gargoylelike serpents. On the east side of the ⓫ **Anexo de las Monjas** (Nunnery Annex), the Chenes facade celebrates the rain god Chaac. In typical style, the doorway represents an entrance into the underworld; figures of Chaac decorate the ornate façade above.

South of the Nunnery Complex is an area where field archaeologists are still excavating (fewer than a quarter of the structures at Chichén Itzá have been fully restored). If you have more than a superficial interest in the site—and can convince the authorities ahead of time of your importance, or at least your interest in archaeology—you can explore this area, which is generally not open to the public. Otherwise, head back toward El Castillo past the ruins of a housing compound called ⓬ **Akab Dzib** and the ⓭ **Templo de los Panales Cuadrados** (Temple of the Square Panels). The latter of these buildings shows more evidence of Toltec influence: instead of weight-bearing Mayan arches—or "false arches"—that traditionally supported stone roofs, this structure has stone columns but no roof. This means that the building was once roofed, Toltec-style, with perishable materials (most likely palm thatch or wood) that have long since disintegrated.

Beyond El Caracol, Casa Roja, and El Osario, the right-hand path follows an ancient sacbé, now collapsed. A mud-and-straw hut, which the Maya called a **na,** has been reproduced here to show the simple implements used before and after the Spanish conquest. On one side of the room are a typical pre-Hispanic table, seat, fire pit, and reed baskets; on the other, the Christian cross and colonial-style table of the post-conquest Maya.

Behind the tiny oval house, several unexcavated mounds still guard their secrets. The path meanders through a small grove of oak and slender bean trees to the building known today as ⓴ **El Mercado.** This market was likely one end of a huge outdoor market whose counterpart structure, on the other side of the grove, is the ⓵ **Plaza de Mil Columnas.** (Plaza of the Thousand Columns). In typical Toltec-Maya style, the roof once covering the parallel rows of round stone columns in this long arcade has disappeared, giving the place a strangely Greek—and distinctly non-Maya—look. But the curvy-nosed Chaacs on the corners of the adjacent ⓶

Templo de los Guerreros are pure Maya. Why their noses are pointing down, like an upside-down "U, " instead of up, as usual, is just another mystery to be solved.

The Templo de los Guerreros shows the influence of Toltec architecture.

WHERE TO STAY AT CHICHÉN ITZÁ

★ **$$$–$$$$** ¶◎| **Mayaland.** This charming property is in a large garden, and close enough to the ruins to have its own entrance (you can even see some of the older structures from the windows). The large number of tour groups that come here, however, will make it less appealing if you're looking for privacy. Colonial-style guest rooms have decorative tiles; ask for one with a balcony, which doesn't cost extra. Bungalows have thatched roofs as well as wide verandas with hammocks. The simple Maya-inspired "huts" near the front of the property, built in the 1930s, are the cheapest option, but are for groups only. ⊠ *Carretera 180, Km 120* ☎ *985/851–0100 or 800/235–4079* 📠 *985/851–0128* 📠📠 *985/851–0129* ⊕ *www.mayaland. com* 🔖 *60 bungalows, 30 rooms, 10 suites* 🝔 *4 restaurants, room service, bars, tennis court, pools, laundry service, parking (free), no-smoking rooms* ▭ *AE, D, MC, V.*

★ **Fodor's Choice** **$$$** ¶◎| **Hacienda Chichén.** A converted 16th-century hacienda with its own entrance to the ruins, this hotel once served as the headquarters for the Carnegie expedition to Chichén Itzá. Rustic-chic, soap-scented cotes are simply but beautifully furnished in colonial Yucatecan style, with bedspreads and dehumidifiers; all of the ground-floor rooms have verandas, but only master suites have hammocks. There's a satellite TV in the library. An enormous (and deep) old pool graces the gardens. Meals are served on the patio overlooking the grounds, or in the air-conditioned restaurant. A big plus is the hotel's intimate size; it's a place for honeymoons and silver anniversaries, not tour groups. ⊠ *Carretera 180, Km 120* ☎ *985/851–0045, 999/ 924–2150 reservations, 877/631–4005* 📠📠 *999/924–5011* ⊕ *www.hacienda chichen.com* 🔖 *24 rooms, 4 suites* 🝔 *In-room: no phone, no TV. In-hotel: 2 restaurants, bar, pool, laundry service, parking (free), no-smoking rooms* ▭ *AE, DC, MC, V.*

Sacred Cenotes

CLOSE UP

To the ancient (and tradition-bound modern) Maya, holes in the ground—be they sinkholes (*cenotes*) or caves—are considered conduits to the world of the spirits. A source of water in a land of no surface rivers, sinkholes are of special importance. The domain of Chaac, god of rain and water, cenotes like Balancanchén, near Chichén Itzá, were used as prayer sites and shrines. Sacred objects and sacrificial victims were thrown in the sacred cenote at Chichén Itzá, and in others near large ceremonial centers in ancient times.

There are at least 2,800 known cenotes in the Yucatán. Rainwater sinks through the peninsula's thin soil and porous limestone to create underground rivers, while leaving the dry surface river-free.

Some pondlike sinkholes are found near ground level; most require a bit more effort to access, however. Near

downtown Valladolid, Cenote Zací is named for the Mayan town conquered by the Spanish. It's a relatively simple saunter down a series of cement steps to reach the cool green water.

Lesser-known sinkholes are yours to discover, especially in the area labeled "zona de cenotes." To explore this area southeast of Mérida, you can hire a guide through the tourism office. Another option is to head directly for the ex-hacienda of Chunkanan, outside the village of the same name, about 30 minutes southeast of Mérida. There former henequen workers will hitch their horses to tiny open railway carts to take you along the unused train tracks. The reward for this bumpy, sometimes dusty ride is a swim in several incredible cenotes.

Almost every local has a "secret" cenote; ask around, and perhaps you'll find a favorite of your own.

$$ ⊡ **El Mesón del Marqués.** On the north side of the main square, this well-preserved, old hacienda house was built around a lovely, colonnaded, open patio. The rooms are less impressive, although comfortable; Nos. 407, 408, and 409 are the newest, and have views of the cathedral. The charming restaurant ($–$$), in a courtyard with an old stone fountain and surrounded by porticoes, serves Yucatecan specialties. Again, the ambience is more impressive than the food itself, although the soups are pretty good. **Pros:** great downtown location; nice outdoor areas. **Cons:** food could be better. ⊠ *Calle 39 No. 203, between Calles 40 and 42* ☎ *985/856–2073 or 985/856–3042* ⊕ *www.mesondelmarques. com* ⟿ *88 rooms, 2 suites* ♿ *In-room: Safe. In-hotel: Restaurant, room service, bar, pool, laundry service, parking (free), no-smoking rooms* ⊟ *AE* ⦿ *EP, CP.*

SIDE TRIP

EK BALAM

★ *30 km (18 mi) north of Valladolid, off Carretera 295.*

⛰ What's most stunning about the large Ek Balam ("black jaguar") site are the elaborately carved and amazingly well-preserved stucco panels of one of the temples, the **Templo de los Frisos.** A giant mask crowns its summit, and its friezes contain wonderful carvings of figures often referred to as "angels" (because they have wings)—but which more likely represented nobles in ceremonial dress.

As is common with ancient Mayan structures, this temple, styled like those in the region of Chenes in the northwest, is superimposed upon earlier ones. The temple was a mausoleum for ruler Ukit Kan Lek Tok, who was buried with priceless funerary objects, including pearls, perforated seashells, jade, mother-of-pearl pendants, and small bone masks with moveable jaws. At the bases at either end of the temple, the name of the leader is inscribed on the forked tongue of a carved serpent, which obviously hadn't had the negative biblical connotation ascribed to the snake in Western culture today. A contemporary of Uxmal and Cobá, the city may have been a satellite city to Chichén Itzá, which rose to power as Ek Balam waned.

Another unusual feature of Ek Balam are the two concentric walls—a rare configuration in Mayan sites—that surround the 45 structures in the main part of the site. They may have provided defense, or perhaps they symbolized more than provided safety for the ruling elite that lived within.

Ek Balam also has a ball court and quite a few freestanding stelae (stone pillars carved with glyphs or images for commemorative purposes). New Age groups sometimes converge on the site for prayers and seminars, but it's usually quite sparsely visited, which adds to the mystery and allure. ⊠$3.50 ⊘Daily 9–5.

WHERE TO STAY

¢ 🔝**Genesis Retreat.** Close to the Ek Balam site, this simple retreat is modeled on the local dwellings of the region. Cabins of stucco, wood, and thatch surround a casually maintained open area with a ritual *temazcal* (Mayan steam lodge) and a small swimming pool. There are two well-behaved dogs, three cats, and a few tame parrots on the property. The owners organize artisan tours of a nearby Mayan village. You'll grind corn for tortillas and learn about weaving and other traditional crafts. Genesis pairs longer-term guests up with a local host family for a cultural exchange—you could learn how to make tortillas, weave hammocks, or build cabanas. You can also rent a bike to tour nearby ruins and sinkholes. There's lots of organic produce from nearby farms on the restaurant menu. **Pros:** well-kept, intimate atmosphere; cultural programs; close to the Ek Balam ruins. **Cons:** most cabins have shared bathrooms; sometimes difficult to make reservations by phone, but Internet responses are always prompt. ⊠*Domicilio Conocido* ☎985/852–7980 *or* 985/858–9375 ⊕*www.genesisretreat.com* ⤳7 cabins ⌂*In-room: No a/c, no phone, no TV. In-hotel: Restaurant, bicycles, Wi-Fi, no-smoking rooms* ▭*No credit cards* ⫯*EP.*

¢ 🔝**María de la Luz.** A worn but still somehow engaging budget hotel, Mary of the Light is on the main plaza. Motel-style buildings are centered on a swimming pool, where there are banana trees and tables for drinking or dining. The plain rooms are nothing to write home about, but consistently attract a diverse and bohemian clientele. The restaurant, where guests tend to gather, serves predictable but tasty Mexican dishes; *pollo pibíl* is a house specialty. You may be tempted to upgrade to the hotel's single suite—but it has the same uneventful decor, with a whirlpool tub and more beds of various sizes jammed in. **Pros:** on the zócalo; big pool; tasty restaurant food. **Cons:** sparse rooms; linens a bit worn; hard beds. ⊠*Calle 42 No. 193C* ☎*985/856–2071 or 985/856–1181* ⊕*www.mariadelaluzhotel.com* ⟳*67 rooms, 2 suites* ⌂*In-room: No phone. In-hotel: Restaurant, bar, pool, parking (free), Wi-Fi* ⊟*MC, V.*

PISTÉ

46 km (29 mi) east of Valladolid; 116 km (72 mi) east of Mérida; 2 km (1½ mi) west of Chichén Itzá.

The town of Pisté serves primarily as a base camp for travelers to Chichén Itzá. Hotels, campgrounds, restaurants, and handicrafts shops tend to be less expensive here than those at the ruins.

EXPLORING

Across from the Dolores Alba hotel is the **Parque Ik Kil** *("place of the winds").* A $6 entrance fee is required if you want to swim in the lovely cenote here, open daily between 8 AM and 6 PM. If you're going to eat in the adjacent restaurant, or sleep overnight, you don't need to pay the entrance fee. ⊠*Carretera Mérida–Puerto Juárez, Km 122* ☎*985/858–1525* ⊟*No credit cards.*

WHERE TO STAY

¢ 🏨**Dolores Alba.** The best low-budget choice near the ruins is this family-
★ run hotel with a small motel feel, a longtime favorite of international travelers. Spartan-ish rooms have hard beds and chunky, colonial-style furniture; but there are also two pools (one with palapas with hammocks) and a family-style restaurant where breakfast, lunch, and dinner are served. The convivial vibe, along with cheap prices, is the big draw here. Free transportation to Chichén Itzá is provided daily. There is a small discount on reservations made online. **Pros:** close to ruins; transport to ruins (though not back from them) is included. **Cons:** restaurant leaves much to be desired; small rooms; furniture and linens look a little past their prime. ⊠*Carretera 180, Km 122, 3 km (2 mi) east of Chichén Itzá* ☎*985/858–1555* ⊕*www.doloresalba.com* ⟳*40 rooms* ⌂*In-room: Safe, no phone, no TV. In-hotel: Restaurant, pools, parking (free)* ⊟*MC, V* �|○|*EP, MAP.*

$$$ 🏨**Hacienda Chichén Resort.** This refurbished hacienda with a butter-yellow exterior, has beautiful gardens, simple, but spacious rooms, and an inviting pool surrounded by palm trees. However, the main draw here is that you can walk to Chichén Itzá in just a couple of minutes. Rooms don't have TV, but there is a TV in a common area. **Pros:** short walk from ruins; beautiful gardens. **Cons:** pricier than at other area hotels; restaurant food just OK. ⊠*Carrertera Mérida-Puerto Júarez, Km 120, Zona Hotelera de Chichén Itzá cerca del Pueblo Pisté* ☎*999/920–8407, 877/631–4005 in U.S.* ⊕*www.haciendachichen.com* ⟳*29 rooms* ⌂*In-room: No phone, no TV. In-hotel: Restaurant, pool, spa, parking (free), no-smoking rooms* ⊟*AE, MC, V.*

$$ ⊞**Hotel Chichén Itzá.** Just over 1½ km (1 mi) from the ruins in the town of Pisté, this two-story hotel surrounding a pool feels like a motel in a very unlikely setting: a large grassy area edged with banana and other tropical trees and flowers. The nicest rooms have contemporary rustic Mexican furnishings of iron and wood, larger bathrooms with tub, and minibars; standard rooms have shower only. The restaurant is open from 7 AM until 10 PM, but there's no room service. **Pros:** minutes from ruins; big pool. **Cons:** mediocre food; rooms amenities vary (check out a few if possible). ⊠*Calle 15 No. 45* ☏ *985/851–0022 or 800/235–4079* ⊕*www.mayaland.com* ⌁*44 rooms* ⌂*In-hotel: Restaurant, bar, pool, laundry service, parking (free), Wi-Fi, no-smoking rooms* ⊟*AE, D, MC, V.*

GRUTAS DE BALANCANCHÉN

⚓ *38 km (24 mi) west of Valladolid; 6 km (4 mi) east of Chichén Itzá;*
🕐 *117 km (72 mi) east of Mérida.*

How often do you get the chance to wander below the earth? The caves translated as both "throne of the jaguar caves" and "caves of the hidden throne" are dank and sometimes slippery slopes to an amazing, rocky underworld. The caverns are lighted to best show off their lumpy limestone stalactites and niche-like side caves. It's a privilege also to view in situ vases, jars, and incense burners once used in sacred rituals. These were discovered in the 1950s, and left right as they were. An arrangement of tiny *metates* (stone mortars for grinding corn) is particularly moving. At the end of the line is the underground cenote where Mayan priests worshiped Chaac, the god of rain and water. Wear comfortable, nonslip walking shoes. The site has a sound-and-light show that recounts Mayan history. The caves are 6 km (4 mi) from Chichén Itzá; you can catch a bus or taxi or arrange a tour at the Mayaland hotel. Although there's a six-person minimum, the ticket vendor will often allow even a pair of visitors to tour. ⌸*$8.50, including tour; sound-and-light show $5; parking $2 extra* ⊙ *Daily 9–5; tours leave daily at 11, 1, and 3 (English); 9, noon, 2, and 4 (Spanish); and 10 (French).*

PROGRESO AND THE NORTH COAST

Various routes lead from Mérida to towns along the coast, which are spread across a distance of 380 km (236 mi). Separate roads connect Mérida with the laid-back fishing village of Celestún, the gateway to an ecological marine reserve that extends south to just beyond the Campeche border. Carretera 261 leads due north from Mérida to the relatively modern but humble shipping port of Progreso, where Méridians spend hot summer days and holiday weekends. To get to some of the small beach towns east of Progreso, head east on Carretera 176 out of Mérida and then cut north on one of the many access roads. Wide, white, and generally shadeless beaches here are peppered with bathers from Mérida during Holy Week and in summer—but are nearly vacant the rest of the year.

The terrain in this part of the peninsula is absolutely flat. Tall trees are scarce, because the region was almost entirely cleared for coconut palms in the early 19th century and again for henequen in the early 20th century. Local people still tend some of the old fields of henequen, even though there is little profit to be made from the rope fiber it produces. Other former plantation fields are wildly overgrown with scrub, and are only identifiable by the low, white, stone walls that used to mark their boundaries. Many bird species make their home in this area, and butterflies swarm in profusion throughout the dry season.

CELESTÚN

90 km (56 mi) west of Mérida.

This tranquil and humble fishing village sits at the end of a spit of land separating the Celestún estuary from the Gulf of Mexico.

Celestún is the point of entry to the **Reserva Ecológica de los Petenes,** a 100,000-acre wildlife reserve with extensive mangrove forests and one of the largest colonies of flamingos in North America. Clouds of the pink birds soar above the estuary all year, but the best months for seeing them in abundance are April through July. This is also the fourth-largest wintering ground for ducks of the Gulf-coast region, and more than 300 other species of birds, as well as a large sea-turtle population, make their home here. Conservation programs sponsored by the United States and Mexico protect the birds, as well as the endangered hawks-bill and loggerhead marine tortoises, and other species such as the blue crab and crocodile. Other endangered species that inhabit the area are the ocelot, the jaguar, and the spider monkey.

The park is set among rocks, islets, and white-sand beaches. There's good fishing here, too, and several cenotes that are wonderful for swimming. Most Mérida travel agencies run boat tours of the *ría* (estuary) in the early morning or late afternoon, but it's not usually necessary to make a reservation in advance.

■ TIP➔**To see the birds, hire a fishing boat at the entrance to town (the boats hang out under the bridge leading into Celestún). A 75-minute tour for up to six people costs about $50, a two-hour tour around $75. Popular with Mexican vacationers, the park's sandy beach is pleasant during the morning but tends to get windy in the afternoon. And, unfortunately, mosquitoes gather in great numbers on the beach at dawn and dusk, particularly during the winter months, making a walk on the beach uncomfortable. Most hotels offer mosquito netting around the beds, but bring along a good cream or spray to keep the bugs away.**

WHERE TO EAT AND STAY

$ ✕ **La Palapa.** Celestún's most popular seafood place under an enormous
SEAFOOD   *palapa* roof is known for its *camarones a la palapa* (fried shrimp smoth-ered in a garlic and cream sauce) and fresh seafood cocktails. Unless it's windy or rainy, most guests dine on the beachfront terrace. The menu has lots of fresh fish (including sea bass and red snapper), as well as crab, squid, and lobster. There are a few beef plates if you're not in the mood for seafood. Although the restaurant's hours are 9 AM

to 6 PM, it sometimes closes early during the low season. ⊠ *Calle 12 No. 105, between Calles 11 and 13* ☎ *988/916–2063* ⊟ *AE, MC, V.*

$$$ 🖾 **Hotel Eco Paraíso Xixim.** On an old coconut plantation outside town, this hotel offers classy comfort in thatch-roof bungalows along a shell-strewn beach. Each unit has two comfortable queen beds, tile floors, and attractive wicker, cedar, and pine furniture. The extra-large porch has twin hammocks and comfortable chairs. Biking and bird-watching tours as well as tours to old haciendas or archaeological sites can be arranged; kayaks are available for rent. Vegetarian food is available for breakfast and dinner, which are included in the room price. Their Web site details their eco initiatives, which include keeping outdoor lighting low so as not to disorient area sea turtles. **Pros:** on beach; good service. **Cons:** a drive from main plaza; no a/c. ⊠ *Camino Viejo a Sisal, Km 10* ☎ *988/916–2100, 800/400–3333 in U.S. and Canada* ⊕ *www.eco paraiso.com* ⟳ *15 cabanas* ⚒ *In-room: No a/c, no phone, safe, no TV. In-hotel: Restaurant, bar, pool, beachfront, no-smoking rooms* ⊟ *AE, MC, V* ⊟ *MAP.*

WORD OF MOUTH

"We rented a car and drove to Celestún, just for the day. It was easy to hook up with a boat/driver in town and zip out to see the flamingos (this was early March). There were lots of other birds as well. We went to Uxmal and really enjoyed it too. We had lunch at a lovely hacienda and toured it. The weekend festivities in Mérida are fun to see." –glover

5

$$ 🖾 **Hotel Manglares.** Every single room at this, the most luxurious hotel in town, has a view of the beach. The more expensive private cabanas have small kitchens and hot tubs. The hotel can help you arrange canoe trips to see flamingos and evening canoe trips. **Pros:** spacious rooms; powerful a/c; on beach. **Cons:** restaurant and bar are still in planning stages; no lobby or public space for socializing. ⊠ *Calle 12 No. 63, Celestún* ☎ *988/916–2561* ⊕ *www.hotelmanglares.com.mx* ⟳ *20 rooms, 4 cabanas* ⚒ *In-room: Safe, Wi-Fi. In-hotel: Pool, beachfront, no-smoking rooms* ⊟ *MC, V* ⊟ *EP.*

¢ 🖾 **Hotel Sol y Mar.** Gerardo Vasquez, the friendly owner of this small hotel across from the town beach, also owns the local paint store—so it's no accident that the walls here are a lovely shade of cool green. In fact, everything in the entry garden seems to be painted green, even the concrete fountain. The spacious rooms are sparsely decorated but have two double beds, a table, chairs, and a tile bathroom. The more expensive rooms downstairs also have air-conditioning, TVs, and tiny refrigerators. Prices go down by about $5 in low season, which is everything except Easter, Christmas, and August. There's no restaurant, but La Palapa is across the street. **Pros:** inexpensive; walking distance to small shops and restaurants. **Cons:** spartan rooms; odd decor in outdoor lobby and bar. ⊠ *Calle 12 No. 104, at Calle 10* ☎ *988/916–2166* ⟳ *15 rooms* ⚒ *In-room: no a/c (some), refrigerator (some), no TV (some)* ⊟ *No credit cards* ⊟ *EP.*

DZIBILCHALTÚN

⟳ *16 km (10 mi) north of Mérida.*

🏛 Dzibilchaltún (dzi-bil-chal-*tun*), which means "the place with writing on flat stones," is not a place you'd travel miles out of your way to see. But since it's located not far off the road, about halfway between Progreso and Mérida, it's convenient and, in its own small way, interesting. Although more than 16 square km (6 square mi) of land here are cluttered with mounds, platforms, piles of rubble, plazas, and stelae, only a few buildings have been excavated. According to archaeologists, the area may have been settled as early as 500 BC and was inhabited until the time of the conquest. At its height, there were around 40,000 people living at the site.

Scientists find Dzibilchaltún fascinating because of the sculpture and ceramics from all periods of Mayan civilization that have been unearthed. Save what's in the museum, though, all you'll see is tiny **Templo de las Siete Muñecas** ("temple of the seven dolls," circa AD 500), one of a half-dozen structures excavated to date. It's a long stroll down a flat dirt track sided by flowering bushes and trees to get to the low, trapezoidal temple exemplifying the late pre-Classic style. During the spring and fall equinoxes, sunbeams fall at the exact center of two windows opposite each other inside one of the temple rooms, an example of the highly precise mathematical calculations for which the Maya are known. Studies have found that a similar phenomenon occurs at the full moon between March 20 and April 20.

Dzibilchaltún's other main attraction is the ruined open chapel built by the Spaniards for the Indians. Actually, to be accurate, the Spanish forced Indian laborers to build it as a place of worship for themselves: a sort of pre-Hispanic "separate but equal" scenario.

⟳ One of the best reasons to visit Dzibilchaltún is **Xlacah Cenote**, the site's sinkhole, whose crystalline water is the color of smoked green glass and is ideal for cooling off in after walking around the ruins. Another reason to visit is the **Museo Pueblo Maya**: small, yet both attractive and impressive. The museum (closed Monday) holds the seven crude dolls that gave the Temple of the Seven Dolls its name, and outside in the garden rest several huge sculptures found on the site. Museo Pueblo Maya also traces the area's Hispanic history and highlights contemporary crafts from the region.

The easiest way to get to Dzibilchaltún is to get a *colectivo* taxi from Mérida's **Parque San Juan** (⊠ *Calles 69 and 62, a few blocks south of Plaza Principal*). The taxis depart whenever they fill up with passengers. Returns are a bit trickier. If a colectivo taxi doesn't show up, you can take a regular taxi back to Mérida (it will cost you about $12 to $15). You can also ask the taxi driver to drop you at the Mérida–Progreso highway, where you can catch a Mérida-bound bus for less than $4. 🎟 *$6.60, including museum* ⊙ *Daily 8–5.*

PROGRESO

16 km (10 mi) north of Dzibilchaltún; 32 km (20 mi) north of Mérida.

The waterfront town closest to Mérida, Progreso is not particularly historic. It's also not terribly picturesque; still, it provokes a certain sentimental fondness for those who know it well. On weekdays during most of the year the beaches are deserted, but when school is out (Easter week, July, and August) and on summer weekends it's bustling with families from Mérida, and new businesses are popping up to cater to them. Low prices are luring more retired Canadians, many of whom rent apartments here between December and April. It's also started attracting cruise ships, and twice-weekly arrivals also bring tourist traffic to town.

Progreso's charm—or lack thereof—seems to hinge on the weather. When the sun is shining, the water appears a translucent green and feels bathtub-warm, and the fine sand makes for lovely long walks. When the wind blows during one of Yucatán's winter *nortes,* the water churns with whitecaps and looks gray and unappealing, and the sand blows in your face. Whether the weather is good or bad, however, everyone ends up eventually at one of the restaurants lining the main street, Calle 19, across from the oceanfront malecón. These all serve up cold beer, seafood cocktails, and freshly grilled fish. There is also a small downtown area, between Calle 80 and Calle 31, with small restaurants that serve simpler fare (like tortas and tacos), shops, banks, and supermarkets.

Although Progreso is close enough to Mérida to make it an easy day trip, several B&Bs that have cropped up over the past few years make this a pleasant place to stay, and a great base for exploring the untouristy coast. Just west of Progreso, the fishing villages of Chelem and Chuburna are beginning to offer walking, kayaking, and cycling tours ending with a boat trip through the mangroves and a freshly prepared ceviche and beer or soft drink for about $33. This is ecotourism in its infancy, and it's best to set this up ahead of time through the Progreso tourism office. Experienced divers can explore sunken ships at the Alacranes Reef, about 120 km (74 mi) offshore, although infrastructure is limited. Pérez Island, part of the reef, supports a large population of sea turtles and seabirds. Arrangements for the boat trip can be made through individuals at the private marina at neighboring Yucaltepén, 6 km (4 mi) from Progreso.

GETTING HERE AND AROUND

Progreso is 32 km (20 mi) north of Mérida via México 261. To drive from Mérida, head north from the Paseo de Montejo and keep going north as you head out of town. It's a straight drive to the beach. Buses for Progreso also leave Mérida from Calle 62 #524, between Calle 65 and Calle 67.

ESSENTIALS

Visitor and Tour Info Progreso Municipal Tourism Office (⊠ *Casa de la Cultura, Calles 80 and 25, Centro* ☎ *969/935–0104* ⊕ *www.ayuntamientode progreso.gob.mx).*

WHERE TO EAT AND STAY

¢ ✕**Eladio's.** This bar and restaurant is a new branch of a classic and
MEXICAN popular Merida joint. Under a tall palapa on the beach you can enjoy
the view and the breeze through tall windows facing the water. Live
music adds to the partylike atmosphere. Tasty appetizers are free with
your drinks, and there are plenty to choose from; this is a good place to
try different Yucatecan dishes such as *longaniza asada,* a local roasted
sausage, and *pollo pibíl,* marinated chicken baked in banana leaves.
Fresh seafood dishes are also on the menu, but these do not come with
the drinks. ⊠ *Av. Malecón s/n , at Calle 80, Centro* ☎*969/935–5670*
⊕*www.eladios.com.mx* ⊟*AE, MC, V.*

$ ✕**Flamingos.** This restaurant facing Progreso's long cement promenade is
SEAFOOD a cut above its neighbors. Service is professional and attentive, and soon
after arriving you'll get at least one free appetizer—maybe black beans
with corn tortillas, or a plate of shredded shark meat stewed with tomatoes. The creamy cilantro soup is a little too cheesy (literally, not figu-
ratively), but the large fish fillets are perfectly breaded and lightly fried.
Breakfast is served after 7 AM. There's a full bar, and although there's
no air-conditioning, large, glassless windows let in the ocean breeze.
⊠*Calle 19 No. 144-D, at Calle 72* ☎*969/935–2122* ⊟*MC, V.*

$-$$ ✕**La Lagunita.** A casual family-owned restaurant, Lagunita is a great
SEAFOOD reason to make a detour to the small fisherman's town of Santa Clara.
The great seafood here manages to attract big crowds, seemingly from
out of nowhere. You'll know you have arrived when you see small
ponds, which are just out front. Appetizers, such as potato salad and
beets, are included with every alcoholic drink you order. The lobster
dish *langosta a la mantequilla* has a delicious cheesy and buttery flavor.
The fresh local fishes, including merlot, are also exquisitely prepared.
Santa Clara is 50 km (31 mi) west of Progreso. ⊠*Calle 18 No. 78-A,
Puerto de Santa Clara* ☎*991/102–2009* ⊟*No credit cards.*

$-$$ ✕**Le Saint Bonnet.** This thatched-roof restaurant and bar on the malecón
SEAFOOD is *the* place for locals. It gets its name from a French partner who has
given all the dishes Gallic monikers; the shrimp St. Bonnet—jumbo
shrimp stuffed with cheese, wrapped with bacon, breaded, fried, and
served with crab sauce—is a perennial favorite. European and Chilean wines complement the meals, and the caramel crepes or chocolate
mousse are perfect for dessert. A live band plays tropical music daily
(except Monday) from 2:30 to 6:30 PM. ⊠*Av. Malecón (Calle 19)
150D, at Calle 28* ☎*969/935–2299* ⊟*AE, MC, V.*

$ ▣**Casa Isidora.** A couple of Canadian English teachers have restored
this grand, 100-year-old house a few blocks from the beach. Each guest
room is very simply decorated, but all have beautiful tile floors and
a cozy, beachy style; some even have small private patios. A quick
breakfast of coffee, toast, and fruit is served in the dining room or
out back, where the small swimming pool is surrounded by cushioned
chaise lounges. Mexican and American bar food and lots of tequilas
are served in the popular, street-side bar. Spanish lessons and Internet use are free for hotel guests. When the hotel is not full of visitors
from Mérida, it's a quiet and peaceful place to spend a morning. **Pros:**

close to beach; cozy, congenial atmosphere. **Cons:** strange bathroom design that bathes toilet with every shower; basic breakfasts. ✉ *Calle 21 No. 116* 📠 *969/935–4595* ⊕ *www.casaisidora.com* ➥ *7 rooms* ⌂ *In-room: No TV, Internet. In-hotel: Restaurant, bar, Internet terminal, pool, laundry service, parking (free), no-smoking rooms* ☐ *AE, MC, V* 🍴 *BP.*

XCAMBO

🔺 *26 km (16 mi) east of Chicxulub, off the Progreso Hwy. at Xtampu.*

Surrounded by a plantation where disease-resistant coconut trees are being developed, the Xcambo (*ish*-cam-bo) site is a couple of miles inland following the turnoff for Xtampu. It's also in the hometown of former governor Victor Cervera Pacheco, who, it is rumored, had given priority to its excavation. Salt, a much-sought-after item of trade in the ancient Mayan world, was produced in this area and made it prosperous. Indeed, the bones of 600 former residents discovered in burial plots showed they had been healthier than the average Mayan. Two plazas have been restored so far, surrounded by rather plain structures. The tallest temple is the **Xcambo,** also known as the Pyramid of the Cross. On a clear day you can see the coast, about a mile away, from the summit. Ceramics found at the site indicate that the city traded with other Mayan groups as far afield as Guatemala, Teotihuácan, and Belize. The Catholic church on the site was built by dismantling these ancient structures, and until recently locals hauled off the cut stones to build fences and foundations. ✉ *Turn off Progreso–Dzilam de Bravo Hwy. at Xtampu* 🎫 *Donation* ⊙ *Daily 8–5.*

PARQUE NATURAL RÍA LAGARTOS

⌚ *115 km (71 mi) north of Valladolid.*

★ This park, which encompasses a long estuary, was developed with ecotourism in mind—although most of the alligators for which it and the village were named have long since been hunted into extinction. The real spectacle these days is the birds; more than 350 species nest and feed in the area, including flocks of flamingos, snowy and red egrets, white ibis, great white herons, cormorants, pelicans, and peregrine falcons. Fishing is good, too, and the protected hawksbill and green turtles lay their eggs on the beach at night.

You can make the 90-km (56-mi) trip from Valladolid (1½ hours by car or 2 hours by bus) as a day trip (add another hour if you're coming from Mérida; it's 3 hours from Cancún). There's a small information center at the entrance to town where Carretera 295 joins the coast road to San Felipe. Unless you're interested exclusively in the birds, it's nice to spend the night in Río Lagartos (the town is called *Río* Lagartos, the park *Ría* Lagartos) or nearby San Felipe, but this is not the place for Type A personalities. There's little to do except take a walk through town or on the beach and grab a meal. Buses leave Mérida and Valladolid regularly from the second-class terminals to either Río Lagartos or, 10 km (6 mi) west of the park, San Felipe.

Bird-Watching in Yucatán

Rise before the sun and head for shallow water to see flamingos engrossed in an intricate mating dance. From late winter into spring, thousands of bright pink, black-tipped flamingos crowd the estuaries of Ría Lagartos, coming from their "summer homes" in nearby Celestún as well as from northern latitudes to mate and raise their chicks. The largest flocks of both flamingos and bird-watching enthusiasts can be found during these months, when thousands of the birds—90% of the entire flamingo population of the western hemisphere—come to Ría Lagartos to nest.

Although the long-legged creatures are the most famous winged beasts found in these two nature reserves, red, white, black, and buttonwood mangrove swamps are home to hundreds of other species. Of Ría Lagartos's estimated 350 different species, one-third are winter-only residents—the avian counterparts of Canadian and northern-U.S. "snowbirds." Twelve of the region's resident species are endemic, found nowhere else on earth. Ría Lagartos Expeditions now leads walks through the low deciduous tropical forest in addition to boat trips through the mangroves.

More than 400 bird species have been sighted in the Yucatán, inland as well as on the coast. Bird-watching expeditions can be organized in Mérida as well as Ría Lagartos and Celestún. November brings hundreds of professional ornithologists and bird-watching aficionados to the Yucatán for a weeklong conference and symposium with films, lectures, and field trips.

The easiest way to book a trip is through the Núñez family at the Isla Contoy restaurant, where you can also eat a delicious dinner of fresh seafood. Call ahead to reserve an English- or Italian-speaking guide through their organization, **Ría Lagartos Expeditions** (☎ *986/862–0000* ⊕ *www. riolagartos-ecotours.com*). This boat trip will take you through the mangrove forests to the flamingo feeding grounds (where, as an added bonus, you can paint your face or body with supposedly therapeutic green mud). A 2½-hour tour, which accommodates five or six people, costs $70; the 3½-hour tour costs $75 (both per boat, not per person). You can take a shorter boat trip for slightly less money, or a two-hour, guided walking-and-boat tour ($50 for one to six passengers), or a night tour in search of crocs (2½ hours, one to four passengers, $70). You can also hire a boat ($20 for one to ten passengers) to take you to an area beach and pick you up at a designated time.

Be aware that mosquitoes are known to gather at dusk in unpleasantly large groups in May, June, and July. So bringing along some spray to fend them off might be a good idea.

WHERE TO EAT AND STAY

$ ✕ **Isla Contoy Restaurante.** Run by the amicable family that guides lagoon
★ tours, this open-sided seafood shanty at the dock serves generous helpings of fish soup, fried fish fillets, shrimp, squid, and crab. If you come with a group, order the combo for four (it can easily feed six, especially if you order a huge ceviche or other appetizer). The delicious platter comes with four shrimp crepes, fish stuffed with seafood, a

seafood skewer, and one each of grilled, breaded, garlic-chile, and battered fish fillets (usually grouper or sea trout, whatever is freshest). There are also a few regional specialties and red-meat dishes. It's open for breakfast, too, and breakfast is included if you stay in one of their four simple rooms (¢) on the beach. ⊠ *Calle 19 No. 134, at Calle 14* ☎ *986/862–0000* ⊕ *www.riolagartos-ecotours.com/restaurant-isla-con toy.html* ⊟ *MC, V.*

¢ 📷 **Hotel San Felipe.** This three-story white hotel in the beach town of San Felipe, 10 km (6 mi) west of Parque Natural Ría Lagartos, is basic (for example, the toilets have no seats), but adequate. Each room has two twin beds or a double—some are mushy, some hard—and walls are decorated with regional scenes painted by the owner. The two most expensive rooms have private terraces with marina views (ask for a hammock) and are worth the small splurge. The owner can arrange fly-fishing expeditions for tarpon. **Pros:** there are oceanside rooms; some rooms have a private balcony; the town of San Felipe is more organized and cleaner than nearby Ría Lagartos. **Cons:** no air-conditioning, reservations are necessary in high season. ⊠ *Calle 9 No. 13, between Calles 14 and 16, San Felipe* ☎ *986/862–2027* ⊕ *sanfelipehotel@hotmail.com* ⤴ *30 rooms* ♿ *In-room: No a/c (some), no TV. In-hotel: Restaurant, parking (free), no-smoking rooms* ⊟ *No credit cards.*

ISLA HOLBOX

141 km (87 mi) northeast of Valladolid.

Tiny Isla Holbox (25 km [16 mi] long) sits at the eastern end of the Ría Lagartos estuary and just across the Quintana Roo state line. A fishing fan's heaven because of the hordes of pompano, bass, barracuda, and sharks just offshore, the island also pleases bird-watchers and seekers of tranquility. Birds fill the mangrove estuaries on the island's leeward side; whale sharks cruise offshore April through September; and sandy beaches are strewn with seashells. Although the water is often murky— the Gulf of Mexico and the Caribbean come together here—it is shallow and warm and there are some nice places to swim. Sandy streets lead to simple seafood restaurants where the fish fillets, conch, octopus, and other delicacies are always fresh.

Isla's lucky population numbers some 1,500 souls, and in the summer it seems there are that many biting bugs per person. Bring plenty of mosquito repellent. The Internet has arrived, and there's one Web café, but there are no ATMs, and most—if not all—businesses accept cash only, so visit an ATM to stock up before you get here.

There are less expensive lodgings for those who eschew conventional beds in favor of fresh air and a hammock. Since it's a small island, it's easy to check several lodgings and make your choice. Hotel owners can help you set up bird-watching, fishing, and whale shark–viewing expeditions.

GETTING HERE AND AROUND

To get to Isla Holbox from Río Lagartos, take Carretera 176 to Kantunilkin and then head north on the unnumbered road for 44 km (27 mi) to Chiquilá. Continue by ferry to the island; schedules vary, but there are normally five crossings a day. The fare is $3 and the trip takes about 35 minutes. A car ferry makes the trip at 11 AM daily, returning at 5 PM. (You can also pay to leave your car in a lot in Chicquilá, in Quintana Roo.)

WHERE TO STAY

$$ ⊡ **Los Mapaches.** A coconut's throw from the beach, this small enclave includes several thatch-roof bungalows and a second-floor, two-bedroom apartment. Each has wooden floors typical of coastal dwellings and a small patio or balcony overlooking small gardens.

WORD OF MOUTH

"We went to Isla Holbox our last time in Mexico and really enjoyed it. Remember, though, Isla Holbox is very laid-back. Ferries do not always run (depending on weather) and staff is not really there to watch out for you. (So check to make sure your sea kayak is not leaking before you set out.)"   —GeordieFoley

For an additional fee you can take Spanish lessons, arrange a fishing expedition, grab a free bike or a golf cart for touring the island, or just lounge in your hammock. Weekly and monthly rates are available. **Pros:** quick walk to downtown; lovely gardens. **Cons:** fills up quickly, so reservations are often necessary. ⊠ *Av. Pedro Joaquin Coldwell s/n* ☎984/875–2090 ⊕*www.losmapaches.com* ⌁*3 bungalows, 2 suites* ⚒*In-room: No phone, kitchen, no TV. In-hotel: Beachfront, bicycles, laundry service, some pets allowed* ▤MC, V.

$$–$$$ ⊡**Villas Delfines.** Somewhat expensive by island standards, this fishermen's lodge consists of pleasant cabins on the beach. Deluxe bungalows have wood floors (rather than cement), larger balconies, and a few more creature comforts, such as hair dryers and safes. All are on stilts with round palapa roofs, and have waterless, "ecofriendly" toilets. You can get your catch grilled in the restaurant ($–$$), and if you're not into fishing, rent a kayak or arrange for a bird-watching trip. It's a 15-minute walk from the village's small main square. **Pros:** spacious rooms; beautiful beach setting; nice Saturday grill. **Cons:** long walk into town (you may need transport). ⊠*Domicilio Conocido* ☎998/884–8606 ⊕ ⌁*20 cabins* ⚒*In-room: No phone, safe (some), no TV. In-hotel: Restaurant, bar, beachfront, bicycles, no-smoking rooms* ▤AE, D, MC, V ⏏BP, EP, MAP.

$$ ⊡**Xaloc.** Each of these rustic (but comfortable) bungalows has a tall, pointy, thatch roof, cool ceramic-tile floors, and shuttered windows. Some are pushed right up next to the two swimming pools, which are lined with white limestone to re-create the look of the sand through the sea. Other bungalows face the garden; all have mosquito netting over the canopy beds to keep away biting bugs. The Maja'che restaurant serves mainly fish, with lots of fresh seasonal fruits. Rent a bike or golf cart to explore the 19-square-km (7-square-mi) island, or a kayak to check out the marine life in incredibly shallow seas. **Pros:** right on beach; comfortable palapa-covered rooms; lovely pools. **Cons:** relatively high prices; some rooms are for adults only, so families with children must book well in advance. ⊠*Calle Chacchi s/n, at Calle Playa Norte* ☎984/875–2160 ☎800/728–9098 *in U.S. and Canada* ⊕*www.mexicoboutiquehotels.com/xaloc* ⌁*18 bungalows* ⚒*In-room: No a/c, no phone, no TV. In-hotel: Restaurant, pools, beachfront, water sports* ▤AE, MC, V ⏏BP, FAP, MAP.

CAMPECHE

Campeche's historic district is a lovely place to spend some time; it's filled with colonial buildings, gardens, museums, and shops, and remnants of the walls and ramparts that once protected the city from pirates lend romance. Campeche City, the state's most accessible spot, makes a good hub for exploring other areas, many of which have only basic restaurants and primitive lodgings. The Edzná archaeological site is a short detour south of Carreteras 180 and 188.

■ TIP→You'll need at least rudimentary Spanish; few people outside the capital speak English. If you plan to venture off the beaten path, pack a Spanish–English dictionary.

CAMPECHE CITY

174 km (108 mi) southeast of Mérida via Mexico 180.

Campeche is a tranquil, picturesque town, where block upon block of buildings with lovely facades, all painted in bright colors that appear to have come from the mind of an artist, meet the sea. Tiny balconies overlook clean, geometrically paved streets, and charming old street lamps illuminate the scene at night.

In colonial days the city center was completely enclosed within a 3-meter-thick (10-foot-thick) wall. Two stone archways (originally there were four)—one facing the sea, the other the land—provided the only access. The defensive walls also served as a de facto class demarcation. Within them lived the ruling elite. Outside were the barrios, with blacks and mulattoes brought as slaves from Cuba and everyone else.

On strategic corners, seven *baluartes,* or bastions, gave militiamen a platform from which to fight off pirates and the other ruffians that continually plagued this beautiful city on the bay. But it wasn't until 1771, when the Fuerte de San Miguel was built on a hilltop outside town, that pirates finally stopped attacking the city.

■ TIP→Campeche's historic center is easily navigable—in fact, it's a walker's paradise. Narrow roads and lack of parking spaces can make driving a bit frustrating, although drivers here are polite and mellow. Streets running roughly north–south are even-numbered, and those running east–west are odd-numbered.

GETTING HERE AND AROUND

Aeroméxico and Mexicana de Aviación fly several times daily from Mexico City to Campeche City. Campeche's Aeropuerto Internacional Alberto Acuña Ongay is 16 km (10 mi) north of downtown. Taxis are the only means of transportation to and from the airport. The fare to downtown Campeche is about $7.

Within Campeche City, the route of interest to most visitors is along Avenida Ruíz Cortínez; the ride on a bus costs the equivalent of about 30¢. There are also fairly frequent buses to points all over the Yucatán Peninsula.

■TIP➡For trips between major destinations within the Yucatán Peninsula, purchase tickets with a credit card by phone through Ticketbus; make sure to ask from which station the bus departs.

Campeche City is about 2 to 2½ hours from Mérida along the 180-km (99-mi) *via corta* (short way), Carretera 180. The alternative route, the 250-km (155-mi) *via ruinas* (ruins route), Carretera 261, takes three to four hours, but passes some major Mayan ruins.

You can hail taxis on the street in Campeche City; there are also stands by the bus stations, the main plaza, and the municipal market. The minimum fare is $2; it's $2.50 from the center to the bus station and $4 to the airport (it's cheaper to go to the airport than from it). After 11 PM, prices may be slightly higher. There's a small fee, less than 50¢, to call for a cab through Radio Taxis; you can also call Taxis Plus any time, day or night.

ESSENTIALS

Bus Contacts ADO (✉*Av. Patricio Trueba at Casa de Justicia 237* ☎*981/ 811–9910 Ext. 2402* ⊕*www.ado.com.mx*). **Ticketbus** (☎*01800/702–8000 toll-free in Mexico* ⊕*www.ticketbus.com.mx*). **Unión de Camioneros** (✉*Calle Chile and Av. Gobernadores* ☎*981/816–3445*).

Currency Exchange Bancomer (✉*Av. 16 de Septiembre 120* ☎*981/816– 6622* ⊕*www.bancomer.com*). **Banorte** (✉*Calle 8 No. 237, between Calles 53 and 55* ☎*981/811–4250* ⊕*www.banorte.com*).

Mail and Shipping Correo (✉*Av. 16 de Septiembre, between Calles 53 and 55* ☎*981/816–2134*). **DHL** (✉*Av. Miguel Alemán 140* ☎*981/816–0382* ⊕*www. dhl.com*).

Medical Assistance Clínica Campeche (✉*Av. Central No. 72, Centro* ☎*981/ 816–5612*). **General emergencies** (☎*Dial 060*). **Hospital Manuel Campos** (✉*Av. Boulevard s/n* ☎*981/811–1709 [Ext. 138 for pharmacy], 981/816–0957*).

Rental Cars Localiza (✉*Hotel Baluartes, Av. 16 de Septiembre 128* ☎*981/ 811–3187* ⊕*www.localizarentacar.com*). **Maya Car Rental** (✉*Del Mar Hotel, Av. Ruíz Cortínez No. 51, at Calle 59* ☎*981/811–1618*).

Visitor and Tour Info Municipal Tourist Office (✉*Calle 55, between Calles 8 and 10* ☎*981/811–3989 or 981/811–3990*). **State Tourism Office** (✉*Av. Ruíz Cortínez s/n, Plaza Moch Couoh, across from Gobierno, Centro* ☎*981/811–9229*).

EXPLORING
TOP ATTRACTIONS

⓬ **Baluarte de San Carlos.** Named for Charles II, King of Spain, this bastion, where Calle 8 curves around and becomes Circuito Baluartes, houses the **Museo de la Ciudad.** The free museum contains a small collection of historical artifacts, including several Spanish suits of armor and a beautifully inscribed silver scepter. Captured pirates were once jailed in the stifling basement dungeon. The unshaded rooftop provides an ocean view that's lovely at sunset. ✉*Calle 8, between Calles 65 and 63, Circuito Baluartes, Centro* ☎*No phone* 🎫*$2.50* ☉*Tues.–Fri. 8–8, Sat. 8–2 and 4–8, Sun. 9–1.*

A STREETCAR NAMED EL GUAPO

Guided trolley tours of historic Campeche City leave from Calle 10 on the Plaza Principal on the hour 9 to noon and 5 to 8. You can buy tickets ahead of time at the adjacent kiosk or once aboard the trolley. (Trips run less frequently in the off-season, and it's always best to double-check schedules at the kiosk.) The one-hour tour costs $7; if English-speakers request it, guides will do their best to speak the language. For the same price, the green "El Guapo" ("the handsome") trolley makes unguided trips to Reducto de San José at 9 AM and 5 PM (also at 10, 11, and noon during vacation periods such as Christmas and Easter). You'll only have about 10 minutes to admire the view, though.

El Guapo and Super Guapo trams (☎ *981/811–3989, number of nearby municipal tourism office; tram service doesn't have its own phone*).

⓫ Calle 59. Some of Campeche's finest homes were built on this city street between calles 8 and 18. Most were two stories high, the ground floors serving as warehouses and the upper floors as residences. These days, behind the delicate grillwork and lace curtains you can glimpse genteel scenes of Campeche life. The best-preserved houses are those between calles 14 and 18; many closer to the sea have been remodeled or destroyed by fire. Campeche's INAH (Instituto Nacional de Antropología e Historia) office, between Calles 16 and 14, is an excellent example of one of Campeche City's fine old homes. Each month INAH displays a different archaeological artifact in its courtyard. Look for the names of the apostles carved into the lintels of houses between calles 16 and 18.

❹ Casa Seis. One of the first colonial homes in Campeche is now a cultural center. It has been fully restored—rooms are furnished with original antiques and a few reproductions. Original frescoes at the tops of the walls remain, and you can see patches of the painted "wallpaper" that once covered the walls, serving to simulate European trends in an environment where wallpaper wouldn't stick due to the humidity. The Moorish courtyard is occasionally used as a space for exhibits and lectures. ⊠ *Calle 57, between Calles 10 and 8, Plaza Principal, Centro* ☎ *981/816–1782* ⌨ *$1* ⊙ *Daily 9–9.*

⓰ Fuerte de San Miguel. Near the city's southwest end, Avenida Ruíz Cortínez winds its way to this hilltop fort with its breathtaking view of the Bay of Campeche. Built between 1779 and 1801 and dedicated to the archangel Michael, the fort was positioned to blast enemy ships with its long-range cannons. As soon as it was completed, pirates stopped attacking the city. In fact, the cannons were fired only once, in 1842, when General Santa Anna used Fuerte de San Miguel to put down a revolt by Yucatecan separatists seeking independence from Mexico. The fort houses the **Museo de la Cultura Maya,** whose exhibits include the skeletons of long-ago Mayan royals, complete with jewelry and pottery, which are arranged just as they were found in Calakmul tombs.

Campeche's History

Campeche City's Gulf location played a pivotal role in its history. Ah-Kim-Pech (Mayan for "lord of the serpent tick," from which the name Campeche is derived) was the capital of an Indian chieftainship here, long before the Spaniards arrived in 1517. In 1540 the conquerors—led by Francisco de Montejo and later by his son—established a real foothold at Campeche (originally called San Francisco de Campeche), using it as a base for the conquest of the peninsula.

At the time, Campeche City was the Gulf's only port and shipyard. So Spanish ships, loaded with cargoes of treasure plundered from Mayan, Aztec, and other indigenous civilizations, dropped anchor here en route from Veracruz to Cuba, New Orleans, and Spain. As news of the riches spread, Campeche's shores were soon overrun with pirates. From the mid-1500s to the early 1700s, such notorious corsairs as Diego the Mulatto, Lorenzillo, Peg Leg, Henry Morgan, and Barbillas swooped in repeatedly from Tris—or Isla de Términos, as Isla del Carmen was then known—pillaging and burning the city and massacring its people.

Finally, after years of appeals to the Spanish crown, Campeche received funds to build a protective wall, with four gates and eight bastions, around the town center. For a while afterward, the city thrived on its exports,

especially *palo de tinte*—a valuable dyewood more precious than gold due to the nascent European textile industry's demand for it—but also hardwoods, chicle, salt, and *henequen* (sisal hemp). But when the port of Sisal opened on the northern Yucatán coast in 1811, Campeche's monopoly on Gulf traffic ended, and its economy quickly declined. During the 19th and 20th centuries, Campeche, like most of the Yucatán Peninsula, had little to do with the rest of Mexico. Left to their own devices, *Campechanos* lived in relative isolation until the petroleum boom of the 1970s brought businessmen from Mexico City, Europe, and the United States to its provincial doorstep.

Campeche City's history still shapes the community today. Remnants of its gates and bastions split the city into two main districts: the historical center (where relatively few people live) and the newer residential areas. Because the city was long preoccupied with defense, the colonial architecture is less flamboyant here than elsewhere in Mexico. The narrow flagstone streets reflect the confines of the city's walls; homes here emphasize the practical over the decorative. Still, government decrees, and an on-and-off beautification program, have helped keep the city's colonial structures in good condition despite the damaging effects of humidity and salt air. An air of antiquity remains.

Other archaeological treasures are funeral vessels, masks, many wonderfully expressive figurines and whistles from Isla de Jaina, stelae and stucco masks from the Mayan ruins, and an excellent pottery collection. Although it's a shame that most information is in Spanish only, many of the pieces speak for themselves. The gift shop sells replicas of artifacts. ⊠ *Av. Francisco Morazán s/n, west of town center, Cerro de Buenavista* ☎ *No phone* ✉ *$2.50* ☉ *Tues.–Sun. 9–7:30.*

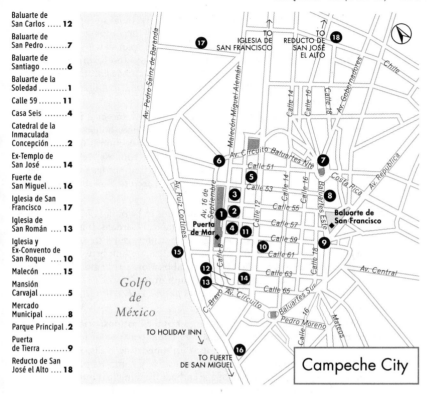

Campeche City

⓯ Malecón. A broad sidewalk, the malecón, more than 4-km (2½-mi) long,
★ runs the length of Campeche's waterfront boulevard, from northeast of
the Debliz hotel to the Justo Sierra Méndez monument at the southwest
edge of downtown. With its landscaping, sculptures, rest areas, and
fountains lit up at night in neon colors, the promenade attracts joggers,
strollers, and families. (Note the separate paths for walking, jogging,
and biking.) On weekend nights, students turn the malecón into a party
zone, and families with young children stay out surprisingly late to
enjoy the cool of the evening.

❷ Parque Principal. Also known as the Plaza de la Independencia, this
central park is small by Mexican standards, and fairly nondescript,
though pleasant. In its center is an old-fashioned kiosk with a pleasing
café-bar where you can sit and watch city residents out for an evening
stroll and listen to the itinerant musicians that often show up to play
traditional ballads in the evenings. ⊠ *Bounded by Calles 10, 8, 55,
and 57, Centro.*

❾ Puerta de Tierra. Old Campeche ends here; the Land Gate is the only
☾ one of the four city gates with its basic structure intact. The stone arch
interrupts a stretch of the partially crenellated wall, 26 feet high and 10
feet thick, that once encircled the city. Walk the wall's full length to the
Baluarte San Juan for excellent views of both the old and new cities.

The staircase leads down to an old well, underground storage area, and dungeon. There's a two-hour light show ($2), accompanied by music and dance, at Puerta de Tierra; it's presented in Spanish with French and English subtitles. Shows are on Tuesday, Friday, and Saturday at 8:30 PM, and daily during spring, summer, and Christmas vacation periods. ✉ *Calles 18 and 59, Centro* ⊘ *Daily 8 AM–9 PM.*

WORTH NOTING

❼ Baluarte de San Pedro. Built in 1686 to protect the city from pirate attacks, this bastion flanked by watchtowers now houses one of the city's few worthwhile handicraft shops. The collection is small but of high quality, and prices are reasonable. On the roof are well-preserved corner watchtowers; you can also check out (but not use) the original 17th-century potty. ✉ *Calles 18 and 51, Circuito Baluartes, Centro* 🕾 *No phone* ✆ *Free* ⊘ *Daily 9–9.*

❻ Baluarte de Santiago. The last of the bastions to be built (1704) has been transformed into the **X'much Haltún Botanical Gardens.** It houses more than 200 plant species, including the enormous ceiba tree, which had spiritual importance to the Maya, symbolizing a link between heaven, earth, and the underworld. The original bastion was demolished at the turn of the 20th century, and then rebuilt in the 1950s. ✉ *Calles 8 and 49, Circuito Baluartes, Centro* 🕾 *No phone* ✆ *Free* ⊘ *Tues.–Fri. 8–2 and 5–8, weekends 8–2.*

❶ Baluarte de la Soledad. This is the largest of the bastions, originally built
★ to protect the **Puerta de Mar,** a sea gate that was one of four original entrances to the city. Because it uses no supporting walls, it resembles a Roman triumphal arch. It has comparatively complete parapets and embrasures that offer views of the cathedral, municipal buildings, and the old houses along Calle 8. Inside is the **Museo de las Estelas** with artifacts that include a well-preserved sculpture of a man wearing an owl mask, columns from Edzná and Isla de Jaina, and at least a dozen well-proportioned Mayan stelae from ruins throughout Campeche. ✉ *Calle 8, between Calles 55 and 57, Centro* 🕾 *No phone* ✆ *$2.50* ⊘ *Tues.–Sat. 8–7:30, Sun. 8–7:30.*

❷ Catedral de la Inmaculada Concepción. It took two centuries (from 1650
★ to 1850) to finish the Cathedral of the Immaculate Conception, and as a result, it incorporates both neoclassical and Renaissance elements. On the simple exterior, sculptures of saints in niches are covered in black netting to discourage pigeons from unintentional desecration. The church's neoclassical interior is also somewhat plain and spare. The high point of its collection, now housed in the side chapel museum, is a magnificent Holy Sepulchre carved from ebony and decorated with stamped silver angels, flowers, and decorative curlicues; each angel holds a symbol of the Stations of the Cross. ✉ *Calle 55, between Calles 8 and 10, Plaza Principal, Centro* 🕾 *No phone* ⊘ *Daily 6 AM–9 PM.*

⓮ Ex-Templo de San José. The Jesuits built this fine baroque church in honor of Saint Joseph just before they were booted out of the New World. Its block-long facade and portal are covered with blue-and-yellow Talavera tiles and crowned with seven narrow stone finials—resembling both the roof combs on many Mayan temples and the combs Spanish

TAKE A TOUR

You can take Xtampak Tours from Campeche to nearby ruins like Edzná, Calakmul, Balamku, and Uxmal. Prices for shared tours range from $15 per person (for a 4-hour tour) to $65 per person (for a 12-hour tour). Some tours include guides and entry fees at the ruins, whereas others only include transport, so ask ahead about what is included in the package. Make your reservations a day in advance.

Rappelling, spelunking, or mountain-bike tours are occasionally offered through Expediciones Ecoturísticos de Campeche. For tours of Isla de Jaina—where archaeologists are

working and where you'll need special permission to visit—contact Hector Solis of Espacios Naúticos. If you like, you can augment the island tour with breakfast, lunch, or swimming at the beach. Espacios Naúticos also offers waterskiing, bay tours, snorkeling, and sportfishing.

Espacios Naúticos
(⊠ *Av. Resurgimiento 120* ☎ *981/816–8082).* **Expediciones Ecoturísticos de Campeche** (⊠ *Calle 12 No. 168A, Centro* ☎ *981/816–6373 or 981/816–1310).* **Xtampak Tours** (⊠ *Calle 57 No. 14, Centro* ☎ *981/811–6473).*

women once wore in their elaborate hairdos. Next door is the **Instituto Campechano,** used for cultural events and art exhibitions. These events and exhibits are regularly held here Tuesday evening at 7 PM; at other times you can ask the guard (who should be somewhere on the grounds) to let you in. From the outside you can admire Campeche's first lighthouse, built in 1864, now perched atop the right-hand tower. ⊠ *Calles 10 and 65, Centro* ☎ *No phone.*

 Iglesia de San Francisco. With its flat, boldly painted facade and bells ensconced under small arches instead of in bell towers, the Church of Saint Francis looks more like a Mexican city hall than a Catholic church. Outside the city center in a residential neighborhood, the beautifully restored temple is Campeche's oldest. It marks the spot where some say the first Mass on the North American continent was held in 1517—though the same claim has been made for Veracruz and Cozumel. One of Cortés's grandsons was baptized here, and the baptismal font still stands. ⊠ *Avs. Miguel Alemán and Mariano Escobedo, San Francisco* ☺ *Daily 8–noon and 5–7.*

 Iglesia de San Román. Like most Franciscan churches, this one is sober and plain; its single bell tower is its only ornamentation. The equally spare interior is brightened a bit by some colorful stained-glass windows, and the carved and inlaid altarpiece serves as a beautiful backdrop for an ebony image of Jesus, the "Black Christ," brought from Italy in about 1575. Although understandably skeptical of Christianity, the Indians whom the Spaniards forced into perpetual servitude eventually came to associate this black Christ figure with miracles. As legend has it, a ship that refused to carry the holy statue was lost at sea, while the ship that accepted him reached Campeche in record time. To this day, the Feast of San Román—when worshippers carry a black-wood Christ and silver filigree cross through the streets—remains a solemn but colorful affair.

⊠*Calles 10 and Bravo, San Román* ⊙*Daily 7–1 and 3–7.*

⑩ **Iglesia y Ex-Convento de San Roque.** The elaborately carved main altarpiece and matching side altars here were restored inch by inch in 2005, and this long, narrow church now adds more than ever to historic Calle 59's old-fashioned beauty. Built in 1565, it was originally called Iglesia de San Francisco for Saint Francis; in addition to a statue of Francis, humbler-looking saints peer out from smaller niches. ⊠*Calles 12 and 59, Centro* ⊙*Daily 8:30–noon and 5–7.*

> **MEN IN THE MARKET**
>
> According to local lore, pirate attacks in Campeche were once so surprising and frequent that, in order to protect women from the dangers of the streets, men went to the market instead of the women. It's said that men going to market is a tradition that is still alive today.

❺ **Mansión Carvajal.** Built in the early 20th century by one of the Yucatán's wealthiest plantation owners, Fernando Carvajal Estrada, this eclectic mansion is a reminder of the city's heyday, when Campeche was the peninsula's only port. Local legend insists that the art-nouveau staircase with Carrara marble steps and iron balustrade, built and delivered in one piece from Italy, was too big and had to be shipped back and redone. These days the mansion is filled with government offices; you'll have to stretch your imagination a bit to picture how it once was. ⊠*Calle 10 No. 584, between Calles 51 and 53, Centro* ☎*981/816–7644* ⊠*Free* ⊙*Weekdays 9–3.*

❽ **Mercado Municipal.** The city's heart is this municipal market, where locals shop for seafood, produce, and housewares in a newly refurbished setting. The clothing section has some nice, inexpensive embroidered and beaded pieces among the jeans and T-shirts. Next to the market is a small yellow bridge aptly named **Puente de los Perros**—where four white plaster dogs guard the area. ⊠*Av. Baluartes Este and Calle 53, Centro* ⊙*Daily dawn–dusk.*

⑱ **Reducto de San José el Alto.** This lofty redoubt, or stronghold, at the
Ⓒ northwest end of town, is home to the **Museo de Armas y Barcos.** Displays in former soldiers' and watchmen's rooms focus on 18th-century weapons of siege and defense. You'll also see manuscripts, religious art, and ships in bottles. The view is terrific from the top of the ramparts, which were once used to spot invading ships. The "Guapo" tram ($7) makes the trip here daily at 9 AM and 5 PM, departing from the east side of the main plaza. Visitors get about 10 minutes to admire the view before returning to the main plaza. ⊠*Av. Escénica s/n, north of downtown, Cerro de Bellavista* ☎*No phone* ⊠*$2.20* ⊙*Tues.–Sun. 8–8.*

WHERE TO EAT

$ ✕**Casa Vieja.** Whether you're having a meal or an evening cocktail,
ECLECTIC try to snag a table on this eatery's outdoor balcony for a fabulous
★ view over Campeche's main plaza. You wouldn't know it from the tiny entrance on the main plaza, but the interior is large and inviting, and the brightly painted walls are crammed with art. There's sometimes live Cuban music in the evening, and yes, that's your waiter dancing with the

singer. (Service is not a strength.) The menu displays a rich mix of international dishes, including some from the owners' native lands: Cuba and Campeche. In addition to pastas, salads, and regional food, you'll find a good selection of aperitifs and digestifs. To get here, look for the stairway on the plaza's east side. ⊠ *Calle 10 No. 319 Altos, between Calles 57 and 55, Centro* ☎ *981/811–8016* ▭ *No credit cards.*

$ ✕ **Cenaduría los Portales.** Campechano families come here to enjoy a light
MEXICAN supper, perhaps a delicious sandwich *claveteado* of honey-and-clove-
★ spiked ham, along with a typical drink such as the delicious *agua de chaya,* a mixture of pineapple water and water flavored with chaya leaf, a leaf used in traditional Mayan cuisine. On weekends, try the *tamal torteado,* a tamale with beans, tomato sauce, turkey, and pork, wrapped in banana leaves—it's not listed on the menu but is available if you ask. Although the place opens at 6 PM, most people come between 8 and midnight. Mark your choices on the paper menu: for tacos, "m" means *masa,* or corn, tortillas; "h" stands for *harina,* or flour. The dining area is a wide colonial veranda with marble flooring and with tables decked out in plastic tablecloths. There's no booze, but a couple doors down there's a beer stall called Cervefrío that's open until around 9 PM. There's a new Internet café nearby called Cyber Hacker that also rents out motorized toy cars. ⊠ *Calle 10 No. 86, at Portales San Francisco, 8 blocks northeast of Plaza Principal, San Francisco* ☎ *981/811–1491* ▭ *MC, V* ⊙ *No lunch.*

$–$$ ✕ **La Pigua.** This is the town's hands-down lunch favorite. The seafood
SEAFOOD is delicious, and the setting is unusual: glass walls replicate an oblong
Fodor'sChoice Mayan house, incorporating the profusion of plants outside as a design
★ element. A truly ambitious meal might start with a plate of stone crab claws, or *camarones al coco* (coconut-encrusted shrimp), followed by fresh local fish, pampano, prepared in one of many ways. For dessert, the classic choice is *ate,* slabs of super-condensed mango, sweet potato, or other fruit or vegetable jelly served with tangy Gouda cheese. ⊠ *Av. Miguel Alemán 179A, Col. San Martin* ☎ *981/811–3365 www.lapigua. com.mx* ▭ *AE, V* ⊙ *Daily noon –10 PM.*

$–$$ ✕ **Marganzo.** This is a local favorite and a great place to stop in for
MEXICAN a breakfast if you want to get an early start sightseeing (they open at 7 AM). They serve everything from cereal to traditional Yucatecan dishes like *panuchos* (pork or chicken baked in banana leaves). The waitresses, dressed in colorful skirts from the region, are very kind about explaining regional dishes to visitors, so take a look at what the people at the table next to you are eating and ask your waitress. Note that you can try plain *agua de chaya* here; in some other restaurants chaya-flavored water is sweetened with pineapple. The lunch and dinner menus also offer good seafood options. ⊠ *Calle 8, No. 267, Col. Centro* ☎ *981/811–3898* ▭ *MC, V.*

WHERE TO STAY

$–$$ ⊞ **Francis Drake.** This small, spiffy hotel sits right in the center of town. Its rooms offer few amenities, but their yellow walls, ocean-blue drapes, and bright patterned curtains and spreads lend a cheerful air. The restaurant is formal, and a bit sterile, and there's no bar or other place for guests to mingle. Still, it's a good place to park it if you're looking to stay inexpensively in the heart of the old city. **Pros:** helpful staff. **Cons:** windows in some rooms open above garage and exhaust enters the room; small bathrooms; traffic noise can be a problem at night; stronger Wi-Fi signal in some rooms than others; no elevator means a bit of a hike to some rooms. ⊠ *Calle 12 No. 207, between Calles 63 and 65, Centro* ☎*981/811–5626 or 981/811–5627* ⊕*www.hotelfrancisdrake.com* ⇱*13 rooms, 12 suites* ⚹*In-room: Internet (some), Wi-Fi. In-hotel: Restaurant, room service, laundry service, parking (free)* ☰*AE, MC, V.*

$$$$ ☷**Hacienda Puerta Campeche.** Finally, Campeche has a hotel worth fawn-
★ ing over. The 17th-century mansions on most of a city block were reconfigured to create this lovely Starwood property just across from *the Puerta de Tierra*, the old city's historic landmark. Many of the original walls and lovely old tile floors have been retained, and the unusual indoor/outdoor swimming pool is surrounded by half-tumbled walls with hints of original paint and with inviting hammocks that hang out over the water. Rooms are sumptuously painted and decorated in classic Starwood style. On Friday and Saturday, enjoy the lounge and a sound-and-light show. You can also arrange to use a small, private, underground room that the staff calls "la cava" for romantic dinners. Even if you don't stay here, Restaurante La Guardia, which serves well-prepared seafood ($$–$$$), is worth a visit. **Pros:** stunning surroundings; calm atmosphere; excellent restaurant. **Cons:** expensive; not central. ⊠ *Calle 59 No. 71, Centro* ☎*981/816–7508, 888/625–5144 in U.S. and Canada* ⊕*www.starwoodhotels.com* ⇱*12 rooms, 3 suites* ⚹*In-room: Safe, refrigerator, DVD (some), Wi-Fi. In-hotel: Restaurant, room service, bar, pool, laundry service, parking (free), no elevator, no-smoking rooms* ☰*AE, MC, V.*

$$$ ☷**Holiday Inn Campeche.** This new and modern hotel was built with business travelers in mind. It's a bit removed from the downtown area, but a short taxi ride will take you there. Rooms are clean and comfortable with white bed spreads, and black, modern furniture; half of them have ocean views. This is one of the few hotels in town to have a pool—it's big and pleasant for families, with a small area for children nearby. ⊠ *Av. Resurgimiento s/n , Col. Prado* ☎*981/127–3700* ⊕*www.ichotelsgroup.com* ⇱*91 rooms* ⚹ *In-room: Safe, Wi-Fi. In-hotel: Restaurant, bar, pool, gym, Wi-Fi, parking (free), no-smoking rooms* ☰*AE, MC, V.*

$–$$ ☷**Hotel Castelmar.** This recently renovated hotel in the heart of the downtown area is an elegant and comfortable place to relax and enjoy Campeche. The building was originally constructed in 1800 as a cartel. Many of the original details, including some of the tiling, the pillars, and the archways, have been preserved, but some of the newest additions, the pool, and the inner courtyard where you can enjoy your breakfast— complete with fountain and plants—also add comfort and charm. The rooms are not all alike—there's even one on the first floor without windows—so take a look before you agree to take one. **Pros:** great downtown location; pretty building and rooms; pools. **Cons:** street noise at night can be a problem; rooms vary. ⊠ *Calle 61, between Calles 8 and 10, Centro* ☎*981/811–1204* ⊕*www.castelmarhotel.com*

⇖*22 rooms, 3 suites* ⬧*In-room: Wi-Fi. In-hotel: Pool, laundry service* ▭*MC, V* ⦿*BP.*

NIGHTLIFE

Each Saturday between 3 and 10 PM, the streets around the main square are closed to traffic and filled with folk and popular dance performances, singers, comics, handicrafts, and food and drink stands. If you're in town on a Saturday, don't miss these weekly festivities, called *Un Centro Histórico para Disfrutar* (A Historic Downtown to Enjoy)—the entertainment is often first-rate and always free. In December, concerts and other cultural events take place as part of the Festival del Centro Histórico.

On Friday and Saturday nights there is lounge music at the Hacienda Puerta Campeche, and it is one of the nicest places in town to have a drink.

There are a few bars and clubs along the malecón. Locals show up around 10 PM to enjoy the cool evening air. **Sole** (⊠ *Malecón s/n, Centro* ☎982/828–0123) is one of the most comfortable. It has a small open-air patio where you can watch projections of music videos and enjoy a drink.

SPORTS AND THE OUTDOORS

Fishing and bird-watching are popular throughout the state of Campeche.

Contact **Fernando Sansores** (⊠ *Calle 30 No. 1, Centro* ☎982/828–0018) at the Snook Inn to arrange area sportfishing or wildlife photo excursions. **Francisco Javier Hernandez Romero** (⊠*La Pigua restaurant, Av. Miguel Alemán 179A, Centro* ☎981/811–3365) can arrange boat or fishing trips to the Reserva Ecológica Peténes.

CHAMPOTÓN

35 km (20 mi) from Campeche City.

Carretera 180 curves through a series of hills before reaching Champotón's immensely satisfying vista of open sea. This is an appealing, if a little dingy and sometimes smelly, untouristy little town with palapas at the water's edge and plenty of swimmers and boats. The Spaniards dubbed the outlying bay the Bahía de la Mala Pelea, or "bay of the evil battle," because it was here that the troops of the Spanish conqueror and explorer Hernández de Córdoba were first trounced, in 1517, by pugnacious locals armed with arrows, slingshots, and darts. The famous battle is commemorated with a small reenactment each year on March 21.

The 17th-century church of Nuestra Señora de la Inmaculada Concepción is the site for a festival honoring the Virgin Mary (Our Lady of the Immaculate Conception). The festival culminates each year on December 8. On that day the local fishermen carry the saint from the church to their boats for a seafaring parade. In the middle of town are the ruins of the Fortín de San Antonio. The Champotón area is ideal for bird-watching and fishing. More than 35 kinds of fish, including shad, snook, and bass, live in Río Champotón. The mangroves and swamps are home to cranes and other waterfowl. The town is primarily an agricultural hub—its most important exports are lumber and honey, as well as coconut, sugarcane, bananas, avocados, corn, and beans.

GETTING HERE AND AROUND

A toll road from Campeche City to Champotón costs $4.50 one-way and shortens the drive from 65 km (40 mi) to 45 km (28 mi). Look for the Carretera 180 CUOTA sign when leaving the city. Carretera 180 continues to Ciudad del Carmen (90 minutes to 2 hours); the bridge toll entering or leaving Ciudad del Carmen is about $3.

ESSENTIALS

Currency Exchange Banamex (⊠ *Calle 29 No. 103* ☎ *01800/226–2639 toll-free in Mexico* ⊕ *www.banamex.com*).

EXPLORING

★ About a dozen small seafood restaurants make up **Los Cockteleros**, an area 5 km (3 mi) north of the center of Champotón. This is where Campechanos head on weekends to munch fried fish and slurp down seafood cocktails. The open-air palapa eateries at the beach are open daily during daylight hours.

Approximately 15 km (9 mi) southwest of Champotón, **Punta Xen** is a beautiful beach popular for its calm, clean water. It's a long stretch of deserted sand interrupted only by birds and seashells. Across the highway are a few good, basic restaurants.

WHERE TO EAT AND STAY

$ ✕ **Las Brisas.** A favorite with locals, this is the best place in town for
SEAFOOD   fresh fish, shrimp, and octopus. Open until 6 PM, Las Brisas is on the main street by the water, overlooking the bay. ⊠ *Av. Eugenio Echeverría Castellot s/n between Calles 18 and 16* ☎ *No phone* ☐ *No credit cards* ⊗ *No dinner.*

$ ⊞ **Snook Inn.** Most patrons are hunters or fishermen who have signed up for trips with the Sansores clan, the hotel's longtime owners and outdoors enthusiasts. The owner, Jorge Sansores, organizes half-day, two-day, and even weeklong fishing and hunting trips. In December the hotel also organizes a fishing tournament. The clean, kidney-shape pool has both a slide and a diving board, and it's surrounded by the two-story, L-shaped, 1960s-era hotel. Simple rooms have remote-control TVs, tile floors, unadorned walls, and hammock hooks in the walls (bring your own hammock). The parking area is quite small. **Pros:** most comfortable hotel in town; the best hunting and fishing tours leave from here. **Cons:** breeze sometimes smells a little fishy; reservations important since hotel sometimes fills up with tours and tournaments. ⊠ *Calle 30 No. 1* ☎ *982/828–0018* ⊕ *www.snookinnhunting.com.mx* ⟿ *19 rooms* ♨ *In-room: Wi-Fi. In-hotel: Restaurant, pool, laundry service, parking (free), no-smoking rooms* ☐ *MC, V.*

EDZNÁ

Fodor'sChoice   *61 km (37 mi) southeast of Campeche City.*

★ A leaf-strewn nature trail winds slowly toward the ancient heart of Edzná.

⛩ Although only 55 km (34 mi)—less than an hour's drive—southeast of

Campeche City, the site sees few tour groups. The scarcity of camera-carrying humans intensifies the feeling of communion with nature, and with the Maya who built this once-flourishing commercial and ceremonial city.

Despite being refreshingly underappreciated by 21st-century travelers, Edzná is considered by archaeologists to be one of the peninsula's most important ruins. A major metropolis in its day, it was situated at a crossroads of sorts between cities in modern-day Guatemala and Chiapas and Yucatán states, and this "out-of-state" influence can be appreciated in its mélange of architectural elements. Roof combs and corbeled arches are reminiscent of those at Yaxchilán and Palenque, in Chiapas; giant stone masks are characteristic of the Petén-style architecture of southern Campeche and northern Guatemala.

Edzná began as a humble agricultural settlement around 300 BC, reaching its pinnacle in the late classic period, between AD 600 and 900, and gradually waning in importance until being all but abandoned in the early 15th century. Today soft breezes blow through groves of slender trees where brilliant orange and black birds spring from branch to branch, gathering seeds. Clouds scuttle across a blue backdrop, perfectly framing the mossy, multistepped remains of once-great structures.

A guide can point out features often missed by the untrained eye, like the remains of arrow-straight sacbés. These raised roads in their day connected one important ceremonial building within the city to the next, and also connected Edzná to trading partners throughout the peninsula.

The best place to survey the site is 102-foot **Pirámide de los Cinco Pisos,** built on the raised platform of the **Gran Acrópolis** (Great Acropolis). The five-story pyramid consists of five levels, terminating in a tiny temple crowned by a roof comb. Hieroglyphs were carved into the vertical face of the 15 steps between each level; some were recemented in place by archaeologists, although not necessarily in the correct order. On these stones, as well as on stelae throughout the site, you can see faint depictions of the opulent attire once worn by the Mayan ruling class—quetzal feathers, jade pectorals, and jaguar-skin skirts.

In 1992 Campeche archaeologist Florentino García Cruz discovered that the Pirámide de los Cinco Pisos was constructed so that on certain dates the setting sun would illuminate the mask of the creator-god, Itzámná, inside one of the pyramid's rooms. This happens annually on May 1, 2, and 3, the beginning of the planting season for the Maya—then and now. It also occurs on August 7, 8, and 9, the days of harvesting and giving thanks. On the pyramid's fifth level, the last to be built, are the ruins of three temples and a ritual steam bath.

West of the Great Acropolis, the Puuc-style **Plataforma de los Cuchillos** (Platform of the Knives) was so named by a 1970 archaeological exploration that found a number of flint knives inside. To the south, four buildings surround a smaller structure called the **Pequeña Acrópolis.** Twin sun-god masks with huge protruding eyes, sharply filed teeth, and oversize tongues flank the **Templo de los Mascarones** (Temple of the Masks, or Building 414), adjacent to the Small Acropolis. The mask at bottom left (east) represents the rising sun, whereas the one on the right represents the setting sun.

If you're not driving, consider taking one of the inexpensive day trips offered by tour operators in Campeche; this is far easier than trying to get to Edzná by municipal buses. ⊠ *Carretera 261 east from Campeche City for 44 km (27 mi) to Cayal, then Carretera 188 southeast for 18 km (11 mi)* 🕾 *No phone* 🎫 *$3.30* ⊙ *Daily 8–5.*

WHERE TO STAY

$$$$ 🏨 **Hacienda Uayamón.** Abandoned in 1913, this former hacienda was
★ resurrected nearly a century later and transformed into a luxury hotel with an elegant restaurant. The original architecture and decor have been carefully preserved: the library has exposed-beam ceilings, cane chairs, sisal carpets, and wooden bookshelves at least 12 feet high. Each casita has a private garden, hot tub, and bathroom, as well as a cozy bedroom. The original *tienda de raya,* or company store, now houses a spa that offers Mayan-influenced massage and other treatments. The remaining two walls of the old machine house shelter the outdoor pool, and candles are still lighted at the ruined chapel. **Pros:** stunning grounds; beautiful, spacious rooms. **Cons:** expensive. ⊠ *9 km (5½ mi) north of Edzná* 🕾 *981/829–7527, 888/625–5144 in U.S. or Canada* ⊕ *www. starwood.com* 🛏 *2 suites, 10 casitas* 🔌 *In-room: Safe. In-hotel: Restaurant, room service, bar, pool, spa, laundry service, parking (free), some pets allowed, no-smoking rooms* 🚭 *AE, MC, V.*

SANTA ROSA XTAMPAK

🔺 *107 km (64 mi) from Campeche City; entrance at Carretera 261, Km 79, travel 30 km (19 mi) down signed side road.*

A fabulous example of the zoomorphic architectural element of Chenes architecture, Xtampak's **Casa de la Boca del Serpiente** (House of the Serpent's Mouth) has a perfectly preserved and integrated zoomorphic entrance. Here the mouth of the creator-god Itzámná stretches wide to reveal a perfectly proportioned inner chamber. The importance of this city during the classic period is shown by the large number of public buildings and ceremonial plazas; archaeologists believe there are around 100 structures here, although only 12 have been cleared. The most exciting find was the colossal **Palacio** in the western plaza. Inside, two inner staircases run the length of the structure, leading to different levels and ending in subterranean chambers. This combination is extremely rare in Mayan temples. ⊠ *East of Hopelchén on Dzibilchaltún–Chencho Rd., watch for sign* 🕾 *No phone* 🎫 *$2.50* ⊙ *Daily 8–5.*

HOCHOB

🔺 *109 km (68 km) southwest of Campeche City; 55 km (34 mi) south of Hopelchén; 15 km (9 mi) west of Dzibilnocac.*

The small Mayan ruin of Hochob is an excellent example of the Chenes architectural style, which flowered from about AD 100 to 1000. Most ruins in this area (central and southeastern Campeche) were built on the highest possible elevation to prevent flooding during the rainy season, and Hochob is no exception. It rests high on a hill overlooking the surrounding valleys. Another indication that these are Chenes ruins is the number of *chultunes,* or cisterns, in the area. Since work began at Hochob in the early 1980s, four temples and palaces have been excavated at the site, including two that have been fully restored. Intricate and perfectly preserved geometric designs cover the temple known as **Estructura II;** these are typical of the Chenes style.

The doorway represents the open mouth of Itzámná, the creator god; above it the eyes bulge; fangs are bared on either side of the base. It takes a bit of imagination to see the structure as a mask; color no doubt originally enhanced the effect. Squinting helps a bit: the figure's "eyes" are said to be squinting as well. But anyone can appreciate the intense geometric relief carvings decorating the facades, including long cascades of Chaac rain-god masks along the sides. Evidence of roof combs can be seen at the top of the building. Ask the guard to show you the series of natural and manmade chultunes that extend back into the forest. ⊠*Southwest of Hopelchén on Dzibalchén–Chencho Rd.* ☎*No phone* 🖃*Free* ☉*Daily 8–5.*

CARRETERA 186 INTO CAMPECHE

Xpujil, Chicanná, Calakmul . . . exotic, far-flung-sounding names dot the map along this stretch of jungly territory. These are places where the creatures of the forest outnumber the tourists: in Calakmul, four- and five-story ceiba trees sway as families of spider monkeys swing through the canopy; in Xpujil, brilliant blue motmots fly from tree to tree in long, swoopy arcs.

The vestiges of at least 10 little-known Mayan cities lie hidden off Carretera 186 between Escárcega and Chetumal. You can see Xpujil, Becán, Hormiguero, and Chicanná in one rather rushed day by starting out early from Chetumal, Quintana Roo, and spending the night in Xpujil. If you plan to visit Calakmul, spend the first night at Xpujil, arriving at Calakmul as soon as the site opens the next day. That provides the best chance to see armadillos, wild turkeys, families of howler and spider monkeys, and other wildlife.

From Chetumal on the coast of Quintana Roo, it's about 140 km (87 mi) to Xpujil. Carretera 186, is a two-lane highway in reasonably good condition. ■TIP➡ **Drive with extreme caution on Highway 186 between Escárcega and the Quintana Roo state border; the road is curvy and narrow in many spots, and it's often under repair. It's best to avoid driving at night, especially on this highway. Military checkpoints pop up here and there, but the machine gun–wielding soldiers are nothing to fear; they'll usually just wave you right on.**

EXPLORING

There are not many good tour guides in the region. Some of the most experienced and enthusiastic are part of a community organization called **Servidores Turísticos Calakmul.** There are bicycle tours, horseback tours, and tours where spotting plants and animals is the main focus; all tours can be customized to meet your interests, including trips that span across several days with overnight stays in the jungle. If your Spanish is shaky, ask for Leticia, who speaks basic English and has years of experience as a guide. ✉ *Av. Calakmul between Okolwitz and Payan* ☎ *983/871–6064* ✒ *ciitacalakmul@prodigy.net.mx.*

Hotel owners Rick Bertram and Diane Lalonde offer tours through their hotel **Río Bec Dreams** (*see Where to Stay below*). They are native English speakers and enthusiastic guides, and will give you a comprehensive trip around the local archaeological sites. They charge $100 for an 8- to 10-hour day, though you need to book this with them in advance since they juggle duties at their hotel with their tour schedules. ✉ *Carretera 186, Escarcega-Chetumal, Km 142* ☎ *983/124–0501* ⊕ *www.riobecdreams.com.*

XPUJIL

🔺 *Carretera 186, Km 150; 300 km (186 mi) southeast of Campeche; 130 km (81 mi) south of Dzibilnocac; 125 km (78 mi) west of Chetumal.*

Xpujil (meaning "cat's tail," and pronounced ish-*poo*-hil) gets its name from the reedy plant that grows in the area. Elaborately carved facades and doorways in the shape of monsters' mouths reflect the Chenes style, while adjacent pyramid towers connected by a long platform show the influence of Río Bec architects. Some of the buildings have lost a lot of their stones, making them resemble "day after" sand castles. In **Edificio I,** all three towers were once crowned by false temples, and at the front of each are the remains of four vaulted rooms, each oriented toward one of the compass points and thought to have been used by priests and royalty. On the back side of the central tower is a huge mask of the rain god Chaac. Quite a few other building groups amid the forests of gum trees and *palo mulato* (so called for its bark with both dark and light patches) have yet to be excavated. 🎟 *$2.20* ⊙ *Daily 8–5.*

WHERE TO STAY

$$ 🏨 **Chicanná Ecovillage Resort.** Rooms in this comfortable jungle lodge are
★ in two-story stucco duplexes with thatch roofs. Each ample unit has a tile floor, an overhead fan, screened windows, a wide porch or balcony with a table and chairs, and one king or two double beds with bright cotton bedspreads. There's a library with a television and VCR, and a small pool filled with rainwater and surrounded by flowering plants. The hotel has no phone or fax; both are available in nearby Xpujil. For reservations, contact the Del Mar Hotel in Campeche City. **Pros:** Convenient to several ruins in the Río Bec region, spacious rooms. **Cons:** Restaurant food is just OK. ✉ *Carretera 186, Km 144, 9 km (5½ mi) north of village of Xpujil* ☎ *01800/560–8612, 981/811–9191 for reservations* ⊕ *www.mayanroutes.com/hotels/calakmul* ⇆ *42 rooms* ⚬ *In-room: No a/c, no phone, no TV. In-hotel: Restaurant, bar, pool, laundry service, parking (free), Wi-Fi, no-smoking rooms* ▭ *AE, MC, V.*

¢ 🏨 **Río Bec Dreams.** From the moment you arrive at this hotel in the
★ middle of the jungle, owners Rick Bertram and Diane Lalonde will make you feel at home. They may invite you to pull up a chair at their bar, flip through books and magazines about the area, and swap stories with them and other guests about your day and your interest in local

ruins. Since archaeologists often stay at the hotel, they are up on the latest gossip about new ideas and discoveries. You can order a meal at the bar; when it's ready, you'll be led to a private table decorated with candles and a bouquet of flowers to enjoy the delicious food. The small, freestanding "jungalows," separated by winding paths, have cozy beds with curtains around them so that you don't have to worry about bugs at night. Ample and very clean bathrooms are shared between units. The two private cabanas are roomier and have a private bathroom, but since there are currently only two (though plans are in the works to build more), you will need to reserve in advance if you prefer more privacy. Also reserve in advance if you are interested in touring any of the local ruins—both Rick and Diane lead tour groups but are happy to slot you in if they have notice. They are experts on what time of year is best to travel, how long it will take to get from one site to another, and even what books to read before you go; they can also provide all services you'd get with a group tour, including transportation and delicious bag lunches. **Pros:** bar is great place to meet people; wonderful restaurant; owners are friendly, attentive, and excellent guides. **Cons:** some rooms lack private bathrooms; no a/c; two (well-behaved) dogs live here. ✉ *Carretera 186, Escarcega-Chetumal, Km 142* ☎ *983/124–0501* ⊕ *www.riobecdreams.com* ↪ *4 shared jungalows, 2 private cabanas* ⬢ *In-room: No a/c, no phone, no TV. In-hotel: Restaurant, bar, no-smoking rooms* ▤ *No credit cards* ❶ *EP.*

BECÁN

★ *Carretera 186, Km 145; 264 km (164 mi) southwest of Campeche City;*
⚠ *7 km (4½ mi) west of Xpujil.*

An interesting feature of this once important city is its defensive moat—unusual among ancient Mayan cities—though barely evident today. The seven ruined gateways, which once permitted the only entrances to the guarded city, may have clued archaeologists to its presence. Becán (usually translated as "canyon of water," referring to the moat) is thought to have been an important city within the Río Bec group, which once encompassed Xpujil, Chicanná, and Río Bec. Most of the site's many buildings date from between about AD 600 and 1000, but since there are no traditionally inscribed stelae listing details of royal births, deaths, battles, and ascendancies to the throne, archaeologists have had to do a lot of guessing about what transpired here.

You can climb several of the structures to get a view of the area, and even spot some of Xpuhil's towers above the treetops. Duck into **Estructura VIII,** where underground passages lead to small subterranean rooms and to a concealed staircase that reaches the top of the temple. One of several buildings surrounding a central plaza, Estructura VIII has lateral towers and a giant zoomorphic mask on its central facade. The building was used for religious rituals, including bloodletting rites during which the elite pierced earlobes and genitals, among other sensitive body parts, in order to present their blood to the gods. ⊙ *Daily 8–5.*

CHICANNÁ

🔺 *Carretera 186, Km 141; 274 km (174 mi) southwest of Campeche City; 3 km (2 mi) east of Becán.*

Thought to have been a satellite community of the larger, more commercial city of Becán, Chicanná ("house of the serpent's mouth") was also in its prime during the late classic period. Of the four buildings surrounding the main plaza, **Estructura II**, on the east side, is the most impressive. On its intricate facade are well-preserved sculpted reliefs and faces with long twisted noses, symbols of Chaac. In typical Chenes style, the doorway represents the mouth of the creator-god Itzámná; surrounding the opening are large crossed eyes, fierce fangs, and earrings to complete the stone mask, which still bears traces of blue and red pigments. 🖼*$3* 🕙*Daily 8–5.*

HORMIGUERO

🔺 *272 km (169 mi) southwest of Campeche City; 14 km (9 mi) southeast of Xpujil.*

Bumping down the badly potholed, 8-km (5-mi) road leading to this site may give you an appreciation for the explorers who first found and excavated it in 1933. Hidden throughout the forest are at least five magnificent temples, two of which have been excavated to reveal ornate facades covered with zoomorphic figures whose mouths are the doorways. The buildings here were constructed roughly between 400 BC and AD 1100 in the Río Bec style, with rounded lateral towers and ornamental stairways, the latter built to give an illusion of height, which they do wonderfully. The facade of **Estructura II**, the largest structure on the site, is beautiful: intricately carved and well preserved. **Estructura V** has some admirable Chaac masks arranged in a cascade atop a pyramid. Nearby is a perfectly round chultun (water-storage tank), and, seemingly emerging from the earth, the eerily etched designs of a still-unexcavated structure.

Hormiguero is Spanish for "anthill," referring both to the looters' tunnels that honeycombed the ruins when archaeologists discovered them and to the number of large anthills in the area. Among the other fauna sharing the jungle here are several species of poisonous snakes. Although these mainly come out at night, you should always be careful of where you walk and, when climbing, where you put your hands. 🖼*$2.50* 🕙*Daily 8–5*

RESERVA DE LA BIOSFERA CALAKMUL

Fodor'sChoice ★   *Entrance at Carretera 186, Km 65; 365 km (227 mi) southwest of Campeche City; 107 km (66 mi) southwest of Xpujil.*

🔺 Vast, lovely, green, and mysterious Calakmul may not stay a secret for much longer. You won't see any tour buses in the parking lot, and on an average day site employees and laborers still outnumber the visitors traipsing along the moss-tinged dirt paths that snake through the jungle. But things are changing. The nearest town, Xpujil, already has Internet service. And the proposed building of a water-retention aqueduct in the same area will, if it becomes a reality, almost surely bring increased tourism—maybe even chain hotels—to the area. So if you're looking for untrammeled Mexican wilderness, don't put it off any longer: the time to visit Calakmul is now.

Calakmul encompasses some 1.8 million acres of land along the Guatemalan border. It was declared a protected biosphere reserve in 1989, and is the second-largest reserve of its kind in Mexico after Sian Ka'an in Quintana Roo. All kinds of flora and fauna thrive here, including wildcats, spider and howler monkeys, and hundreds of exotic birds, orchid varieties, butterflies, and reptiles. (There's no shortage of insects, either, so don't forget the bug repellent.)

The centerpiece of the reserve, however, is the ruined Mayan city that shares the name Calakmul (which translates as "two adjacent towers"). Although Carretera 186 runs right through the reserve, you'll need to drive about 1½ hours from the highway along a 50-km (31-mi) authorized entry road to get to the site. Although structures here are still being excavated, the dense surrounding jungle is being left in its natural state: as you walk among the ruined palaces and tumbled stelae, you'll hear the guttural calls of howler monkeys, and see massive strangler figs enveloping equally massive trees.

This magnificent city, now in ruins, wasn't always so lonely. Anthropologists estimate that in its heyday (between AD 542 and 695) the region was inhabited by more than 50,000 Maya; archaeologists have mapped more than 6,250 structures and found 180 stelae. Perhaps the most monumental discovery thus far has been that of the remains of royal ruler Garra del Jaguar (Jaguar Claw); his body was wrapped (but not embalmed) in a shroud of palm leaf, lime, and fine cloth, and locked away in a royal tomb in about AD 700. In an adjacent crypt, a young woman wearing fine jewelry and an elaborately painted wood-and-stucco headdress was entombed, together with a child. Their identity remains a mystery. The artifacts and skeletal remains have been moved to the Maya Museum in Campeche City.

Unlike those at Chichén Itzá (which also peaked in importance during the classic era) the pyramids and palaces throughout Calakmul can be climbed to achieve soaring vistas. You can choose to explore the site along a short, medium, or long path, but all three eventually lead to magnificent **Templo II** and **Templo VII**—twin pyramids separated by an immense plaza. Templo II, at 175 feet, is the peninsula's tallest Mayan building. Scientists are studying a huge, intact stucco frieze deep within this structure, but it's not currently open to visitors.

Arrangements for an English-speaking Calakmul tour guide should be made beforehand with Servidores Turísticos Calakmul, Río Bec Dreams, or through Chicanná Ecovillage near Xpujil. Camping is permitted with the Servidores Turisíicos Calakmul; be sure to tip the caretakers at the entrance gate. You can set up camp near the second checkpoint. Even if day-tripping, though, you'll need to bring your own food and water; the only place to buy a meal is near the entrance, and you may want to carry a bottle of water and a snack, as the walk to the ruins is long.

✉ *97 km (60 mi) east of Escárcega to turnoff at Cohuás, then 50 km (31 mi) south to Calakmul* ☎ *No phone* 🎫 *$4 per car, more for larger vehicles, plus $4 per person* ⊗ *Daily 8–5.*

SPANISH VOCABULARY

	ENGLISH	SPANISH	PRONUNCIATION
BASICS			
	Yes/no	Sí/no	see/no
	Please	Por favor	pore fah-**vore**
	May I?	¿Me permite?	may pair-**mee**-tay
	Thank you (very much)	(Muchas) gracias	(**moo**-chas) **grah**-see-as
	You're welcome	De nada	day **nah**-dah
	Excuse me	Con permiso	con pair-**mee**-so
	Pardon me	¿Perdón?	pair-**dohn**
	Could you tell me?	¿Podría decirme?	po-dree-ah deh-**seer**-meh
	I'm sorry	Lo siento	lo see-**en**-toh
	Good morning!	¡Buenos días!	**bway**-nohs **dee**-ahs
	Good afternoon!	¡Buenas tardes!	**bway**-nahs **tar**-dess
	Good evening!	¡Buenas noches!	**bway**-nahs **no**-chess
	Good-bye!	¡Adiós!/¡Hasta luego!	ah-dee-**ohss**/**ah**-stah **lwe**-go
	Mr./Mrs.	Señor/Señora	sen-**yor**/sen-**yohr**-ah
	Miss	Señorita	sen-yo-**ree**-tah
	Pleased to meet you	Mucho gusto	**moo**-cho **goose**-toh
	How are you?	¿Cómo está usted?	**ko**-mo es-**tah** oo-**sted**
	Very well, thank you.	Muy bien, gracias.	**moo**-ee bee-**en**, **grah**-see-as
	And you?	¿Y usted?	ee oos-**ted**
	Hello (on the telephone)	Diga	**dee**-gah
NUMBERS			
	1	un, uno	oon, **oo**-no
	2	dos	dos
	3	tres	tress
	4	cuatro	**kwah**-tro
	5	cinco	**sink**-oh

ENGLISH	SPANISH	PRONUNCIATION
6	seis	**saice**
7	siete	see-**et**-eh
8	ocho	**o**-cho
9	nueve	new-**eh**-vey
10	diez	dee-**es**
11	once	**ohn**-seh
12	doce	**doh**-seh
13	trece	**treh**-seh
14	catorce	ka-**tohr**-seh
15	quince	**keen**-seh
16	dieciséis	dee-**es**-ee-**saice**
17	diecisiete	dee-**es**-ee-see-**et**-eh
18	dieciocho	dee-**es**-ee-**o**-cho
19	diecinueve	**dee**-**es**-ee-new-**ev**-eh
20	veinte	**vain**-teh
21	veinte y uno/ veintiuno	**vain**-te-**oo**-noh
30	treinta	**train**-tah
32	treinta y dos	train-tay-**dohs**
40	cuarenta	kwah-**ren**-tah
43	cuarenta y tres	kwah-**ren**-tay-**tress**
50	cincuenta	seen-**kwen**-tah
54	cincuenta y cuatro	seen-**kwen**-tay **kwah**-tro
60	sesenta	sess-**en**-tah
65	sesenta y cinco	sess-**en**-tay **seen**-ko
70	setenta	set-**en**-tah
76	setenta y seis	set-**en**-tay **saice**
80	ochenta	oh-**chen**-tah
87	ochenta y siete	oh-**chen**-tay see-**yet**-eh
90	noventa	no-**ven**-tah

ENGLISH	SPANISH	PRONUNCIATION
98	noventa y ocho	no-**ven**-tah-**o**-choh
100	cien	see-**en**
101	ciento uno	see-**en**-toh **oo**-noh
200	doscientos	doh-see-**en**-tohss
500	quinientos	keen-**yen**-tohss
700	setecientos	set-eh-see-**en**-tohss
900	novecientos	no-veh-see-**en**-tohss
1,000	mil	meel
2,000	dos mil	dohs meel
1,000,000	un millón	oon meel-**yohn**

COLORS

black	negro	**neh**-groh
blue	azul	ah-**sool**
brown	café	kah-**feh**
green	verde	**ver**-deh
pink	rosa	**ro**-sah
purple	morado	mo-**rah**-doh
orange	naranja	na-**rahn**-hah
red	rojo	**roh**-hoh
white	blanco	**blahn**-koh
yellow	amarillo	ah-mah-**ree**-yoh

DAYS OF THE WEEK

Sunday	domingo	doe-**meen**-goh
Monday	lunes	**loo**-ness
Tuesday	martes	**mahr**-tess
Wednesday	miércoles	me-**air**-koh-less
Thursday	jueves	hoo-**ev**-ess
Friday	viernes	vee-**air**-ness
Saturday	sábado	**sah**-bah-doh

	ENGLISH	SPANISH	PRONUNCIATION
MONTHS			
	January	enero	eh-**neh**-roh
	February	febrero	feh-**breh**-roh
	March	marzo	**mahr**-soh
	April	abril	ah-**breel**
	May	mayo	**my**-oh
	June	junio	**hoo**-nee-oh
	July	julio	**hoo**-lee-yoh
	August	agosto	ah-**ghost**-toh
	September	septiembre	sep-tee-**em**-breh
	October	octubre	oak-**too**-breh
	November	noviembre	no-vee-**em**-breh
	December	diciembre	dee-see-**em**-breh
USEFUL PHRASES			
	Do you speak English?	¿Habla usted inglés?	**ah**-blah oos-**ted** in-**glehs**
	I don't speak Spanish	No hablo español	no **ah**-bloh es-pahn-**yol**
	I don't understand (you)	No entiendo	no en-tee-**en**-doh
	I understand (you)	Entiendo	en-tee-**en**-doh
	I don't know	No sé	no seh
	I am American/British	Soy americano (americana)/inglés(a)	soy ah-meh-ree- **kah**-no (ah-meh-ree- **kah**-nah)/in-**glehs(ah)**
	What's your name?	¿Cómo se llama usted?	koh-mo seh **yah**-mah oos-**ted**
	My name is . . .	Me llamo . . .	may **yah**-moh
	What time is it?	¿Qué hora es?	keh **o**-rah es
	It is one, two, three . . . o'clock.	Es la una./Son las dos, tres . . .	es la **oo**-nah/sohnahs dohs, tress
	Yes, please/No, thank you	Sí, por favor/No, gracias	**see** pohr fah-**vor**/no **grah**-see-us
	How?	¿Cómo?	**koh**-mo

ENGLISH	SPANISH	PRONUNCIATION
When?	¿Cuándo?	**kwahn**-doh
This/Next week	Esta semana/ la semana que entra	**es**-teh seh-**mah**- nah/ lah seh-**mah**-nah keh **en**-trah
This/Next month	Este mes/el próximo mes	**es**-teh mehs/el **proke**-see-mo mehs
This/Next year	Este año/el año que viene	**es**-teh **ahn**-yo/el **ahn**-yo keh vee-**yen**-ay
Yesterday/today/ tomorrow	Ayer/hoy/mañana	ah-**yehr**/oy/mahn-**yah**-nah
This morning/ afternoon	Esta mañana/ tarde	**es**-tah mahn-**yah**- nah/ **tar**-deh
Tonight	Esta noche	**es**-tah **no**-cheh
What?	¿Qué?	keh
What is it?	¿Qué es esto?	keh es **es**-toh
Why?	¿Por qué?	pore **keh**
Who?	¿Quién?	kee-**yen**
Where is . . . ?	¿Dónde está . . . ?	**dohn**-deh es-**tah**
the train station?	la estación del tren?	la es-tah-see-on del trehn
the subway station?	la estación del tren subterráneo?	la es-ta-see-**on** del trehn la es-ta-see-**on** soob-teh-**rrahn**-eh-oh
the bus stop?	la parada del autobus?	la pah-**rah**-dah del ow-toh-**boos**
the post office?	la oficina de correos?	la oh-fee-**see**- nah deh koh-**rreh**-os
the bank?	el banco?	el **bahn**-koh
the hotel?	el hotel?	el oh-**tel**
the store?	la tienda?	la tee-**en**-dah
the cashier?	la caja?	la **kah**-hah
the museum?	el museo?	el moo-**seh**-oh
the hospital?	el hospital?	el ohss-pee-**tal**
the elevator?	el ascensor?	el ah-**sen**-sohr
the bathroom?	el baño?	el **bahn**-yoh

ENGLISH	SPANISH	PRONUNCIATION
Here/there	Aquí/allá	ah-**key**/ah-**yah**
Open/closed	Abierto/cerrado	ah-bee-**er**-toh/ ser-**ah**-doh
Left/right	Izquierda/derecha	iss-key-**er**-dah/ dare-**eh**-chah
Straight ahead	Derecho	dare-**eh**-choh
Is it near/far?	¿Está cerca/lejos?	es-**tah sehr**-kah/ **leh**-hoss
I'd like . . .	Quisiera . . .	kee-see-ehr-ah
a room	un cuarto/una habitación	oon **kwahr**-toh/ **oo**-nah ah-bee- tah-see-**on**
the key	la llave	lah **yah**-veh
a newspaper	un periódico	oon pehr-ee-**oh**- dee-koh
a stamp	un sello de correo	oon **seh**-yo deh korr-ee-oh
I'd like to buy . . .	Quisiera comprar . . .	kee-see-**ehr**-ah kohm-**prahr**
cigarettes	cigarrillos	ce-ga-**ree**-yohs
matches	cerillos	ser-**ee**-ohs
a dictionary	un diccionario	oon deek-see-oh- **nah**-ree-oh
soap	jabón	hah-**bohn**
sunglasses	gafas de sol	**ga**-fahs deh sohl
suntan lotion	Loción bronceadora	loh-see-**ohn** brohn- seh-ah-**do**-rah
a map	un mapa	oon **mah**-pah
a magazine	una revista	**oon**-ah reh-**veess**-tah
paper	papel	pah-**pel**
envelopes	sobres	**so**-brehs
a postcard	una tarjeta postal	**oon**-ah tar-**het**-ah post-**ahl**
How much is it?	¿Cuánto cuesta?	**kwahn**-toh **kwes**-tah
It's expensive/	Está caro/barato	es-**tah kah**-roh/
cheap		bah-**rah**-toh

ENGLISH	SPANISH	PRONUNCIATION
A little/a lot	Un poquito/ mucho	oon poh-**kee**-toh/ **moo**-choh
More/less	Más/menos	mahss/**men**-ohss
Enough/too much/too little	Suficiente/ demasiado/ muy poco	soo-fee-see-**en**-teh/ deh-mah-see-**ah**- doh/ **moo**-ee **poh**-koh
Telephone	Teléfono	tel-**ef**-oh-no
Telegram	Telegrama	teh-leh-**grah**-mah
I am ill	Estoy enfermo(a)	es-**toy** en-**fehr**- moh(mah)
Please call a	Por favor llame a	pohr fah-**vor ya**-meh
doctor	un medico	ah oon **med**-ee-koh

ON THE ROAD

Avenue	Avenida	ah-ven-**ee**-dah
Broad, tree-lined boulevard	Bulevar	boo-leh-**var**
Fertile plain	Vega	**veh**-gah
Highway	Carretera	car-reh-**ter**-ah
Mountain pass	Puerto	poo-**ehr**-toh
Street	Calle	**cah**-yeh
Waterfront promenade	Rambla	**rahm**-blah
Wharf	Embarcadero	em-bar-cah-**deh**-ro

IN TOWN

Cathedral	Catedral	cah-teh-**dral**
Church	Templo/Iglesia	**tem**-plo/ ee-**glehs**- see-ah
City hall	Casa de gobierno	kah-sah deh go-bee-**ehr**-no
Door, gate	Puerta portón	poo-**ehr**-tah por-**ton**
Entrance/exit	Entrada/salida	en-**trah**-dah/sah-**lee**- dah

ENGLISH	SPANISH	PRONUNCIATION
Inn, rustic bar, or restaurant	Taverna	tah-**vehr**-nah
Main square	Plaza principal	plah-thah prin- see-**pahl**

DINING OUT

Can you	¿Puede	**pweh**-deh rreh-koh-
recommend a good	recomendarme un	mehn-**dahr**-me oon
restaurant?	buen restaurante?	bwehn rrehs-tow- **rahn**-teh?
Where is it located?	¿Dónde está situado?	**dohn**-deh ehs-**tah** see-**twah**-doh?
Do I need reservations?	¿Se necesita una reservación?	seh neh-seh-**see**-tah **oo**-nah rreh-sehr- bah-**syohn**?
I'd like to reserve a	Quisiera reservar	kee-**syeh**-rah rreh-
table . . .	una mesa . . .	sehr-**bahr oo**-nah **meh**-sah . . .
for two people.	para dos personas.	**pah**-rah dohs pehr- **soh**-nahs
for this evening.	para esta noche.	**pah**-rah **ehs**-tah **noh**-cheh
for 8 PM	para las ocho de la noche.	**pah**-rah lahs **oh**-choh deh lah **noh**-cheh
A bottle of . . .	Una botella de . . .	**oo**-nah bo-**teh**- yah deh
A cup of . . .	Una taza de . . .	**oo**-nah **tah**-thah deh
A glass of . . .	Un vaso de . . .	oon **vah**-so deh
Ashtray	Un cenicero	oon sen-ee-**seh**-roh
Bill/check	La cuenta	lah **kwen**-tah
Bread	El pan	el pahn
Breakfast	El desayuno	el deh-sah-**yoon**-oh
Butter	La mantequilla	lah man-teh-**key**-yah
Cheers!	¡Salud!	sah-**lood**
Cocktail	Un aperitivo	oon ah-pehr-ee-**tee**-voh
Dinner	La cena	lah **seh**-nah

ENGLISH	SPANISH	PRONUNCIATION
Dish	Un plato	oon **plah**-toh
Menu of the day	Menú del día	meh-**noo** del **dee**-ah
Enjoy!	¡Buen provecho!	bwehn pro-**veh**-cho
Fixed-price menu	Menú fijo o turistico	meh-**noo** **fee**-hoh oh too-**ree**-stee-coh
Fork	El tenedor	el ten-eh-**dor**
Is the tip	¿Está incluida la	es-**tah** in-cloo-**ee**-dah
included?	propina?	lah pro-**pee**-nah
Knife	El cuchillo	el koo-**chee**-yo
Large portion of savory snacks	Raciónes	rah-see-**oh**-nehs
Lunch	La comida	lah koh-**mee**-dah
Menu	La carta, el menú	lah **cart**-ah, el meh-**noo**
Napkin	La servilleta	lah sehr-vee-**yet**-ah
Pepper	La pimienta	lah pee-me-**en**-tah
Please give me	Por favor déme	pore fah-**vor deh**-meh
Salt	La sal	lah sahl
Savory snacks	Tapas	**tah**-pahs
Spoon	Una cuchara	**oo**-nah koo-**chah**-rah
Sugar	El azúcar	el ah-**thu**-kar
Waiter!/Waitress!	¡Por favor Señor/ Señorita!	pohr fah-**vor** sen- **yor**/ sen-yor-**ee**-tah

Travel Smart Cancun

WORD OF MOUTH

"Phone cards can be bought at any convenience store (7/11, Oxxo,etc) and many kiosks that sell beverages and sweets—they are actually very easy to obtain and use. Some have written instructions in English. If you get the basic ones for public phones, you don't even need instructions, they're so easy to use. Just find a public phone, stick the card in, wait for the dial tone, and dial your number (0, then country code first). Really so easy, and so much cheaper than hotel calls."

—Junejuly

GETTING HERE AND AROUND

Cancún is the region's air transportation hub, and many travelers base themselves here and take day or overnight excursions. Other travelers fly in and out of Cancún, but base themselves in Playa del Carmen. There are many direct flights from Europe, Canada, and U.S. cities. Cozumel also has an airport that receives a number of direct flights from the U.S. You'll need to fly through Mexico City to reach Mérida and Campeche from most U.S. cities. The peninsula is flat, and the roads are for the most part easy to drive. (There's a four-lane toll highway between Mérida and Cancún.) First-class and deluxe buses are comfortable, plentiful, and affordable.

■ AIR TRAVEL

Cancún is 3½ hours from New York and Chicago, 2½ hours from Miami, 4½ hours from Los Angeles, 3 hours from Dallas, 11¾ hours from London, and 18 hours from Sydney. Add another 1 to 4 hours if you change planes at one of the hub airports. Flights to Cozumel and Mérida are comparable in length, but are more likely to have a change along the way.

There are direct flights to Cancún from hub airports such as New York, Boston, Washington, D.C., Houston, Dallas, Miami, Chicago, Los Angeles, Orlando, Ft. Lauderdale, Charlotte, and Atlanta. From other cities, you must generally change planes. Some flights go to Mexico City, where you must pass through customs before transferring to a domestic flight to Cancún. This applies to air travel from the United States, Canada, the United Kingdom, Australia, and New Zealand. Be sure to have all your documents in order for entry into the United States, otherwise you may be turned back.

Most of the larger U.S. airlines no longer offer meals on flights to the Yucatán Peninsula. The flights are considered short-haul flights because there's a stopover at a hub airport (where you can purchase your own overpriced meals). The snacks provided on such flights are measly at best, so you may want to bring food on board with you. Aeroméxico and Mexicana both provide full meals.

All flights to and within Mexico are no-smoking.

Charter flights, especially those leaving from Cancún, are notorious for last-minute changes. Be sure to ask for an updated telephone number from your charter company before you leave, so you can call to check for any changes in flight departures. Most recommend that you call within 48 hours. This check-in also applies for the regular airlines, although their departure times are more regular. Their changes are usually due to weather conditions rather than seat sales.

Airline-Security Issues Transportation Security Administration (⊕ *www.tsa.gov*) has answers for almost every question that might come up.

AIRPORTS

Cancún Aeropuerto Internacional (CUN) is the area's major gateway, though some people now choose to fly directly to Cozumel (CZM). The inland Hector José Vavarrette Muñoz Airport (MID), in Mérida, is smaller but closer to the major Mayan ruins. Campeche and Chetumal have even smaller airports served primarily by domestic carriers. The ruins at Palenque and Chichén Itzá also have airstrips that handle small planes; there's a new airport at Chichén (CZA), handling smaller craft as well as 747s via Azteca, Mexicana, and other major airlines.

Airfares to Cancún are generally cheaper than fares to Mérida and Cozumel. Car rentals are a bit less expensive in Mérida than in Cancún and Cozumel, but not enough to warrant a four-hour drive from Cancún if it's your hub.

In peak season, lines can be long and slow-moving; plan accordingly.

It's 20 to 30 minutes from the Hotel Zone to Cancún International or from downtown Mérida or Campeche to their airports. Allow 1½ hours from Playa del Carmen to the Cancún airport. The Cozumel airport is less than 10 minutes from downtown.

Airport Information Contacts Cancún Aeropuerto Internacional (☏No phone ⊕www.cancun-airport.com). **Cozumel Aeropuerto Internacional** (☏987/872–2081 ⊕www.asur.com.mx). **Aeropuerto Internacional de Mérida** (☏999/946–1530 ⊕www.asur.com.mx).

GROUND TRANSPORTATION

Some of the major hotels send shuttles to pick up arriving guests; it's worth checking into before you arrive. Private taxis from the airport charge reasonable rates within Cancún, but will charge up to $60 or more to destinations along the Riviera Maya. Airport shuttle vans, which charge set rates based on your destination, sometimes take forever before filling up and getting under way. There are taxi and shuttle desks in the baggage-claim area; go to the ones with posted prices.

From the Riviera Maya to and from the airport, it's worth looking for a shuttle service, as a private taxi can be prohibitively expensive. Some of the shuttle services can be arranged beforehand via phone or the Internet. Cancún Valet rents per van, rather than per person, for up to 10 passengers, making it a good value for couples, families, and groups. Prices from the airport to the Hotel Zone, Playa del Carmen, and Tulum, as well as intermittent points are reasonable, e.g., $40 to Cancún ($75 round-trip) or $65 to Playa del Carmen ($125 round-trip). Cancún Airport Transportation charges $32 per couple or individual, one-way, to the Hotel Zone ($60 to Playa). Canún Valet also rents cell phones for use in Mexico.

Contacts Cancún Airport Transportation (☏888/479–9095). **Cancún Valet** (⊕www.cancunvalet.com).

FLIGHTS

You can reach the Yucatán either by U.S., Mexican, or regional carriers. The most convenient flight from the United States is a nonstop on a domestic or Mexican airline. Flying within the Yucatán is neither cost-effective nor convenient; given the additional time needed for check-in, you might as well take a bus to your destination—for example, Mérida—unless you are continuing on to another destination by plane. Select your hub city for exploring before making your reservation from abroad. There are more flights to business-oriented Ciudad del Carmen, in Campeche state, for example, than to the tiny airport in the more touristic capital, Campeche City.

Since all the major airlines listed here fly to Cancún, and often have the cheapest and most frequent flights there, it's worthwhile to consider it as a jumping-off point even if you don't plan on visiting the city. Aeroméxico, American, Continental, and Mexicana also fly to Cozumel. Aeroméxico, American, Continental, Delta, and Mexicana fly to Mérida.

Airline Contacts Aeroméxico (☏800/237–6639 in U.S. and Canada, 01800/021–4010 or 55/5133–4010 in Mexico ⊕www.aeromexico.com). **American Airlines** (☏800/433–7300 ⊕www.aa.com). **Continental Airlines** (☏800/523–3273 for U.S. and Mexico reservations, 800/231–0856 for international reservations ⊕www.continental.com). **Delta Airlines** (☏800/221–1212 for U.S. reservations, 800/241–4141 for international reservations ⊕www.delta.com). **Mexicana** (☏800/531–7921 in U.S., 866/281–3049 in Canada, 01800/502–2000 in Mexico ⊕www.mexicana.com).

∎ BOAT TRAVEL

The Yucatán is served by a number of ferries and boats. Most popular are the efficient speedboats that run between Playa del Carmen and Cozumel or from Puerto Juárez, Punta Sam, and Isla Mujeres.

Smaller and slower boat carriers are also available in many places.

Most carriers follow schedules, with the exception of boats going to the smaller, less-visited islands. However, departure times can vary with the weather and the number of passengers. Visitcancun.com and Travelyucatan.com have information on water taxis and ferries, though you should always confirm the details before heading down to the docks.

▌BUS TRAVEL

The Mexican bus network is extensive and also the best means of getting around. Service is frequent, and tickets can be purchased on the spot (except during holidays and on long weekends, when advance purchase is crucial). Bring something to eat on long trips in case you don't like the restaurant where the bus stops; bring toilet tissue; and wear a sweater, as the air-conditioning is often set on high. Most buses play videos or television continually until midnight, so bring earplugs if you are bothered by noise. Smoking is prohibited on Mexican buses.

Mexican bus companies offer several classes of service: first-class (*primera clase*) and deluxe or executive-class (*de lujo* or *ejecutivo*) Mexican buses are generally timely and comfortable, air-conditioned coaches with bathrooms, movies, reclining seats with seat belts, and refreshments. They take the fastest route (usually on safer, well-paved toll roads) and make few stops between points. Less desirable, second-class vehicles (*segunda clase*) connect smaller, secondary routes; they also run along some long-distance routes, often taking slower, local roads. They're tolerable, but are usually cramped and make many stops. The class of travel will be listed on your printed ticket—if you see *económico* printed next to *servicio,* you've been booked on a second-class bus. At many bus stations, one counter will represent several lines and classes of service, and mistakes do happen. ADO

(Autobuses del Oriente) is the Yucatán's principal first-class bus company. Most bus tickets, including first-class or executive- and second-class, can be reserved in advance in person at ticket offices. ADO allows you to reserve tickets online 48 hours in advance. ADO and ADO GL (deluxe service) travel between the Yucatán and Mexico City as well as other destinations in southern Mexico, especially Oaxaca, Veracruz, and Puebla.

Bus travel in the Yucatán, as throughout Mexico, is inexpensive by U.S. standards, with rates averaging $2 to $6 per hour depending on the level of luxury (or lack of it). Schedules are posted at bus stations; the bus leaves more or less around the listed time. Often, if all the seats have been sold, the bus will leave early.

Typical times and fares on first-class buses are Cancún to Mérida: 3½ hours, $22; Cancún to Campeche: 7 hours, $33; Mérida to Campeche: 2½ hours, $12; and Cancún to Mexico City: 23 hours, $110.

Bus Contacts ADO (☎ *998/884–4352, 01800/702–8000 toll-free in Mexico, or 800/900–0287 in the U.S.* ⊕ *www.ticketbus. com.mx).*

▌CAR TRAVEL

Renting a car is generally expensive in and around Cancún; if you're not traveling far afield, don't bother, as you will be able to arrange taxi service to nearby sights through your hotel. However, taxis for longer trips—to Playa del Carmen, for instance—can get expensive, so renting a car for a day or two of exploring may be more economical. Pancake-flat Yucatán makes for fairly easy driving, although side roads may be unsigned; four-wheel drive vehicles aren't necessary. Ask for a child's car seat when booking. You won't need a car on Isla Mujeres, which is too small to make driving practical. Again, a rental isn't necessary in Playa del Carmen because the downtown area is quite small and the main street is blocked off to vehicles. Cars are actually a burden in

Mérida and Campeche City, because of the narrow cobbled streets and the lack of parking spaces. You'll need a car in Cozumel only if you wish to explore the eastern side of the island.

Although consolidators like Travelocity.com may offer great deals, it's a good idea to book directly through a major rental company's Web site, as consolidator sites will sometimes allow you to make a booking even when no cars are available.

Car-rental agencies in Mexico require you to purchase CDW coverage (starts at $11 per day), regardless of any coverage afforded by your credit-card company (insurance fees are often included in quoted rates). Additional theft protection and personal injury policies are optional.

Be sure that you have been provided with proof of such insurance; if you drive without it, you're not only liable for damages, but you're also breaking the law. If you're in a car accident and you don't have insurance, you may be placed in jail until you are proven innocent. If anyone is injured you'll remain in jail until you make retribution to all injured parties and their families—which will likely cost you thousands of dollars. Mexican laws seem to favor nationals.

Technically, you can decline the agency-mandated insurance—though the agent won't be happy about it—if you are absolutely certain you are fully covered by your credit-card company. However, we wouldn't recommend it. Getting into a car accident in Mexico would be harrowing enough without having to navigate the bureaucracy of your credit-card company to clear things up with Mexican authorities. Buying insurance makes renting a car in Mexico one of the most expensive parts of the trip, but in this case it's better to be safe than frugal.

Before setting out on any car trip, check your vehicle's fuel, oil, fluids, tires, and lights. Gas stations and mechanics can be hard to find, especially in more remote areas. Consult a map and have your route in mind as you drive. Be aware that Mexican drivers often think nothing of tailgating, speeding, and weaving in and out of traffic. Drive defensively and keep your cool. When stopped for traffic or at a red light, always leave sufficient room between your car and the one ahead so you can maneuver to safety if necessary. On the highway, a left turn signal in Mexico means the driver is signaling those behind that it's safe to pass.

In Mexico the minimum driving age is 18, but most rental-car agencies have a minimum age requirement between 21 and 25; some have a surcharge for drivers under 25. Your own driver's license is acceptable; there's no reason to get an international driver's license.

GASOLINE

Pemex, Mexico's government-owned petroleum monopoly, franchises all gas stations, so prices throughout the Yucatán—and the country—are the same. Prices tend to be slightly less than those in the United States. Gas is always sold in liters. Some stations accept credit cards and a few have ATMs, but don't count on it—make sure you have pesos handy. Ask for a *recibo* if you want a receipt. Premium unleaded gas (called *premium*), the red pump, and regular unleaded gas (*magna*), the green pump, are available nationwide. Fuel quality is generally lower than that in the United States and Europe, but it has improved enough so that your car will run acceptably.

There are no self-service stations in Mexico. Ask the attendant to fill your tank—*lleno* (YAY-noh), *por favor*—or ask for a specific amount in pesos to avoid being overcharged. Check to make sure that the attendant has set the meter back to zero and that the price is shown. Watch the attendant check the oil as well—to make sure you actually need it—and watch while he pours it into your car. Never pay before the gas is pumped, even if the attendant asks you to. Always tip your attendant a few pesos. Finally, keep your gas tank full, because gas stations are not plentiful in this area. If you run out of gas in a small village and there's no gas station for miles, ask if there's a store that sells gas from containers.

PARKING

A circle with a diagonal line superimposed on the letter *E* (for *estacionamiento*) means "no parking." When in doubt, park your car in a parking lot. Tip the parking attendant or security guard and ask him to look after your car. Never park your car overnight on the street. Never leave anything of value in an unattended car.

ROAD CONDITIONS

The road system in the Yucatán Peninsula is extensive and generally in good repair. Carretera 307 parallels most of the Caribbean coast from Punta Sam, north of Cancún, to Tulum; here it turns inward for a stretch before returning to the coast at Chetumal and the Belize border. Carretera 180 runs west from Cancún to Valladolid, Chichén Itzá, and Mérida, then turns southwest to Campeche, Ciudad del Carmen, and on to Villahermosa. From Mérida, the winding, more scenic Carretera 261 also leads to some of the more off-the-beaten-track archaeological sites on the way south to Campeche and Escárcega, where it joins Carretera 186 going east to Chetumal. These highways are two-lane roads. Carretera 295 (from the north coast to Valladolid and Felipe Carrillo Puerto) is also a good two-lane road.

The *autopista,* or *carretera de cuota,* a four-lane toll highway between Cancún and Mérida, was completed in 1993. It runs roughly parallel to Carretera 180 and cuts driving time between Cancún and Mérida—otherwise about 4½ hours—by about 1 hour. Tolls between Mérida and Cancún total about $27, and the stretches between highway exits are long. Be careful when driving on this road, as it retains the heat from the sun and can make your tires blow if they have low pressure or worn threads.

Many secondary roads are in bad condition—unpaved, unmarked, and full of potholes. If you must take one of these roads, the best course is to allow plenty of daylight hours and never travel at night. Slow down when approaching towns and villages—which you are forced to do by the *topes* (speed bumps)—and because of the added presence of children and animals, as well as adults. People selling oranges, candy, or other food will almost certainly approach your car.

ROADSIDE EMERGENCIES

The Mexican Tourism Ministry operates a fleet of some 350 pickup trucks, known as Angeles Verdes, or the Green Angels, a 40-year-old organization that assists motorists on major highways. You can call the Green Angels directly or call the Ministry of Tourism's hotline and they will dispatch them. The bilingual drivers provide mechanical help, first aid, radio-telephone communication, basic supplies and small parts, towing, and tourist information. Services are free, and spare parts, fuel, and lubricants are provided at cost. Tips are always appreciated.

The Green Angels patrol fixed sections of the major highways twice daily 8 AM to dusk, later on holiday weekends. If your car breaks down, pull as far as possible off the road, lift the hood, hail a passing vehicle, and ask the driver to notify the patrol. Most bus and truck drivers will be quite helpful. Do not accept rides from strangers. If you witness an accident, do not stop to help, but instead find the nearest official.

**Emergency Service Contacts Ange-
les Verdes** (☎ *078 nationwide three-digit Angeles Verdes and tourist emergency line, 55/3002–6300 Ministry of Tourism hotline*).

RULES OF THE ROAD

There are two absolutely essential points to remember about driving in Mexico. First and foremost is to carry Mexican auto insurance. If you injure anyone in an accident, you could well be jailed—whether it was your fault or not—unless you have insurance. Second, if you enter Mexico with a car, you must leave with it. In recent years the high rate of U.S. vehicles being sold illegally in Mexico has caused the Mexican government to enact stringent regulations for bringing a car into the country. You must be in your foreign vehicle at all times when it is driven. You cannot lend it to another person. Do not, under any circumstances, let a national drive your car. It's illegal for Mexicans to drive foreign cars; if a national driving your car is caught, the car will be impounded by customs and you will receive a stiff fine. Newer models of vans, SUVs, and pickup trucks can be impossible to get back once impounded.

You must cross the border with the following documents: title or registration for your vehicle; a birth certificate or passport; a credit card (AE, DC, MC, or V); and a valid driver's license with a photo. The title-holder, driver, and credit-card owner must be one and the same—that is, if your spouse's name is on the title of the car and yours isn't, you cannot be the one to bring the car into the country. For financed, leased, rental, or company cars, you must bring a notarized letter of permission from the bank, lien holder, rental agency, or company. When you submit your paperwork at the border and pay the approximately $27 charge on your credit card, you'll receive a car permit and a sticker to put on your vehicle. The permit is valid for the same amount of time as your tourist visa, which is up to 180 days. You may go back and forth across the border during this six-month period, as long as you check with immigration and bring all your permit paperwork with you. If you're planning to stay and keep your car in Mexico for longer than six months, however, you will have to get a new permit before the original one expires.

One way to minimize hassle when you cross the border with a car is to have your paperwork done in advance at a branch of Sanborn's Mexico Auto Insurance; look in the Yellow Pages to find an office in almost every town on the U.S.–Mexico border. You'll still have to go through some of the procedures at the border, but all your paperwork will be in order, and Sanborn's express window will ensure that you get through relatively quickly. There's a $10 charge for this service on top of the $10 per day and up for auto insurance. The fact that you drove in with a car is stamped on your tourist card, which you must give to immigration authorities at departure. If an emergency arises and you must fly home, there are complicated customs procedures to face.

When you sign up for Mexican car insurance, you should receive a booklet on Mexican rules of the road. It really is a good idea to read it to avoid breaking laws that differ from those of your country. If an oncoming vehicle flicks its lights at you in daytime, slow down: it could mean trouble ahead. When approaching a narrow bridge, the first vehicle to flash its lights has right of way. One-way streets are common. One-way traffic is indicated by an arrow; two-way, by a double-pointed arrow. Other road signs follow the widespread system of international symbols.

Mileage and speed limits are given in kilometers: 100 KPH and 80 KPH (62 MPH and 50 MPH, respectively) are the most common maximums. A few of the toll roads allow 110 KPH (68 MPH). In cities and small towns, observe the posted speed limits, which can be as low as 20 KPH (12 MPH). Seat belts are required by law throughout Mexico.

Drunk driving laws are fairly harsh in Mexico, and if you're caught you'll go to jail immediately. It's hard to know what the country's blood-alcohol limit really is. Everyone seems to have a different idea about it; this means it's probably being handled in a discretionary way, which is nerve-racking, to say the least. The best way to avoid any problems is simply to not drink and drive. There's no right on red. Foreigners must pay speeding penalties on the spot, which can be steep; sometimes you're better off offering a little *mordida* (bribe, though don't refer to it as such) to the officer—just take out a couple hundred pesos, hold it out inquiringly, and see if the problem goes away.

If you encounter a police checkpoint, stay calm. These are simply routine checks for weapons and drugs; customarily they'll check out the car's registration, look in the backseat, the trunk, and at the undercarriage with a mirror. Basic Spanish does help during these stops, though a smile and polite demeanor will go a long way.

Contact **Sanborn's Mexican Auto Insurance** (☎800/222-0158 ⊕ *www.sanbornsinsurance. com*).

SAFETY ON THE ROAD

Never drive at night in remote and rural areas. Although there are few *banditos* on the roads here, there are large potholes, free-roaming animals, cars with no working lights, and road-hogging trucks, and getting assistance is difficult. If you must travel at night, use the toll roads whenever possible; although costly, they're much safer.

Some of the biggest hassles on the road might be from police who pull you over for supposedly breaking the law, or for being a good prospect for a scam. Remember to be polite—displays of anger will only make matters worse—and be aware that a police officer might be pulling you over for something you didn't do. Although efforts are being made to fight corruption, it's still a fact of life in Mexico, and the $5 (and up) it costs to get your license back is definitely supplementary income for the officer who pulled you over with no intention of taking you down to police headquarters.

▌CRUISE SHIP TRAVEL

Cozumel and Playa del Carmen have become increasingly popular ports for Caribbean cruises. The last few years have seen many changes in the cruise business. Several companies have merged and several more are suffering financial difficulties. Due to heavy traffic, Cozumel and Playa del Carmen have limited the number of ships coming into their ports. Carnival and Cunard leave from Galveston, New Orleans, and Miami, whereas Norwegian departs from Houston, New Orleans, Miami, and Charleston. Holland America, Cunard, Carnival, Princess, Royal Caribbean, and Celebrity Cruises dock at Cozumel. Princess and Carnival lines, among others, call at the Puerto Costa Maya in Mahahual, an increasingly popular destination on the southern Yucatán Peninsula.

Cruise Line Contacts **Carnival Cruise Line** (☎305/599-2600 or 888/227-6482 ⊕*www. carnival.com*). **Cunard Line** (☎661/753-1000 or 800/728-6273 ⊕*www.cunard.com*). **Norwegian Cruise Line** (☎866/234-7350 ⊕*www.ncl.com*). **Princess Cruises** (☎661/753-0000 or 800/774-6237 ⊕*www. princess.com*). **Royal Caribbean International** (☎305/539-6000 or 866/562-7625 ⊕*www. royalcaribbean.com*).

ESSENTIALS

▮ ACCOMMODATIONS

The price and quality of accommodations in the Yucatán Peninsula vary from super-luxurious, international-class hotels, and all-inclusive resorts to modest budget properties, seedy places with shared bathrooms, and *cabañas* (beach huts). You may find appealing bargains while you're on the road, but if your comfort threshold is high, look for an English-speaking staff, guaranteed dollar rates, and toll-free reservation numbers. Mexico doesn't have an official star-rating system, but the usual number of stars (five being the ultimate) denotes the most luxury and amenities, while a two-star hotel might have a ceiling fan only and TV with local channels only. "Gran turismo" is a special category of hotel that may or may not have all the accoutrements of a five-star hotel (such as minibars) but is nonetheless at the top of the heap, both in price and level of service and sophistication.

Properties are assigned price categories based on the range from their least-expensive standard double room at high season (excluding holidays) to the most expensive. We always list the facilities that are available—but we don't specify whether they cost extra; when pricing accommodations, always ask what's included and what costs extra. Lodgings are denoted in the text with a house icon 🏠.

▮**TIP**→Assume that hotels operate on the European Plan (**EP**, no meals) unless we specify that they use the Breakfast Plan (**BP**, with full breakfast), Continental Plan (**CP**, Continental breakfast), Full American Plan (**FAP**, all meals), or Modified American Plan (**MAP**, breakfast and dinner), or are all-inclusive (**AI**, all meals and most drinks and activities).

WORD OF MOUTH

Did the resort look as good in real life as it did in the photos? Did you sleep like a baby, or were the walls paper-thin? Did you get your money's worth? Rate hotels in User Reviews or start a discussion about your favorite places in Travel Talk on www.fodors.com. Your comments might even appear in our books. Yes, you, too, can be a correspondent!

APARTMENT AND HOUSE RENTALS

Local rental agencies can be found in Isla Mujeres, Cozumel, and Playa del Carmen. They specialize in renting out apartments, condos, villas, and private homes.

Rental Agency Contacts A1 Vacations (☎No phone ⊕ www.a1vacations.com). **Akumal Villas** (☎984/875–9088 ⊕ www.akumal-villas.com). **Real Estate Yucatán** (☎678/528–1775 ⊕ www.realestateyucatan.com). **Coldwell Banker Caribbean Realty** (☎910/543–0019 in U.S.). **Cozumel Vacation Rentals** (☎512/371–3062 in U.S. ⊕ www.islacozumel.net/homes). **Cozumel Villas** (☎866/564–4427 or 406/686–9169 ⊕ www.cozumelvillas.com). **Lost Oasis Property Rentals** (☎998/888–0429, 831/274–6277in U.S. ⊕ www.lostoasis.net). **Playa Beach Rentals** (☎984/873–2952, 205/332–3458in U.S. ⊕ www.playabeachrentals.com). **Turquoise Waters** (☎877/254–9791 ⊕ www.turquoisewater.com). **Vacation Home Rentals Worldwide** (☎201/767–9393 or 800/633–3284 ⊕ www.vhrww.com). **Villas & Apartments Abroad** (☎212/213–6435 ⊕ www.vaanyc.com). **Villas International** (☎415/499–9490 or 800/221–2260 ⊕ www.villasintl.com). **Villas of Distinction** (☎800/289–0900 ⊕ www.villasofdistinction.com).

HOTELS

Hotel rates are subject to the 10% to 15% value-added tax, in addition to a 2% hotel tax. Service charges and meals generally aren't included in the hotel rates. Hotels of three stars or less often include tax in their quoted rates; make sure to ask and to take this into account when comparing properties.

The Mexican government categorizes hotels, based on qualitative evaluations, into *gran turismo* (superdeluxe, or five-star-plus, properties, of which there are fewer than 50 nationwide), and five-star down to one-star. Anything less than two stars generally doesn't advertise the fact, and even budget travelers are unlikely to stay at a one-star lodging. Keep in mind that many hotels that might otherwise be rated higher have opted for a lower category to avoid higher interest rates on loans and financing, and that a rustic chic resort with plenty of charm may receive a lower rating for lack of certain amenities only, like air-conditioning.

High- versus low-season rates can vary significantly. In the off-season, Cancún hotels can cost one-third to one-half what they cost during peak season. Keep in mind, however, that this is also the time that many hotels undergo necessary repairs or renovations.

Hotels in this guide have private bathrooms with showers, unless stated otherwise; bathtubs aren't common in inexpensive hotels and properties in smaller towns.

Reservations are easy to make over the Internet. If you call hotels in the larger urban areas, there will be someone who speaks English. In more remote regions you will have to make your reservations in Spanish. Be sure to book online hotel reservations at least two days in advance of your stay, and always print out your confirmation. Although major resorts are generally efficient at keeping up with online bookings, there's often a lag, and the reservation desks that handle such things may be closed on weekends.

It's essential to reserve in advance if you're traveling to the resort areas during high season or holiday periods, and it's recommended, though not always necessary, to do so elsewhere during high season. Overbooking is a common practice in some parts, especially in Cancún. To protect yourself, get a confirmation in writing, via fax or e-mail.

General Hotel Contacts Cancún Hotel Association (✉ *Av. García de la Torre 6, Sm 15* ☎ *998/881–8730* ⊕ *www.ahqr.com.mx*). **Cozumel Island Hotel Association** (✉ *Calle 2 Norte 299* ☎ *987/872–7585* ⊕ *www. islacozumel.com.mx*). **Hotels Tulum** (⊕ *www. hotelstulum.com*). **HolboxIsland.com** (⊕ *www. holboxisland.com*).

∎ COMMUNICATIONS

INTERNET

If you're traveling with your laptop, watch it carefully. The biggest danger, aside from theft, is the constantly fluctuating electricity, which will eventually damage your hard drive. Invest in a Mexican surge protector (available at most electronics stores for about $50) that can handle the frequent brownouts and fluctuations in voltage. The surge protectors you use at home probably won't give you much protection. If possible, leave repairs until you are back home; although there are many competent techies here as elsewhere, language may be a barrier.

Internet is widely available; there are net "cafés" all over the place—with and without coffee. Connections are fast in Cancún, not so fast elsewhere. Despite controversy over needing more cell towers everywhere, Cozumel is being totally wired for Wi-Fi now.

In Cancún free Wi-Fi is available in many large hotels, at least in public areas. Cost for in-room connection runs $15 to $25 per day—yes, it's shocking, especially when in other parts of the country Wi-Fi is a free perk offered by many hotels. The cost for public Internet is as much as 10 pesos a minute (for those with super-fast connection). For slower connections, the charge is usually more like 10 pesos for 10 minutes.

LOCAL DO'S AND TABOOS

CUSTOMS OF THE COUNTRY

In the United States, being direct, efficient, and succinct are highly valued traits. In Mexico, communication tends to be subtler, so this style can be perceived as rude and aggressive. People will be far less helpful if you lose your temper or complain loudly. Remember that there's rarely a stigma attached to being late. Try to accept the slower pace here gracefully.

GREETINGS

Business people and strangers shake hands upon greeting each other or being introduced; friends may give a kiss on one cheek. It's traditional to use the formal form of you (*usted*) rather than the informal tú when addressing elders, subordinates, superiors, and strangers. When taking your leave, say *adíos* (good-bye) or *hasta luego* (see you later).

SIGHTSEEING

Although shorts are permissible in churches, short shorts and skimpy tops are frowned upon. During church services you can stand at the back and look. Say *con permiso* (pardon me) to get past people in a crowd.

OUT ON THE TOWN

Mexicans call waiters *joven* (literally, young man) no matter how old they are (it's the equivalent of the word "maid" being used for the old woman who cleans rooms). Call a female waitress *señorita* ("miss") or *señora* (ma'am). Ask for *la cuenta, por favor* (the check, please); it's considered rude to bring it before the customer asks for it. Mexicans dress nicely for a night out, though in tourist areas dress codes are upheld mainly at sophisticated discos. Some restaurants have smoking sections; in smaller establishments you can usually smoke with abandon anywhere.

DOING BUSINESS

A handshake is an appropriate greeting, along with a friendly inquiry about family members. With established clients, don't be surprised if you are welcomed with a kiss on the cheek or full hug with a pat on the back. Mexicans love business cards; without them you may have trouble being taken seriously. Always be respectful of colleagues and keep confrontations private. When invited to dinner at the home of a customer or business associate, it's not necessary to bring a gift.

LANGUAGE

Spanish is the official language, although various dialects of Mayan are spoken in rural areas. In this heavily touristed region people speak good to moderate English. At the very least, shopkeepers will know the numbers for bargaining purposes. As in most other foreign countries, knowing the mother tongue has a way of opening doors, so learn some Spanish words and phrases. Mexicans welcome even the most halting attempts to use Spanish.

If you've been schooled in Castilian grammar, you'll find Mexican Spanish to be different. For example, it replaces the *vosotros* form of the second-person plural with the more formal *ustedes*. As for pronunciation, the lisped Castilian "c" or "z" is dismissed as a sign of affectation.

LANGUAGE-STUDY PROGRAMS

Playa del Carmen's Playalingua del Caribe language center can help you find affordable lodging. Language Link runs schools in Cancún and Playa del Carmen.

Playalingua del Caribe (⊠ *Calle 20 Norte between Avs. 5A and 10A, Playa del Carmen* ☎ *984/873-3876* ⊕ *www.playalingua.com*). **Language Link** (⊡ *Box 3006, Peoria, IL 61612* ☎ *309/673-9220, 800/552-2051 toll-free in U.S.* ⊕ *www.langlink.com*).

Internet Café Contacts **Cybercafes** (⊕ *www. cybercafes.com*) lists about 170 Internet cafés in Mexico.

PHONES

The good news is that you can now make a direct-dial telephone call from virtually any point on earth. The bad news? You can't always do so cheaply. Calling from a hotel is almost always the most expensive option; hotels usually add huge surcharges to all calls, particularly international ones. Calling cards usually keep costs to a minimum, use your international calling card or purchase a Ladatel card to use at a pay phone—although hearing above ambient noise can be a problem. And then there are mobile phones (⇨ *below*), which are sometimes more prevalent—particularly in the developing world—than land lines; as expensive as mobile-phone calls can be, they are still usually a much cheaper option than calling from your hotel.

The country code for Mexico is 52. When calling a Mexico number from abroad, dial the country code and then all of the numbers listed for the entry.

CALLING WITHIN MEXICO

Towns and cities throughout Mexico now have standardized three-digit area codes (LADAs) and seven-digit phone numbers. (In Mexico City, Monterrey, and Guadalajara the area code is two digits followed by an eight-digit local number.) While increasingly rare, numbers in brochures and other literature—even business cards—are sometimes written in the old style, with five or six digits. To call national long-distance, dial 01, the area code, and the seven-digit number.

Directory assistance is 040 for telephone lines run by Telmex, the former government-owned telephone monopoly that still holds near-monopoly status in Mexico. While you can reach 040 from other phone lines, operators generally do not give you any information, except, perhaps, the directory-assistance line for the provider you are using. For international assistance, dial 00 first for an international operator and most likely you'll get one who speaks English; tell the operator in what city, state, and country you require directory assistance, and he or she will connect you.

CALLING OUTSIDE MEXICO

To make an international call, dial 00 before the country code, area code, and number. The country code for the United States and Canada is 1, the United Kingdom 44, Australia 61, New Zealand 64, and South Africa 27.

The cheapest method for making local or long-distance calls is to buy a prepaid phone card and dial direct (⇨ *see Calling Cards*). Another option is to find a *caseta de larga distancia,* a telephone service usually operated out of a store such as a papelería, pharmacy, restaurant, or other small business; look for the phone symbol on the door. These are few and far between in Cancún, however. *Casetas* may cost more to use than pay phones, but you have a better chance of immediate success. To make a direct long-distance call, tell the person on duty the number you'd like to call, and she or he will give you a rate and dial for you. Rates seem to vary widely, so shop around.

Sometimes you can make collect calls from casetas, and sometimes you cannot, depending on the individual operator and possibly your degree of visible desperation. Casetas will generally charge 50¢ to $1.50 to place a collect call (some charge by the minute); it's usually better to call *por cobrar* (collect) from a pay phone— but be sure to avoid phones near tourist areas that advertise, in English, "Call the U.S. or Canada here!" These charge an outrageous fee per minute. If in doubt, dial the operator and ask for rates.

Access Code Contacts **AT&T Direct** (☎ *01800/112–2020 or 001800/462–4240 toll-free in Mexico*). **MCI WorldPhone** (☎ *01800/674–7000*). **Sprint International Access** (☎ *001800/877–8000 toll-free in Mexico*).

CALLING CARDS

In most parts of the country, pay phones (predominantly operated by Telmex) accept only prepaid cards (*tarjetas Lada*), sold in 30-, 50-, or 100-peso denominations at newsstands, pharmacies, minimarkets, or grocery stores; coin-only pay phones are few and far between. There are pay phones are all over the place—on street corners, in bus stations, and so on. They usually have two unmarked slots, one for a Ladatel (a Spanish acronym for "long-distance direct dialing") card and the other for a credit card. These are primarily for Mexican bank cards, but some accept Visa or MasterCard, though *not* U.S. phone credit cards.

To use a Ladatel card, simply insert it in the appropriate slot, dial 001 (for calls to the States) or 01 (for long-distance calls within Mexico) and the area code and number you're trying to reach. Local calls may also be placed with the card. Credit is deleted from the card as you use it, and your balance is displayed on a small screen on the phone.

MOBILE PHONES

If you have a multiband phone (some countries use frequencies different from those used in the United States) and your service provider uses the world-standard GSM network (as do T-Mobile, Cingular, and Verizon), you can probably use your phone abroad. Roaming fees can be steep, however: 99¢ a minute is considered reasonable. And you normally pay the toll charges for incoming calls. It's almost always cheaper to send a text message than to make a call, since text messages have a very low set fee (often less than 5¢).

If you just want to make local calls, consider buying a new SIM card (note that your provider may have to unlock your phone for you to use a different SIM card) and a prepaid service plan in the destination. You'll then have a local number and can make local calls at local rates. If your trip is extensive, you could also simply buy a new cell phone in your destination, as the initial cost will be offset over time.

■TIP➔If you travel internationally frequently, save one of your old mobile phones or buy a cheap one on the Internet; ask your cell-phone company to unlock it for you, and take it with you as a travel phone, buying a new SIM card with pay-as-you-go service in each destination.

Mobile Phone Contacts Daystar (☎ 888/908–4100 ⊕ *www.daystarwireless. com*) rents cell phones at $6 per day, with incoming calls at 22¢ a minute and outgoing at $1.19.

TOLL-FREE NUMBERS

Toll-free numbers in Mexico start with an 800 prefix. To reach them, you need to dial 01 before the number. In this guide, Mexico-only toll-free numbers appear as follows: 01800/123–4567. Some toll-free numbers use 95 instead of 01 to connect. Some hotels will charge for 800 numbers made from guest rooms. The 800 numbers listed simply 800/123–4567 are U.S. numbers and generally work north of the border only. Those that do work to access a U.S. company from Mexico may or may not be free; those that aren't should give you the chance to hang up before being charged. Directory assistance is 040.

■ CUSTOMS AND DUTIES

Upon entering Mexico, you'll be given a baggage-declaration form—you can fill out one per family. Most airports have a random bag-inspection scheme in place. When you pick up your bags you'll approach something that looks like a stoplight; hand your form to the attendant, press the button, and if you get a green light you (and the rest of your family) may proceed. If you get a red light, you may be subject to further questioning or inspection. You're allowed to bring in three liters of spirits or wine for personal use; 400 cigarettes, 50 cigars, or 250 grams of tobacco; a reasonable amount of perfume for personal use; one movie camera and one regular camera and 12 rolls of film for each; and gift items not to exceed a total of $300. If driving across the U.S. border, gift items must not exceed $50. You aren't allowed to bring firearms or ammunition, meat, vegetables, plants, fruit, or flowers into the country. You can bring in one of each of the following items without paying taxes: a cell phone, a beeper, a radio or tape recorder, a musical instrument, a laptop computer, and a portable copier or printer. Compact discs are limited to 20 and DVDs to five.

Mexico also allows you to bring one cat, one dog, or up to four canaries into the country if you have these two things: (1) a pet health certificate signed by a registered veterinarian in the United States and issued not more than 72 hours before the animal enters Mexico; and (2) a pet-vaccination certificate showing that the animal has been treated for rabies, hepatitis, pip, and leptospirosis.

For more information or information on bringing other animals or more than one type of animal, contact a Mexican consulate. Aduana Mexico (Mexican Customs) has an informative Web site, though everything is in Spanish. You can also get customs information from a Mexican consulate; many major American cities have them as well as border towns. To find the consulate nearest you, check the Ministry of Foreign Affairs Web site, select Consular Services from the menu on the left, and scroll down.

Consulate Contacts Aduana Mexico (⊕ www.aduanas.gob.mx). **U.S. Customs and Border Protection** (⊕ www.cbp.gov). **Ministry of Foreign Affairs** (⊕ portal.sre.gob.mx/usa).

DAY TOURS AND GUIDES

In the states of Quintana Roo, Yucatán, and to a lesser extent, Campeche, tour guides are stationed outside the more popular ruins. Official guides will be wearing a name tag and identification issued by INAH, Instituto Nacional de Antropología e Historia (National Institute of Anthropology and History).

These guides have taken courses in guiding as well as area- and site-specific history courses. If possible, ask friends who have used guide services or the local tourism office for a recommendation. At the smaller ruins, guides are usually part of the research or maintenance teams and can give you an excellent tour.

Guides in Campeche may be booked through the Campeche tourist office. Costs vary. At the smaller sites a $3 to $10 tip (for one or two people) will suffice, depending on how long you spend with the guide. At the larger ruins the fees can run as high as $30, but the price can be shared among a group of people. Those charging more are scam artists. The larger ruins tend to have the more competitive and aggressive guides. Turn them down with a very firm *No, gracias,* and if they persist, lose them at the entrance gate.

EATING OUT

The restaurants we list are the cream of the crop in each price category.

For information on food-related health issues, see Health below.

MEALS AND MEALTIMES

Desayuno can be either a breakfast sweet roll and coffee or milk or a full breakfast of an egg dish such as *huevos à la mexicana* (scrambled eggs with chopped tomato, onion, and chiles), *huevos rancheros* (fried eggs on a tortilla covered with salsa), or *huevos con jamón* (scrambled eggs with ham), plus juice and toast or tortillas. Traditionally, lunch is called *comida* or *almuerzo* and is the biggest meal of the day. Traditional businesses close between 2 PM and 4 PM for this meal. It usually includes soup, a main dish, and dessert. Regional specialties include *pan de cazón* (baby shark shredded and layered with tortillas, black beans and tomato sauce), in Campeche; *pollo pibíl* (chicken baked in banana leaves), in Mérida; and *tikinchic* (fish in a sour-orange sauce), on the coast. Restaurants in tourist areas also serve American-style food such as hamburgers, pizza, and pasta. The lighter evening meal is called *cena*.

Most restaurants are open daily for lunch and dinner during high season (December through April), but hours may be reduced during the rest of the year. It's always a good idea to phone ahead.

Unless otherwise noted, the restaurants listed in this guide are open daily for lunch and dinner.

PAYING

Most small restaurants do not accept credit cards. Larger restaurants and those catering to tourists take credit cards, but their prices reflect the fee placed on all credit-card transactions.

For guidelines on tipping, see Tipping below.

RESERVATIONS AND DRESS

Regardless of where you are, it's a good idea to make a reservation if you can. In Cancún, for example, reservations are expected at the nicer restaurants. We only mention them specifically when reservations are essential (there's no other way you'll ever get a table) or when they are not accepted. For popular restaurants, book as far ahead as you can (often 30 days), and reconfirm as soon as you arrive. (Large parties should always call ahead to check the reservations policy.) We mention dress only when men are required to wear a jacket or a jacket and tie.

Some restaurants accept online reservations, although it's always wise to confirm by phone.

WINES, BEER, AND SPIRITS

Almost all restaurants in the region serve beer and some Mexican label spirits. Larger restaurants have beer, wine, and spirits. The Mexican wine industry is relatively small, but notable producers include L.A. Cetto, Bodegas de Santo Tomás, Pedro Domecq, and Monte Xanic; as well as offering Mexican vintages, restaurants may offer Chilean, Spanish, Italian, and French wines at reasonable prices. You pay more for imported liquor

> **WORD OF MOUTH**
>
> Was the service stellar or not up to snuff? Did the food give you shivers of delight or leave you cold? Did the prices and portions make you happy or sad? Rate restaurants and write your own reviews in Travel Ratings or start a discussion about your favorite places in Travel Talk on www.fodors.com. Your comments might even appear in our books. Yes, you, too, can be a correspondent!

such as vodka, brandy, and whiskey; some brands of tequila and rum are less expensive. Take the opportunity to try some of the higher-end, small-batch tequila—it's a completely different experience from what you might be used to. Some small lunch places called *loncherias* don't sell alcohol. Almost all corner stores sell beer, brandy, cheap wine, and tequila; grocery stores carry all brands of beer, wine, and spirits. Liquor stores are rare and usually carry specialty items. You must be 18 to buy liquor, but this rule is often overlooked.

▌ELECTRICITY

Electrical converters are not necessary, because Mexico operates on the 60-cycle, 120-volt system; however, many outlets have not been updated to accommodate three-prong and polarized plugs (those with one larger prong), so bring an adapter. Some older hotels have outlets for round pin attachment plugs instead of modern flat ones, although most have been upgraded. If your room has one of these ancient plugs, ask at the front desk for an adapter. As brownouts and power surges can be a problem, it's recommended that those with laptop computers bring a power-surge protector.

Contacts Steve Kropla's Help for World Travelers (⊕ *www.kropla.com*) has information on electrical and telephone plugs around the world.

■ EMERGENCIES

It's helpful, albeit daunting, to know ahead of time that you're not protected by the laws of your native land once you're on Mexican soil. However, if you get into a scrape with the law, you can call the Citizens' Emergency Center in the United States. In Mexico, you can also call INFOTUR, the 24-hour English-speaking hotline of the Mexico Ministry of Tourism (Sectur). The hotline can provide immediate assistance as well as general, non-emergency guidance. In Mérida and environs, contact the tourist police (☎999/930–3200 *Ext. 462*), although getting an English speaker is hit or miss. In an emergency, call ☎060 from any phone.

Consulates and Embassies U.S. Consul (✉*Paseo de Monejo 453, at Av. Colón, Centro, Mérida* ☎999/925–5011). **U.S. Consul** (✉*Segundo Nivel No. 320–323, Plaza Caracol Dos, Blvd. Kukulkán, Zona Hotelera, Cancún* ☎998/883–0272). **U.S. Embassy** (✉*Paseo de la Reforma 305, Col. Cuauhtémoc, Mexico City* ☎55/5080–2000 ⊕*mexico.usembassy. gov/eng*).

General Emergency Contacts Air Ambulance Network (☎800/327–1966 or 01800/010–00271 ⊕*www.airambulance network.com*). **Angeles Verdes** (*Emergency roadside assistance in Mexico City* ☎078). **Citizens' Emergency Center** (☎202/647–5226 weekdays 8:15 AM– 10 PM EST and Sat. 9 AM–5 PM, 202/647–4512 after hrs and Sun.). **Global Life Flight** (☎01800/305–9400 or 01800/361–1600 toll-free in Mexico, 800/554–9729 in U.S. and Canada ⊕*www.globallifeflight.com*). **INFOTUR** (☎800/482–9832 in U.S., 01800/903–9200 toll-free in Mexico ⊕*www.sectur.gob.mx*).

■ HEALTH

According to the U.S. government's National Centers for Disease Control and Prevention (CDC) there's a limited risk of malaria in certain rural areas of the Yucatán Peninsula, especially the states of Campeche and Quintana Roo. Dengue fever is also a limited risk along the Caribbean coast. Travelers in mostly urban areas need not worry, nor do travelers who rarely leave artificial resort environs.

To safeguard yourself against mosquito-borne diseases like malaria and dengue, use mosquito nets, wear clothing that covers the body, apply repellent containing DEET, and use spray for flying insects in living and sleeping areas. You might consider taking antimalarial pills, but the side effects are quite strong, and the current strain of Mexican malaria can be cured with the right medication. There's no vaccine to combat dengue.

Health Warnings National Centers for Disease Control & Prevention (*CDC* ☎877/394–8747 international travelers' health line ⊕*www.cdc.gov/travel*). **World Health Organization** (*WHO;* ⊕*www.who.int*).

FOOD AND DRINK

Despite concerns raised by the H1N1 influenza outbreak of early 2009, in Mexico the biggest health risk is *turista* (traveler's diarrhea) caused by consuming contaminated fruit, vegetables, or water. The usual suspects are ice, uncooked food, and unpasteurized milk and milk products.

Drink only bottled water or water that has been boiled for at least 10 minutes, even when you're brushing your teeth. At restaurants off the beaten path, be sure to ask for *agua mineral* (mineral water) or *agua purificada* (purified water). When ordering cold drinks at questionable establishments, skip the ice: *sin hielo.* (You can usually identify ice made commercially from purified water by its uniform shape and the hole in the center.) Hotels with water-purification systems will post signs to that effect in the rooms; even then, be wary. Although salads in tourist-oriented areas have usually been hygienically prepared, when in doubt don't eat any raw vegetables that haven't been, or can't be, peeled (e.g., lettuce and tomatoes).

REMEDIES

Mild cases of turista may respond to Imodium (known generically as loperamide or Lomotil) or Pepto-Bismol (not as strong), both of which you can buy over the counter; keep in mind, though, that these drugs can complicate more serious illnesses. Drink plenty of bottled water or tea; chamomile tea (*te de manzanilla*) is a good remedy, and it's readily available in restaurants throughout Mexico.

In severe cases, rehydrate with Gatorade or a salt-sugar solution (½ teaspoon salt and 4 tablespoons sugar per quart of water). If your fever and diarrhea last three days or longer, see a doctor—you may have picked up a parasite that requires prescription medication.

PESTS

It's best to be cautious and go indoors at dusk (called the "mosquito hour" by locals). An excellent brand of *repelente de insectos* (insect repellent) called Autan is readily available; do not use it on children under age two. If you want to bring a mosquito repellent from home, make sure it has at least 10% DEET or it won't be effective. If you're hiking in the jungle or near standing water, wear repellent and/or long pants and sleeves; if you're camping in the jungle, use a mosquito net and invest in a package of mosquito coils (sold in most stores).

Another local flying pest is the *tabaño,* a type of deer fly, which resembles a common household fly with yellow stripes. Some people swell up after being bitten, but taking an antihistamine can help. Some people may also react to ant bites. Watch out for the small red ants, in particular, as their bites can be quite irritating.

Scorpions also live in the region; their sting is similar to a bee sting. They are rarely fatal, but can cause strong reactions in small children and the elderly. Clean all cuts carefully (especially those produced by coral), as the rate of infection is much higher here.

The Yucatán has many poisonous snakes; in particular, the coral snake, easily identified by its black and red markings, should be avoided at all costs, since its bite is fatal. If you're planning any jungle hikes, be sure to wear hard-sole shoes and stay on the path. For more remote areas, hire a guide and make sure there's an antivenom kit accompanying you on the trip.

SUNBURN

More common hazards to travelers in the Yucatán are sunburn and heat exhaustion. The sun is strong here; it takes fewer than 20 minutes to get a serious sunburn. When practical, avoid the sun between 11 AM and 3 PM. Wear a hat and use sunscreen. You should drink more fluid than you do at home—Mexico is probably hotter than what you're used to and you will perspire more. Rest in the afternoon and stay out of the sun to avoid heat exhaustion. The first signs of dehydration and heat exhaustion are dizziness, extreme irritability, and fatigue.

TRIP INSURANCE

Consider buying trip insurance with medical-only coverage. Neither Medicare nor some private insurers cover medical expenses anywhere outside of the United States. Medical-only policies typically reimburse you for medical care (excluding that related to pre-existing conditions) and hospitalization abroad, and provide for evacuation. You still have to pay the bills and await reimbursement from the insurer, though.

Another option is to sign up with a medical-evacuation assistance company. A membership in one of these companies gets you doctor referrals, emergency evacuation or repatriation, 24-hour hotlines for medical consultation, and other assistance. International SOS Assistance Emergency and AirMed International provide evacuation services and medical referrals. MedjetAssist offers medical evacuation.

Medical Assistance Companies AirMed International (⊕ *www.airmed.com*). **International SOS Assistance Emergency** (⊕ *www.*

intsos.com). **MedjetAssist** (⊕ *www.medjet assist.com*).

Medical-Only Insurers **International Medical Group** (⊕ *www.imglobal.com*). **International SOS** (⊕ *www.internationalsos.com*). **Wallach & Company** (⊕ *www.wallach.com*).

▌ HOURS OF OPERATION

In well-traveled places such as Cancún, Isla Mujeres, Playa del Carmen, Mérida, and Cozumel, businesses generally are open during posted hours. In more off-the-beaten-path areas, neighbors can tell you when the owner will return.

Most banks are open weekdays 9 to 5, but some will exchange money only until early afternoon. Many are open Saturday until noon or 1 PM. Most businesses are open weekdays 9 to 2 and 4 to 7.

Some gas stations are open 24 hours, although those off main highways usually close from midnight until 6 AM, or even earlier.

Most museums throughout Mexico are closed on Monday and open 8 to 5 the rest of the week. But it's best to call ahead or ask at your hotel. Hours of sights and attractions in this book are denoted by a clock icon ⊙.

The larger pharmacies in Cancún and Cozumel are usually open daily 8 AM to 10 PM, and those in Cancún, Campeche, and Mérida have at least one 24-hour pharmacy. Smaller pharmacies are often closed on Sunday.

Tourist-oriented stores in Cancún, Mérida, Playa del Carmen, and Cozumel are usually open 10 to 9 Monday through Saturday and on Sunday afternoon. Shops in more traditional areas may close weekdays between 1 PM and 4 PM, opening again in the evening. They are generally closed Sunday.

HOLIDAYS

The lively celebration of holidays in Mexico interrupts most daily business, including banks, government offices, and to a lesser extent shops and services, so plan your trip accordingly: New Year's Day; February 5, Constitution Day; May 5, Anniversary of the Battle of Puebla; September 1, the State of the Union Address; September 16, Independence Day; October 12, Day of the Race; November 1, Day of the Dead; November 20, Revolution Day; December 12, Feast of Our Lady of Guadalupe; and Christmas Day.

Banks and government offices close during Holy Week (the Sunday before Easter until Easter Sunday), especially the Thursday and Friday before Easter Sunday. Some private offices close from Christmas to New Year's Day; government offices usually have reduced hours and staff.

▌ MAIL

Mail can be sent from your hotel or the *oficina de correos*, or local post office. Be forewarned, however, that mail service to, within, and from Mexico is notoriously slow and can take anywhere from 10 days to, well, never. Don't send anything of value to or from Mexico via mail, including cash, checks, or credit-card numbers.

It costs 9.50 pesos to send a postcard or letter weighing under 20 grams to the United States; it's 10.50 to Canada, 13 to Europe and 14.50 to Australia.

To receive mail in Mexico, you can have it sent to your hotel or use *poste restante* at the post office. In the latter case, the address must include the words A/C LISTA DE CORREOS (general delivery), followed by the city, state, postal code, and country. To use this service, you must first register with the post office at which you wish to receive your mail. Mail is held for 10 days, and a list of recipients is posted daily. Postal codes for the main Yucatán destinations are as follows: Cancún, 77500; Isla Mujeres, 77400; Cozumel, 77600; Campeche, 24000; Mérida, 97000. Keep in mind that the postal service in Mexico is very slow; it can take up to 12 weeks for mail to arrive.

Holders of American Express cards or traveler's checks can have mail sent to them in care of the local American Express office. For a list of offices worldwide, write for the *Traveler's Companion* from American Express.

SHIPPING PACKAGES

Hotel concierges can recommend international carriers, such as DHL, Estafeta, or Federal Express, which give your package a tracking number and ensure its arrival back home.

Despite the promises, *overnight* courier service is rare in Mexico. It's not the fault of the courier service, which may indeed have the package there overnight. Delays occur at customs. Depending on the time of year, all courier packages are opened and inspected. This can slow everything down. You can expect one- to three-day service in Cancún and two- to four-day service elsewhere. Never send cash through the courier services. MexPost is the Mexican postal system's version of courier service and is found at the larger post offices. Although cheaper than FedEx and DHL, it's also slightly less reliable.

Express Services DHL (☎ *01800/765–6345* ⊕ *www.dhl.com*). **Estafeta** (☎ *01800/903–3500* ⊕ *www.estafeta.com*). **Federal Express** (☎ *01800/900–1100* ⊕ *www.fedex.com*).

▍ MONEY

Because the value of the currency fluctuates, and upper-end accommodations and some tours quote prices in U.S. dollars, most prices in this book are in dollars.

U.S. dollar bills (but not coins) are widely accepted in many parts of the Yucatán, particularly in Cancún and Cozumel, where you'll often find prices in shops quoted in dollars. However, you may get your change in pesos. Many tourist shops and market vendors, as well as virtually all hotel service personnel, also accept dollars. Wherever you are, though, watch out for bad exchange rates—you'll generally

do better paying in pesos. Hotels, restaurants, passenger bus lines, and market vendors readily accept dollars but usually do not offer a good exchange rate. Many businesses and most highway toll booths do not accept dollars. If you run out of pesos, then by all means use U.S. dollars, pay with a credit card, or make a withdrawal from an ATM.

Cancún is one of the most expensive destinations in Mexico. Cozumel is on par with Cancún, and Isla Mujeres in turn is slightly less expensive than Cozumel. You're likely to get the best value for your money in Mérida and the other Yucatán cities less frequented by visitors, like Campeche. For obvious reasons, if you stay at international chain hotels and eat at restaurants designed with tourists in mind (especially hotel restaurants), you will find the Yucatán's prices are similar to those of other popular international destinations.

Peak-season sample costs for Cancún (about half these prices for Campeche, Progreso, and other nontouristy places): cup of coffee, 15 pesos to 25 pesos; bottle of beer (in a bar/restaurant), 25 pesos to 50 pesos; plate of tacos with trimmings, 40 pesos to 100 pesos; grilled fish platter at a tourist restaurant, 75 pesos to 250 pesos; 2-km (1-mi) taxi ride, 20 to 50 pesos.

Prices throughout this guide are given for adults. Substantially reduced fees are almost always available for children, students, and senior citizens.

ATMS AND BANKS

Your own bank will probably charge a fee for using ATMs abroad; the foreign bank you use may also charge a fee. Nevertheless, you'll usually get a better rate of exchange at an ATM than you will at a currency-exchange office or even when changing money in a bank. And extracting funds as you need them is a safer option than carrying around a large amount of cash.

■**TIP→PIN numbers with more than four digits are not recognized at ATMs in many countries. If yours has five or more, remember to change it before you leave.**

ATMs (*cajeros automáticos*) are now commonplace. Cirrus and Plus are the most frequently found networks. Rural towns, however, often lack banking facilities. Unless you're in a major city or resort area, treat ATMs as you would gas stations—don't assume you'll be able to find one in a pinch (in smaller towns, even when they're present, machines are often out of order or out of cash). Many, but not all, gas stations have ATMs. All airports have ATMs but many bus stations do not.

Before you leave home, ask what the transaction fee will be for withdrawing money in Mexico (it can be up to $5 a pop). Ask your bank if it has an agreement with a Mexican bank to waive or charge lower fees for cash withdrawals. For example, Bank of America account holders can withdraw money from Santander-Serfin ATMs free of charge.

Be sure to also alert your bank's customer-protection division to let them know you will be using your card in Mexico—otherwise they may assume that the card's been stolen and put a hold on your account.

CREDIT CARDS

Throughout this guide, the following abbreviations are used: **AE**, American Express; **D**, Discover; **DC**, Diners Club; **MC**, MasterCard; and **V**, Visa.

It's a good idea to inform your credit-card company before you travel to Mexico, especially if you don't travel internationally very often. Otherwise, the credit-card company might put a hold on your card owing to unusual activity—not a good thing halfway through your trip. Record all your credit-card numbers—as well as the phone numbers to call if your cards are lost or stolen—in a safe place, so you're prepared should something go wrong. Both MasterCard and Visa have general numbers you can call (collect if you're abroad) if your card is lost, but

you're better off calling the number of your issuing bank, since MasterCard and Visa usually just transfer you to your bank; your bank's number is usually printed on your card.

If you plan to use your credit card for cash advances, you'll need to apply for a PIN at least two weeks before your trip. Although it's usually cheaper (and safer) to use a credit card abroad for large purchases (so you can cancel payments or be reimbursed if there's a problem), not all companies offer this service on foreign transactions. Note that some credit-card companies *and* the banks that issue them add substantial percentages to all foreign transactions, whether they're in a foreign currency or not. Check on these fees before leaving home, so there won't be any surprises when you get the bill.

Credit cards are accepted in most tourist areas. Smaller, less expensive restaurants and shops, however, tend to take only cash. In general, credit cards aren't accepted in small towns and villages, except in hotels. Diners Club is usually accepted only in major chains; the most widely accepted cards are MasterCard and Visa. When shopping, you can usually get better prices if you pay with cash.

In Mexico the decision to pay cash or use a credit card might depend on whether the establishment in which you're making a purchase finds bargaining for prices acceptable. To avoid fraud, it's wise to make sure that "pesos" or the initials M.N., *moneda nacional* (national currency) is clearly marked on all credit-card receipts.

Before you leave for Mexico, be sure to find out the lost-card telephone numbers of your credit-card issuer's banks that work in Mexico. (Foreign toll-free numbers often don't work in Mexico. U.S. and Canada toll-free numbers are normally reached by dialing 001–880 instead of 1–800 before the seven-digit number.) Carry these numbers separately from your wallet so you'll have them if you need to call to report lost or stolen cards.

Reporting Lost Cards American Express (☎ *800/528-4800 in U.S., 800/268-9824 from abroad* ⊕ *www.americanexpress.com*). **Diners Club** (☎ *800/234-6377 in U.S., 702/797-5532 collect from abroad* ⊕ *www. dinersclub.com*). **Discover** (☎ *800/347-2683 in U.S., 801/902-3100 collect from abroad* ⊕ *www.discovercard.com*). **MasterCard** (☎ *800/622-7747 in U.S., 636/722-7111 collect from abroad, 55/5480-8000 Mexico City* ⊕ *www.mastercard.com*). **Visa** (☎ *800/847-2911 in U.S., 410/581-9994 collect from abroad* ⊕ *www.visa.com*).

CURRENCY AND EXCHANGE

The approximate exchange rate at this writing was 13.39 pesos to US$1. Check with your bank, the financial pages of your local newspaper, or ⊕ *www.xe.com* for current exchange rates.

Mexican currency comes in denominations of 10-, 20-, 50-, 100-, 200-, 500-, and 1,000-peso bills. The latter are not very common, and many establishments refuse to accept them due to a lack of change. Coins come in denominations of 1, 2, 5, 10, 20, and 100 pesos. Many of the coins are very similar, so check carefully. Of the older coins you may occasionally see a 10 or 20 or more often a 50 *centavo* (cent) piece.

Most banks only change money on weekdays until noon (though they stay open until 5), whereas *casas de cambio* (private exchange offices) generally stay open until 6 or 9 and often operate on weekends. Bring your photo ID or passport when you exchange money. Bank rates are regulated by the federal government, but vary slightly from bank to bank, while casas de cambio have slightly more variable rates. Exchange houses in the airports and in areas with heavy tourist traffic tend to have the worst rates, although unless you're changing large sums of money, convenience may heavily outweigh this difference. Some hotels also exchange U.S. dollars and traveler's checks, but for providing you with this convenience they give a poorer exchange rate than banks.

■**TIP**➔ Many shop and restaurant owners are unable to make change for large bills. Enough of these encounters may compel you to request *billetes chicos* (small bills) when you exchange money and to horde change.

Currency Conversion Contacts Google (⊕ *www.google.com*). **Oanda.com** (⊕ *www. oanda.com*). **XE.com** (⊕ *www.xe.com*).

▮ PACKING

Pack light, because you may want to save space for purchases: the Yucatán is filled with bargains on clothing, leather goods, jewelry, pottery, and other crafts.

Bring lightweight clothes, sundresses, bathing suits, sun hats or visors, and cover-ups for the Caribbean beach towns, but also pack a light jacket or sweater to wear in the chilly, air-conditioned restaurants, or to tide you over during a rainstorm or an unusual cool spell. For trips to rural areas or Mérida, where dress is typically more conservative and shorts are considered inappropriate, make sure you have at least one pair of slacks. Comfortable walking shoes with rubber soles are a good idea, both for climbing ruins and for walking around cities. Lightweight rain gear and an umbrella are a good idea during the rainy season. Cancún is the dressiest spot on the peninsula, but even fancy restaurants don't require men to wear jackets.

Pack sunscreen and sunglasses for the Yucatán's strong sun. Other handy items—especially if you're using budget hotels and restaurants or going off the beaten path—include toilet paper, facial tissues, a plastic water bottle, and a flashlight (for occasional power outages or use at campsites). Snorkelers should consider bringing their own equipment unless traveling light is a priority; reef shoes with rubber soles for rocky underwater surfaces are also advised. Bring prescription drugs in the original, current pill bottle or with a current prescription to avoid problems at customs. Don't count on purchasing necessary OTC or prescription meds (such as sleeping pills); the same brands are not always available in Mexico.

▮ PASSPORTS AND VISAS

A tourist visa is required for all visitors to Mexico. If you're arriving by plane, the standard tourist visa forms will be given to you on the plane. They're also available through travel agents and Mexican consulates and at the border if you're entering by land. In addition to having your visa form, you must prove your citizenship.

▮**TIP➔ You're given a portion of the tourist card form upon entering Mexico. Keep track of this documentation throughout your trip: you will need it when you depart. You'll be asked to hand it, your ticket, and your passport to airline representatives at the gate when boarding for departure.** If you lose your tourist card, plan to spend some time (and about $60) sorting it out with Mexican officials at the airport before your flight out.

U.S. Homeland Security regulations require U.S. citizens of all ages returning by air to have a valid U.S. passport. Those returning by land or sea are required to present either a government-issue photo ID and a certified copy of your birth certificate or a U.S. Passport Card (available as of mid-2008).

Minors traveling with one parent need notarized permission from the absent parent. You're allowed to stay 180 days as a tourist; frequently, though, immigration officials will give you less. Be sure to ask for as much time as you think you'll need up to 180 days; going to a Mexican immigration office to extend a visa can easily take a whole day; plus, you'll have to pay an extension fee.

U.S. Passport Information U.S. Department of State (☎ 877/487–2778 ⊕ travel.state.gov/ passport).

U.S. Passport and Visa Expediters
A. Briggs Passport & Visa Expeditors (☎ 800/806–0581 or 202/338–0111 ⊕ www. abriggs.com). **American Passport Express** (☎ 800/455–5166 or 800/841–6778 ⊕ www. americanpassport.com). **Passport Express** (☎ 800/362–8196 ⊕ www.passport express.com). **Travel Document Systems** (☎ 800/874–5100 or 202/638–3800 ⊕ www. traveldocs.com). **Travel the World Visas** (☎ 866/886–8472 ⊕ www.world-visa.com).

▮ RESTROOMS

Expect to find reasonably clean flushing toilets and running water at public restrooms in the major tourist destinations and at tourist attractions; toilet tissue and soap are usually, but not always, on hand. Although many markets, bus and train stations, and the like have public facilities, you usually have to pay about five pesos for the privilege of using them. Remember that unless otherwise indicated you should put your used toilet paper in the wastebasket next to the toilet; many plumbing systems in Mexico still can't handle accumulations of toilet paper.

Find a Loo The Bathroom Diaries (⊕ www. thebathroomdiaries.com) is flush with unsanitized info on restrooms the world over—each one located, reviewed, and rated.

▮ SAFETY

Unfortunately Mexico has seen a dramatic increase in violence—much of which is drug-related—over the past few years, but most of this has been concentrated in the capital, along border zones, and in less-touristed areas. The Yucatán remains one of the safest areas in Mexico.

But even in resort areas like Cancún and Cozumel you should use common sense. Make use of hotel safes when available, and carry your own baggage whenever possible unless you're checking into a hotel. Leave expensive jewelry at home, since it often entices thieves and will mark you as a turista who can afford to be robbed.

When traveling with all your money, be sure to keep an eye on your belongings at all times and distribute your cash and any valuables between different bags and items of clothing. Do not reach for your money stash in public. If you carry a purse, choose one with a zipper and a thick strap that you can drape across your body; adjust the length so that the purse sits in front of you at or above hip level.

There have been reports of travelers being victimized after imbibing drinks that have been drugged in Cancún nightclubs. Never drink alone with strangers. Avoid driving on desolate streets, and don't travel at night, pick up hitchhikers, or hitchhike yourself.

Use ATMs during the day and in big, enclosed commercial areas. Avoid the glass-enclosed street variety of banks where you may be more vulnerable to thieves who force you to withdraw money for them.

Bear in mind that reporting a crime to the police is often a frustrating experience unless you speak excellent Spanish and have a great deal of patience. If you're victimized, contact your local consular agent or the consular section of your country's embassy in Mexico City.

A woman traveling alone will be the subject of much curiosity, since traditional Mexican women do not generally choose to travel unaccompanied. There has been an increase in reported rapes in Cancún in recent years. Many of them are acquaintance rapes, but crimes against tourists perpetrated by strangers do happen. Don't walk on deserted beaches alone, and make sure your hotel room is securely locked when you retire. Part of the machismo culture is being flirtatious and showing off in front of *compadres,* and lone women are likely to be subjected to catcalls, although this is less true in the Yucatán than in other parts of Mexico.

Although annoying, it's essentially harmless. The best way to get rid of unwanted attention is to simply ignore the advances. It's best not to enter into a discussion with harassers, even if you speak Spanish.

When the suitor is persistent say "no" to whatever is said, walk briskly, and leave immediately for a safe place, such as a nearby store. Dressing conservatively may help—clothing such as brief tops or shorts may be inappropriate in more conservative rural areas—but don't count on it. Never go topless on the beach unless it's a recognized nude beach with lots of other people. Mexicans, in general, do not sunbathe nude, and men may misinterpret your doing so as an invitation.

■TIP→**Distribute your cash, credit cards, IDs, and other valuables between a deep front pocket, an inside jacket or vest pocket, and a hidden money pouch. Don't reach for the money pouch once you're in public.**

Contact Transportation Security Administration (*TSA* ⊕ *www.tsa.gov*).

▌TAXES

An air-departure tax of around $48, or the peso equivalent, must be paid at the airport for international flights from Mexico. This charge is almost always pre-paid as part of your ticket; if for some reason, it's not included or only partially included, you must pay the remainder in cash at the airport. Check with your airline if you're not sure they included the tax in the ticket price.

Hotels in the state of Quintana Roo charge a 12% tax, which is a combined 10% Value Added Tax with the 2% hotel tax; in Yucatán and Campeche, expect a 17% tax, since the V.A.T. is 15% in these states.

Mexico has a value-added tax (V.A.T.), or IVA (*impuesto de valor agregado*), of 15% (10% along the Cancún–Chetumal corridor). Many establishments already include the IVA in the quoted price. When comparing hotel prices, it's important to know whether yours includes IVA and any service charge. Occasionally (and illegally) it may be waived for cash purchases; this is nothing for you to worry about.

In June 2008, those who travel to Mexico by air or cruise ship will be eligible to be reimbursed for the value-added tax they were charged on purchases made at stores throughout the country. There are, of course, some restrictions. You must have paid by credit card (from outside of Mexico), or cash, and your purchases must have totaled $115 (1,200 pesos). While purchasing, you must show your passport and get a receipt and a refund form. Then you visit a kiosk at the Cancún airport to receive your refund in the form of a credit that can be applied to more shopping (no meals or hotel stays); up to half in Mexican pesos (to a max of 10,000 pesos), and the remainder will be credited to your credit cards or bank accounts.

▌ TIME

Mexico has three time zones. Baja California (norte) is on Pacific Standard Time. Baja California Sur and the northwest states are on Mountain Time. The rest of the country is on Central Standard Time, which is two hours ahead of Pacific Time. Cancún and all of the areas covered in this book are on Central Standard Time.

Time Zones Timeanddate.com (⊕ *www.time anddate.com/worldclock).*

▌ TIPPING

When tipping in Mexico, remember that the minimum wage is just a bit more than $5 a day and that many in the tourism industry don't earn much more. There are also Mexicans who think in dollars and know, for example, that in the U.S. porters are tipped $1 to $2 a bag. Many of them expect the peso equivalent from foreigners. Though dollars are widely accepted in Cancún and Cozumel, you should always tip using local currency whenever possible, so that service personnel aren't stuck going to the bank to exchange dollars for pesos.

What follows are some guidelines. Naturally, larger tips are always welcome:

porters and bellhops, 10 pesos per bag at airports and moderate and inexpensive hotels and 20 pesos per person per bag at expensive hotels; maids, 10 pesos per night (all hotels); waiters, 10% to 15% of the bill, depending on service, and less in simpler restaurants (anywhere you are, make sure a service charge hasn't already been added, a practice that's particularly common in resorts); bartenders, 10% to 15% of the bill, depending on service (and, perhaps, on how many drinks you've had); taxi drivers, 5 to 10 pesos only if the driver helps you with your bags. Tipping cabbies isn't usual, and they often overcharge tourists when possible. Tip tour guides 50 pesos per half day, 100 for a full day; drivers about half as much. Gas-station attendants expect 3 to 5 pesos unless they check the oil, tires, and so on, in which case tip more; parking attendants, 5 to 10 pesos, even if it's for valet parking at a theater or restaurant that charges for the service.

▌ TOURS

Mayaland Tours leads custom tours as well as guided eight-day trips that hit the highlights of archaeology (Chichén Itzá, Uxmal, and the Ruta Puuc sites) with forays into Campeche and Río Lagartos. California Native includes guide service, accommodations, breakfast, and most lunches in its seven-day trip with stops at Mérida, Izamal, Chichén Itzá, Ek Balam, Uxmal, and Edzná. Originally organized by birders and naturalists, Ecoturismo Yucatán, based in Mérida, now leads a large variety of guided tours hitting peninsula highlights of archaeology and culture as well as specialized tours. EcoColors and Alltournative are recommended for sustainable adventure tours on the coast, offering archaeological and nature tours.

Recommended Companies Alltournative (⊠ *Calle 5 between Calles 12 and 14, and Calle 5 between Calles 2 and 4, Playa del Carmen* ☎ *984/803–9999, 800/507–1092 from U.S. and Canada* ⊕ *www.alltournative.*

com). **California Native** (⊠ 6701 W. 87th Pl., Los Angeles, CA ☎ 800/926–1140 or 310/642–1140 ⊕ www.calnative.com). **Ecotour** (⊠ Calle Camaron 32, SMNZ 32, Cancún ☎ 866/978–6225 ⊕ www.ecotravelmexico. com). **Ecoturismo Yucatán** (⊠ Calle 3. No. 235 x 32A y 34, Col. Pensiones, 97219 ☎ 999/920–2772 ⊕ www.ecoyuc.com. mx). **Mayaland** (☎ 998/887–2495 Cancún, 800/235–4079 in U.S. ⊕ www.mayaland.com).

SPECIAL-INTEREST TOURS
ADVENTURE

Contacts **Green Tortoise Adventure Travel** (⊠ 494 Broadway, San Francisco, CA ☎ 800/867–8647 or 415/956–7500 ⊕ www. greentortoise.com). **TrekAmerica** (⊡ Box 189, Rockaway, NJ07866 ☎ 800/873–5872 ⊕ www. trekamerica.com).

ART AND ARCHAEOLOGY

Contacts **Far Horizons Archaeological & Cultural Trips** (⊡ Box 2546, San Anselmo, C 94979 ☎ 800/552–4575 or 415/482–8400 ⊕ www.farhorizons.com). **The Mayan Traveler** (☎ 800/451–8017 or 281/367–3386 ⊕ www. themayantraveler.com).

BIKING

■ TIP➔Most airlines accommodate bikes as luggage, provided they're dismantled and boxed.

Contacts **Aventuras Tropicales de Sian** (⊠ 37 S. Clearwater Rd., Grand Marais, MN ☎ 218/388–9455 ⊕ www.boreal.org/yucatan). **Backroads** (⊠ 801 Cedar St., Berkeley, CA ☎ 800/462–2848 ⊕ www.backroads.com).

BIRD-WATCHING

Contacts **Ecoturismo Yucatán** (⊠ Calle 3 Nos. 235 x 32A y 34, Col. Pensiones, 97219 ☎ 999/920–2772 ⊕ www.ecoyuc.com.mx).

DIVING

Contacts **Aqua Dreams Travel** (⊠ 4708 SE 8th Ct., #3, Cape Coral, FL ☎ 888/322–3483 toll-free, 239/540–4512 ⊕ www.aquadreams. com).

ECOTOURS

Contacts **Alltournative** (⊠ Calle 5 between Calles 12 and 14, Playa del Carmen ☎ 994/803–9999, 800/507–1092 from U.S.

and Canada ⊕ www.alltournative.com). **Ecoturismo Yucatán** (⊠ Calle 3 No. 235, between Calles 32A and 34, Col. Pensiones, Mérida ☎ 999/920–2772 or 999/925–2187 ⊕ www. ecoyuc.com). **Emerald Planet** (⊠ 1706 Constitution Ct., Fort Collins, CO ☎ 970/372–5922 ⊕ www.emeraldplanet.com).

FISHING

Contacts **Costa de Cocos** (⊠ 2 km [1 mi] outside of Xcalak, Quintana Roo ⊕ www. costadecocos.com). **Fishing International** (⊠ 5510 Skylane Blvd., Suite 200, Santa Rosa, CA ☎ 800/950–4242 or 707/542–4242 ☎ 707/526–3474 ⊕ www.fishinginternational. com). **Ecocolors** (⊠ Calle Camaron 32, Sm. 27, Cancún ☎ 988/884–9580 ⊕ www.eco travelmexico.com).

LANGUAGE PROGRAMS

Contacts **Institute of Modern Spanish** (⊠ Calle 15 Nos. 500B X 16A y 18 Col. Maya, Mérida, Yucatán ☎ 877/463–7432 in U.S. ⊕ www.modernspanish.com). **Spanish Institute of Mérida** (⊠ Calle 60 No. 358 centro, Mérida, Yucatán ☎ 999/925–4475 or 800/539–9710, 512/377–6112 in U.S. ⊕ www. simerida.com).

■ VISITOR INFO

ONLINE TRAVEL TOOLS

The official Web site for Mexico tourism has information on tourist attractions and activities, and an overview of Mexican history and culture. Yucatan Today and Loco Gringo have comprehensive information on nightlife, hotel listings, archaeological sites, area history, and other useful information for travelers.

Tourist Board Offices Mexico Tourism Board (☎ 800/446–3942 in U.S. or Canada ⊕ www.visitmexico.com).

All About Cancún, Cozumel, and the Yucatán Peninsula ⊕ www.yucatantoday. com; ⊕ www.locogringo.com. Also try ⊕ www. cozumelmycozumel.com, ⊕ www.cancun.bz, and ⊕ www.travelyucatan.com.

INDEX

Photo Credits: 4, *cancuncd.com*. 6, *Angelo Cavalli/age fotostock*. 7 (left), *Georgie Holland/age fotostock*. 7 (right), *Guillermo Aldana/Mexico Tourism Board*. 12, *Mark Newman/age fotostock*. 13 (left), *cancuncd.com*. 13 (right), 14, *Stefano Morini/Cancun Convention and Visitors Bureau. Bruce Herman/ Mexico Tourism Board*. 15 (left), *Doug Scott/age fotostock*. 15 (right), *Alvaro Leiva/age fotostock*. 16, *Stefano Morini/Cancun Convention and Visitors Bureau*. 17, *Bruce Herman/Mexico Tourism Board*. 18, *Jon Arnold/Agency Jon Arnold Images/age fotostock*. **Chapter 1: Cancun:** 19, *Angelo Cavalli/age fotostock*. 20 (top and bottom), *Corbis*. 21, *Mary Magruder/viestiphoto.com*. 23, *Walter Bibikow/ viesti-photo.com* **Chapter 2: Isla Mujeres:** 87 and 88 (top), *Bruce Herman/Mexico Tourism Board*. 88 (bottom left), *Stefano Morini/Cancun Convention and Visitors Bureau*. 88 (bottom right), *Walter Bibikow/viestiphoto.com*. 89, *Jack Milchanowski/age fotostock*. **Chapter 3: Cozumel:** 117, *Miguel A. Núñez/Cancun Convention and Visitors Bureau*. 118 (top), *cancuncd.com*. 118 (bottom), *Bruce Herman/Mexico Tourism Board*. 119, *Robert Winslow/viestiphoto.com*. 148 and 149, *cancuncd.com*. 151 (top and bottom), *Georgie Holland/age fotostock*. 152, *cancuncd.com*. 153, *Georgie Holland/ age fotostock*. **Chapter 4: The Caribbean Coast:** 157, *Stefano Morini/Cancun Convention and Visitors Bureau*. 158 (left and right), *Bruce Herman/Mexico Tourism Board*. 159 (top), *Philip Coblentz/ Brand X Pictures*. 159 (bottom), *Bruce Herman/Mexico Tourism Board*. 192, *Campeche Tourism*. 193, *Philip Baird/anthroarcheart.org*. 194 (top), *Ken Welsh/age fotostock*. 194 (bottom), *SuperStock/ age foto-stock*. 195, *Philip Coblentz/Brand X Pictures*. **Chapter 5: Yucatán & Campeche States:** 223, *Bruno Perousse/age fotostock*. 224, *Guillermo Aldana/Mexico Tourism Board*. 268, *David Davis/Shutterstock*. 269, *Corbis*. 270 (top), *José A. Granados/Cancun CVB*. 271 (top), *Gonzalo Azumendi/age fotostock*. 271 (center), *Philip Baird/anthroarcheart.org*. 271 (bottom), *Mexico Tourism Board*. 272 (top), *Corbis*. 272 (bottom), *Bruno Perousse/age fotostock*. 273 (top inset), *Luis Castañeda/age fotostock*. 273 (top image), *José A. Granados/Cancun CVB*. 273 (bottom), *Joe Viesti/Viestiphoto.com*. 274, *Marco/viestiphoto.com*. 275, *Joe Viesti/viestiphoto.com*.

NOTES

NOTES

ABOUT OUR WRITERS

After earning a degree in the history of Mexico from the University of California–Berkeley seven years ago, Michele Joyce moved to Mexico City to teach a summer history course. She has lived in the capital ever since, and travels around the country as often as possible, notepad and camera in hand. She recently earned her master's degree in art history from Mexico City's Casa Lamm. She works with husband, Gustavo Cota, drawing on his local knowledge. The pair worked on the Yucatán and Campeche chapter of this edition.

As a freelance journalist and author, Marlise Kast has contributed to more than 50 publications including *Forbes, Surfer, San Diego Magazine,* and *New York Post.* Her passion for traveling has taken her to 60 countries and lead her to establish short-term residency in Switzerland, the Dominican Republic, Spain, and Costa Rica. Following the release of her memoir *Tabloid Prodigy,* Marlise co-authored *Fodor's 2009 Guide to San Diego, Fodor's Mexico 2009,* and *Day & Overnight Hikes on California's Pacific Crest Trail.* She recently completed a 13-month surfing and snowboarding expedition through 28 countries. Now based in San Diego, she is currently working on her next full-length manuscript. Marlise contributed to Cancún, Isla Mujeres, and the Caribbean Coast.

A native of "Alta" California, Coco Krumme has traveled extensively in Mexico and Latin America. She lived in Argentina while working as a journalist for the *Buenos Aires Herald,* and recently co-authored the Fearless Critic restaurant guide to Washington, D.C. Coco contributed to Travel Smart.

Recipient of the prestigious Pluma de Plata award for writing on Mexico, the Golondrina award for her coverage of Cozumel, and the Cancún International Journalism awards for her coverage of Cozumel, Maribeth Mellin has spent nearly three decades exploring Mexico. Her home in California is filled with folk art and photos from Latin America; books she has authored on Mexico, Peru, Argentina, and Costa Rica line her office shelves. She writes a weekly column, "Mexico: The Real Deal," for the San Diego News Network, and her recent articles and photos have appeared in Alaska Airlines magazine, Endless Vacation, Postcards, Concierge.com, and TravelAge West. Maribeth authored the Cozumel chapter of this book.